INTRODUCTION TO GEOLOGY

VOLUME I

PRINCIPLES

INTRODUCTION TO GEOLOGY

VOLUME I
PRINCIPLES

H. H. READ
F.R.S., F.R.S.E., F.G.S., D.Sc., A.R.C.S.

Formerly Professor of Geology in Imperial College of Science and Technology, University of London

JANET WATSON
Ph.D., A.R.C.S., D.I.C.

Professor of Geology in the University of London, Imperial College, London

First Edition 1962
Reprinted 1963, 1964, 1965
Second Edition 1968
Reprinted 1969, 1970, 1973, 1974, 1977, 1978, 1979

Published by
THE MACMILLAN PRESS LTD
London and Basingstoke
Associated companies in Delhi Dublin
Hong Kong Johannesburg Lagos Melbourne
New York Singapore and Tokyo

ISBN 0 333 04727 3 (hard cover)
0 333 11693 3 (paper cover)

Printed in Hong Kong

PREFACE

THIS book has evolved out of a cooperative effort begun some years ago by several members of the staff of the Geology Department of Imperial College, London. Although we made a completely new start when we took over the project, we have nevertheless had the assistance of some of our colleagues in the preparation of certain chapters. Especially we wish to express our gratitude to Dr. F. G. H. Blyth for allowing us to use material for Chapter 2, The Earth, and to Dr. Gilbert Wilson who generously placed at our disposal his original draft for Chapter 8, Geological Structures. We should emphasise, of course, that our colleagues cannot be held responsible for the use we have finally made of their contributions. We are also greatly indebted to Mr. J. A. Gee, Photographer of the Geology Department of Imperial College, for his invaluable technical assistance with the illustration of this work. Our thanks are due to Iranian Oil Services, Ltd., for allowing us to reproduce the magnificent aerial photograph of Figure 264, and we wish to acknowledge permission from the Director of H.M. Geological Survey to use the photographs reproduced in Figures 72, 85, 124, 135, 137 and 338, of which copyright is reserved by the Crown. Further, Figures 186, 193, 197 and 203 are taken from the *Introduction to Geology* by E. B. Bailey and J. Weir (Macmillan, 1939).

In preparing a comprehensive work of this kind we have, consciously or unconsciously, been influenced by methods, statements, illustrations and so forth that have appeared in other publications. So far as we are able, we have acknowledged our indebtedness but, if we have failed to do this, we wish now to express our general gratitude.

H. H. READ
J. WATSON

Imperial College, London
January 1962

PREFACE TO SECOND EDITION

In this second edition important changes or additions have been made in the chapters dealing with the Earth, Surface Processes, Vulcanicity, Metamorphism and Earth-history. Throughout the book we have endeavoured to remove inconsistencies and obscurities by making many small changes in both text and figures. About a score of illustrations have been replaced or considerably modified; certain of the new drawings of common fossils are based on the magnificent illustrations in the Handbooks on British Fossils issued by the British Museum (Natural History) and referred to in Chapter 6. The reading lists and bibliographies have been brought up to date but, as in the first edition, a deliberate selection has been made from the vast output of recent work. By these changes we trust that the usefulness of the original book may be increased in this new edition.

H. H. READ
JANET WATSON

Imperial College, London
August 1967

CONTENTS

CONTENTS

x CONTENTS

1

THE SCIENCE OF GEOLOGY

THE science of Geology deals with all matters concerning the earth. It provides descriptions of the materials — the rocks — of which the earth is made and discusses their origins. It traces the effects of various forces upon these rocks, forces deriving their energy from the earth itself or from the sun. It studies the way in which the rocks are arranged in the accessible part of the earth. It is very much concerned with the types of former life found in the rocks and with the evolution and habitats of this life. It endeavours to determine the limits of land and sea during past ages and so to trace an unending succession of lost geographies. All branches of this broad science are interconnected and interdependent; further, they draw copiously upon the physical, chemical and biological sciences.

The fundamental aim of geology is thus to furnish a detailed history of the earth; *geology is earth-history*. The documents from which this history is to be read are the rocks themselves which, by the way they were made and their relations to one another, provide a record of thousands of millions of years of astonishingly varied events.

The geologist, then, deals with *rocks*. These are the solid portions of the outer parts of the earth, and each rock possesses a certain individuality and maintains its characters over a greater or lesser extent. Rocks are not necessarily hard and tough. A bed of modern peat is just as much a rock to the geologist as a seam of coal derived from an old peat bed; soft mud and running sand are rocks just as much as the hardened mud called shale and the compacted sand called sandstone. Most rocks are made of *minerals*, which are inorganic substances with a definite chemical composition and a definite atomic structure. The great variety among rocks is the result of the differences in the nature, properties, sizes, shapes and arrangements of the constituent minerals, all these variations expressing a diversity of origins of the rocks, as illustrated in Fig. 1.

Study of the rocks reveals the evolution of the accessible parts of the earth. This evolution is not yet finished; the geological processes that can be examined in action at the present time and over the present surface of the earth appear to be in a general way similar to those that have operated since geological history began. It is in fact found that some of the oldest known rocks were formed in the same

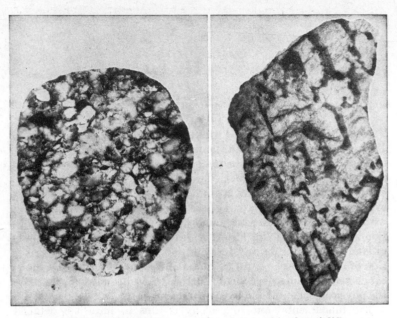

A

B

FIG. 1. *Two rocks with the same mineral composition but of different origins.* A. *Arkose*, formed by the accumulation of transported fragments of quartz and feldspar at the earth's surface. B. *Graphic Granite*, formed by the simultaneous crystallisation of quartz and feldspar deep in the crust.

ways as certain modern ones. The present can thus be used to interpret the past; this, the *Principle of Uniformitarianism*, is the first fundamental doctrine of geology. We can illustrate it like this; shingle can be observed forming on a modern beach and the knowledge gained in this observation can be used to conclude that a similar but ancient rock might have been formed on an ancient beach. Again, lava pouring from a volcano into the sea is seen to consolidate in characteristic shapes; some ancient lavas with the same shapes can reasonably be interpreted as having consolidated in water or wet mud. Uniformitarianism must clearly be applied in a critical fashion; similar-looking rocks may result from different processes and, besides, certain processes operate at levels so deep within the earth that they can never be observed in action.

By actual observation it can often be established what were the original characters and shapes of bodies of rock. It can be shown that the mud and sand brought down into the sea by a river are spread out as a flat layer in the estuary, or that a body of salt, produced by the drying-up of a salt lake, has a thin disc-like shape. Inspection of

2

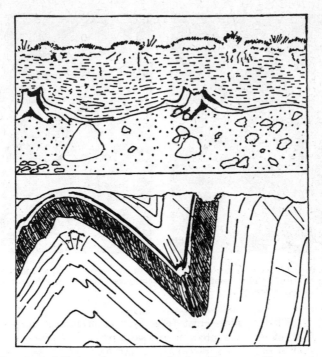

Fig. 2. A folded coal seam records the subsequent history of an original bed of peat.

older muds and sands, now often compacted into shales and sandstones, shows that they have been disturbed. That rocks originally deposited in water now make dry land indicates movement of the earth's outer parts, and that these movements are often violent is proved by folding and buckling of the originally flattish layers (Fig. 2). In the study of the rocks, then, we have to deal not only with their *primary* characters as indicating their manner of formation but also those *secondary* characters imposed on them during their subsequent history.

By such movements, rocks come to occupy different positions from those in which they were first formed. A rock such as a mud, first made at the earth's surface under atmospheric temperature and pressure, may later become deeply buried and thus subjected to high temperatures and great pressures. Another rock, granite for example, formed deep within the earth, may be raised to the surface. In both instances, the original environment has been markedly changed and it is found that the rocks have reacted to these changes. The surface mud may be transformed into a rock of quite different appearance

3

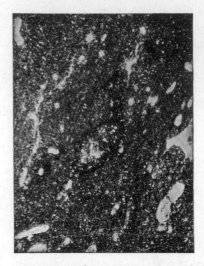
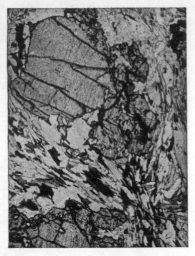

A   B

FIG. 3. Reaction in rocks to change in environment: A, a thin slice of mud; B, a thin slice of mica-schist composed of the minerals garnet, mica and quartz.

which is called a mica-schist (Fig. 3); the originally deep-seated granite is broken down into mud and sand by surface processes. *This reaction to changes in environment is the basis of the second great principle of geology.* The reactions proceed in such a way that a new harmony or *equilibrium* is established fitted to the new environment. To use the example already employed (Fig. 3), the mud, composed of tiny wet flakes of 'clay-minerals', is in a state of equilibrium, or *stable*, under surface conditions of temperature and pressure; the mica-schist, made of large grains of the minerals garnet, mica and quartz arranged in parallel, is the stable form under deep-seated conditions of high temperature and great pressure.

These reactions to changed conditions may be exceedingly slow: a freshly quarried granite block, for example, may appear to remain whole and solid for thousands of years but, eventually, it will crumble and decay. Almost trivial processes, whose annual product can scarcely be observed, will produce great results when operating over the immense spans of time involved in earth-history. A small stream, given time, will carve for itself a great valley. The geologist requires, and has, enormous time for the history he sees recorded in the rocks.

It has been implied throughout the foregoing that rocks are of different ages and that the present state of the outer parts and surface of the earth is short-lived. In the seas of to-day there are being laid down the raw materials of modern rocks, mud and sand, which have been worn in many cases off shales and sandstones that make the existing lands, and thence carried to the sea by rivers. On the principle of uniformitarianism, these shales and sandstones have themselves been derived from still older rocks. This history can be pushed back to the earliest geological times, thousands of millions of years ago, and the geologist, as the historian of the earth, is much concerned with dating his documents, the rocks. He arranges the rocks in order of relative ages and, on occasion, can date them in terms of millions of years. One of the rules that he applies here follows from the principle of uniformitarianism; a layer of rock, formed by the laying down of mineral fragments, must obviously be younger than the rock on which it rests. This rule is known as the *law of superposition* and was first established by William Smith (1769–1839). With its aid, applied critically, all the layered rocks accessible to us are being steadily fitted into their proper positions in the great succession of the rocks.

Many of the rocks contain *fossils*, which are the remains of organisms entombed in them when they were being made. Throughout the great period of time, some 600 million years at least, during which life is recorded in the rocks, organic evolution has gone on. The types of fossils found in the succession of rocks have changed continuously until the present-day fauna and flora have been evolved. It follows from this circumstance that each layer or *stratum* (Latin, 'something spread') in the succession is characterised by a particular kind or group of fossils which enables any layer to be placed correctly in the relative time sequence (Fig. 4). This is expressed in the second of William Smith's laws, that of *strata identified by fossils*.

A fictitious example combines William Smith's two laws; mud has been deposited in successive layers on the floor of the North Sea at least since Roman times; a deep and old layer might contain a bolt from a Roman galley, a higher and therefore younger layer a coin from a galleon of the Spanish Armada and the highest and youngest layer a piece of a modern aeroplane; we can date the layers as 55 B.C., A.D. 1588 and A.D. 1967. In doing so, we apply William Smith's two laws, however unusual our fossils in this case may be.

Fossils are also of great importance in supplying evidence on the conditions under which the strata containing them were formed. Remains of marine organisms in a rock indicate that it was laid down in a sea; a bed containing nothing but the remains of land reptiles or of land plants must have been formed on land. A study of all the characters of a stratum of rock — its composition, form, the arrangement of its constituents, its fossil contents and all that can be found out about it — leads to an opinion as to how and where it was made.

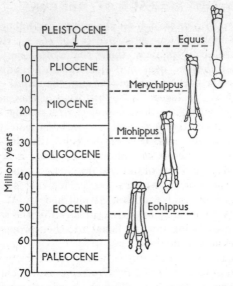

FIG. 4. A dated succession of Tertiary rocks with forelimbs of fossil horses characteristic of the different layers.

These total characters of a rock give its *facies*. The geography of the present lands and seas controls the distribution of the facies of the present time — the facies of ice-sheets, high mountains, plains, deserts, lakes and rivers, estuaries, beaches, shallow seas, deep seas and so on. In these and many other environments, the appropriate facies are being formed. One prime aim of geology is to provide a great number of maps showing the past geography — the *palaeogeography* — at many times in the geological history of the earth. This is done in the same way as that used by a modern geographer, by mapping the distribution of the facies, as indicating the environments of their formation, of any one time in the past.

Geology can be studied for its own sake — for fun or for love. We may be satisfied to build up, with patient observation and inspired guess, the countless episodes in the past of our planet. We may be *pure geologists*. But there is another side to geology. Most of the raw materials of modern industry come from the earth. Coal, petroleum, iron-ore, the ores of the useful metals, the precious metals, a host of industrial minerals, salt and fertilisers, refractories and abrasives, all are derived from the earth. Soil is geological material, building stones and all kinds of materials of construction are mineral or rock products. There is therefore a great field of *economic or applied geology*. But, of course, there is only one way of studying the rocks, whether

6

they happen to be useful or not, though the emphasis in this study may vary.

This study is based more on observation than on experiment. Facts are accumulated concerning the rocks and, in due time, hypotheses are advanced to explain the facts. Since rocks occur outside the laboratory, the fundamental basis of geology is field-work, the investigation of rocks as they make the outer solid part of the earth; a geological map of some kind is made. Now, the geologist is able to examine relatively little of this part; most of it is hidden beneath the oceans, and exposures on the land, whether natural or artificial, are sporadic and discontinuous. This leads to a certain nebulosity (woolliness the so-called exact scientists may call it) about much geological thinking — but, nevertheless, a geological argument on a geological matter is always the best kind of argument.

It now remains to divide up this broad science into manageable portions and to introduce the plan of study followed in this book.

(a) In this volume, dealing with the principles of earth-history, a beginning (Chapter 2) is made with *geophysics and geochemistry*. The size, shape, density and other physical properties of the globe are considered. Its internal constitution is discussed, the data used being supplied by the study of earthquakes or *seismology*. Seismic and other geophysical methods of investigating the outer parts of the earth are summarised and their application to the search for useful materials such as oil, ores and water is indicated. An account is then given of the broad chemical features of the earth. Finally, theories concerning its origin and early history are outlined and methods of finding the absolute ages of its constituents described.

(b) The smallest units that the geologist usually deals with are *minerals*, and their study is *mineralogy*. The chief rock-forming minerals are examined in Chapter 3, but their occurrence in rocks is left to later pages.

(c) One of the great classes of rocks is the *sedimentary rocks*, formed by the mechanical and chemical breaking up of older rocks exposed to agencies acting at the earth's surface; usually the worn-off material is deposited at the surface from a moving medium of some kind under normal temperature and pressure. In order to understand the sedimentary rocks it is necessary, on sound uniformitarian lines, to understand the surface processes that provide their raw material, the *sediments*. The geological agents of erosion and deposition operating at the present surface of the earth are studied in turn (Chapter 4). This study is, in fact, that of the geological environments of the present-day surface — it is often called *Physical Geology*.

This having been done, we are equipped to deal with the *sedimentary rocks* themselves (Chapter 5), their chief types, their form in space and their succession in time. The typical form of a sedimentary rock is a layer, bed or *stratum* and they are often called the *stratified rocks*. The study of their succession and their interpretation as historical records is *stratigraphy*, a branch of the wider subject of *historical geology*. The immense span of geological time is of necessity divided into manageable portions.

As we have seen, invaluable help is given in stratigraphy by *fossils*. The study of fossils is *palaeontology* (Chapter 6); the chief groups of fossils are described, and the uses of fossils, both in pure and applied geology, are set out.

(*d*) The second great class of rocks is the *igneous rocks*, which are formed by the consolidation of molten rock-substance called *magma*. Surface manifestations of magma are provided by *volcanoes* and the manifold types of *vulcanicity* and its products are dealt with in Chapter 7. The *volcanic rocks* as described here include all those that can reasonably be related to surface magmatic activity.

(*e*) We have seen that most rocks do not retain their original form and position undisturbed, but have been moved, folded or broken subsequent to their formation. The elucidation of the history of rocks as it is recorded in their final architecture — their geometrical arrangement in space — is the subject-matter of *structural geology* (Chapter 8). The *geological map*, also dealt with in this chapter, gives a two-dimensional representation of the structure as it is revealed at the surface of the earth.

(*f*) Besides the sedimentary and volcanic rocks, there are two other great classes of rocks, the metamorphic and the plutonic. The *metamorphic rocks* (Chapter 9) are produced from any pre-existing rocks by the action of high temperatures and strong pressures at deep levels in the earth. The *plutonic rocks* (Chapter 10) are also of deep-seated origin and include both igneous rocks which solidified at depth and types transitional to metamorphic rocks.

(*g*) A specialised group of rocks make the *mineral deposits* useful to man (Chapter 11). Here, attention is directed chiefly to the deposits of metalliferous ores, and other mineral resources such as coal, oil, salt and water are dealt with at appropriate places elsewhere.

(*h*) Finally, in Chapter 12, we consider the inter-relation between all the rocks and processes discussed in earlier chapters. We see how the evolution of sedimentary, volcanic, metamorphic and plutonic rocks is linked to produce the *pattern of earth history*. The basis of this pattern and the illustration of it form the subject matter of a companion volume.

It has been emphasised that geology is fundamentally an observational or field science. Minerals, rocks and fossils can be examined in the laboratory but their geology — their mode of occurrence, their mutual relations and arrangement as indicating their history — must be studied out of doors. The student must see to this.

READING LIST ON THE HISTORY OF GEOLOGY

The development of geological ideas can be obtained from:

Geikie, Sir Archibald, 1897, *The Founders of Geology*. This is a readable account for ordinary people.

Zittel, K. A. von (translated by M. M. Ogilvie-Gordon), 1901, *History of Geology and Palaeontology to the End of the Nineteenth Century*. Technical, best left to the experts, or consulted when occasion arises.

Adams, F. D., 1949, *The Birth and Development of the Geological Sciences*. Can be enjoyed by the ordinary reader.

Read, H. H., 1949, *Geology: an Introduction to Earth History*, Home University Library. Chapter I gives a twenty-five page summary in popular form.

2

THE EARTH

Iт will be as well to know something of the physical and chemical properties of the earth as a whole before entering on the examination of such parts as are accessible to geological observation. The two sciences that are drawn upon in this chapter are **geophysics** and **geochemistry** which deal respectively with the physics and chemistry of the globe. Much of what follows is well-grounded and factual, but there are also more speculative discussions on such topics as the constitution of the earth, its origin, age and evolution.

GEOPHYSICS

Size and shape of the earth. The earth is a nearly spherical body, with an equatorial radius of 6378 kms. (3965 miles) and a polar radius only 21 kms. less. This slight departure from an ideal sphere is a consequence of centrifugal forces produced by the earth's rotation.

The determination of the *shape* of the earth is the province of *geodesy*. One method of doing this is now outlined. Any section of the planet which contains the polar axis is approximately an ellipse, and the shape of such a section is found from accurate astronomical observations of latitude made at points whose distance apart, along a meridian, can be measured. A distance of, say, 100 or 200 miles north and south is measured by triangulation on the surface and the angle subtended at the centre of the earth by this arc is found by observing the difference in latitude between the two ends. From these data the earth's radius for that particular arc can be calculated. If an arc measured near the equator is compared with one in a more northerly or southerly latitude, the difference between the calculated radii for the two arcs gives information from which the shape of the elliptical section can be found.

Surface relief of the earth. The shape of the earth, measured in the way just described, takes no direct account of the relief of the surface where, after all, the geologist works. It may be remarked that the difference in level between the highest mountain and the floor of the deepest sea is some 20 kms., a figure that is not greatly different from that between the polar and equatorial radii of the earth. This has of course no particular significance, but the figure of 20 kms. serves to show how minute the surface irregularities are when viewed on a global scale. The geologist deals with a very thin skin of the earth. The surface area of the globe is about 510 million sq. kms. or nearly 197 million sq. miles. Of this more than two-thirds is occupied by the *oceans*, the rest by the *continents*. As we shall see later, the ocean floors and the continental masses have profoundly different geological compositions. Around the margins of the land masses is a platform, of varying width and covered by no great depth of water, that is geologically related to the continents. It is accordingly called the *continental shelf*. If we add its area to that of the lands, then we obtain a figure of about 35 per cent for the continental surface of the earth.

The topographical extremes of height and depth are respectively 8840 metres (29,140 feet) at Everest, and 11,055 metres (36,204 feet)

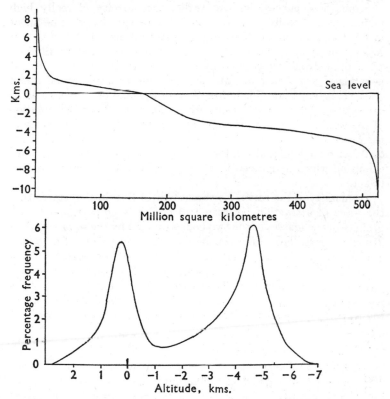

FIG. 5. Frequency distribution of levels of the lithosphere, the solid surface of the earth.

in the Mariana trench off New Guinea. A curve can be constructed to show the areas of land and sea-floor that lie between different heights and depths. These areas can be measured for successive intervals of, say, one kilometre, and from these measuremonts the *hypsometric curve* shown in Fig. 5 above can be drawn. It must be clearly understood that the curve shows only the relationship between areas and heights of the earth's solid surface and is not a section across the continental margins. Perhaps the distribution of the different levels is better expressed in the frequency diagram of Fig. 5 below. This shows two well-marked maxima, one at about 100 metres above sea-level, the other about 4700 metres below it. Put numerically, roughly 30 per cent of the surface lies between 1 km. above and 1 km. below sea-level, and 40 per cent lies between 4 and 6 kms. below sea-level.

From these curves, we can realise the scarcity of really high mountains and really deep seas. Such features are found to be linear in form and we speak of mountain *belts* and oceanic *trenches*. For reasons given later, these linear features are to be related to different kinds of deformation suffered by the outer skin of the earth. In the next place, the occurrence of one maximum of levels round about sea-level means that wide inundations of the land or extensive withdrawals of the sea may result from relatively slight deformation of the earth. Further, changes in the amount of water locked up in the ice-sheets of any time may lead to marked modification of the distribution of land and sea. Finally, these curves express a temporary condition which is doomed to alter as geological processes continue to act.

The density of the earth. Newton's Law of Gravitation states that the force of attraction between two bodies is proportional to the product of the masses of the two bodies divided by the square of their distance apart. This force can be measured by means of a torsion balance or an ordinary balance. Suppose the force exerted by a sphere of mass M on another sphere of mass m when their centres are a distance D apart is P. The earth of mass E exerts a force on m which is the weight of m — we may call this W; the distance apart of the centres in this case is R, the radius of the earth. We therefore have

$$P = \frac{M \times m}{D^2} \quad \text{and} \quad W = \frac{E \times m}{R^2}$$

and
$$\frac{P}{W} = \frac{M \times m}{D^2} \times \frac{R^2}{E \times m} = \frac{MR^2}{D^2E},$$

whence $E = \dfrac{MR^2W}{PD^2}$. The quantities on the right of this equation can be determined and the mass of the earth obtained. Independent determinations have shown that this mass is 5.98×10^{27} grammes. The volume of the earth is estimated at 1.08×10^{21} cubic metres, so that its mean density is 5.527 grammes per cubic centimetre.

Since the density of most rocks occurring at the earth's surface does not exceed 3 — the common rock granite, for example, has an average density of 2.67 — there must be material of higher density at lower levels within the earth. This high density could be due to a change either in physical state of the material or in its chemical composition. Information about the interior of the earth has come from the study of earthquakes and is discussed later in this chapter.

Magnetism. The earth can be regarded as a permanent magnet. The direction, and the vertical and horizontal components, of the earth's total magnetic field have been determined at innumerable places by the use of suitably suspended magnetic needles. At the magnetic poles, the magnetic needle stands vertical; these magnetic poles are situated some 18° of latitude from the geographical poles and a line joining them passes about 1200 kms. distant from the centre of the earth. Not only does the earth's magnetic field change with position but also with time. Further, local variations arise from the irregular distribution of bodies of magnetic rocks or minerals as explained on p. 37.

When certain rocks are formed, magnetic particles in them act as little magnets and are lined up in the earth's magnetic field existing at the time and place of their formation. When such rocks are finally consolidated, the magnetic field becomes as it were fossilised in them and so the direction of the earth's field at many times in its past history can be determined. If it is found that the direction of magnetisation of a rock is not agreeable with its present position at the earth's surface then certain explanations of great geological interest are forthcoming. This study of *palaeomagnetism* is concerned, for example, in the debate as to whether or not the continents are fixed in position (see later, p. 644).

Temperature within the earth. The existence of hot springs and the obvious heated condition of lavas early indicated that the earth was hotter below its surface. Measurements in deep boreholes and mines confirmed that the temperature of the rocks increased with depth. The *geothermal gradient* is the vertical distance over which the rock-temperature increases by 1° C. Though this gradient cannot be measured very accurately, it seems that its real value must vary greatly at different places, depending most likely on the local geological conditions and history. In Britain, for example, values between 22 and 74 metres have been obtained, whereas in South Africa they are between 76 and 144 metres. All these values refer to the mere outer skin of the earth, 6 kms. at the most. At greater depths it is possible that the gradient is low and it has been suggested that, even in the deepest parts of the earth, the temperature does not exceed a few thousand degrees.

It is a hazardous business to produce any kind of curve relating depth and temperature within the earth. The variables are too many, there being, among others, the thermal conductivity of the rocks, the heat produced by the decay of the irregularly distributed radioactive minerals and the irregular distribution of other heat sources. It can be suggested, nevertheless, that the temperature at a depth of 30 kms. might be of the order of a few hundred degrees, say 500, a temperature not sufficient to melt the rocks making this part of the earth. In belts of abnormal mobility, especially where the crust is unusually thick (pp. 24–6), temperatures at this depth may reach about 800° C.

It was early considered that the increase of temperature with depth would lead to the fusion of the materials making the interior of the earth, even though the melting points of minerals increase with pressure. There thus arose the notion of a fluid *core* contained within a solid *crust*. These terms, core and crust, have now acquired special meanings developed from the study of earthquakes. This study we now take up.

SEISMOLOGY

The investigation of earthquakes and the transmission of earthquake waves through the earth is known as *seismology*. An earthquake shock generates elastic vibrations or 'waves', which move out in all directions from the point of origin, or *focus*, of the earthquake.

The rocks forming the outer parts of the earth are traversed by many fractures along which they have been broken and moved. Such fractures are known as *faults*. They are very numerous in the outer few kilometres of the earth, and some probably persist to much greater depths. Stresses accumulate in the earth from various causes and eventually reach an intensity which brings about the local rupturing of the rocks. When such a break occurs and movement takes place on the fault, the rock mass on one side of the fracture slips past that on the other and the earth locally receives a jolt or shock. A homely analogy is the shock felt in your arms when you snap a stout stick. Although a fault-movement may be small in itself, the masses

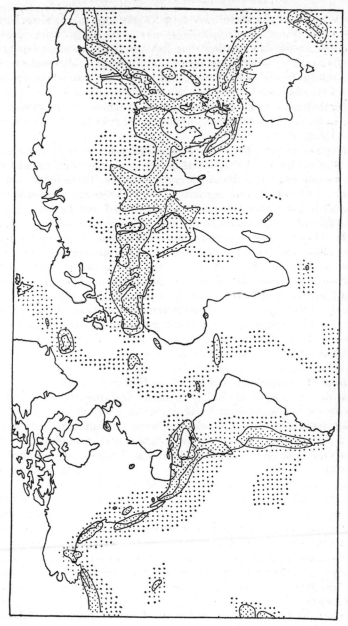

Fig. 6. Map of earthquake centres.

15

of rock involved are often very large. According to the extent of these two factors, the resulting shocks may range from small tremors to severe earthquakes that may produce extensive damage if they happen to affect large centres of population. Movements on faults tend to recur; a fault which has once been active may move again, so that successive earthquakes are often produced at intervals in a particular area. There are thus areas in which earthquakes are prone to occur, while others experience few shocks and these only of small intensity.

When the distribution of modern earthquake centres is plotted on a map of the world (Fig. 6), it is seen that they tend to cluster along certain zones or belts of the earth's surface. These belts, as we see later, correspond to the regions of the more recently formed fold-mountain chains where the rocks are crumpled and faulted, or to major lines of faulting such as the Rift Valley system of Africa (pp. 491–2). They are belts of crustal instability where adjustments are taking place. Two main belts of seismic activity are conspicuous: (1) the *circum-Pacific belt*, which follows the west coasts of North and South America, passes through the Aleutian Islands and south to Japan, East China, the East Indies and New Zealand; (2) the *Mediterranean-Himalayan belt*, which runs from Spain and Morocco through the Alpine arc to the Balkans and Asia Minor, thence past the Himalayan ranges to Burma and the East Indies, to link up there with the first belt. It is estimated that more than 80 per cent of recorded earthquakes have occurred in these two belts.

Effects of earthquakes. We have seen that earthquakes represent stages in the growth of faults. In many instances there is clear evidence of the movement involved, as in 1899 off the coast of Alaska, when part of the sea-floor received an uplift amounting in places to 15 metres. Again, in the Japanese earthquake of 1891 at Midori, the land on one side of a fault was lifted 6 metres and displaced 4 metres horizontally relative to the other side, forming a fault scarp and severing roads and field-boundaries.

The earthquakes which affected parts of Greece in the summer of 1953 were due to movements mainly on submarine faults. Apart from the damage done, one visible effect of the earthquakes was to stir up mud on the sea-floor, so that from the air the waters of the Mediterranean in the region appeared greyish and turbid. Tidal waves or *tsunamis* are often generated when a submarine shock occurs, and may inundate low-lying coasts situated well away from the earthquake centre.

The earthquake which partly destroyed San Francisco in 1906 has been the subject of much study. It was due to movement on a major

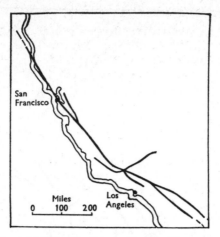

FIG. 7. Map of the San Andreas and related faults, California.

fracture, the *San Andreas fault* (Fig. 7). The trace of this fault at the surface can be distinctly seen in aerial photographs, and its course can be followed at intervals for several hundreds of miles north or south of the city. The movement was mainly a horizontal one, opposite sides of the fault being shifted relative to each other through distances up to 7 metres. This is a large displacement for a single earthquake, and very extensive damage was done. The horizontal nature of the movement was shown by sheared and tilted buildings, by displaced fences and by severed water-pipes and other supply mains. Surface streams were offset along the fault-trace in a number of places; such a stream on approaching the fault now turns and follows it for a few yards before continuing its old course on the other side of the fault.

During an earthquake fissures in the ground may be opened up near to the focus of activity; the walls of the fissure sometimes remain separated, at other times they may close up again, and it is alleged that animals have been engulfed in this way. Soft sediments such as make coastal mud-flats are especially liable to disturbance and fissuring, or if subjected to lateral compression they may locally be thrown into folds. Bridges and other structures erected in such areas suffer accordingly. Evidence of compression is also found in the telescoping of water-pipes and sewers.

Where it is desirable to construct important buildings so that they may have a high resistance to earthquake shocks, special designs are employed, so that the building may move as a whole without being broken. An example of this is the British Embassy in Tokyo, built

17

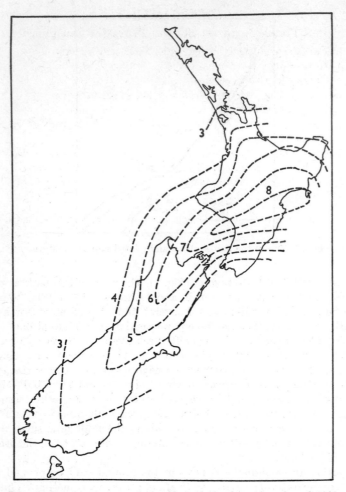

FIG. 8. Isoseismal map of the New Zealand earthquake of 1921
(after Bullen).

about 1930, for which a strong framed structure was used, giving a
large degree of immunity from damage in an earthquake-prone area.

Earthquake maps. After a severe shock has occurred, its intensity
in different parts of the area affected may be estimated from the
effects produced on people and objects, and from the damage to
buildings which has resulted. The damage is assessed according to a
scale of intensity; one well-known scale — of which there are several
versions — is given opposite:

18

ROSSI-FOREL SCALE OF SEISMIC INTENSITY (Simplified)

1. Earthquake noticed by experienced observers only.
2. Noticed by a few people at rest.
3. Generally felt by people at rest.
4. Felt by people in motion; doors and windows rattle.
5. Felt generally; furniture disturbed.
6. Hanging objects such as chandeliers made to swing; clocks stopped; sleepers awakened.
7. Causes panic; moveable objects overthrown; church bells ring.
8. Damage to buildings; chimneys fall and walls are cracked.
9. Some buildings destroyed.
10. Widespread damage.

The damage done or intensity felt, at many points in the area, can then be recorded by numbers on a map and lines of equal intensity — *isoseismal lines* — can be drawn, rather like contour lines. Such a map is shown in Fig. 8. On this map, the *epicentre* is the point on the surface situated above the centre or *focus* of the earthquake. The innermost isoseismals surrounding an epicentre often tend to have an elliptical form, though this is not always the case, and the long axis of such an ellipse then corresponds to the trend of the fault which generated the shock.

Earthquake waves and records. The elastic vibrations generated when a fault-slip takes place travel out in all directions from the earthquake focus. They are of three kinds (Fig. 9):

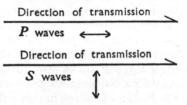

FIG. 9. Earthquake vibrations.

Body Waves travelling through the Earth

(1) *Primary* or *compressional waves*, (*P* waves), consisting of longitudinal vibrations which give an oscillatory movement to particles in the direction in which the waves are propagated.

(2) *Secondary*, *shear-* or *distortional* waves, (*S* waves), which are transverse vibrations with an oscillatory movement at right angles to their path.

Surface Waves

(3) Waves of long period which travel around the periphery of the earth and are called *L* waves, after Love who discovered them.

The *P* waves have the greatest velocity and are the first to arrive at a recording station at a given distance from the focus; the *S* waves are a little slower, and the *L* waves the slowest of the three groups.

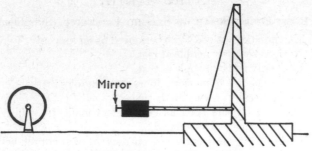

FIG. 10. Seismograph.

But the L waves have the largest amplitude and are those that do the most damage. The vibrations are detected by instruments known as *seismographs*, the principle of which is shown in Fig. 10. A frame, mounted on masonry or concrete let into the ground, carries a delicately suspended lever or beam, on which a heavy mass is mounted. Owing to the inertia of this mass, a movement is imparted to the beam when vibrations are transmitted from the ground to the frame of the instrument. The movement is magnified by the reflection of a ray of light which falls on a mirror attached to the end of the beam. The reflected ray makes a trace on a rotating drum which carries a cylinder of photographic paper, on which are marked time-breaks at minute and hour intervals. The magnified oscillations of the beam are thus recorded on the drum, and the times at which they begin and end can be read off the record. A typical record or *seismogram* for a distant earthquake is shown in Fig. 11; on it the arrivals of the P, S and L waves, in that order, are clearly distinguishable.

In order to record completely the movement of the ground at a station, two instruments are required to receive the horizontal components of the vibrations in two directions at right angles (horizontal seismographs), and a third to record the vertical component of movement (vertical seismograph). From the recordings made by such a group of instruments, the distance and direction of an epicentre can be computed. A single instrument at a station will give the *distance* of an epicentre; the *position* of the latter can be plotted from three such stations.

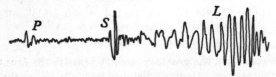

FIG. 11. Seismogram.

The velocity of elastic waves. Before we attempt to use earthquake records to reveal the constitution of the earth, it is necessary to consider what are the physical properties of a material that control the velocity of elastic waves transmitted through it. We are here concerned only with the body waves which, as already stated, are of two types, compressional and shear. The properties in question are (1) the density, D, (2) the bulk-modulus, K, or the resistance to change of volume without change of shape and (3) the rigidity-modulus, N, or the resistance to change of shape without change of volume. It can be shown that for compressional waves, the velocity is equal to $\sqrt{\left(\dfrac{K + \frac{4}{3}N}{D}\right)}$ and for shear-waves the velocity is $\sqrt{(N/D)}$. From this it is seen that compressional waves travel faster than shear-waves in the same medium. Further, in fluids there can be no shear-waves since the rigidity is zero, and the velocity of compressional waves transmitted will be $\sqrt{(K/D)}$.

From these statements we can draw certain conclusions of interest. We see why the compressional P waves are received first at the recording station. Further, if it is found that some part of the earth does not transmit shear-vibrations, then we can infer that that part has the elastic properties of a fluid at the earth's surface. It is not thereby proved to be a fluid; the part may be made of some material in a special physical state not yet known to science. But so far as our present knowledge goes, fluids cannot transmit shear-waves. Of possibly greatest importance to the geologist is the fact that for any given rock, the bulk- and rigidity-moduli and the density can be measured and from these values there can be calculated the velocities at which the rock in question would transmit compressional and shear-waves. From this, suggestions can be made concerning the nature of the rocks making the outer parts of the earth, due regard being had to the pressures and temperatures thought to prevail within the earth.

The interpretation of earthquake records: the core, mantle and crust. A big advance in the understanding of earthquakes was made early in this century when R. D. Oldham showed that the 'preliminary tremors' which arrived before the 'main shock' were in fact the P and S waves, which were followed by the large oscillations of the L waves. From further study of many earthquake records remarkable results emerged. It was found that P and S waves were not transmitted to stations situated at distances greater than 105° of arc away from an epicentre — the distance is measured around the earth, as shown in Fig. 12 — but, at 142° of arc from the epicentre, the P waves were found to appear again, in modified form and without

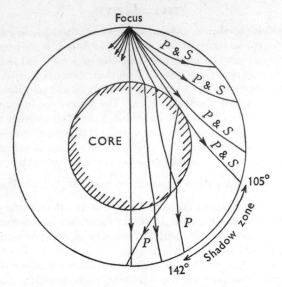

FIG. 12. Transmission of earthquake waves through the earth.

the *S* vibrations. Thus, between 105° and 142° — the *shadow zone* — no *P* or *S* waves arrive; the *P* waves which reach points at 142° and onwards are, however, late in arriving, suggesting that they have been slowed down on their way through the earth. The curve showing the relation between depth in the earth and velocity of the waves transmitted is given in Fig. 13.

Oldham argued that the slowing down of the *P* waves just mentioned was due to their having passed through matter of different composition from that near the surface. This material evidently lay at a greater depth than that penetrated by the waves received at

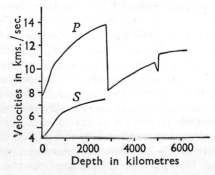

FIG. 13. Earthquake waves: velocity-depth curves (after Jeffreys).

22

105°, and could be due to the presence of a *core* of different composition within the earth. Further, as shear or S waves were not transmitted beyond the 105° distance from the epicentre, the material of this core would appear to have no rigidity. As we have seen, shear-waves are not transmitted by fluids at the surface and Oldham therefore suggested that the earth possessed a central core of material in a fluid condition, surrounded by a solid outer shell. Many subsequent observations have confirmed the basis for this deduction, and the radius of the core has been calculated as about 3500 kms. The boundary between the core and the overlying material is called the *Weichert-Gutenberg Discontinuity*.

From the consideration of the density of the earth, further deductions about the nature of the core can be made. As we have seen, the rocks of the accessible parts of the earth have an average density of under 3, whereas the mean density of the whole earth is about 5·5. The core must therefore be heavy, and its mean density has been calculated to be about 12. Since iron (density at the surface 7·8) is the most abundant heavy metal, it is reasonable to conclude that it is a main constituent of the core, regard being paid to the high pressures in the interior of the earth. Further, certain meteorites, known as *siderites* or *irons*, are made of an iron-nickel alloy and these, considered as samples of solar material, suggest that nickel (density 8·2) also enters into the composition of the earth's core. It must be stated at once, however, that some geophysicists consider that the contrasting physical properties of earth-shells result from differences in physical state of the materials, and not from differences in composition. Nevertheless, the general opinion is that the core is composed of a mixture of nickel and iron in a fluid state under conditions of high temperatures and pressures; it has no rigidity. From its presumed composition it is referred to as the *nife*, from the chemical symbols for nickel and iron.

After the discoveries related above, the structure of the *outer parts of the earth* was investigated with the aid of records of earthquakes relatively near the seismographs. In 1909 the Serbian seismologist A. Mohorovičić found that *two* sets of P and S waves were recorded at some stations. There was a difference in travel times of the first and second impulses of P and also in those of S, and Mohorovičić concluded that the additional impulses had travelled by some route other than the direct path from epicentre to recorder. This would be explained if there were a discontinuity in the material composing the earth, as illustrated in Fig. 14. In this diagram, the main P and S waves are shown travelling in a deeper layer; on reaching the upper boundary of this layer, they are refracted along it and move through

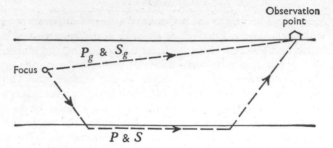

FIG. 14. Mohorovičić diagram for two paths of P and S waves.

the lower layer with a higher velocity than those, P_g and S_g, following the direct path. It should be understood that the path shown in the diagram is one of many possible routes, and that only a small fraction of the energy dissipated by an earthquake follows one particular route.

The discontinuity just mentioned is of great importance in the structure of the earth. It defines the *base of the crust*, and is known as the Mohorovičić or M Discontinuity (often referred to in conversation as the 'Moho'). The depth of the M Discontinuity below the continents averages about 35 kms., but is found to be in general greater below mountain areas; beneath the oceans this discontinuity lies at about 10–11 kms. below sea-level or some 5 kms. below the floor of the ocean. Between it and the core is the *mantle*.

So far, then, we have arrived at the conclusions that the earth is made of three parts, the central *core*, separated by the Weichert-Gutenberg Discontinuity from the *mantle* which in turn is separated by the M Discontinuity from the *crust*. We may now examine the evidence provided by earthquake records for the composition of the mantle and crust.

The *mantle* shows a sudden increase in the velocity of earthquake waves in comparison with those travelling in the crust (see Table, p. 25), and these velocities increase steadily with depth, the increase corresponding to a rise in density from 3·3 at the outer part of the mantle to about 5·7 at its base. So far as the mantle is concerned, laboratory results show that three rocks have the physical properties reasonably consistent with the earthquake velocities observed in it. They are *eclogite*, made of the minerals garnet and pyroxene, *dunite* or olivine-rock, and *peridotite*, a rock composed largely of olivine with some pyroxene. The minerals mentioned are silicates of iron and magnesium and they, and the rocks in question, are described in later pages. From the nature of the case, no definite decision can be

24

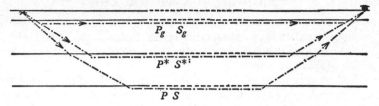

FIG. 15. Paths of waves from near earthquake (based on Jeffreys).

made, but a peridotite rich in olivine appears to meet the requirements best. Somewhat similar material is represented among the meteorites by the group known as *chrondites*.

Evidence relating to the composition of the *crust* comes from the study of the seismograms of earthquakes occurring at less than some 500 miles from the recording stations — these are the 'near' earthquakes. After the discoveries of Mohorovičić, a third onset of P and S waves was recognised by Conrad and by Jeffreys in certain seismograms. The waves of these pulses, labelled P^* and S^*, had velocities intermediate between those of the two sets of associated P and S waves and were interpreted as travelling in a layer immediately above the M Discontinuity. The crustal structure indicated is now thought to be characteristic of continental regions.

The velocities of the three sets of vibrations have now been determined from many observations; those given by Jeffreys, together with the symbols used for the three sets of waves, are as follows:

$$\text{CRUST} \begin{cases} P_g & 5\cdot57 \text{ kms./sec.} \qquad S_g \quad 3\cdot36 \text{ kms./sec.} \\ P^* & 6\cdot50 \qquad\qquad\qquad\ \ S^* \quad 3\cdot74 \end{cases}$$
$$\text{MANTLE } P \quad 7\cdot76 \qquad\qquad\qquad\qquad S \quad 4\cdot36$$

The P and S waves travel below the M Discontinuity and, as already explained, their velocities suggest that the mantle is peridotitic in composition. The other two sets of waves travel in the continental crust and are held to indicate that this consists of two layers separated by another discontinuity at which refraction occurs, as shown in Fig. 15. When the velocities in the crust are compared with those calculated for rocks tested in the laboratory, it is found that P_g and S_g correspond to the velocities for granite and P^* and S^* to those for basalt. Though other rocks also have suitable velocities, granite and basalt are the two most abundant and widely occurring kinds of rocks among the igneous group, a geological fact that influences any interpretation. Basalt is rather heavier than granite, with a density of 2·95 as against about 2·7 for granite; it may be noted that peridotite has a density of about 3·0. It has been suggested from

25

these considerations that an *upper, granitic, layer* overlies a *middle, possibly basaltic, layer*, these two layers making the crust, which is separated by the M Discontinuity from the *lower, peridotite, layer* which makes the mantle.

The granitic layer of the continental crust is often referred to by the general term *sial*, expressing the predominance of silica and alumina in rocks of granitic composition. The basaltic crustal layer has been termed *sima*, the name being derived in a similar way from silica and magnesia. These terms should not be taken to imply that each layer is of uniform composition. The sialic layer is known from direct observation to contain material of many different types: the sima is also probably inhomogeneous and may pass gradually into the sial by increases in the proportions of granitic components.

Consideration of the paths of the three sets of waves represented in Fig. 15 shows that although the deeper waves travel faster, they have to travel the extra distances from the focus down to their particular layer and then up again to the recorder. Since the extra distances to be travelled are constant for any one earthquake, the velocities in the lower layers can be calculated and, from this, the handicap due to extra travel. From data of this type, the thicknesses of the crustal layers can be obtained. The *total thickness of the continental crust* is usually between 25 and 40 km. The crust is thick, as already noted, below mountainous areas and also below mobile orogenic zones and tends to be thinner below regions with a long history of stability. The sialic layer usually forms the upper 10–20 km. of the continental crust.

Beneath the great ocean basins, the M Discontinuity is shown by seismic studies to lie much nearer the surface than it does beneath the continents. The *thickness of the oceanic crust* averages some 5 km. From the velocities of P and S waves it is inferred that, apart from a variable cover of sediments, the oceanic crust is essentially basaltic in composition. The sialic layer of the continental crust thins abruptly at the continental slope (Figs. 20, 118) and does not extend continuously into the floors of the ocean basins proper.

The structure of the earth. From the results of seismology discussed above, we can now obtain the picture of the broad structure of the earth as a whole given in Fig. 16. The three main units are the core, the mantle and the crust.

The *core*, or *nife*, is thought to consist of nickel-iron with low rigidity that behaves like a fluid towards shear-waves. Its density may be about 12, and its temperature a few thousand degrees. The *Weichert-Gutenberg Discontinuity* limits the core and at it the velocity of compressional waves penetrating from the mantle falls abruptly.

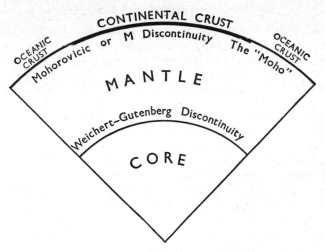

Fig. 16. Proposed constitution of the earth.

The *mantle* is the shell bounded at its base by the Weichert-Gutenberg Discontinuity and at its top by the *Mohorovičić or M Discontinuity*. The outer parts of the mantle are thought to be made of peridotite and in it the velocity of compressional waves increases with depth, corresponding to a density rise from 3·3 to 5·7 at its base.

The *crust* has as its lower limit the M Discontinuity. In the continental masses, it is believed to consist of two parts — the *sial* of broadly granitic composition, and the *sima* of basaltic composition (Fig. 20). The thickness of the crust varies, averaging about 35 kms. The sial is rigid and has considerable strength; it forms the continents, is thickened under the mountain masses, but is largely absent from the deep ocean floors such as that of the Pacific. The underlying sima is denser, hotter and of less rigidity. Though capable of transmitting shear-waves, it yields to long-continued stresses. An imperfect analogy, by way of illustration of this point, may be drawn from the behaviour of a stick of sealing wax which, hung up with a weight suspended from one end, will gradually become elongated under the pull of the weight.

A discontinuous *sedimentary cover*, variable in thickness and composition, forms an outer pellicle on continental sial and oceanic sima alike. This sedimentary veneer is made of material derived from the primary rocks by the ceaseless activity of the surface agents of erosion and deposition. This apparently insignificant skin is of immense importance to man, a surface dweller. It may be noted that

27

the sedimentary cover and the crust together amount to no more than 0·5 per cent of the radius of the earth.

Finally, two more zones, the *hydrosphere* and the *atmosphere*, may be mentioned. The hydrosphere comprises the seas, lakes and rivers; the atmosphere forms the gaseous envelope surrounding the earth.

Normal and deep-focus earthquakes. The depths of focus of earthquakes can be determined from the data that are used to calculate the thicknesses of the crustal layers (p. 26). Most shocks originate at depths not greater than 50 kms. and give rise to what may be called *normal* or *shallow-focus* earthquakes. There is, however, a group of earthquakes of great interest that have foci going down to depths as great as 700 kms. These *deep-focus* earthquakes are characterised by a number of properties, among which may be mentioned a large time interval between the P and S waves and only a minor development of the surface waves. They have a highly significant distribution — around the Pacific Ocean but with the important exception of the North American border. The cause of both shallow and deep-focus earthquakes appears to be the same and this implies stress and sudden rupture at depths within the earth up to one tenth of its radius, where the temperature may well be high and the strength of the rocks small. The distribution of the deep-focus earthquakes and the arrangement of their focal depths suggest that they arise by movements on low-angled planes of thrusting — the movement being directed away from the continental masses in the regions affected, as shown in Fig. 17.

Isostasy. We can now return to consider the relationships between sial and sima in the great continental areas or crustal blocks. We have seen that the continents are most likely formed of sial, and the evidence of seismology suggests that this is everywhere underlain by a denser material, the sima. The sial and the upper part of the sima together constitute a strong composite shell which is sometimes called the *lithosphere*; the material underlying the lithosphere probably has low strength and little rigidity, and can be called the *asthenosphere* (from the Greek, *sthenos*, strength, *a*, not). It is uncertain as yet how much of the sima belongs to this weak zone. These stronger and weaker parts of the earth do not necessarily correspond to any of the layers revealed by seismology, since we are here dealing with strengths.

We have noted that beneath large topographical features such as mountain ranges, the crust is found to be thicker. From a consideration of the nature of mountains there arose the concept of *isostasy* — a state of balance between topographical masses and the underlying

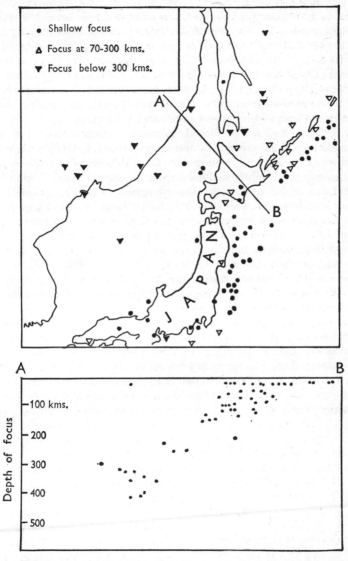

FIG. 17. Deep focus earthquakes: above, epicentres in the Japanese area; below, depth of focus along the line AB (after Gutenberg and Richter).

supporting material. We shall therefore trace briefly the development of ideas on this subject.

An early notion was that mountains were simply an extra mass superimposed on an otherwise uniform crust. It is possible to compute the gravitational attraction of such a mass on neighbouring bodies, and its actual attraction can be found experimentally. This was first done for Chimborazo in Equador (Bouguer, 1749) and Schichallion in Scotland (Maskelyne, 1774). In both cases, the measured attraction was found to differ from the value calculated on the assumption that a mountain is an additional mass above a level surface.

In 1855, J. E. Pratt published his results of measurements of the deflection of the plumb-line by the mass of Everest. The plumb-line, whether in the form of a plummet or the bubble-tube of a surveying instrument, was slightly deflected from its normal position, that is, pulled out of the vertical, by the attraction of the mountain. The deflections, however, were only one-third of what would be expected if the mountain were treated as an extra mass superimposed on the crust. In explanation, Pratt suggested that the density of the crust *beneath* the mountain must be less than that underlying the plains to the south, where his observations were made. Such a body of material of low density would account for the smaller deflection actually found. In 1864, Pratt published his *Theory of Compensation*, in which he proposed that vertical columns of matter in the crust, having different densities according to their heights, extended downwards to a depth, called the *level of compensation*, at which their weight was balanced by the upward pressure of the supporting substratum. This concept is illustrated in Fig. 18A; by analogy, we may note that columns of different materials such as ice, wood, cork, etc., but of the same weight and cross-section, would float in water with their bases at the same level. Pratt's theory necessitates lateral variation in density in the earth's crust, that is, from one column to another.

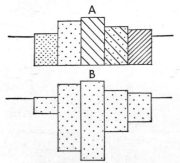

FIG. 18. Isostasy: A, Pratt's hypothesis; B, Airy's hypothesis.

A rival explanation of the facts was put forward, also in 1855, by Sir George Airy who considered the earth to have a thin solid crust supported by a weak, not necessarily fluid, substratum. The term crust as used by Airy would correspond roughly to the present-day sial. Airy showed that the elastic resistance of this crust to bending might be so small that any extra load added to it, such as a mountain mass, would push it down till the load was balanced by the upward pressure of the material below. In other words, the material immediately below a mountain is of lower density than surrounding material at the same level and, as we should now say, mountains have 'roots'. This concept is illustrated in Fig. 18B, where columns of different height but of the same average density float at different levels in the supporting fluid. Note that the heights of the columns *above* water-level are the same in both concepts. Thus Airy postulated a uniform average density for mountains, with varying thicknesses for different parts, while Pratt assumed varying densities above a uniform 'depth of compensation'.

A large mountain plateau, like that of Tibet and the Himalayas, with an average height of $2\frac{1}{2}$ miles, would necessarily sink some distance into the heavier substratum, displacing the latter and causing an outflow of its material towards regions of lighter load. The total mass of the plateau would equal the mass of matter displaced in the substratum. Accordingly, at some distance south of the Himalayas, where the deflection of the plumb-line as given by calculation from the visible mountain mass should have been pronounced, it was actually found to be nil. In other words, the attractive effect of the mass was *compensated* by the deficiency of density arising from the displaced matter of the substratum. Later, the term *isostasy* was coined by C. E. Dutton (1899) to denote a state of balance at some level in the earth's crust. Dutton argued that the loss of altitude arising as a mountain mass was denuded would be partly made good by the rise of the eroded mass due to the slow inflow of material below the area — the isostatic balance was restored. The basic concept of a supporting medium below the outer crust was thus established long before modern seismology demonstrated the Mohorovičić discontinuity and the existence of earthshells of different compositions.

In 1931 and 1938, W. Heiskanen re-stated the Airy hypothesis of isostasy and put it on a workable basis. This version has received confirmation from work in the Alps and, with some modifications, enters present-day concepts. It gives a rather better agreement between observed and calculated values of gravity than does the Pratt hypothesis. This difference between the observed and calculated values of gravity at any place is known as the *gravity anomaly* for that place; it can be positive or negative according to which of the two values is the greater. Gravity is determined by accurately timing the swings of a pendulum.

The work of Vening Meinesz in 1931 and onwards in making gravity determinations over the sea-floor from submarines, notably off the East Indies and in the Atlantic, has greatly increased our knowledge of the distribution of gravity anomalies over large areas, and has revealed the existence of tracts having high *negative anomalies*, corresponding to deficiency of mass. The results of Vening Meinesz' observations off the East Indies are summarised in Fig. 19. From this it can be seen that a narrow belt — less than 200 kms. wide and some 4000 kms. long — characterised by negative anomalies runs parallel to the Sumatra-Java-Flores arc of islands. This negative belt is flanked on either side by bands of positive anomalies. The arrangement is clearly one of marked isostatic inequilibrium; it has been interpreted as due to a *down-buckling* by which light sialic material is thickened in the strip to give the negative anomalies, and a complementary up-arching of dense simatic material along its flanks to produce there the positive anomalies. On this interpretation the anomalies result from a horizontal compression in the crust with the forcing-down of the light sial into the heavy sima — it will be recalled that this region is one in which deep-focus earthquakes are well-known and that these are likely to arise from movement along low-angled thrust-planes. Whatever the mechanism of their formation, the zones of isostatic inequilibrium are zones of instability and they contrast with the stable areas of the crust, such as the Canadian shield, where most gravity anomalies can be directly related to variation in the nature of the local rocks.

It is believed that large topographic features, such as continents, mountain plateaux, and oceanic basins, exist by virtue of isostatic balance; that is, the larger irregularities of the crust are compensated. But smaller mountains and valleys are not so compensated; they exist because of the rigidity of the sial, which is strong enough to support local irregularities of loading. But, none-the-less, any geological change disturbs the equilibrium. When a region of high altitude is being eroded, and sediment is carried by rivers and other agents and deposited outside the area of erosion, the resulting transference of load — removal at one place and deposition at another — tends to upset the isostatic equilibrium. This must be slowly restored by flow in the underlying sima from regions of increasing load to those of diminishing load. A case in point is that of the carving of deep valleys through the Himalayas, a comparatively youthful mountain range, by streams flowing south. Several deep gorges through the mountains have been cut by these streams and geological evidence has shown that while they were cutting their valleys down, the area was slowly rising. Thus, as the mountain load was reduced by erosion and transferred to the Gangetic plain

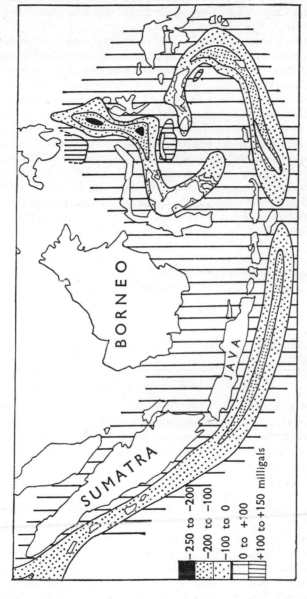

Fig. 19. Gravity map of the East Indies (after Vening Meinesz).

-250 to -200
-200 to -100
-100 to 0
0 to +100
+100 to +150 milligals

33

where the river-transported sediment was deposited, the weaker sima underlying the sial was responding and tending to restore isostatic balance.

Another example is found in the vertical movements which have affected areas once covered by the great ice-sheets of the Pleistocene Period (p. 293). When the ice, several kilometres thick, as in Greenland at the present day, covered the land-areas of the northern hemisphere, its weight constituted a load which depressed the crust below it into the underlying substratum. At the close of the glaciation, the load was taken off during the melting out of the ice-sheets, and the depressed areas began to rise again. This was a very slow process and one probably continuing to the present day. Evidence of this rise of the land relative to the sea is provided by the raised beaches which exist around many of the coasts of Britain and elsewhere. The beaches were formed at the margins of the late-glacial or post-glacial seas, and were then elevated to their present positions when isostatic uplift took place.

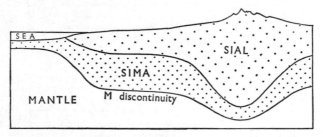

Fig. 20. Sialic continents floating isostatically in sima.

Origin and history of the continental masses. From what has been said already, the continents appear to be masses of sialic material buoyed up in a simatic substratum — the conditions being those shown in Fig. 20. The general opinion is that the sialic material was originally continuous and the problem therefore arises of its present concentration into the disconnected continental bodies. Various suggestions have been put forward as solutions of this problem. It is proposed that, during the immense span of earth-history, the original thin sialic layer has been folded and crumpled together to form thick discontinuous bodies. Another view is that a sort of sialic scum has been collected into the continental masses by deeper-seated convection currents, and yet another theory supposes that part of the original sialic layer has been abstracted from the earth by the escape of the moon. A radically different proposal denies that the sialic layer was ever continuous. The problem of the discontinuous continents is one of the greatest in geology and seems incapable of solution at present.

A further problem is that of the *permanence* of the continental masses. The ancient marine sediments which are found far in the interior of the continents — even in the high Himalayan ranges — are essentially deposits of fairly shallow seas. Few, if any, deposits of the true ocean basins are found in the continents. Most geologists favour the view that the evolution of the continental masses has followed a different course from that of the great ocean basins and that oceanic crust has not been extensively transformed into continental crust or *vice versa*. This view, however, does not imply that the continents and oceans have necessarily remained in fixed positions. The hypothesis of *continental drift* envisages the lateral movement of sialic rafts over the simatic substratum, bringing about progressive changes in the positions of the continents relative to each other and to the north and south poles. At some periods, the continents appear to have been massed into one or two very large bodies; at others, they were dispersed over the globe. These ideas will be discussed later when the arguments for and against them will be better appreciated (pp. 643–8 and Volume 2).

Mobile and stable regions of the crust. We have seen that the extreme heights and depths of the earth's surface are arranged in linear belts which make mountain chains and oceanic trenches. Features of these types, together with some other distinctive topographical forms such as island arcs, are at the present day linked into two systems which encircle the globe; these are the *circum-Pacific* and *Alpine-Himalayan* belts already referred to. Both belts are characterised by geophysical anomalies of various kinds. They are regions of seismic activity; they include the sites of all the recorded deep-focus earthquakes; they often show positive or negative gravity anomalies; and they are frequently subject to volcanic activity. It is evident that their topographical peculiarities are only the superficial expression of a state of instability affecting the crust and the underlying mantle. We may term the circum-Pacific and Alpine-Himalayan zones *mobile belts* in contrast to the relatively *stable* tracts which make the remainder of the crust.

Geological evidence shows that mobile belts of the type represented today by the circum-Pacific and Alpine-Himalayan belts pass through a prolonged evolution, of which the early stages are marked by the accumulation of considerable thicknesses of sediment and the later stages by the upheaval of this sediment to make high mountain-belts. Mountain-building of this type is termed *orogenesis*; it is one of the most important geological processes we shall have to consider and its effects will be mentioned repeatedly in later chapters.

APPLIED GEOPHYSICS

Geophysical prospecting. As we have seen, the rocks of the crust vary in their physical properties such as density, magnetism, rigidity, compressibility and so forth. By the use of suitable instruments at the earth's surface, some of the variations can be measured and the results interpreted to give information concerning the distribution and arrangement of certain types of rocks at deeper levels. The application of geophysics to the search for useful mineral deposits is called *geophysical prospecting*; between two and three hundred million dollars a year are spent on such investigations. Four chief methods are employed, depending on gravity, magnetism, the reflection and refraction of artificial earthquake waves, and the electrical conductivity of rocks. A significant variation in the physical properties of the rocks of the area under investigation is called an *anomaly* (cf. p. 31).

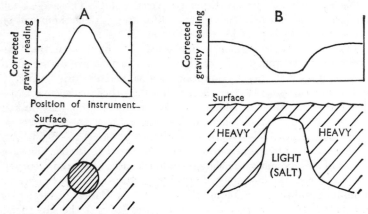

Fig. 21. Gravity surveying: A, over a buried heavy sphere; B, over a light salt plug.

Gravity method. Variations in the value of gravity measured at the surface, whilst depending fundamentally on latitude, topography and the broad constitution of the earth, are also produced by irregularities in the distribution of rocks of different densities within relatively shallow depths of the crust. By making the appropriate corrections, the effects of this irregular distribution can be separated out and used to provide information concerning the nature and arrangement of concealed rocks. Folding of the rocks of the crust may arch up dense rocks or crease down light rocks; the presence of a volcanic plug or a dome of salt will modify the value of gravity over the area; a fracture or fault in the strata may bring rocks of different densities together. By systematic measurement of gravity with the use of instruments known as *gravity meters* or *gravimeters* — essentially spring-balances — the gravity anomalies resulting from these and other geological factors can be mapped and the distribution of density over the investigated field determined. The geophysical data thus obtained are ready for interpretation as exemplified in Fig. 21.

The *intensity* of the gravitational field is measured in *milligals*, a milligal being a thousandth part of a gal (after Galileo), which is an acceleration of 1 cm./sec./sec. A milligal is about one millionth of the normal gravitational acceleration at the earth's surface, and many anomalies of interest to geologists are not more than 10 milligals in size.

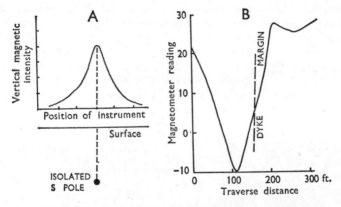

FIG. 22. Magnetic surveying: A, variation in magnetic intensity over an idealised south pole; B, variation across the contact of the Armathwaite dyke, of igneous rock (*right*) with sedimentary rocks (*left*). (After Bruckshaw.)

Magnetic methods. Some minerals, for example magnetite (Fe_3O_4), pyrrhotite (Fe_nS_{n+1}) and ilmenite ($FeO.TiO_2$), are highly magnetic and may be common enough in certain types of igneous rocks to make the rocks themselves appreciably so. The location of bodies of magnetic ore, or the arrangement of a hidden mass of magnetic igneous rock, may be determined by the systematic mapping of the magnetic field over the area under investigation. The unit of measurement of the intensity of the magnetic field is the gamma, equal to 10^{-5} gauss, a gauss being a force of one dyne acting on a unit pole. The instruments used in magnetic prospecting are essentially

pivoted magnets, such as the simple *dip-needle* and the more complicated *magnetometer* or *variometer*. An example of the results is given
in Fig. 22. Corrections of the observed values are applied for the daily
variations in the earth's field and for the much greater changes due
to magnetic storms. Nowadays, rapid magnetic surveys are made by
the use of airborne magnetometers, towed behind an aeroplane or
built into its tail. In such surveys, the powerful magnetic field of the
earth is for the most part masked, so that anomalies of a small order
can be detected. The interpretation of a magnetic anomaly largely
depends on a knowledge of the regional and local geology.

Seismic prospecting. Artificial earthquake waves are used for
finding the depths of buried surfaces. Where a surface separates two
kinds of rocks having different physical properties, the behaviour of
elastic vibrations which are reflected from it gives information from
which its depth can be found. The vibrations are generated by
exploding a charge placed in a bore-hole a little below ground-level,
and detectors, fundamentally the same as seismographs, are set at
different distances from the point of explosion. By means of electrical
timing, the travel-times are obtained for waves which go down to
the buried surface and back again, to be picked up by the detectors
or *geophones*. From these travel-times, the depth can be calculated.
This *reflection-shooting* method has been used in Great Britain in
recent years in the search for petroleum, and has led not only to the

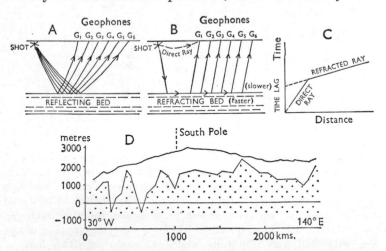

FIG. 23. Seismic surveying: A, reflection shooting; B, refraction
shooting; C, time-distance curve; D, Seismic traverse across Antarctica
showing thickness of the ice-sheet (based on Pratt, *Trans-antarctic
Expedition 1958*).

discovery of oil, as at Eakring near Nottingham, and at several localities in the North Sea, but also to a more detailed knowledge of the underground structure of many areas. The same method was employed by the Commonwealth Transantarctic Expedition in 1958 to determine the thickness of the Antarctic ice-sheet. The principle is illustrated in Fig. 23.

Not all the wave-energy is reflected at a buried boundary surface. Some is transmitted along *refracted* paths. When the angle of incidence is the critical angle for the two layers, the wave travels along the surface between them and is refracted up again to the geophones. A *time-distance* curve (Fig. 23) is thus obtained, made up of two parts: one is due to the wave travelling direct from the explosion-point to the nearest geophone, and the other is due to refracted waves picked up by the array of geophones. From this curve, the time-lag is obtained, and since the velocities in the two layers are determined, the depth of the boundary surface can be calculated. We may refer back to the determination of the thickness of the crustal layers from observations of natural earthquakes. Boundary surfaces that are not horizontal are investigated by *refraction-shooting* of this kind both up and down the surface.

Electrical methods. The electrical conductivity, or its reciprocal the *resistivity*, varies in different rocks, the differences arising not only from the inherent characters of the rocks but also from their position with respect to the earth's surface. The resistivity is the electrical resistance of a centimetre cube to current flowing parallel to one edge. The *effective resistivity* of a rock depends overwhelmingly on the pore-liquids contained in it, since the minerals themselves are insulators. The resistivity is smaller in rocks with much liquid in their pores and is also smaller when this liquid is salt. Since loose sediments, gravels sands and the like, contain much water in their pores, and are therefore much better conductors than the compact bedrock on which they may lie, *resistivity surveys* are especially valuable in finding the thickness of such a cover on bedrock. This is often of great importance in engineering geology in connection with the siting of dams and other heavy structures. The electrical currents used in these methods are either natural or, more often, artificial. In the latter case, the current is passed through shallow layers of rocks from two metal spikes, the *electrodes*, driven into the ground; its paths between the electrodes take up the pattern shown in Fig. 24. The resistivity is obtained by placing a second pair of electrodes suitably disposed between the other two and measuring the voltage drop between them. Two methods are available in resistivity surveys, the first for vertical variations and the second for horizontal. In the

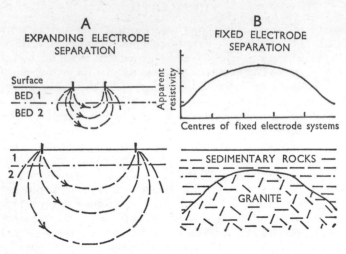

FIG. 24. Resistivity Surveying: A, expanding electrode separation; B, fixed electrode separation.

first method, distances between the electrodes can be regularly increased along a line about a fixed centre — as the *electrode separation* is increased, the current reaches deeper and the resistivity can be obtained for different levels so that, by a routine calculation, the depth of a boundary surface can be obtained. In the second method, the electrodes are moved over the area under investigation with their separation kept constant. In this way lateral differences in resistivity are observed and the shape of the boundary surface can be obtained (Fig. 24).

Many ore-deposits consisting of metallic sulphides have been discovered by the use of *electromagnetic methods*. In one of these, an alternating current is passed through a loop of cable lying on the ground and sets up induction currents in any conducting bodies of ore in the vicinity. These induced currents are measured at the surface and provide information that enables the ore-body to be located. Recently, the induction method has been used in *airborne electro-magnetic* surveys, a transmitting coil being contour-flown in a helicopter.

Natural currents of *electrochemical origin* produced by the oxidation of certain masses of metallic sulphide ores lying not far below the surface can be detected at the surface and so lead to the discovery of the ore-body.

In *electrical well-logging* the technique already mentioned of resistivity survey using electrodes a constant distance apart is employed to determine the resistivities of all the various beds encountered in a bore-hole. Instead of being horizontal, the traverse is now vertical,

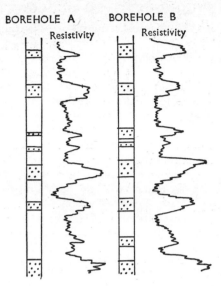

FIG. 25. Correlation by electrical well-logging.

the electrodes being lowered down the hole (Fig. 25). The resistivities are measured continuously and the continuous record — the *Schlumberger log* — thus obtained can be compared with that for neighbouring holes. In this way a means is provided of matching or *correlating* the beds met in the different holes. *Self-potential logging* utilises the different natural potentials of different beds in the borehole. In this method, one electrode is fixed at the top of the bore-hole and a second lowered down it, the voltage differences being measured on a continuous record.

GEOCHEMISTRY

Geochemistry deals with two main topics: first, the chemical composition of the earth as a whole and of its constituent parts, the earth shells, the rocks and the minerals, and all the naturally occurring earth materials, and second, the chemical processes that control the distribution of the elements in space and time. This second topic is touched upon in later pages and now we are to be concerned with the chemical composition of the earth and of its major parts.

Chemical composition of the earth. We have seen that the earth can be divided into its various shells or zones, these being from within outwards, the core, mantle, crust, hydrosphere and atmosphere. Suggestions were made on the constitution of these shells and

41

now we can discuss the chemical composition of certain of them and of the earth as a whole.

The *core,* some 3500 kms. radius, is considered to be made of nickel-iron alloy and its composition may be taken as 90·78 per cent iron, 8·59 per cent nickel, 0·63 per cent cobalt — this being the average composition of iron meteorites as estimated by Brown and Patterson. The *mantle*, about 3000 kms. thick, has been assumed to be of peridotite. Suggestions have been advanced that in its deepest parts it may be mixed with a nickel-iron alloy of core type or may even be of a kind of oxide-sulphide matte similar to that formed in some smelting processes. Objections can be raised against both these suggestions and, for our immediate purpose, we may take a mantle composition of peridotite. For comparison, we give in the Table below the average composition of 23 analysed crustal peridotites according to Nockolds. Coming to the *crust*, we have seen that it is likely to be made of simatic and sialic materials differing in relative proportions in different segments of the crust. In the Table below are given the averages of 198 basalts and 546 granites computed by Daly; these averages can be taken as approximations to the composition of the two crustal layers. The discontinuous and thin sedimentary cover forming the outermost skin of the crust has been estimated by Poldervaart to have the composition given in the Table. On the assumption that the crust is isostatically adjusted and that the various crustal columns have the constitutions proposed by seismologists, Poldervaart has also suggested that the chemical composition of the crust may be that given in the Table. These different sets of figures are worth examining from various aspects, some of which we now consider.

	SiO_2	TiO_2	Al_2O_3	Fe_2O_3	FeO	MnO	MgO	CaO	Na_2O	K_2O	P_2O_5	CO_2
Peridotite	43·9	0·8	4·0	2·5	9·9	0·2	34·3	3·5	0·6	0·2	0·1	—
Basalt	49·9	1·4	16·0	5·4	6·5	0·3	6·3	9·1	3·2	1·5	0·4	—
Granite	70·8	0·4	14·6	1·6	1·8	0·1	0·9	2·0	3·5	4·1	0·2	—
Sediment	44·5	0·6	10·9	4·0	0·9	0·3	2·6	19·7	1·1	1·9	0·1	13·4
Crust	55·2	1·6	15·3	2·8	5·8	0·2	5·2	8·8	2·9	1·9	0·3	—

Many estimates of the chemical composition of the *earth as a whole* have been made, these being based on different assumptions concerning the constitution and dimensions of core, mantle and crust. Mason has pointed out that core and mantle together amount to over 99 per cent of the earth's mass and, taking the core to have the composition of iron-meteorites and the mantle of peridotite with some sulphide, he has provided the following figures, in percentages of elements, for the whole earth.

Fe 35, O 28, Mg 17, Si 13, Ni 2·7, S 2·7, Ca 0·61, Al 0·44
Co 0·2, Na 0·14, Mn 0·09, K 0·07, Ti 0·04, P 0·08, Cr 0·01

It should be noted that from this estimate, four elements make up 93 per cent of the whole earth, a dozen more occur in small amounts and the rest must be in minute quantities. Since geologists are primarily concerned with the crust, it is worth while giving Mason's estimate of the order of relative abundance of the fourteen most common elements in the crust. It is: O Si Al Fe Ca Na K Mg Ti H P Mn S C.

We can follow this up by looking at the distribution of the elements in the outer part of the crust accessible to the observations of geologists. As already mentioned in Chapter 1, the standard classes of rocks are the igneous (including plutonic), sedimentary and metamorphic — the last two being ultimately derived from the first. Accordingly, the average composition of the igneous rocks can be taken to represent that of the accessible part of the crust. Many thousands of chemical analyses of igneous rocks have been made. Taking into consideration the areas at the surface which are occupied by different igneous rocks and thus deriving a weighted average, Clarke and Washington calculated the average composition of such rocks, expressed in oxides as usually returned in a chemical analysis; this average is given in the table below.

Average Igneous Rock		Weight Percentage		Volume Percentage
SiO_2	59·12	O	46·60	93·77
Al_2O_3	15·34	Si	27·72	0·86
Fe_2O_3	3·08	Al	8·13	0·47
FeO	3·80	Fe	5·00	0·43
MgO	3·49	Ca	3·63	1·03
CaO	5·08	Na	2·83	1·32
Na_2O	3·84	K	2·59	1·83
K_2O	3·13	Mg	2·09	0·29
H_2O	1·15		98·59	100·00
TiO_2	1·05			
P_2O_5	0·30			
MnO	0·12			

This average can be subjected to a certain amount of criticism but its main outlines are fundamentally correct. It reveals that eight oxides make together almost 97 per cent of the average igneous rock, an abundance broadly true for the outer crust as a whole. Expressed in terms of elements, this becomes still more evident, as shown in the table. The eight elements, O, Si, Al, Fe, Ca, Na, K and Mg account for nearly 99 per cent by weight of the average crustal rock; their percentages by volume can be calculated by use of their atomic radii (see p. 55), and these proportions are also given. Several comments on these remarkable figures are necessary.

First, the predominance of oxygen, both by weight and especially by volume, means that the accessible crust is largely made of atoms of this element between which are arranged the seven less abundant elements on the list. Secondly, the common mineral constituents of the surface rocks must accordingly be oxygen compounds, either silicates or oxides of the six common metallic elements. Lastly, elements other than the common eight must occur in minute quantity — we can therefore classify the elements into two groups:

Major Elements — O Si Al Fe Ca Na K Mg
Trace Elements — all others.

The relative abundance of the trace elements can be assessed in various ways, especially by spectrographic analysis. The estimated abundance of the more common trace elements is the following:

Ti 0·44, H 0·14, P 0·12, Mn 0·10, S 0·05, C 0·03, Cl 0·03 per cent.

It will be noted that so far in this discussion of relative abundance, most of the elements, especially the metals, that are useful and indeed essential for modern industry, are absent. These useful metals must be concentrated by natural processes before they can become available to man as bodies of ore — such processes of concentration are described in Chapter 11. The estimated abundance of some representative useful metals is as follows: Cr ·02, Ni ·008, Cu ·007, Sn ·004, Co ·002, Pb ·002, As ·0005, U ·0004, Hg ·00005, Ag ·00001, Au ·0000005 per cent. The scarcity of such metals as copper, tin, lead, silver and gold should be noted.

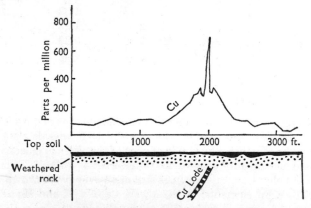

Fig. 26. Geochemical anomaly in soils above a concealed copper deposit, Northern Rhodesia (after Tombs).

Recently geochemical methods have been employed in the search for deposits of these useful metals — such methods constitute *geochemical prospecting* and are especially useful in mineral exploration in areas, such as the tropics, where the bedrocks may be obscured beneath a cover of vegetation or thick soil. Systematic estimates by rapidly applied tests are made of certain trace elements in the rocks, soils, stream-waters, river-deposits or vegetation of promising areas. As a result, *geochemical anomalies* may be revealed in which there is shown an abnormal concentration of particular trace elements as compared with the regional background amounts. The tests are easily carried out and are capable of detecting minute amounts of the trace elements; for example, such quantities of copper or zinc as small as ·002 parts per million can be determined in a few minutes. An example of a geochemical anomaly in the soils above a concealed copper deposit in Northern Rhodesia, revealed by geochemical prospecting, is given in Fig. 26. Geochemical soil-surveys and geochemical drainage surveys are now being commonly used.

We may recall that one of the fundamental principles of geology is that changes in the environment of a rock lead to reactions to restore equilibrium. Geochemistry is much concerned with the laws that control these reactions; it studies the distribution and migration of their constituent elements as rocks become subjected to a succession of geological processes. A grand *geochemical cycle* can be made to represent the changes that go on as rocks are subjected in the depths of the crust to high temperatures and pressures, resulting possibly in fusion, the migration of this fused material into higher levels and its solidification there, with subsequent upheaval to the surface where conditions of low temperatures and pressures prevail and sediments are formed — these sediments eventually return to the depths and the cycle is closed. If such broadly-sketched cycles have any value, it will be better appreciated when much more has been said about rocks, their origins and the geological processes that may operate on them.

EARLY HISTORY OF THE EARTH

The broad physical and chemical constitution of the earth has now been suggested and we may briefly examine some of the many theories of the origin of the solar system in so far as the production of a planet like our earth is involved.

In 1796, *Laplace* suggested that the primitive sun was a contracting mass of gas and dust, which threw off rings of matter from its equator as its speed of rotation increased. From these rings the planets were eventually formed. Laplace's hypothesis held the field for over a century, but when treated mathematically it was shown to be untenable; among many other defects, it failed to explain the distribution of angular momentum in the solar system. The planets possess about 98 per cent of the whole angular momentum, the sun only 2 per cent. This state of affairs would not be brought about by any process of steady contraction.

Towards the close of the last century, two American scientists, T. C. Chamberlin and F. R. Moulton, proposed their *Planetesimal Hypothesis*, according to which the planets of the solar system were formed by the aggregation of fragments — *planetesimals* — derived from the disruption of two stars on their near approach to one another. One of the two stars was the primitive sun, on which tides were raised by the approach of the other star, and matter was pulled out from the tidal bulge. This theory was later modified by J. S. Jeans and H. Jeffreys, who substituted a grazing collision of the two stars for the near approach in the earlier theory. As a result of such a grazing contact, a filament of gaseous matter at high temperature would be drawn out from the sun and given a rotation about its parent by the gravitational effect of the other star before this passed out of range. The gaseous filament would cool rapidly and collect into knots which eventually formed the planets.

This hypothesis, often referred to as the *Tidal Disruption Theory*, and its predecessor have in the last score of years met with difficulties. These again arise in connection with the angular momentum of the system and the improbably high velocity of approach of the two stars which would be necessary to impart the right momentum to the planets. In order to overcome these difficulties, R. A. Lyttleton suggested that the collision out of which the solar system was born was between a *double star* — the primitive sun and a companion moving around it — and a third star. Hoyle has recently proposed a further modification in assuming that the companion star exploded and became a *nova*; all the fragments resulting from the explosion were lost to the system except an incandescent gaseous filament which condensed to form the planets, assisted by accretion from interstellar matter. Hoyle considers that at the high temperatures involved in this process, elements of low atomic weight would become transmuted to others of higher atomic weight, such as magnesium, aluminium, silicon, iron and lead, and thus provide matter of the right composition for the formation of the earth and the other planets.

Another approach has been made by American physicists, notably H. C. Urey; Urey visualises the development of stars from a *contracting cloud of interstellar dust and gas*. Of these stars, the sun was one. Residual gas and dust formed a disc around the primitive sun in the plane of the present ecliptic. The disc was unstable and broke up into large masses increasing in size with increasing distance from the sun. The further growth of these planetary bodies proceeded by the accumulation of large and small planetesimals at a low temperature. The planetesimals were mixtures of silicates with some metallic iron, water and ammonia, accumulated from the fine dust of the primitive planetary bodies. Condensation of water and ammonia provided coagulating agents and served to promote the process. One of the objects so formed, at a low temperature, was the moon. Later, adiabatic compression of the gases of the primitive planets raised the temperatures of their interiors. According to Urey's theory, the earth and the other planets were formed at much lower temperatures than is generally thought to have been the case. Urey suggests, also, that the earth has acquired its nickel-iron core during geological time from a roughly uniform mixture of iron and silicates: the iron has gradually sunk through the mantle towards the centre, and the present core is in a liquid state. Meteorites may be the remains of planetesimals which failed to accumulate into a planet — they consist, as we have seen, of iron, nickel and silicates.

In the theory of Von Weizsächer, the primitive sun is considered to have moved into a *dense cloud of solid particles and gas* in turbulent motion, and to have attracted this material into a gigantic envelope about it. Von Weizsächer proposes that the planets are formed by condensation within this envelope. The passage of stars through diffuse nebular clouds is not an unlikely event and this theory has much to commend it.

Whether the earth was born of solid planetesimals or of gaseous material, it is likely that at some stage it was a hot homogeneous molten mass surrounded by a gaseous envelope. Its composition, as we have seen, was dominantly Fe, O, Mg, Si, with less abundant Ni, S, Ca, Al and Na. There was insufficient oxygen to give oxidised compounds throughout, so that the heavy, less-easily oxidised elements such as Fe and Ni concentrated in the interior, and the more-easily oxidised ones in the outer parts. Thus a *primary differentiation* gave a liquid FeNi core with a liquid silicate shell about it. As cooling proceeded, solidification in the mantle began at its base by the crystallisation of the heavy high-temperature minerals, olivine and pyroxene, rich in Fe and Mg and poor in Si. An enrichment of the crustal material in Al, Ca, Na, Si and K consequently took place. With solidification of this material, the *second differentiation* concluded with the formation of an outer thin granitic layer resting on a basaltic layer below. We have already mentioned possible ways in which this original thin sialic crustal skin might have been collected into the thick discontinuous continental masses.

The primitive atmosphere most likely consisted of the residual parts of the primary gaseous envelope reinforced by gases expelled from the liquid layers as they crystallised. It is suggested that it consisted largely of H_2O and CO_2; free atmospheric oxygen may have been subsequently produced by photochemical reactions. When the critical temperature and pressure of water had been reached, the first rains fell upon the earth, the hydrosphere was initiated and the geological history of the earth began.

THE AGE OF THE EARTH AND OF ITS COMPONENTS

The age of the universe is not the direct concern of the geologist and all we need do here is to record that on various astronomical and geochemical grounds this age is considered to lie between 3000 and 5000 million years, the latter figure resulting from the recent reassessment of certain astronomical data. Determinations of the age of some meteorites give figures averaging 4500 million years. The time since the formation of the earth's crust is suggested to be about 4000 million years. These are ages outside the geologist's time-span, and what he is more immediately interested in is the accurate dating, in terms of years, of crustal rocks. Before considering methods of achieving this end, we may mention that the absolute age of the oldest dated rock is possibly 3,500 million years — this gives a minimum age for the formation of the earth's crust.

Various geological methods, now discredited, have been proposed for measuring the duration of geological time. If we could estimate the volume of the sedimentary rocks and the rate of the erosion or sedimentation that was responsible for them, we could calculate the age of the oldest sediment. Again, assuming that the ocean was originally fresh, we could suggest its age by estimating its volume and its sodium content and the amount of sodium annually carried into it by rivers. Innumerable criticisms of such methods immediately arise, apart from the inaccuracy of the assumptions and estimates involved. The chief of these is that it is by no means certain that the rate of geological processes such as erosion and deposition is constant. Indeed, there is evidence of local rhythms in earth-history, short periods of rapid erosion, for example, alternating with long periods of gentle erosion.

These two examples have served to make it clear that what is needed is some change that is going on at a constant rate which has not varied in the past, and of which it is possible to measure the total effect as well as the rate of change. Radioactive disintegration is such a process and provides a means of measuring geological time that is of great promise. The *half-life period* of a radioactive element is the time taken for it to be reduced to one half as a consequence of radioactive decay.

At present, three transformations are employed in *radiometric* or *isotopic* age-determinations, (1) uranium and thorium into lead and helium, (2) potassium into argon and (3) rubidium into strontium. There is no need here to give details of the complex chemical and physical operations that are involved in age-determinations and the following brief statement is sufficient for our purpose.

Uranium, consisting of a mixture of two isotopes, U^{238} and U^{235}, breaks down with the emission of various particles or rays into lead isotopes with the atomic weights of 206 and 207, together with helium. Thorium undergoes a similar transformation with the liberation of helium and the formation of lead of atomic weight 208. These transformations may be represented thus:

$$U^{238} \rightarrow Pb^{206} + 8He^4 + energy$$
$$U^{235} \rightarrow Pb^{207} + 7He^4 + energy$$
$$Th^{232} \rightarrow Pb^{208} + 6He^4 + energy$$

No known change in the physical environment seems to be able to alter the rate of these transformations. This rate is known and therefore the determination of the amount of uranium and thorium and of their stable derivatives, Pb^{208}, Pb^{207} and Pb^{206}, or helium, gives the data for calculating the age of a mineral containing uranium and thorium. Many corrections and refinements are of course necessary to yield the most reliable results.

The second transformation, that of potassium of atomic weight 40 into argon of the same atomic weight, is becoming of increasing value in age determinations, especially of igneous rocks. Common constituents of many of these rocks are the potassium-bearing minerals, feldspar and micas. The micas, especially the varieties lepidolite and biotite, are also used in the rubidium-strontium method in which the transformation is from rubidium of atomic weight 87 to strontium also of 87.

Organic matter, such as wood, can be dated up to an age of about 70,000 years by the determination of the ratio of radiocarbon — carbon of atomic weight 14 — to ordinary carbon of atomic weight 12, found in the material. This method is useful in dating archeological periods and, for the geologist, episodes in recent geological history.

In every case where the age of a mineral has been estimated by one of these methods, the geologist has still to determine what is the *geological age* of the dated material. This he does by the standard methods of geological study dealt with later in this book. As an example, the relations of an igneous rock, whose feldspar or mica has been dated, to the surrounding rocks provide evidence of an approximate geological age. Thus, the small Shap granite in the English Lake District has recently been determined by the K–Ar and Rb–Sr methods to be 380–95 million years old; geologically, this granite is found to intrude and bake rocks that the geologist refers to the Silurian division of geological time and the date of the intrusion is therefore post-Silurian; further, rocks dated by their fossils as Carboniferous lie unchanged on the granite which is therefore pre-Carboniferous. Between the Silurian and Carboniferous divisions of time there comes the Devonian period — it is inferred that some part of the Devonian is 380–95 million years old. By the development of these methods, the divisions of geological time have been approximately dated in terms of millions of years, as we see later on p. 293.

Moreover, it must always be remembered that what are being dated by the radioactive decay methods are minerals, and that a given rock may have a long and complex history during which the formation of its constituent minerals may be separated by great periods of time. Thus, in a metamorphic rock from the Eastern United States, the constituent zircon has been found to be 1100 million years old and the constituent biotite 300 million years old. Two widely separated episodes in the history of the rock are revealed. It is clear that investigations along these lines, now only in their infancy, may contribute greatly to the understanding of the events recorded in a rock. Geological control of the interpretation of age-determinations is always necessary.

Two proposed dates are worth mentioning. First, the oldest rock containing evidence of former life by the presence in it of undoubted fossils, is reckoned to be about 600 million years old. Second, as we have seen, the oldest rocks so far dated with reasonable accuracy are about 3500 million years old and we may conclude that *geological history began well over* 3500 *million years ago.*

SELECTED BIBLIOGRAPHY AND READING LIST

Geophysics

Clark, D., 1954, *Plane and Geodetic Surveying*, 4th edit., Constable, London, vol. 1.

Dobrin, M. B., 1952, *Introduction to Geophysical Prospecting*, McGraw-Hill, London.

Gutenberg, B., Editor, 1951, *Internal Constitution of the Earth*, 2nd edit., Dover Publications. Covers the field of the physics of the Earth.

Gutenberg, B., and C. F. Richter, 1954, *Seismicity of the Earth*, 2nd edit., Princeton Univ. Press.

Howell, B. F., 1959, *Introduction to Geophysics*, McGraw-Hill, London.

Jeffreys, H., 1959, *The Earth*, 4th edit., Cambridge Univ. Press, London. The latest edition of a standard work.

Benioff, H., 1955, Seismic evidence for crustal structure and tectonic activity, *The Crust of the Earth*, Spec. Paper 62, Geol. Soc. America, p. 61.

Blackett, P. M. S. and others, 1960, 'An analysis of rock-magnetic data', *Proc. Roy. Soc. A*, vol. 256, p. 291.

Bruckshaw, J. McG., 1948, 'The application of geophysics to geology', *Proc. Geol. Assoc.*, vol. 59, p. 113.

Meinesz, F. A. Vening, 1948, 'Major tectonic phenomena and the hypothesis of convection currents in the earth' (William Smith Lecture), *Quart. Journ. Geol. Soc.*, vol. 103, p. 191.

Oldham, R. D., 1900, 'On the propagation of earthquake motion to great distances', *Phil. Trans. A*, vol. 194, p. 135. A fundamental paper in seismology.

Smith, D. Taylor, 1954–5, Geophysical methods of oil prospecting, *Petroleum*, Oct., Dec., 1954, March, June, 1955.

Wager, L. R., 1937, 'The Arun River drainage pattern and the rise of the Himalaya', *Geographical Journal*, vol. 89, p. 239.

Geochemistry

Breger, I. A., 1963, *Organic Geochemistry*, Pergamon Press.

Clarke, F. W., 1924, 'Data of Geochemistry', *Bull. 770, United States Geol. Survey*. The final edition of the classic application of chemistry to geological processes and materials.

Hawkes, H. E. and J. S. Webb, 1962, *Geochemistry in Mineral Exploration*, Harper and Row, New York.

Mason, B., 1958, *Principles of geochemistry*, 2nd edit., Wiley, New York.

Nockolds, S. R., 1954, 'Average chemical composition of some igneous rocks', *Bull. Geol. Soc. America*, vol. 65, p. 1007.

Poldervaart, A., 1955, 'Chemistry of the earth's crust', *The Crust of the Earth*, Spec. Paper 62, Geol. Soc. America, p. 119.

Origin and age of the earth

Chamberlin, T. C., 1906, 'The Planetesimal Hypothesis', in Chamberlin, T. C., and R. D. Salisbury, *Geology: Earth History*, Murray, London, vol. II, chap. 1, p. 38. The first full statement, with illustrations.

Faul, H., Editor, 1954, *Nuclear Geology*, Wiley, New York.

Hoyle, F., 1950, The nature of the universe.

Libby, W. F., 1952, *Radio-carbon Dating*, Univ. of Chicago Press.

Urey, H. C., 1952, *The planets, their origin and development*, Oxford Univ. Press, London.

Holmes, A., 1959, 'A revised geological time-scale', *Trans. Edinburgh Geol. Soc.*, vol. 17, part 3, p. 183.

3

MINERALOGY

Rocks and minerals. As we saw in the first pages of this book, the rocks that the geologist deals with are aggregates of minerals, and the variety among rocks arises from the differences in the relative abundance and in the properties and relationships of their constituent minerals. For the geologist, minerals are thus of fundamental importance in that their study as constituents of rocks helps him in his main purpose, the interpretation of these records of earth-history. This study is **mineralogy**.

Definition of mineral. A mineral is a naturally formed, inorganic, substance which possesses a definite chemical composition and a definite atomic structure. But though minerals are definite chemical compounds or elements, expressible by a chemical formula, some restricted latitude is allowed. This follows from the remainder of the definition, the requirement of a definite atomic structure. Minerals are made up of atoms arranged in a regular three-dimensional pattern, which is significant for each mineral. But a particular pattern is not violently distorted or destroyed if the places of some of its atoms are taken by others of rather similar kind. Thus, the common mineral olivine has the chemical formula $(MgFe)_2SiO_4$ as established by innumerable chemical analyses; for all olivines the arrangement of the atoms is the same, but in different olivines different numbers of Mg atoms have been substituted by Fe atoms — the total number of atoms of Mg and Fe in all olivines has the same ratio to that of Si and O. This substitution of atoms by somewhat similar ones results in *isomorphism*, and is elaborated later. Finally, our definition includes *both* definite chemical composition *and* definite atomic structure. There are many examples of different minerals having the same chemical composition — their differences arise from their different atomic structures on which depend the diagnostic physical characters. A good example of this *polymorphism* is provided by the two minerals, diamond and graphite, both made of carbon atoms which are, however, arranged in quite different ways. The different arrangement of the same atoms controls the physical properties of the two minerals; the great strength of the bonding in the hardest known mineral, diamond, contrasts with the flimsy structure of the soft flaky mineral graphite. As we shall see repeatedly, the internal

52

atomic arrangement of the constituent atoms of a mineral has naturally a fundamental influence on its physical properties.

ATOMIC STRUCTURE OF MINERALS

As one consequence of their orderly internal structure, minerals often occur as *crystals*, that is, in forms bounded by plane surfaces arranged in a regular symmetrical manner. In 1665, Robert Hooke, Curator of Experiments to the Royal Society, showed that the various shapes of alum crystals could be reproduced by piling shot in regular patterns and thus foreshadowed both the atomic theory of matter and the structural architecture of crystals. More than a century later, in 1784, Haüy of the University of Paris, suggested that crystals were

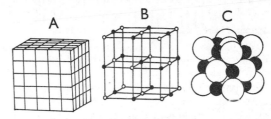

FIG. 27. A, Haüy's cube of rock-salt made up of cleavage cubes; B, Unit cell of rock-salt, sodium ions black, chlorine ions circles; C, Unit cell of rock-salt, with spheres proportional to the ionic radii of sodium (black) and chlorine (open).

built up of solid bricks or 'integral molecules', different arrangements of the bricks producing the different crystal forms shown by any one mineral. As another consequence of their internal structure, many minerals break into *cleavage-fragments* with a shape characteristic for each mineral. Haüy supposed that his 'integral molecules' were exceedingly minute cleavage-fragments (Fig. 27A). Later, with the development of the atomic theory, Haüy's concept of solid bricks was superseded by an open three-dimensional framework, the *space-lattice*, an arrangement of *points* representing the positions of atoms or groups of atoms. The smallest complete unit of the space-lattice is now called the *unit-cell*. Haüy's 'integral molecule' has become the unit-cell (Fig. 27B). During the nineteenth century, geometrical aspects of space-lattices were extensively studied, and speculations on the atomic arrangements compatible with the geometrical arrangements were made. But it was not until 1912 that Von Laue, by using crystals as three-dimensional diffraction gratings for X-rays, demonstrated the true nature of crystal structure.

Von Laue passed a narrow beam of X-rays through a crystal on to

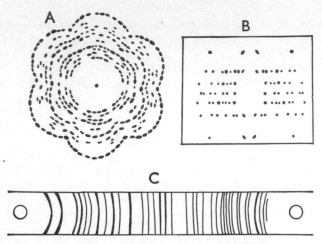

FIG. 28. A, Laue diagram of a hexagonal mineral, beryl; B, rotation diagram of an orthorhombic mineral; C, powder diagram of quartz.

a photographic plate (Fig. 28A); on the developed plate appeared a large number of spots, of differing intensities, arranged in a symmetrical pattern, the result of the diffraction of the rays by the various atomic planes present in the crystal edifice. The interpretation of the Laue pattern is a complicated process and more direct methods of investigating crystal structure are now available.

One of these is the *powder method* in which monochromatic X-rays, falling upon a cylinder made of minute, randomly orientated grains of the powdered crystal, are diffracted, the pattern being recorded on a circular photographic film (Fig. 28C). Since the minute crystal grains have all possible orientations, diffraction takes place on all the atomic planes present in the mineral. Most of the rays are scattered and produce no effect on the film but, for reasons which need not be gone into, grains showing a certain favourable orientation provide reflections from their internal planes which are of sufficient intensity to be recorded on the film. The pattern of lines appearing on the film is typical for each mineral and thus the powder method is especially useful in the identification of very fine-grained material. Another method of structural analysis, the *rotation method*, provides, like the powder method, data from which the dimensions of the unit-cell can be determined. A tiny crystal is rotated or oscillated about a vertical axis in a horizontal beam of monochromatic X-rays. As the crystal revolves, diffractions take place at successive atomic planes and are recorded on a circular photographic film (Fig. 28B).

The photographs obtained by these experiments show, as indicated crudely in Fig. 28, a number of spots or lines which have, first, a definite arrangement or spacing and, second, varying degrees of intensity. From the *positions* of the spots or lines, the size and shape of the unit-cell can be determined — the unit-cell, it will be remembered, being the basic pattern of the lattice whose repetition builds up the mineral. The lengths of the edges of the unit-cell, and other structural measurements, are given in Ångstrom units, one Ångstrom or Å being 10^{-8} cms. The *intensities* of the spots or lines depend upon the arrangement of the atoms of the constituent elements in the unit-cell, that is, on the way in which they are grouped around each geometrical point of the space-lattice. The constituent atoms may be arranged in several different ways in the one type of unit-cell; we can illustrate this point, and at the same time acquire a knowledge of symmetry, by examining the structure of a few common minerals. We shall see, too, that there are various types of unit-cells.

Atomic structure and crystal symmetry. According to the modern views, based on the Rutherford-Bohr theory of the structure of the atom developed in the early part of this century, an atom is considered to be constructed of a central *nucleus*, made up of *protons* and *neutrons*, which is surrounded by a number of smaller units called *electrons*. The protons carry positive electrical charges which equal the sum of the negative charges carried by the electrons, the whole atom being electrically neutral. The electrons revolve in orbits around the nucleus, so that the atom is a kind of minute model of our solar system. The size of the atom is determined by the radius of the orbit of the outermost electrons of the system and it becomes convenient in representing the structure of a mineral to use spheres differing in size according to the different sizes of the constituent atoms. This is illustrated in Fig. 27 which depicts the structure of rock-salt; the radius of Na is 0·98Å, that of chlorine is 1·81Å, so that the unit-cell can be considered to be packed with spheres of these two sizes in orderly arrangement. As we see later (p. 89), the atoms making a mineral can be held together in various ways. The commonest manner of this *bonding* in the rock-forming minerals is the *ionic*, in which each atom has lost or gained one or more electrons and has thereby become an *ion* and is no longer electrically neutral. In rock-salt, the Na ions have a single positive charge, the Cl ions a single negative charge, but the whole structure is electrically neutral since each ion is appropriately surrounded by ions of opposite charge.

We now examine the arrangement of the sodium and chlorine ions in the rock-salt structure in greater detail (Fig. 29). The Cl ions are situated at the corners of a cube and at the centres of the faces of the

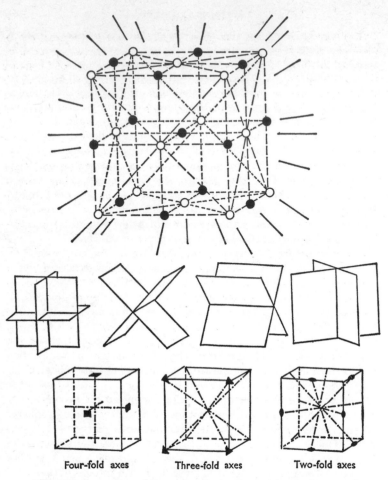

Four-fold axes   Three-fold axes   Two-fold axes

FIG. 29. Symmetry of the rock-salt structure: (*above*), planes and axes of symmetry; (*middle*), the planes dissected; (*below*), the axes dissected (the axes of symmetry can be best seen by lining up with a straight edge the appropriate rays shown in the upper diagram).

cube — the arrangement being that of a *face-centred cube*. The Na ions lie at the middle points of the cube edges and at the centre of the cube; their pattern is of course also that of a face-centred cube. Each face of the cube shown in the figure has the same number of ions arranged in the same way and there is no reason for selecting any particular face as front, side or top of the cube. In other words, the unit-cell of rock-salt is cubic, its edges are all equal and inter-changeable; its dimensions have been found to be 5·6402Å.

The regularity of the arrangement of the ions in the unit-cell of rock-salt gives the *symmetry of the structure*. This symmetry can be assessed in terms of three criteria. *First*, inspection of Fig. 29 shows that there are certain planes passing through the structure which divide it so that one half is the mirror image of the other half; these *planes of symmetry* are indicated and dissected for greater clarity in Fig. 29. *Second*, it will be seen that the structural edifice as a whole can be rotated around certain lines so that it presents the same appearance to the viewer more than once during a complete revolution. Thus, rotation about a line parallel to any one of the cube edges would cause the structure to take up the same position four times in a complete turn; this is expressed by saying the structure has 3 *axes*

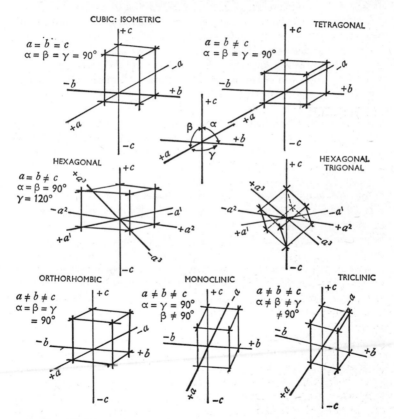

Fig. 30. Nomenclature of unit-cell types; crystallographic axes, notation connected with them and axial ratios. The top central small diagram gives the basic notation.

of four-fold symmetry. In addition, the structure has 4 axes of three-fold symmetry, rotation about which repeats the structure three times and 6 axes of two-fold symmetry with a two-times repetition, as indicated in the figure. *Third*, the structure has a *centre of symmetry*, in that the pattern of ions met along any line passing through any particular ion is the same on both sides of this ion. The symmetry of the atomic structure of rock-salt can therefore be expressed as: Planes of symmetry 9 : Axes of symmetry 3^{IV} 4^{III} 6^{II} : a Centre of symmetry.

Though many minerals have cubic unit-cells, their constituent ions may not be packed into them in the same arrangement as that shown by those of rock-salt, and such minerals will accordingly have different symmetries. Thus, zinc-blende, ZnS, and pyrite, FeS_2, both have cubic unit-cells but their structures differ from one another and from that of rock-salt. These structures are difficult to represent in diagrams but, as we see immediately, they are expressed in the shapes of the crystals of the minerals. From these crystals the symmetry can be readily determined, as shown later: for zinc-blende, it is Planes 6 : Axes 3^{II} 4^{III} : no Centre; for pyrite Planes 3 : Axes 3^{II} 4^{III} : a Centre.

These three minerals, rock-salt, blende and pyrite, with very different atomic arrangements, all possess a cubic unit-cell, defined by three equal edges meeting at right angles. Other minerals have other kinds of unit-cells. There are seven kinds of true or *primitive unit-cells* as shown in Fig. 30. The three edges of the unit-cells meeting at a point can be used as axes of reference to locate any structural plane in the edifice. Attention should be directed to the details of Fig. 30, such as the nomenclature of the cell-types, of the axes and of the angles between them; the *axial ratio* should also be noted; it is further illustrated under Tetragonal, Hexagonal and Orthorhombic in Fig. 35.

Atomic structure and crystal form. It has just been mentioned that as one consequence of their orderly internal structure, minerals often occur as *crystals*, that is, bodies bounded by plane surfaces or *faces* arranged in a symmetrical manner. When a mineral is formed, or *crystallises*, the atoms arrange themselves in the appropriate structural pattern unless, as in glasses, they are hindered by high viscosity.

The *faces* which bound a crystal are parallel to planes in the atomic edifice. The best-developed and most commonly occurring faces are those parallel to the structural planes which have the *highest reticular density* — that is, in which there lie the greatest number of lattice-points or ions. Further, it is obvious that growth will take place preferentially along rather than across planes which are widely separated from their parallel neighbours. Thus, in rock-

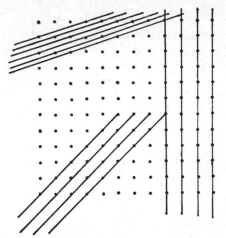

Fig. 31. Possible crystal faces and reticular density.

salt as shown in Fig. 31, other things being equal, we should expect crystal faces parallel to the sides of the unit-cell to occur more commonly and in better development than others.

It has already been mentioned that the position of any plane in the crystal edifice can be indicated by using the three edges of the unit-cell as axes of reference (Fig. 30). *Crystallographic notation* is a concise method of doing this in which *index numbers* or *indices* are used. In

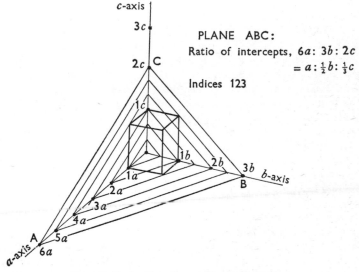

PLANE ABC:
Ratio of intercepts, $6a : 3b : 2c$
$= a : \frac{1}{2}b : \frac{1}{3}c$

Indices 123

Fig. 32. Derivation of crystallographic indices.

59

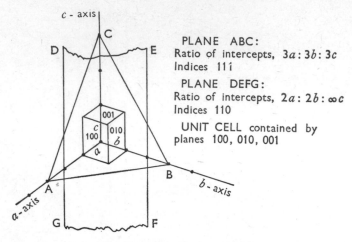

PLANE ABC:
Ratio of intercepts, $3a : 3b : 3c$
Indices 11ī

PLANE DEFG:
Ratio of intercepts, $2a : 2b : \infty c$
Indices 110

UNIT CELL contained by
planes 100, 010, 001

FIG. 33. Indices of various faces.

Fig. 32, a lattice is made up of repeated unit-cells with edges a, b, c, produced to form the a, b and c axes. The position of a plane, such as ABC, can be defined by the *ratio of the intercepts* made by the plane on the axes, the unit of measurement along each axis being the length of the appropriate cell-side: the plane ABC gives the ratio a, $\frac{1}{2}$b, $\frac{1}{3}$c. The more usual way of denoting the plane is to use the reciprocals of the intercepts; these are the *indices* and for the plane ABC are thus 123. These indices can be derived directly from Fig. 32 by noting the number of planes of ABC character that are crossed between two lattice-points along the a, b and c axes in turn. Along a, 1 plane is crossed, along b 2 planes, along c 3 planes, and the indices are accordingly 123 (read one, two, three). Further cases can now be considered (Fig. 33). First, a plane lying so that it intercepts the axes at unit distance along each will obviously have the symbol 111. Second, a plane parallel to an axis makes an infinite intercept along that axis, or to put it another way, no planes are crossed along that axis, and accordingly 0 (nought) appears in the appropriate place in the symbol; thus a plane parallel to the c-axis and to the diagonal of the unit-cell has the symbol 110. Lastly, if a plane is parallel to two axes, its symbol will be of the type 100, 010, 001, according to whether it intercepts the a, b or c axis.

It follows from the structural edifice of a crystal that the *indices* of all possible crystal faces *are rational whole numbers*. The commonest and best-developed faces usually have small indices; it is generally true, for example, that a face such as 111 is more commonly encountered than one such as 974. As another consequence of the

60

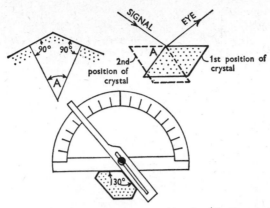

FIG. 34. The interfacial angle A; measured by the reflecting goniometer
(*above*) and contact goniometer (*below*).

structural foundation, the angle between particular faces is constant
for any one mineral. This *Law of the Constancy of Interfacial Angles* is
important in the identification and description of minerals from their
crystal shapes. The angle determined is actually that between the
perpendiculars to two intersecting faces; it is obtained by using
goniometers, either the contact-goniometer or the reflecting goniometer, the principles of which are illustrated in Fig. 34.

THE CLASSIFICATION OF CRYSTALS

We have already seen, as shown in Fig. 30, that there are seven kinds
of primitive unit-cells, the fundamental building units of crystals.
Accordingly, the first classification of crystals is into the *Crystal
Systems* by their primitive unit-cell types (Fig. 35). The extended
edges of the unit-cells can be used as *crystallographic axes* for the
location of crystal planes. In the next place, we have noted that one
particular kind of unit-cell can be packed with the constituent atoms
in various ways and thus produce a number of different symmetries
in the one crystal system. This provides the second step in the
classification of crystals, that into the *symmetry classes*. There are
mathematically possible thirty-two of these symmetry classes, but all
the minerals dealt with in this book fall into eleven classes.

There is no need here to give elaborate descriptions of the crystal
systems and symmetry classes, and it is sufficient to comment on the
information contained in Fig. 35, which should be carefully studied
and collated. First, note that the crystal systems are arranged in order
of decreasing symmetry, from the Cubic or Isometric with many planes
and axes of symmetry down to the Triclinic which has only a centre of
symmetry. Next, with regard to the crystallographic axes, compare

ISOMETRIC

$a^1 = a^2 = a^3$
$a^1 \wedge a^2 \wedge a^3 = 90°$

Cube (100)
Octahedron (111)

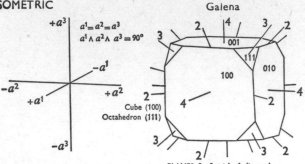

Galena

PLANES 9, 3 axial, 6 diagonal
AXES 13, 3 4-fold, 4 3-fold, 6 2-fold
CENTRE

Pyrite

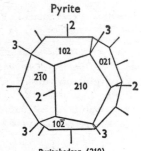

Pyritohedron (210)
PLANES 3 axial
AXES 7, 4 3-fold, 3 2-fold
CENTRE

Tetrahedrite

Tetrahedron (111)
PLANES 6 diagonal
AXES 7, 4 3-fold, 3 2-fold
[or 1 4-fold inversion axis
4 3-fold axes]
NO CENTRE

TETRAGONAL

$a^1 = a^2 \neq c$
$a^1 \wedge a^2 \wedge c = 90°$

$a : c = 1$: axial ratio

Zircon

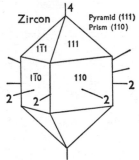

Pyramid (111)
Prism (110)

PLANES 5, 3 axial, 2 vertical diagonal
AXES 5, 1 4-fold, 4 2-fold
CENTRE

FIG. 35. The crystal systems

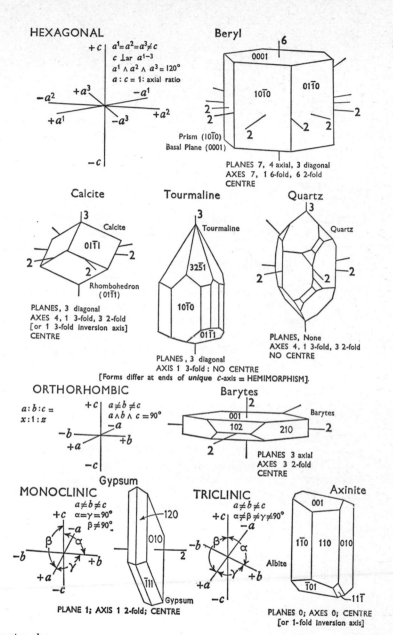

HEXAGONAL

$a^1 = a^2 = a^3 \neq c$
$c \perp$ar a^{1-3}
$a^1 \wedge a^2 \wedge a^3 = 120°$
$a : c = 1$: axial ratio

Beryl

0001

$10\bar{1}0$ $01\bar{1}0$

Prism ($10\bar{1}0$)
Basal Plane (0001)

PLANES 7, 4 axial, 3 diagonal
AXES 7, 1 6-fold, 6 2-fold
CENTRE

Calcite

Calcite

$01\bar{1}1$

Rhombohedron
($01\bar{1}1$)

PLANES, 3 diagonal
AXES 4, 1 3-fold, 3 2-fold
[or 1 3-fold inversion axis]
CENTRE

Tourmaline

Tourmaline

$32\bar{5}1$

$10\bar{1}0$

$01\bar{1}1$

PLANES, 3 diagonal
AXIS 1 3-fold : NO CENTRE
[Forms differ at ends of *unique* *c*-axis = HEMIMORPHISM].

Quartz

Quartz

PLANES, None
AXES 4, 1 3-fold, 3 2-fold
NO CENTRE

ORTHORHOMBIC

$a : b : c =$
$x : 1 : z$

$a \neq b \neq c$
$a \wedge b \wedge c = 90°$

Barytes

001
102 210

Barytes

PLANES 3 axial
AXES 3 2-fold
CENTRE

MONOCLINIC

$a \neq b \neq c$
$\alpha = \gamma = 90°$
$\beta \neq 90°$

Gypsum

120

010

$\bar{1}11$

Gypsum

PLANE 1; AXIS 1 2-fold; CENTRE

TRICLINIC

$a \neq b \neq c$
$\alpha \neq \beta \neq \gamma \neq 90°$

Albite

Axinite

001

$1\bar{1}0$ 110 010

$\bar{1}01$

$11\bar{1}$

PLANES 0; AXES 0; CENTRE
[or 1-fold inversion axis]

and symmetry classes.

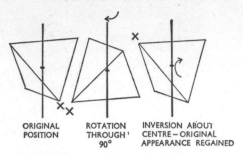

ORIGINAL POSITION — ROTATION THROUGH 90° — INVERSION ABOUT CENTRE – ORIGINAL APPEARANCE REGAINED

FIG. 36. Inversion-axis.

them with the edges of the unit-cells drawn in Fig. 30. The nomenclature of the crystallographic axes should be studied, their lettering, and that of the angles between them, and the convention concerning positive and negative directions along them. Instead of the extension of the unit-cell edges it is convenient to employ three equal horizontal interchangeable axes in the hexagonal and trigonal systems, the fourth axis being perpendicular to the plane containing these three. Further, the eleven symmetry classes dealt with are given names from common minerals occurring in them. The symmetry of each class is tabulated. In the drawings of crystals illustrating each symmetry class it is convenient to show axes of symmetry rather than planes and this necessitates a few new terms for describing symmetry. Thus, in the Tetrahedrite Class, a four-fold *inversion axis* (Fig. 36) indicates that rotation through 90° about this vertical axis, combined with inversion about a point at the centre of the crystal, results in the same appearance — in a complete turn this occurs 4 times. Again, a one-fold inversion axis is the same criterion of symmetry as a centre of symmetry, a two-fold inversion axis is equivalent to a plane of symmetry, and a three-fold inversion axis to an ordinary three-fold axis together with a centre of symmetry. In drawings of crystals a minus sign over an axis indicates an inversion axis.

We have already mentioned the *faces*, the smooth surfaces bounding a crystal. If the faces of a crystal are all of one kind then a *form* is produced; thus all faces of a cube of rock-salt are alike and the cube is a crystal form. Some forms such as the cube can enclose space by themselves and are said to be *closed*; other forms called *open* cannot enclose space by themselves and additional forms must be present to complete the crystal. A crystal that consists of two or more forms is called a *combination*. The names of some of the common forms in the different symmetry classes are given in the drawings of crystals of minerals shown in Figs. 35, 37. Indices are placed on some of the crystal faces of the crystals shown and should be studied and verified.

64

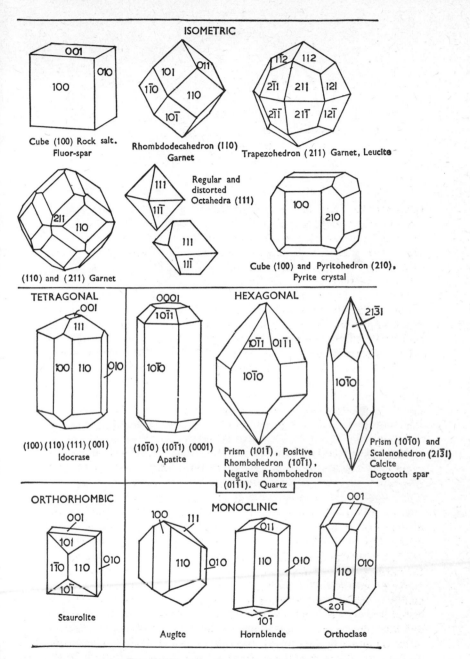

FIG. 37. Crystals of some common minerals.

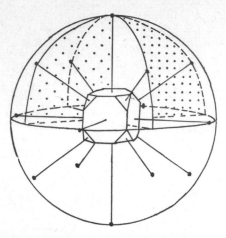

FIG. 38. Spherical projection of a combination of cube and octahedron. The dotted plane projects as a semicircle on the upper
hemisphere.

Spherical and stereographic projections. Information about the
solid geometry of crystals can be recorded in various ways — by
listing the index numbers of the faces developed, by making accurate
drawings conforming to certain conventions and by means of various
types of projections. A convenient introduction to this last method is
supplied by a consideration of the *spherical projection* (Fig. 38). In
this three-dimensional projection, the crystal is supposed to lie at the
centre of a sphere and the crystallographic directions to be recorded
are projected on to the surface of this sphere. By convention, the
crystal is so placed that the *c*-axis is vertical and the *a*-axis faces the
observer. A little consideration will show that the projection of plane
structures will appear on the sphere as lines. Planes passing through
the centre of the sphere produce *great circles*, other planes produce
small circles. Linear structures appear on the projection as points,
and the geometry of crystals is generally recorded by plotting points
which represent the projections of the normals to the crystal faces;
these points are termed the *poles* to the faces. The angle between the
poles of adjacent faces measured around the surface of the sphere
gives the interfacial angle.

A *stereographic projection* gives a two-dimensional representation
of the original three-dimensional structure and can be derived from
the spherical projection by projecting the lines and points plotted on
one hemisphere of the latter on to the equatorial plane (Fig. 39).
For crystallographic work, the *upper hemisphere* is chosen for
projection and each point is projected along a line joining it to the

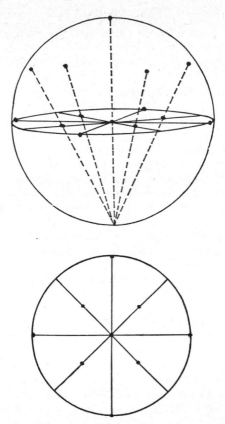

FIG. 39. Stereographic projection and its relation to spherical projection; combination of cube and octahedron as in FIG. 38.

south pole of the sphere. For the representation of geological structures projection is from the lower hemisphere (pp. 449–50).

The clumsy method of constructing a stereographic projection via a spherical projection is not used in practice. Instead, points are plotted by means of a ready-made *stereographic net* on which are marked the projections of great and small circles drawn at fixed angles to each other. The net is so drawn that the angular relations of structures projected on to the original sphere are preserved with little distortion.

The finished projection giving a representation of the crystal faces shows a pattern of points marking the poles to the faces. In the example given, the crystal belongs to the cubic system; the a and b crystallographic axes correspond to the north-south and east-west axes of the projection respectively, and the vertical c-axis

67

emerges at the centre of the projection. The pole of (100) lies on the circumference at the points of emergence of the north-south axis and the positions of poles to the other faces should be located and checked.

Crystallographic and geometrical symmetry. So far crystals have been represented as having perfect geometrical symmetry, all the faces of each form having the same size and shape and being equidistant from the centre of the crystal. Natural crystals, however, rarely show this perfect geometrical arrangement, since the supply of material may be very different to different faces. But this lack of geometrical symmetry does not, of course, alter the crystallographic symmetry since this depends on the constant internal atomic structure. The arrangement of ions is the same for all parallel planes equally spaced so that the sizes of crystal faces and their distances from the centre of the crystal are irrelevant in this connection. The *perfect* and the *distorted* octahedra of magnetite, Fe_3O_4, shown in Fig. 37, would be found on measurement to have identical interfacial angles between any two intersecting faces — this, obviously, expressing the identical atomic structures of the two specimens of the one mineral.

A variety of factors controls the shape, or *habit*, of a crystal. Among these are variation in the supply of material, the speed of growth, quiescent or disturbed conditions, the degree of saturation of the solution and the presence in it of impurities. For example, rock-salt crystallises in cubes from a pure solution but in octahedra from one containing 10 per cent urea. Descriptive names are given to particular habits, such as *tabular*, *acicular* or needle-like, *fibrous*, *capillary* or hair-like, *bladed*, *columnar*, *foliaceous* or leaf-like, *lamellar* and so on.

Ideal and real crystals. So far we have considered crystals to be *ideal*, that is to have uniform atomic arrangements throughout their extent, with identical symmetries in each smallest portion of the structural edifice. But the actual crystals that occur in nature are only rarely ideal and now we may examine some of the departures from the ideal structural arrangements shown by such *real* crystals.

First, however, we may note that the very existence of boundary surfaces to crystals is a departure from the ideal, uniformly extending, lattice-pattern. Conditions at the boundary surfaces must be different from those farther within the crystal. The faces of real crystals have been shown to be not perfect planes but to be made up of a number of surfaces with steps only a few Ångstroms high between them. The overgrowth of one mineral on another is controlled by the state of the boundary surface of the host. Further, boundary conditions between the crystal and the medium in which it is growing may decide the forms present in the crystal and their relative development — that is their *crystal habit* — as already noted in the preceding section.

Imperfections in the structural edifice of real crystals may arise in two main ways. First, defects may be produced by the disorientation of small units each with perfect structure, the result being a *mosaic*. The boundaries between the units are called *dislocations*, though structural discontinuties would be a better term for them. Other defects are caused by the impersistence or local 'warping' of certain atomic layers in an otherwise perfect structure. The second group of imperfections in real crystals is the result of the random filling of lattice positions by atoms or ions. It is considered that some atoms may move through the more rigid parts of the crystal structure and take up new and random positions — such crystals possess abnormally high electrical conductivity. Of greater interest to geologists are the defects in *mixed crystals*, in which the cations for example may occupy random cation sites in the structure — we have already mentioned an example in the olivines in which Fe^{+2} and Mg^{+2} may be distributed in any ratio over the cation positions. Another type of disorder is the consequence of some of the atomic positions remaining unfilled. We may illustrate this by the mineral pyrrhotite, iron sulphide, whose composition is more often given by some such formula as $Fe_{1-x}S$ or Fe_nS_{n+1} rather than by FeS. Practically all the analyses of pyrrhotite show this deficiency of Fe which is attributed to vacant sites in the Fe^{+2} lattice, the S positions being all occupied; the electrical neutrality is achieved by a smaller number of Fe^{+3} ions being present. Other defects in this class result from the enclosure of small atoms in a structure of large ones, or by the almost accidental entanglement of foreign atoms as, for example, the embedded carbon atoms in γFe that result in austenite.

The degree of *disorder* in a lattice may profoundly affect the properties of a crystal; for example, the alloy $AuCu_3$ is soft plastic and ductile in its ordered condition but brittle and hard when disordered. A general rule is that *order* increases with the lowering of the temperature of formation of the crystal structure. At high temperatures, rapid growth takes place, the atoms as it were are not properly sorted out, and a certain amount of disorder arises in the structure; at lower temperatures, stresses set up on cooling force atoms of a similar size to migrate into discrete groups, a process known as *exsolution*. We meet order and disorder again when we deal with specific minerals, such as the forms of silica (p. 100) and the feldspars (p. 101).

TWINNED CRYSTALS

Many minerals occur in *twinned crystals* which are constructed in such a way that the two parts have a definite orientation one to the other and thus share some crystallographic direction or plane. The twinned crystal of rutile, TiO_2, drawn in Fig. 40, is made up of two halves united on a definite crystallographic plane, 101; one half is a reflection of the other half in this plane which is called the *twin-plane*. A twin-plane is thus a plane of symmetry for the whole twin — a plane of symmetry of the single crystal cannot be a twin-plane since, by definition, it already divides the crystal into two symmetrical parts. In the rutile twin of Fig. 40, the twin may be considered as

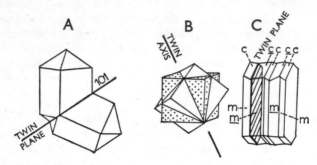

FIG. 40. Twinning: A, contact-twin of rutile (TiO_2), twin-plane 101; B, penetration-twin of fluorspar (CaF_2), twin-axis the 3-fold symmetry axis; C, repeated twin of albite feldspar, twin-plane 010, *m* indicates prism faces, *c* basal pinacoids.

produced by rotation of one half through 180° about a line, the *twin-axis*, perpendicular to the twin-plane. Of course, no such rotation has taken place, and the explanation of the appearance is most likely that the twinned crystal began to grow from a sheet of atoms in the twin-plane — growth on the two sides of this sheet, while conforming to the rutile structure, proceeded with different orientations. It follows from the atomic structural arrangement of crystals that such twin-planes must always be possible faces of the crystal and twin-axes must be parallel to some possible edge or perpendicular to some possible crystal plane. The twin-plane is usually, but not always, also the *composition-plane*, on which the two halves of the twin are joined.

Twins are of various types; *simple, repeated* or *polysynthetic, penetration* and *complex*, to name a few. Some of these types are shown in Fig. 40.

CLEAVAGE, GLIDING AND FRACTURE IN MINERALS

Early in this chapter it was remarked that Haüy proposed that crystals were built up of 'integral molecules' or exceedingly minute *cleavage-fragments*. Haüy had one day accidentally dropped a fine crystal of calcite, $CaCO_3$, which broke into innumerable cleavage-fragments each one a rhombohedron; with these unit-bricks he could reconstruct the original crystal. This property of cleavage of minerals depends on the internal atomic structure. The *cleavage-plane* is one in which the atoms are closely packed or have a high reticular density

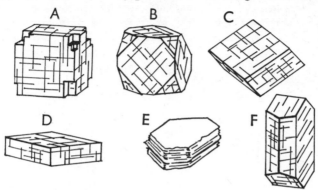

FIG. 41. Cleavage. A, cubic cleavage shown by galena, PbS; B, octahedral cleavage, fluorspar; C, rhombohedral cleavage, calcite; D, prismatic cleavage, barytes, $BaSO_4$; E, basal pinacoidal cleavage, mica; F, feldspar showing two cleavages, one parallel to the side pinacoid, 010, and the other parallel to the basal pinacoid, 001.

and which is widely separated from its parallel neighbours; the cohesion is thus strong in the plane and weak at right angles to it and the mineral preferentially breaks along it.

The cleavage-plane must necessarily be parallel to possible faces of the crystal. Cleavage is therefore described by stating the crystallographic planes along which it occurs and by adding whether it is perfect, good, difficult, poor and so on. The cleavage-planes obey, of course, the symmetry requirements of the atomic arrangement of the mineral. Thus, in rock-salt, all faces of the cube are possible cleavage-faces so that the cleavage-fragment is a cube; in fluorspar, CaF_2, the octahedral faces are all cleavage-faces and the cleavage-fragment is an octahedron (Fig. 41). The perfect cleavage of the micas, silicates of AlKMgFe, takes place parallel to strong Si_4O_{10} sheets which are loosely connected by K ions. Other examples of the dependence of cleavage on the atomic structure are given in the description of other silicate minerals in later pages. Cleavage is an important diagnostic character of a mineral, both in hand-specimen and, as we see later, under the microscope.

When the structural edifice of minerals is subjected to pressure, relief is found by gliding of certain layers of atoms past one another with the production of *glide-planes* which often give rise to *partings* in the crystal. If the moved layers take up a twin position, *secondary twinning* results; for example, when calcite is ground down to make a thin slice for microscopic examination, excellent secondary twinning and enhanced cleavages are produced.

Certain minerals break along surfaces that are neither cleavage-planes nor partings. This manner of *fracture* may be characteristic of particular minerals. Thus quartz (SiO_2) and flint and the natural glasses break with a *conchoidal fracture*, marked by curving or concentric undulations decreasing towards the point of percussion; conchoidal fracture is often well shown on prehistoric flint implements. Other minerals break with a *splintery, even* or *uneven, hackly* or *earthy* fracture.

HARDNESS AND STRENGTH OF MINERALS

The hardness and cohesiveness of minerals depend upon the strength of the bonds between the constituent ions, as illustrated by diamond and graphite mentioned in an earlier page. In a general way, *hardness* increases with a greater density of the atomic packing and a decreasing size of the ions. A rough *scale of hardness* is that of *Mohs* who proposed ten minerals arranged in order of increasing hardness as standards: they are talc, gypsum, calcite, fluorspar, apatite, orthoclase, quartz, topaz, corundum and diamond. These minerals, however, do not increase in hardness in any systematic or regular manner.

Since hardness depends on the atomic structure of a mineral it will vary in different directions in the crystal. An extreme case of this is provided by the mineral kyanite, Al_2SiO_5, which occurs in bladed crystals with a hardness of 5 in Mohs' scale parallel to their length and of 7 across their length; an alternative name for kyanite is disthene (Greek = two strengths).

The *tenacity* of a mineral is indicated by its resistance to breaking, crushing or bending It can be described by such terms as *sectile* (e.g. gypsum), *malleable* (e.g. gold), *flexible* (e.g. talc), *elastic* (e.g. mica) or *brittle* (e.g. pyrite).

SPECIFIC GRAVITY OF MINERALS

The specific gravity of a mineral is the *ratio* of its weight to that of an equal volume of water at 4° C. The specific gravity depends on the kind of constituent atoms and the way they are packed in the unit-cell. These two controls are illustrated in the following comparisons:

	Specific Gravity
1. Diamond, C, (dense packing)	3·52
Graphite, C, (looser packing)	2·3
2. Calcite, CaCO₃, trigonal	2·71
Aragonite, CaCO₃, orthorhombic	2·94
3. Anhydrite, CaSO₄, (Atomic Weight, Ca 40·08)	2·93
Barytes, BaSO₄ (Atomic Weight, Ba 137·36)	4·5
Anglesite, PbSO₄ (Atomic Weight, Pb 207·21)	6·3

If the specific gravity of a mineral is known and the dimensions of the unit-cell determined, the molecular weight of the compound can be calculated directly.

The specific gravity is an important determinative character of minerals and therefore of rocks. With the expected exception of minerals containing heavy metals such as Pb, Ba, etc., the 'sparry', non-metallic-looking minerals have specific gravities about 2·6–2·8, the metallic-looking minerals about 5. The student should make himself familiar with the relative weights of comparable pieces of the common minerals and rocks.

The specific gravity of minerals is determined in a number of ways depending upon the accuracy aimed at and the material available. It is given by $W_a/(W_a - W_w)$, where W_a is the weight in air and W_w the weight in water of the specimen under investigation. It can be measured by the use of an ordinary balance, of a pycnometer or specific gravity bottle, or by the special apparatus usually available in geological laboratories, such as Walker's steel-yard, Jolly's spring-balance and the fine modern Berman balance.

Heavy liquids are employed not only in the determination of specific gravity but also for separating minerals of different densities. Two liquids, whose specific gravities straddle that of the mineral, are mixed so that the mineral neither floats nor sinks in the mixture; the specific gravity of the mixture, and therefore of the mineral, is found by the use of the pycnometer or a Westphal balance. Heavy liquids are especially used for separating out the small amount of minerals of high specific gravity — the *heavy minerals* or *residues* or *accessories* — in rocks. The rock is crushed to give single mineral grains and the powder placed in a separating funnel containing a heavy liquid: the heavy minerals sink in the liquid and are drawn off at the bottom of the funnel. Other methods of separation, such as *elutriation*, also depend on the differing specific gravities of minerals, and are described later on p. 247.

Heavy liquids employed in these operations include: bromoform, Sp. Gr. 2·9, methylene iodide, Sp. Gr. 3·33, thallium formate and malonate (Clerici's solution) Sp. Gr. 4·0.

RADIOACTIVE, MAGNETIC AND ELECTRICAL PROPERTIES OF MINERALS

Radioactivity of minerals containing uranium and thorium has already been mentioned in connection with the radiometric determination of the ages of such minerals (p. 49), as have also the *magnetic* properties of certain minerals in the brief account of magnetic methods of geophysical prospecting. The different magnetic susceptibilities of different minerals are utilised in the laboratory in the separation of minerals by the electro-magnet and also in processes of ore-dressing or purification in the mining industry. A few important ore-minerals are good *conductors of electricity*, a circumstance utilised in their separation from useless non-conductors in industrial processes. Certain minerals develop electrical charges when heated or cooled; tourmaline, a complex borosilicate of aluminium, is an example of such *pyroelectric* minerals — it becomes positively charged at one end and negatively charged at the other end of its vertical trigonal axis. *Piezoelectric* minerals become electrically charged when subjected to pressure. This property is possessed by crystals with no centre of symmetry and is well shown by quartz, SiO_2. Great numbers of suitably oriented quartz-plates are used as oscillator-plates for frequency control in radio and telephone systems.

OPTICAL PROPERTIES OF MINERALS

By virtue of the arrangements and characters of their constituent atoms, minerals possess a number of properties depending upon light. As we shall see, these *optical properties* are especially important in connection with the rock-forming minerals, those that make up the common rocks of the earth's crust. The optical properties considered here are the colour of minerals, their refractive index, double refraction and their general behaviour when examined by the petrographical microscope.

Colour of minerals. The *colour* of a mineral depends on the absorption of some of the vibrations of white light and the reflection of others, these latter giving a sensation of a certain colour to the eye. A pure mineral possesses its own inherent colour, but this is often modified by the presence of traces of impurities.

The inherent colour depends on the nature of the constituent ions. Minerals with Al Na K Ca Mg Ba are colourless or light-coloured, those with Fe Cr Mn Co Ni Ti Va are coloured, often deeply. We can illustrate this by the group of silicates of composition $Ca_2(Mg, Fe)_5Si_8O_{22}(OH)_2$ which belong to the common rock-forming minerals known as the amphiboles; members of this group free from or low in Fe, such as tremolite, are pale-coloured or white, those rich in Fe, such as actinolite, are dark green. With regard to individual elements, the ways they are arranged in the atomic structure or their different valencies also affect the colours of the minerals containing them. Carbon atoms arranged in the strong compact diamond structure give a colourless mineral, in the flimsy graphite structure a black one. Minerals with divalent Fe are commonly green, with trivalent Fe red, brown or yellow, with both, blue or deep green.

The presence of impurities markedly affects the colour of minerals, as illustrated by the gem minerals of composition Al_2O_3; ruby, sapphire, and oriental amethyst, oriental emerald and oriental topaz, are all differently coloured varieties of this one mineral, corundum — traces of chromium or other colour-making ions being responsible.

The colour of a finely powdered mineral is called its *streak* and is of high diagnostic value. Thus, magnetite (Fe_3O_4) and hematite (Fe_2O_3) may both be black in mass, but the streak of magnetite is black, that of hematite is cherry-red.

Minerals vary in the amount of light they transmit and grade from transparent to translucent to opaque. But many apparently opaque minerals become translucent when they are cut into very thin slices, as we see in later pages. Further, certain minerals may absorb different quantities and qualities of light along different crystallographic directions. This property of *pleochroism* is important in the identification of rock-forming minerals under the microscope and is referred to later (p. 81). It can be illustrated now by the mineral tourmaline which in thin sections may appear almost black when light passes through it vibrating perpendicular to the vertical crystallographic axis and light green in a position at right angles to this.

Refractive index of minerals. A ray of light passing through the air on to the surface of a mineral is in part *reflected* back into the air and in part *refracted* into the mineral. The reflected ray makes the same angle with the normal to the surface as the incident ray. The refracted ray is bent so that the angle of refraction is less than the angle of incidence (Fig. 42). The amount of refraction is directly proportional to the velocities of light in the air and in the mineral and the ratio between these two velocities is called the *refractive index*. As shown in Fig. 42, the refractive index is the ratio of the distances travelled by the ray in unit time in air and in the mineral, and is

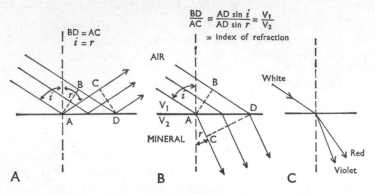

FIG. 42. A, Reflection; B, refraction; C, dispersion.

clearly given by the ratio of the sine of the angle of incidence to the sine of the angle of refraction. Refractive index is related, as shown by Sir Laurence Bragg, to the atomic arrangement of the mineral, especially the shape of the molecules and the interatomic spacing. It is therefore characteristic for each mineral and is accordingly an important diagnostic quantity. The refractive index of a mineral varies with the colour of the light, that for red light being less than that for violet light; the difference between these two values for the two ends of the spectrum gives the *dispersion* (Fig. 42). Diamond depends for its brilliancy on its high refractive index and strong dispersion — the refractive index for red light being 2·40735, for violet light 2·46476, the dispersion thus being 0·05741.

The *determination of the refractive index* of a mineral, whether absolute or relative to other minerals, is done by the examination of the mineral either in grains immersed in liquid or in *thin slices* embedded in Canada Balsam as a mount. A *thin slice* is a parallel-sided plate of a mineral or rock of a thickness of about 30 microns, 1/30 of a millimetre. It is prepared by grinding a perfectly flat surface on a chip of rock and cementing this surface to a glass plate with Canada Balsam; the chip is then ground down again to the required thinness and covered by a thin glass coverslip.

The appearance of a mineral when viewed by a petrological microscope depends on the relative refractive indices of the mineral and the mount, or of the mineral and the adjacent minerals. If the difference is considerable, the mineral appears to stand out from its neighbours, it has an emphasised darker border and its surface seems rough and pitted; if the difference is small, the mineral is inconspicuous. Thus, cryolite, Na_3AlF_6, with refractive index 1·339, is practically invisible when put into water, refractive index 1·335.

76

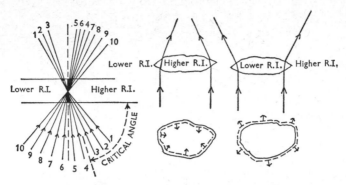

Fig. 43. Explanations of the Becke Line effect: (*left*), using the critical angle; (*right*), using the mineral grain as a lens.

H. G. Wells' invisible man made himself so by making his refractive index equal that of air — to remain invisible he had to keep out of the rain. By mixing suitable liquids, the refractive index of the mixture can be so adjusted that a given mineral immersed in it becomes invisible; the refractive index of the mixture, and therefore of the mineral, can then be determined by a *refractometer*, such as the Abbé, Herbert Smith, or Tully, available in most geological laboratories. Suitable *immersion liquids* and their refractive indices are: kerosene 1·448, clove oil 1·53, α-monobromnapthalene 1·658, methylene iodide 1·740 and methylene iodide saturated with sulphur 1·778; a series of liquids, in which refractive indices advance by a small regular interval, can be prepared or can be purchased ready made. The examination of relative refractive indices utilises the *Becke Effect* or *Becke Line* (see Fig. 43). As shown in this figure, light coming from below the thin slice or mount is concentrated towards the material with the higher refractive index. This concentration gives a bright line, the Becke Line, which appears to move into the mineral with the higher refractive index as the objective of the microscope is raised. A simple method of determining relative refractive indices thus becomes available. When the absolute refractive index is being determined by the immersion method, a stage is reached when *colour fringes* appear around the edges of the grains, especially well developed when inclined illumination is used; one edge of a grain is red, the other blue, indicating that for some intermediate colour such as yellow, the refractive index of the mineral grain equals that of the oil in which it is immersed.

Single and double refraction. From the account of the atomic structure of minerals already given, it is to be expected that, in general, light will not be able to travel with equal velocities in all

77

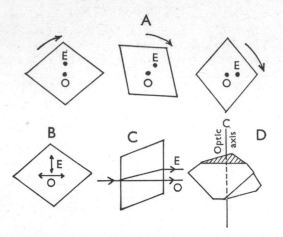

FIG. 44. A, Experiments with calcite cleavage rhombs to illustrate double refraction, O =ordinary ray, E =extraordinary ray; B, directions of vibration of O and E; C, paths of O and E; D, the optic axis in calcite.

directions within a crystal. In certain special cases, however, the velocity is constant and thus the refractive index is the same for all directions of transmission. Such minerals are *singly refracting* or *isotropic* and belong to the *cubic system*. In minerals that belong to any crystal system other than the cubic, the refractive index varies with the direction of transmission in the crystal; such minerals are *doubly refracting* or *anisotropic*. We can explore double refraction by experiments with a cleavage-fragment of *iceland spar*, the transparent variety of calcite, $CaCO_3$, which shows this property especially well. The student is advised to perform these simple experiments for himself.

We have seen that the cleavage-fragment of calcite is a rhombohedron in which the vertical crystallographic axis *c* joins the two corners at which three obtuse angles meet (Fig. 35). If the rhomb is laid over a dot, two images of the dot are seen (Fig. 44); on rotation of the rhomb, one dot remains stationary and the other revolves around it. The stationary dot is produced by the *ordinary ray*, the movable dot by the *extraordinary ray*. These two rays obviously travel through the rhomb with different velocities and have different refractive indices. Examination by a tourmaline plate, which transmits light vibrating in a single plane, that is, *polarised* light, shows that the ordinary ray consists of light vibrating parallel to the long diagonal of the rhomb face, the extraordinary ray of light vibrating parallel to the short diagonal.

This property of double refraction of calcite is used in the *nicol prism* or *nicol*. This prism is so constructed that only the extraordinary ray leaves it; the direction of vibration of the light of this ray is, as we have just seen, parallel to the short diagonal of the rhomb face at the end of the nicol.

When a dot is viewed through a parallel-sided plate made by grinding down the two corners of the cleavage-rhomb of calcite at which the *c*-crystallographic axis emerges only one image is seen (Fig. 44). Light travelling along this axis is not doubly refracted, the ordinary and extraordinary rays travel with the same velocity and their refractive indices are the same. Experiments show that there is only one direction along which this occurs; calcite is said therefore to be *uniaxial*, and the *c*-crystallographic axis is the *optic axis*. Further experiments show that the refractive index for the ordinary ray is constant, whilst that for the extraordinary ray varies with its direction of transmission, reaching a minimum at right angles to the *c*-axis. The two values for calcite are:

R.I.$_e$ extraordinary ray, 1·486.
R.I.$_\omega$ ordinary ray,   1·658.

Minerals such as calcite which have R.I.$_e$ less than R.I.$_\omega$ are said to be *negative*. The opposite condition is seen in some other uniaxial minerals, such as quartz, and these are *positive*.

All minerals crystallising in the tetragonal, hexagonal and trigonal systems are uniaxial. Those belonging to the orthorhombic, monoclinic and triclinic systems are *biaxial*, as there are two directions in such crystals along which no double refraction occurs.

The following classification of minerals is now obtained:

ISOTROPIC MINERALS   — Cubic Minerals
ANISOTROPIC MINERALS — (i) *Uniaxial* — Tetragonal, Hexagonal and Trigonal minerals.
                    (ii) *Biaxial* — Orthorhombic, Monoclinic, and Triclinic Minerals.

The petrological microscope. A special kind of microscope is used for the examination of thin slices and grains of minerals and rocks. In this, two devices for producing polarised light are fitted, these being nicol prisms in the older type of microscope or special filters in the newer; we may call these devices of whatever type the *polars*. One, the *polariser*, is fitted below the microscope stage and the other, the *analyser*, is inserted in the tube of the microscope between the objective and the eye-piece. Both polariser and analyser can be removed, so that the slice can be viewed first in *ordinary light*, second in *polarised light* when the polariser is in position and third between *crossed polars* when both polariser and analyser are inserted. In this last condition, the direction of vibration of the polarised light transmitted by the polariser is at right angles to that transmitted by the analyser, so that if nothing is on the microscope stage blackness results.

The examination of minerals by the petrological microscope. In this book dealing with general geology, it is not necessary to go beyond the simple methods of identification of minerals in thin slices. It is convenient to classify the observations to be made under the three headings mentioned in the preceding paragraph: those using ordinary light, those using polarised light and those between crossed polars. Methods involving convergent light are described in the specialised books on optical mineralogy.

In ordinary light (Fig. 45). Minerals viewed in thin slices with both polariser and analyser removed are mostly *transparent*; a few, notably the iron-oxides such as magnetite and ilmenite, are *opaque*. Some are *colourless*, such as quartz and the feldspars, others are *coloured*. Different sections of coloured minerals, biotite and hornblende for example, may show different colours or different depths or shades of the same colour, due to the pleochroism and absorption of the mineral in question (see later, p. 81). The *refractive index* of a mineral

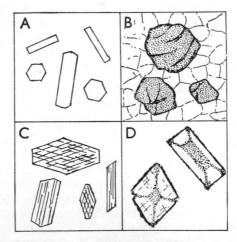

Fig. 45. Minerals in ordinary light; A, form of apatite, hexagonal basal and rectangular longitudinal sections; B, difference in refractive index between garnet (R.I. 1.81) and quartz (R.I. 1.54), resulting in high relief of the former; c, cleavages in hornblende; D, inclusions in andalusite.

relative to adjacent minerals or to the Canada Balsam mount can be judged by its appearance; a mineral with a markedly different refractive index will appear to stand out with well-marked borders and a pitted surface — thus garnet (R.I. = 1·81) is conspicuous when set in quartz (R.I. = 1·54). If a large enough number of sections of a given mineral are available in a thin slice, conclusions may be drawn on its *crystal form*; thus apatite, crystallising in the hexagonal system, provides in slice many sections that are hexagonal (cross sections) or oblong (longitudinal sections). The shapes of minerals are of course also dependent on the presence of other minerals in the slice which may have interfered with their free growth — this matter of the fabric or texture of minerals in rocks is dealt with in later chapters. *Cleavage* appears in slice as one or more sets of parallel cracks, depending on the direction in which the crystal is cut by the slice. Sections of hornblende, for example, show one set of cleavages when cut parallel to the vertical crystallographic axis and two sets meeting at about 120° when cut at right angles to this (Fig. 45). Lastly, some minerals show in slice *inclusions* arranged in a definite pattern which may be diagnostic. The variety of andalusite known as chiastolite is characterised by inclusions arranged in a cross-shaped pattern (Fig. 45).

In polarised light (Fig. 46). With the polariser inserted below the microscope-stage, the main observation that may be made is that of *pleochroism*, already mentioned. Pleochroism is shown by a change in the colour and quantity of light transmitted by the mineral according to the direction in which the polarised light travels through the

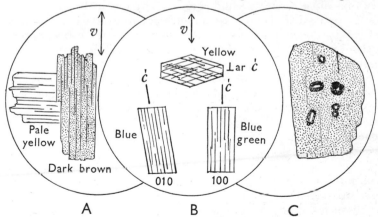

Fig. 46. Minerals in polarised light; A, pleochroism in biotite; B, pleochroism in hornblende; C, pleochroic haloes around zircon grains in a biotite plate.

section. The polariser or the microscope-stage is rotated in the observation of pleochroism. The mica biotite can be used in illustration; when the light transmitted vibrates parallel with the strong biotite cleavage, the mineral is deep brown, when across the cleavage, the mineral is pale yellow (Fig. 46).

All sections of isotropic minerals will necessarily show the same colour and absorption; cubic minerals are thus *non-pleochroic*. In uniaxial minerals, sections at right angles to the vertical crystallographic axis are non-pleochroic, those parallel to this axis may show the greatest differences in colour and absorption. Biaxial minerals may show three shades or colours; for example, hornblende may vary from yellow to blue-green to blue depending on the direction of transmission of the polarised light (Fig. 46).

Certain minerals, such as biotite and cordierite, may contain minute inclusions of radioactive minerals from which emanations have been emitted that have altered the host mineral immediately surrounding them. Such altered zones or *pleochroic haloes* are often more strongly pleochroic than the main portion of the mineral (Fig. 46).

Under crossed polars. When the polars of a petrological microscope are *crossed*, the polarised light coming from the polariser is entirely rejected by the analyser and darkness results. This condition may or may not be modified by the presence of mineral sections on the microscope-stage — this we now examine.

It will be recalled that *isotropic* minerals are singly refracting. Light from the polariser therefore passes unaltered through all sections of such minerals and is rejected by the analyser. The dark field produced by crossed polars remains undisturbed. All sections of *cubic minerals* thus *give blackness between crossed polars*; natural glasses and a few non-crystalline minerals such as opal are also isotropic.

Anisotropic minerals are doubly refracting, so that a ray of light passing through them is split up into two rays, travelling with different velocities and vibrating at right angles to one another, along the *vibration-directions*. When these vibration-directions of the mineral are parallel to the vibration planes of the polars, the positions of these being given by the cross-wires of the microscope, blackness or *extinction* results: polarised light leaving the polariser continues unchanged through the mineral plate and is thrown out by the analyser. This *extinction* occurs four times during the complete rotation of the microscope-stage.

The vibration-directions of a mineral bear of course a definite relation to the crystallographic axes and to the atomic structure of

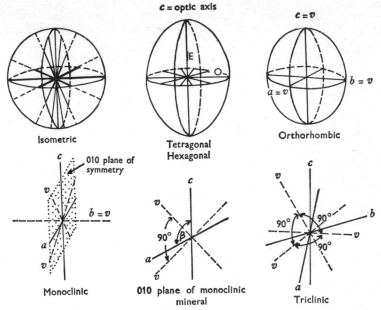

FIG. 47. Vibration directions, *v*, in the different crystal systems.

the mineral. This *optical orientation* (Fig. 47) for the various crystal systems is given in the following table:

Cubic System: three equal vibration axes, all directions alike.

Tetragonal, Hexagonal and Trigonal Systems: vibrations taking place perpendicular to the optic axis (= vertical crystallographic axis) are all equal.

Orthorhombic System: the vibration axes coincide with the crystallographic axes.

Monoclinic System: one vibration axis coincides with the *b* crystallographic axis, the other two lie in the plane of symmetry at right angles to one another.

Triclinic System: the three vibration directions, of course at right angles to one another, may be in any position with respect to the crystallographic axes.

In thin slices of minerals there are usually seen crystal edges or cleavages of determinable crystallographic orientation. The position of extinction with regard to these is an important observation. The *extinction angle* is the angle between a vibration-direction and a crystallographic direction in a given section of the mineral. Extinction is said to be *straight* if it occurs when a crystallographic direction or

83

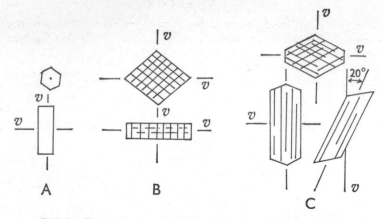

FIG. 48. Extinction in the different crystal systems: A, apatite, hexagonal, vertical sections extinguish straight, hexagonal basal sections are isotropic; B, barytes, orthorhombic, symmetrical extinction on 001, straight extinction on 100 (compare the cleavage fragment in FIG. 41D); C, hornblende, monoclinic, symmetrical extinction on some sections perpendicular to the b-axis, e.g. 001, straight on 100, inclined on 010. v = vibration direction.

cleavage is parallel to the cross-wires of the microscope, or *inclined* if the crystallographic direction makes an angle with the cross-wires when the mineral is in the position of extinction; in *symmetrical* extinction the cross-wires bisect the angles between two sets of cleavages or edges. The extinctions characteristic of each crystal system are summarised below and illustrated in Fig. 48. They can be deduced of course from Fig. 47 and its accompanying table of vibration directions.

Cubic System: All sections isotropic.

Tetragonal, Hexagonal and Trigonal Systems: basal sections, perpendicular to the optic axis c, are isotropic; vertical sections give straight extinction.

Orthorhombic System: sections parallel to two crystallographic axes give straight extinction.

Monoclinic System: sections at right angles to the plane of symmetry give straight extinction, parallel to this plane inclined extinction.

Triclinic System: all sections give inclined extinction.

In positions intermediate between the extinction positions, the mineral sections show *polarisation-* or *interference-colours* produced by the interference of the two rays emerging from the analyser. Light entering the mineral section from the polariser is resolved into two

84

vibrations at right angles parallel to the vibration-directions of the
section; these two rays, on entering the analyser are broken up into
two vibrations which are suppressed, and
into two which emerge and interfere to
give the polarisation-colour (Fig. 49).
During their passage through the mineral section, these two emergent rays
have acquired a phase-difference that
can be expressed in terms of the wave-
length of the light-vibrations. Depending
on this phase-difference, certain colour-
components of white light are suppressed
and certain pass on to give the polarisation-colour observed. The polarisation-
colour of a given mineral section depends
on the thickness of the slice and on the
birefringence of the mineral, this being
the difference between the refractive
indices of the two rays traversing the
mineral plate and, of course, varying
with the direction in which the crystal is
cut by the plane of the thin slice. Polarisation-colours are described by reference
to *Newton's Scale*, which may be reproduced by a *quartz-wedge* examined
between crossed polars. Newton's Scale
is summarised in Fig. 50. It is clear from
this that thickening of the mineral sec-

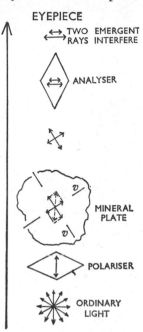

FIG. 49. Passage of light
through the petrological microscope.

tion raises the polarisation-colour in this Scale; increased birefringence
has the same effect.

Some examples will make these points clearer (Fig. 51). In quartz,
a uniaxial mineral, the extraordinary ray with refractive index 1·553
vibrates parallel to the optic axis or the c-crystallographic axis, the
ordinary ray with refractive index 1·544 vibrates at right angles to
the optic axis. Quartz sections cut parallel to the optic axis accordingly have a birefringence of 0·009 and, in slices of the standard
thickness of 30 microns, give a yellow of the First Order in Newton's
Scale as their polarisation-colour; sections cut perpendicular to the
optic axis, as previously explained, are isotropic; their birefringence
is nil as no double refraction takes place. Zircon, also uniaxial, has
maximum and minimum refractive indices of 1·985 and 1·925
respectively, its maximum birefringence is consequently 0·060 and it
gives in sections parallel to the optic axis, high polarisation-colours

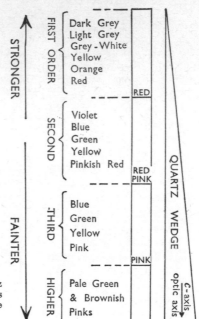

FIG. 50. The quartz wedge and Newton's scale of interference colours.

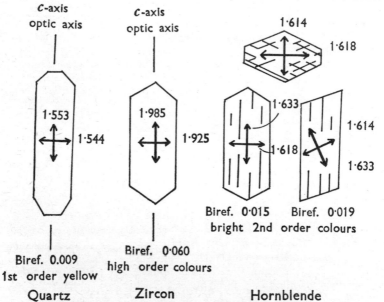

FIG. 51. Birefringence and vibration directions in quartz, zircon and hornblende.

86

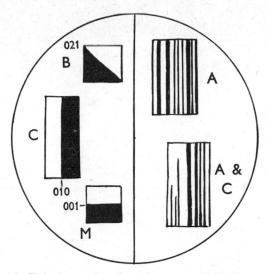

Fig. 52. Twinning under the microscope. (*Left*), in orthoclase feldspar; c, Carlsbad Law, composition plane 010; B, Baveno Law, twin-plane 021; M, Manebach Law, twin-plane 001. (*Right*), in plagioclase feldspar; A, repeated twinning on Albite Law, twin-plane 010 (see Fig. 40c); A and c combined twinning on Albite and Carlsbad laws.

of the Fourth Order. As an example of a biaxial mineral, hornblende may be taken. The three refractive indices, α the least, β the intermediate and γ the greatest, corresponding to the three vibration directions in a certain specimen were found to be $\alpha = 1 \cdot 614$, $\beta = 1 \cdot 618$, $\gamma = 1 \cdot 633$; three sections could be cut each containing two vibration directions and these would have birefringences of $0 \cdot 004$, $0 \cdot 015$, $0 \cdot 019$ — the first section would show low First Order polarisation colours, the other two bright Second Order colours.

It will be recalled that in *twinned crystals* the two or more parts had different orientations. In thin slices of twinned crystals this is revealed by different positions of extinction and by different polarisation-colours in the parts of the twin. Twinning as shown in thin slices is often an important diagnostic character of minerals as, for example, in the feldspars (Fig. 52).

CRYSTAL CHEMISTRY

The Structure of the Atom and Atomic Bonding

Earlier in this chapter we referred briefly to the structure of atoms, their sizes and the way in which they were linked together to form minerals. These topics are now examined in greater detail.

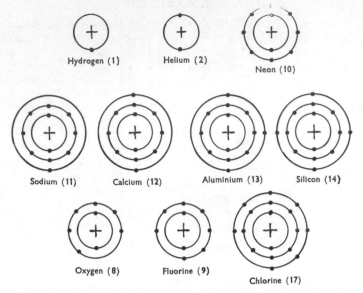

Hydrogen (1)   Helium (2)

Neon (10)

Sodium (11)   Calcium (12)   Aluminium (13)   Silicon (14)

Oxygen (8)   Fluorine (9)

Chlorine (17)

Fig. 53. Electronic structure of various atoms (atomic numbers in brackets after name of element).

As we have seen, the atom is considered to be composed of a nucleus, made up of protons each with a positive charge and neutrons, around which revolve electrons, each with a negative charge, the whole structure being electrically neutral. The number of electrons varies from one in hydrogen to 92 in uranium, this number being called the *atomic number* of the element concerned. The orbits or shells in which the electrons can revolve are 7, designated for convenience K L M N O P Q or 1 2 3 4 5 6 7, from that nearest the nucleus outwards; these shells can hold different numbers of electrons, thus K is filled with 2, L with 8, M can accommodate 1 to 18, N 1 to 32, O 1 to 32, P 1 to 9 and Q 2. The further subdivision of the shells is not our concern. The chemical and crystallographic properties of the atom are controlled fundamentally by the *valency electrons*, those in the outer shell of the element in question. When the outer shell is filled, the structure is stable, as in the inert gases (Fig. 53). In order to become stable, elements can lose electrons from the outer shell so as to empty it or they can acquire electrons to fill the shell. Metals have few electrons in their outer shell and so lose them, non-metals may have many electrons with only a few vacant positions in this shell and so collect others to become stable. Examples of metallic and non-metallic atomic formations are given in Fig. 53.

There are a number of ways in which atoms can be joined or *bonded* in minerals so as to produce the stable inert-gas structure with a full complement of electrons in their outer shell. The more important of these bonds are now examined.

The ionic bond. In this type of bonding, the few electrons in the

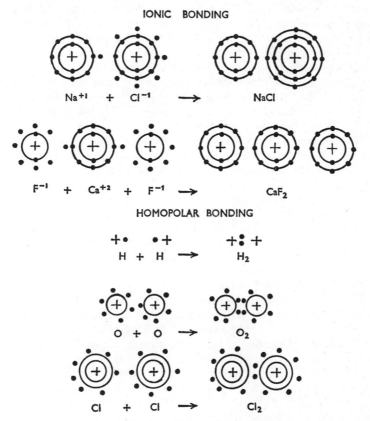

FIG. 54. Ionic and homopolar bonding.

outer shell of an element such as a metal are transferred to the few vacant sites in the outer shell of another element, such as a non-metal. The atoms thus become *ions*, having lost or gained one or more peripheral electrons, and are no longer electrically neutral. The atoms that lose electrons form *cations*, such as hydrogen and the metals, and are styled *electropositive*; those that gain electrons give the *electronegative anions*, such as oxygen, fluorine, chlorine and sulphur. The charge on cation or anion is equal to that of the electrons lost or gained.

We can illustrate the ionic bond in minerals by reference to two common species, rock-salt NaCl and fluorspar CaF_2. The electronic structures of Na, Cl, Ca and F are given in Fig. 54. Consider rock-salt first: when conditions become suitable for production of sodium chloride, the atom Na, with one valency electron in its outer shell, loses it to the atom Cl which has one vacant site in its outer shell and the electropositive cation unites by attraction with the electronegative anion to make rock-salt, NaCl. Both ions now have eight electrons in their outer shell and the stable inert-gas structure is achieved. Now consider fluorspar: the electropositive Ca has two available valency electrons, the electronegative F has one vacant site in its outer shell: to form fluorspar, CaF_2, two ions of fluorine are therefore bonded to one of calcium, the M shell of calcium now becoming the outermost with the eight-electron stable pattern and the L-shells of the two fluorine ions becoming filled also to produce this eight-electron shell.

The ionic bond does not give any highly directional property to a mineral so that many minerals bonded in this way have high crystal symmetry. Further, such minerals are usually of moderate hardness and medium specific gravity and possess fairly high melting and boiling points.

Homopolar or covalent bond. In many compounds the link between the atoms is achieved by the sharing of one or more electrons between two atoms; this gives the *homopolar* or *covalent bond*. The resulting chemical structure is a strong one, minerals so bonded are very stable and insoluble, and some possess high melting and boiling points.

Examples of homopolar bonding are given in Fig. 54. The atom of H has one electron in the K shell; in the H molecule these 2 electrons are shared between 2 atoms to achieve the inert-gas structure of helium. The O atom has 2 electrons in the K shell, 6 in the L shell; in a molecule of O, 2 electrons from each of 2 atoms are shared, so that the stable inert-gas structure with 8 electrons in the L shell results. The Cl atom has 7 electrons in the outer shell; to produce the inert-gas structure one electron is shared between 2 Cl atoms. An excellent example of one kind of homopolar bonding is given by diamond, C. The carbon atom has 4 outer electrons and thus needs 4 to give the stable eight-configuration in its L shell. In diamond, each C atom is surrounded by 4 other atoms arranged at the corners of a tetrahedron and has 4 homopolar bonds with these. The resulting structure is clearly one of great strength and stability and controls the physical properties of the mineral. Lastly, the Si atom, with the

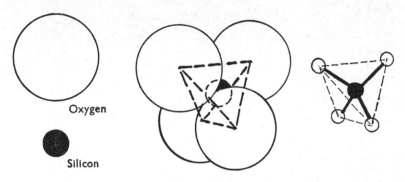

Oxygen

Silicon

FIG. 55. The SiO_4-tetrahedron.

electronic configuration of 2 electrons in the K shell, 8 in L, 4 in M, has 4 vacancies in its outermost shell, the O atom has 2 vacancies in its L shell, so that a very stable unit is formed by a structure which has Si at the centre and 4 oxygen atoms at the corners of a tetrahedron. This unit is the *SiO_4-tetrahedron* (Fig. 55) and is fundamental in the structure of the common mineral silicates, as we see later.

Other types of bonds. Some minerals have both ionic and homopolar bonding. Thus in calcite, $CaCO_3$, the bonds between O and C in the complex ion of the carbonate radicle are homopolar, those between the Ca ions and this radicle are ionic.

Two other types of bonding may be mentioned. First, in the *metallic bond*, the structural units are the nuclei bound together by an aggregate of clouds of electrons, no outer electron being tied to any particular nucleus. The characteristic properties of metals, such as their high plasticity, tenacity, ductility and conductivity, their low hardness, melting point and boiling point, are correlated with this metallic structure. Second, in the *Van der Waals bond*, the linkage results from the attraction due to weak residual charges on the surfaces of the molecules. This bond is not alone responsible for the coherence of any mineral and is usually masked by the other types of attraction. When present, it may be correlated with a strong cleavage in a mineral as, for example, in graphite made up of homopolar-bonded sheets of C atoms loosely linked across the cleavage by the Van der Waals bond.

Ionic radii. The atomic radius of an element is, as we have seen, the radius of the sphere formed by its outermost shell. But it is the *ionic radius* that is usually considered by geologists when dealing with the common minerals in which ionic bonding is typical. A cation, formed by an atom losing its outer shell, will have a *smaller* radius than the atom; thus it has been found that the atomic radius of Na is 1·86Å

91

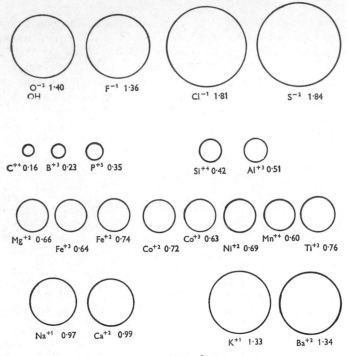

FIG. 56. Ionic Radii, in Ångstrom units.

whilst the ionic radius of Na^{+1} is 0·97Å. On the other hand, the anion has completed its outermost shell and its radius is in general *larger* than that of the atom; thus the atomic radius of O is 0·60Å, the ionic radius of O^{-2} is 1·40Å.

The space in a mineral structure is controlled by the forces of attraction and repulsion operating between the ions and their neighbours. As two ions approach, a force of repulsion suddenly sets in when the ions become a certain distance apart and closer approach is impossible. As we have done already throughout this chapter, the ions can therefore be symbolised as spheres of characteristic size in contact with one another; the distance between the centres of two adjacent spheres is the sum of the ionic radii of the two ions. These ionic radii can be determined by various methods.

In ionic crystals, each cation is surrounded by a number of anions, this number being called the *co-ordination number*. Its value depends on the radii of the ions in question. For example, in sodium chloride, NaCl, the sizes of the Na and Cl ions are such that each Na ion is surrounded by six Cl ions, situated at the corners of an octahedron the centre of which is a Na ion: this is a case of six-fold co-ordination. Other elements occurring in six-fold co-ordination include Al, Fe, Mg, Ti. Reference has been made above to the fundamental unit of silicate structure, the SiO_4-tetrahedron (Fig. 55); the four large O ions are packed together so that there is just room for the small Si ion in between them — the Si ion is in four-fold co-ordination. The ionic radius of Al is only a little larger than that of Si, so that it can play the role of Si in four-fold co-ordination; Al can thus occur in six- or four-fold co-ordination.

In Fig. 56 there are given the ionic radii of cations and anions, important in mineralogy, arranged in various ways.

Isomorphism. Isomorphism, the substitution of one ion by another in the structure, was mentioned in the early pages of this chapter. This substitution is particularly easy in the case of ions of approximately the same radius and charge. Thus, Fe^{+2}, ionic radius 0·74, is replaced by Mg^{+2}, ionic radius 0·66; Al^{+3}, 0·51, by Fe^{+3}, 0·64; Na^{+1}, 0·97, by Ca^{+2}, 0·99. Substitution takes place also among similarly-sized anions as, for example, O^{-2}, ionic radius 1·40, OH^{-1}, 1·40, and F^{-1}, 1·36.

Especially important in the rock-forming silicate minerals is the substitution, already mentioned, of Si^{+4}, ionic radius 0·42, by Al^{+3}, ionic radius 0·51, in four-fold co-ordination. The substitution of the Al with a charge of +3 for Si, +4, disturbs the electrically neutral condition of the structure, so that an additional cation is required to make the positive cation charges again equal to the negative anion charges. We may illustrate this by the common minerals, the feldspars; in orthoclase, $K^{+1}Al^{+3}Si^{+4}_3O_8^{-2}$, with a fundamental structural pattern of Si_4O_8, a quarter of the Si has been substituted by Al and one K ion introduced to give neutrality, the positive charges, on the cations, $1 + 3 + 3 \times 4 = 16$, balancing the negative charge $8 \times 2 = 16$, on the O ions.

THE STRUCTURE OF SILICATE MINERALS

As we have seen, the fundamental structural unit of the silicates is a tetrahedron in which a Si cation occupies the centre and four O ions the corners — this is the SiO_4-tetrahedron (Fig. 55). The units can occur separately and be linked together into a silicate structure by cations, or they can be linked by sharing O ions between different units in different ways. Metallic cations can be accommodated in the structure according to their ionic sizes and valencies. By these means the variety of the silicate minerals is produced. Five structural types of these silicate minerals are distinguished, as follow:

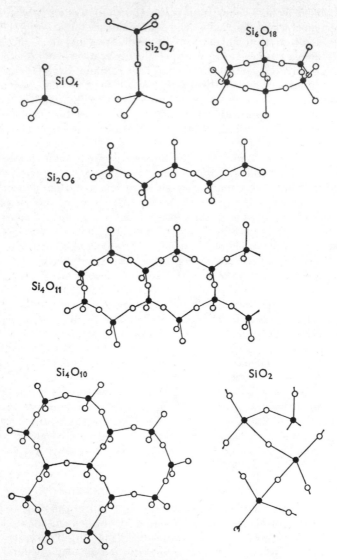

FIG. 57. Structure of Silicates: black circles silicon, open circles oxygen.

Nesosilicates. In these the SiO_4-tetrahedra remain separate units, with no shared O ions — the units are 'islands' (*nesos* = island) in the edifice and are tied together by the metallic cations between them. In the SiO_4-unit, the Si has 4 positive valencies, the four O ions have together 8 negative valencies so there is an excess of 4 negative valencies which is to be neutralised by linkage with appropriate cations. As an illustration of this balance we may consider the *olivine group*, an isomorphous series with the two end members, forsterite $Mg_2(SiO_4)$ and fayalite $Fe_2(SiO_4)$. In these, each SiO_4-tetrahedron is linked to two divalent ions, Mg^{+2} or Fe^{+2} and the 4 negative excess valencies are satisfied. Each O ion is linked with one Si and three Mg (or Fe), these last being in six-fold co-ordination. Other nesosilicates are *garnets* of formula type $Al_2Mg_3(SiO_4)_3$, with much isomorphous replacements among the cations, and zircon, $Zr(SiO_4)$.

Sorosilicates. In this class of silicates, the tetrahedra form separate groups (*soros* = group) in which they share one or more of their O ions. In the simplest case, two tetrahedra share a common O (see Fig. 57), the group becoming Si_2O_7. The charge on such a group is -6, so that to be in equilibrium the structure requires 3 divalent cations; these bind the Si_2O_7 groups together. An example of this simple case is provided by the mineral *melilite*, $Ca_2Mg(Si_2O_7)$. When the group is formed by the sharing of O ions by more than two tetrahedra, *ring structures or ring groups* result with the general composition Si_nO_{3n}. Three tetrahedra joined in this way give the ring group Si_3O_9 and can be illustrated by the mineral wollastonite $Ca_3[Si_3O_9]$. Six tetrahedra so joined (see Fig. 57) have the group composition of Si_6O_{18} and are illustrated by beryl $Be_3Al_2[Si_6O_{18}]$. In beryl, the piles of Si_6O_{18}-rings are linked laterally by Be^{+2} ions in four-fold co-ordination and Al^{+3} ions in six-fold co-ordination. These stacks of rings are parallel to the c-axis of the beryl crystal and through them run 'tunnels' down which gases have been passed. Another sorosilicate is *cordierite*, $Mg_2Al_3[AlSi_5O_{18}]$ in which an Al ion replaces a Si ion in the four-fold co-ordination position.

Inosilicates. The SiO_4-tetrahedra may be joined together to form straight *chains* bonded to one another by the metallic cations and giving a structure characterising the inosilicates (*inos* = fibre). There are two variations characterised by two important groups of rock-forming minerals, the *single chain* of the pyroxene family, and the *double chain* of the amphibole family.

In the *single chain*, the SiO_4-tetrahedra are linked by sharing two O ions each and the tetrahedra have their apexes oriented as shown in Fig. 57. This arrangement gives the general composition $n(Si_2O_6)$

D2

with a charge of -4 in excess. In a simple pyroxene, the mineral *diopside* $CaMg[Si_2O_6]$, this excess negative charge is balanced by two cations Ca^{+2} and Mg^{+2}, the Ca being in eight-fold co-ordination and the Mg in six-fold co-ordination with the oxygen ions. The chains run parallel to the c-axis of the mineral. In other members of the pyroxene family, part of the Si may be replaced by Al in four-fold co-ordination; besides, Al in six-fold co-ordination may act as a cation linking the chains together and then taking the place of Mg^{+2} or Fe^{+2}. Many isomorphous substitutions are found among this very varied family.

In the *double chain* or *ribbon structure*, two single chains lie side by side connected by alternate tetrahedra sharing an O ion, with the apexes of the tetrahedra arranged as shown in Fig. 57. The general composition is accordingly one O less than two single chains, that is nSi_4O_{11}. As we have seen, the amphibole family possess this double chain type of structure and we may take one member, *tremolite* $Ca_2Mg_5[Si_4O_{11}]_2(OH)_2$, as an example. The double chains run parallel to the length of the crystal, which is the c-axis, and are held together laterally by the cations Ca^{+2} in eight-fold co-ordination and Mg^{+2} in six-fold. All amphiboles contain hydroxyl OH^{-1} as an essential component and, in some, F^{-1} occurs in place of some hydroxyl: note that the ionic radii of O, OH and F are very alike (see p. 92). The hydroxyl and fluorine are fitted into the spaces in the structure shown in Fig. 57. As in the pyroxenes, Al can replace some of the Si in the chains in the amphiboles; such a replacement requires additions to the cations to attain equilibrium, and Al^{+3} may substitute for Mg^{+2}, or such ions as Na^{+1} may be added. Again, isomorphous substitution by cations of similar size and charge takes place in the amphiboles; the substitution of Fe^{+2} or Mn^{+2} for Mg^{+2}, Fe^{+2} Mg^{+2} or $2Na^{+1}$ for Ca^{+2}, and so on gives rise to the great variety of the members of this family.

Phyllosilicates. We have so far examined structures in which the tetrahedra are joined by sharing one or two O ions; now we have the case in which three oxygens of each tetrahedron are shared with its neighbours to form two-dimensional networks or sheets (Fig. 57). This structure characterises the phyllosilicates (*phyllon* = leaf), such as the micas, chlorites, talc and the clay-minerals. The sheets are tied together by the cations and have a Si : O ratio of 4 : 10 giving Si_4O_{10}. We may examine the structure of the white mica, *muscovite*, in a little detail. The formula for a muscovite can be stated as $KAl_2[(AlSi_3)O_{10}](OH)_2$ in which it will be noted that a quarter of the Si has been replaced by Al, this change being balanced by bringing in K^{+1}. The muscovite structure is made up of pairs of Si_4O_{10}-sheets, with apexes of the tetrahedra of both sheets pointed inwards; the pair of sheets is held together by Al ions, with which OH is linked. The pairs of sheets are separated by the K ions in twelve-fold co-ordination. The bonding in this K-layer is weak and the perfect cleavage of muscovite takes place along this layer, parallel to the sheet-structure. In other micas, such as *biotite*, Mg or Fe occupy the Al positions.

Tectosilicates. In this, the last group of silicates, all the corners of the tetrahedra are linked to other tetrahedra to give a three-dimensional framework. Each oxygen is shared between two tetrahedra so that the general composition is reduced from SiO_4 to SiO_2; the charges on such a framework are balanced. Quartz, SiO_2, has the tectosilicate structure. In silicates belonging to this class, some of the Si^{+4} is replaced by Al^{+3}, requiring additional positive ions to restore electrical equilibrium. This can be illustrated by reference to the *feldspars* (see ante, p. 93), the most important of the rock-forming minerals, and is elaborated later (p. 101).

Other tectosilicates include the feldspathoids and the zeolites. Quartz SiO_2 may be theoretically grouped here as having a framework structure in which no substitution of Si ions has taken place.

The foregoing account of silicate structures is summarised in the table below.

Classification	Structure	Composition Si:O ratio	Charge	Example
A. Nesosilicates	Independent SiO_4-tetrahedra	SiO_4 1:4	-4	Olivine $(MgFe)_2SiO_4$
B. Sorosilicates	(i) Two tetrahedra sharing one O	Si_2O_7 2:7	-6	Melilite Ca_2Mg (Si_2O_7)
	(ii) Ring structures	Si_nO_{3n} 1:3	$-2n$	Beryl Be_3Al_2 $[Si_6O_{18}]$
C. Inosilicates	(i) Single chains, each tetrahedron sharing two O ions	Si_2O_6 1:3	-4	Pyroxenes e.g. diopside, $CaMg[Si_2O_6]$
	(ii) Double chains, tetrahedra sharing alternately 2 and 3 O ions	Si_4O_{11} 4:11	-6	Amphiboles e.g. tremolite, $Ca_3Mg_5[Si_4O_{11}]_2 \cdot (OH)_2$
D. Phyllosilicates	Sheets of tetrahedra each sharing 3 oxygens	Si_4O_{10} 2:5	-4	Muscovite KAl_2 $[(AlSi_3)O_{10}].(OH)_2$
E. Tectosilicates	Three-dimensional framework of tetrahedra, each sharing all 4 oxygens	SiO_2 1:2	0	Quartz SiO_2 Orthoclase $KAlSi_3O_8$

General physical properties of the silicate minerals in relation to structure. The structural complexity of the five groups of silicate minerals established above increases from that of the independent SiO_4-tetrahedra of the nesosilicates to that of the three-dimensional

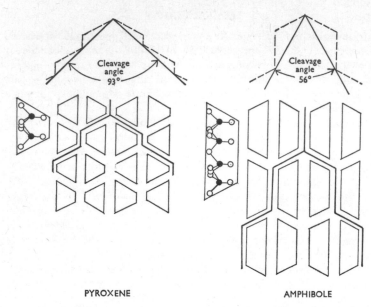

PYROXENE   AMPHIBOLE

FIG. 58. Relation of cleavage to structure in pyroxene (*left*), and amphibole (*right*). The chains of SiO_4-tetrahedra are viewed end-on; note that the cleavage planes are in fact made up of a series of steps.

frameworks of the tectosilicates. Comparable with these structural changes are certain general trends in physical properties. The *specific gravity* in general decreases with increasing structural complexity: olivines and the pyroxenes have average specific gravities of 3·2, feldspars and quartz 2·6. *Refractive index* similarly decreases, that for olivine and the pyroxenes being around 1·7, of feldspars and quartz 1·5. There are, of course, a large number of other factors controlling these properties. *Cleavage*, as we have seen, takes place along those planes across which the bonding is weakest. Nesosilicates and sorosilicates have in general poorly developed cleavages, if any. Chain structures in such inosilicates as the pyroxenes and amphiboles control the two directions of cleavage shown by these minerals — the cleavages pass between the chains and intersect at angles characteristic for the two groups of minerals, as shown in Fig. 58. In minerals with sheet structures there is often, as we have seen, a perfect cleavage parallel to the sheets, as in the micas. In quartz the bonds are evenly distributed in all directions and the mineral has no cleavage: other tectosilicates such as the feldspars possess a cleavage controlled by patterns in the framework.

Finally, it may be noted that the *temperature of formation* of the silicate minerals appears to decrease with increasing structural complexity. Olivine crystallises from a melt at a much higher temperature than do quartz or feldspar.

THE ROCK-FORMING MINERALS

As we saw in Chapter 2, the average igneous rock has 46·60 per cent oxygen, 27·72 per cent silicon and 24·27 per cent Al Fe Ca Mg Na K — these eight elements making nearly 99 per cent of the whole. The common minerals of the igneous rocks are accordingly silica, as quartz, and silicates. In spite of the great variety in composition of the igneous rocks and of the large number of mineral silicates known, it is found that seven families of minerals make up something like 99 per cent of these rocks. These rock-forming minerals of the igneous rocks are quartz, the feldspars and feldspathoids, the micas, the amphiboles, the pyroxenes and the olivine family.

The common minerals of the sedimentary rocks are of two origins, those persisting from the parent rock and those formed by chemical reactions from these. Quartz and feldspars are the common inherited minerals; the secondary minerals are especially the clay-minerals — hydrous aluminium silicates with sheet structures — and the carbonates, calcite $CaCO_3$, and dolomite $CaCO_3. MgCO_3$, which form the limestones of chemical or organic origin. The soluble products of chemical reactions at the earth's surface are transported to the sea or to inland lakes; under suitable conditions these solutions may be concentrated to give deposits of evaporates such as rock-salt.

The common minerals developed in the metamorphic rocks in response to changed conditions of temperature, pressure and chemical environment belong to the same families as those found in the igneous rocks. Quartz and feldspars are abundant, as are pyroxenes and amphiboles amongst the inosilicates. Phyllosilicates are particularly characteristic of metamorphic rocks, such families as the micas and chlorites being responsible for the typical textures of many of these rocks: less common phyllosilicates are talc and serpentine. Nesosilicates are represented by members of the olivine family and by the typically metamorphic families of the garnets, epidotes and the aluminium silicates, andalusite, kyanite and sillimanite. There occur also a number of less common silicates in the metamorphic rocks and besides, the carbonates, calcite and dolomite, are the main components of metamorphosed limestones.

Some properties of the common rock-forming minerals. This chapter on mineralogy now finishes with summary statements on the chief rock-forming minerals mentioned above. No attempt is made at completeness especially on the diagnostic side, but some emphasis is placed on chemical composition, structure and manner of formation. The ore-minerals are listed in Chapter 11 and the evaporate minerals in Chapter 4. We begin with the seven great families, quartz, feldspars, feldspathoids, micas, amphiboles, pyroxenes and olivines, pass on to the other common silicates and finish with the non-silicate minerals.

Quartz and other forms of silica. We may notice three minerals with the composition SiO_2, quartz, tridymite and cristobalite, quartz being of course the commonest of the three and, indeed, of all minerals. The three SiO_2 minerals are built up of SiO_4-tetrahedra linked together in three different ways to form three-dimensional frameworks. The packing is denser in quartz than in tridymite and cristobalite, a circumstance reflected in the densities and refractive indices of the three minerals, thus:

Density:	Quartz 2·65	Tridymite 2·26	Cristobalite 2·32
Refractive Index:	— 1·55	— 1·47	— 1·49

Quartz, tridymite and cristobalite are stable over different temperature ranges, quartz below 870°, tridymite 870–1470° C, and cristobalite 1470°–1713° C, this last temperature being the melting point of silica. Further, tridymite and cristobalite are not stable at high pressures, quartz is. As was to be expected, therefore, quartz is typical of the deep-seated plutonic rocks, whilst tridymite and cristobalite are found only in volcanic surface lavas. Quartz itself can exist in two modifications; high-temperature or β-quartz forms between 570° and 870° C, but at about 573° C it inverts to low-temperature or α-quartz. By certain criteria, such as form and twinning, it can be shown that the quartz of igneous rocks was originally the β-type, whilst that of quartz veins crystallised in the α-form. It is concluded from this that the quartz-bearing igneous rocks consolidated above 573° C, the quartz veins below this temperature. These temperatures are at atmospheric pressure.

Additional facts concerning quartz are: crystal system trigonal (rhombohedral) (see Figs. 35 and 37); common crystal form, hexagonal prism terminated by two equally developed rhombohedra; colourless or coloured by impurities; conchoidal fracture; hardness 7; specific gravity 2·65; refractive indices 1·544–1·553, birefringence ·009 (see Fig. 51); optically positive, uniaxial.

The feldspar family. As we have seen, the feldspars are tectosilicates in which Si^{+4} of the SiO_2-units is partly replaced by Al^{+3}, necessitating the introduction of cations to restore electrical equilibrium. On this basis, the three main components of the Feldspar Family can be developed as follows: equilibrium is restored in the Si_4O_8-unit

(1) on the substitution of 1 Al^{+3} for 1 Si^{+4}, by the introduction of 1 K^{+1} giving $KAlSi_3O_8$, the potassium feldspar ORTHOCLASE,
(2) on the substitution of 1 Al^{+3} for 1 Si^{+4} by the introduction of 1 Na^{+1} giving $NaAlSi_3O_8$, the sodium feldspar ALBITE,
(3) on the substitution of 2 Al^{+3} for 2 Si^{+4} by the introduction of Ca^{+2} giving $CaAl_2Si_2O_8$, the calcium feldspar ANORTHITE.

The structure of the feldspars is a three-dimensional framework of SiO_4- and AlO_4-tetrahedra with the cations K, Na and Ca in the interstices; when the cation is large, as K, the crystal symmetry is monoclinic, when small, as Na and Ca, it is triclinic.

Orthoclase, $KAlSi_3O_8$, is monoclinic; there is another *potash-feldspar, microcline*, of the same composition but pseudo-monoclinic, its axial lengths and crystal angles differing very slightly from those of orthoclase. It is possible that these two potash-feldspars differ in their structure, orthoclase having Al and Si randomly distributed, microcline having them ordered. Between albite, $NaAlSi_3O_8$, and anorthite, $CaAl_2Si_2O_8$, there exists a series of solid-solution mixtures produced by the substitution of NaSi for CaAl: this isomorphous series is the *plagioclase-feldspars* or *soda-lime feldspars*. Another series, the *alkali feldspars*, exists between orthoclase and albite giving the intermediate species of *soda-orthoclase*, (K,Na) $AlSi_3O_8$ which is monoclinic, and *anorthoclase*, (Na, K) $AlSi_3O_8$, triclinic. Substitution of Na by Ca is easy in the plagioclases since the two cations are about the same size; substitution of K by Na is more difficult because of the great size-difference between the two cations, and alkali feldspars are less abundant; no substitution of K by Ca seems possible and no feldspar mixtures between orthoclase and anorthite are known. This information concerning the composition and classification of the feldspars is given in Fig. 59. The compositions in oxide percentages of the pure end-members of the feldspar series are given below:

	K_2O	Na_2O	CaO	Al_2O_3	SiO_2
Orthoclase	16·9	—	—	18·4	64·7
Albite	—	11·8	—	19·5	68·7
Anorthite	—	—	20·1	36·7	43·2

We have seen that microcline and orthoclase differ in the perfection of their atomic structure — similar differences are found in all the main feldspar types and have been related to the temperatures of

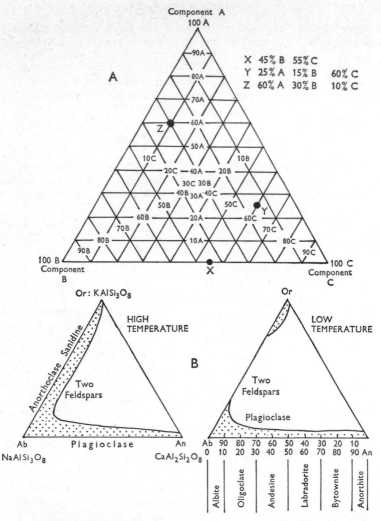

FIG. 59. A, Three-component Compositional Diagram. Verify the compositions indicated by points x, y and z, B. Composition diagram of the feldspars with classification indicated. Note that at all temperatures a solid solution series exists between Ab and An but only at high temperatures between Or and Ab.

their formation. Thus, for the potassium feldspars, a high temperature form, *sanidine*, with considerable disorder in its lattice structure, characterises high temperature lavas; *orthoclase*, with a partly ordered lattice structure, appears in lower-temperature lavas and

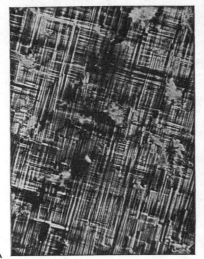

A   B

FIG. 60. A, Microcline, with small perthitic patches: polars crossed,
× 25; B, vein perthite in orthoclase: polars crossed, × 20.

igneous rocks consolidated at no great depth, and the well-ordered
microcline characterises the more deep-seated rocks. Similarly, high
and low temperature forms of albite and of anorthite exist, very
slight differences in optical properties distinguishing the two forms in
each case.

Natural feldspars are never pure end members. Orthoclase may
contain a small amount of albite and this often appears as *perthite
intergrowths*. The plagioclase forms wisps, films and patches regularly
orientated in the potassium feldspar host. In the formation of most
examples of perthite, unmixing or *exsolution* (p. 69) at lower
temperature has occurred in a homogeneous high-temperature
crystal; at high temperature, the NaK ions may have a random
distribution which gives place, at lower temperature, to an orderly
arrangement of Na-rich and K-rich parts. In *antiperthite*, orthoclase
wisps occur in the plagioclase host.

The general properties of the feldspars (Fig. 60) are these. Their
colour is whitish, greyish or pale shades of red. Their hardness is
about 6, specific gravity 2·5–2·74. Though, as we have seen, they
crystallise in different systems, their crystals are alike in habit, the
prism (110), side pinacoid (010) and basal pinacoid (001) being
dominant (see Fig. 37). Two principal cleavages are developed,
parallel to (010) and (001) and thus at right angles or nearly so.
Twinning is common, simple in orthoclase, repeated in plagioclase —

103

its appearance in thin sections is shown in Fig. 52 (see also Fig. 40). Orthoclase has refractive indices of 1·518–1·526; microcline has slightly higher refractive indices and shows between crossed nicols a characteristic 'cross-hatched' appearance.

The plagioclase feldspars show a continuous gradation in physical properties, the end-terms being given in the following table:

	Spec. Grav.	Cleavage angle	Refractive Index	Maximum extinction in zone ⊥ 010
Albite	2·605	86° 24′	1·525–1·536	−18°
Anorthite	2·765	85° 50′	1·576–1·588	+60°

The feldspathoids. The feldspathoids (Fig. 61) are alkali-aluminium tectosilicates with their SiO_4- and AlO_4-tetrahedra linked in the same way as in the feldspars, from which they differ in having a lower Si : Al ratio. The two chief feldspathoids are *nepheline* (artificial nepheline is $NaAlSiO_4$) and *leucite* $KAlSi_2O_6$, and their relations to the analogous feldspars may be represented as:

$$NaAlSiO_4 + 2SiO_2 \rightarrow NaAlSi_3O_8$$
$$\text{(nepheline)} \quad \text{(silica)} \quad \text{(albite)}$$

$$KAlSi_2O_6 + SiO_2 \rightarrow KAlSi_3O_8$$
$$\text{(leucite)} \quad \text{(silica)} \quad \text{(orthoclase)}$$

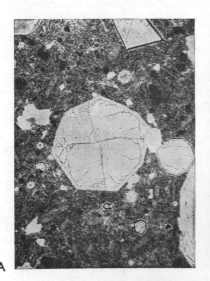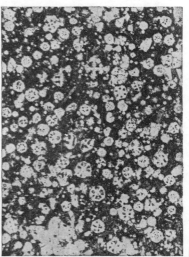

A   B

FIG. 61. A, Leucite in leucite-basalt, × 20; B, Leucites showing inclusions, in leucite-basalt, × 20.

Most feldspathoid is the result of crystallisation from a rock melt or magma (see p. 364) which, as was to be expected from the foregoing equations, must be one relatively poor in silica and rich in alkalies.

The artificial nepheline composition is never attained by natural *nepheline* which can be considered to be an isomorphous mixture of $NaAlSiO_4$, $KAlSiO_4$ and $SiSiO_4$, that is, SiO_2 — its general composition can be stated as $(NaK)(AlSi)_2O_4$. Nepheline is the commonest feldspathoid, occurring in volcanic and more deep-seated igneous rocks. It crystallises in the hexagonal system, a common combination being hexagonal prism and basal plane; it has a distinct prismatic cleavage. Nepheline is colourless or whitish, often with a greasy lustre, its hardness is 5–5·6, specific gravity 2·5–2·6, refractive indices 1·541–1·538, and the mineral is uniaxial negative.

COMPOSITION OF FELDSPATHOIDS

	Na_2O	K_2O	Al_2O_3	SiO_2	Cl
Nepheline, $NaAlSiO_4$ (artificial)	21·8	—	35·9	42·3	—
Leucite, $KAlSi_2O_6$	—	21·5	23·5	55·0	—
Sodalite, $3(NaAlSiO_4)$. NaCl.	25·6	—	31·6	37·2	7·3

Leucite, $KAlSi_2O_6$, is confined to the volcanic rocks of a few regions. It crystallises as trapezohedra (211) in such high-temperature lavas, but on cooling below about 600° it becomes pseudo-cubic and shows complex twinning between crossed nicols. Leucite is white or grey in colour, its hardness is 5·5–6, specific gravity 2·5; its refractive index is 1·508–1·509, and it may be isotropic, or show twinning bands and low polarisation-colours; symmetrically arranged inclusions in the equant crystals can often be observed in thin sections.

Three other feldspathoids may be mentioned and their composition, to be compared with nepheline, given:

Sodalite $3(NaAlSiO_4)$.NaCl
Hauyne $3(NaAlSiO_4)$.CaSO_4
Cancrinite $4(NaAlSiO_4)$.CaCO_3.H_2O.

These minerals may accompany nepheline or leucite in alkali-rich igneous rocks.

The micas. The two most important micas are muscovite and biotite, less common species being paragonite and phlogopite. The compositions of these minerals are:

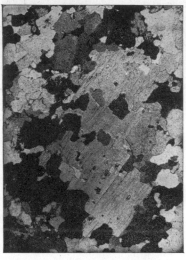

A   B

FIG. 62. A, Biotite, showing form, cleavage, pleochroism and
pleochroic haloes, × 20; B, Muscovite, a large plate showing cleavage:
polars crossed, × 20.

Muscovite $KAl_2[(AlSi_3)O_{10}].(OH)_2$
Paragonite $NaAl_2[(AlSi_3)O_{10}].(OH)_2$
Biotite $K(Mg, Fe)_3[(AlSi_3)O_{10}].(OH)_2$
Phlogopite $KMg_3[(AlSi_3)O_{10}].(OH)_2$

The micas are the chief representatives of the phyllosilicates, those
with sheet or layer-lattice structure. Muscovite has been used to
exemplify this sheet-structure, as set out before on p. 96.

In muscovite it will be noted that a quarter of the Si has been
replaced by Al, the charge being balanced by bringing in K^{+1}. In
paragonite, this K is replaced by Na. In biotite Mg and Fe take the
place of Al, and in phlogopite Mg alone. The manner of co-ordination
of the hydroxyl (OH) ions is used to group the micas into two classes.
In the *dioctahedral* micas, such as muscovite and paragonite, there are
two Al ions to each octahedron of OH ions, in the *trioctahedral* micas,
biotite and phlogopite, there are three Mg ions to each OH octahedron.

Muscovite (white mica) and biotite (black mica) are abundant
rock-forming minerals (Fig. 62). Both occur commonly in igneous
rocks, especially in the granitic types, and are essential components
of many metamorphic rocks such as mica-gneisses, mica-schists and
micaceous hornfelses. Detrital micas coat the bedding planes of many
sedimentary rocks such as sandstones.

As a consequence of their sheet-structure, all micas possess a perfect basal cleavage giving elastic plates. All crystallise in the monoclinic system but the forms approximate to those of the hexagonal system. Their average hardness is 2·5, their specific gravity ranges from 2·7 to 3·1. In thin section, muscovite is colourless, biaxial, its lowest refractive index is about 1·560, its highest about 1·600. Biotite in thin section is strongly pleochroic in brown, reddish brown and yellow; its refractive indices range from about 1·584 to 1·648; it is almost uniaxial.

Sericite is a group name applied to a fine scaly form of white mica, usually taken to be of muscovite composition but not necessarily so.

The amphiboles. The amphiboles comprise a number of isomorphous series of inosilicates in which extensive replacement of ions leads to complex chemical compositions. The general formula can be given as $(WXY)_{7-8}(Z_4O_{11})_2(O, OH, F)_2$ and the chemical complexities to be expected will be realised when we state that W can be Ca or Na, X can be Mg, Fe^{+2} Mn^{+2}, Y can be Ti, Al, Fe^{+3} and Z can be Si and Al; besides this, it will be noted that F and OH enter the structure in varying degrees. We have used a common amphibole, the mineral tremolite $Ca_2Mg_5[Si_4O_{11}]_2(OH)_2$, to illustrate the double-chain variety of the inosilicate structure (see p. 96 and fig. 57). The double chains run parallel to the length of the tremolite crystal, which is the c-axis, and are held together laterally by cations Ca^{+2} and Mg^{+2}. The bonding along the chains is stronger than between them, resulting in the elongation of amphiboles into fibres or prisms parallel to the c-axis and in the development of a good prismatic cleavage (see Fig. 58).

Five isomorphous series of amphiboles of varying importance are given below. Of these, anthophyllite is orthorhombic in crystallisation, the others monoclinic.

Anthophyllite Series: $(Mg, Fe)_7(Si_4O_{11})_2(OH)_2$, with Mg dominant over Fe

Cummingtonite Series:
    Cummingtonite $(Mg, Fe)_7(Si_4O_{11})_2(OH)_2$
    Grunerite $(Fe, Mg)_7(Si_4O_{11})_2(OH)_2$

Tremolite Series:
    Tremolite $Ca_2Mg_5(Si_4O_{11})_2(OH)_2$
    Actinolite $Ca_2(Mg, Fe)_5(Si_4O_{11})_2(OH)_2$

Hornblende Series: $(Ca, Na, Mg, Fe, Al)_{7-8}[(Al, Si)_4O_{11}]_2(OH)_2$

Alkali Amphibole Series:
    Arfvedsonite $Na_3Mg_4[(AlSi)_4O_{11}]_2(OH)_2$
    Glaucophane $Na_2(Mg, Fe)_3(AlFe^{+3})_2(Si_4O_{11})_2(OH)_2$
    Riebeckite $Na_2Fe^{+2}_3Fe^{+3}_2(Si_4O_{11})_2(OH)_2$

A
B

FIG. 63. A, Hornblende, showing form and cleavage in transverse and longitudinal sections, × 15; B, Tremolite, in elongated prismatic crystals showing cleavage, × 30.

Members of the anthophyllite, cummingtonite and tremolite series occur in metamorphic rocks of appropriate compositions. Hornblende, the commonest amphibole, appears as a primary constituent of deep-seated igneous rocks and is common in metamorphic derivatives of such rocks. Arfvedsonite and riebeckite crystallise from magmas rich in silica and soda, and glaucophane commonly in metamorphosed rocks of a similar composition.

Brief notes on the more important amphibole species are now given (Fig. 63). All show a perfect prismatic cleavage visible in thin sections as two sets of cleavage cracks intersecting at about 120°. Those occurring in metamorphic rocks form elongated crystals, blades or fibres, the extreme development being seen in *asbestos*. In thin section, *tremolite* is colourless, *actinolite* pleochroic in shades of yellow and green; refractive indices increase from tremolite, e.g. 1·599–1·625 to actinolite, e.g. 1·628–1·655. *Common hornblende* occurs in prismatic crystals, being combinations of prism (110), clinopinacoid (010), clinodome (011) and hemiorthodome (10$\bar{1}$), (see Fig. 37); simple twinning on 100 is commonly seen; in thin section hornblende is pleochroic in shades of yellow, green or brown, six-sided transverse sections showing two sets of cleavages meeting at 120°, longitudinal sections showing one set of cleavages and extinguishing at 18–20°; refractive indices are fairly high, e.g. 1·629–1·653. The *alkali*

108

amphiboles are usually strongly pleochroic in blue, green and yellow, and occur in prismatic, fibrous or granular forms.

The pyroxenes. The pyroxenes are inosilicates with a single chain structure, the SiO_4-tetrahedra being linked by sharing two O ions each and the tetrahedra having their apexes oriented as shown in Fig. 57. This arrangement gives the general composition $n(Si_2O_6)$ with a charge of -4 in excess, which is balanced in different pyroxenes by different positive ions. The general pyroxene formula can be written as $(W)_{1-y}(XY)_{1+y}(Si_2O_6)$, where W may be Na or Ca, X may be Mg, Fe^{+2}, Li or Mn, Y may be Al, Fe^{+3} or Ti; part of the Si may be replaced by Al in four-fold co-ordination.

The pyroxenes form a number of isomorphous series which can be placed in two groups, the orthopyroxenes crystallising in the orthorhombic system and the clinopyroxenes crystallising in the monoclinic system. The chief series are:

> *Orthopyroxenes. Enstatite-Hypersthene Series:*
>   Enstatite $MgSiO_3$
>   Hypersthene $(Mg, Fe)SiO_3$
> *Clinopyroxenes*
> *Diopside-Hedenbergite Series*:
>   Diopside $CaMgSi_2O_6$
>   Hedenbergite $CaFeSi_2O_6$
> *Augite Series* (aluminous):
>   Augite $(Ca, Mg, Fe, Al)_2.(Al, Si)_2O_6$
>   Pigeonite $(Ca, Mg)(Mg, Fe)(Si_2O_6)$
> *Alkali-pyroxene Series:*
>   Acmite, Aegirine $NaFe^{+3}(Si_2O_6)$
>   Jadeite $NaAl(Si_2O_6)$

The orthopyroxenes occur as constituents of basic and ultrabasic igneous rocks (see p. 407) and of highly metamorphosed rocks of various origins. The diopside-hedenbergite series is commonly found in metamorphosed impure calcareous rocks, and diopside itself is often of primary magmatic crystallisation. Augite is a common constituent of many igneous rocks and also of certain highly metamorphosed rocks. Acmite crystallises from soda-rich magmas.

The chain structure of the pyroxenes controls their cleavage (see fig. 58), the cleavages passing between the chains and thus being prismatic; the characteristic cleavage angle is about 90°. In thin slices, these cleavages appear in transverse sections as two sets of cracks at right angles and in prismatic sections as one set parallel to the length.

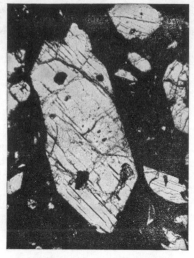

A   B

FIG. 64. A, Hypersthene, prismatic crystals, in norite, ×15; B, Augite, oblique transverse section showing cleavage, in basalt, ×15.

Some physical properties of the commonest pyroxenes are now given (Fig. 64). The *orthopyroxenes*, $MgSiO_3 - FeSiO_3$, comprise two common minerals, enstatite with up to 15 per cent $FeSiO_3$ and hypersthene with 15–60 per cent $FeSiO_3$. These two species show a gradation in physical properties, the specific gravity, depth of colour and pleochroism, refractive indices and birefringence increasing with the iron content. Thus, typical values of refractive index for enstatite are 1·656–1·665, for hypersthene, 1·673–1·683 to 1·715–1·731. Hypersthene shows marked pleochroism in pink, yellow and green and often contains tiny platy inclusions arranged in varying sets of parallel planes — these are called *schiller-plates*. In the *diopside-hedenbergite* series of non-aluminous clinopyroxenes, the specific gravity and refractive index increase, the birefringence decreases and the extinction angle on the clinopinacoid increases as more Fe is substituted for Mg in the diopside lattice. Thus a sample diopside has specific gravity 3·2–3·28, refractive index 1·673–1·703, and a sample hedenbergite specific gravity 3·7, refractive index 1·739–1·757. Common *augite* forms black or greenish-black crystals made up of the prism (110), clinopinacoid (010), orthopinacoid (100) and negative hemipyramid (111), often twinned on (100); in thin slices, augite is pale brownish-green non-pleochroic; a typical specimen gave refractive indices, α 1·698, β 1·704, γ 1·723. The specific gravity

110

of augite is 3·2–3·5. The *alkali pyroxenes* have higher refractive indices than augite or diopside, show a strong birefringence and are markedly pleochroic in browns and greens.

The olivines. As we have already seen on p. 95, the olivine group of minerals are nesosilicates forming an isomorphous series between forsterite $Mg_2(SiO_4)$ and fayalite $Fe_2(SiO_4)$, common olivine being represented as $(Mg, Fe)_2 (SiO_4)$. Each SiO_4-tetrahedron of the nesosilicate structure is linked to two divalent ions, Mg^{+2} or Fe^{+2}, and each 0 ion is linked with 1 Si and 3 Mg or Fe, these last being in six-fold co-ordination. This tight structure of the olivines, in common with other nesosilicates, expresses itself in equant compact crystals with high specific gravity and high refractive index. Some values for forsterite, common olivine and fayalite are:

$$Forsterite: 3·2 \quad \beta\ 1·661$$
$$Olivine: \quad\quad\quad \beta\ 1·681–1·706$$
$$Fayalite: \quad 4·3 \quad \beta\ 1·864$$

Forsterite is found in thermally altered impure limestones (see p. 524), according to the reaction:

$$2(CaCO_3.MgCO_3)+SiO_2 \rightarrow 2CaCO_3+Mg_2SiO_4+2CO_2$$
$$\text{dolomite} \quad\quad \text{quartz} \quad\quad \text{calcite} \quad \text{forsterite}$$

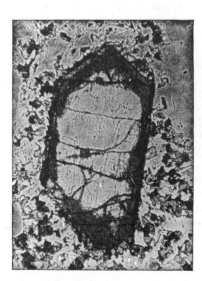
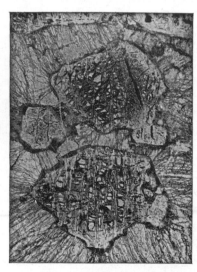

A   B

Fig. 65. A, Olivine, longitudinal section showing form, parting and marginal alteration, in basalt, × 30; B, Olivine, much serpentinised, in troctolite, × 20; the volume increase on serpentinisation has caused radial cracks in the feldspar.

Common olivine, $(Mg, Fe)_2SiO_4$, forms in the early high-temperature stages of the crystallisation of magmas relatively poor in silica and may accumulate by sinking to build igneous rocks very rich in olivine, such as the peridotites.

Olivine crystallises in the orthorhombic system; in thin slice it is colourless and shows no cleavages; its refractive index is high and birefringence strong. It is commonly altered to serpentine with the disengagement of black iron-oxide particles (Fig. 65).

OTHER COMMON SILICATES

The seven great families of minerals especially characteristic of igneous rocks have now been described and we may pass on to review briefly other silicates that occur fairly abundantly or significantly in various kinds of rocks. These additional silicates may conveniently be considered in their structural groups, tectosilicates to nesosilicates.

Tectosilicates. The silicates with a structure similar to that of quartz, feldspars and feldspathoids that we deal with here are (i) the Zeolites (ii) the Scapolites.

The Zeolites. All members of the zeolite family conform to the composition $n(SiO_2)$ as required by their linked framework structure; Al replaces part of the Si and the resulting negative charges on the framework are balanced by cations such as Na K or Ca which lie in open spaces in the structure. Water molecules are also accommodated in these spaces and their presence in the wide spacing of the structure results in certain special characters of this group of minerals. Thus, the H_2O group, together with the alkali ions, can be exchanged without disrupting the zeolite structure, thus giving these minerals their 'base exchange' property (see also p. 115). Two zeolites, for example, are related in composition thus:

$$natrolite \ Na_2Al_2Si_3O_{10}.2H_2O$$
$$scolecite \ CaAl_2Si_3O_{10}.3H_2O$$

Replacement of 2 $Na^{+1} + 2H_2O$ by 1 $Ca^{+2} + 3H_2O$ does not destroy the structure. Further, the water in zeolites is given off with frothing on heating the minerals, a circumstance that underlies their name, Greek *zein* to boil. When their water has been completely evacuated, zeolites can act as *molecular sieves*, permitting the selective entry or passage of other substances according to their molecular sizes relative to the dimensions of the zeolite structure concerned.

In composition, the zeolites are in many ways analogous to the feldspars, CaAl being replacable by NaSi. In general, they result from the hydration of feldspars and similar minerals in igneous rocks, and occur for example filling steam-holes, cavities and fissures in

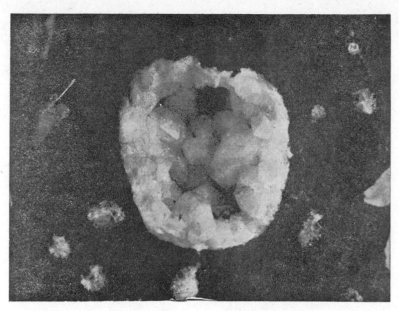

Fig. 66. Zeolites filling amygdales in Tertiary basalts.
Above, Gmelinite, a soda-rich species from Antrim, × 5.
Below, Mesolite, a NaCa species from Ireland, × 2.

113

lavas (Fig. 66). They are formed during the final stages in the consolidation of igneous magmas and are often associated with ore-
deposits of the same origin. The chief species that may be mentioned
are:

Cubic Zeolite.	Analcime: $Na(AlSi_2)O_6.H_2O$
Fibrous Zeolites.	Natrolite $Na_2(Al_2Si_3O_{10}).2H_2O$
	Scolecite $Ca(Al_2Si_3O_{10}).3H_2O$
	Thomsonite $NaCa_2(Al_5Si_5O_{20}).6H_2O$
Other Zeolites.	Heulandite $Ca_2(Al_4Si_{14}O_{36}).12H_2O$
	Phillipsite $(K, Ca)(Al_2Si_4O_{12})4\frac{1}{2}H_2O$
	Stilbite $(Na, Ca)(Al_2Si_6O_{16}).6H_2O$

The Scapolites. The scapolites resemble the plagioclase feldspars
in composition and structure but have interspersed anions so that
they can be described as 'double salts' of plagioclase and NaCl or
$CaCO_3$. Common scapolite is a mixture of two end-members of an
isomorphous series, namely:

Marialite $3(NaAlSi_3O_8).NaCl$	*cf.* 3 albite + NaCl
Meionite $3(CaAl_2Si_2O_8).CaCO_3$	*cf.* 3 anorthite + $CaCO_3$

Scapolite crystallises in the tetragonal system and is accordingly
optically uniaxial, its cleavage is prismatic. It occurs in metamorphic
rocks of suitable composition or as an alteration-product of lime-
rich plagioclases.

Phyllosilicates. We have seen that the common phyllosilicates are
the micas, with a sheet-structure expressing itself in a perfect basal
cleavage. Additional phyllosilicates that have to be briefly considered
here are various 'flaky' minerals such as chlorite, talc, serpentine,
the clay-minerals, and still more briefly, chloritoid and glauconite.

The *chlorites* are related in composition to the micas, but contain
no alkalies. They may be considered to be hydrous silicates of Al Fe
and Mg, the properties of different types varying with the Fe : Mg
ratio; an approximate formula is $(Mg, Fe)_5.Al(AlSi_3)O_{10}.(OH)_8$.
The chlorites are monoclinic, greenish in colour, with a perfect basal
cleavage, and hardness of 2. In thin slice, they are moderately
pleochroic in shades of yellow and green, with moderate refractive
index and very low birefringence, often shown by anomalous inky-
blue polarisation colours. Chlorite is a common constituent of the
metamorphic rocks.

Talc is a hydrous magnesium silicate, $Mg_3Si_4O_{10}.(OH)_2$, occurring
in white or greenish compact masses of flakes showing a perfect
basal cleavage. It is soft (H = 1) and its specific gravity is 2·7–2·8.
Talc is formed from magnesium-rich rocks by metamorphism of

various kinds or by the action of magmatic waters. *Steatite* is massive compact talc.

Serpentine, either as a mineral or a rock, is another hydrous magnesian silicate, $Mg_6Si_4O_{10}(OH)_8$, occurring in massive granular, platy or fibrous associations, of varied colours; its hardness is 3–4, specific gravity 2·5–2·6. Two varieties may be mentioned, a fibrous form *chrysotile* and a bladed form *antigorite* (see also p. 605). Serpentine is produced by the modification of magnesium-rich rocks during metamorphism of one kind or another.

The *clay-minerals* are a group of hydrous aluminous phyllosilicates that constitute the clay fraction of the sediments and sedimentary rocks and are produced by the modification of other aluminous silicates. They form exceedingly small flakes with the Si_4O_{10}-sheet structure. The principal clay-minerals or groups of minerals are:

Kaolinite $Al_4Si_4O_{10}(OH)_8$

Montmorillonite $Al_4(Si_4O_{10})_2.xH_2O$

Illite $K_yAl_4(Si_{8-y}Al_y)O_{20}.(OH)_4$

Illite has a structure intermediate between that of muscovite and that of montmorillonite and the series muscovite-illite-montmorillonite may represent a reversible genetic sequence.

The clay-minerals have a high *base-exchange capacity*, that is, the property of exchanging some of their cations (especially) for others brought into contact with them in solutions. This is important in a number of surface-processes, such as weathering or rock-decay, the modification of the composition of underground water by, for example, the exchange of Na for Ca or Mg, and in making available plant food in soils. Some of these topics are dealt with in later pages.

FIG. 67. Chloritoid in phyllite, × 15.

Chloritoid is the chief member of a group of phyllosilicates known as the *brittle micas*, since they resemble the micas in form, cleavage and structure, but their cleavage flakes are non-elastic and brittle. Chloritoid may have a composition represented by $FeAl_2SiO_5.(OH)_2$ in which 2/5 of the Fe^{+2} may be replaced by Mg and less than 1/5 by Mn. Chloritoid occurs in metamorphic rocks of sedimentary origin, especially those of clayey composition metamorphosed under strong stress (Fig. 67).

Glauconite is essentially a hydrous silicate of Fe and K, though Al Mg and Ca are often present. Its composition might be represented by $K_2(MgFe)_2Al_6(Si_4O_{10})_3 (OH)_{12}$. Glauconite occurs as green grains in the 'greensands' and is being formed in oceanic sediments at the present day. It may arise by the alteration of FeMg-silicates, especially biotite.

Sorosilicates (Fig. 68). The chief sorosilicates have already been mentioned in the account of this type of silicate structure. It will be recalled that the SiO_4-tetrahedra here form separate groups by sharing one or more of their O ions.

The mineral *melilite*, $Ca_2Mg[Si_2O_7]$, is an example of the simplest case, two tetrahedra sharing a common O, the group becoming Si_2O_7. Some substitution of Na for Ca, and Al for Si or Mg may take place. Melilite is not a common mineral, occurring in lavas low in silica and without feldspar; it is also a common constituent of slags.

When the sorosilicate group is formed by the sharing of O ions by more than two tetrahedra, ring structures are formed with the general composition Si_nO_{3n}. *Wollastonite*, $Ca_3[Si_3O_9]$ illustrates the joining of three tetrahedra in this way. Wollastonite occurs in tabular crystals or fibres, with a good cleavage parallel to the front pinacoid. It is whitish or greyish, with hardness 4·5–5 and specific gravity 2·8–2·9. It occurs as a product of the thermal metamorphism of impure limestone.

In *beryl*, $Be_3Al_2[Si_6O_{18}]$, six tetrahedra are joined to give the group composition of Si_6O_{18} (Fig. 57). Beryl crystallises in the hexagonal system, crystals commonly being prismatic with terminations of pyramid and basal pinacoid. Colour is usually greenish, hardness 7·5–8, specific gravity 2·7; gem varieties are *emerald*, green, and *aquamarine*, pale blue. Beryl occurs as an accessory constituent of silica-rich igneous rocks, especially pegmatites (p. 574), and in metamorphic rocks of various kinds.

Another sorosilicate is *cordierite*, $Mg_2Al_3[AlSi_5O_{18}]$ in which an Al ion replaces a Si ion in the four-fold co-ordination position. Iron may replace magnesium in varying amounts. Cordierite is ortho-rhombic, its colour various shades of blue, hardness 7–7·5, specific

A
B

FIG. 68. A, Cordierite, transverse section showing complex sector twinning, in hornfels, Aberdeenshire, × 20; B, Tourmaline showing longitudinal and transverse sections, × 30.

gravity 2·6–2·7. In thin slices cordierite is colourless, with refractive indices near those of quartz and balsam, and birefringence slightly higher than that of quartz. Sector-twinning (Fig. 68A) is often seen and pleochroic haloes around zircon inclusions are common. Cordierite occurs in metamorphic rocks formed at high temperatures and as a constituent of rocks resulting from the consolidation of magmas that have been contaminated with sediments of clay composition.

The last sorosilicate to be mentioned is *tourmaline*, with a general formula of $XY_3B_3Al_3[(Al, Si)_3O_5]_3$ $(OH, F)_4$ where X may be Na or Ca and Y may be Mg, Fe or Li. Varieties arise according to which metals are present; common tourmaline contains Na, Ca, Mg, Fe^{+2} and Fe^{+3}. Tourmaline crystallises in the rhombohedral hemimorphic class (Fig. 35) of the hexagonal system and commonly forms prismatic crystals three-sided in cross-section, needles or aggregated grains. It is usually black in colour, its hardness is 7–7·5 and specific gravity 2·98–3·2. Under the microscope (Fig. 68B), tourmaline is usually dark brown, green or yellow, with strong pleochroism in these colours. Its refractive index is high, e.g. 1·642–1·622, and birefringence is moderate; it is uniaxial, optically negative. Tourmaline occurs as an accessory constituent of igneous rocks rich in silica, especially pegmatites, and as a result of gas action at igneous contacts and in certain metamorphic rocks.

117

A   B

FIG. 69. A, Garnet, showing form, high refractive index, absence of
cleavage, × 30; B, Idocrase, showing zoning, × 15.

Nesosilicates. It will be recalled that this group of silicates is
characterised by a structure of independent SiO_4-tetrahedra linked
together by metallic cations. The SiO_4-group has itself an excess of
four negative charges which are neutralised by the appropriate
cations; the Si : O ratio is 1 : 4. A number of important mineral
families are nesosilicates — those considered here are the garnets,
idocrase (Fig. 69), zircon, topaz and the epidotes; with the normal
nesosilicates we can take a group comprising staurolite and the
aluminium silicate family, sillimanite, andalusite and kyanite.

The *Garnets* have the general formula of $X^{+2}{}_3Y^{+3}{}_2(SiO_4)_3$ where
$X^{+2} = Ca$, Mg, Fe, Mn and $Y^{+3} = Fe$, Al, Cr, Ti. Two mixed series
can be separated which, with their chief species, are now given:

Almandine Series: $(Mg, Fe, Mn)_3Al_2[SiO_4]_3$
    Pyrope $Mg_3Al_2[SiO_4]_3$
    Almandine $Fe_3Al_2[SiO_4]_3$
    Spessartine $Mn_3Al_2[SiO_4]_3$
Andradite Series: $Ca_3(Al, Fe, Cr)_2[SiO_4]_3$
    Grossular $Ca_3Al_2[SiO_4]_3$
    Andradite $Ca_3Fe_2[SiO_4]_3$
    Uvarovite $Ca_3Cr_2[SiO_4]_3$

All garnets are cubic, common forms being rhombdodecahedron
(110) or trapezohedron (211). The colour depends on the composition;

grossular is pale green, uvarovite emerald-green, or reddish brown. The hardness ranges from 6·5 to 7·5, gravity from 3·5–4·3. The refractive index is very high, 1·74 to 1·94 (Fig. 69A); garnet is usually isotropic, but sometimes shows interference colours attributed to strain. Garnets are common members of metamorphic rocks, the composition of the garnet depending on that of the rock containing it.

Idocrase or *vesuvianite* is a complex silicate often occurring with garnet in metamorphosed limestones. Its structure appears to contain both SiO_4 and Si_2O_7 groups and its formula might be given as

$$Ca_{10}Al_4(MgFe)_2(Si_2O_7)_2(SiO_4)_5(OH)_4.$$

Idocrase crystallises in the tetragonal system, is brown, green or yellow in colour, with hardness 6·5, specific gravity 3·35–3·45. In thin slice, it is often seen to be zoned (Fig. 69B), and it shows high refractive index and very low birefringence.

Zircon, $ZrSiO_4$, is a tetragonal mineral, giving prismatic crystals, usually colourless and without cleavage. Its hardness is 7·5, specific gravity 4·7. Its refractive index and birefringence are very high, and the mineral is optically positive (see Fig. 51). Zircon occurs as a primary constituent of igneous rocks, and in metamorphic rocks, and is a common accessory component in many sedimentary rocks such as sandstones.

Topaz is a fluo-silicate of aluminium, $Al_2F_2SiO_4$, in which part of the F may be replaced by OH. It crystallises in the orthorhombic system in prismatic crystals with perfect basal cleavage; hardness 8, specific gravity 3·5–3·6. Topaz occurs in silica-rich igneous rocks, pegmatites and veins carrying tin oxide (see Fig. 368).

The *epidotes* are common minerals with the general formula $X^{+2}_2Y^{+3}_3(SiO_4)_3(OH)$, where $X^{+2} = Ca$, Fe and $Y^{+3} = Al$, Fe, Mn, Ce. They may contain both SiO_4 and Si_2O_7 structural groups. They may be classified into two groups according to their crystal system, thus:

Orthorhombic: Zoisite. $Ca_2Al_3(SiO_4)_3.OH$
Monoclinic: Clinozoisite. $Ca_2Al_3(SiO_4)_3.OH$
        Epidote. $Ca_2(AlFe)_3(SiO_4)_3.OH$

Zoisite forms prismatic crystals or granular masses, grey or green in colour, and has a high refractive index and gives abnormal inky-blue polarisation colours in certain sections. Clinozoisite is similar but the abnormal polarisation-colours are not shown. Epidote shows a perfect basal cleavage and is coloured in shades of green; hardness 6–7, specific gravity 3·25–3·5. In thin slice epidote may be markedly

E

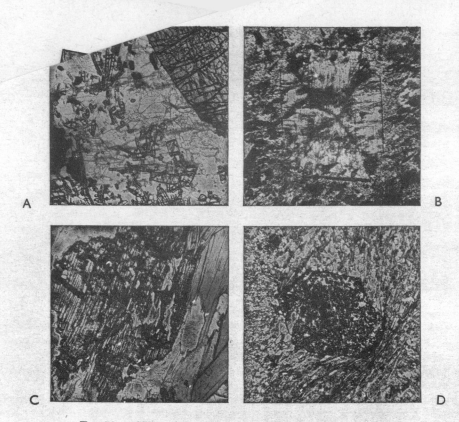

A   B

C   D

Fig. 70. A, Sillimanite, small crystals showing form and cleavage,
× 15; B, Andalusite, transverse section showing form, cleavage and
inclusions, × 20; C, Kyanite, showing form and cleavage, × 15;
D, Staurolite, transverse section showing form, × 20.

pleochroic and shows a high refractive index and strong birefringence.
The epidotes are common constituents of metamorphic rocks derived
from impure limestones or from igneous rocks rich in lime-plagioclase.

In the normal type of nesosilicates that we have so far considered
all the O atoms are accommodated in the SiO_4-tetrahedra so that the
Si : O ratio is 1 : 4 or more. The remainder of the nesosilicates that
we now deal with have, as is required, independent SiO_4-tetrahedra
in their structure but there are O atoms outside them and the Si : O
ratio is 1 : 5 or less. These are the low silicon silicates or 'sub-
silicates', and those we mention here are important minerals especially in metamorphic rocks. They are sphene, the aluminium silicates —
sillimanite, andalusite and kyanite — and staurolite (Fig. 70).

The composition of *sphene* can be written $CaTiO(SiO_4)$. The

120

mineral crystallises in the monoclinic system in wedge-shaped crystals, brown, black or grey in colour. Hardness is 5–5·5 and specific gravity 3·54. In thin slices, sphene is often pleochroic from colourless to a shade of red, and shows very high refractive index and birefringence. Sphene occurs as a primary constituent in igneous rocks and in metamorphic rocks of various origins.

The *aluminium silicates* (Fig. 70) have the composition Al_2SiO_5, the mineral species being:

sillimanite,	orthorhombic
andalusite,	orthorhombic
kyanite,	triclinic.

In sillimanite and andalusite, part of the Al is in six-fold co-ordination and the AlO_6 groups are arranged in vertical chains; in kyanite all the Al is in six-fold co-ordination and the O atoms form a pseudo-cubic face-centred lattice.

Sillimanite forms long needles or fibres, with a perfect (010) cleavage; its hardness is 6–7, specific gravity 3·23. In thin slice, sillimanite is colourless and shows high refractive index, and rather high birefringence.

Andalusite forms prismatic crystals or granular masses, grey or purple in colour; hardness 7·5, specific gravity 3·1–3·3. In thin slice it is colourless or shows a patchy pink pleochroism; its refractive index is moderately high, birefringence weak. *Kyanite* usually occurs in long-bladed crystals, white or light blue in colour, and showing several cleavages. Its hardness varies on different faces, 4–7 (p. 72), its specific gravity is 3·6–3·7. In thin slice, kyanite is colourless and shows good cleavage; its refractive index is high, birefringence low; some prismatic sections show oblique extinction up to 30° — andalusite and sillimanite prismatic sections extinguish straight. The aluminium silicates occur in metamorphic rocks of clay-composition, the species present depending on the conditions of metamorphism, as shown in p. 535.

Staurolite (Fig. 70) is essentially an iron aluminium silicate, probably $FeAl_4Si_2O_{10}(OH)_2$; this formula can be written as

$$2(Al_2SiO_5).Fe(OH)_2$$

which agrees with the structure of staurolite which is found to be that of alternate layers of kyanite Al_2SiO_5 and iron hydroxide, $Fe(OH)_2$; some Mg and Mn are also present. Staurolite is orthorhombic, its prismatic crystals being commonly in penetration twins. Its colour is brown or black, hardness 7–7·5, specific gravity 3·7. In thin slice, staurolite is yellow and markedly pleochroic, its refractive index is high and its birefringence low. Staurolite occurs in meta-morphosed rocks of clay composition, where it is often accompanied by kyanite and garnet.

NON-SILICATE MINERALS

Half-a-dozen non-silicate minerals are now mentioned to complete our brief survey. These are, first, the apatite family which have structures something like that of a silicate, then the very important mineral carbonates which compose the common limestones, then a group of oxides, the spinels, corundum and iron oxides, and lastly an element, graphite.

Apatites are phosphates of calcium with some F, Cl or OH; their composition can be represented as $Ca_5(F, Cl, OH).[PO_4]_3$, in which F may be replaced to any extent by Cl or OH. In the apatite structure, the PO_4-groups form tetrahedra somewhat analogous to the SiO_4-tetrahedra of the silicates. Common apatite is hexagonal, with pris-matic crystal habit, green or yellow in colour, hardness 5, specific gravity 3·17–3·20. Apatite occurs in igneous rocks in small hexagonal prisms with high refractive index and low birefringence; it is uniaxial negative.

The *carbonate minerals* that we consider here are calcite, $CaCO_3$ and dolomite $CaCO_3.MgCO_3$. Both crystallise in the trigonal system and have a perfect rhombohedral cleavage; they are uniaxial nega-tive. In the structure of calcite, Ca ions are situated at the corners of a rhombohedron and the CO_3 radicles form as it were separate islands arranged in horizontal planes and with their centres midway along the rhombohedral edges. Physical properties differ markedly parallel and perpendicular to the horizontal plane just mentioned, e.g. the two refractive indices for calcite are 1·658 and 1·486 (see ante, p. 78–9).

Calcite often forms good crystals of diverse habits or occurs in lamellar, fibrous or granular fashion; it is usually colourless or white, with hardness 3 and specific gravity 2·71. Calcite is the dominant component of the limestones, both of chemical and organic origin, and of their metamorphic derivatives. *Dolomite* occurs often in rhombohedral crystals or granular masses, white yellow or brown in colour. Its hardness is 3·5–4, specific gravity 2·8–2·9. Dolomites form extensive beds by the alteration, *dolomitisation*, of original calcite limestones by percolating magnesium-carbonate solutions.

The distinctions between calcite and dolomite may be assembled. Calcite rarely occurs as the rhombohedron, dolomite commonly so; calcite effervesces with cold dilute acid, dolomite only with warm acid; calcite boiled for fifteen minutes in a solution of aluminium or

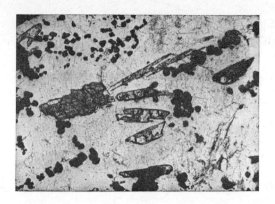

FIG. 71. Spinel, small opaque grains, and corundum, prismatic crystals with high refractive index, in cordierite-hornfels, Aberdeenshire, × 20.

ferric chloride and logwood is stained pink, dolomite is not (Lemberg's Test); the refractive index for the ray vibrating parallel to the short diagonal of the cleavage-rhomb of calcite is 1·566, of dolomite 1·588.

The *oxide minerals* we mention here can be grouped into two sets (1) the trigonal oxides, X_2O_3, such as corundum Al_2O_3, hematite Fe_2O_3 and ilmenite $(FeTi)_2O_3$ and (2) the cubic spinel family, XY_2O_4, including spinel $MgAl_2O_4$, magnetite $Fe^{+2}Fe^{+3}_2O_4$ and chromite $FeCr_2O_4$.

Corundum occurs in pyramidal crystals, usually grey or greenish, hardness 9, specific gravity 3·9–4·1. It is found in silica-poor contact-metamorphosed clay-rocks (Fig. 71), in metamorphosed limestones and in various igneous rocks, and as residues in gravels derived from such primary sources. *Hematite* and *ilmenite* are important economic minerals (Chapter 11). In the *spinel* family, there is an isomorphous series between spinel proper $MgAl_2O_4$ and chromite $FeCr_2O_4$ and other series occur between other end-members belonging to this family, in which Fe^{+3} can replace Al or Cr only to a limited extent, whereas Cr can replace Al in any proportion. Magnetite is dealt with as an economic mineral (p. 589). The spinels (Fig. 71) occur in octahedral crystals, of varying colour according to their composition. Spinel proper is a high-temperature mineral, chromite occurs as a constituent of igneous rocks relatively poor in silica.

The only element mineral we need mention is *graphite*, carbon, C, which crystallises in lamellae with a perfect basal cleavage, expressing the manner in which the C atoms are arranged. It is black and opaque, with a black streak. Graphite occurs in fissure veins, bedded masses or disseminations, often metamorphosed (see p. 606).

123

FURTHER READING AND REFERENCE

Berry, L. G. and Brian Mason, 1959, *Mineralogy: Concepts, Descriptions, Determinations*, Freeman, San Francisco. A modern general textbook, but optical properties not dealt with in any detail.

Bragg, W. L. and G. F. Claringbull, 1965, *Atomic structure of minerals*, Bell.

Bunn, C. W., 1961, *Chemical crystallography*, 2nd Edit., Clarendon Press, Oxford. An advanced treatment, but parts are relevant to this chapter.

Deer, W. A., R. A. Howie and J. Zussman, 1966, *An Introduction to the Rock-forming Minerals*, Longmans, Green, London.

Evans, R. C., 1963, *An introduction to crystal chemistry*, 2nd edit., Cambridge Univ. Press.

Grivor'ev, D. P., 1965, *Ontogeny of Minerals*.

Kerr, P. F., 1959, *Optical Mineralogy*, McGraw-Hill, London. Useful for the determination of minerals in thin sections of rocks.

Phillips, F. C., 1963, *An introduction to crystallography*, Longmans, Green, London.

Read, H. H., 1962, *Rutley's Elements of mineralogy*, 25th edit., Murby (Allen and Unwin), London. Useful for the determination of minerals.

4

SURFACE PROCESSES

INTRODUCTION

The geologist is interested in the processes which go on near the earth's surface for two reasons — he wishes to understand how the details of that surface were produced and, more important, he sees being made there the raw materials for the great group of sedimentary rocks. In surface processes, Uniformitarianism finds the key to much of earth-history.

The present surface of the earth is the result of two operations, the one of *denudation*, destruction or wearing-away and the other of *deposition*, construction or building-up. In broad terms, denudation prevails on the land areas, deposition on the sea-floors. The surfaces of denudation and deposition at any one moment together make the surface of the solid earth, the lithosphere.

The deposits we are to study are called *sediments* and their deposition is *sedimentation*. For our purpose sediments are defined as *accumulations of materials on the surface of the lithosphere brought about by geological agents working there*.

These geological agents rarely act singly though one may be dominant in a particular area of the earth's surface and its products be there clearly defined. For purposes of description, however, it is best to consider the agents separately. First, we have to deal with the reactions that take place in the rocks where they meet the atmosphere. Having been formed elsewhere, these rocks are now clearly out of equilibrium and, by the second great principle of geology, become modified when exposed to the surface conditions of rapid changes of temperature, to frost and to rain. They are, in short, exposed to the weather and they undergo *weathering*, with the production of a blanket of variable thickness of altered rock. Through weathering, the face of the earth becomes continuously changed and great sequences of geological and biological operations initiated. Weathering, then, is our first topic among surface processes.

The weathered covering may remain in position as a *residual deposit*. Among such deposits are many of geological significance but the most important are the *soils*, both ancient and modern.

Not all the rain falling on the earth's surface runs off — some soaks into the ground to build up the store of underground-water or *groundwater*. This groundwater nourishes the springs and, less romantically, it produces supplies of water for human use. Besides, rocks near the surface undergo innumerable transformations in which groundwater is concerned.

Most of the products of weathering are moved in a number of ways from the place of their formation. Their removal continually exposes fresh surfaces to weathering and the rocks are gradually worn away or *denuded*, with the production of a variety of land-forms appropriate to the *erosive* agent at work. *Mass-movements* of the weathered material, loosened by groundwater, may take place downhill under the influence of gravity. The more important transporting agents are, however, *air, water and ice in motion* — the winds, rivers, lakes, seas, glaciers and ice-sheets. The relative importance of these agents will clearly depend upon the climate in which they act. Not only the style of weathering but also the means of transport will vary in different parts of the world, as they have most likely done in the past. We consider in turn the geological work of the *wind*, the action of *moving water* on the land as rainwash, rivers and lakes, the processes that take place in the *estuaries*, then the *seas* and all that goes on in them and, finally, the geological action of *ice-masses*, the glaciers and ice-sheets.

From all this, we acquire a knowledge of the many environments of sedimentation of the present time and of the diagnostic characters of the sediments deposited in them. We are here really surveying the *facies distribution of today* so that we can proceed to reconstruct the facies distribution of past ages.

WEATHERING

The rocks exposed to weathering were for the most part formed deep within the crust, under conditions of temperature and pressure greater than those at the earth's surface. Their original minerals were the products of *endothermic* or heat-absorbing reactions, and are characterised by close ionic packing. Under surface conditions, many of these become unstable and reactions go on to restore equilibrium. As was to be expected from the theorem of Le Chatelier — which states that whenever changes in the external conditions of a system in equilibrium occur, changes within the system take place, when possible, which tend to counteract the effects of the external changes — the chemical reactions of weathering are dominantly *exothermic* or heat-expelling, with the production of new minerals of relatively loose ionic packing. The total amount of these new products is increased by the disintegration of the rock into smaller and smaller pieces so that the surface areas exposed to chemical change are greater. Weathering, therefore, proceeds by two kinds of processes, the first a disintegration of the rock by *mechanical* means, the second a decomposition by *chemical* means. These two processes are of course not clearly separable in nature. But under different climatic conditions one or the other may predominate, and it is convenient to treat them separately.

MECHANICAL WEATHERING

A physical breaking-up of rocks into small fragments or a disintegration into their constituent mineral grains is brought about possibly by changes in temperature and certainly by frost-action. Some further breaking-up is due to other agents which are mentioned later. Besides this true weathering, rocks are broken up by the wind, running water, the sea or glacial ice, and such breaking-up is best considered when these processes are dealt with.

Effects of changes of temperature. The coefficient of cubical expansion of different minerals may be very different; thus that for quartz is twice that for orthoclase. Further, for any particular anisotropic mineral it follows from the nature of its atomic edifice that its linear coefficient of expansion will differ according to the direction within the crystal; for quartz, the linear coefficient of expansion perpendicular to the c-axis is more than twice that parallel to this axis. These facts are considered by some geologists to have a bearing on the disintegration of those rocks that consist of coarse aggregations of different minerals arranged in different directions. When such aggregations are heated in the sun's rays or cooled at night or by a sudden rainfall, a complex system of strains may be set up by unequal expansions and contractions. Intergranular cracks may develop and the rocks may thus be weakened, cracked and finally disintegrated into small grains. It is as well to state that lengthy experiments to test the validity of this purely physical method of disintegration have failed to supply any supporting evidence.

But temperature changes do help in the breaking-up of rocks. A primitive method of quarrying, *fire-setting*, mentioned in the Book of Job, is to light fires on flat rock-surfaces; the outer layer of rock near the fire expands and parts from the cold rock below it and can then be broken loose. Something of the same kind may happen to bare rock-surfaces in regions of high temperature. It is likely, however, that the actual planes of parting are initiated by the removal of the load on a deep-seated rock as it comes to the surface; the rock tends to expand upwards. Sometimes rocks break into

E2

curved parallel-sided slabs, like enormous onion-skins — this process is termed *exfoliation*. Experimental work, again, has shown that unaided temperature-changes lead to but little exfoliation but that the process is greatly accelerated if the rock is periodically wetted. The electrical structure of water-molecules causes them to line up in such a way as to exert a force on the enclosing rock, a process strongly influenced by temperature. Exfoliation is thus probably the result of temperature changes combined with chemical activity — we meet a variant of it in *spheroidal weathering* later. A great sheet of rock may be weathered into a collection of gigantic spherical boulders, spectacular examples being afforded by the granite hills around Rhodes' Grave in Rhodesia. On a larger scale, dome-shaped hills, as in the 'Dome-Gneiss' country of Bihar, India, or the sugar-loaf forms provided by the *inselbergen* or *bornhardts* of southern Africa, may result from exfoliation.

The ice-wedge. Frost-action becomes an exceedingly powerful agent in surface disintegration in those regions where alternate freezing and thawing of water in the rock-pores or fissures takes place. The change from water to ice involves a volume increase of about 9 per cent and, under ideal conditions, would result in a bursting pressure of about a ton per square inch. Hence the freezing of water in the crevices of rocks forces the pieces apart and, when the ice melts, the exposed rock-surface tends to disintegrate. We see comparable results in Britain in spring in the state of an arable field after an autumn ploughing.

This frost-action is referred to as the *ice-wedge*. It is the principal agent of weathering on high Alpine peaks such as the Matterhorn and is largely responsible for their spectacularly jagged outlines. Angular slabs may be wedged off and accumulate on the lower slopes of the mountains in great heaps of *talus*. The *screes* of Wastwater in the English Lake District are classic illustrations of the results of ice-wedging. Much of the blocky material accumulating at the bases of steep cliffs and called *slide-rock* by the Americans is supplied by the ice-wedge. These piles of frost-riven slabs are very unstable and their material is constantly on the move downhill. This leads to great difficulties in maintaining roads or railways on them and it has on occasion been found to be more economical to by-pass them by tunnelling into the bedrock.

In many cold countries building-stones must be chosen according to their power to resist granular disintegration by frost-action. Special tests, including repeated wetting, freezing and thawing, have been devised to determine the reliability of building-stones under such conditions.

Some other agents of mechanical weathering. A number of other processes of rock disintegration may be briefly noted. Rock-shattering caused by *lightning* striking high peaks during thunderstorms is probably not uncommon, but first-hand evidence is rarely available. *Plants and animals* assist the disintegration and decomposition of rocks in various ways. The widening of crevices by growing roots, the loosening and mixing of soil by burrowing animals and the manifold activities of the most destructive of all animals, man, may be mentioned. Much organic weathering is essentially chemical and this is discussed later. Whilst a plant cover helps to retain moisture on or near the rock surfaces, it acts also as a protective cover and slows down the removal of weathered material.

As the load on a rock is removed by erosion, the underlying rock tends to expand and crack. This *release of load* leads to the formation in homogeneous rocks of a sheeted structure of more or less horizontal subparallel fractures; we have referred to such structures in connection with exfoliation. *Chemical action* promotes mechanical break-up, since its products are generally more bulky than the parent minerals. Lastly, the *crystallisation of salts* brought from below by solutions rising to the surface exerts a disruptive pressure.

By all these processes of mechanical weathering, the rocks at the earth's surface are prepared for the maximum activity of chemical weathering — this activity we now examine.

CHEMICAL WEATHERING

Processes and products. Dry air by itself can perform little or no chemical weathering — water is necessary, though not in great quantity. This is supplied by rain and snow which in falling through the air take up oxygen, carbon dioxide and other atmospheric gases. Rain-water itself is not chemically neutral but is partially ionised with H^+ and OH^- ions. Once under the ground, the water acquires also various organic acids produced by the decay of plant and animal matter. Water so charged, moving slowly over the immense total surface provided by a much disintegrated rock, is capable of sustained chemical work.

The atmosphere has three chief constituents, nitrogen, oxygen and the inert gases, mainly argon, the percentage by volume being N 78·122, O 20·941, A etc. 0·937. In addition, it contains minor and varying amounts of other substances, such as water vapour, nitrogen oxides, sulphur dioxide, sulphuretted hydrogen, ammonia, carbon monoxide and, most important, carbon dioxide. Solid impurities are dusts of various origins, soot and sodium chloride, the chief of the so-called 'cyclic salts' blown in from the sea. As rain falls through the air the various constituents, major and minor, are dissolved to different degrees. Nitrous and nitric acids are formed from the nitrogen oxides, sulphuric acid from sulphur dioxide, and weak solutions of ammonia, ammonium sulphate and sodium chloride are produced — all these being of interest to the agricultural scientist. Of special interest to the geologist is the solution of oxygen and carbon dioxide. The differing solubilities of nitrogen, oxygen and carbon dioxide are shown in the table below from which it will be noted that the two active gases, oxygen and carbon dioxide, are markedly concentrated in rain-water. Oxidation and the formation of carbonates are likely to be promoted.

	N	O	CO_2
	(percentage by volume)		
Normal air:	78	21	0·03
Air from Rain-water:	63·49	34·05	2·46

The products of organic decay grouped as 'humus complexes' play an important role in chemical weathering that is not yet fully understood. It seems clear, at least, that these colloids and colloidal solutions promote the decomposition of rocks by contributing carbon dioxide, nitric acid, sulphuric acid and other decay-products to rain-water and, also, by their marked capacity for base-exchange and adsorption of cations.

From the nature of things, the processes and products of chemical weathering brought about by the variety of reagents already mentioned will be complex and interdependent. Solution, hydration, hydrolysis, oxidation, reduction, the formation of carbonates, attack by alkaline and acid solutions, the leaching out of more soluble products and many other operations may go on in different combinations, depending on the parent rock and the environment of the weathering. It is best from the geological side to illustrate these processes by reference to specific minerals and rocks.

We may first deal with the weathering of the common igneous rocks since these provide the raw materials for most sediments. The chief minerals of the parent rocks are quartz, feldspars and the FeMg silicates, micas, amphiboles, pyroxenes and olivines, collectively known as the *ferromagnesian* minerals. *Quartz* is an obdurate mineral, of simple atoms strongly bonded, and resists both mechanical and chemical weathering. Like all minerals, however, it is slowly dissolved in weathering solutions and some corrosion of quartz grains in sediments is commonly observed. Because of its resistance, quartz may be weathered out of a rock, transported and deposited several times — in technical terms, it may go through several *sedimentary cycles.* The commonest constituents of igneous rocks, the *feldspars*, alkali-calc-aluminium silicates, with their more diversified chemical composition, succumb more easily to chemical weathering than quartz. By processes of ionic solution, hydration and hydrolysis, the feldspar lattices are completely wrecked. The strong bases K, Na and Ca are extracted, and reaction of the Al and Si with OH gives colloidal aggregates that crystallise into the phyllosilicate clay-minerals (p. 115), especially kaolinite. These hydrous alumino-silicates are the new minerals stable under weathering conditions. The bases are largely removed in solution as carbonates, sodium and calcium carbonates passing freely into the local drainage systems, but much of the K being adsorbed by the clay-minerals and so retained.

The *ferromagnesian silicates* are least resistant to chemical weathering and are converted into clay-minerals (which, since Fe and Mg are available, belong mainly to the montmorillonite and illite groups) together with silica and soluble carbonates of Mg, Ca and Fe. Of these, the iron carbonate is readily oxidised to give reddish hematite, Fe_2O_3, which in turn is hydrated to produce indefinite hydrated iron oxides of the limonite group or *ochres*.

The minerals of the igneous rocks can be arranged in a rough order of *increasing resistance* to chemical weathering: this order is:

olivine, calcic feldspar, pyroxenes and amphiboles,
sodic feldspar, biotite, potash-feldspar, muscovite, quartz.

This differential resistance underlies the diversity of the sediments and hence of the sedimentary rocks, as we see in later pages.

When we were dealing with exfoliation due to physical action it was mentioned that some spheroidal forms were better attributed to chemical weathering. This *spheroidal weathering* is especially well shown by coarse igneous rocks that are traversed by fracture planes called *joints* (Chapter 8). Such planes are commonly in three sets roughly at right angles to each other. Chemical decomposition begins along the joints and is concentrated at the corners of the roughly cubical blocks outlined by them. As a result, the decomposition advances into the block so as to leave a relatively unaltered spherical core surrounded by concentric shells of weathered rock, increasingly altered outwards.

To generalise the foregoing, the usual weathering products of igneous rocks are resistant quartz grains and some colloidal silica, the clay-minerals some with adsorbed K, and iron hydroxides, together with solutions of carbonates of Ca, Mg and Na. The common sedimentary rock, *limestone*, made of calcium carbonate, reacts to the weather in such spectacular fashion as to require separate description.

FIG. 72. Grikes in limestone, Malham Cove, Yorkshire. (Crown Copyright: by Permission of the Controller of H.M. Stationery Office.)

Weathering of limestone. We have seen in the foregoing that rain-water is enriched in CO_2 and that it can acquire more from weathering processes taking place near the surface. Such solutions of carbonic acid H_2CO_3 react with the calcite, $CaCO_3$, of limestones to produce the soluble bicarbonate, $Ca(HCO_3)_2$. The effects of this solution are spectacular. Exposed limestone surfaces become etched, and joint-fractures traversing the rock become widened. These enlarged fissures are called *grikes* in England and the paving-stone-like surfaces between them are *clints* (Fig. 72). Where the limestone is intensely fretted by solution the French word *lapiaz* is used and extensive areas of such jagged rock-surfaces are described by the German word *Karrenfeld*.

Solution of the limestone is particularly marked at the intersection of grikes and here are formed large solution-holes, *swallow-holes, pots* or *dolinas*, into which streams may cascade. Smaller, partly closed, pots are often marked by conical depressions in the overlying soil cover. The pots commonly lead to extensive systems of *caves* or *caverns* which have been partly dissolved and partly eroded by underground streams (Fig. 73). Some limestone regions are honey-combed by such enlarged stream courses, the whole drainage of the area having gone underground.

The land-forms developed by this chemical weathering of limestone

132

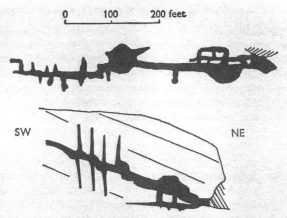

FIG. 73. Plan (*above*) and section (*below*) of Rochefort Cave east of Dinant, Belgium, (based on Martel). Shape of the cave is controlled by planes of bedding and jointing.

country are so characteristic that such regions are said to have *Karst topography*, after the Karst area of Istria and Dalmatia. In England similar features are beautifully developed in the Pennine area of West Yorkshire. The Burren of Co. Clare, Ireland, the Causses of France and the 'cockpit country' of Jamaica provide further excellent examples of karst topography.

CONTROLS OF WEATHERING

A weathered covering is continually being formed over the sound bedrock below. Under certain circumstances, as for example those of rapid chemical decay without removal of the products, the depth of the decayed rock may be considerable — in Brazil nearly 400 feet, in the Transvaal 200 feet. Decomposition commonly follows fractures or joints wherein the descending water is canalised, so that narrow zones of weathered material may penetrate downwards between blocks of relatively unaltered rock. The variations in thickness, degree and arrangement of weathered material are clearly of importance in civil engineering and mining, where it is often necessary to explore the weathered ground by pitting, boring or resistivity surveying (see ante p. 39).

The thickness of the weathered layer depends on several factors. Obviously, the chemical composition of the parent rock, the way in which its constituents are bound together, and the presence in it of fissures, joints, crevices or pores are all of fundamental importance. Secondly, the climate of the area is decisive, especially the amount and style of the rainfall, the prevalence of frost and the incidence of

133

temperature changes. Lastly, the topography and relief affect the drainage of the area and so control the removal of the weathering products as they are formed.

From their nature, it is obvious that all processes of weathering cannot operate equally in all parts of the earth's surface. Frost effects will be of small account in tropical regions, chemical processes demanding water will be unimportant in deserts. Mechanical effects will obviously be dominant at high latitudes, at high altitudes and in arid regions; decomposition will be dominant in the humid tropics.

The nature of ancient weathering products may therefore supply a clue to the topography and climate of past times. It may be useful to distinguish the following broad *belts of weathering* of today.

Sub-arctic: mechanical weathering, largely frost action.
Temperate: mechanical and chemical weathering act together.
Desert: mechanical weathering by temperature changes.
Tropical: chemical weathering producing thick residual deposits.

RESIDUAL DEPOSITS

One of two things may happen to the weathered covering; it may remain where it has been made and give a *residual deposit* or it may be *transported* to be deposited in some other place. Clearly, since we are dealing with a set of interconnected processes, part may remain and part may be transported. We deal first with the residual deposits of weathering.

The general characters of weathering products have been indicated in previous paragraphs. They will be for the most part clays and sandy clays of many different types, depending upon the original bedrock and the degree and kind of the chemical weathering that has affected it. We have to consider especially two important groups of residues, first the *laterites* and *bauxites*, the results of chemical decay carried to extremes in the humid tropics, and second, the *soils*. Besides these, we briefly note other residual deposits such as *terra rossa*, *clay-with-flints*, and certain *feldspathic sands*.

Laterite and bauxite. Laterite and bauxite are clays enriched in ferric and aluminium hydroxides that have a widespread occurrence in the present-day humid tropics as a weathered mantle to rocks of all kinds. They are dirty white, grey, brown, yellow or red in colour, and massive, earthy, granular or pisolitic (p. 250) in texture; soft in depth, they harden when exposed to the air and become covered with a clinker-like crust. The laterites and bauxites are composed of varying proportions of ferric hydroxide and aluminium hydroxides, such as diaspore (AlOOH), boehmite (AlOOH) or gibbsite [Al(OH)$_3$], with small amounts of silica. The Al : Fe ratio varies, Fe being dominant in laterite proper, Al in bauxite. Laterites in the wider sense include both true sedentary deposits formed *in situ* and transported re-deposited types — these latter, the detrital laterites, naturally contain some admixture of clay and other transported materials.

In the foregoing we have given the impression that all high-AlFe residual deposits were formed by tropical weathering carried to completion. It was implied that all kinds of rocks had had their silica, alkaline-earths and alkalies removed by leaching, with the accumulation of AlFe hydroxides as residuals. It is known that the solubility of silica increases in waters of pH5 to pH9, whereas aluminium hydroxide is practically insoluble over the same interval. But difficulties arise when the details of the process are examined and, further, it is not certain that all lateritic and bauxitic clays are of pure weathering origin. These points are now considered.

In the first place, there has been discussion concerning the movement of the weathering solutions. Some geologists consider that a *seasonal* tropical climate is essential for laterisation. A rainy period is followed by a dry period during which the solutions, drawn up from below, precipitate the FeAl hydroxides. Others compare the process of accumulation of these hydroxides to that of *illuviation* taking place in the B zone of soils (p. 136); in this process the FeAl hydroxides are carried down to a deeper layer, leaving an overlying depleted layer (the A zone of soils) to be removed by later uplift and erosion. In the second place, it may be noted that, though many modern laterite-bauxite deposits are taken to be the result of weathering through the agency of atmospheric waters, it has also been argued that heated waters of deeper-seated volcanic or even plutonic origin are responsible for certain older deposits. Such an explanation has been applied to the French bauxites and to some of those of the southern United States.

Minor residual deposits. The solution of soluble surface rocks such as limestones may lead to the concentration of insoluble impurities as residual deposits. As an example, *terra rossa*, a red irony clay composed of ferric oxide and aluminium hydroxide with alkaline-earth compounds, accumulates on the limestones of the Karst country of Dalmatia (p. 133). It seems likely that much of the *clay-with-flints* which occurs on the surface of the Chalk of Southern England is of residual origin. Another residual deposit that may be mentioned, since it may have a climatic significance, is *feldspathic sand* or *arkosic sand* resulting from the rapid mechanical disintegration of coarse rocks like granite, formed mainly of quartz and feldspar. In the Gobi desert, large areas of the desert floor are covered by a coarse sand of quartz, feldspar and granite chips.

Soils

The most valuable and widespread of the residual deposits of the present day are the *soils* formed by the prolonged activity of organisms, organic material, water and air at the upper surface of the weathered mantle. The soils — 'the stuff in which plants grow' — are composed of the mineral products of weathering such as sand and clay, together with organic material, *humus*, arising from the decay of plant and animal matter, and air and water. The nature of a soil depends fundamentally on the climate, and especially on the amount and kind of rainfall and the range of temperature; other factors are the composition of the bedrock, the style of the topography and the time allowed for the soil to form. The arrangement of the great soil belts of the world shows the control of climates in their formation.

Undisturbed soils show a series of layers of different components and colours down to the underlying rock. This *soil-profile* in a moist temperate climate such as that of Britain can be divided into three parts. The upper few inches, the A or *eluvial* (washed-out) horizon, consists of a dark humus-rich layer below which comes a light-coloured layer resulting from the washing-out by rain-water of clay-particles, humus, and of iron and aluminium compounds. These materials are accumulated in the underlying B or *illuvial* (washed-in)

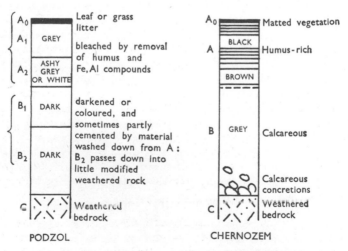

Fig. 74. Soil-profiles of Podzol and Chernozem.

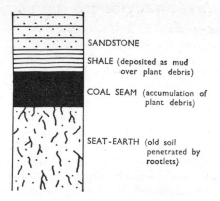

SANDSTONE

SHALE (deposited as mud over plant debris)

COAL SEAM (accumulation of plant debris)

SEAT-EARTH (old soil penetrated by rootlets)

FIG. 75. Section of Seat-earth and Coal Seam.

layer which is often brightly coloured by iron hydroxides or darkened by humus. This B layer passes down into the C layer composed of the weathered underlying rock. Two soil profiles are given in Fig. 74. The *podzols* are formed in regions with a rainfall high enough to wash down the AlFe compounds into the B layer; we have already noted that this process of *podzolization* has been suggested as an explanation of the formation of laterite-bauxite clays. The *chernozem* or *black earth* soils show a black humus-rich A layer, with a lower layer rich in carbonate; the rainfall is insufficient to remove the carbonate which becomes concentrated in the B layer. American soil-scientists have erected two main classes of soils; the first is the *pedalfers* (*pedon*, soil, AlFe) corresponding to the podzols, the second is the *pedocals*, with calcium carbonate accumulating in the B horizon, as in the chernozems. This carbonate may give rise to concretions of *caliche*.

Ancient soils are rarely preserved in the geological record; one example is considered to be the '*Dirt Bed*' intercalated in the Jurassic (see p. 293) limestone of Purbeck in Dorset. The *fireclays*, *ganisters* or *seat-earths* which underlie coal-seams are usually regarded as still more ancient soils, though of swampy type, in which grew the forests that provided the raw material for the *coals*. These seat-earths have been impoverished in the constituents required for the nourishment of the coal-forming vegetation (Fig. 75).

THE GEOLOGICAL WORK OF UNDERGROUND WATER

Rain, when it reaches the earth's surface, will either pass into the streams and rivers, sink into the ground or be returned to the atmosphere by evaporation and by transpiration by plants. The total precipitation is thus divided into the *run-off*, the *percolation* and the *evaporation-loss*. The ratio of these three quantities depends on the amount and rate of the rainfall, the slope of the ground, the vegetation, the air temperature and humidity, air-currents, the texture of the soil cover, the porosity and permeability of the rocks beneath. A moment's reflection will reveal the varying incidence of these factors; as an example, a rapid downpour of rain falling on a steep slope of impervious rock devoid of vegetation would largely run off. In general, much more than half the rainfall is returned to the atmosphere as evaporation-loss; of the remainder, more than half runs off so that the percolation is a relatively small quantity.

This quantity that infiltrates into the ground is called the *groundwater* and is of great importance in many geological processes; we have already discussed the role of groundwater in chemical weathering.

Porosity and permeability. In connection with groundwater or with any other liquid in the crust, two physical properties of rocks are of fundamental importance — these are *porosity* and *permeability*, by no means the same thing.

The *porosity* of a rock is the ratio of the space not occupied by solid rock to the bulk volume of the sample. It is expressed as a percentage; 10 per cent is an average porosity, below 5 per cent is low, above 15 per cent is high. The spaces or *voids* in rocks are of several origins. In a fragmental rock, the size, shape and arrangement of the components control the volume of the *pore-spaces* between grains (Fig. 76). A sand-bank, for example, of spherical grains of uniform size has a high porosity, theoretically nearly 50 per cent in one style of packing. The packing in of finer material between the large grains, or the presence of a cement binding the grains together, reduces the porosity (Fig. 76). Voids of other kinds may result from the removal of rock-material in solution, from the replacement of one mineral by another, as in some dolomitic limestones, or from the presence of partings such as joints and bedding-planes. Pores and cavities in fossils provide spaces for the accumulation of oil in certain Canadian oil-fields. The oil-geologist distinguishes, in addition to the true porosity we have discussed so far, an *effective porosity* provided by interconnected voids that allow oil to be drawn into a well.

The *permeability* of a rock is its capacity for transmitting fluids. This permeability obviously varies with the viscosity of the fluid, the hydrostatic pressure or *head* of the system, and with the properties of the rock. It can be shown that, other things being equal, permeability varies with the square of the mean diameter of the grains. A coarse-grained sand with a high porosity, e.g. 35 per cent, may have a high permeability and transmit water readily — in one example at the

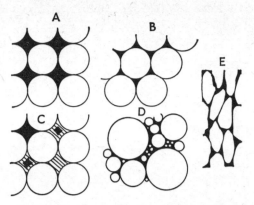

FIG. 76. Various Packings and their effects on Porosity: pore-space indicated by solid black, cement by lined ornament. A and B, two packings of equal spheres; C, effect of cementation in reducing porosity; D, packing of unequal spheres; E, packing of flat grains.

rate of several feet a day under a relatively small head. Clay may have as high a porosity as sand but its permeability is practically nil — the voids are not connected, and as their surface-area is relatively large, retardation by friction is at a maximum. The presence of joints and fissures allows water to be transmitted rapidly — a rate of 9½ miles in 70 hours has been measured in the Chalk, a rock with only minute pores but traversed by many fissures.

With respect to the behaviour of groundwater or oil, therefore, we can recognise two physical classes of rocks, *pervious* and *impervious*. Pervious rocks allow water to pass through them and are exemplified by gravels, sands, sandstones and jointed limestones and other fissured rocks. Impervious rocks, such as clay, shales, slates and compact unjointed rocks generally, act as barriers to the movement of groundwater. A water-bearing bed is called an *aquifer*; a rock carrying oil is the *reservoir rock* of the oil-geologist.

The water-table. The upper layers of soil or surface-rocks are not always saturated with water: evaporation removes some and seeping downwards by gravity takes the water to a lower level. But, at some level, the rocks are saturated with water and the upper surface of this saturated zone is called the *water-table* (Fig. 77). How far the

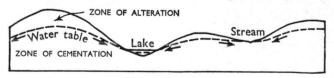

FIG. 77. The Water-table.

139

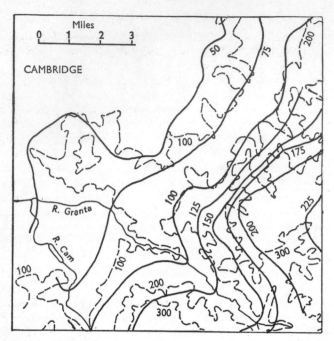

FIG. 78. Contour-map of the water-table in the Chalk southeast of Cambridge: topographic contours broken lines, water-table contours solid lines — both sets in feet (after Bernard Smith).

saturated zone extends downwards is not known at all accurately; some deep mines are dry, and at a few thousand feet depth all the pores and fissures in the rocks must be closed by earth-pressures.

The height of the water-table at any place is given by the level at which water stands in a well there — a well representing an extra-large void in the rock. By the collection of the data furnished by wells, or by a resistivity survey (p. 39), the shape of the water-table in an area can be determined and represented, like any other surface, by contour-lines on a map (Fig. 78). It is found that in flat country, the water-table is flat, in undulating country it is undulating but with more gentle curves than those of the surface of the ground (Fig. 77). This is to be expected — the groundwater drains into the valleys but takes time to flow through the rocks, so that in an area of uniformly distributed rainfall its upper surface would bulge up under the topographic highs. A well can be considered as a circular valley and if water is continuously pumped from the well, the water-table is lowered round about it, giving a *cone of depression* comparable with the depressions in the topographic lows. The flow of ground-

140

water is at right angles to the contours of the water-table. Depending upon its level in relation to a given stream, groundwater may feed the stream or the stream-water feed the groundwater.

The height of the water-table fluctuates with the rainfall. After heavy rain it rises, maybe after a time-lag of weeks or months depending on the permeability of the aquifer. On the Western Front during the First World War, the level of the mine-galleries was suddenly changed to put them above the highest water-table. In time of drought, the water-table is lowered. These movements are of course recorded in levels of the wells of the area and, also, in the behaviour of its springs. In pervious rocks at a sea-coast the fresh groundwater lies upon the denser salt water and the water-table rises and falls with the tides — fluctuations being recorded in *ebbing wells*. Another variation in height is shown by the *capillary fringe*, a few inches or feet in height, that overlies the true water-table; its variation depends on the varying sizes of the pores of the rocks.

There is a marked contrast between the condition of affairs above the water-table and below it. Above it, in the *Zone of Alteration* or of *Aeration*, the water present is moving (*vadose* or wandering water) and chemically active, being charged with O, CO_2, organic acids and a variety of weathering products. The chemical weathering performed in the zone has already been described. Below the water-table, in the *Zone of Cementation*, the groundwater moves very sluggishly, has lost much of its O and CO_2 and has dissolved material from the upper zone. This material tends to come out of solution and to be deposited in the pores and spaces in the rocks, so that loosely consolidated sediments such as sands and gravels become *cemented* together into much harder rocks. These two different operations of groundwater are of great importance in certain types of ore-deposits (p. 606).

Springs and wells. So far we have dealt with the water-table as if it were developed in uniform rocks. But the crust is not uniform, either in rock-types or in the geological accidents that have happened to them. One result of this variation in rocks and structures is the appearance of *springs*, the points of emergence of groundwater. Springs are of many origins, some related to the arrangement of pervious and impervious layers, others to structures such as folding, faulting and jointing of the rocks.

A *stratum spring* (Fig. 79A) issues at the contact of a pervious bed with an underlying impervious bed; an *overflow-spring* (B) is formed at the contact of the water-bearing bed with an overlying impervious layer. *Valley-springs* (C) arise where the water-table is cut by a valley; such springs may cease to flow when the water-table is lowered and are *intermittent*. A special type of intermittent spring is the *bourne* (D)

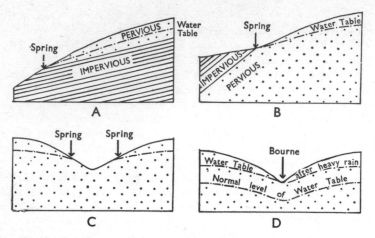

FIG. 79. Springs. A, stratum spring; B, overflow spring; C, valley spring; D, bourne.

which flows only after a considerable winter rainfall has raised the water-table above its normal level. A *perched water-table* is the result of the presence of a minor local impervious bed in the main aquifer (Fig. 80). If a well in a perched water-table is deepened and the impervious layer pierced, the perched supply may drain away below, as happened at Kessingland, Lowestoft, under conditions shown in Fig. 80B.

So far we have dealt with horizontal beds. Tilting of a series of beds of differing permeabilities may put part of an aquifer under hydraulic pressure so that water drawn from such a part rises above the local level of the water-table and may reach the surface as an *artesian* or *flowing well*. The conditions for artesian supplies are shown in Fig. 81.

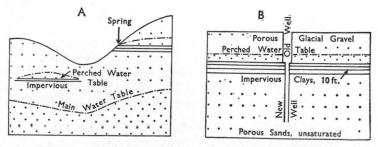

FIG. 80. Perched Water Table. A, diagrammatic; B, Kessingland Well, perched water drained on deepening of well (after Bernard Smith).

142

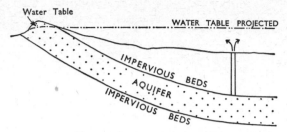

FIG. 81. Artesian Conditions.

A water-bearing layer, sealed off above and below by impervious layers, is bent or tilted so that the water-table in the parts of it that crop out at the surface is higher than the top of the wells, an *artesian slope* resulting.

Two artesian slopes unite to make an *artesian basin*. Among the famous artesian basins is that of London (Fig. 82) where at one time

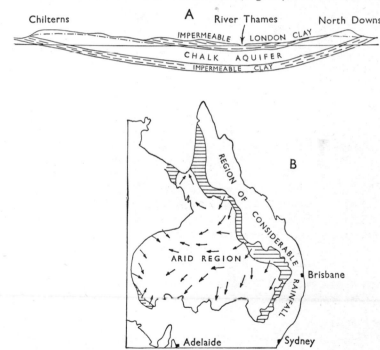

FIG. 82. Artesian Basins. A, section across the London Artesian Basin; B, map of the artesian basin of eastern Australia (based on Edgeworth David); outcrop of aquifer lined, migration of ground-water in aquifer shown by arrows.

143

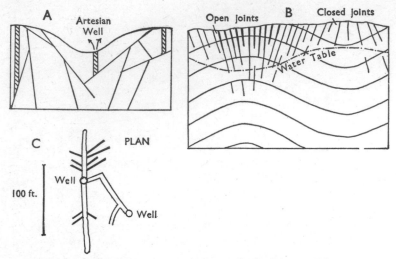

FIG. 83. Joint-springs. A, joints giving artesian conditions; B, relation of flexures in the Chalk to joints and the position of the water table (after Bernard Smith); C, plan of headings driven from shafts to intersect joint-fissures in the Chalk, Worthing (after H.M. Geological Survey).

flowing wells were common — the fountains in Trafalgar Square being so supplied. Over-exploitation has lowered the water-table in the aquifer so that artesian conditions are destroyed and dirty Thames water is being drawn into the wells.

In desert regions, the water-table though deep down may be locally cut by the ground-surface; where this happens *oases* are formed. For example, the water-table in the Libyan desert was shown by Ball to form an almost flat surface gently sloping to the north-east. Ball foretold from these data the heights of the oases of Selima and Laqia, west of Wadi Halfa in the North Sudan — when these heights were later measured a very close agreement with Ball's forecast was found. The importance of a knowledge of the water-table was emphasised in the Libyan campaign where military strategy sometimes depended on a water-supply being guaranteed by the army geologists.

Springs related to structures in the rocks are joint-springs and fault-springs. *Joint-springs* (Fig. 83) issue where the water contained in such fractures in the rocks comes to the surface. Faults, planes on which movement of crustal blocks has taken place, may bring about an arrangement of pervious and impervious layers so that water is stored (Fig. 84). Water is impounded by the fault and may proceed up the fracture to the surface and produce a *fault-spring*.

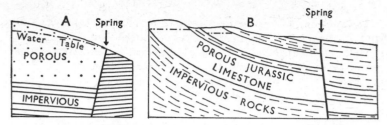

Fig. 84. Fault-springs; A, diagrammatic; B, Boxwell Spring, Gloucestershire: here, water held in the Great Oolite rises to the surface along a fault which throws this Jurassic limestone against impermeable marl.

Mineral veins often follow fault-planes and act as impermeable partitions so that the water-table stands at different heights on the two sides. The famous holy well at Holywell in Flintshire, North Wales, was made dry in 1917 by a mining tunnel breaking through such a partition some miles away from the well. Artesian conditions are produced if the joints or faults are suitably disposed, as indicated in Figs. 83 and 84.

The chemical action of groundwater. The geological action of groundwater is two-fold. Its *mechanical action* leads to movement of lubricated rocks under gravity and will be dealt with later in this chapter; here the *chemical processes* connected with groundwater are considered. These processes can be grouped under *solution, replacement* and *deposition*, which of these dominates naturally depending on the position of the groundwater with respect to the water-table.

Solution by groundwater takes place especially in the Zone of Alteration above the water-table. The results produced in the rocks of this zone have been dealt with in connection with weathering. It is proposed now to consider how the groundwater itself is modified by solution of the rocks it traverses. Groundwater is in general a solution of bicarbonate, sulphates and chlorides of Ca, Mg, K and Na. Chlorides are of local importance and the dominant salts in solution are the carbonates and sulphates, especially of calcium. Groundwater as delivered to wells or springs is therefore *hard* as compared with pure water which is *soft. Temporary hardness* due to carbonate is removed by boiling, but the *permanent hardness* due to the sulphate requires chemical treatment, such as a base-exchange process in which Na is exchanged for Ca and Mg.

In special conditions the water from a well or spring may contain unusual quantities of some particular substance and so provide a *mineral well.* Examples of these are brine springs, sulphuretted hydrogen springs and chalybeate wells, these delivering irony waters.

145

To be of use to man or his beasts or his plants, water must not contain more than a certain amount of particular salts. The solubility of CaMg carbonates is so small that their effect on potability is small. Sulphates of Mg and Na, because of their purgative properties, must be present in only small amount if the water is to be used by man or animals. Plants cannot thrive on water containing minute amounts of sodium carbonate. But the most important component in water, from the utilisation viewpoint, is sodium chloride, common salt; the tolerance for man has been estimated to be as high as 4–5 parts NaCl per 1000, and for cattle and sheep much higher, possibly 14–19 parts. These figures have a significance in the utilisation of deep artesian water drawn from basins below desert regions. For example, in the Australian artesian basin, the water obtained from deep bores in the desert is just drinkable by man and beasts but is of no use for irrigation purposes; during its long passage through the aquifer it has acquired a high content of salts.

Replacement takes place when the groundwater, holding dissolved material, exchanges certain substances for others which it extracts from the rocks. Fossil shells made of calcite, $CaCO_3$, are replaced by silica, SiO_2, or pyrite, FeS_2, or siderite, $FeCO_3$. Fossil trees are found that have their woody tissue perfectly replaced by opal, $SiO_2.Aq.$ Such operations are called *petrifaction*.

Deposition occurs dominantly in the Zone of Cementation but is, of course, not confined to this. It follows from a number of causes — simple evaporation, loss of gases due to release of pressure or by agitation of the water, lowering of the temperature, activity of lowly plants, interaction between different solutions and so forth. Around the orifices of springs, deposits of various minerals may be formed.

In limestone regions, as we saw on p. 132, extensive systems of caves may be formed by solution below the water-table. If the caves are drained by the underground river finding a lower course, then deposition of calcite may take place in them with the production of *stalactites* and *stalagmites* (Fig. 85). Solutions of the soluble calcium bicarbonate percolate through the overlying limestone and drip from the roof of the cave. Where they drip from a thin skin of calcite is deposited owing to the breaking up of the bicarbonate $CaH_2C_2O_6$ on the loss of CO_2. Successive coatings of calcite give pendent *stalactites*, and surplus solutions falling to the floor cause *stalagmites* to grow upwards; often the two meet to form pillars or, where solutions flow down the walls of caves, fantastic curtains of calcite. For these cave deposits, the Americans use the expressive term *dripstone*.

Calcite is often deposited from springs issuing from limestone, and *encrustations* of the mineral are formed on objects placed in the

spring waters, as in the celebrated 'petrifying' springs of Carlsbad, Knaresboro and elsewhere. In Tuscany, thick layers of calcite are formed from calcareous springs; this material is known as *tufa* or *travertine*.

Other springs deposit other minerals. Chalybeate springs deposit hydrated iron oxides or *ochres*. In regions of recent volcanic activity, deposits of *siliceous sinter* made of some form of silica are built up around the orifices of geysers (p. 382).

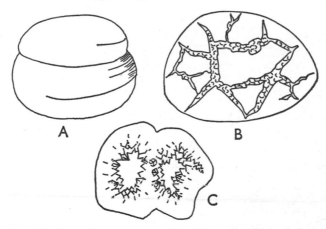

Fig. 86. Concretions. A, concretion of impure calcium carbonate with indications of original bedding planes, in the Magnesian Limestone, a mixture of calcium and magnesium carbonates; B, septarian nodule of impure calcium carbonate, cut through to show shrinkage cracks filled with coarse calcite crystals, from the London Clay; C, geode, broken open, to show cavity lined with quartz crystals.

147

Concretions. Groundwater may take up material evenly distributed through a rock and re-deposit it around some kind of nucleus to form a *concretion* (Fig. 86). The bedding of the host-rock passes through concretions undisturbed, and it is thus obvious that they are formed after the deposition of the host. Examples of concretions are pyrite, FeS_2, nodules in chalk and impure calcareous *septaria* in clays; in these latter, the shrinkage-cracks are often filled with reasonably pure calcite. Some *flint*, $SiO_2.Aq$, nodules are true concretions occurring in chalk, but others are irregular replacement bodies. In certain limestones, concretions of silica which, on being broken open, show internal cavities lined with quartz-crystals, are occasionally found — they are known as *geodes* and most likely started to form in cavities made by fossil shells; as they grew and expanded, they burst the shell into pieces.

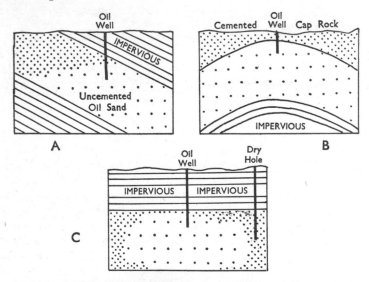

FIG. 87. Effect of cementation in the production of oil-traps.

Cementation. An important operation going on below the water-table is *cementation*, the deposition of mineral matter between the constituent grains of the rocks. The durability, appearance and properties of many rocks depend as much on the cement as on the original grains. Common cementing materials are silica, calcite and iron oxides. The deposition of the cement decreases the pore-space of the rock. The degree of cementation and the distribution of the cement are thus clearly important controls in the amount, localisation and movement of liquids, such as water and oil, in rocks — illustrations of such controls are given in Fig. 87.

Vadose, connate and juvenile waters. Underground-water is not all derived from the rain and it is customary to distinguish three types, though their clear identification is not always possible. *Vadose* ('wandering') water is that portion undoubtedly contributed by the rain and unquestionably forms the usual groundwater that we have been considering. *Connate* ('born together') water is that trapped in sediments when they were deposited and remaining in them when they were converted into sedimentary rocks. Certain salt waters associated with oil-accumulations are thought to be of connate origin. *Juvenile* water is new water coming from deep within the crust and rising in connection with volcanic activity.

MASS-MOVEMENTS UNDER GRAVITY

As weathering and erosion continue to act on the surface-rocks, their state of mechanical equilibrium may become so disturbed that they move under the action of gravity. These *mass-movements under gravity* are now examined. Some of these movements are very slow, some extremely rapid; some are performed by plastic deformation of the whole rock-mass, others by bodily transport. We can conveniently separate two classes, *slow* and *rapid* mass-movements.

Slow mass-movements are exemplified by the various forms of *creep*. The loosened weathered mantle moves slowly downhill by *soil-creep*. This almost imperceptible movement may be revealed by tilted fence-posts and especially by trees which, in an endeavour to keep themselves upright, often show a knee or bend convex down the slope. By such downhill movements, suitably placed beds of the under-lying, partly weathered, bedrock may be turned over in the direction of creep; this *terminal curvature* (Fig. 88), until recognised as such, may give a wrong idea of the attitude of the bedrock — its recognition is especially important in determining the arrangement of the strata exposed in shallow holes or pits. Weathered material obtained from a particular bed or a mineral vein high up a slope moves down lower — a travel that has to be allowed for in locating the outcrop in question (Fig. 88).

A special type of slow mass-movement is *solifluction* defined as the slow flowage from higher to lower ground of masses of waste saturated with water. Solifluction is best developed in polar regions of *permafrost*, perennially frozen ground, but it is by no means confined to such regions. In permafrost areas, the ice near the surface melts in the summers, but the melt-water is unable to percolate downwards

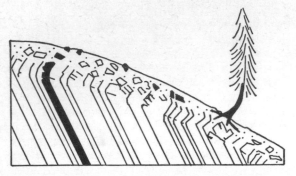

Fig. 88. Creep. Downhill movement of weathered material is indicated by the shape of the tree trunk, terminal curvature and transport of fragments from the ore-body (black).

because of the barrier of still-frozen ground below. A saturated layer thus forms which, since there is no percolation, assumes a slushy, slurry-like, condition and moves slowly down the gentlest of slopes. Even in dead-flat ground, the original arrangement of a deposit, such as the alternation of sand and gravel layers, may become completely disordered by solifluction. Often elongated pebbles in a solifluction-deposit are found to be standing on end, having been ejected by repeated thawing and freezing. It is possible that the 'Coombe Rock' on the Chalk of the south of England, made up of irregular fragments of chalk, is a solifluction-deposit that has flowed down and out of the valleys of the region.

In *periglacial* regions — that is those regions surrounding an ice-sheet — other frost-phenomena besides solifluction occur. *Frost-heaving* due to repeated thawing and freezing produces a much greater disturbance in the weathered or loose surface-material than can be accounted for by the simple expansion of water on freezing — it may rather be due to the vertical growth of ice-crystals, perpendicular to the general cooling-surface. Lenses of ice formed in wet ground may bulge up the material above them to produce mounds, *ice-blisters* or *pingoes*. Other bodies of ice take the form of *ice-wedges*, inserted into the underlying rock; when such wedges melt, their moulds are filled with material from above. *Stone-polygons* are remarkable arrangements of stones with the larger up-ended slabs forming a polygonal border to finer-grained material inside them. Various explanations, none satisfactory, have been given for the formation of these poly-gons — they are thought to be due to repeated thawing and freezing leading to a sorting of the materials and the gradual ejection and rotation of the larger pieces, or to convectional flow in the thawed

150

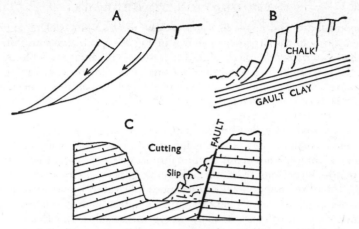

Fig. 89. A, shearing slide; B, bedding-plane landslip, jointed Chalk slipping on wetted Gault clay (e.g. Folkestone Warren); c, landslide on fault plane.

slush, or to their location on shrinkage-fractures produced during periods of low temperature. Another type of sorting is seen in the *stone-strips*, *soil-strips* or *stone-runs*, parallel ridges of large and small stones leading downhill.

Rapid mass-movements are recorded in flows and slides of various kinds. We can distinguish the *flows*, in which continuous deformation takes place throughout the moving mass, from the *slides* which move as a whole on a definite surface.

The *flows* are often divided into *mudflows*, *earthflows* and *debris-avalanches* — their mechanism is similar but their climatic settings may be different. In semi-arid regions, large masses of fine material may accumulate on hill-slopes and adjacent valley-floors; when this unconsolidated material is suddenly soaked with water it may move downward as a *mudflow*. In the Western States gigantic masses of the weathered mantle have moved down slopes and deployed upon the lower ground. In high mountain-regions such as the Alps and Himalayas, large-scale *earthflows* and *debris-avalanches* occur where unusual deepening of the valleys has taken place with the consequent increase in instability of the valley walls.

The planes on which *slides*, *landslides* or *landslips* move are of two types, curved shear-surfaces or structural planes such as bedding, joints or faults. The first type is seen in soft rocks, such as clays or sands, when they stand in steep sea-cliffs or the walls of cuttings. A crack opens on the cliff-top some distance back from the cliff-edge and initiates the slide. Movement takes place on a curved surface,

F   151

spoon-shaped and concave upwards, the moving block being tilted backwards in the process, as shown in Fig. 89. Such slides are often called *shearing-slides* or *slumps*. They were exceedingly troublesome in the construction of the Panama Canal, one slide necessitating the removal of eleven million cubic yards of unwanted material; in these soft rocks continuous deformation of the mudflow type often accompanies the true slumping.

Landslips, controlled by the structure of the rocks, occur when a potential plane of movement is inclined towards the valley or cliff-face. Bedding-planes are of the first importance, especially where they separate a pervious from an underlying impervious rock (Fig. 89). The top of the impervious bed becomes lubricated by water seeping down through the overlying bed and sliding results. Notable bedding-plane slides are those of the Rossberg in the Alps, the Folkestone Warren in Kent and the Gros Ventre in Wyoming. Sliding on lubricated joint-planes suitably inclined is illustrated by the Turtle Mountain landslide in Alberta. Fault-planes are often coated with slippery clay 'gouge' and may give conditions favourable for landslides if intersected by cuttings or by the topography.

Landslide-topography is characterised by its irregular surface of large and small hummocky forms that are occasionally arranged in a crude wave-pattern. Blocks of all sizes, (*Chaos* on some maps of landslide-areas), are mingled together, with the result that such areas closely resemble glacial morainic accumulations (p. 227). In the field, their correct interpretation depends on relating the moved masses to their nearby source and matching their rock-contents with rocks exposed there.

WIND-ACTION

We now consider the more active modes of transport of weathered material. As soon as the transporting agent ceases to act, sedimentation may begin; we may connect, therefore, certain types of sediment with certain types of transport. We make a start by considering processes of transport and sedimentation in which the *wind* is concerned.

The wind is an important geological agent, especially where the weathering products are not protected by grasses or forests, or are not held together by moisture. Its effects may have been more widespread in early times, before the evolution of land-plants. The degree of wind-activity is subject to a climatic control and is greatest in arid or semi-arid regions. In the more humid belts, supplies of material upon which the wind can act will be limited to the drying sand along rivers and beaches and on old lake-floors.

The geological processes connected with wind are *destructive*, leading to denudation, and *constructive*, leading to deposition.

DENUDATION BY WIND

Sand and dust. With regard to the movement of geological material by the wind, we have to note a fundamental distinction between sand and dust. This distinction depends upon a property of falling bodies called the *terminal velocity*. A grain let fall through the air moves at first with the acceleration due to gravity and then the acceleration decreases till the grain falls at a steady speed, the terminal velocity. The reason for this is that as the speed increases, the resistance of the air increases until it neutralises the acceleration. The terminal velocity varies with the size of the particles, their shape and density; for our present purpose, since we are dealing mostly with quartz-grains more or less spherical, it depends on the diameter of the particles. Some values of the terminal velocity are:

diameter 0·01 mm. terminal velocity 0·01 metres per sec.
diameter 0·10 mm. terminal velocity 0·6 metres per sec.
diameter 0·20 mm. terminal velocity 1 metre per sec.
diameter 1·00 mm. terminal velocity 8 metres per sec.

Now a wind is made up of innumerable currents moving in all directions, its overall velocity increasing with height from the ground. The currents we are particularly interested in are those moving vertically, up and down, and these have been found on average to have a velocity about one-fifth of the mean velocity of the wind. Grains with a terminal velocity less than that of the vertical component will be carried aloft and remain in suspension, and grains with a greater terminal velocity will keep near to the ground. Gale velocities are abnormal, and the average speed of the usual winds is about 5 metres per second: from the values given above, this average wind would move grains of 0·20 mm. diameter. It has been found by observations of many deposits resulting from wind-action, that their grain-size lies, in fact, between 0·15 and 0·30 mm. Such deposits are *sands*; for our present purpose, a *sand-grain* is one of such a size that its terminal velocity is about equal to the upward component of the average wind — its diameter averages 0·20 mm. But there are other deposits due to the action of the wind that are made of much finer grains — these are the *dusts*, of grains less than 0·06 mm. diameter and with a terminal velocity so small that they are sorted out from the sand and carried away in suspension by the normal wind.

Movement of dust. As we have just seen, the finest material or dust provided by mechanical weathering is small enough to remain suspended in moving air; dust is present in all atmospheres. The notorious *dust-storms* of the Libyan desert are caused by movements of the air resulting from temperature-differences. Once the dust has reached the more rapidly moving upper levels of the atmosphere, it is carried away and may be deposited at great distances from its source. Dust blown from the Sahara frequently falls in southern Europe and as far north as the Baltic. Fine dust often falls on ships in the Atlantic. Immense quantities of dust are windborne annually: Udden has reckoned that 850,000,000 tons of dust are carried in the Mississippi Valley some 1440 miles each year. The removal by wind of the fine soils in the 'Dust Bowl' of the Middle Western States has devastated vast areas of farmland. This *soil-erosion* is widespread also in Africa and China and presents great problems in soil conservation. It operates even in Britain where some of the light soils, such as those of the Fens and Breckland in the eastern counties of England, may be subject to 'blowing' or wind-denudation.

Movement of sand. Usually the grains of weathered material are too large to be carried in suspension in the wind and they move for the most part by a process of leaping or *saltation* and, for a lesser part, by a kind of *surface-creep* induced by this saltation. Moving grains striking a surface of loose sand hit out other grains; the impact of the airborne grains thus moves the surface-grains by knocking them along (Fig. 90). Bagnold, who in his classic *Physics of Blown Sand and*

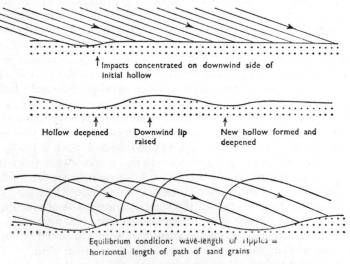

Fɪɢ. 90. Sand Ripples and Sand Movement. Three stages in the development of stable ripples (based on R. A. Bagnold).

Desert Dunes has produced the fundamental research on this subject, estimates that about ⅕ to ¼ of the total movement is due to this surface-creep.

Bagnold has observed that the saltating grain meets the ground again at a small and relatively constant angle, about 15°. No surface of sand is perfectly smooth so that there may be unequal numbers of impacts on nearby areas — the result is the formation of small ridges and hollows. These incipient irregularities are developed into *sand-ripples* (Fig. 90) due to the attainment of a state of equilibrium under the irregular bombardment when the wave-length of the ripples and the horizontal length of the path of the saltating grains become equal.

Sand-blasting. Sand driven by the wind keeps low — less than a couple of metres — and does its greatest erosive work at ground-level. As it is blown along, it impinges on rock-outcrops and this natural *sand-blast*, acting in a way similar to that of the artificial sand-blast used in etching glass, erodes and polishes the surfaces encountered. Softer parts of the rocks are worn away, the harder parts project, as is well illustrated by the pedestal of the Sphinx made of layers of varying hardnesses. Joints are enlarged, and projecting rock-masses are undercut with the formation of *rock-mushrooms* or *pedestal-rocks*. Groove-like hollows, separated by sharp ridges called *yardangs*, are produced by wind-erosion accentuating ridges and furrows already in existence (Fig. 91). Loose stones tend to be polished and worn away first on one surface till they overbalance, and then on another. In this way they periodically present a fresh side to the driving sand and so develop a characteristic three-sided or three-edged shape; such Brazil-nut-shaped stones are called *dreikanter* or *ventifacts* (Fig. 91).

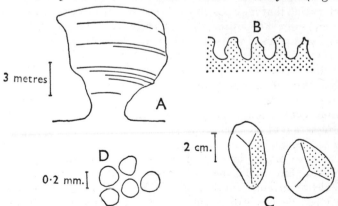

Fig. 91. Sand Blast Action. A, rock mushroom; B, yardangs; C, dreikanters, in plan; D, millet-seed sand grains.

Wade observed in the Eastern Desert of Egypt that 78 per cent of the dreikanter there had their long axis perpendicular to the dominant wind-direction.

The action of the natural sand-blast affects its ammunition; the sand-grains, even the smaller grades, may become rounded giving *millet-seed sand* and are often polished or frosted due to the multitude of impacts (Fig. 91). It must be emphasised that grains transported by the wind have in general been sorted and rounded and reduced to about their present size by some other agent such as that of the waves on a sea-shore — the wind trims them and may change their shape but does not markedly affect their size.

Deflation. Deflation is that aspect of wind-denudation that is concerned with the blowing away of loose material. Wind-action sorts out the unconsolidated surface-material into residual blocks and pebbles that it cannot move, into sand which it rolls and knocks along and into dust which it blows away. Various kinds of desert-surfaces result from this selective deflation. Expanses of bare polished rock, as in the *hammada* deserts of the Sudan, may be produced, or a gravelly stony desert or *desert-pavement*, or the sandy *ergs* of the Sahara. Much of the surface of the Egyptian Desert is of bare rock or of gravel-spreads — *lag-gravels* — from which all the sand has been moved away to lie in sheltered places. In areas where equilibrium has been reached under the prevailing conditions, the surface of the desert may be made of a mosaic of close-packed pebbles from which all the fine grains have been removed; this is the *desert-pavement*, often one pebble thick but so packed that it is able to bear great loads. The pebbles are often coated with *desert-varnish*, a brown or black patina that may possibly be deposited from organic material in the air; however deposited, desert-varnish has been proved to require tens of thousands of years for its formation, thus providing a measure of the stability of some desert-surfaces.

Deflation may lead to the excavation of wide *basins* and *depressions* in fine-grained unconsolidated or weathered surface-rocks. These depressions may reach down to the water-table and form oases — further excavation is stopped by the wetting and consequent consolidation of the surface-material. Many oases in Egypt, such as that of Kharga, may be explained as due to deflation.

The sand moved by any one current of wind will be of uniform grain-size; but wind is made of a great number of very irregular and turbulent currents varying at rapid intervals, so that a wind-controlled deposit will consist of a number of well-sorted units in very intricate arrangements — some of these arrangements we now examine.

DEPOSITION BY WIND

Sooner or later the two fractions, dust and sand, moved by the wind come to rest as its velocity slackens off. These deposits resulting from wind-action are called *windborne* or *eolian*.

Dust deposits. Dust settles outside the desert area where it becomes anchored by moisture or vegetation and may accumulate to form thick deposits. It is a property of fine particles that, once deposited and left undisturbed, they are difficult to shift by wind- or water-currents. The deposition of dust at the present day is of great interest because in China there is a very important dust-deposit formed, geologically speaking, but yesterday. This deposit is the *loess* which in China covers an area the size of France to a thickness of some hundreds of feet. Barbour has recorded that the 'Winter-storm winds today in North China are from the northwest, are cold and extremely dry, and whenever strong are the cause of severe dust-storms'. The material moved in these storms is exactly like that making the loess.

Loess is a yellowish or brownish fine-grained loam made up of very small angular particles of quartz, feldspar, calcite and other minerals, the products of mechanical disintegration. In it are found the shells of snails and bones of animals. When followed towards Mongolia, the loess loams pass into coarser, more sandy, deposits which soon show clear evidence of their origin by wind-action. The dust which makes the loess of China has therefore most likely been blown from the Gobi Desert. Other extensive deposits of loess representing the dust exported from adjacent deserts are found in the Sudan where they provide the 'cotton soils'.

Deposits comparable with loess in character, such as the *adobe* of North America and some of the *brick-earths* of England and Central Europe, obtained their material from the fine rock-flour produced by ice-abrasion during the recent glaciation. They occur in the *peri-glacial* areas around the sites of the ice-sheets of that time. It is these windborne deposits that are becoming windborne once again in the 'Dust Bowl'.

Sand deposits. The windborne sand, perhaps after many temporary halts, accumulates as *sand-drifts* and *sand-dunes*. Obstacles acting as wind-breaks give rise to sand-shadows and drifts, and areas of damp ground may arrest the driving sand. In perfectly flat country, true sand-dunes are formed where the moving sand meets existing sand-patches. The forms of the various accumulations depend on the local conditions of topography, sand-supply and wind-velocity and constancy. Blown sand may occur in confused heaps, sand-seas,

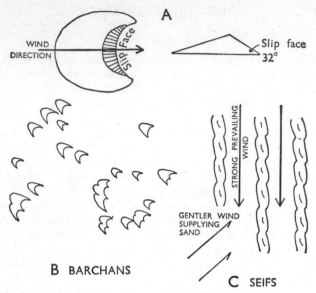

FIG. 92. Sand Dunes. A, Barchan in plan and profile; B, group of barchans; C, seif dunes.

crescentic *barchans* or elongated *seifs*. The barchans result from the action of a unidirectional wind, the seifs from the combined action of persistent gentle winds that supply the sand which is then trimmed into long ridges by strong winds from another quarter (Fig. 92).

The wide variation in the strength, composition and direction of the wind results in characteristic internal arrangements in sand-dunes. Bagnold has shown that in accumulations of constant size and shape, the rate of removal or deposition per unit at any point is proportional to the tangent of the angle of inclination of the surface. Consequently, there is neither removal nor deposition at the summit of the heap and the rate of either is greatest where the surface is steepest. The rate of deposition is greatest just over the summit down the lee-slope. The upper part of this slope therefore builds up rapidly so that the slope steepens. The lee-slope cannot, however, become steeper than about 34°, the angle of rest of dry sand. When it approaches this angle the sand avalanches or shears away along a *slip-plane* inclined at an angle a degree or two short of 34°. With the establishment of the slip-plane the dune has acquired a permanent feature. Sand driven up the windward slope once more topples over the crest to build up the lee-slope until a second avalanche produces a slip-plane a few millimetres in advance of the first. The dune thus moves in a series of jerks recorded by a set of slip-planes inclined at about 32°.

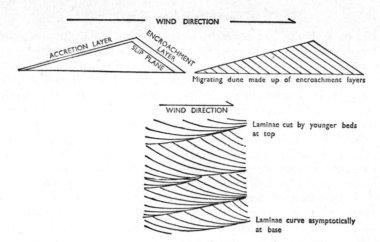

FIG. 93. Dune Bedding.

The laminae of sand bounded by these planes, the *encroachment-layers*, make up the bulk of a moving barchan (Fig. 93). Only at its top will layers of ordinary depositional character be formed; these *accretion-layers* are laid down as thin, gently-sloping laminae when the wind cannot carry away as much sand as it brings (Fig. 93). In longitudinal dunes the slip-surface forms on the side away from the prevailing cross-wind, so that in symmetrical dunes of this kind it may change from side to side as the wind shifts.

Dunes of all types are thus built of a series of layers lying at an angle. A strong wind, or the ordinary process of dune-migration, intermittently removes some of the upper part of the accumulation and new layers are often deposited at an angle to the first set. This arrangement is an example of *current-bedding, cross-bedding* or *false-bedding* (Fig. 93).

For desert travellers, the structure of sand-dunes is of more than academic interest. The sand-grains of the accretion-layers are packed as a result of saltation with the greatest possible density and when the layer is subjected to pressure by a lorry passing over it, its volume is increased by dilatation and it becomes rigid and firm. The encroachment-layers, on the other hand, are quicksands resulting from the irregular piling-up of avalanched grains, and the dune-surface can therefore vary with disconcerting abruptness.

A typical eolian sand forming in a desert environment would, according to Thompson, be expected to show a marked diversity of direction and inclination of its laminae which would be steeply inclined concentric shells. Few horizontal laminae are to be expected and there should be a marked divergence in direction and amount of truncating surfaces in a small area. Ripple-marks should be of asymmetric form, of great wave-length and small amplitude. Frosting and pitting of the sand-grains are probably valid criteria for an eolian origin, but size and sorting are not conclusive. To this evidence might be added that provided by wind-facetted pebbles and the existence of wind-eroded surfaces below the sand-deposit.

Not all eolian deposits are necessarily made of quartz sand, although quartz, the most obdurate of minerals, is by far their commonest component. In Bermuda, shelly dunes occur, and in India certain limestones were probably formed by the wind-drifting of calcareous sand derived from organic material. Salt dunes are known and magnificent dunes of gypsum ($CaSO_4.2H_2O$) are displayed in White Sands National Park, New Mexico. Finally, in Greenland there are well developed snow-dunes giving a topography exactly like that of the dune areas of the Sahara.

Often it is necessary to anchor moving sand. This is attempted by planting with marram grass followed by conifers, by covering the sand with a clay-plaster, or by laying wicker-mats and building wind-breaks.

THE GEOLOGICAL ACTION OF RUNNING WATER

Notwithstanding the universality of the wind, it is *moving water* that plays the dominant part in the transport of the weathering-products and in the denudation of the earth's surface. We realise this when we reflect upon such a commonplace matter as the muddiness of rivers or on such a stupendous phenomenon as the cutting of the gorges of the Indus and Brahmaputra through the highest mountain-ranges of the world. The scale of activity is given by noting that the Mississippi carries two million tons of material to the sea every day.

Rain-action. Our first example of the action of moving water is provided by the rain-water running down a slope. Even in temperate regions, rain may wash the finest weathering-products to the foot of the slope to accumulate there as *rain-wash*. Where the rain is torrential, as for example in Central Africa, thousands of tons of good soil may be lost for ever by an hour's deluge; such *sheet-erosion* is a serious problem in soil conservation.

Thaws may lead to the washing-down of material, often half frozen, on to the lower ground, as illustrated in the *coombe-deposits* of the Chalk districts of southern England (p. 150). If a slope of clay containing sporadic blocks of hard rock is washed by rain, *earth-*

pillars may be produced by the blocks protecting the column of clay underneath them. The classic example is at Bozen in Tyrol where pillars as high as seventy feet are produced; less spectacular examples occur in the valley of the Findhorn in Moray, Scotland.

Stream-development. Sheet-erosion by rain-water running down a slope is unlikely to proceed in a uniform manner. The sheet of rain-water is guided into depressions and areas unprotected by a plant-cover where its erosive action becomes concentrated to produce *rills* of irregular depths running down the slope. Master rills develop by the flooding into them of water from the lesser rills and a drainage-system is established. The main streams flowing directly down the slope are joined by *tributaries* from the side, the junctions being *accordant*, that is, without change of gradient. With the continuance of stream-erosion and valley-development, less and less of the original surface remains intact.

When the weathered mantle is loose and unprotected, the erosion pattern becomes quickly established and *gully-erosion* may result in times of heavy sudden rainfall. Soil-erosion of any type may be combatted by strip-cropping, contour-ploughing or terrace-cultivation of some kind.

Surface-water may contribute a spectacular part to the river-water, but a more steady and reliable quota comes from springs and

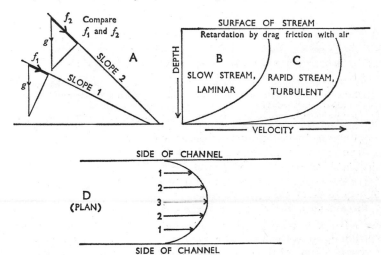

Fig. 94. Stream Flow. A, effect of slope on the component of gravity along the stream course; B, C, relations of velocity and depth of stream, laminar and turbulent flow; D, retardation at the sides of the channel.

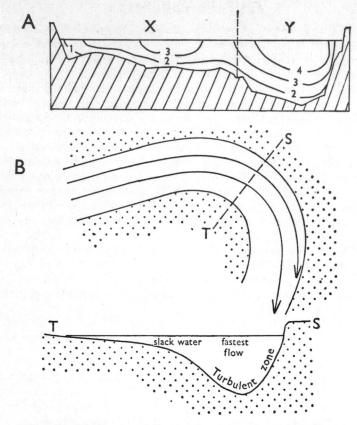

Fig. 95. Velocity in relation to the shape of a stream-channel. A, section across the Danube near Vienna showing control of velocities by shape and depth of the river channel; the two sectors x and y have the same cross-section area — note the greater velocity in the deeper sector; 1, 2, 3 and 4 indicate regularly increasing velocities (based on Harlacher); B, stream energy at a bend.

the groundwater. As we have seen, these waters, percolating through the weathered mantle, have dissolved a variety of salts which they deliver to the river.

Stream-flow. Before the geological work done by rivers is dealt with, it is necessary to examine the way their water moves. As with motion down any other inclined plane, the force moving a particle of water in a river is the component of gravity in the direction of flow (Fig. 94A). The magnitude of this component increases with the slope or *gradient* of the river. Opposed to this driving force is the internal friction of the water and more especially the frictional resistance

162

exerted at the bed and walls of the channel (Fig. 94D). There is thus a limit to the speed of a river. In slow-moving streams, the velocity increases steadily upwards from the river-bed; on the bed itself there is a skin of motionless water and above it the water moves smoothly in laminae along straight paths parallel to the bed — this is *laminar flow* (Fig. 94B). When the river moves fast, this steady laminar flow is upset and especially so when irregularities such as pebbles or boulders occur on the bed; eddies then move in various directions and the flow is *turbulent* (Fig. 94C).

From what has been said in the previous paragraph it is obvious that the energy of a river increases with the gradient and the volume of water and decreases with the frictional resistance. The depth of a river, with the same volume of water, controls the friction and therefore the energy, as illustrated in Fig. 95A. Finally, we can examine the conditions at a bend (Fig. 95B). The velocity on the outside of the bend increases, that on the inside decreases; the water is thrown against the outside — the energy available thus increases at that position and more work can be done there.

Erosion by rivers. Erosion by rivers can be performed on the weathered mantle simply by the hydraulic pressure of the moving water, just as loose surface-material is sluiced away by a hose in hydraulic mining. For cutting into harder rock, the river-water is armed with detritus of various grades — silt, sand, gravel and boulders of resistant rocks — and with these it abrades its bed. This vertical filing action is called *corrasion*. During it, friction between the pebbles themselves and between them and the river-bed leads to the formation of fine-grained ground-down material. The pebbles are split, cracked and chipped and finer material caught between them is crushed. In suitable rocks, grooves and flutings may be cut in the river-bed by a kind of sand-blasting action analogous to that we have already noted in connection with wind-erosion.

The tools for corrasion are supplied by rain-wash, gullying, frost, slumping of the river banks and many other processes. The *eroding power* will depend on the momentum (mass × velocity) of the tools: greatest erosion will obviously take place when the river is in flood and its water moving rapidly. The speed of *wearing down of the river-bed* will clearly be controlled by the amount of run-off, the gradient of the river, the nature of the tools and of the bedrock. It varies along the course of the river. In the *mountain-track* of torrents and steep gullies, erosion is active; lower down, in the *valley-track* of the middle portion of gorges and open valleys, erosion and deposition alternate; in the *plain-track* of the lower reaches where the river winds through a wide plain built up of its own detritus, deposition is dominant —

we meet these three divisions under other names later (p. 179). There is a limit below which a river cannot erode its bed; this ultimate *base-level* is the ocean, but *temporary base-levels* are provided by lakes or by resistant rock-bars crossing the course of the stream.

River-valleys. Corrasion digs a deep trench, which is widened by weathering of the walls, by rain-wash, gullying and slumping in of the sides. A river-valley thus results from two processes, *down-cutting* and *broadening*, with the consequence that its cross-section is V-shaped. Lateral erosion by the stream helps in the widening of its valley. The detail of river-valleys depends on the nature and arrangement of the rocks traversed, and on their hardness, toughness and stability. Open valleys are formed in soft rocks, narrow valleys or gorges in hard, more resistant, rocks.

Pot-holes are produced in the rocks of the river-bed by the swirling action of sands and pebbles caused by eddies; initial hollows or depressions at points of weakness are deepened into pot-shaped holes often several feet across. The efficacy of *pot-hole erosion* is often underestimated. In some streams, the coalescence of pot-holes leads to the formation of narrow deep *gorges*, as in the River Greta in West Yorkshire.

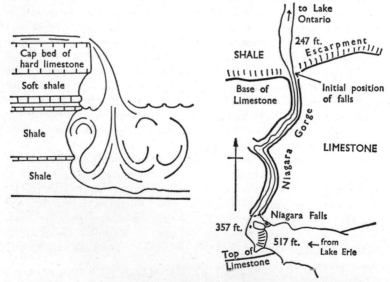

Fig. 96. Niagara Falls. (*Left*), section showing the geological conditions producing a cap-bed waterfall. (*Right*), plan of the Niagara Gorge eroded in soft shale capped by hard limestone, recording the recession of Niagara Falls from the escarpment.

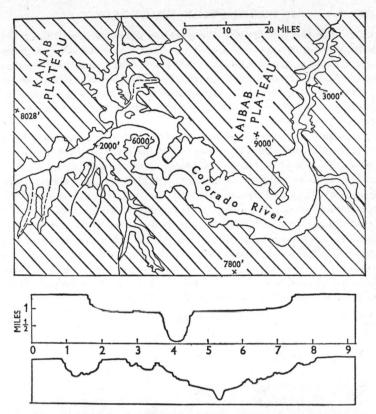

FIG. 97. The Grand Canyon of the Colorado River. The rim of the canyon and the surrounding plateau are made of Kaibab Limestone (lined). The sections across the canyon are drawn on the same vertical and horizontal scales.

When layers of rocks of differing toughness are suitably arranged across a river *rapids* and *waterfalls* result. Alternations of thin beds of soft and hard rock give rise to *rapids* by the preferential erosion of the softer layers. Thicker alternations lead to the formation of *waterfalls* by the holding-up of erosion by a strong thick bed. A capbed waterfall of this type is exemplified by the Niagara Falls (Fig. 96). Here a hard limestone bed lies on soft shales which are readily eroded away to leave a lip of limestone. This lip is constantly undermined by the violent erosion in the plunge-pool below it, and a gorge seven miles long has been formed as the fall has retreated upstream.

Spectacular *canyons* are formed under certain conditions — the

165

stability of the valley-walls, the elevation of the area, and the rapid cutting down by a powerful body of water. The ideal example is the *Grand Canyon* of the Colorado, 200 miles long, some twelve miles across and a mile or more deep (Fig. 97). The Colorado River rises in the rainy Rockies and flows rapidly into an arid land of high elevation built up of horizontal layers of rock that can for the most part stand up in vertical cliffs.

Transport by rivers. The material transported downstream by a river is called its *load*. It consists of two main parts, the first carried in solution, the second in the solid state by mechanical means.

The *load in solution* is mainly provided by the spring-water contribution, aided by solution of the valley-rocks and of the mechanical load. It consists of the soluble products of chemical weathering, such as colloidal silica, hydroxides of Al and Fe, carbonates, sulphates and chlorides of Ca and Mg, Na and K. Any particular chemical character of a river-water will depend upon the rocks of its drainage basin: typical analyses are given in the Table below. The load in solution is carried to the sea or, in the conditions of interior drainage, to an inland lake — we consider its fate later.

ANALYSES OF RIVER-WATERS

	A	B	C
CO_2	34·98	13·02	39·53
SO_4	15·37	28·61	14·72
Cl	6·21	19·92	4·57
NO_2	1·60	—	—
PO_4	—	—	—
Ca	20·50	10·35	28·57
Mg	5·38	3·14	1·82
Na ⎱	8·33	19·75	3·28
K ⎰		2·17	1·55
SiO_2	7·05	3·04	2·36
Al_2O_3	0·45	— ⎱	
Fe_2O_3	0·13	— ⎰	3·60
	100·00	100·00	100·00

A. Mississippi, New Orleans.
B. Colorado River, Yuma, Arizona.
C. Thames, Kew.

The *mechanical load* is transported by three mechanisms. A first portion travels in *suspension* in the water due to its turbulent flow;

very fine particles may not settle in the river at all and so be carried to the sea — this subfraction is called the *permanent suspended load*. Coarser particles make up the *temporary suspended load*. Since gravity as well as turbulence is active, the particles of the suspended load are coarser towards the bottom of the river. A second fraction of the load is *rolled along* the river-bed, spherical particles moving more easily in this way. The third portion of the load moves by *saltation* in a series of short leaps — the grains move up into a higher-velocity layer so that they are carried a short distance forward before falling back to the bed. The load of a river is thus constituted as follows:

$$
\text{LOAD}
\begin{cases}
\text{Solution Load} \\
\text{Suspended Load} \\
\text{Saltated Load} \\
\text{Rolled Load}
\end{cases}
\left.
\begin{array}{c}
\\
\\
\text{BED LOAD or} \\
\text{TRACTION LOAD}
\end{array}
\right.
$$

The *capacity* of a river is the total load that it can carry and is largely dependent on the volume, as in the case of the Mississippi. The *competency* is indicated by the maximum diameter of grain that can be moved and, clearly, varies with the velocity, possibly with the square of this. River physicists are interested in measuring the load of rivers. The average annual discharge can be ascertained, and the average amounts of dissolved and suspended material in a given volume of river-water measured; the size of the traction load can only be estimated.

The consequence of these different transportation operations is that the load becomes roughly sorted out and, when it is dropped on the decrease of the speed of the river, it provides three more or less distinct fractions; the coarse river-gravel made up of partly rounded rock-fragments, the river-sand of grains of the obdurate minerals, chiefly quartz, and the river-muds made of the finest particles of old minerals, and of new minerals, especially clay-minerals, formed during chemical weathering on the surrounding land.

The grains transported undergo two processes, *abrasion* and *sorting*. The *abrasion* reduces the size of the grain; the coarser the material the more rapid being the reduction. Abrasion depends on the original shape and size of the grains, their physical properties such as hardness and cleavage and the distance and manner of their transportation. It is considered that abrasion is very slow in the finest grades of material and that several episodes of transport are necessary to produce significant effects. Sand-grains do not become well-rounded in the presence of coarse material. The greater viscosity of water as compared with that of air is considered to result in the formation of a cushion between grains so that the smaller sizes cannot

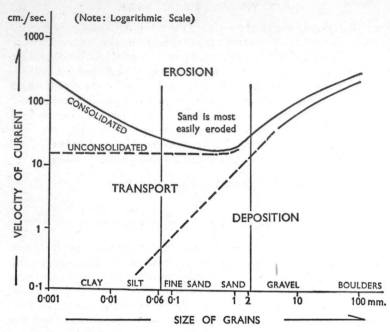

become rounded. In general terms, with travel down the river, the
size of grains decreases, their sphericity and roundness increase.
Investigations on the sands of several rivers do indeed show that
sands become finer lower down the river, but the significance of this
may concern *sorting* rather than abrasion.

Sorting of the transported materials depends upon their size, shape
and specific gravity. In the suspended load, smaller grains will *bypass*
the larger, the irregular the spherical, the light the heavy — selective
sorting thus takes place. The effect of shape is seen in the great
distances travelled by thin cleavage-flakes of mica.

The transporting power of a river is considered to vary as the fifth
or sixth power of its velocity: by doubling its velocity, the transporting power may be increased some thirty to sixty-fold. In flood,
rivers may perform immense geological work. The general relationships between velocity and grain-size as they affect erosion, transport
and deposition are given in Fig. 98.

Deposition by rivers. We have seen that the energy of a river
depends on its gradient, the volume of its water, and the frictional
forces opposed to the movement of water. Deposition of portions of

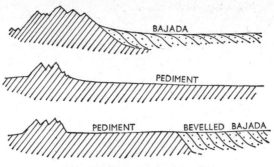

FIG. 99. Pediment and Bajada.

the mechanical load takes place therefore when the gradient (and consequently the speed) is lessened, the volume decreased or the friction increased.

Sheet-flood action. Deposition due to a sudden decrease in velocity occurs typically where a stream flowing swiftly down a steep mountain-slope debouches on to the flatter ground of a main valley or plain — that is, on to the *piedmont*, the foot of the mountains.

In arid regions, the sudden checking of velocity due to change of gradient leads to *sheet-floods* from intermittent streams which are responsible for deposition and erosion on a grand scale. The material deposited by a sheet-flood is made up of a multitude of small fan-like delta units each with fairly well-defined fronts. This deposition may be only temporary and the view is advanced that sheet-floods may act as powerful transporting or, even, eroding agencies. If the drainage is towards a central depression, deposition may take place continually to build up a gently sloping cover of detritus in the piedmont-area; if the drainage is to the sea, then erosion may be the main activity of sheet-floods. Removal of the weathered material is the essential control.

We may distinguish two forms arising in semi-arid regions in which sheet-floods are involved:

(a) the erosion-form, the *pediment* or *rock-fan*, the smooth surface of bare rock, covered by only a veneer of detrital material, on which the desert-mountains appear to stand, and

(b) the deposition-form, the *bajada*, made up of a series of fan-shaped detrital accumulations along the base of the mountain-range (Fig. 99).

We examine the bajada more closely. Each fan-unit is the work of a single stream issuing from the mountains on to the plains; opposite large canyons are large and broad fans of low gradient (up to 3°),

169

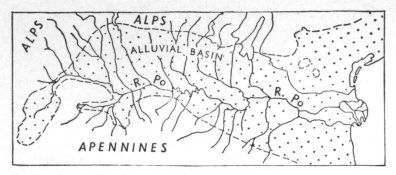

Fig. 100. The Po alluvial basin.

opposite small steep ravines are small fans as steep as 30°. The margin of the bajada with the mountains will be an undulating one, and the detritus of the fans may merge at this margin into the slumped slide-rock of the mountain-face. The outwash material making the fans is very irregular in grain-size and badly sorted; large boulders in clay, and pebbles in sand, are characteristic. Due to the nature of the floods causing them, the layers of detrital material will be wedge-shaped and lenticular, and successive layers, the result of a succession of floods, may vary markedly in grain-size and arrangement of material.

Sheet-floods are not of course the only agency or even the dominant agency in fan formation nor are these built only in arid regions. The essential conditions for the production of really big groups of fans appear to be instability in the crust whereby the necessary topographic contrast between mountainous highland and piedmont lowland is provided. There is an abundance of examples of this essential condition. We may select that given by the Po valley where the main stream has been pushed south by the growth of broad fans laid down by the smaller streams issuing from the Alps until it abuts against the narrower fans built up by the still smaller streams coming from the Apennines (Fig. 100). On large fans, erosion is taking place along the main distributaries which, in some cases, have incised themselves hundreds of feet into the detrital deposits.

Isolated conspicuous fans are called *alluvial cones*; in these the coarser materials are near the mountains, the finer at the edge of the cone.

Fluvial deposits. Rivers which have stabilised their positions in their valleys deposit sediments in their *channels* and over their *flood-plains* — the areas covered by their flood-waters. Along the course of the river, variation in velocity is common, so that deposition

170

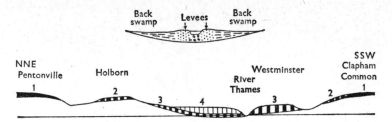

FIG. 101. Alluvial Deposits. (*Above*), levees and back swamps; (*below*), diagrammatic section across the Thames valley, showing the succession of terraces, 1 to 4, the vertical scale is greatly exaggerated.

of portions of the load constantly occurs, though this deposition may be only temporary. The *channel-deposits* are irregular lenses of gravels, sands, silts and clays; conspicuous among them are *gravel-bars* formed in the slack water on the inside of bends (cf. the energy picture, Fig. 95). When the river floods, its waters escape from its bed, their velocity is lowered and their load consequently becomes spread as a layer over the flood-plain. The coarser material comes to rest nearest the river-bed and may build up natural embankments, *levees*, along the sides (Fig. 101); behind the levees are *back-swamps*, covered by scarcely moving water, in which deposition of the fine fraction of the load takes place. The succession of floods leads to the building-up of a considerable thickness of *alluvium* or *alluvial deposits*.

Along many rivers, especially those in parts of the world which have been recently covered by thick ice-sheets (p. 219), alluvium forms a series of terraces one above the other on the valley sides. The highest of these *alluvial terraces* is clearly the oldest and was formed when the river flowed at its highest level, the lowest terrace or flood-plain is being made at the present day (Fig. 101). This arrangement of terraces may be the result of several causes; they may, for example, be due to the spasmodic rejuvenation of the river by uplift so that it received a series of impulses to renewed erosive activity, or else they may be formed by ordinary meandering (see below) or they may be controlled by the shape of the rock-floor of the valley.

Inequalities in the alluvium of a river may cause a slight bend in its course. Any bend tends to increase in amplitude by deposition on its inner side and erosion on its outer side, in accordance with the energy-pattern of the water as it moves round the bend (Fig. 95). These crude curves and loops are termed *meanders*, after the classical River Meander of Troy. The larger the stream, the larger are the meanders. They form a *meander-belt*, some twenty times as wide as the river, which swings back and forth across the flood-plain and so slowly

171

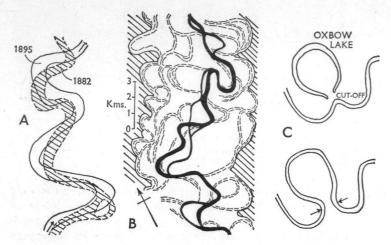

Fig. 102. Meanders. A, the Mississippi below Vicksburg, showing the migration of meanders downstream; B, the Rhine valley near Karlsruhe showing the present channel (black) and earlier meanders; C, formation of cut-off and ox-bow lake.

widens the valley. Each meander tends to move slowly downstream since erosion on the downstream side of the bend is greater than on the upstream. When the loop of the meander becomes large it is liable to be *cut-off* across its neck, leaving an abandoned separated portion which may remain as an *oxbow-lake* or *mort-lake*. The continuous change in the shape of the river in the meander-belt is illustrated by old parish or county boundaries, established centuries ago on the then course of the river, being now completely different from its present course. Some features of meanders are illustrated in Fig. 102.

As we have just seen, conditions in a river and over its flood-plain continuously change with space and time so that river-deposits in general, the *fluvial deposits*, are exceedingly variable and show patterns of contrasting sediments of gravel, sand, silt and mud grades. Alluvial deposits can be made up of elongated strings of the coarse materials representing the channel and levee deposits or more regular seams of finer muds of the flood-plain. The materials naturally vary in degree of sorting and rounding. They often show current-bedding, with the laminae inclined downstream; between the current-bedded layers, more or less horizontal intercalations are common. Pebbles may be arranged in *imbricate* fashion (Fig. 150), like tiles on a roof, and indicate the direction of current-movement. Organic remains in transport by rivers will be battered and comminuted so

172

that, except in the finest fluvial sediments, they stand little chance of being preserved.

DELTAS

Most of the mechanical load of a river is carried on to the sea or to a lake where, the velocity being checked, much of it is deposited as *deltaic sediments* in a Δ-shaped area, with the apex of the Δ upstream. The lower parts of the delta are built outwards into the sea or lake by the successive tipping of the load in that direction; marked cross-bedding is common in such deposits. The level sub-aerial surface of the delta is a continuation of the flood-plain of the river, extended and built up by the work of the bifurcating *distributaries* running across it. Modern deltaic deposits will accordingly be made up of irregular coarse sands of fluvial type and more regular clays and muds. In tropical deltas, such as that of the Niger, where vegetation runs riot, layers of plant-debris, often resting on swamp soils, will be found. This accumulation of vegetable matter can be compared with those ancient deposits from which coals were formed.

The tripartite nature of certain deltaic deposits. The classic account of one type of deltaic sedimentation was given in 1885 by G. K. Gilbert of the United States Geological Survey. When the river enters a lake the coarsest part of the mechanical load, moved by rolling or saltation, comes to rest and builds out a platform with a face sloping at about the angle of repose of the coarse material. The finer part of the load, borne in suspension, is carried beyond this face and sinks slowly to the bottom, the coarser part of the fine material nearest the face and the finest part farther away. 'As the delta is built lakeward, the steeply inclined layers of the delta face are superimposed over the more level strata of the lake bottom and in turn come to support the gently inclined layers of the delta plain, so that any vertical section of a normal delta exhibits at the top a zone of coarse material, bedded with a gentle lakeward inclination, then a zone of similar coarse material, the laminations of which incline at a high angle, and at bottom a zone of fine material, the laminations of which are gently inclined and unite by curves with those of the Middle Zone' (Gilbert). If a lake is drained, deltas built out into it should show this tripartite structure in section.

We reproduce in Fig. 103 Gilbert's drawing illustrating the parts and succession of such a delta. He observed these structures in the deltas along the shores of the ancient Lake Bonneville (p. 189). In Fig. 103 is included a drawing of the deltaic deposits laid down in the Ritomsee in Switzerland. The slopes of the fronts of deltas in the Lake of Geneva are as follows: Rhone, 12°; Drance, 31–35°; Vevey

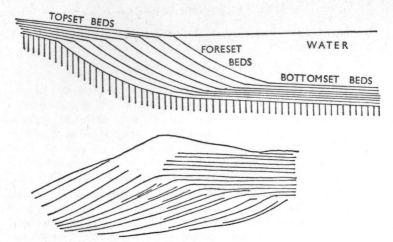

Fig. 103. (*Above*), Gilbert's tripartite division of a delta. (*Below*), topset and foreset beds in a delta in the Ritomsee, Switzerland, from a photograph, after Collet.

31°; Baye de Montreux, 29–33°; it should be noted that the Rhone carries very fine alluvial material, the other streams much coarser, a difference reflected in the angles of repose. Occasionally the material with the steeper slopes becomes unstable and sliding and slumping take place so that the regularity of the deltaic layers is disturbed. The three sets of deltaic beds distinguished by Gilbert and illustrated in Fig. 103 are now known as *topset, foreset* and *bottomset*.

Mixed sedimentation in deltas. A whole delta, as distinct from the part which forms the land delta of topographic maps, is clearly a combination of sediments of terrestrial and marine or lake-origins. The outer and lower parts of the delta are built below the water-level, the upper and inner parts are a continuation of the alluvial deposits of the river. The subaqueous portion of the delta is revealed by the contours of the sea- or lake-floor beyond the land-delta, as is illustrated in the classic *Nile Delta* shown in Fig. 104. In this delta the submarine plain slopes at an angle of less than one in a thousand till it reaches a depth of 50 metres at about 40 kms. from the shore. Beyond the depth of 50 metres, the slope increases gently to some 100 kms. from the coast but more rapidly below 200 metres where there is a descent to 1000 metres depth in a space of 30 kms. This descent indicates the foreset beds which slope at 26 per 1000 or at about 1½°. Beyond the foreset slope is a wide flat expanse of bottom-set beds extending to depths of 2000 metres.

Borings in modern deltas reveal extraordinary thicknesses in some examples thousands of metres, of shallow-water deposits; it is

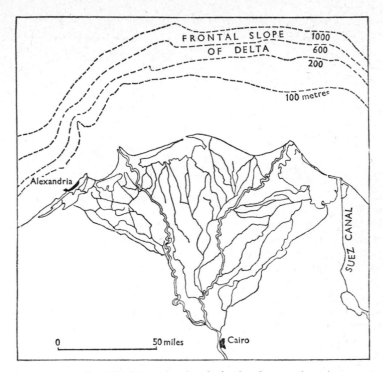

Fig. 104. The Nile Delta, showing the land and seaward portions.

clear that the floor of the delta region must be subsiding. Recurring subsidence and deposition in the middle part of a large delta thus result not only in the interbedding of marine and non-marine sediments but in a great thickening of the deltaic deposits as a whole. A large delta 'is a thick lens, with a relatively thin non-marine inner

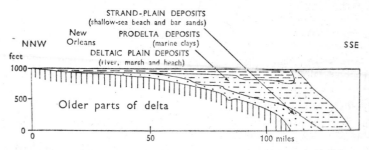

Fig. 105. Section of the latest deposits of the Mississippi delta (after Fisk and Macfarlan).

175

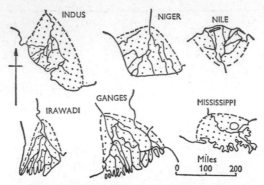

FIG. 106. Six deltas, all to the same scale.

portion, a correspondingly thin outer marine portion, and a thick central zone composed of alternating marine and continental sediments' (Russell and Russell). This is exemplified in Fig. 105 a north-south section of the Mississippi Delta which we examine in a little detail below.

Rivers carrying various grades of load may enter bodies of water of various depths and with varying conditions of waves and currents. Deltaic deposits, therefore, often depart considerably in form from the ideal tripartite type. Fine material of the bottomset beds may be widely dispersed by currents, whilst still waters will favour the growth of foreset beds. A broad sub-aerial plain will be built up where wave-action is poor and many loaded rivers drain to a shallow sea. The size of deltas will likewise vary greatly. The scope for variation will be realised by recalling such examples as the tiny deltas in small lakes and reservoirs, the classic delta of the Nile, the current-trimmed delta of the Rhine, the gigantic Indian and Chinese deltas and the very remarkable delta of the Mississippi. It is important for British students in particular to realise the immense size of some modern deltas (Fig. 106).

The measurement of the rate of growth of deltas is of interest to geologists and of great importance to engineers concerned in the maintenance of reservoirs and lakes. The dozen great reservoirs in Algeria have their volume decreased by 1 per cent annually through sedimentation. The Rhine carries into Lake Constance 2,790,000 cubic metres per year, equivalent to 456 cubic metres per square kilometre of the basin.

The Mississippi Delta provides us with a final example of a tremendous delta of somewhat unusual form. This delta (Fig. 107) is over 12,000 sq. miles (31,000 sq. kms.) in size and is growing seaward at about 1 mile in 16 years, this rate being increased by cultivation and

176

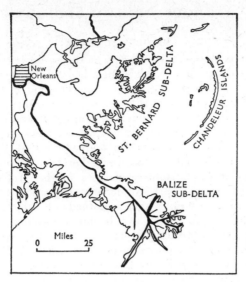

FIG. 107. The Mississippi delta (after Russell and Russell).

deforestation in the drainage area and by the prevention of flooding. It is characterised by the *bird's claw* projection from the main deltaic area. This projection, *the Balize sub-delta*, has been formed in recent times (its surface bears no Indian Mounds) by the building of levees of coarse material along the bifurcating current-channels. In the slack shallow waters between the framework of levees, there is deposited finer material which gradually builds up into swamps and marshes. A rim of beach- and bar-deposits, resulting from wave-action, fringes the Balize sub-delta and beyond these in the Gulf of Mexico are the submarine deltaic deposits. There is little resemblance therefore between the Mississippi type of deltaic accumulation and the classic tripartite bottomset, foreset and topset beds. The pattern of the Mississippi delta, as Russell and Russell have emphasised, is that of a pile of mighty superimposed leaves, the veins being represented by the levee-deposits, the intervein areas by the swamp and similar deposits and the outline of each leaf being indicated by the beach and bar deposits. To the north of the Balize sub-delta there is seen a very much larger unit, the *St. Bernard sub-delta*, which has clearly been drowned by subsidence; the higher levees appear as 'double islands', the lower parts of the sub-delta are completely drowned and the outer rim of beach and bar now form the Chandeleur Islands. Over much of the area of original deltaic sedimentation, shallow-water marine deposits are now accumulating.

THE FLUVIAL CYCLE

In an earlier page, we have noted that the ocean is the base-level below which rivers cannot erode their beds. *Temporary base-levels* are provided by lake-basins or by rock-bars crossing the river and are doomed to obliteration as the river-work proceeds. If the longitudinal profile of a normal river from source to mouth is constructed it will be a more or less smooth curve, concave upwards, gentler near its mouth or base-level and steeper towards its source (Fig. 108). Tributaries to the main stream show similar longitudinal profiles meeting that of the main stream accordantly. Irregularities in the profile are more numerous in its upper part. All such irregularities, even those so great as the Niagara Falls, will be smoothed out if the river has time enough. Lakes in its course will be filled, rapids and waterfalls eroded; local steep stretches will be preferentially eroded, gentle stretches will receive deposits to build up the bed. When all the irregularities are removed and the profile is perfectly smooth, the river is said to be *at grade, graded* or *in equilibrium* with the controls along its course; the profile is then a *profile of equilibrium*, theoretically hyperbolic in form. Though rivers are only approximately in equilibrium, they are nevertheless just able, under average conditions to transport the load delivered at any point along their course.

Temporary base-levels are responsible for temporary profiles and

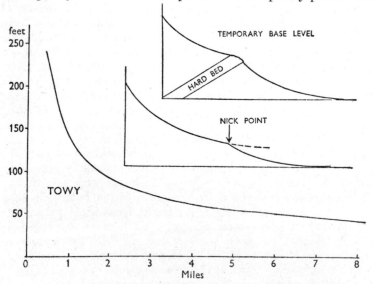

FIG. 108. Profiles of River Valleys (the Towy after O. T. Jones).

when the base-level, such as a waterfall, is removed, a new profile begins to form. The old and the new profiles, of different curvatures, meet at a *nick-point* (Fig. 108).

Given time and opportunity, a river will wear down its valley to the level of its mouth — a condition known as *base-levelled*. This condition is never achieved, but an approach to it is seen in the *peneplain*, where the valley-system forms a broad and rolling country of low relief, with very gentle slopes, and the rivers meander through great alluvial plains. Isolated residual hills rising from the peneplain are called *monadnocks*.

The *fluvial cycle* is the badly chosen name given to the series of progressive changes in land-forms due to river-action. It is marked by *stages*, the position reached in the series and registered by the forms produced. Three stages were recognised by W. M. Davis in the normal fluvial cycle of the humid regions of the globe; to these he gave the equally badly chosen names *youth*, *maturity* and *old-age*. They correspond in a general way to the forms of the mountain-, valley- and plain-tracks of the river that were mentioned earlier on p. 163.

The *stage of youth* is initiated by rapid uplift of the region concerned. It is recorded by steep gradients, giving rapid erosion, with downward-cutting dominating over weathering-back so that V-shaped valleys or narrow gorges result. Waterfalls and rapids and lakes are often common in the system and the river is clearly not at grade. No flood-plain is present and a great deal of the original surface between the streams — the *interfluves* — remains relatively untouched.

In the *stage of maturity*, the gradient is moderate, down-cutting is not so marked, the valley is wider and deeper. Irregularities such as waterfalls and lakes have been obliterated and the stream is graded. Adjustment of the stream is nearly perfect and normally it is just able to carry its load. The interfluves are now largely made of the new valley-slopes, much of the original surface has gone and the relief of the region is considerable. The flood-plain is beginning to form and meandering is starting across it.

In *old-age*, the gradient is still lower, the valley is shallower and wider, and lateral cutting is the main erosion-process. The divides between the streams are reduced. Broad flood-plains are formed across which strong meander-belts wander. The condition of *base-levelling* or *peneplanation* is almost reached.

Accidents to the fluvial cycle. A *consequent* river is one which is the consequence of the formation of an inclined surface such as an uptilted coastal plain or the slope of a new volcano. As erosion of this surface proceeds, new drainage-channels may be formed depending on the

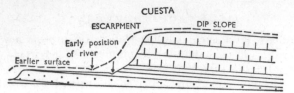

FIG. 109. Escarpment, dip-slope and cuesta.

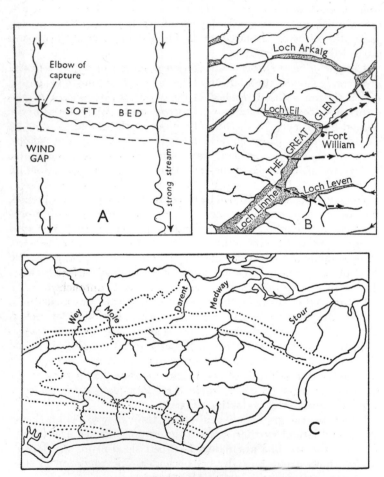

FIG. 110. River Capture. A, diagrammatic conditions of river capture; B, capture of eastward-flowing rivers in the western Highlands of Scotland by the Great Glen, eroded along a major fault (after George); C, The Weald, radial streams initiated on a Chalk dome have adapted themselves to the underlying strata (indicated by dotted lines). Note capture of the headwaters of the Darent by the Medway.

weakness of certain underlying layers of rock — such streams are called *subsequent*. A river which has stable relations to the rocks of its basin is said to be *adjusted*. Erosion by a subsequent stream running on a weak layer between harder layers suitably inclined may result in a number of land-forms that have received special names. Among these we may mention *escarpment* and *dip-slope*, which together form a *cuesta* (Fig. 109).

Consequent rivers initiated on a slope do not grow equally in parallel straight lines. Minor accidents, inequalities of surface, of bedrock or of slope, lead to the increase in size of certain of the streams which enlarge their basins by *capturing* other streams. Tributaries of the active rivers cut into the basins of their neighbours and *behead* them (Fig. 110). Inequalities in the rocks of the valleys especially help in this *piracy* — a stream flowing in soft, easily-eroded rocks captures those that are compelled to erode hard rocks, as is illustrated by the rivers of Yorkshire and the Weald.

A series of consequent rivers initiated on a certain layer of rock may in course of time remove this layer to reveal another set of rocks arranged in a quite different pattern. Such a *superimposed drainage-system* is illustrated by the rivers of the English Lake District (Fig. 111) or of the Weald.

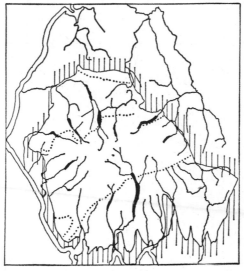

FIG. 111. Superimposed Drainage. In the English Lake District, radial drainage, initiated on a dome of Carboniferous Limestone (vertical lined) has superimposed itself on the underlying older rocks trending north-east and south-west (dotted lines).

Drastic interference with the equilibrium of a river system results from regional elevation or depression. Elevation of the region results in the *rejuvenation* of the rivers traversing it, and a new cycle begins. The rivers start active erosion again and dig down in their flood-plains to produce *entrenched meanders* on the sites of the existing meanders. Erosion may also produce a valley of a more youthful aspect in one more mature, giving a *valley-in-valley*. Depression of the land results in the *drowning* of river-systems and the dismember-ment of their components. The pattern of river-erosion is found to continue on the sea-floor.

LAKE-PROCESSES

We may now examine the geological operations connected with the last portion of terrestrial waters, *lakes*. As mentioned in the previous section of this chapter, lakes are a sign of youth or immaturity in a river-system and, since the main operation that goes on in them is *deposition*, they are doomed eventually to disappear. In most cases, the lake is part of the drainage-system and has an effluent. Its function as a gigantic settling-tank can be appreciated by comparing, for example, the muddy water entering a reservoir — an artificial lake — with the clear water escaping over the spillway or, for another example, the turbid condition of the Rhone when it enters the Lake

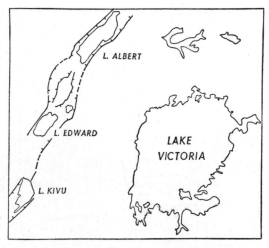

Fig. 112. Lakes of East Africa. Lake Victoria occupies a broad down-warp, Lakes Albert, Edward and Kivu are situated in the rift-valley let down between parallel faults.

of Geneva with its clarity where it leaves. The waters of Lake
Ontario, last in the sequence of the Great Lakes, are the clearest —
most of the mechanical load has been dropped already.

Origins of lake basins. Lakes occupy basins of many different

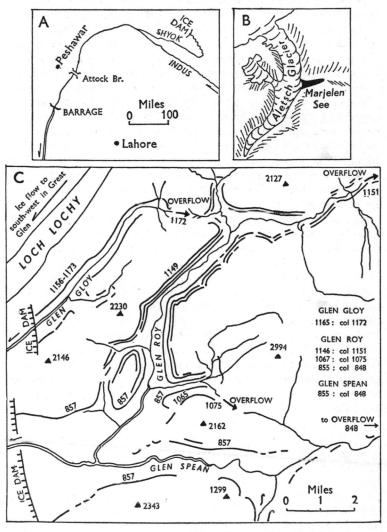

FIG. 113. Glacial Lakes. A, The River Shyok and the Indus; B, the
Marjelen See impounded by the Aletsch glacier; C, the Parallel Roads
of Glen Roy (heights in feet).

origins. They may be *tectonic* in origin, formed as a result of crustal movements; depression of segments of the crust between parallel fractures has provided the Rift-Lakes of East Africa (Fig. 112) and the Dead Sea in the sunken Jordan valley; broad warps produce depressions occupied by wide relatively shallow lakes exemplified by Lough Neagh in Northern Ireland and Lake Victoria in East Africa. Some small lakes occupy *volcanic craters*. *Oxbow-lakes* are formed by cut-off meanders. Innumerable lakes are related to glaciation (p. 231) in some manner; many occupy *hollows in glacial deposits* or *rock-basins* excavated by glacial erosion. Other lakes are impounded by a *barrier* of some kind, as for example a lava-stream, land-slip, a glacial deposit or a gravel bar formed by wave-action. One of the most interesting of these barriers is a glacier. The Marjelen See in Switzerland is held up in a tributary valley by the Aletsch glacier that occupies the main valley (Fig. 113). In recent years, the gorge of the River Shyok, a tributary of the Indus, has been periodically blocked by the Khumdan Glacier moving across it; in 1932, this ice-barrier was 500 feet high and over 1000 feet thick. When the lake formed above the glacier-barrier bursts the ice-dam, a great flood of water causes immense damage lower down the valley and menaces the great Sukkur barrage and the Attock Bridge 900 miles away on the Indus (Fig. 113). During the recent Ice-age exactly similar temporary lakes were formed in the glaciated regions. Examples are provided in the Cleveland Hills and the various levels of one such lake are recorded in Glen Roy in western Scotland by its old shores one above the other — the famous Parallel Roads of Glen Roy (Fig. 113). Surplus water from these lakes escaped by carving *glacial overflows* or spillways which now appear as trenches across ridges.

Sedimentation in lakes. As we have seen, much of the mechanical load is deposited in lakes and forms the major part of the *lacustrine deposits*; if the lake has an outlet the load in solution passes on, but where there is no outlet, this material too is finally deposited. Deltas are built out by the incoming rivers and their flood-plain deposits extend until, given time, the site of the lake becomes a level alluvial plain. If the lake is large, *gravels*, *sands* and *clays* will be deposited at appropriate positions. With these there is usually a considerable amount of organic material such as drifted vegetable matter. Diatoms, unicellular plants which have a siliceous framework, live in lake-water and their tests may accumulate to give a layer rich in their siliceous remains — this is *diatomite*, an important industrial material used as an absorbent, a filtering medium and for insulating and many other purposes. Other organisms, such as molluscs and plants like *Chara*, build calcareous shells or frameworks and these may contribute an important quota to the mud being deposited; the result is a *lake-marl*, a mixture of clay, calcium carbonate and plant-debris. In certain shallow lakes and fresh-water swamps, the muds are sufficiently rich in ferric hydroxides, especially the mineral *goethite*, $HFeO_2$, to constitute *bog iron-ore*; sometimes iron carbonate as the mineral *siderite*, $FeCO_3$, is precipitated under similar conditions, and certain lake-muds are rich in iron sulphides.

What sediments are formed, and what processes of denudation or deposition are in operation, depend on the size and position of the lake and the stage reached in its extinction. In the largest lakes, waves and currents are active and shore-processes continue on a scale not much different from those of the sea. In small or almost obliterated lakes plant-growth may be the dominant factor in sedimentation.

The mud-laden river-water tends, on entering a lake, to sink to the bottom beneath the lighter and cleaner surface layers. On occasion, processes resembling those of rivers go on far out into the lake. The furrow of the Rhone in the Lake of Geneva is a trench flanked by two banks, steep towards the trench and gentle away from it, which are analogous to the levees of ordinary rivers and are thought to be built up by the slowing-down of the river-current where it mixes with the lake-waters.

Bare rock, gravel, sand or mud, may make the floor of large lakes at depths of less than about twenty-five metres, but beyond this depth mud predominates. Lakes of no great size often show, when drained, a narrow gravel margin and extensive mud-flats. Mansfeld Lake in Germany revealed alternations of humus-rich and lime-rich muds with abundant molluscan shells. Lime may be supplied by shells, by the break-up of calcium bicarbonate in the water as a result of summer heating of the surface layers or by the assimilation of this compound by lake-plants. The presence of calcareous rocks in the drainage-basins is also important; no marls have been recorded from the Highland lochs of Scotland except in the island of Lismore which is made of limestone.

Seasonal deposition: varves. Many lake-processes are seasonal in operation. The volume of water entering a lake is often greater in spring or summer than in winter when the source areas are under snow or frost. Summer warming of lake-water reduces their density and so promotes deposition of the fine load. In the deep part of the Lake of Zurich, Nipkow found that a year's deposit was made up of two layers. The winter layer is dark and rich in organic debris and iron sulphide; it is largely due to an alga which flourishes in winter

and on decomposition gives sulphuretted hydrogen which precipitates iron in the lake-waters as iron sulphide. The light-grey
summer layer is rich in small crystals or powder of calcium carbonate
derived from lime-secreting plants.

Lamination in lake-sediments, thus, often records seasonal variations either in the volume and grain-size of the detritus or in the
kind of organic activity. If we obtained a columnar sample of
bottom-deposits from the Lake of Zurich we should be able, by
counting summer and winter layers, to estimate the number of years
taken for the deposition of a given thickness of sediment. Ancient
lacustrine sediments sometimes show a banding considered to be of
seasonal type and proposals have been made for dating certain events
in earth-history by its use. The most celebrated are banded or
varved clays deposited in temporary lakes formed during the retreat
of the ice-sheets which covered north-west Europe and northern
America in geologically recent times. Their name comes from a
Swedish word *varv*, meaning a turn in the hand of a watch, or a lap in
a race. A *varve* is defined by Antevs as 'a distinctly marked *annual*
deposit of a sediment regardless of its origin'. Geological processes, as
we have seen, are generally to be measured in terms of millions of
years. Before we attempt to measure events in terms of *single* years,
it will be as well to establish the interpretation of varves as solidly as
space permits. This is essentially an exercise in the uniformitarian
method.

Lake Louise, in Alberta, is a small lake which drains by a stream a
mile long the silt-laden melt-water of the Victoria Glacier. This
stream has built out a delta and deposits material on this and over
the lake-floor; the outlet-stream is almost clear. Measurements of the
incoming suspended load for one year indicate that if evenly distributed on the lake-floor it would form a layer ⅛ inch thick. Since
much more sediment is brought to the lake in summer than in winter,
it can be deduced that the deposit should be banded. In summer, the
coarse detritus should settle quickly and the fine material remain
suspended; this deduction is borne out by the fact that the lake-
waters become turbid and greenish in late summer. In winter, the
fine material should settle, and in fact the water becomes clear and
blue by spring. The beauty of this study is that it was tested by the
collection of core samples from the lake-sediments. These samples
showed a faint but definite banding, the bands running five or six
to the inch and each band having 'a coarser, lighter-coloured lower
portion which passes upwards into a finer, darker-coloured upper
part' (W. A. Johnston). The bipartite nature and thickness of the
bands agree with expectation; it is geologically reasonable to inter-

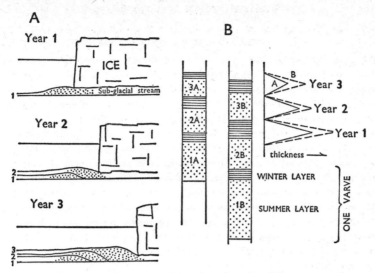

FIG. 114. Varves. A, varve formation, deposits of three successive years from a sub-glacial stream issuing from a retreating glacier. B, varve correlation: the patterns of the thicknesses of successive contemporaneous varves at the two localities are the same.

pret them as seasonal varves, and studies of other glacier-fed lakes confirm the interpretation.

The remarkable geological episodes recorded by the varved clays of Scandinavia and North America are not our concern at this moment; we need only examine their characters as lacustrine sediments. It can be shown that the clays, though the most extensive, are only part of each year's deposits; we may illustrate this by an example from Finland. Sauramo demonstrated that his Varve No. 485 gradually changes in character and thickness. At a locality Littalia it is represented by 0·2 cms. of clay. At Toijala, 17 miles away it is 0·4 cms. of silty clay, at Vasilahti another 26 miles away it is 1 cm. of silt and another 3 miles on it has thickened to 30 cms. of sand. It is clear that in this traverse we are approaching the source of the sediment. In fact, many varves have been traced into a core or knot of coarse deltaic material and we should presumably see similar transitions from the floor to the head of Lake Louise if the lake were drained. It is geologically sound to interpret the varve series as the deposits of a sub-glacial river which laid down coarse detritus at the mouth of its ice-tunnel, sand within a few hundred yards of its entry into the lake and a spread of the finest silt and clay for perhaps a hundred miles over the lake-floor (Fig. 114).

LAGOONAL AND SWAMP SEDIMENTATION·

As along the sea-coasts, the indented shores of large lakes become simplified and straightened out by the closing of the embayments by sand and gravel bars. The cut-off portions formed in this way are controlled by a regime entirely different from that of the open lake. Wave- or current-action is scarcely known, the temperature is higher than in the open lake-waters and the floor is shallower or rapidly becomes shallower; all these favour an abundance of aquatic life, especially of plants. The land-derived sediment in the lagoon becomes mixed with a high proportion of plant-material of one kind or another. Diatoms contribute their siliceous frameworks; *Chara* segregates calcium carbonate to form a marl which, when mixed with plant-matter, gives a soft ooze; where decomposed plant-debris is especially abundant a black mud is formed in place of the marl; there is often too a contribution of sand blown from dunes around the lagoon-shores.

In the normal history of lakes there must also come a time when plant-growth provides the bulk of the sediment. Whilst marls may form in the deeper parts of the shallower lakes, there will be a plant belt around their margins. This plant-belt and especially its matted and rotting debris act as a filter to incoming muddy waters so that lake-sediments may be almost entirely of organic origin. Finally, lakes and lagoons are replaced by *swamps*. Mats of plants grow from the shores outwards, their landward parts become firmer and their lakeward parts develop till quaking bogs give place to swamps.

Marshes and swamps form upon a variety of flattish surfaces — river-terraces, flood-plains, deltas, lake-sites, lagoon-floors — and in fresh and in sea-waters. *Accumulations of vegetable matter* in these and other environments are of great interest and are here briefly noted. In polar regions, turf and peat cover the enormous expanses of the tundras. Wherever there is high precipitation and low evaporation in the more temperate areas, *peat* forms and increases in thickness with the growth of new plants on the remains of the old. In the tropics the remains of the riotous vegetation, though rapidly destroyed in most situations, are able to accumulate in areas of impeded drainage. The peat of any situation may be contaminated with sedimentary material proper to the site concerned.

DEPOSITION IN SALT LAKES

We have now to consider the special sediments laid down in lakes which have no outlets. Under these conditions of *interior drainage* not only the mechanical load but also the chemical load is trapped.

As rivers bring in their load in solution and evaporation proceeds from the lake-surface, its waters become concentrated salt solutions which eventually precipitate various salts to form *saline residues* or *evaporates*. Salt lakes may be rich in sodium chloride, sodium sulphate, alkali carbonates, borax or other soluble salts, according to the nature of the rocks of the drainage basin, and their deposits are therefore varied. In addition to the *terrestrial* salt lakes of interior drainage systems, we may mention *marine* salt lakes formed when bodies of sea-water are by geological accidents shut off from the open ocean.

It is only in the arid and desert zones of the earth that present-day evaporates are forming on any large scale. Obviously, both low rainfall and high air-temperatures are necessary. In polar regions where the first requirement is satisfied small salt deposits have been recorded. In the warm-arid climatic belts lying between the tropical and temperate zones evaporates are forming on a large and complex scale: it is interesting to note that the salt-content of the sea is greatest in these same belts.

In the western part of the United States there recently existed two gigantic lakes (Fig. 115) whose shrunken remnants now appear as a multitude of small and disconnected salt basins. A remnant of the first of these old lakes — known to geologists as *Lake Bonneville* — is the Great Salt Lake of Utah. Its waters are many times as concentrated as the sea, though not unlike sea-water in type. Tributary streams are found to bring in calcium carbonate, sodium chloride, magnesium sulphate and other compounds. No carbonate, however, is found in the lake-water and this material must clearly have been deposited; it appears, in fact at many places along the shore of the lake and widespread carbonate deposits occur on the floor of the dried-up parts of Lake Bonneville. In very shallow parts of the Great Salt Lake, sodium chloride — *rock-salt* or *halite* — is separating out and sodium sulphate — the mineral *mirabilite* — is thrown down in winter.

The second of the old lakes of Western America, *Lake Lahonton*, is now represented by scattered remnants in the Great Basin region of Nevada. Each remnant has special characters related to the composition of the rocks of its drainage-system, but all are alkaline and thus entirely different from sea-water. The inflowing waters are generally rich in calcium carbonate, and there are thick layers of *calc-tufa* on the old lake-floor. Many of the relict lakes periodically dry up and deposit sodium carbonates — *thermonatrite* ($Na_2CO_3.H_2O$), *natron* ($Na_2CO_3, 10H_2O$) and *trona* ($Na_2CO_3NaHCO_3.2H_2O$) — with admixture of sodium sulphate and sodium chloride. Similar *natron lakes* or *soda-lakes* occur in Armenia, Egypt, Venezuela and elsewhere.

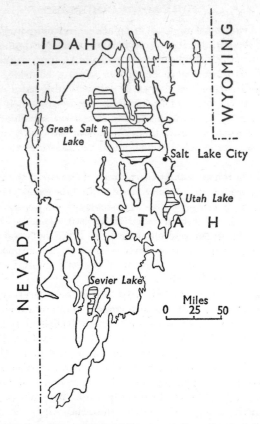

FIG. 115. Lake Bonneville and its present-day relics (ruled).

The shallow ephemeral lakes of the Nevada basin are examples of *playa-lakes* — vast sheets of water which appear in low ground after sudden and violent rain-storms in deserts. These lakes, which may cover hundreds of square miles to a depth of only a few inches, soon turn to sheets of liquid mud and dry out to give mud-flats often coated with efflorescences of salt. While still soft, the mud may record rare showers as *rain-pits* and may receive the tracks of desert animals. On drying out, it shrinks to produce polygonal *sun-cracks* and all these structures may be preserved when the next flood covers them with a layer of new mud. In Nevada and elsewhere, some playa-deposits are characterised by unusual materials such as borax, sodium nitrate or ammonium salts derived from special, perhaps volcanic, sources.

190

Analyses of water of salt lakes reveal, in addition to the substances so far mentioned, salts of potassium, magnesium and bromine. We can use the data from the River Jordan and the Dead Sea to illustrate this. Jordan water is rich in sulphates and carbonates which are largely precipitated on entering the Dead Sea. Dead Sea water is rich in chlorides and contains such a high proportion of magnesium, potassium and calcium chlorides that it is probable sodium chloride is being laid down on the lake-floor; the residual solutions form a *bittern* and if the Dead Sea were to dry up these bittern salts would be deposited. Deposits of such salts are rare.

Deposition in marine salt lakes. The lakes formed by shutting off of portions of sea-water are of a more uniform kind. Their original sea-water contains on the average about 3·5 per cent of dissolved matter of which the greater part is common salt, sodium chloride (p. 201).

Experimental data on the evaporation of sea-water were provided nearly a century ago by the classic investigation of Usiglio (Fig. 116). No deposition took place till nearly half the water had evaporated. The order of deposition was, first, ferric oxide in small amount and calcium carbonate, then hydrous calcium sulphate, then sodium

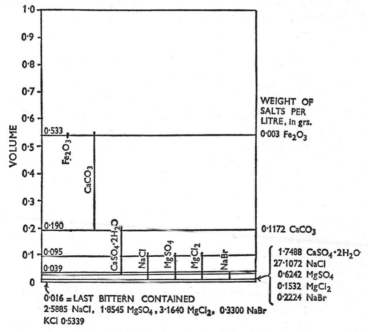

FIG. 116. Usiglio's experiments on the evaporation of sea-water.

chloride — the mother liquor being enriched in the bittern salts such as magnesium sulphate and chloride, potassium chloride and sodium bromide. In terms of minerals this order reflects relative solubility, as is seen by quoting the solubilities in grams per hundred cubic centimetres of water at 18° C: calcite, 0·0013, gypsum 10·4, rock-salt 35·86.

Usiglio's experiments point to an important geological conclusion. Both isolation and concentration are necessary for deposition. The water must be reduced to half before calcite is deposited, to one-fifth before gypsum and to one-tenth before rock-salt (Fig. 116). Such concentration can only take place in the warm-arid belts.

Deposition in the Caspian. The Caspian Sea began as a remnant of the ocean, but it has for long received the waters of the Volga and other rivers. Its waters are therefore now intermediate between those of the sea and the rivers, and are rich in sulphate as well as chloride. Opening on to the east of the sea is the *Gulf of Karabugas* which provides a classic example of a salt lagoon and has been employed in many discussions on ancient salt deposits (Fig. 117).

The gulf has a mean depth of only fifteen metres and is connected with the Caspian by a narrow strait no more than a metre or two deep. Water-level in the gulf is slightly lower than that in the Cas-

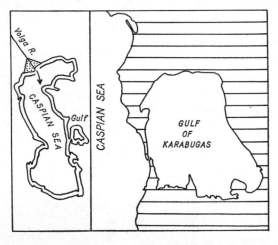

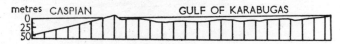

FIG. 117. The Caspian and the Gulf of Karabugas; (*below*), section midway across the gulf.

pian, and a continuous current carries in water. Each day some 350,000 tons of salt enter the lagoon whence no return is possible, and accordingly the saline content of the Gulf is steadily increasing as water evaporates from the surface. Calcium sulphate is being deposited and layers of gypsum appear round the margin and on the lagoon floor. In the centre of the Gulf sodium sulphate, $Na_2SO_4.10H_2O$, is deposited in winter and if present conditions continue, sodium chloride should begin to come down in a couple of centuries.

The Persian Gulf. In the desert coastal plains or *sabhkas* which fringe the Persian Gulf, marine evaporates are being formed by a mechanism rather different from that outlined above. Gypsum, anhydrite, rock-salt and dolomite are being precipitated within recently-deposited carbonate sediments from very saline groundwaters. These *connate brines* are drawn into the porous sediments from the sea, rise towards the surface by capillary action and become concentrated by evaporation. The salts which they carry are deposited within the host sediments as cementing material and successive replacements, and as crusts on the surface, building up layers rich in evaporate minerals. Deposition of this type is a *diagenetic* process (p. 255) which operates in the period following deposition of the host-sediments. It clearly depends on the concentration of groundwaters derived from the sea by evaporation in arid conditions and is therefore likely to take place in the hot deserts of the world.

Ancient salt-deposits are often thousands of feet thick and, in view of the 3·5 per cent of salts in sea-water, a problem arises as to how such thicknesses have accumulated. Extreme thicknesses are often demonstrably produced after deposition by the squeezing-together of material from an originally thinner layer to give lenses, domes or plugs of salt. This distortion is aided by the high mobility and the low specific gravity of rock-salt. Nevertheless, some of the original deposits, whether formed by the 'evaporating dish' or sabhka mechanisms, must have been remarkably thick.

SEDIMENTATION IN ESTUARIES

In an estuary, as in a marine delta, the meeting of river and sea provides a special set of conditions for sedimentation. There is a contest between fluvial and marine controls, between the outflowing fresh water and inflowing sea-water each with its own density and load. The contest between tidal and river currents is interrupted during the ebb by long periods when they act together. This alternation of opposed and co-operating currents controls estuarine deposition and erosion. When the tide is flowing in, the outflowing river is slowed, checked and finally reversed. The load in suspension, mostly mud with a little silt and sand, is deposited and eventually builds up the *mud-flats* characteristic of estuaries and revealed between tide-marks. When the tide flows out, the outflowing river and tidal waters become concentrated into channels with a consequent restriction of their erosive action. The area of estuarine deposition is thus great, of estuarine erosion narrowly limited.

Where the river-water meets the salt water, the surface-condition of the tiny particles of clay is changed so that they clot or *flocculate* into larger composite particles and so sink more readily. With these clay-aggregates goes down slightly coarser material of the silt grade, 0·05 to 0·1 mm. in diameter, proper to the velocity at such localities. *Estuarine muds and silts* are often finely laminated due to slight hardening at low tides of the thin layers deposited during high tides. Ripple-marks, sun-cracks, footprints and marks of animals and birds impressed on a layer are preserved by the next layer put down at high tide. These muds contain abundant organic matter and plenty of finely-divided iron compounds; bacterial decay is active and iron sulphides are formed which colour the muds black. Variations in currents due, for example, to a winter storm, cause the sporadic deposition of pebble bars and sand banks. Because the water is so muddy, organisms will not flourish sufficiently to give rise to layers composed of their remains alone. If the estuary is bordered by dunes there may be a small contribution of blown sand to the estuarine deposits. Sollas' description of the Severn estuary as a sea of more or less diluted mud exemplifies the estuarine environment as one separate from that of river or sea. Their special character is the predominance of very fine-grained material deposited in very shallow waters.

In the estuaries along the North Sea coast of Germany *tidal flats* are laid bare that have been extensively studied. The dominant muddy sediment is a 'soft unctuous water-soaked slime' (W. Hantzschel) — it has the very expressive German name of *Schlick* — and is composed of fine silt and clay with a small amount of quartz sand, together with tiny shell-fragments, plant-debris, remains of diatoms, foraminifera and ostracods, and abundant excrement of worms and molluscs. Its blue-black colour is due to finely-divided iron sulphides. Hantzschel emphasises the 're-working' of these estuarine muds — material deposited may be moved and distributed again and again by shifting currents; small chunks of laminated mud may be transported and redeposited with the lamination vertical.

GEOLOGICAL PROCESSES IN THE SEA

Most of the load of rivers is carried to the broad sea where sedimentation of great importance takes place. This importance arises from the fact that marine sediments are the commonest types of raw materials for the sedimentary rocks. The present land-surface, even the higher parts of the Alps and Himalayas, is largely made of marine rocks. An understanding of present-day marine processes is clearly desirable for the interpretation of the older marine deposits, the common sedimentary rocks; but this understanding is difficult to come by. The sea covers nearly three-quarters of the globe and though direct observations can be made along its margins, these are trifling when we realise that nearly 80 per cent of the sea is deeper than 3000 metres. The detailed investigation of what goes on in the sea, what is the form of the ocean-floor and of what this is made and of a host of other fundamental marine problems, has always been a matter of great difficulty. But modern methods are beginning to supply data in increasing quantity. Such techniques as echo-sounding, coring at great depths, submarine photography, radio-fixing and the like, added to geophysical investigations of standard type, have led in recent years to remarkable advances in our knowledge of some parts of the ocean. The old broad generalisations are being replaced by detailed, if at present restricted, bodies of fact. In what follows, we base our summary especially on the work of the Lamont Geological Observatory, Columbia University, New York.

THE FORM OF THE OCEAN FLOOR

Various elaborate classifications of the oceans and seas, mostly on a geographical basis, have been proposed; an example is that into the great and deep oceans, the subsidiary seas near to or mainly within the land-masses, and the minor bays and straits marginal to the seas. A classification of more significance to the geologist depends on the depths of the sea-waters, as controlling the geological processes going on there. We can thus view the seas in two broad categories, the *shallow seas* at the margins of the present continents, the *deep seas* of the ocean-basins going down to abysmal depths. The shallow seas are scenes of great activity and in some such environment most of the common types of marine rocks have been deposited. In the deep seas, conditions are more uniform and the less common sediments are formed.

The shallow or *epicontinental seas cover the continental shelves* (Fig. 118), the platforms that slope gently seawards from the margins of the land. The width of the continental shelf varies greatly,

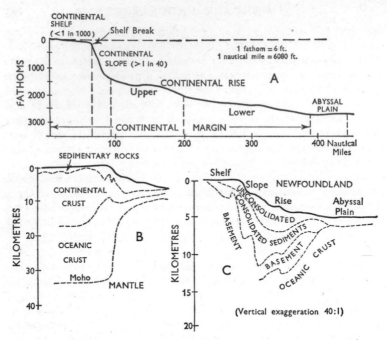

FIG. 118. The Ocean Floor. A, Divisions of the ocean floor of the western North Atlantic; B, constitution of the crust of the ocean margins, generalised; C, the constitution off Newfoundland, deduced from geophysical observations (after Heezen et alia, 1959).

averaging about fifty miles. It may reach several hundred miles in width off great rivers, lowland areas or lands that have been recently glaciated; it is very narrow, a mile or two, along some coasts such as that of western South America that are made of recently folded rocks running parallel with the coast (Pacific type of coast of some geographers). The relief of much of the continental shelf is subdued, with low rises and shallow depressions, but in certain sectors it may be more rugged, as off California where it reflects the 'basin-and-range' topography of the adjacent lands.

The seaward margin of the shelf, the *shelf-break*, is fixed at a change in slope; the slope of the shelf is less than 1 in 1000 — at the break the gradient becomes greater than 1 in 40. The shelf-break may be as deep as 600 feet or as shallow as half this: perhaps it averages 400 feet (120 metres).

This shelf-break marks the beginning of the *continental slope* (Fig. 118) which may continue with a gradient of more than 1 in 40 to depths of as much as 1750 fms. (1 fm. = 1 fathom = 6 feet) — its seaward limit can be set at where it flattens out to a gradient of less than 1 in 40. In the North Atlantic, the continental slope is succeeded oceanwards by the *continental rise*, a few hundred miles wide and having a gradient of from 1 in 100 to 1 in 700; it ranges down to depths of 2800 fms. (Heezen et alia).

The three foregoing elements — the continental shelf, slope and rise — together constitute the *continental margin*. This may be further diversified by such forms as escarpments, plateaus, ridges and trenches. We pass on to consider the most spectacular feature of this part of the sea-floor — the *submarine canyons*. .

Submarine canyons occur off all coasts but are best known from those of North America. They begin in the continental shelf towards its edge, become well established down the continental slope and may cross the continental rise to reach depths of 2000 metres. They may

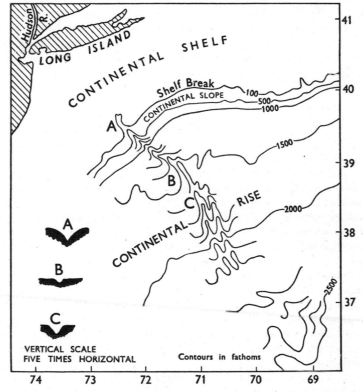

FIG. 119. Hudson Submarine Canyon, contour map and cross-sections of the canyon (after Heezen et alia, 1959).

198 INTRODUCTION TO GEOLOGY

be incised to a depth of 1000 metres and may show almost vertical walls of a corresponding height. Their steepest gradients are at their heads where they cut into the continental slope. Tributaries are often developed and join the main canyon for the most part accordantly. The rocks in which the canyons have been cut are fairly well-consolidated sediments; a Californian canyon is cut in granite but it is likely that its course follows a fault-zone in which the massive rock has been fractured and weakened. We may illustrate submarine canyons by the Hudson Canyon presented in Fig. 119; from this it will be seen that this canyon indents the continental shelf at the hundred-fathom line to form a gorge in the slope that is steep and narrow at first and then becomes more gentle and less canyon-like. Another gorge section appears where it crosses the continental rise, beyond which it seems to give place to a broad submarine delta.

The origin of submarine canyons has given rise to much debate. Many were cut during the Pleistocene Period (p. 293), since Pliocene rocks have been found in their walls and post-Pleistocene muds have been revealed by borings in them. It is considered by many geologists that their formation is related in some way to the Pleistocene glaciation (p. 219). The locking-up of water in the extended ice-sheets of that period led to a general lowering of the sea-level. During this time of lowered sea-level, the canyons were eroded, but whether this erosion was sub-aerial or submarine is a matter for discussion. On one view, the lowering of sea-level is considered to have been so great that the sea-floor was made dry to depths of 2000 metres or more so that the canyons could be cut by normal river-erosion across it. On various geological grounds, such a lowering is not favoured and submarine erosion during a much more moderate fall is preferred. The submarine erosive agent is considered to have been *turbidity-currents* (p. 216), currents of water charged with suspended sediment stirred up during on-shore storms or by slumping. Such denser water moved along the bottom of the continental shelf and, where its erosive action could become concentrated in depressions, began to excavate the canyon system. This excavation process was helped in its development by slumping and sliding-in of the valley-walls.

As we have just seen, Pliocene rocks are found in the walls of some submarine canyons and, in those off the east coast of North America, extensive sequences of Cretaceous and Tertiary rocks have been proved. The continental shelf and slope, therefore, do not simply constitute a gigantic delta built out into the sea by land-waste; the continental slope is likely to be in part an erosional feature covered by only a thin layer of modern sediments.

The *constitution* of the continental margin as a whole has been interpreted from numerous geophysical measurements and is diagrammatically shown in the lower part of Fig. 118. A kind of *trough* appears to be formed by a tongue of sialic continental rocks that thins out seawards at the edge of the continental margin. The trough is filled with a thick lens of sedimentary rocks, the upper portion being unconsolidated, and appears to be a filled trench (p. 200). The great change in crustal structure at the bottom of the continental slope is very evident.

Beyond the continental margin, the sea-floor descends to the *ocean-basins*. The floor of these is found to be in many places highly diversified, with broad plains, hill-peaks, scarps, valleys and deep troughs. We can distinguish several different topographic types of this part of the ocean-floor. Broad *abyssal plains* extend over great areas from the foot of the continental margin and, with a slope of less than 1 in a 1000, must be the flattest surfaces of the lithosphere. The plains connect with one another through gaps. *Abyssal hills* are often found along the seaward margins of the plains and form a collection of small eminences each a few hundred fathoms high and a few miles wide. For the North Atlantic, it has been suggested by Heezen, Tharp and Ewing that the abyssal plains are those portions of original abyssal hill topography that have been covered by deposits from turbidity-currents. It is estimated from geophysical measurements that beneath the abyssal plains there may be a kilometre of sediments and sedimentary rocks resting on 3–4 kms. of basaltic material before the M discontinuity is reached. *Oceanic rises* are large structures, covering hundreds of square miles and rising for a few hundred fathoms from the abyssal floor; their topographic detail is varied and they can be illustrated by the Rockall Rise in the eastern North Atlantic. More isolated elevations are the *seamounts*, large conical peaks, rising as much as 2000 fms. from the adjacent ocean-floor and with bases a thousand square miles or more in area. Their tops are covered by 500–800 fms. of water and in some examples are known to be flat. In this they are comparable with the *guyots* charted in the Pacific. It is a matter for discussion whether seamounts and guyots are of tectonic origin or are volcanic cones truncated by marine erosion.

It has been found by Heezen and Ewing that a continuous *mid-oceanic ridge* runs at the centre of the Atlantic, Indian and South Pacific oceans for some 40,000 miles (Fig. 120). This astounding feature can be sampled by its best-known portion, the *Mid-Atlantic Ridge*. The ridge rises by a series of crude steps into a high plateau, 1750 fms. in depth, which in turn culminates in a central mountainous belt in places as much as 1000 fms. higher. This central belt is trenched

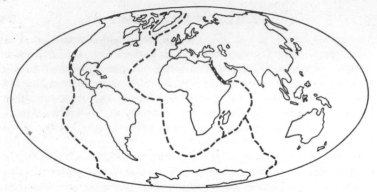

FIG. 120. The mid-oceanic ridge system.

by a narrow central valley dropping 900 fms. below the mountains on its flanks. Dredging has revealed that the rocks making the central part of the Ridge are basic and ultrabasic igneous rocks like those of the oceanic islands. Further, earthquake epicentres in the North Atlantic are concentrated along the centre line of the Ridge. It thus appears reasonable to interpret this gigantic feature as due to *rift-faulting* (p. 491) affecting a broad arch of the ocean-floor subjected to tensional stresses.

The last major features of the sea-floor that we have to deal with are the *trenches*, profound depressions in the floor some two or three hundred kilometres across (125 miles) and several thousand kilometres (1500 miles) in length. They descend to tremendous depths — the Aleutian Trench being more than 7500 metres deep — and their bottoms are as much as 3000 metres below the level of the adjacent sea-floor. The distribution of the trenches is significant: they occur along the borders of continents parallel to *island arcs* of recent geological formation (Fig. 377). Like these, they are to be considered the result of modern crustal movements.

THE COMPOSITION OF SEA-WATER

As water runs from the lands it delivers its load in solution to the sea. Sea-water is saturated for certain compounds and any excess delivered to it is precipitated. Further, some of the dissolved substances provided by rivers are used by marine organisms and so become depleted — an example is given by the $CaCO_3$ used in the making of molluscan shells. Substances that are not so used or that are particularly soluble are concentrated in sea-water and give it its saltiness. The salts present are those whose constituents are not readily precipitated or adsorbed. We may illustrate this point by reference to the behaviour of the alkalies during weathering: the average igneous rock, the primary source of sediments, has about equal amounts of Na and K, whereas sea-water has nearly thirty times as much Na as K, the latter having been adsorbed by and retained in the clay-sediments. It is likely that all elements are present in sea-water and, though most occur in traces only, their total amounts are gigantic since the volume of the oceans is so great; thus it has been estimated that 9 million tons of gold are present in the seas.

River-waters normally contain minute traces of the heavy metals such as Cu, V or Se and, if we consider the vast period of time throughout which rivers have been emptying into the sea, we should expect the concentration of such elements in sea-water to be relatively high; in fact, it is minute, for Cu 0·001 g/ton, V, 0·0003, Se, 0·004. Obviously some process is operating to remove these elements from the sea and it is possible that they are adsorbed by such colloidal precipitates as ferric hydroxide and with them become incorporated in the bottom-sediments. This is fortunate, as these heavy metals are poisonous to life, and if it were not for their continuous abstraction the sea might have long since become uninhabitable.

The composition of the chief substances dissolved in sea-water is given in various ways in the Table below.

COMPOSITION OF SEA-WATER (DITTMAR)

	In 1000 gms. Sea-water	% of all Salts		
NaCl	27·213	77·758	Na	30·593
$MgCl_2$	3·807	10·878	Mg	3·725
$MgSO_4$	1·658	4·737	Ca	1·197
$CaSO_4$	1·260	3·600	K	1·106
K_2SO_4	·0·863	2·465		
$CaCO_3$ etc.	0·123	0·345	Cl	55·292
$MgBr_2$	0·076	0·217	Br	0·188
			SO_4	7·692
	35·000	100·000	CO_3	0·207
				100·000

This *composition* of the dissolved salts is exceedingly uniform over the oceans, and so much so that the determination of one constituent, say chloride, determines the composition of the whole. But the *concentration* of the salts is not so uniform. This quantity is given as the *salinity*, which is the quantity of salts expressed in parts per thousand when all carbonate has been converted into oxide, Br and I into Cl, and organic material oxidised; the salinity so expressed turns out to be a little less than the concentration obtained by evaporation to dryness. The salinity varies with the rainfall over the oceans, the evaporation, the contribution of fresh water by rivers or melting ice, and the kind of connection between different parts of the ocean. Some salinities of different seas will illustrate these controls: Red Sea 38·8, Persian Gulf 36·7, Mediterranean 37–39, Bering Sea 30·3, Black Sea 18, Baltic Sea 7·8.

Air dissolved in sea-water is necessary for marine life. The different constituents of air have different solubilities and appear in different ratios in sea-water. Oxygen and carbon dioxide are more soluble than nitrogen: oxygen constitutes 1/5 of the atmosphere, but 1/3 of air in sea-water, CO_2 which constitutes 0·3 per cent of air increases to 2 per cent in sea-water. There is an important variation in the relative amounts of O and CO_2 with depths of sea-water. In the upper layers, plant-activity dependent on light breaks up CO_2 with the consequent saturation of these layers with O. In such an oxidation environment, organic material would be broken down into CO_2 and H_2O. Lower down, beyond the reach of sunlight, where plant-activity is less, CO_2 increases whilst the O is used in the decay of organic debris falling through the water. In the deeper layers of the Baltic, for example, the dissolved gases have as much as 25 per cent CO_2 in their composition.

Usually, movement of the water prevents the complete depletion of the oxygen, but in *stagnant basins* stirring and circulation of the waters are impeded, the bottom-waters are devoid of oxygen and processes take place in a reducing environment. Such basins are exemplified by some of the deep fiords of Norway which communicate with the Atlantic over a shallow sill; an extreme example is that of the *Black Sea* which is more than 7000 feet deep but connects with the Mediterranean by the Bosphorus, ½ mile wide and 130 feet deep. The surface layer of the Black Sea is replenished with river-water, is rich in oxygen and teems with life. Below are the oxygen-free stagnant layers in which life is absent, apart from sulphur bacteria. Organic remains falling through such waters are not completely decomposed and accumulate on the sea-bottom where as much as 35 per cent of organic material has been recorded in the sediments. In this reducing environment, H_2S and sulphides such as FeS_2 are formed, the latter, with the organic material, colouring the accumulating muds black. Organisms entombed in such an environment may be perfectly preserved. This *black mud*, rich in organic material, is called *sapropel* and is believed to be the parent material of *petroleum* (p. 279).

MOVEMENTS OF THE OCEAN-WATERS

Sea-waters are moved in three ways, by currents, tides and waves.

Currents. *Convection-currents* are the result of density differences produced by variations in temperature, pressure or salinity. Cold and dense water from polar regions drifts at depth towards the equator, whence lighter tropical waters move on the surface towards the poles. Denser water of high salinity flows as a deep current from the Mediterranean through the Straits of Gibraltar, whilst above it lighter Atlantic water moves in. *Drift-currents* or *surface-currents* are produced by the frictional drag of the wind, their pattern being controlled by the wind-belts of the earth and the shape of the continents. In the Atlantic, for example, a broad equatorial stream moves westward, divides on meeting the continents and gives currents moving eastward in higher latitudes, as exemplified by the Gulf Stream and North Atlantic Current.

Tides. Tides result from the oscillation of masses of water under the attraction of the moon and, in lesser degree, the sun. As the earth rotates, the position of the tidal bulge moves from east to west. The tidal rise is small in the open sea, but with suitable configurations of land and sea the bulge is piled up with the production of *tidal currents* that can move as rapidly as 15 miles per hour. At Liverpool a rise of 40 feet is usual, in the Bay of Fundy, 50 feet. In narrow estuaries like the Severn, the tide moves up as a wall of water, the *bore*.

Waves. Waves are the result of friction produced by wind passing over the sea's surface. Their height depends on the strength of the wind, the breadth and depth of the sea, the form of the coast-line and the *fetch* — the distance of free play of the wind. In a symmetrical wave, each particle of water moves in a circular orbit whose diameter is equal to the height of the wave (Fig. 121); because of friction, the orbits become smaller at depth until, at a level known as the *wave-base*, the disturbance dies out. Even in storms, the wave-base is generally only a few hundred feet in depth, but the *swells*, the waves of long wave-length persisting after the wind has died down, may produce a much deeper disturbance. The

FIG. 121. Motion of water particles in a wave.

position of the wave-base is important in connection with the movement and sorting of sediment on the continental shelf.

When a wave reaches shallow water its wave-length becomes smaller and its height greater. When the depth of water about equals the height of the wave, the wave falls forward as a *breaker*; this produces a fresh wave which in turn becomes a breaker and so on till the shore is reached. Water returns by a *backwash* or *undertow* which has less energy than the breaker and accordingly moves only finer material. Waves meeting the shore obliquely are bent till they are almost parallel with it. Breakers which meet the shore at an angle produce a *longshore drift* of sediment.

In shallow water, the orbits of particles moving in the wave-form are flattened. At the bottom of the orbits, particles move to and fro parallel to the sea-floor and may produce *ripple-marks* in fine material, arranged roughly perpendicular to the direction of wave-motion.

The *force of waves* can be very great. Stevenson measured pressures of 611 lbs/sq. foot on the Scottish coasts in summer, 2086 lbs/sq. foot in winter; over 6000 lbs/sq. foot has been recorded during a gale at Skerryvore. Gigantic blocks can therefore be shifted by wave-action and much marine erosion accomplished.

MARINE EROSION

The erosive action by the sea is naturally greatest and most diversified at the coasts but some erosion occurs on the sea-floor. We can thus distinguish coastal erosion and bottom-erosion.

Coastal erosion. Sea-water has a solvent action on the coastal rocks, especially of course if these are limestones, but its main geological work is *mechanical*. This is obviously greatest where the motion of the sea is greatest, where currents, tides and waves are most active. The actual force of the breakers may tear off pieces of rock from the cliffs. Compression and expansion of air imprisoned in crevices in the rocks may wedge off or suck out portions of rock (Fig. 122) and may eventually lead to the driving of passages

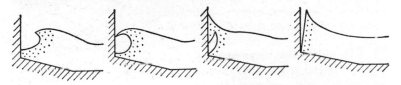

Fig. 122. Successive positions of a wave breaking against a cliff, showing the compression of imprisoned air and its sudden release, leading to the sucking-out of fragments (after R. A. Bagnold).

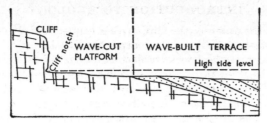

FIG. 123. Cliff and shore-platform.

through the cliff-rocks to the surface; such passages are *blow-holes*. Most marine mechanical erosion is performed by the horizontal sawing action of pieces of rocks, dislodged from the cliff, battering at its base as they are moved by the waves. This action is confined to a narrow vertical range. As the waves cut in, a *cliff* is formed at the landward edge of a *wave-cut platform* or *shore-platform*; the material broken away and used as tools is spread out seawards and extends this platform as a *wave-built terrace* (Fig. 123).

The *detail of the coast* produced by marine erosion is controlled by a variety of factors. The height of the *cliff* naturally depends on the height of the land being eroded. Rapid erosion will give steep cliffs; slow erosion, permitting sub-aerial agents of denudation to have a

FIG. 124. Natural arch, sea-stack and cliff-detail, Macduff, Banff-shire. (Crown Copyright: by Permission of the Controller of H.M. Stationery Office.)

share in the shaping of the cliff, gives a gentler cliff. The nature of the rocks concerned obviously controls the rate and style of marine erosion. Hard resistant rocks project as *headlands*, softer rocks make re-entrant *bays*. As the waves approach a coast they converge on the headlands and spread out in the bays; their erosive energy is therefore concentrated on the headlands which are preferentially eroded — a straight coast-line is the resultant stable form. The existence of *planes of weakness* in the coastal rocks controls much of the detail. Joints, bedding-planes, zones of fracturing produced by faulting provide weak planes that are preferentially eroded by wave-action. The attitude of such planes affects the stability of the cliffs; under certain arrangements, as for example bedding or jointing inclined seawards, *landslips* may occur as we have already seen in an earlier page. The details of a coast thus result from many circumstances: some special forms are *stacks, caves, arches, blow-holes* and *geos* (Fig. 124).

Bottom-erosion. We have already discussed the possibility that the deep submarine canyons are eroded by turbidity-currents. It is likely, too, that swift currents running through narrow straits may exert considerable erosive action. But where areas of bare rock or of coarse fragmental material are recorded on the sea-floor it may not be correct to ascribe these conditions to bottom-erosion; there may have been no deposition or only deposition of coarse materials in such areas. Bottom-erosion is intimately connected with transport of material in the sea and accordingly is best considered with that process in the next section of this account.

TRANSPORT BY THE SEA

It is believed that most of the material transported by the sea is supplied by the rivers, only a small quantity coming from the direct erosion of the coastal rocks. The material provided is in a variety of shapes and sizes depending upon its previous history, and during marine transport it becomes further modified by abrasion and sorting. Its final characters when deposited may thus be partly inherited and partly acquired.

The mechanisms of transport in the sea are similar to those already described in connection with rivers, namely, suspension, rolling and saltation. We may refer back to Fig. 98 in which is shown the relation between the size of particles and velocity of movement as controlling erosion, deposition and transport of grains. Though, as there shown, clay-particles once deposited are difficult to move again, much material of this size is brought into the sea by rivers and more is stirred and churned up by wave-action. Clay may remain suspended and attain an enormous distribution before it is deposited by coagulation into larger particles through flocculation (p. 194) or organic activity. Larger grains are kept in suspension by turbulence in the sea-water. The size of grain transported will depend largely on the speed of the current operating. As a consequence various kinds of *sorting* may take place; in particular the fine material may be removed to leave a coarser residual deposit so that the original grade-size of a bottom-sediment may become markedly modified. Vast quantities of material are moved by turbidity-currents, and spread over extensive areas of the floors of the deep ocean. This material may be coarse, since the density of the turbidity-current is greater than that of clear water, so that coarse sands and silts may be carried into deep water.

Wave-action is a spectacular though restricted agent of transportation. Not only do waves churn up material in readiness to be carried away, but they continually move it up and down the foreshore. Material of all grades is moved up by the breakers but only the finer is taken down again by the less powerful backwash. A sorting thus takes place and the finest material may be gradually passed out into deep water. Abrasion continually takes place with reduction of the fragments. Rounding of the pebbles may be good and, in the opinion of some, equal to that performed by wind — the greater rounding shown by dune-sands may indeed be the consequence of selective blowing away from the beaches of already rounded sands. As already noted in connection with the formation of waves (p. 204) *longshore* transport or *drift* occurs when waves approach the shore obliquely.

MARINE DEPOSITION

Material for marine sediments is obtained in a variety of ways. As we have just seen, most is supplied by rivers and much is made available by the marine erosion of the coasts. A small quota comes from glaciers and ice-sheets that end in the ocean, another small but interesting contribution is blown into the sea from the land areas, a little is provided by volcanic eruptions and still less from extra-terrestrial sources. Besides these *detrital* components, materials of *organic* origin make up some very important marine sediments formed by the accumulation of the remains of creatures that have extracted substances for their shells etc., from the sea-water. Lastly, some ingredients of marine sediments are of *chemical* origin, being precipitated under suitable conditions of concentration.

In an earlier page reference has been made to the *shallow seas* covering the continental shelves and the *deep seas* of the ocean basins. It is obvious that material derived from the land will be deposited for

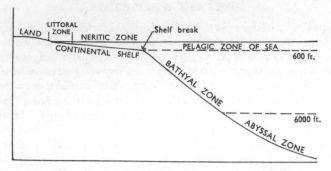

FIG. 125. Classification of environments of marine deposition.

the most part in the shallow seas and that only the finest clay or colloidal particles will be transported into the deep seas proper. In these deep seas, therefore, any deposits forming on their floors will be only slightly adulterated by land-derived, or *terrigenous* material; they will be dominantly of sea-derived, or *pelagic* origin. A marine deposit is a balance struck between terrigenous and pelagic sources, and although the deepest parts of the oceans are usually the furthest from land, deposition is not always evenly controlled by depth. It is the custom, nevertheless, to classify the *environments of marine deposition* on a depth basis. This classification is given in Fig. 125 and elaborated in the next paragraphs.

The main divisions adopted here are four; from the coast seawards these are the *littoral, neritic, bathyal* and *abyssal* zones.

The *littoral zone* is that between tide-marks, from low-tide mark to the level reached by the highest storm-waves. It is a region dominated by stormy wave and tidal action; most of its deposits are coarse, shingle gravels and sands, though muds are found in estuaries and lagoons.

The *neritic zone* reaches from low-water mark out to the shelf-break at the edge of the continental shelf. It is the region of the shallow or epicontinental seas whose waters are agitated by waves, tides and currents and, accordingly, conditions vary rapidly within it. Life is abundant and diverse, adapting itself to the variable conditions. Similarly, deposits are of great variety and exemplify the common rocks that now make the continents. Typical deposits are sands, shelly sands, greensands, calcareous muds and terrigenous deposits generally; organic sediments are represented by accumulations of shells (*neritos* = a mussel). Corals and other organisms may build up their own littoral and neritic zones as reefs. The keynote of the neritic zone is clearly its variability.

The *bathyal zone*, from the continental shelf-break down to an

arbitrary depth of 6000 feet, is on the whole a much more uniform
environment. It includes the upper parts of the continental slope and
is gently swept by ocean-currents. Its deposits are for the most part
the finest terrigenous material, muds of various colours and kinds
with areas of coarse material supplied by turbidity-currents, mixed
with varying amounts of pelagic organic material coming from the
upper layers of the ocean-waters. Bathyal deposits are clearly likely
to be uniform over great areas.

The *abyssal zone* constitutes the deep sea proper, from 6000 feet
down to the abyssal depths. It is almost beyond the reach of terrigenous material and its remarkable deposits are formed from the
remains of pelagic organisms, wind-blown dust often of volcanic
origin and meteoritic fragments from outer space. Typical deposits of
the abyssal zone are the oozes and the Red Clay. It may be stressed
once again that it is distance from land rather than depth that
controls the deposits of the abysses.

Littoral deposits. Certain deposits strictly included within the
littoral group, such as those of estuaries, lagoons and deltas, have
already been noted and now we are to deal with the accumulations of
relatively coarse materials that make the *beaches* and the many kinds
of *sand-banks*.

Beaches are the layers and banks of gravel and sand formed largely
by wave-action between tide-marks. The materials making them are
usually of hard resistant rocks derived in many cases from the local
cliffs, though longshore drift may contribute non-local material. They
vary in grade from boulders beneath cliffs of hard rocks to shingle
and sand on more gentle coasts. Other beaches are made of shell-
fragments as on the islands of the Pacific. The steepness of the beach
depends to some degree on the size of its constituents, the steeper
being made of coarser fragments. The beach begins at the *berm*, a
steepish bank thrown up by wave-action about high-water mark and
separating the gentle *foreshore* below it from the irregular *backshore*
above it. *Storm-beaches* occur higher up, above normal beach level.
Behind the backshore there may be a belt of *dunes* (*links* in Scotland)
of sand blown inland from the dried-out beach. The beach-material
has been worked over by the waves and is usually graded with the
coarsest highest up the beach. The shapes of the pebbles depend to
some extent on the nature and structures of the rocks provided, hard
massive rocks giving well-rounded pebbles. The beach as a whole is
found to be made up of lenses of sand or gravel which slope at gentle
angles seawards. Individual lenses show a good sorting. The fluctuations of shore processes lead to the pile of lenses showing irregular or
cross-bedding. In the finer materials of the foreshore *ripple-marks* are

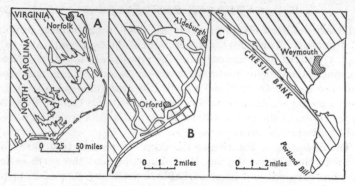

FIG. 126. Simplification of coasts by the formation of shingle banks.
A, North Carolina; B, Orford Ness, Suffolk; C, Chesil Bank, Dorset.

produced; in the finest, *suncracks* due to drying-out, *rain-pits* and the *tracks* of birds and animals may be recorded.

On a gently sloping shore, breakers break some way out and their rotating action may build up a *bar* of shingle offshore parallel to the coast. This bar may rise above sea-level to enclose a lagoon or it may curve across a bay to connect the headlands as a *baymouth bar* (*ayre* in Shetland). A bar connecting an island to the mainland is called a *tombolo*. Shore-drift produces a *spit* where the tidal currents leave a headland and move into a bay; the spit may develop a *hook* at its end as a result of the sweeping round of the dominant waves there. The tendency of shore deposition is to cut off bays and to simplify the coast-line. These shore features are illustrated in Fig. 126.

Neritic or shelf-sediments. As already noted, the keynote of marine sedimentation in the epicontinental seas is variability. The simple statement that marine sediments decrease in grain-size seawards is only locally and exceptionally true. The flat continental shelf is swept by strong currents and, as a consequence, winnowing of the materials making the sea-floor is an important process in determining the type of sediment formed. The finest constituents may be swept away and transported over the continental slope into the deep sea, leaving behind coarse *residual* sediments far from the land. Further, great areas of bare rock in the neritic zone may be swept free of any sediment. Perhaps the most typical shelf-sediment forming today is a coarse well-sorted *sand*, often ripple-marked and current-bedded. Opposite the mouths of large rivers or in quiet lagoon-like areas, *muds* may accumulate. In other quiet areas, material of organic origin may be sufficiently abundant to form *calcareous muds* and, in waters free from land-derived material, shells may give rise to *shell-sands*. Flocculation of iron compounds brought in by the rivers leads

210

to the deposition of *siderite, chamosite* and other iron-bearing minerals along with the sediments. A special type of iron-bearing sand is the *greensand*, so coloured by the green mineral glauconite, a hydrated silicate of K and Fe; glauconitic sands are formed by the decomposition of ferromagnesian silicates, such as biotite, in the presence of organic material and appear to favour sea-floors of moderate depth and swept by strong currents.

We may now examine the marine deposits of *organic origin* a little more closely. An abundance of creatures that live in the sea make their shells and skeletons of calcium carbonate which they extract from the load in solution contributed to the sea-water. Algae, foraminifera, corals, crinoids, sea-urchins, molluscs and other living creatures take part in providing the raw materials. The growth of molluscs and other shelled animals, the efficiency of chemical reactions and the concentration of calcium carbonate in the water will all be helped by warm tropical waters. Shells, fragments of shells, *shell-sand* and *shell-mud* accumulate where little or no land-derived detritus is deposited, and this accumulation is worked over by solutions rich in calcium carbonate — the raw materials for the making of limestones are provided.

Calcareous deposits may be built up in place by the growth of generations of sedentary organisms such as corals and algae. These accumulations are *coral-reefs*; their growth, often in mid-ocean, especially the Pacific, and the fact that reef-corals cannot survive in deep waters, present a problem that is best considered in a later page (p. 213).

In certain warm and shallow seas and lagoons, calcium carbonate is being precipitated from sea-water without the intervention of organisms; sometimes it is precipitated as a succession of coatings around a tiny nucleus which is being trundled up and down between tide-marks. The result is an accumulation of spheres of calcite resembling fish-roe and called *oolites* (Fig. 149). Under some circumstances, *dolomite*, $MgCO_3.CaCO_3$, may be precipitated with the calcite directly from sea-water but in most magnesian limestones or dolomite rocks the dolomite has developed later by replacement of calcium by magnesium (p. 257).

We may illustrate the foregoing summary of the general characters of shelf deposits by reference to the sedimentation that is taking place at present off the east coasts of North America. Off the glaciated lands of the north Atlantic seaboard, shelf-sedimentation is controlled by the nature of the glacial deposits that cover large parts of the floor. These deposits, originally consisting of confused mixtures of boulders, stones, sand and the finest rock-flour, have been worked over and sorted by current action. Near the coast the coarser residuals form a belt of gravel, farther out comes a zone of sand and silt and then one of mud representing the finest materials washed from the inner zones. Beyond this mud-zone, near the edge of the shelf, the floor is covered with well-sorted sand, interpreted by Stetson as the residuals of sand-dunes formed there when the sea-level was much lower during the Pleistocene glaciation (p. 219). Farther south along the shelf, off the coasts of the Atlantic States, there is found an extensive spread of fine sand interpreted as the reworked products of the weathering of the rocks of the coastal plain during the same period of low sea-level. In these two sections of the shelf we see illustrated some of the controls of modern shelf-deposits. Still farther south, off Florida and the Bahamas, terrigenous material is in small quantity and much of this is of calcium carbonate composition; in the warm sub-tropical seas, calcareous organisms flourish, the sea-water is saturated with calcium carbonate, so that extensive deposits of limy sediments such as shell-banks, calcareous sands and muds are laid down, with local coral-reefs.

CORAL-REEFS

Coral-reefs have already been mentioned as organic marine deposits and, since they are formed not only against the shore and on the shelf but, besides, rise out of the oceanic depths, they can conveniently be considered in this place. The interest of coral-reefs to the geologist derives basically from the restricted habitats of reef-building corals and associated organisms such as calcareous algae. Corals (p. 307) flourish only under strict conditions of temperature and depth of water, which must be saline, clear and clean and furnished with oxygen and, of course, with abundant food. The optimum temperature is between 25° and 30° C; the colonial corals cannot live in water deeper than about 75 metres and grow most luxuriantly only a few metres below sea-level. Dirty water inhibits strong growth in that it cuts off the sunlight, so that corals are absent or stunted opposite large rivers that bring both mud and fresh water into the sea. Oxygen and food are abundantly provided by the agitation of the sea-water by waves and currents. The distribution of coral-reefs bears out these requirements; they occur in a zone some 30° north and south of the equator and preferentially off the eastern coasts of the land-masses (see Fig. 213); in these positions, the westerly equatorial currents have become warmed and laden with oxygen and food. From the depth-control of coral-growth, sinking or elevation of the reef with reference to sea-level would kill off the corals. Again, it is clear that some sort of foundation at the suitable depth must be available for coral-growth.

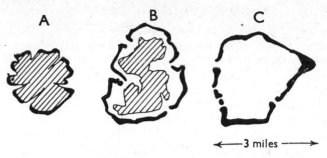

<----- 3 miles ----->

Fig. 127. Coral Reefs. A, fringing reef; B, barrier reef; C, atoll: coral
rock in black, old land lined.

Charles Darwin long ago provided the basic classification of coral-
reefs (Fig. 127) into *fringing reefs, barrier reefs* and *atolls*. *Fringing
reefs* are attached directly to the rocky coasts; the corals grow out
seawards towards their food supply, and towards the coast the coral
deposits are mixed with much terrigenous material. *Barrier reefs* are
built on the continental shelf at varying distances from the shore from
which they are separated by the *lagoon*. This may be more than 100
metres in depth. The classic example of this kind of reef is the Great
Barrier Reef of Australia that runs for a thousand miles at a distance
of 20 to 100 miles off the Queensland coast. Borings made into it
disclosed some 500 feet of coral-rock resting on a sand foundation of
unknown thickness. Fine calcareous deposits mixed with land-
derived detritus are forming in the lagoon. The *atoll* is an irregular
ring-shaped reef, broken by passes and enclosing a lagoon which is of
no great depth, perhaps 45 metres on an average. The outer, upper,
part of the atoll is naturally the scene of most vigorous coral-growth
and often forms an overhanging rim from which pieces of coral-rock
break off to supplement the talus slope below. This talus slope is steep
and falls rapidly to the ocean depths. Inwards from the growing
coral, the *reef-flat* slopes gently into the lagoon; it is made of coral-
rock smoothed over by algal growths or of limy sands and coral-
rubble. On the lagoon-floor, fine-grained calcareous sands and silts
are laid down. The local tides and currents, as controlling the food
and oxygen supply, modify the atoll shape.

The origin of atolls has been a topic of much discussion for more
than a century. Charles Darwin in 1842 put forward the classic
subsidence theory, based upon the study of a gradational series of
reef-forms from fringing reef to atoll, as illustrated in Fig. 128. This
series was interpreted as indicating a gradual subsidence of the sea-
floor during which the corals were able to maintain their position of
maximum growth. Put crudely, they could keep their heads just

213

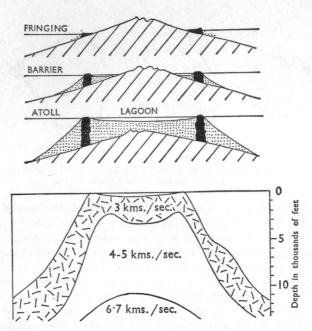

FIG. 128. Darwin's Origin of Atolls. (*Above*), three stages in the subsidence of an oceanic island, coral reef black, coral debris and talus dotted, old land lined. (*Below*), results of a geophysical survey of Funafuti, showing velocities of transmission of seismic waves; top layer corresponds to coral rock, lower layers to volcanic rocks (based on Gaskell).

below the water — if subsidence was too rapid they were drowned and, in fact, drowned coral-reefs are well known. On Darwin's theory, a volcanic island in the Pacific would start with a fringing reef which would become a barrier reef with subsidence and, with complete submergence of the island, an atoll. John Murray, in 1880, proposed a rival theory of *antecedent platforms* in which no change of sea-level was involved. Submarine volcanic activity built up banks to within the critical depth, or this depth was reached by organic deposition on banks not quite high enough. When a coral-colony was established, it would grow upwards and outwards to give the atoll form. The lagoon was the result of decay and erosion of the dead corals in the central area of the colony; the infilling of the lagoon is one of the weaknesses of the Darwin theory.

Murray's theory required the presence in the coral-seas of a large number of eminences at a suitable height, about 200 feet below sea-level. Though, as we have seen, guyots and seamounts of various kinds are now known, this remains a major criticism of the antecedent platform theory. It is overcome by the *glacial control* theory which depends on the general lowering of sea-level during the Pleistocene ice-age by the locking-up of water in the gigantic ice-sheets of that time. During this period of lowered sea-level, maybe 300 feet lower, many volcanic oceanic islands would be planed off by marine erosion; as the ice-sheets melted and the sea-level rose, colonising corals were able to keep pace with the rising sea-level and to build up atolls and barrier reefs at the edges of the platforms. Difficulties of recolonisation might be met by Kuenen's suggestion that coral-reefs were present before the levelling and so the very slow process of migration was not necessary.

Tests of these theories should be forthcoming from deep borings on reefs. The early Funafuti boring was too near the seaward edge of the atoll to give a decisive answer but more recently many significant results have been obtained from there and elsewhere. A seismic survey of Funafuti is illustrated in Fig. 128. On Eniwetok atoll, shallow-water atoll sediments, going back in date to the Eocene, have been proved to be some 4000 feet thick and to rest on basic volcanic rocks. The presence of thick sediments of a similar kind on Bikini atoll has been proved by boring and confirmed by geophysical methods. It thus appears that a combination of the submergence and glacial-control theories may best explain the formation of atolls.

BATHYAL OR SLOPE-DEPOSITS

On certain parts of the continental shelves, as we have seen, mud is being deposited but the more usual environment of the *marine muds* is on the continental slopes and down into the deep seas. Such muds do not show evidence of normal current action or intermittent emergence as do some estuarine or lagoonal muds. The *muds* are blue, green, red, yellow or some other colour, depending on their sources, and represent the finest land-derived material. Muds are, however, diluted with varying amounts of pelagic material, such as foraminifera, which contribute calcium carbonate to the deposit. In the deep Mediterranean, a sea into which few mud-laden rivers flow, such foraminiferal material accumulates as calcareous mud. Coral-muds are derived from reef-areas on the shelf, such as the Bahamas; other muds are rich in volcanic dust and some others are coloured green with iron compounds such as glauconite. The *black muds* have already been considered in connection with foul-bottom basins such as the Black Sea (p. 202).

DEPOSITION BY TURBIDITY-CURRENTS

Turbidity-currents have been discussed as possible agents of erosion of submarine canyons (p. 197). It has been mentioned also (p. 207) that such currents are capable of transporting vast quantities of coarse material and spreading it out over the floors of the deep oceans. It appears likely that the current that broke the submarine cables south of Newfoundland during the earthquake of November 18, 1929, moved at a speed of 60 miles an hour down the continental slope at a depth of 12,000 feet. Such velocities are sufficient to move large blocks and to leave coarse deposits spread over enormous areas. We may look into deposition by slumping and turbidity-currents a little more closely.

The loose sediment on the continental shelf may, when deposition is rapid, pile up until it becomes unstable. The top of the pile then *slumps* or slides down the shelving sea-floor till it comes to rest as a crumpled mass in deeper water. The top of the *slump-sheet* is flattened off by currents and normal deposition continues until the top of the unstable pile slumps again. In this way, alternations of evenly-bedded and distorted or contorted sediments accumulate.

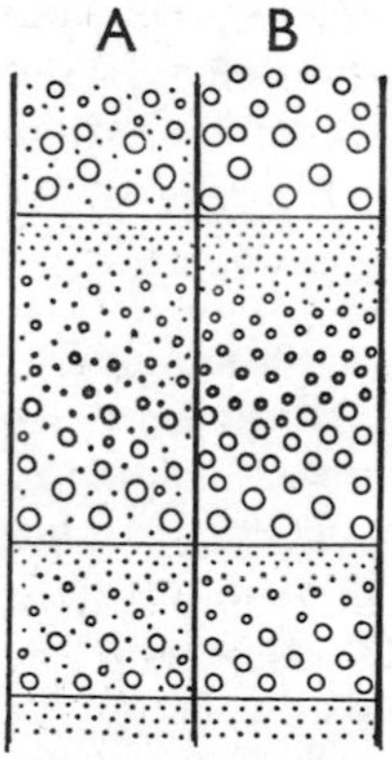

Under some conditions the loose sediment, instead of sliding en masse, is churned up into a thick suspension of mud and sand in water which flows as a *turbidity-current* down the sea-floor. As the current slows down, the heavier part of its load comes to rest first and the finer particles settle out more slowly. A turbidity-current thus lays down a *graded bed* passing upwards from coarser to fine material (Fig. 129). It is believed that extensive plains — some of the abyssal plains noted on p. 199 — are floored with deposits from turbidity-currents. Cores obtained in such situations show in many examples an alternation of coarse graded beds and thin layers of typical abyssal sediments such as Red Clay (p. 217). This association of coarse deposits with the finest abyssal material is difficult to explain without invoking turbidity-currents. Other examples of this association show the interbedding of abyssal deposits with coarse calcareous sands containing fossils typical of a shallow-water environment.

FIG. 129. Graded Bedding. A, produced by turbidity currents; B, produced by slackening current. Note better sorting in B.

ABYSSAL OR PELAGIC DEPOSITS

Although coarse deposits from turbidity-currents may cover large, areas of the deep-sea floor, the more normal abyssal deposits are quite different, their character depending mainly on their remoteness from land. Only the finest land-derived detritus reaches them and a major constituent is pelagic in origin, supplied by organisms in the upper layers of the water. Deposition is so slow that certain ingredients usually diluted in more rapidly-formed sediments become conspicuous. The depth of the sea also exerts an influence on the character of the deposits. The siliceous and calcareous skeletons of pelagic organisms are, given time, dissolved as they fall through the water. As calcium carbonate is more soluble than silica, *calcareous oozes*, made from the skeletons of lime-secreting animals, accumulate in waters not more than about 3600 metres in depth. *Siliceous oozes* occur at depths of 3900–5300 metres, while at greater depths even siliceous remains are dissolved and a red clay accumulates.

The oozes. The main pelagic organisms that build their shells of calcium carbonate are *foraminifera* (p. 302) and *pteropods* (p. 319). Their minute shells rain down in immense numbers to form a slimy *Globigerina ooze* or *pteropod ooze*. A considerable quantity of colloidal clay-particles is of course included, but a deposit with over 30 per cent of organic material is usually reckoned as an ooze. *Globigerina* ooze covers over 50 million square miles. It is dominated by foraminifera of the families Globigerinidae and Globorotalidae, with primitive plant remains known as *coccoliths* and *rhabdoliths*. Pteropod ooze is less widely developed and occurs at an average depth of only 2000 metres.

The siliceous oozes derive their material from *radiolaria*, which are minute animals (p. 304) and *diatoms*, which are pelagic plants (p. 345). *Radiolarian ooze* covers some 5 million square miles in the tropical Pacific. Even at great depths many radiolarian tests are still not dissolved, and enter the Red Clay. *Diatom ooze* is developed in the polar regions, especially around Antarctica.

The Red Clay. The *Red Clay* occurs at depths greater than 4000 metres especially in the Pacific, where half the ocean floor is covered by this deposit. It consists of very fine-grained material coloured chocolate or red by manganese or ferric compounds, and made up of clay-minerals most likely of terrigenous origin. Other major constituents may be waterlogged and decomposed pumice, volcanic ash and, in the shallower developments, radiolaria. Meteorite dust and spherules are abundant. Among more fantastic components are large numbers of the earbones of whales and the teeth of sharks — some of the latter belonging to species now extinct. These components illustrate the extreme slowness of deposition of the Red Clay — it has been estimated to be of the order of a millimetre or two in 1000 years. Nodules, concretions and grains of manganese oxide are sometimes so abundant as to constitute a possible source of manganese. Lastly, the Red Clay and, to a lesser degree, other pelagic deposits are many times more radioactive than the igneous rocks of the continents, possibly as a result of adsorption of radioactive elements on the clay-particles.

MOVEMENTS OF SEA-LEVEL

The sea-level is not constant and may change as a result of a number of geological processes. As we have seen, abstraction of the water to make ice-sheets and its return on these melting will affect the level of the sea. Isostatic adjustments to changes of load, such as the growth or decay of ice-masses or the accumulation of masses of sediment, alter the levels of the land and the sea-floor. Earth-movements may uplift or depress large or small segments of the crust and so disturb the relative levels of land and sea. These processes, with some less important ones not mentioned, can act independently of one another and at very different rates — the result is that it is often difficult to disentangle the sequence of the changes of sea-level that follow from complex operations such as the growth, fluctuation and waning of ice-sheets. Some *local instability* may produce changes in the level of a restricted part of a coast as recorded for example, in the borings by marine molluscs of the columns of the temple of Jupiter Serapis at Pozzuoli near Naples. Changes of *widespread* or worldwide extent are called *eustatic* movements of sea-level.

Submergence is recorded by the existence of such land accumulations as forests and peats now below high-water mark. Submerged forests occur around the coasts of Cheshire and Lancashire, and peat is dredged from the floor of the North Sea. Human records — Roman roads, old mooring rings and the like — are in places now below the sea. Submergence is indicated by *drowned* coast-lines, highly indented and embayed, when the sea meets a highly developed land topography; river-systems are drowned and dismembered. The *ria* coast, typified by that of south-west Ireland, provides a special case of drowned topography. Lastly, it will be recalled that Darwin's theory of atoll formation postulates a general submergence of large areas of the ocean-floors.

Emergence is revealed by marine evidences high above present high-water mark. Especially important here are *raised beaches*, marked often by erosional features such as marine platforms, cliffs and sea-stacks at various heights above sea-level. Around the coasts of Scotland, a raised beach is well developed at about 100 feet above O.D. and others at lower levels; these record successive stands of the sea in recent times.

GEOLOGICAL WORK OF ICE MASSES

The last surface agent that we have to deal with is *ice*, in the great masses that constitute *glaciers* and *ice-sheets*. As much as 10 per cent of the present land-areas is covered by ice and, in the recent past, this percentage was very much greater. During this *Pleistocene* (p. 293) *Glaciation*, gigantic ice-sheets extended millions of square miles over northern Europe and America and have left their varied records over the regions where modern civilisation has developed. Moreover, glaciation on ice-sheet scales has occurred at several times in geological history and, on occasion, in very extraordinary places. Accordingly, on uniformitarian principles, it is necessary to consider the work done by present-day ice-masses.

The formation of glaciers. In high latitudes or at high altitudes, precipitation is as *snow* which collects in the *snowfields* above the *snowline*. At the equator the present snowline is about 18,000 feet, in latitudes of about 20° N or S it reaches its maximum height of about 20,000 feet and then declines towards the poles. Depending on the local meteorological conditions the snowline may reach sea-level in 60° N or S latitudes. For a snowfield to form there must of course be snow; in northern Siberia the precipitation is so small that no permanent snow accumulates. With adequate snowfall and low summer temperature, the snowfield gradually increases in thickness and the snow itself undergoes a series of changes.

Snow falls as flakes made of skeletal crystals belonging to the hexagonal system, exemplified by the frost-patterns seen on windows. This is gradually changed into an aggregate of granular ice pellets called *névé* or *firn*; in Britain, examples of névé are found in the drifts that linger into summer in the north-facing crevices of Highland mountains. The grain-size of névé is about 1 mm., and both grain-size and density increase with depth in the glacier. An Alpine névé covered by the accumulations of twelve years, attained a grain-size of 3–4 mms. and a density of 0·702. In the dry glaciers of polar regions, névé is formed by sublimation; in more temperate zones, water plays a dominant role, the snow-crystals being changed into ellipsoidal grains by removal at their edges and deposition around their centres. Water supplied by daily changes of temperature, and by melting due to the pressure of overlying snow, seeps through the névé and crystallises out as a cement to the grains. Some air remains entangled and gives the névé a white colour. A banding may be produced by the expulsion of air from, or infiltration of water into certain layers, often determined by annual events. The névé layer on a normal glacier is about 100 feet thick. Below this level the névé is transformed by compaction and recrystallisation to *glacier-ice* formed of solid, interlocking grains. Glacier-ice is compact and blue-grey in colour, as the intergranular air has been squeezed out. Its porosity is low and its density has increased to 0·9. The grain-size shows characteristic variations; it increases towards the snout of a glacier, is greater in large glaciers than in small, in gently sloping than in steep glaciers and reaches its maximum, 10 cms. or so, in stagnant ice-bodies. In addition to bands of clear ice, a glacier may show *annual dirt-bands*, containing dust blown from the rock-slopes laid bare each summer.

Observations have been made on the *fabric* of various parts of ice-masses. In the upper parts of the névé, ice-crystals have been found to be orientated with their vertical crystallographic axes perpendicular to the ice-surface. This regular arrangement disappears with depth. In glacier-ice, the crystals become arranged so that their basal planes lie preferentially in the direction of flow.

As snow piles up in the snow-field, its weight begins to press the excess ice outwards. In mountainous regions, this excess moves down the valleys as tongue-like *glaciers* which advance till the supply of ice equals the wastage. Where a glacier leaves the snow-field a great crevasse called the *bergschrund* is opened up (p. 224). In high latitudes, the ice may reach the sea and *icebergs* may break off and float away, a process known as *calving*.

We can view a glacier or ice-sheet as made up of two sections, one of *accumulation*, where the snowfall exceeds wastage, and the other of *ablation*, where wastage exceeds supply. The two sections are separated by the *névé* or *firn line*. When the supply from above is sufficient to make good the wastage, the glacier is in equilibrium; at the present time, most ice-bodies are shrinking.

The amount of ablation depends on the climate, altitude and exposure of the ice-body. Wastage is due to melting and evaporation, with some assistance from corrosion by running water and wind. The most important process is one of *thinning* below the névé line and the retreat of the snout is the result of this process. Finally, a glacier is reduced to a number of isolated segments, separated by rock-areas.

On the surfaces of the wet glaciers of temperate regions, *super-glacial* streams are common. They often plunge into crevasses to form well-like hollows or *moulins* reaching down to bedrock. Inside the glacier, *englacial* streams follow irregular channels, and *subglacial* streams flow beneath it. All these streams unite with the melt-waters at the end of the glacier to bear away immense quantities of silt and rock-flour.

Glacier-movement. The *mechanism of glacier-movement* is a difficult and complex problem. In parts of a glacier, the ice is brittle and breaks or shears under tension or compression. In other parts, although each ice-particle is a crystalline solid, the movement is thought to be like that of a viscous liquid such as pitch. Many glaciers are sinuous and are able to negotiate bends in their valleys. Ice, therefore has considerable *rigidity* or *strength*, but under pressure it is *deformed* and will *flow*.

Observation shows that fractures or *crevasses* in glaciers do not exceed a couple of hundred feet in depth. Ice at greater depths is capable of flowing and shows a striping due to differential movement. Accordingly, we can distinguish two zones in a glacier (Fig. 130):

 (i) The upper *zone of fracture*, up to about 200 feet thick, in which ice breaks under tension to give crevasses.
(ii) The lower *zone of flow* in which the ice behaves as a viscous body.

The névé and ice of the upper zone are passively carried along by the movement of the lower zone. Towards the end of the glacier, the original upper zone is removed by thinning and the lower zone comes under upper-zone conditions and can be inspected: ice with flowage-bands now develops crevasses.

Broadly speaking, there are two groups of ideas — not mutually exclusive — on the mechanism of glacier motion. The first concerns movement by the translation of rigid blocks of ice along *thrust-planes*. Such planes displace dirt-bands and may be accompanied by drag-folding (p. 457) and brecciation (p. 489). They are often found near the bed of a glacier, and at steps in the valley-floor the ice yields more easily on upwardly-inclined planes; similar up-thrusting may occur at the terminus where moving ice comes up against the dead end.

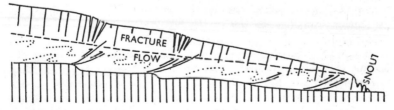

Fig. 130. Diagrammatic section down a valley glacier, showing zones of fracture and flow, and crevasses and thrusts at valley steps.

The second mechanism of movement concerns the *movement of ice-grains*. Such movement is witnessed by the distortion of air bubbles and by the preferred orientation of ice-crystals already mentioned. Ice-crystals show a strong glide-plane (p. 71) parallel to the basal plane. Crystals may grow with this plane parallel to the direction of movement, or they may be rotated or recrystallised to take up this position. These processes produce a distinctive fabric and allow slipping on the glide-planes to take place. The ice-mass is thus deformed by a *quasi-viscous creep*. The rate of creep increases with the load, that is, with the thickness of the glacier, and with temperature.

However caused, glaciers move. Friction of a valley-glacier against its floor and walls causes a *differential flow*, the upper and central parts moving faster than the marginal and basal parts. The velocity, as we have seen, depends especially on the gradient, the thickness and the temperature of the ice, increasing as these increase. Alpine glaciers may move 80–150 metres in a year, Greenland glaciers as much as 33 metres in a day, the very cold Antarctic glaciers only a few millimetres a day. It is important to remember that the motive force of glaciers and ice-sheets is gravity. If an ice-sheet is thick enough it can transport blocks to high altitudes: we see an example in the Pleistocene Scandinavian ice-sheet which, with its centre over the Baltic, moved blocks to the tops of the Scandinavian mountains. The base of a glacier, however, can ride up and down over irregular surfaces, and glacial erosion is therefore not limited, as river-erosion is, by the existence of a base-level.

Classification of ice-bodies. Agassiz, the founder of glaciology as a science, applied concepts based on his study of Alpine glaciers to the continental glaciation of the Pleistocene, since little or nothing was then known of an ice-sheet. But continental ice-sheets are not simply very large valley-glaciers — the setting and controls are fundamentally different in the two cases. We can accordingly separate out: (1) *mountain-glaciers*, where mountain-slopes dominate the glacier, with rock-slopes high above the glacier as in the Alps, (2) *ice-sheets*, where little or no rock shows and the ice-masses form flattish domes or shields covering practically the whole of a land-surface, as in Greenland.

It will be convenient to elaborate this classification. Among the mountain-glaciers we can distinguish: (i) the *corrie-glacier* that occupies the bowl-shaped depression of a corrie, (ii) the *valley-glacier* of Alpine type, but better developed in Alaska, the Himalayas and New Zealand, that flows down the valleys leading from the high snowfield, and (iii) the *piedmont-glacier*, formed by the coalescence of several valley-glaciers as they debouch from the mountains on to the level ground at their foot, and typified by the Malaspina Glacier in Alaska. *Ice-caps* are small ice-sheets transitional from the mountain glaciers into the great continental *ice-sheets* that cover hundreds of thousands of square miles.

Corrie-glaciers. Snow-banks collected in a depression on a slope are attended in summer by excessive frost-action about their receding margins. Some of the broken-up material is removed by melt-water and the depression is deepened and recessed by this process of *nivation*. Solifluction and other periglacial activities (p. 149) are noted

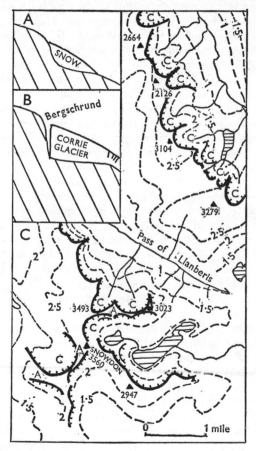

FIG. 131. The Bergschrund and Corries. A and B, development of the bergschrund; c, the corries (cwms) of Snowdonia, indicated by C, arêtes indicated by A. Contours in thousands of feet, corrie lakes lined.

around these incipient corries. Such a snow-bank may become large enough to flow and start erosive work; the depression is enlarged into a true *corrie, cwm* or *cirque,* a bowl-, amphitheatre- or arm-chair-shaped hollow bitten into the mountain-slope and often occupying the whole head of a valley (Fig. 131). When abandoned by the ice, this natural quarry into the hillside is found to be backed by a steep unglaciated wall that may be thousands of feet high. The corrie may contain a *corrie-lake* or *tarn,* occupying a hollow in the rocks or dammed up in part by an accumulation of glacial debris.

The steep unglaciated back wall of a corrie is difficult to explain. It has been ascribed to weathering but there is no horizontal niche to correspond with a névé level. The importance of the *bergschrund* (p. 220) in corrie-formation was recognised by W. D. Johnson in 1904. Johnson was lowered and then climbed 150 feet down the great crevasse of the Mt. Lyell glacier. He found that the bergschrund reached rock and had a twenty-foot rock-wall on the side towards the mountain. The wall was frost-rifted, blocks broken from it were tilted towards the ice and similar blocks were embedded in the ice. The rock-wall was wet by day, frozen by night. In the winter, the bergschrund fills with snow which grips the loose rock; in summer this snow draws away from the wall and transfers the rock-fragments to the corrie-glacier. Each winter, the bergschrund gapes a little higher up the mountainside. On this interpretation, therefore, rock is excavated from near or at the base of the corrie-wall.

Corries were magnificently developed during the Pleistocene glaciation in the 3000 feet plateau of the Scottish Highlands, as in the Cairngorms, Ben Mor Assynt and in the Cuillins in Skye. Other fine examples are seen in the English Lake District (Skiddaw) and in Snowdonia in Wales (Fig. 131). Corries are often said to develop preferentially on the northern sides of the mountains; this is only a partial truth — some of the best in Scotland face south-westwards (Glen Clova).

By the growth of corries on the margins of high plateaux, the upland becomes *scalloped* and a *remnant tableland* is produced. *Corrie-recession* may proceed so far as to destroy the tableland completely, the final remnant being represented by the *fretted uplands.* Coalescence of corries gives comb-like ridges, the *arêtes,* with conspicuous *aiguilles; horn*-mountains are formed at the junctions of such comb-ridges. Two corries attacking an arête from opposite sides result in a *col* with a hyperbolic curve.

Valley-glaciers. The valley-glacier occupies a previously existing valley, normally cut by river-action, which it modifies in significant ways. The ice of the valley-glacier is subjected to various compres-

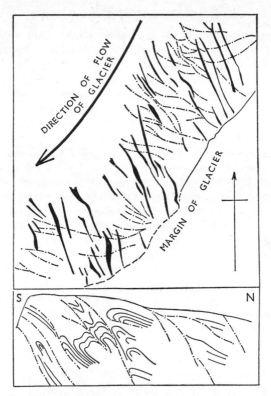

FIG. 132. The Rhone Glacier near Belvedere Hotel. (*Upper*), map
showing opened tensional crevasses (black) and outcrops of thrust-
planes (dot and dash). (*Lower*), section showing thrust-planes and
deformed flowbands (after George Slater).

sions and tensions which produce recognisable structures in it. As an
example of such structures we may summarise the results obtained by
Slater from the mapping, often in three dimensions, of portions of the
Rhone Glacier. Near the Belvedere Hotel, Slater investigated a zone
of *compression* characterised by a set of thrust-blocks recorded as
ridges on the surface of the glacier. The arrangement of the thrusts
(Fig. 132) depended upon the slower movement of the margin
relative to the interior of the glacier and upon the shape of the valley.
Tension-fractures formed gaping *marginal crevasses* oblique to the
general line of movement (Fig. 132).

As already noted, other tension-crevasses break across the line of
flow, the most important being the *bergschrund* or mountain-crevasse
formed where the moving ice of the glacier parts company from the

névé frozen to the rocks at the head of the valley. *Changes in gradient* give rise to crevasses across the glacier by curving the glacier-profile so that it is subject to tension; combined with this curving is the drag on the base of the zone of fracture due to the increased creep in the zone of flow caused by the change in gradient. A much-crevassed steep zone is termed an *ice-fall,* the upstanding masses bounded by the fracture-planes being *séracs.* The differential movement of valley-glaciers — the centre moving more rapidly than the margins — has been demonstrated many times by observations on lines of cairns or stakes set up across the glacier.

Transport by valley-glaciers. Valley-glaciers are dominated by mountain-slopes and from these frost-riven material slides down on to the glacier or is carried down by avalanches to build up a moving scree of loose material called a *lateral moraine* (Fig. 133). This material appears as a ridge along the margins of the glacier, since it protects the ice below it from ablation; in course of time, some of the loose stones slide down from the ridge across the ice and broaden the moraine. Where two valley-glaciers meet, the lateral moraine of one joins that of the other and both move forward as a *medial moraine.* A glacier that has received several tributaries will show on its surface a corresponding number of medial moraines as parallel banks of rock-

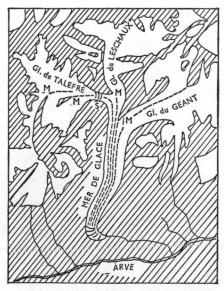

FIG. 133. Formation of medial moraines in Alpine glaciers. M indicates junction of two lateral moraines, S crevassed area.

debris moving down the valley. Consideration of their origin will show that these banks must continue down through the glacier and may reach bedrock In the lower parts of the glacier where ablation is taking place, the surface may be covered with debris, giving an *ablation-moraine*, and slowing down the ice-wastage; the medial and lateral moraines contribute to this cover.

Some of the *superglacial* material may fall into crevasses and be carried along in the ice as *englacial* material and some reaches the bottom to be *subglacial* material. When the glacier melts, the englacial material is let down on to the subglacial and together they form the *ground-moraine*. Enormous loads can be carried by the glacier; possibly when there is more rock-debris than ice the glacier may be slowed down or brought to a halt. Some of the transported material reaches the terminus to build up a *terminal moraine* or *end-moraine*, a confused system of morainic material, ice and melt-waters, subject to disturbance from variations in the movements of the glacier. Water melting from the glacier washes out the finer material and leaves sandy or bouldery deposits, tipped and false-bedded. Not much of the material will be ice-scratched (p. 228); it is frost-action that erodes most in the Alps, for example; the valley-glaciers act mainly as transporters.

Erosion by valley-glaciers. As the tongues of ice move down the valleys, *erosion* is effected. Much of our knowledge of the erosion-forms comes of course from the examination of the results of the Pleistocene Glaciation.

The sole of the glacier is shod with frozen-in blocks of rocks of all sizes, and between the sole and the underlying rock-floor finer material is to be expected. This finer material acts as an abrasive and the underlying rock is scratched and polished. The scratches produced by this process are *glacial striae* (Fig. 134). They provide evidence of the two possible directions in which the ice responsible for them was moving. Certain rocks, such as limestones, may receive a fine *glacial polish* with striae well developed on the polished surface. Hard rocks, such as quartz-veins, retain glacial striae when those on the softer rocks have been weathered away. It is asserted that the actual direction of ice-movement can be told from striae by observation of their detailed shape (e.g. *nailhead striae*) or by their feel to the fingers. *Crossed striae* are of fairly frequent occurrence. Their interpretation is difficult; they may be due to ice-movements of very different ages or they may more probably result from eddies in the ice of one period. *Friction-cracks* and *chattermarks* are crescentic markings or gouges formed especially on the glaciated surfaces of hard rocks. It is believed that friction-cracks are inclined towards

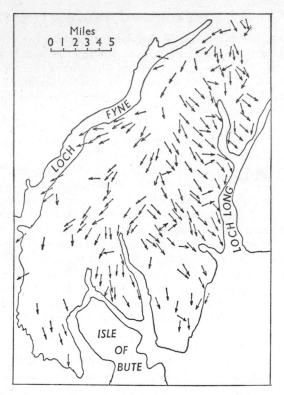

FIG. 134. Map of Glacial Striae in Cowal, Argyllshire (after Clough, Geological Survey).

the direction of glacier-movement. Glacial abrasion naturally picks out the weak places in the bedrock and *fluted* and *grooved* surfaces may be formed by the removal of this broken-out material.

During abrasion, the stones used as tools by the glacier become trimmed into sub-angular shapes, that of a 'facetted flat-iron' being said to be characteristic (Fig. 147). They are often striated but, as they change their position in the ice, their striae run in various directions. It should be remembered that only a small proportion of the stones carried by a glacier will be striated.

We may now deal with the larger-scale erosion phenomena of valley-glaciers. Passage of a glacier over the steep bedding-planes of a rock which has been weakened by weathering may bend over the planes to produce another example of *terminal curvature* (p. 150). This structure is liable to be confused with hill-creep (p. 149) and, like it, may give a wrong impression of the inclination of the beds in a

228

FIG. 135. Roches moutonnées, Ardnamurchan, Scotland. (Crown Copyright: by Permission of the Controller of H.M. Stationery Office.)

shallow exposure. Small projecting crags in the path of the glacier become 'stream-lined' or ice-moulded to give *roches moutonnées* (Fig. 135); their upstream side is rounded off, their lee side is made steep by the *plucking* away of unsupported blocks, especially where vertical joints are suitably placed. Their plan is a truncated oval. Roches moutonnées thus provide evidence of the direction of ice-movement — viewed in this direction a moutonnée countryside appears smooth, in the reverse direction it seems to be made up of small steep crags. Larger crags may form a protection from the moving ice and so preserve a tail in their lee. This *crag-and-tail* is beautifully seen in the Midland Valley of Scotland; Edinburgh Castle Rock stood in the way of Pleistocene ice coming from the west, the ice-stream was split and gouged out the valleys of Princes Street to the north and Grassmarket and Cowgate to the south, leaving the protected tail running down to Holyrood (Fig. 136).

Valley-glaciers *modify the river-cut valleys* down which they flow. The characteristic features that mark such glaciated valleys are of course best displayed by valleys occupied by ice during the Pleistocene Glaciation. In some valleys vacated by valley-glaciers there occurs a series of *steps*, level portions of the valley-floor being separated from each other by narrow steep rises. Lakes, occupying

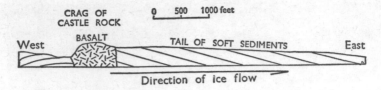

CRAG OF
CASTLE ROCK
0 500 1000 feet
BASALT
West
TAIL OF SOFT SEDIMENTS
East
Direction of ice flow

FIG. 136. Crag and Tail, Edinburgh.

eroded hollows, may occur on the steps and a string of such lakes provides the *paternoster lakes*, so called because they are reminiscent of beads on a rosary. The origin of the steps is a difficult problem: they are most likely due to the plucking of jointed rock at the back of the steps. Initial irregularities in the valley-floor may be emphasised by plucking at the steep parts due to the full weight of the ice being carried over them on upward thrusts from the gentler areas (p. 221). As the glacier retreats, corrie-conditions may set in at the steps which thus become still more accentuated.

The V-shaped cross-section of the original river-cut valley is modified into a broad-bottomed *U-shape*, typical of glaciated valleys, by side or lateral erosion by the glacier (Fig. 137). It may be remarked that erosion by plucking and allied processes is much more effective than that by direct abrasion of rock-surfaces. In the Alps,

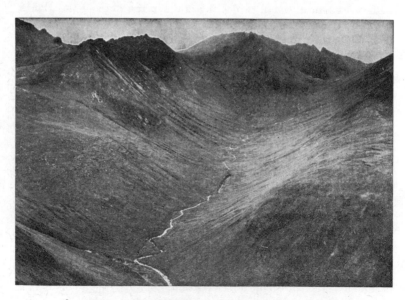

FIG. 137. U-shaped valley, Glen Rosa, Arran. (Aerofilms).

the U-shaped valley is often cut in a broader flatter older valley, so
giving high-level summer-meadows or *alps* — examples are those of
Murren and Wengen on either side of the Lauterbrunnental. The
development of the U-shaped valley straightens out the old valley
by persistent ice-erosion of the valley *spurs* which become *bevelled* or
truncated. Since glacial erosion depends on the volume of the ice, the
main valleys of a system are *over-deepened* and *over-widened* in comparison with the tributary valleys. This over-deepening is especially
marked when the main valley happened to coincide with the general
direction of ice-movement and may lead to the excavation of the
floor below sea-level. After glaciation, therefore, an originally accordant river-valley system becomes markedly discordant. The
tributary valleys *hang* to the main valley and their streams enter it
over a steep cliff in cascades and waterfalls.

Belts of softer or shattered rock are naturally readily eroded by
glacial action. The weathered and broken material is removed to
leave *rock-basins*, often occupied by lakes of various sizes. The Great
Glen of Scotland has been eroded along a broad shatter-belt and
many Scottish lochs are in over-deepened rock-basins. For example,
Loch Ericht, depth 512 feet, width ½ mile, length 14¼ miles, occupies
a hollow excavated in a fault-zone of weakened rock; Loch Loyal is
deepest where it is narrowest, that is, where ice-erosion was particularly concentrated. Loch Morar, with a water-surface only a few
feet above sea-level, has a depth of over 1000 ft. These facts are
consistent only with glacial over-deepening.

A *fjord* is a glaciated trough-shaped valley that is partly filled by
the sea. Franz Joseph Fjord in East Greenland is 100 miles long, 8
miles wide and in places its floor is ½ mile below sea-level. Fjords
usually have a pronounced sill or threshold at their seaward ends and
their landward portion is an over-deepened basin similar to many of
the Scottish lochs.

Depositon by valley-glaciers. As the glacier wastes away, its load
comes to rest. This deposit is *glacial drift*, a term usually taken to
include the deposits of glacier-lakes and streams. It is convenient to
discuss many of the deposits of ice-sheets together with those of
valley-glaciers.

The *lateral* and *medial moraines* are not usually well preserved.
The lateral moraines are partly supported by the ice and, when this
melts, the morainic material slides into the valley and is largely lost
in scree and landslip. The medial moraines, held steeply sided in the
ice, also slump outwards and lose their individuality. The *terminal* or
end-moraines, as already noted, are ridge-like accumulations of drift
formed in various ways such as the shoving-up of material in front of

the ice, by the plastering of slabs of drift in successive layers and by pure dumping from the melting ice at periods of glacier still-stand. According to their material, they may be described as *rubble-, block-* or *boulder-moraine*. Festoons of terminal moraines may mark the expanded foot of a glacier as at Lake Garda, Italy.

The *ground-moraine* is formed by the slow collapse of the ice as it melts and is more typically developed in ice-sheet glaciation. The superglacial and ablation-material, made of the spread-out moraines just mentioned, with the englacial load is let down to rest on top of the subglacial material. The ground-moraine as a whole is thus often composed of two parts. The *lower part* consists of ground-up rock-flour with boulders of all sizes and is compacted and hard; the *upper part* is looser, more porous drift, the finer material having been largely washed away. The stones in the lower part are often striated and ice-moulded; in the upper part they are larger and less ice-worn. The two layers may be so different and distinct as to give the impression that they record two separate epochs of glacial deposition.

Boulder-clay or *till* is a widespread drift deposit consisting of an unsorted mixture of rock-flour, sand and boulders (see Fig. 158). It is laid down by mountain-glaciers and, on a still larger scale, by ice-sheets. It may be confused with land-slip debris, mudflow or solifluc-tion deposits but usually its make-up and geological relations are sufficient to identify it. Till may be modified by water-action by which the finer material is removed, or it may be diversified by sandy and gravelly layers deposited from englacial streams. The lithological character of till naturally depends on the rocks over which or past which the ice has travelled. Sandstone bedrocks give a sandy drift, chalk a chalky drift and so on. Observation shows that the stones in boulder-clay possess a *fabric* — the *till-fabric* — in which a significant number lie with their longest axes parallel to the direction of flow of the ice (see Fig. 151); it is suggested that such oriented stones slid along the bottom of the glacier until they became embedded, with their orientation preserved, in the ground-moraine. Study of the till-fabric may give an accurate idea of the direction of ice-movement.

Boulders or *erratics* in the drift may often be identifiable as de-rived from a particular rock-outcrop and hence supply evidence of the *general* movement of the ice which brought them. *Erratic blocks* are conspicuous erratics often perched in spectacular situations. Occasionally, erratics left by the Pleistocene ice-sheets have been employed to locate mineral-deposits by following the trail of ore-bearing erratics back to their source, as in Finland and Canada (Fig. 138).

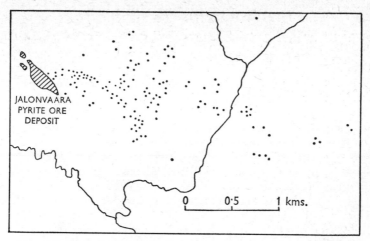

FIG. 138. Trail of glacially transported boulders of ore-bearing rock derived from the Jalonvaara pyrite deposit, Finland (after Sauramo).

Thick deposits of ground-moraine often show *drumlin* forms. Drumlins are small elongated oval hills of drift giving in mass a 'basket of eggs' topography (Fig. 139). Their lengths may reach a mile, widths up to half a mile and their height above the local

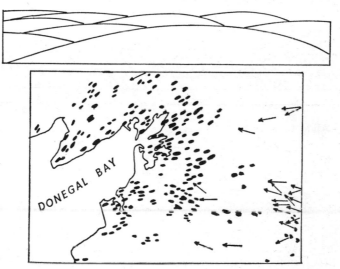

FIG. 139. Drumlins in Co. Donegal, Ireland (after Wright). (*Upper*), characteristic 'basket of eggs' topography. (*Lower*), map showing elongation of drumlins in the direction of ice-flow, as indicated by glacial striae (arrows).

233

ground-level may be several hundred feet. Their long axes are found to be in the direction of ice-flow and their blunter ends are upstream. Drumlins may occur singly or in great patterned groups that may reveal details of the direction of ice-flow (Fig. 139). They may be interpreted as accumulations of boulder-clay, anchored perhaps on a rock base or core, or by particularly stony pockets of drift; such accumulations become stagnant and are over-ridden and moulded by the moving cleaner ice — they are stream-lined in the direction of flow. Certain glaciologists believe that the arrangement of drift-deposits, especially the *disturbed* drift, is a model or 'pseudomorph' of the structures that actually occurred in the ice.

The blanket of ground-moraine is very irregular in thickness, from a few feet to several hundred feet. Its upper surface is irregular, undulating or of drumlin-form, due to uneven deposition from ice unevenly charged with debris. The lower surface is that of the *pre-glacial topography*, which thus becomes more or less buried. Deep river-channels may be filled in with boulder-clay and the river forced to find a new post-glacial course. The *buried channels* are a hazard in mining or tunnelling in regions affected by the Pleistocene glaciation and their location, by boring or geophysical investigation, may be necessary. An important buried channel is illustrated in Fig. 140.

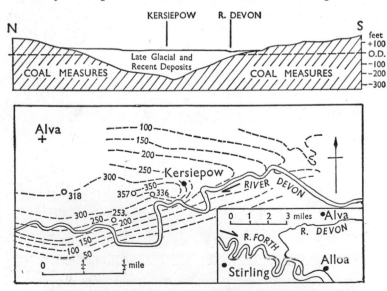

FIG. 140. Buried channel of the River Devon, Clackmannanshire, Scotland; contours show depth to solid rock (after Blyth and Parthasarathy).

WATER-ACTION IN GLACIAL DEPOSITION:
FLUVIOGLACIAL DEPOSITS

In the ablation area of a glacier, melt-waters collect in streams that flow on, in or under the ice or along the ice-margin or, finally, away from the glacier-front. Deposition of different kinds takes place from these streams and makes the *fluvioglacial deposits* that we now survey.

Water flowing in ice-tunnels deposits *sands and gravels* where its velocity is checked and these deposits will appear as impersistent lenses, seams and courses in the till. Where the streams, armed with abrasive tools, reach the wall- or bed-rock they may erode pot-holes or undercut steeper rock-surfaces. Englacial streams coming to the surface in the ablation area may spread out and deposit their load which also appears in the final till as sand- or gravel-seams. Such seams are important in the construction of earth-dams, etc., in till areas.

More important, and more interesting, deposits of fluvioglacial sand and gravel are the *kames* and *eskers*; these are built up against an ice-wall and may be called therefore *ice-contact deposits* since much of their shape depends on that of the now-vanished ice.

Kame-terraces are built by streams running between the valley-wall and the glacier (Fig. 141). They appear as short discontinuous terraces along the valley-side. There may be two or more at different levels recording stages in the retreat of the glacier responsible. *Kames* have the form of low knolls, ridges or confused heaps and are made of coarse sands and gravels rapidly varying in grade and structures. They are believed to be formed from crevasse-fillings in stagnant ice-masses or by small deltaic cones formed along the ice-margin.

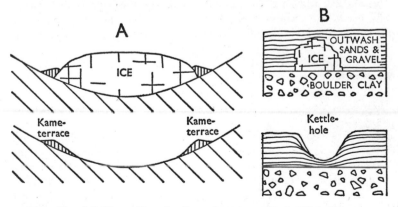

FIG. 141. Formation of A, kame-terrace, and B, kettle-hole.

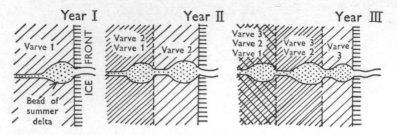

FIG. 142. Formation of a beaded esker and its associated varves during the retreat of an ice-front (see also FIG. 114).

Kame-terraces and other sheets of fluvioglacial deposits often show rounded depressions, usually about thirty feet deep and a few hundred yards across, that have no outlets. These *kettle-holes* result from the melting of isolated masses of ice enclosed in the drifts and are especially characteristic of the terminal portions of the glacier (Fig. 141).

Eskers (Fig. 142) are winding ridges of current-bedded sand, gravel and boulders, up to 100 feet high and many miles long. A Quebec example is about 150 miles long. Eskers have steep sides and narrow flattish tops; they occasionally show branching tributary ridges. The esker-system broadly follows the general direction of flow of the last ice of a glaciated region. Their origin is reasonably connected with deposition by subglacial streams. Fairly smooth-topped types may be the deposits laid down in such a stream traversing a stagnant ice-body. Others, known as *beaded eskers*, are connected with a retreating ice-front; these are the deposits of a subglacial stream entering a body of water held up against the ice-front. They are normally at right angles to this front and are interpreted as deltaic deposits of fluvioglacial origin. The *beads*, or high parts, of the beaded esker are the *summer deltas*, the lower parts in between the beads being the winter deposits. Laterally, the beads pass into finer deposits laid down farther from the entrance of the stream into the lake. These finer deposits are the *varves* that we have already described and illustrated in Fig. 114; we may recall the variation in thickness shown by varve No. 485 in Finland.

Beyond the terminal moraines of some glaciers and ice-sheets there may be built up an accumulation of material deposited by melt-waters from the ice-body. This deposit forms the *outwash-fan* or *apron*. Streams leaving the glacier are overloaded and choked with sediment and build up deposits whose thickness may attain some hundreds of feet. The streams are braided and constantly change their positions. The coarsest material is nearest the ice, the finer is farther away. The heads of some outwash-fans are built up against the ice of stagnant glaciers and then the ice contact-slope is preserved

236

as a relatively steep bank. Outwash-aprons are often pitted with innumerable kettle-holes, and so produce *pitted outwash-plains*.

Piedmont-glaciers. Piedmont-glaciers occur today in regions of high precipitation and strong relief where mountains have a flat expanse — the piedmont — at their feet. A number of valley-glaciers protruding from the mountain-valleys unite on the piedmont to form

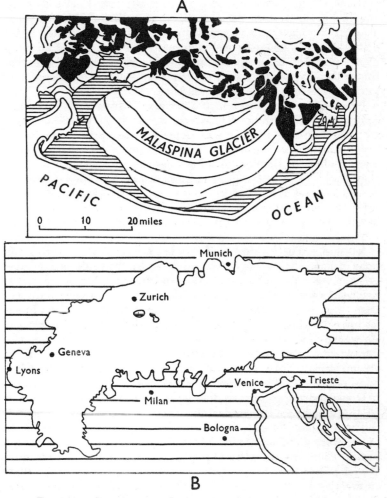

Fig. 143. A, The Malaspina Piedmont glacier, Alaska; black, mountain peaks protruding through the ice; B, the Alpine ice-cap during the Pleistocene glaciation.

a great 'lake' of ice, the piedmont-glacier. The typical example of a piedmont-glacier is the Malaspina in Alaska (Fig. 143) produced by the coalescence on the coastal plain of valley-glaciers emerging from the Mt. St. Elias ranges. The whole mass of ice is in motion but so slowly that no crevasses are formed and the glacier can easily be crossed by sledge. The surface is largely covered by hummocky moraine much of which supports forests. Sporadic movements of portions of the glacier lead to trees, vegetation and old soils being engulfed in the ice as englacial material. If melting of this piedmont-glacier takes place, this vegetable matter will be intercalated in the drift and might be erroneously interpreted as evidence of an inter-glacial period. During the Pleistocene glaciation it is probable that the valley-glaciers of the Alps and the Caucasus coalesced into piedmont-glaciers at the mountain-foot.

Ice-caps. Ice-caps cover high plateaux in Iceland, Norway and Spitzbergen. They are small ice-sheets in that they are not dominated by mountain-slopes; they may represent an early stage in the development of an ice-sheet. The formation of ice-caps depends more on altitude than latitude. From the margins of their high plateaux they discharge by outlet glaciers through passes to the lower lands. Since little rock is exposed in the ice-cap, the ice is relatively clean, little morainic material is carried and the terminal moraines of the outlet glaciers are accordingly small and largely made of angular unstriated fragments.

Ice-sheets. The greatest masses of ice, the *ice-sheets*, covering millions of square miles, are developed either by the continued enlargement of ice-caps such as that now covering Spitzbergen or by the extension of valley- and piedmont-glaciers until only isolated rock-peaks still protrude through the ice cover. Such rock-islands in the ice are called in Greenland *nunatakkr* (usually in English *nunataks*). As already noted, the movement of the ice-body now becomes dependent on the position and altitude of the dome of ice. The Pleistocene glaciation was largely a glaciation by ice-sheets, so that it is appropriate to deal briefly with the two present-day ice-sheets, those of Greenland and Antarctica. The erosional and depositional work of ice-sheets has already been dealt with.

The *Greenland Ice-sheet* is a flat dome of ice with a marginal ribbon of nunataks and land usually 5–25 miles wide but up to 100 miles in places. There are really three broad domes or high points from which the ice moves to the coast and discharges itself through the valleys transecting the high marginal mountains. The following impressive figures are those provided by the Victor expeditions of 1949–51 and 1952.

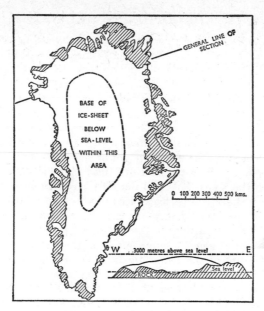

Fig. 144. The Greenland Ice-sheet (after Haller).

Surface-area of ice-sheet	1,726,400 km.²
Mean height	2,135 m. above sea-level
Mean height of bedrock	620 m. above sea-level
Mean thickness of ice	1,515 m.
Volume	2·6 × 10⁶ km.³

The Victor expeditions were able by geophysical means to measure the thickness of the ice at a network of some 400 stations and Fig. 144 is based on their results. From these it will be seen that the ice-sheet thickens towards the central axis of Greenland so that its base in this part goes down below sea-level. The ice-sheet is thus filling and over-filling a basin, the excess ice escaping through gaps in the mountain-rim. As already noted, the prime mover is the weight of the ice-body, the ice spreading out from the high points of the dome. The rate of movement in the main ice-sheet is from 10 to 30 cms. per day. In the outlet-glaciers of the coastal belt enormous velocities are reached, of the order of 40 cm. to 1·30 metres an hour, and in many places the glaciers can be seen to move. As the inland ice approaches this belt, great crevasses are opened up. In the outlet-glaciers, the crevasses may be healed, but they still provide planes of weakness for the calving of icebergs when the glaciers enter the fjords.

The *Antarctic Ice-sheet* is many times bigger than the Greenland

Ice-sheet and attains a surface-area of 13½ million square kilometres (5 million square miles), one and a half times the area of the U.S.A. Estimates of its volume vary: one suggests 28·5 millions of cubic kilometres (Wegmann). Recent measurements by the Commonwealth Transantarctic Expedition show that the thickness of the ice is very variable and that a rugged mountainous land is buried beneath the ice-sheet (see Fig. 23). The upper surface of the ice-sheet forms a fairly smooth high plateau, with an average elevation of some 6000 feet and a maximum height of nearly 10,000 feet. Undulations may perhaps be controlled by land-forms below. The ice-shed lies between the South Pole and the Pacific coast-line and from this divide the great body of very cold ice radiates slowly to the sea. Over most of its margin, the ice-sheet reaches the sea, but at intervals high mountains block its path, as in the Ross Sea area; through portals in these, great outlet glaciers move out from the ice-sheet. A very remarkable feature of the Antarctic Ice-sheet is the development of enormous expanses of *shelf-ice*, typified especially by the *Ross Shelf-Ice*, but also by the Filchner Shelf-Ice in the Weddell Sea and the Shackleton Shelf-Ice off Queen Mary Land. The Ross Shelf-Ice is some 500 miles long, up to 300 miles wide and presents ice-cliffs up to 280 feet high at its seaward face. It may be as thick as 1000 feet. It is afloat, and is formed by the pushing out into deep water of the inland ice covered by its own névé built by direct snowfall and by drifting by strong katabatic winds. Great tabular icebergs break off along vertical joints in the shelf-ice. By this mechanism of shelf-ice formation it is possible for ice-sheets to advance hundreds of miles across deep seas. Like all ice-bodies of the present day, the Antarctic Ice-sheet is shrinking — in this case due to low precipitation over the great central area of the ice-sheet which may thus be gradually spreading itself out thinner. The excessively cold Antarctic Ice-sheet should not be used to explain the more temperate ice-sheets responsible for the Pleistocene Glaciation.

ENVIRONMENTS OF DEPOSITION OF SEDIMENTS

The deposition of sediments in many kinds of environments is the aspect of surface-processes that is of the greatest importance to the geologist. He is much concerned with ancient sediments — the sedimentary rocks — as records of their environments of deposition and his main aim is to reconstruct the conditions under which the sedimentary rocks of one particular time were accumulated.

The places where sediments accumulate constitute their *environments of deposition*. From the foregoing pages, we may contrast the land-environments, where denudation rather than sedimentation is dominant, with the marine environments where the reverse holds. Besides this two-fold grouping, there are a number of amphibious environments, such as the deltaic, that combine land- and sea-conditions. The environments of deposition control the *facies* of the sediments, that is, the sum total of all their characters, lithological and faunal. These environments may be tabulated as below; such a table is of course capable of great elaboration.

ENVIRONMENTS OF DEPOSITION

A. Land	*B. Mixed or Amphibious*
Desert	Lagoonal
Glacial	Deltaic
Fluvial	Estuarine
Piedmont	Beach, Littoral
Valley-flat	
Lacustrine	*C. Sea*
Fresh-water Lakes	Shallow-water, Neritic or Shelf
Salt-water Lakes	Deeper-water, Bathyal or Slope
Swamps	Deep-sea, Abyssal, Pelagic.

An environment of deposition is highly dynamic, since its character depends on a combination of mechanical, chemical and organic agents and processes. Detritus originating outside the basin of deposition constitutes the *allochthonous* component of the sediments; within the basin, materials formed by inorganic and organic precipitation are *autochthonous* components. Usually, allochthonous and autochthonous components are deposited together to make the sediment.

As we have seen, the nature of the *allochthonous components* depends on the processes of weathering and transport which they have undergone. Their primary composition is determined by their *provenance*, the original rocks from which they were derived, but these primary characters may be profoundly modified by weathering. In the basin of deposition, the transporting agents control the size-frequency of the particles deposited at any one place or time, the rate of deposition and whether deposition is permanent or whether the detritus is *reworked*.

Chemical activity in the region of deposition depends on the environment and, besides, on the rate of deposition and burial. Rapid deposition covers the lower layers before they can be much affected, slow deposition permits reworking during which profound chemical changes can happen. Clay-minerals are especially sensitive to change in environment.

The *autochthonous components* originate in the basin of deposition by inorganic precipitation, organic precipitation or by the accumulation of organic debris. We have already seen examples of these processes in the deposition of calcium carbonate, iron hydroxide and the evaporates generally, in the formation of shelly deposits and the growth of reefs.

We may recall that there is another component of many sediments which is of great importance in their subsequent history. This is *connate water* included in the pores of aqueous deposits. Unstable minerals may continue to react with this water after the sediment has been laid down and so begin the great series of post-depositional changes which are considered in a later page (p. 255).

FURTHER READING AND REFERENCE

General Works

Clarke, F. W., 1924, 'The Data of Geochemistry', *Bull. 770, United States Geological Survey.*

Cotton, C. A., 1942, *Geomorphology,* 3rd Edit., Whitcombe and Tombs.

Davis, W. M., 1954, *Geographical Essays,* Dover Publications.

Dury, G. H., 1959, *The Face of the Earth,* Pelican Books.

Holmes, A., 1965, *Principles of Physical Geology,* 2nd edit., Nelson.

King, L. C., 1967, *The morphology of the Earth,* 2nd Edit., Oliver and Boyd.

Trask, P. D., Editor, 1939, *Recent Marine Sediments,* Amer. Assoc. Petr. Geologists.

Special Books and Papers

Goldich, S. S., 1938, 'A study of rock weathering', *Journ. Geol.,* vol. 46, p. 17.

Brade-Birks, S. G., 1944, *Good Soil,* English Universities Press.

Tolman, C. F., 1927, *Groundwater,* McGraw-Hill.

Sharpe, C. F. S., 1938, *Landslides and Related Phenomena,* Columbia Univ. Press.

'Effects of Permafrost and related topics', *Journ. Geology,* vol. 57, no. 2, 1949.

Hollingworth, S. E., 1934, 'Some solifluction phenomena', *Proc. Geol. Assoc.,* vol. 45, p. 167.

Bagnold, R. A., 1941, *The physics of blown sand and desert dunes,* Methuen.

Bagnold, R. A., 1941, *Libyan Sands,* Hodder and Stoughton.

Leopold, L. B., M. G. Wolman and J. P. Miller, 1964, *Fluvial processes in geomorphology,* Freeman.

Gilbert, G. K., 1890, 'Lake Bonneville', *Mon. 1, United States Geol. Survey.*

Shearman D. J. 1966, 'Origin of marine evaporites by diagenesis,' *Trans. I.M.M.*, Section B, Vol. 75, p. B208.

Fisk, H. N., and E. McFarlan, 1955, 'Late Quaternary Deltaic Deposits of the Mississippi River', *The Crust of the Earth, Spec. Paper 62, Geol. Soc. Amer.*, p. 279.

Antevs, E., 1922, *The recession of the last icesheet in New England*, American Geogr. Soc. Research Series, 11 (varves).

Sauramo, M., 1923, 'Quaternary Varved Sediments in Southern Finland', *Bull. Comm. Géol. Finlande*, no. 60 (varves).

Kuenen, P. H., 1950, *Marine Geology*, Wiley.

Shepard, F. P., 1964, *Submarine Geology*, 2nd Edit., Harper.

Kuenen, P. H., 'Origin and classification of submarine canyons', *Bull. Geol. Soc. America*, vol. 64, p. 295.

Davis, W. M., 1928, *The Coral Reef Problem*, Amer. Geographical Soc., Special Publication, no. 9.

Heezen, B. C., M. Tharp and M. Ewing, 1959, 'The floors of the oceans', *Spec. Paper 65, Geol. Soc. America*.

Flint, R. F., 1947, *Glacial geology and the Pleistocene Epoch*, Wiley, New York.

5

THE SEDIMENTARY ROCKS

INTRODUCTION

IN the previous chapter, emphasis was properly laid on the processes operating to produce the sediments, the raw materials of the sedimentary rocks. We have now to deal with the products of these processes. Many of these have been mentioned or even briefly discussed in the preceding chapter, and some special features of them have been attached to some appropriate process. It is the purpose of this present chapter to describe more systematically the lithology and geology of the sedimentary rocks, that is, their physical and chemical characters and their arrangements in space and time.

The surface-processes that we have studied are held to have produced the same kinds of sediments in the past as they do today. We must of course accept this uniformitarian doctrine, but at the same time make certain reservations. While a process may remain the same in mechanism, its speed may vary at different times in earth-history. In the making of any given sediment, a complexity of processes may be involved and as a result of the infinite choice of patterns in this complexity no two rocks are exactly alike; uniformitarianism thus becomes a generalisation. Further, sedimentary material may be involved in a succession of processes and the products modified accordingly. It is possible, too, that the geological history of the earth is so long that an evolution in physical processes may have taken place. Certainly the types, habitats and geological consequences of organisms have changed fundamentally during the later portions of that history. Whilst we must accept uniformitarianism, we must allow every rock to tell its own story.

SEDIMENTARY DIFFERENTIATION

In the previous chapter we saw that chemical and mechanical weathering affects the different mineral constituents of rocks in varying degrees and in dissimilar ways. The weathered material is transported by diverse agencies and during transport undergoes a variety of further changes. The final deposition of the varied sediments takes place under a number of controls and in many different environments. As a result of these complex selective operations, a profound mechanical and chemical sorting of the parent material occurs which can be described as *sedimentary differentiation*. This provides a reasonable basis for the classification of the sediments.

The typical minerals of the common igneous rocks have been arranged (p. 131) in an order of stability under weathering conditions; beginning with the least stable, this order is approximately olivine, anorthite, pyroxenes, amphiboles, albite, biotite, potash-feldspar, muscovite and quartz. The less stable minerals are converted into new minerals such as the clay-minerals, hydroxides, carbonates etc. that are stable under surface conditions; the more stable minerals, especially quartz, persist in the sediment. A sediment therefore contains varying amounts of *new* minerals and of *inherited* minerals. Depending on the amount and type of the new minerals, the sediments can be divided into groups recording the sedimentary differentiation. Goldschmidt's names for these groups are given below, together with their dominant chemical constituents:

	Resistates	Si
	Hydrolysates	Al
MINERALS OF THE	Oxidates	Fe
IGNEOUS ROCKS	Carbonates	Ca, Mg
	Evaporates	Na, K
	Reduzates	C

The significant points about these groups are now examined. First, the *resistates*, concentrations of the obdurate minerals, are essentially composed of quartz and are represented by the common sands and sandstones. Original feldspars are mostly converted into clay-minerals but survive in feldspathic sandstones and other feldspar-bearing sedimentary rocks. The *hydrolysates* show a concentration of alumina, in the clay minerals, and provide the ordinary clays; some potassium is adsorbed or co-precipitated in these. The *oxidates* are represented by iron and manganese hydroxides, derived from the breakdown of the primary ferromagnesian minerals. The cations Na, K, Ca, and Mg, derived from the decomposition of feldspars and ferromagnesian minerals, are transported in solution. The calcium is precipitated as the *carbonate* in the limestones; the more soluble magnesium carbonate reacts with limestones to give dolomite. The most soluble materials are eventually precipitated as the *evaporates*, such as rock-salt, gypsum, anhydrite and salts of potassium and magnesium, produced and preserved under special geological conditions. To these five groups, Rankama and Sahama have added a sixth, the *reduzates*, formed under reducing conditions and typified by the coals and by clayey sediments containing sulphides of iron and manganese.

Sedimentary differentiation provides a number of reasonably distinct groups of sediments that can be used as a basis for a geological classification of the sedimentary rocks. It can be baldly stated that no classification of these rocks is entirely satisfactory, since the physical and chemical factors are so closely interlocked. As a start, we can distinguish two broad classes: one contains those sediments made by the accumulation of pieces of minerals or rocks, the other contains the sediments precipitated from a solution or produced by organic agencies. The first class, called *detrital* sediments, is illustrated by the resistate sands, made of fragments of inherited quartz, and the hydrolysate clays, made of newly formed but transported particles of clay-minerals. This detrital class is often incorrectly called *clastic* (clastos = broken); this latter term should be restricted to sediments made from fragments of parent rocks or minerals and would not include newly-formed components such as clay-minerals. The second class of sedimentary rocks contains the carbonate rocks, the evaporates and the coals, which can be referred to as the *chemical-organic* sediments. Proceeding further with our classification, we may subdivide the detrital sediments into three groups depending on the size of their constituent particles — giving the pebbly or *psephitic* sediments, the sandy or *psammitic* and the clayey or *pelitic*. These three groups are in line with everyday practice; geologically and mineralogically, too, they are fairly sharply distinct. The chemical-organic sediments are best classified by their chemical composition into the carbonate, siliceous, ferruginous, aluminous, phosphatic, saline and carbonaceous groups. It is at once obvious that there are many defects in this system and, after the sediments have been examined, we shall be able to present a classification into which the geological controls enter more directly.

We can therefore make a first classification of sediments and sedimentary rocks as given in the Table below. A variety of rock-names appears in this; these rocks, and the many important transitional types not there listed, will be defined and described in later pages. Before this is done, there are a few matters to be attended to.

FIRST CLASSIFICATION OF SEDIMENTARY ROCKS

A. *Detrital* (subdivided by grain-size)
  1. Coarse: *psephites* — gravel, conglomerate, breccia
  2. Medium: *psammites* — sand, sandstone, greywacke, arkose
  3. Fine: *pelites* — mud, clay, shale

B. *Chemical-Organic* (subdivided by composition)
  1. Carbonate: lime-mud, shell-sand, limestone, dolomite
  2. Siliceous: diatomite, radiolarite, flint, chert

3. Ferruginous: iron carbonates, silicates, oxides, sulphides
4. Aluminous: laterite, bauxite
5. Phosphatic: phosphorite
6. Saline: rock-salt, gypsum, anhydrite
7. Carbonaceous: peat, lignite, coals, bitumens.

Sedimentary rocks possess characteristic *textures* and *structures* of great importance in the interpretation of their manner of formation, and these characters are now dealt with. In addition, the processes of conversion of a sediment into a sedimentary rock — processes grouped as *diagenesis* — are clearly important for adequate description of the rock-types.

TEXTURES AND STRUCTURES OF THE SEDIMENTARY ROCKS

It will be useful to show how the terms texture and structure are used in this book. *Texture* refers to the characters of the constituent grains or units and their relations to one another (e.g. the diagenetic textures in Fig. 156); *structure* is a larger-scale feature resulting from from the way in which textural groups are related.

TEXTURE

Textures of the sedimentary rocks have to do with the size and sorting of the grains, their shapes and arrangement, and the resulting physical properties such as porosity and permeability. The last two topics have been dealt with in the previous chapter (pp. 138–9).

Size, as we have seen, is the basis of the classification of the detrital rocks and is illustrated by their raw materials, gravel (diameter >2 mm.) sand ($2-\frac{1}{16}$mm.) silt and clay ($<\frac{1}{16}$mm.). In any given sediment or sedimentary rock, the grains differ in size within different limits and the determination of the relative amounts of the various sizes present may be an important matter. This *mechanical analysis* is done by first breaking down the sediment or sedimentary rock into its constituent grains and then sorting these into their different grades by sieving or by elutriation. In elutriation, the grains are sorted by passing currents of water of different velocities through the glass vessel of an *elutriator* shown in Fig. 145. The results of mechanical analysis are presented either as a *histogram*, a 'frequency-distribution pyramid', a *frequency-curve* or by a *cumulative curve*. Examples of an analysis plotted in two of these ways are shown in Fig. 146.

I

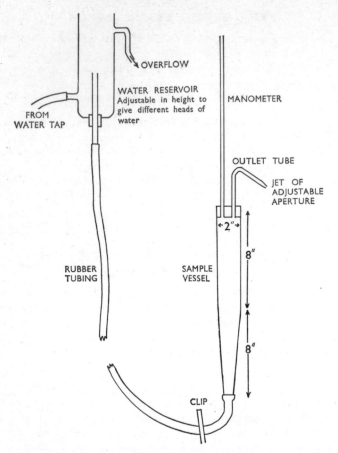

FROM
WATER TAP

OVERFLOW

WATER RESERVOIR
Adjustable in height to
give different heads of
water

MANOMETER

OUTLET TUBE

JET OF
ADJUSTABLE
APERTURE

←2"→

8"

RUBBER
TUBING

SAMPLE
VESSEL

8"

CLIP

Fig. 145. The Elutriator. A weighed amount of the prepared sample is placed in the sample vessel, the size of the jet and the height of the reservoir adjusted to give the velocity required to separate a particular grade, this being washed through the outlet tube, collected, dried and weighed.

The *shape* of the grains of a sediment is an important textural character since it may give a clue to the manner of its accumulation. Angular grains cannot have moved far, rounded grains or dreikanter pebbles may be indicative of deposition by the wind, the stones in glacial deposits may have a significant flat-iron shape. Illustrations of typical grain-shapes are given in Fig. 147. The *sphericity* of a pebble or grain is given by the ratio of the diameter of a sphere, having the same volume as that of the pebble, to the diameter of a sphere circumscribing the pebble (Fig. 148). Sphericity may be an

248

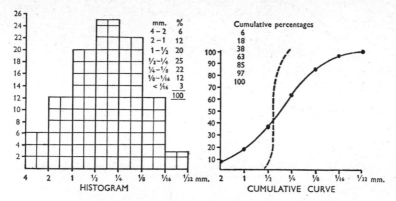

Fig. 146. Plotting mechanical analyses. (*Left*), the *histogram*, in which the area of the vertical bar for any grade is proportional to its quantity — this should be verified by counting the number of squares in each bar. (*Right*), the *cumulative curve* for the same analysis, constructed by plotting the cumulative percentages against grades; the broken curve represents a well-sorted sand; note that the horizontal scales are logarithmic.

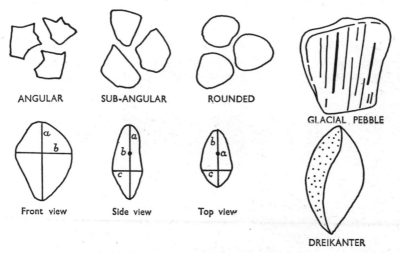

Fig. 147. Shapes of grains and pebbles; *a*, *b*, *c*, are length, breadth, thickness, *a* is perpendicular to *b*, *c* is perpendicular to the plane containing *a* and *b*.

$b/a > 2/3$, $c/b < 2/3$ gives 'discs'
$b/a > 2/3$, $c/b > 2/3$ gives 'spheres'
$b/a < 2/3$, $c/b < 2/3$ gives 'blades'
$b/a < 2/3$, $c/b > 2/3$ gives 'rods'.

249

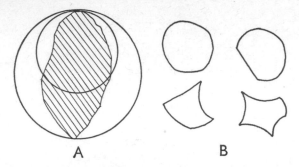

A   B

FIG. 148. A, Sphericity; B, Roundness as a function of convex, concave and plane surfaces.

important criterion for the origin of a sediment: certain modern beach-gravels have a sphericity of 0·71–0·76 (Pettijohn, Flinn).

A grain-shape of particular interest and one we have already met is the *oolitic* form (Fig. 149). It will be recalled that an oolite is a spherical or ellipsoidal grain of calcite made up of successive coatings deposited around a nucleus as it was trundled between tide-marks on a tropical beach in water saturated with calcium carbonate. *Pisolites* are larger grains, often bean- or disc-shaped, formed especially around calcareous springs.

The arrangement in space of the constituent particles of a sedimentary rock provides its *fabric*. In some rocks this fabric has a pattern given by a *preferred orientation* of grains or pebbles. Plates of clay-minerals or flakes of detrital micas are deposited so that they lie

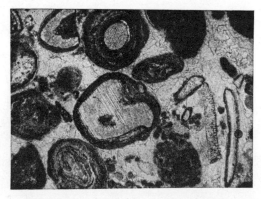

FIG. 149. Oolitic texture in a thin slice of Colwall Limestone, Malvern, × 15.

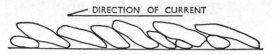

FIG. 150. Imbricate fabric in pebbles.

parallel to one another. Pebbles transported by current-action often come to rest overlapping like tiles on a roof and so giving an indication of the direction of the current responsible; this *imbricate texture* is illustrated in Fig. 150. Long axes of non-spherical pebbles are often aligned in the direction of the operative currents. Observations on grain- or pebble-orientation are graphically displayed by plotting the position of, say, the longest axis on equiareal polar co-ordinate paper or a Schmidt net. Clustering of dots in the diagram indicates the degree and attitude of any preferred orientation, as illustrated in Fig. 151 which deals with the fabric of a boulder-clay.

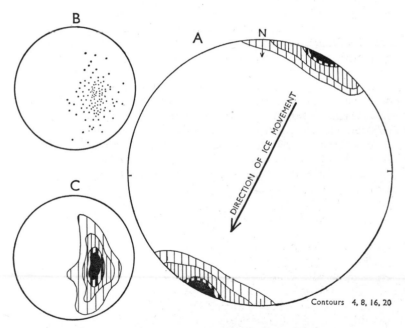

FIG. 151. A, Till fabric; preferred orientation of boulders in a New York boulder-clay (after C. D. Holmes). B, and C, explanation of the contouring of a stereographic plot (see also FIGS. 38 and 39), B, projections of long axes of a group of objects, C, the same contoured by counting the percentage of the points in unit areas of the diagram.

Structure

The most important structures of the sedimentary rocks are *bedding* and the *bedding-plane*. The character of the bedding of a sedimentary rock may reveal the circumstance and environment in which the sediment was deposited. Moreover, bedding-planes are formed more or less horizontal so that their final attitude may record any later deformation that the beds have undergone. Bedding and the bedding-plane are thus of fundamental importance in stratigraphical and structural geology.

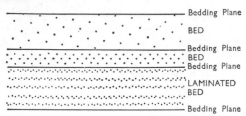

Fig. 152. Beds and bedding planes.

A *bed* (Fig. 152) represents the product of a single act of sedimentation. Many beds were built up from the bottom on a flat floor and have a flattish, practically horizontal, upper surface. A bed is thus a sheet of sedimentary material of very great extension in comparison to its thickness, and is bounded top and bottom by *bedding-planes*. The upper bedding-plane marks a pause, of varying duration, in the sedimentation at that place; during this pause, the upper surface may be hardened, dried, cracked or marked in some way so that it comes to form a sharp separation-plane from the next younger bed laid down on it. This next bed cannot be absolutely identical with the one below it so that, as sedimentation continues, a succession of individualised beds is built up giving a *stratification* to the series. A collection of beds of one general lithological type is called a *formation*; examples are the Chalk, Wenlock Limestone, Lingula Flags.

A bed may show a number of laminae of slightly different characters due to minor fluctuations in the supply and nature of the sediment. These *laminations* (Fig. 152) are usually parallel to the bounding bedding-planes of their bed.

Bedding is of four main types, *regular bedding*, *current bedding*, *graded bedding and slump-bedding*, all illustrated in Fig. 153. *Regular beds* are separated by parallel bedding-planes and their laminations are parallel to these planes. *Current-bedding* has already been mentioned in connection with wind-processes and delta-building and its

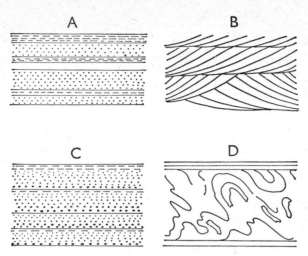

FIG. 153. Types of bedding; A, regular bedding; B, current-bedding; C, graded bedding; D, slump bedding.

manner of formation explained. Its geometry is controlled by two sets of planes, depositional and erosional. The curved *deposition-planes* separate the successive laminae of deposition and are inclined down-current so that, under favourable circumstances, the directions of the *palaeocurrents* can be determined (Fig. 154). In their complete form, deposition laminae are sigmoid in cross-section, but their upper portions are often truncated by *erosion-planes* on which the next current-bedded deposit is laid down. This contrast of asymptotic bottom and truncated top provides a valuable means of determining the original stratigraphical order in disturbed or overturned beds, as we illustrate later.

In *graded bedding* (see Fig. 129), the size of the grains making the bed varies regularly from coarse at the bottom to fine at the top and thus provides another method of determining the 'way-up' of a bed. Graded bedding commonly results from the settling through deep water of vast quantities of detritus brought there by turbidity-currents operating on an unstable submarine slope, as explained on p. 216. The movement of sediment-laden water in turbidity-currents produces various *sole-markings* on the lower bedding-plane of the graded bed. These are preserved as casts on the bottom of the bed; examples of such erosional markings are illustrated in Fig. 155. They provide another way of determining the palaeocurrent direction, since they are aligned parallel to the responsible current-flow. Graded beds of another kind are the varves described on p. 186.

253

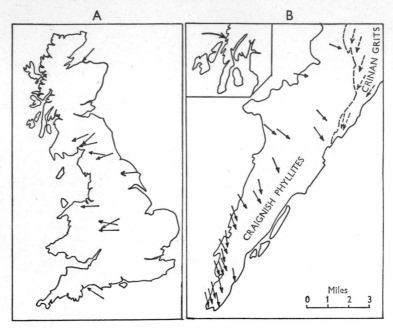

FIG. 154. Palaeocurrents. A, direction of winds during the New Red
Sandstone period as determined from current bedding observations in
dune sandstones (after Shotton; see also p. 647). B, directions of water
currents at two horizons in the Dalradian rocks of south-west
Scotland (after Knill); broken arrows show the direction of flow of
turbidity currents.

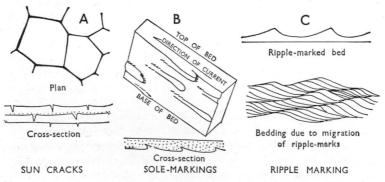

FIG. 155. A, suncracks; B, sole-markings, as casts on the base of the
bed; C, ripple mark.

254

In *slump-bedding* or, better, *slump-structure*, the bedding is disturbed in various ways by the sliding of incoherent masses of mixed sediments on the sea-floor. Layers of different sediments become broken-up, folded into one another and often complexly mixed. Slump-sheets are often associated with graded beds and both structures can be attributed to instability in the environment of sedimentation.

Two minor structures appearing on bedding-planes may be recalled. *Ripple-mark* is produced on the surface of a suitable sediment when the current of air or water passing over it reaches a certain speed and begins to move the grains of the sediment. The ripple-mark is made of long subparallel ridges running roughly at right angles to the current-direction. The ratio of length to amplitude of the marks is called the *ripple-index* and is held to be characteristic in value for water or wind-made ripple-marks (Fig. 155). All fossil ripple-marks are considered to have been produced by water-currents. The last structures that need be mentioned are *sun-cracks* due to shrinkage of the surface portion of a deposit with the formation of polygons separated by shallow cracks (Fig. 155).

LITHIFICATION AND DIAGENESIS

Lithification is the process of conversion of sediments into sedimentary rocks, rocks here being used in its popular sense as something hard and solid. Many of the processes of *diagenesis* lead to lithification. Diagenesis itself may be defined as comprising all those changes that take place in a sediment near the earth's surface at low temperature and pressure and without crustal movement being directly involved. It continues the history of the sediment immediately after its deposition and, with increasing temperature and pressure, it passes into metamorphism.

The main diagenetic processes are such physical operations as dewatering, compaction and welding, and chemical operations such as desalting, recrystallisation, cementation, formation of concretions and replacement. Physical and chemical operations are of course often not sharply separated.

Many sediments when deposited contain great quantities of water, this water being that which we have already called *connate* (p. 149); some of the Mississippi muds have over 60 per cent of pore-space filled with water. Such water may contain dissolved and colloidal matter. Pressure of the overlying layers of sediment expels most of the connate water — this *dewatering* decreases the pore-space and leads to hardening and *compaction* of the sediment. In suitable

12

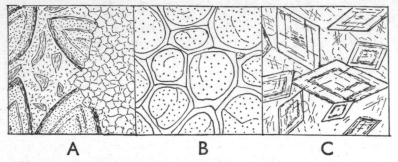

A   B   C

Fig. 156. Diagenesis. A, recrystallisation with destruction of original organic textures in a limestone; B, outgrowths of new silica on original grains of quartz in the Penrith Sandstone, Cumberland, England; C, dolomitisation of a calcite limestone.

sediments, such as the muds, *welding* of the particles enhances the degree of lithification.

Chemical processes go on in the sediment by the activity of solutions, either native to the sediment or introduced from its immediate neighbourhood. Some of these processes have already been described in connection with groundwater (p. 145). Changes take place that depend of course on the nature of the sediment. In the first place, marine sediments *lose their salt* by leaching — marine rocks contain no sodium chloride as such. In the presence of connate water and under slightly increased temperature and pressure, a sediment of suitable composition may *recrystallise*; thus, recrystallisation of the calcite making an accumulation of shelly debris may lead to the production of a coarse crystalline limestone with the disappearance of all evidence for the organic nature of the original material (Fig. 156A). In the hydrolysates, the clays, it is likely that much of the material is deposited in the colloidal state; on diagenesis, this crystallises as discrete clay-minerals, often with varying amounts of potassium replacing the aluminium in their structure.

Cementation, already noted in connection with groundwater, is an important process of lithification, the deposition of the cement in the pore-spaces of a loose sediment converting it into a hard rock. The chief cementing materials, deposited from solutions traversing the pervious sediments, are calcite and other carbonates, silica and iron hydrates. Cementation obviously decreases the porosity of the rock, as already illustrated in Fig. 76.

During diagenesis, minerals styled *authigenic* are produced by 'growth on the spot' (Pettijohn). Chief among these minerals are quartz, carbonates, feldspars, clay-minerals, chlorite, gypsum, anhydrite, barytes and pyrite — these occur often as sizeable crystals sporadically distributed in a rock of different composition. *Secondary outgrowths* in optical continuity with primary grains are illustrated by the quartzes in the Penrith Sandstone of Cumberland (Fig. 156B).

As was noted in the previous chapter when the operations of groundwater were dealt with, another result of the movement of solutions through a porous rock is the production of *concretions* (Fig. 86). Material evenly distributed in small amount through a rock may be concentrated by solution and redeposition to give practically pure nodules or lumps. *Replacement* may take place in the formation of concretions as illustrated by the preservation in flint of a fossil shell originally made of calcite. Replacement is indicated, too, in the retention of bedding-planes passing undisturbed through concretions. An important operation of replacement is *dolomitisation*, the conversion of calcite into dolomite, $CaCO_3.MgCO_3$, a process beginning in the sea and continuing during diagenesis (Fig. 156c).

Water moving through a sediment or sedimentary rock may dissolve certain mineral constituents. Thus, a calcareous sand may be *decalcified* and in a similar way fossils made of calcite may disappear from a once fossiliferous rock.

THE PSEPHITES: GRAVEL, CONGLOMERATE, BRECCIA, TILLITE

The psephitic or coarse detrital rocks are characterised by the dominance of pebbles over 2 mm. in size — the pebbles are usually much bigger and may reach feet across. Two main classes may be distinguished (1) the *conglomerates* with rounded pebbles and (2) the *breccias* with angular pebbles; a third rock-type, boulder-clay or tillite, is described here for convenience.

Conglomerates. Conglomerates are gravels, the pebbles of which are bound together by finer material or by a cement such as silica, calcium carbonate or ferruginous compounds (Fig. 157). The nature of the pebbles depends on the rocks from which they were originally derived and upon the history and geological setting of the area of their deposition. We can separate two groups of differing geological significance, the *oligomict conglomerates* and the *polymict conglomerates*.

The *oligomict conglomerates* are formed mainly of pebbles of a single obdurate rock such as quartz, quartzite or chert, that are well rounded and usually small in size; these rocks are well-sorted deposits — therefore *monomodal* with one dominant grain-size — and of no great thickness. They are typical of shore-lines of seas advancing slowly on the land. They represent a *stable* deposit, in that nothing much

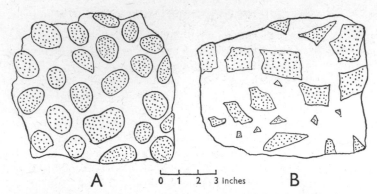

A   0   1   2   3 inches   B

Fig. 157. Psephites. A, conglomerate of rounded flint pebbles in a siliceous matrix; B, breccia of angular flint pebbles in a siliceous matrix.

chemically or physically can happen to them in their own environment.

The *polymict conglomerates* have large and small pebbles of a mixture of rocks, many of unstable types such as limestones and coarse igneous rocks. The pebbles are not well rounded and show a variety of grain-sizes — the rocks are therefore said to be *polymodal*. The matrix between the pebbles consists of unsorted angular grains of rocks similar to those making the pebbles. Since the pebbles could still undergo a considerable amount of physical and chemical change, polymict conglomerates are *unstable*. These conglomerates occur in thick beds, often intercalated with sandstones of a type similar to their matrix, and are clearly formed by rapid deposition of material denuded from nearby high mountains. They can be exemplified by the conglomerates of the Old Red Sandstone of Scotland.

Breccias. The angularity of the pebbles of breccias shows that their material cannot have moved far. Indeed, the parent material of many sedimentary breccias is *scree*. As an example we may give the North of England rock locally called *brockram*, made up of angular fragments of limestone in a sandy matrix and representing a consolidated scree of Permian age. Slumping, as we have seen, may give rise to breccias — *slump-breccias* — and many of the rocks called *pebbly mudstones* belong here.

Boulder-clay or tillite. Boulder-clay or till (p. 232) differs from the ordinary psephitic rock by having relatively few pebbles scattered through an unbedded fine-grained matrix (Fig. 158). As we have already noted, the pebbles often have a characteristic shape — the facetted flat-iron — and occasionally, but not always, show scratches on their surfaces. The grade-size of till components varies from that

258

FIG. 158. Boulder-clay, Harlech, North Wales.

of large blocks down to that of the finest rock-flour; the distribution of sizes agrees with that found in the products experimentally yielded by crushing and grinding operations. The boulders often show a *till-fabric* (Fig. 151), with their longest axes preferentially aligned in the direction of ice-movement and their shortest axes perpendicular to the floor over which the ice has passed. The composition of boulders and matrix depends of course on the rocks eroded by the ice; in many tills the matrix is essentially ground-up raw unweathered rock.

Tillite is hardened consolidated boulder-clay and is represented by thick deposits formed at various times in geological history. It shows random blocks of many sizes and materials in a ground-mass that is often recrystallised and, on occasion, highly modified by metamorphism.

259

THE PSAMMITES: SAND, SANDSTONE, GREYWACKE, ARKOSE

The psammites are the medium-grained detrital rocks, with grains less than 2 mm. in diameter and going down to $\frac{1}{16}$ mm. Their dominant component is naturally quartz and the term sand almost automatically means a quartz-sand. Detrital rocks of the specified grain-size may of course be formed of other components such as calcite, gypsum or snow — but these rocks should have the appropriate prefix in their names. Some psammites contain notable amounts of feldspar or lesser amounts of such minerals as micas or clay-minerals or, under special conditions, concentrations of heavy minerals such as magnetite, zircon, garnet and so forth.

The same classification can be applied to the psammites as to the psephites, and for the same genetic reasons. Two main classes are therefore separable:

OLIGOMICT: sand quartz-sand, sandstone, orthoquartzite — stable deposits, mature and well-sorted.

POLYMICT: grit, greywacke, arkose — unstable deposits, immature and badly sorted.

The chief members of these classes are now described and their variants briefly mentioned.

Sandstones. The oligomict *sands* are predominantly made up of quartz grains which are usually moderately or well rounded and well sorted — as was to be expected from their origin by prolonged chemical and mechanical decay along the margins of shallow seas. The obdurate quartz-grains represent the stable product and can survive several cycles of re-working. Consistent with their environment of deposition, the sands often show well-developed current-bedding.

The original almost pure quartz-sands are converted into *quartzitic sandstones* or *orthoquartzites* by cementation of various kinds (Fig. 159). The commonest cement is *silica*, others are calcite and, more rarely, dolomite.

Other 'sandstones', not necessarily belonging by origin to the oligomict class, that may be mentioned for completeness are the following. *Feldspathic sandstones* contain a small amount of feldspar grains; *micaceous sandstones* show the collection of mica plates on narrowly spaced bedding-planes — the rock readily splits along these planes and is accordingly called a *flagstone*; *greensands* include a variable content of the green mineral *glauconite* (p. 116).

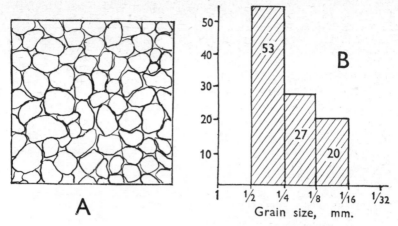

FIG. 159. A, Orthoquartzite; quartz grains with cement of calcite;
B, Histogram of typical orthoquartzite.

Other varieties of sandstone are characterised by some particular cementing material as in the common *ferruginous sandstones*, yellow, red or green in colour according to their iron hydrate cement, and the rarer sandstones cemented by barytes, fluorspar or gypsum. Finally we may mention *millet-seed sandstone* produced by wind-action, and *ganister*, a fine-grained sandstone made up of angular quartz-grains cemented by silica and used as a refractory material (p. 137).

Greywackes. In contrast to the pure oligomict sandstones, the *polymict greywackes* are badly sorted deposits, polymodal, with angular fragments of minerals and rocks bonded together by interstitial finer, and still unsorted, material of the same kind. This matrix is readily reconstituted to form sericite and chlorite. Many of the fragments of the greywackes are of unstable minerals such as the feldspars or ferromagnesian silicates or of rocks, and the greywackes are obviously the result of the rapid deposition, often by the agency of turbidity-currents, of incompletely sorted and weathered material.

Greywacke is a rather fine-grained, often dense, compact rock, dark grey in colour, and often showing graded bedding (Fig. 160). The variety of the constituent grains, their angular shapes and lack of sorting can often be determined in the hand-specimen. *Grit* is an old rock-name best applied nowadays to coarse greywackes in which the angular constituent grains are easily recognisable.

Arkoses. *Arkoses* (Fig. 160) are quite different rocks from the greywackes, both in lithology and origin. They are coarse rocks, pinkish or pale grey in colour, made up dominantly of quartz and

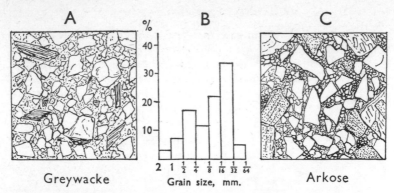

FIG. 160. A, greywacke; B, histogram of typical greywacke; C,
arkose. Angular grains of quartz (clear), feldspar (dotted) and of rocks.

feldspar, the latter often amounting to one-third or more of the whole. These constituents are moderately well-sorted and often partially rounded. Together with mica flakes, they are cemented in a ferruginous or calcitic cement. Current-bedding of a torrential type is often present.

Arkoses are associated with analogous polymict conglomerates to make great thicknesses of strata clearly formed by the rapid erosion and deposition of uplifted lands containing much granite exposed at their surface. Most typical arkoses are terrestrial, being deposited as coalescing alluvial fans by streams issuing from high mountains.

In a later page, the three contrasted psammitic rocks, ortho-quartzite, greywacke and arkose, will be related more closely to their geological position both of time and place.

THE PELITES: MUD, CLAY, SHALE

The pelites are the finest-grained detrital rocks, the constituents of which belong to several categories but agree in being less than say $\frac{1}{16}$ mm. in size. These constituents are first, the newly-formed clay-minerals — sheet-lattice hydrated aluminium silicates — resulting from the decay of the less stable components of the original rocks, second, the true inherited material represented by very fine pieces of quartz with less abundant feldspar and mica and, third, new minerals such as iron hydroxides, quartz, hydromicas, sericitic and chloritic minerals produced by the crystallisation of colloidal material or by diagenetic reconstructions of allied material.

It will be recalled that the important clay-minerals are: kaolinite, $Al_4Si_4O_{10}.(OH)_8$, montmorillonite, $Al_4(Si_4O_{10})_2.2H_2O$ and illite, $K_yAl_4(Si_{8-y}Al_y)O_{20}.(OH)_4$ and the hydromicas generally. It is considered that each of these dominated the mud deposited in a particular environment — as, for example, kaolinite in fresh-water continental deposits, and hydromicas in lagoonal and marine deposits. But since the clay-minerals easily undergo diagenetic changes and since, moreover, they can hardly be distinguished by ordinary microscopic methods of investigation, it is sufficient for our purpose to consider them simply as clay-minerals.

As we have seen, *muds* when deposited contain a great deal of water. When the mud is covered by succeeding layers, some of this water is squeezed out and the rock becomes compacted and partially reconstituted into clay. *Clay* forms a fine-grained structureless mass, white when pure but usually coloured brown, grey, green, red or black, the colour depending upon the presence of iron compounds or carbonaceous material. It has a characteristic smell, and absorbs water to become plastic. As more water is squeezed out and further compaction and reconstruction take place, the clay passes through structureless *mudstone* into laminated *shale*. In shale, a finely laminated structure parallel to the bedding-planes of the rock produces a fissility in this direction.

A few special varieties of pelites may be mentioned. *Oil-shale* is a black or brown shale, which gives a curved shaving when cut with a knife. It contains natural hydrocarbons and is mined in the Midland Valley of Scotland as a raw material for crude oil and ammonia. Many clays contain concretions of pyrite, FeS_2, which readily decompose to give sulphuric acid — this reacting with sericitic mica in the shales produces alum $KAl(SO_4)_2.12H_2O$, to give *alum-shales* as in the Jurassic rocks of Yorkshire. *Fuller's Earth* is a clay, containing a large amount of montmorillonite, which falls to powder in water; it is used in the refining of oils and fats, a use depending upon the absorbent qualities of the sheet-lattice components. *Black shales* are rich in organic matter and in pyrite, and are usually exceedingly finely laminated, giving *paper-shales*; they are derived from muds deposited in partially enclosed basins, such as the Black Sea of today, under conditions of oxygen-deficiency so that organic material is preserved and sulphides remain unoxidised (p. 202). *Fireclays* occur below coal-seams and are regarded as old soils, 'seat-earths', from which the plants providing the raw materials for the coal have extracted their food — the seat-earth has thereby been deprived of alkalies, lime and magnesia and in many cases is now a valuable refractory material. Fireclay is a grey unbedded clay, frequently containing rootlets, and is composed mostly of clay-minerals with some quartz. *Silts* are rich in very fine particles of inherited minerals such as quartz.

Pelites are of course transitional to other lithological types and names such as *semi-pelite* have been given to some of the transitional rocks. *Marl* is a calcareous shale or clay, with an admixture of calcium carbonate, *clay-ironstone* (p. 269) is rich in siderite, Fe_2CO_3, *siliceous shale* in silica. These rocks, together with the black shales, provide examples of transitions to the chemical-organic class of sedimentary rocks next described.

THE CARBONATE ROCKS: LIMESTONE, SHELL SAND, LIME MUD, DOLOMITE

The carbonates concerned in these rocks are calcite, $CaCO_3$, and dolomite, $CaCO_3.MgCO_3$, calcite being the main component of the limestones and dolomite of the rock of the same name. The calcium carbonate brought in solution into the lakes or the sea is utilised by organisms for the construction of their shells or skeletons and most of the raw material of limestones is primarily of organic origin. Limestones due to the direct precipitation of calcite from solutions are relatively rare. As a result of organic activities, magnesium is dominant over calcium in sea-water, few organisms having any notable amount of magnesium carbonate in their shells. Likewise, primary deposits of dolomite of chemical origin are scanty. Most dolomite-rock is secondary in origin due, as was mentioned under diagenesis, to replacement by dolomite mineral of original calcite limestones, the magnesium carbonate being derived primarily from sea-water.

In addition to their dominant carbonate constituents, limestones and dolomites have varying amounts of detrital material, such as quartz-grains and clay-particles, which provide passages to the psammitic and pelitic rocks.

All the *limestones* (Fig. 161) agree in being made mostly of calcite but they show an immense variety depending on the sources of the calcite. In some limestones, such as the reef-limestones, the calcite is provided by shells and skeletons of organisms accumulating where these grew; in others such material has been mechanically transported and deposited like any other detrital particles and in all limestones a great deal of precipitation and reprecipitation of the soluble calcite has gone on. All three sources have contributed in varying degrees to make the limestones.

The *reef-limestones* are not composed mainly of coral material but are usually of mixed organic ingredients of which lime-secreting algae provide the dominant part. These limestones form mounds of unbedded, often cavernous, rock flanked by well-bedded limestone,

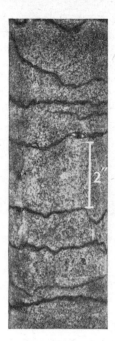

A

B

FIG. 161. A, Organic limestone, polished slab showing fragments of crinoids in a calcareous matrix. B, Stylolites in limestone, ascribed to differential solution at original plane surfaces, with the concentration of insoluble residues along the interlocking margins.

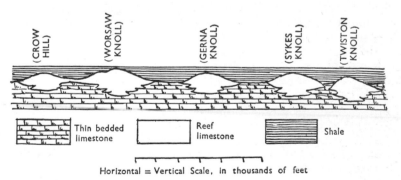

Horizontal = Vertical Scale, in thousands of feet

Fig. 162. Reef knolls in Carboniferous Limestone, Clitheroe, Lancashire (based on Parkinson).

265

in the manner shown in Fig. 162. Such *reef-knolls* or *bioherms* are often reservoirs for oil, but in many examples the reef-rock has been cemented by the deposition of new calcite and hence its porosity has been lowered. From their origin, bioherms are often richly fossiliferous, in contrast to their flanking limestones deposited in deeper, less hospitable, water. *Algal limestones*, produced by the activity of lime-secreting water-plants, are prominent members of many limestone formations such as, for example, the Carboniferous Limestone of Britain. Other limestones may be formed dominantly of the remains of one particular animal — whether these have been transported or not — and are then given the appropriate name such as *shelly limestone, coral limestone, crinoidal limestone, Productus limestone, echinoderm limestone, Trigonia limestone* and so forth. Foraminifera contribute very largely to some limestones, such as the *Nummulitic Limestone* of the Mediterranean region of which the Pyramids were made. Another limestone that can be considered here is *chalk*, a soft white fine-grained rather friable rock composed of tests of the foraminifera *Globigerina*, coccoliths, sponge spicules and radiolaria skeletons — these two last made of silica — set in a fine calcite-mud. Chalk occurs in thick beds in the Cretaceous (*creta* = chalk) rocks of Europe.

The detrital limestones, formed by the deposition of mechanically transported shelly debris, can be compared to the detrital muds, sands and gravels, in so far as their raw materials are concerned. *Lithographic stone* is a consolidated calcite-mud, with an exceedingly fine and even grain. Coarser limestones are partially or completely cemented shell-sands or shell-fragments, the calcite being often deposited in optical continuity with that of the fragments. Many of the limestones already named are partly of this detrital origin. Since limestones are important reservoir-rocks for oil, the amount of their cement is a fundamental property.

Oolites and *pisolites* have been described earlier in this chapter when the shapes of grains of sediments were being discussed. The *oolitic limestones* are some of the most important building stones; in Britain examples are the Bath Stone and Portland Stone, white or cream even-grained rocks. It will be recalled that oolites appear to require a rather special mechanism for their formation (p. 211). Other *chemical limestones* are not of much account; they include deposits from calcareous springs, such as *pisolite, tufa* and *travertine*, and from other waters charged with calcium bicarbonate that give the *stalactites* and *stalagmites* of limestone caves already described (p. 146). Of these chemical limestones, *travertine* alone has any industrial importance; it is a cream-coloured rock, porous and cellular in structure, and is quarried in Italy for use in interior building. Some of the tufa-deposits are beautifully banded by impurities or inclusions and then supply the decorative stone known as '*onyx marble*'.

As already noted, the calcite of limestones may be mixed with varying amounts of other components, mostly of detrital origin, and thus provide types intermediate to other rocks. These transitional varieties receive appropriate names such as *sandy, clayey* or *argillaceous, bituminous, phosphatic* or *ferruginous* limestones. *Stinkstone* or *fetid limestone* has a small content of sulphuretted hydrogen which becomes obvious when the rock is hammered.

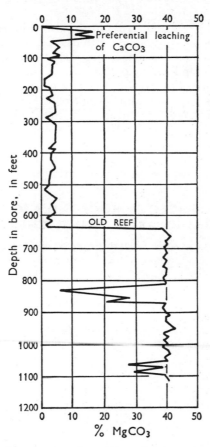

Fig. 163. *The Funafuti Bore:* variation of $MgCO_3$ content with depth.

Dolomite, as already noted, is rarely a primary deposit and all important developments of the rock are the result of replacement of calcite limestones by the double carbonate, dolomite, $CaCO_3.MgCO_3$. This replacement is performed by the reaction of the magnesian salts contained in sea-water with the calcium carbonate. By it, the primary structures and textures of the limestone are more or less obliterated, fossil shells are destroyed and large-scale crystallisation of dolomite mineral, often in rhomb-forms, takes place (Fig. 156c). Many reef-limestones have been dolomitised and, since a reduction in volume of over 12 per cent takes place during the process, such dolomite reefs become still more suitable as potential reservoir rocks for oil.

A classic example of the replacement of calcite by dolomite is provided by the cores obtained in the deep boring on the atoll of Funafuti and investigated by Judd (p. 215). The variation in the amount of magnesium carbonate with depth in the bore is shown in Fig. 163. The enrichment in magnesium carbonate near the surface can be attributed to the leaching out of calcium carbonate; the sudden change at a depth of nearly 700 feet to almost pure dolomite may indicate that the upper coral-rock is built on an older dolomitised reef.

Dolomite is a massive granular saccharoidal rock, whitish when pure but more often coloured yellow, buff or brown by iron carbonate — *ankerite* is a transitional form between dolomite and siderite, $FeCO_3$. *Magnesian limestone* contains up to 10 per cent dolomite molecule which is held in solid solution in the calcite.

THE SILICEOUS ROCKS: DIATOMITE, RADIOLARITE, FLINT, CHERT

The siliceous rocks of non-clastic origin comprise a number of types in which chemical or organic processes are involved in different ratios. First, we may consider the definitely organic siliceous rocks, *diatomite* and *radiolarite*, made up respectively of accumulations of the opaline tests of the algae diatoms, and the siliceous frameworks of radiolaria. *Diatomite* (p. 184) is a soft friable rock, white, yellow or grey in colour, and very light in weight; it occurs in beds deposited on the floors of lakes, being especially abundant where nearby volcanoes have supplied siliceous solutions for prolific diatom growth. *Radiolarite* or *radiolarian earth* is an accumulation of the skeletons of radiolaria, similar in appearance to diatomite. A second type of siliceous rock is *siliceous sinter*, of chemical origin, deposited around the orifices of geysers and, on that account, sometimes called *geyserite*; it is a loose, porous usually pale-coloured rock.

The most important of the siliceous rocks are *flint* and *chert*, the origin of which is a subject for much discussion. *Flint* is compact, cryptocrystalline silica of a black colour or various shades of grey, breaking with a conchoidal fracture and affording sharp cutting-edges. *Chert* resembles flint in appearance but breaks with a more or less flat fracture, rather different from that of flint. We may mention also *jasper*, an impure opaque form of cryptocrystalline silica usually red, brown or yellow in colour. Flint and chert occur as nodules, sheets or bands in limestones such as the Chalk and the Carboniferous Limestone. The discussion on their origin is concerned with whether they are syngenetic or epigenetic, that is whether they were formed at the same time as the rocks associated with them or later. As an example of the evidence, we may consider the flint occurring in the English Chalk; Hawkins (personal communication) has found flint showing impressions of the *soft* parts of echinoderms and therefore likely to be syngenetic as a silica gel on the sea-floor of the time; but much flint replaces calcite fossil-shells or coats vertical joint-planes traversing the chalk and must therefore be an epigenetic replacement. Much chert, but not all, is considered to be of replacement origin. The debate continues: it is likely that some flint is deposited as a syngenetic gel, some collected as later concretions, some transported in solution and redeposited, and some the result of replacement of limestones by silica. As so often in geology, there is no unique answer to any given problem.

THE FERRUGINOUS ROCKS: CARBONATES, SILICATES, OXIDES, SULPHIDES

Red and green sandstones cemented by iron hydroxides have already been mentioned, but the rocks now to be considered contain much more iron and indeed furnish the bulk of industrial iron ore. These iron-bearing sedimentary rocks (Fig. 164) can be dealt with according to their dominant iron-mineral but, of course, mixtures of the different minerals are abundant. The groups are those characterised by (1) iron carbonate, (2) hydrated iron silicate, (3) iron oxides and hydroxides and (4) iron sulphides.

Iron carbonate, siderite, $FeCO_3$, makes beds and concretions of differing degrees of purity formed by primary precipitation, especially in the Coal Measures of Western Europe and America. *Clay-ironstone* is an impure variety of sideritic rock, brownish due to alteration, and *blackband ironstone* consists of a mixture of siderite, iron oxides and sand, clay and coal in varying proportions — it is black in colour. These rocks are dense and compact, and rather heavy as sedimentary rocks go. The great Lake Superior iron-ore deposits were most likely

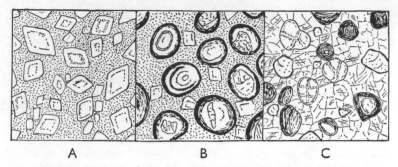

A	B	C

FIG. 164. *Ferruginous Rocks.* A, Chamosite mudstone with rhombs
of siderite; B, Oolites of chamosite, zoned with magnetite and with
siderite nuclei, in a base of chamositic mudstone and siderite
rhombs; C, Glauconitic ironstone, grains of fresh and altered glauconite and of quartz, cemented by siderite.

originally bedded siderite rocks that have been altered and metamorphosed to iron oxides; the primary source of the iron is a subject of
discussion, especially as to whether or not contemporary volcanism
made a contribution. A second group of siderite rocks results from
the replacement of an original limestone by iron carbonate, often
with the preservation of original textures, as in some oolitic siderites.
Such replacement is an example of *metasomatism* (p. 504).

The most important of the *hydrated iron silicates* making the
sedimentary rocks is *chamosite* ($Fe_3Al_2Si_2O_{16}.Aq.$). This silicate,
mixed with other iron-minerals, especially siderite, and with sand
and mud, forms ironstones typified by the Jurassic iron-ores of the
English Midlands. These rocks are chamosite mudstones and
chamosite-siderite mudstones, interbedded with siderite mudstones
and sideritic limestones, and associated with limonitic and hematitic
rocks. The chamosite makes a fine-grained ground-mass in which
siderite appears as rhombs or aggregates. It is considered by some
that the chamosite is of primary sedimentary origin, oolites of this
mineral being formed in exactly the same way as the more common
calcite oolites; others hold that both the chamosite and siderite in
these rocks are replacements of primary calcite.

Glauconite, dominantly a hydrous silicate of iron and potassium,
occurs abundantly in certain sandstones, the *greensands*, and may be
present in sufficient amount to constitute a *glauconite ironstone*.

Among the oxide-hydroxide group of iron-bearing sediments may
be mentioned *hematite-oolites* and *limonite-oolites*, presumably of
original precipitation origin. *Bog iron-ore*, composed of limonite in
varying admixture with clayey material, is deposited in marshes and
lakes as nodules, lumps and lenticular beds.

The *iron sulphides*, marcasite and pyrite, of sedimentary origin, occur disseminated in many sedimentary rocks. In special environments, as for example that of the black-shale deposition already noted on p. 263, iron sulphide may become concentrated into aggregates and lenticular beds.

THE ALUMINOUS ROCKS: BAUXITE AND LATERITE

When we considered the residual deposits of weathering in the previous chapter, we dealt particularly with *bauxite* and *laterite*, the residual clays enriched in aluminium and ferric hydroxides, that are widespread in the present-day humid tropics (p. 134). It was noted that whilst many bauxite-laterites were the result of tropical weathering carried to completion, others were believed to be enriched in FeAl hydroxides drawn up from below or carried down from above, whilst the classic French deposits were considered to have been formed by heated volcanic waters. The AlFe deposits, like many others, may arise in different ways.

There is no need to repeat here the descriptions of bauxite and laterite, their chemical compositions, their mineralogy and variations that have already been provided (p. 134). Laterite, if sufficiently rich in iron, is mined as an iron-ore, as in Guinea; elsewhere in the tropics it is used as building-material or road-metal. Bauxite is the principal ore of aluminium. Deposits formed in modern times occur in the tropical regions of Africa, India and America. Other mined bauxite-deposits are much older, such as those of Russia, France (Les Baux from which the name bauxite is derived) and the southern United States. It may be mentioned here that workable deposits of hydrated oxides of manganese are associated with laterites in India, Brazil, Ghana and Arkansas. Manganese-bearing minerals of the bedrocks are decomposed in the same way as the iron-bearing minerals, but partial separation of the two products takes place because of their different affinities for oxygen.

THE PHOSPHATIC ROCKS: PHOSPHORITE

The phosphatic sedimentary rocks derive their phosphate content from organic sources; the organs of many animals and their bones and teeth contain varying amounts of calcium phosphate and their excrementa are comparatively rich in phosphate. *Coprolites* are nodules of fossil excrement of reptiles and mammals, and *bone-beds* show a concentration of the phosphatic hard parts of animals — but these rocks are relatively unimportant. The chief phosphate rock is *phosphorite*, an earthy or compact rock, often nodular or concretionary in structure, composed of calcium phosphate, usually mixed with calcite. Phosphorite is the result of diverse processes. It may form extensive thin beds, associated with marine rocks that often indicate deposition under Black Sea conditions (p. 202), and is clearly then of primary sedimentary origin. Other phosphorite beds represent transported and redeposited material. Again, phosphorite may be of replacement-origin as demonstrated on oceanic islands where reef-limestones are replaced by phosphates leached out from the *guano* overlying them. The proportion of phosphate present in the sedimentary beds may be increased by the leaching out of the intermingled calcite.

THE SALINE ROCKS: ROCK-SALT, GYPSUM, ANHYDRITE

The production of evaporates by deposition from the brines of salt lakes and lagoons in warm arid regions has already been dealt with in detail (p. 189). It will be recalled that the order of deposition of the salts is the reverse of their solubilities and that complex modifications may take place in these soluble and reactive materials. To illustrate the succession of deposition we may use the famous Stassfurt deposits of Germany: from the top down these are:

Shales, sandstones and clays

(2) $\begin{cases} \text{Rock-salt, NaCl, variable} \\ \text{Anhydrite, } CaSO_4, \text{ 30–80 metres} \end{cases}$

Salt clay, 5–10 metres.

(1) $\begin{cases} \text{Carnallite } (KCl.MgCl_2.6H_2O) \text{ Zone, 15–40 metres,} \\ \quad \text{with kainite } (KCl.MgSO_4.3H_2O), \text{ sylvinite } (KCl), \\ \quad \text{etc.} \\ \text{Kieserite } (MgSO_4.H_2O) \text{ Zone} \\ \text{Polyhalite } (K_2SO_4.MgSO_4.2CaSO_4.2H_2O) \text{ Zone} \\ \text{Older rock-salt and anhydrite, interlayered.} \\ \text{Anhydrite and gypsum.} \end{cases}$ $\left.\begin{array}{c} \\ \\ \\ \end{array}\right\}$ BITTERNS

The chief of these minerals or rocks are now described. *Rock-salt*, NaCl, crystallises in the Cubic System, the common crystals being cubes, but as a rock it occurs massive and granular. The cleavage of rock-salt is perfect cubic, hardness 2–2·5, Sp. Gr. 2·2. When pure, it is colourless or white, but often shows yellow, reddish or purplish tints. It is readily recognised by its taste and solubility. *Anhydrite*, $CaSO_4$, is orthorhombic in crystallisation, and gives prismatic or tabular crystals but is commonly fibrous, lamellar, granular or

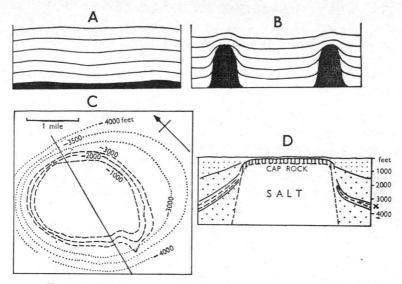

FIG. 165. *Salt Domes.* A, original position of salt bed (black) in a sedimentary series; B, salt domes produced by migration upwards of salt. C and D, Damon Mound, Texas. C, map, broken lines indicate contours on the salt, dotted lines on the index bed, x, in D; D, section.

compact. Its colour is white, often with a grey, bluish or reddish tint; its hardness is 3–3·5, specific gravity 2·93. *Gypsum*, $CaSO_4.2H_2O$, is a monoclinic mineral, common crystals being made up of prism, clinopinacoid and negative hemipyramid, often twinned; it occurs commonly in laminated, granular, compact or fibrous forms. Its cleavage is perfect parallel to the clinopinacoid, its hardness is 1·5–2, the mineral being easily scratched by the finger nail, its specific gravity is 2·3. Crystals of gypsum are colourless; the massive varieties are colourless or white, grey, yellowish or red. The bittern minerals are a matter for the specialist.

In the Stassfurt deposits, anhydrite, gypsum and rock-salt occur in very thin alternating layers which have been interpreted as annual deposits. In many saline deposits, it has been established that original anhydrite has been later patchily converted into gypsum.

Beds of salt differ from other rocks in their reaction to pressures; salt flows whilst other rocks fracture or fold when subjected to crustal movements. Salt glaciers have been described from Iran, and intrusive plugs of salt — the *salt domes* — are of great importance in the Gulf states of the United States, since they have provided the proper conditions for the accumulation of vast reservoirs of oil (Fig. 165).

273

In addition to the important saline rocks already noted, other evaporates, as noted on p. 189, are formed by deposition in salt lakes whose waters have derived a variety of substances from the rocks of their drainage areas. Among these deposits may be recalled those largely composed of *sodium sulphate*, the minerals thenardite (Na_2SO_4), mirabilite ($Na_2SO_4.10H_2O$) and glauberite ($Na_2SO_4.CaSO_4$) as in the Great Salt Lake of Utah. Other deposits are rich in *sodium carbonate*, the minerals natron ($Na_2CO_3.10H_2O$) and trona ($Na_2CO_3.NaHCO_3.2H_2O$), as in the soda-lakes of Egypt and California. *Borates*, such as borax ($Na_2B_4O_7.10H_2O$), kernite ($Na_2B_4O_7.4H_2O$), colemanite ($Ca_2B_6O_{11}.5H_2O$) and ulexite ($NaCaB_5O_9.8H_2O$) occur in the playa deposits, 'alkaline flats' and borax-marshes of California.

THE CARBONACEOUS OR HYDROCARBON ROCKS: COALS, BITUMENS

Rocks composed essentially of hydrocarbons can be considered in two easily separable groups, the coals and the bitumens — both terms being used in rather a broad sense.

COALS

The *coals* are a group of bedded rocks clearly formed by the accumulation of vegetable matter. The original plant material has been subjected in different degrees to physical and chemical modification and a *coal-series* can be established in which the various members are arranged in an order of increasing modification. This modification is, first, biochemical decay, followed by the action of heat and pressure. *Peat* can be taken as the starting point; the stages of increasing modification are represented by *lignite* and *bituminous coal* and the final stage by *anthracite*. The modification is marked chemically by the gradual elimination of volatiles and water with the consequent increase in the carbon content, and physically by increased compaction, greater hardness, loss of plant-structures and increased specific gravity. The chemical changes are essentially reduction and the coals have been called *reduzates*. Some of these changes are represented in Fig. 166; the position of a given coal in the coal-series determines its *rank*.

The description of the rocks making the coal-series can start with peat, formed at the present day as an accumulation of bog plants, especially mosses, that even when tens of feet thick still exhibits its vegetable character. By decay and reconstruction the bottom layers of a peat-bank become compacted, darkened and hardened and their carbon content is increased. *Lignite* or *brown coal* represents a further

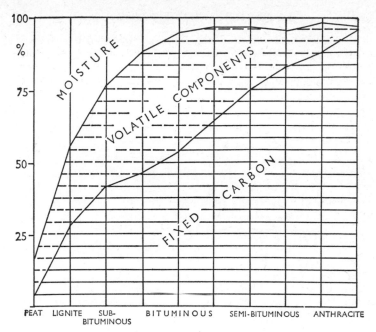

FIG. 166. *The Coal Series.*

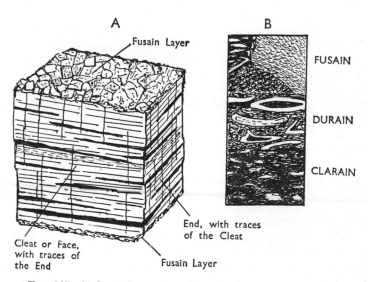

A
Fusain Layer
FUSAIN
DURAIN
CLARAIN
B
End, with traces
of the Cleat
Cleat or Face,
with traces of
the End
Fusain Layer

FIG. 167. *Coal.* A, shape of a piece of coal, determined by the fusain layers, cleat and end; B, constituent layers of coal in thin section.

275

stage in the transformation; it is brown or black in colour and though compact still shows plant fragments. It forms thick beds accumulated during recent geological periods.

Bituminous coal is exemplified by most ordinary house-coals. Most coal of this rank breaks up into pieces of a characteristic shape, roughly cuboidal (Fig. 167) and with characteristic properties. The shape is controlled by two sets of joints or planes of weakness which are roughly at right angles to one another and to the bedding of the coal, this being given by a series of parallel narrow bands of coal of differing qualities. The top and bottom bedding-planes of the piece of coal are formed by *fusain* layers, along which the coal has broken because they are soft and powdery — the fusain layers in fact make coal dirty and they soil the fingers; fusain looks like chips of charcoal and shows a cellular texture, a property permitting it to contain gas or mineral matter such as pyrite or calcite. A banded coal with many fusain layers is likely therefore to be rich in *mineral ash* and, altogether, fusain is not a desirable ingredient of coal. The other bands are seen on the joint-faces formed by the *cleat* and *end*, and are of three main kinds. The first is called the *durain* band, dull hard lustre-less coal, found in thin section to be made up of the more resistant parts of plants such as spore-cases. *Clarain* bands are brighter in appearance and are a mixture of resistant plant-debris embedded in a structureless material, like a consolidated jelly, produced by the complete decay of the vegetable matter. *Vitrain* occurs in banded coals as lenses and streaks of bright glassy-looking substance, breaking with a conchoidal fracture, and showing as gold streaks in thin sections of coal. It resembles the jellified matrix of the clarain layers.

The quality of a bituminous coal as regards its ash-content, crushing strength, size of fragments, coking-properties, gas-yield, etc. will obviously depend upon the relative abundance of the four constituents just described.

Anthracite is an unbanded type of coal, black or brownish black in colour, and does not soil the fingers. It usually has a brilliant lustre and breaks with a conchoidal fracture; its hardness may be over two in Mohs' scale and its specific gravity may reach 1·8. It is less easily kindled than other coals, burns with little flame and then gives out much heat. Coals of lower rank are found to pass laterally into anthracite as illustrated in the South Wales Coalfield (Fig. 168) and there has been considerable discussion on the origin of anthracite in particular. Assuming that all anthracite was originally of bituminous-coal rank, it is suggested that it may be due to increase of heat by intrusion of igneous rocks, folding and dislocation or greater depth of

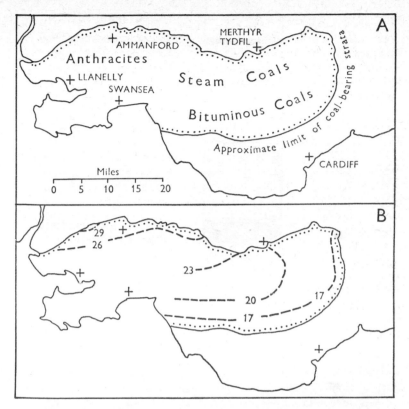

FIG. 168. Variation in rank of coal in the South Wales Coalfield.
A, general variation; B, variation in the Nine Foot Vein, expressed by
contours of equal carbon-hydrogen ratio (based on H.M. Geological
Survey).

burial. Other suggestions are that it is formed of plant-remains
originally different from those giving bituminous coal, or that the
vegetable matter has been differently sorted or has been subjected to
different degrees and styles of decomposition. The problem has not
yet been solved even in a well-explored coal-field such as that of
South Wales.

Coal occurs in beds or *seams*, averaging perhaps six feet in thickness and some extending over thousands of square miles. The seam
often forms a member of a sedimentary *rhythm* or *cyclothem*, illustrated and interpreted by an example from the British Coal Measures
in Fig. 169. The keynote of this rhythm is the slow, spasmodic subsidence of vast swamp-areas round about sea-level. From this interpretation and from the purity of coal-seams and the nature of the

277

ROCKS		INTERPRETATION
Coal seam	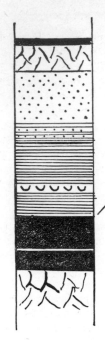	Spread of swamp forest.
Seat-earth		Basin floor built up to
(fireclay or		swamp level
ganister)		
		Warping in basin leads
Sandstone		to local rejuvenation of
		streams and transport
Shale and		of sand
sandstone bands		
Shales with		Rapid subsidence, forests
occasional		drowned by incursion of
'mussel band'		mud-laden waters,
		usually fresh
Coal seam		Steady gentle subsidence
Dirt parting		allowing accumulation of
Coal seam		great thickness of vegetable
		matter
Seat-earth		Swamp soil

FIG. 169. Coal Measure Rhythm or Cyclothem.

seat-earth on which many of them rest, it is concluded that coal is formed from vegetation that accumulated more or less where it grew — this interpretation is the *growth-in-place* theory of coal-formation.

This theory applies reasonably well to practically all coal-seams. There are, however, coals that are more reasonably considered to be the result of the accumulation of *drifted* vegetable-debris. Examples of such coals are the *cannels*. Cannel is a dense, lustreless, greyish-black coal with a conchoidal fracture. It ignites in a candle flame and burns with a smoky candle-like flame. Under the microscope, cannel is seen to be composed of spore and pollen remains with what are thought to be those of oil-bearing algae. Cannel contains a considerable amount of ash and occasionally shows fish-scales and other fossil-fragments. These characters, combined with the circumstance that it occurs in lenticular beds in bituminous coal-seams and often fills *wash-outs* or contemporaneous stream-channels in the swamp, support the interpretation of cannel as a drift-coal.

BITUMENS

The bitumens are composed of a number of hydrocarbons of which the paraffins, C_nH_{2n+2}, the naphthenes, C_nH_{2n}, and the benzenes, e.g., C_6H_6, are the chief. They vary from gases or liquid oils to solids. *Crude petroleum* is a liquid, brown or black in colour and often with a greenish tinge, and is usually lighter than water and has a characteristic odour. *Asphalt* is a brown or black pitch-like substance, soft but when solid enough having a conchoidal fracture. It occurs where oxidation of petroleum has taken place (e.g. in the Pitch Lake of Trinidad) and occasionally impregnates porous rocks to give *asphalt-rocks*. A number of other solid bitumens have been given special names, such as elaterite, ozokerite and the like, but these need not be described further. *Natural gas* is important in some oil-fields, such as the newly-discovered North Sea occurrences off Britain, and can be exploited for domestic and industrial use.

It is generally agreed that the bitumens are produced from original organic material entrapped in sediments. These *source-rocks* are the *sapropelites*, muds containing much organic matter believed to be largely of algal origin (compare cannel, p. 278) deposited in a reducing environment, like that of the present-day Black Sea (p. 202). This organic material is largely of a fatty or carbohydrate nature and is transformed into hydrocarbons by complex chemical adjustments. Under suitable conditions, the petroleum thus generated migrates into *reservoir-rocks*, such as the porous jointed or fractured sandstones and limestones, to form *oil-pools* located on favourable geological structures, domes, gentle folds etc. as illustrated later in Fig. 374.

BASIS OF A GEOLOGICAL CLASSIFICATION OF THE SEDIMENTARY ROCKS

During the foregoing description of the sedimentary rocks it will have become obvious that, besides the lithological classification employed, there could be devised another classification, on geological lines, in which the environments and conditions of sedimentation were the controlling factors. For example there are among psammites at least three types, the pure sandstones, greywackes and arkoses, indicative of different environments of sedimentation. The final nature of any sediment depends on a variety of controls, some operating in the area of sedimentation, some external thereto; relief, climate, style duration and speed of weathering, transport and deposition — all these factors and many more are significant for the final product. All these controls vary according to the place where the sedimentation occurs and to its timing in relation to events going on in the adjacent segment of the crust. Time and place provide the history of a sediment and when they enter into a classification of the sedimentary rocks the classification becomes a geological one.

K

We can use the threefold division of the psammites just recalled to illustrate the basis of the geological classification of the sedimentary rocks. We have already noted that the pure sandstones or ortho-quartzites are formed by long-continued sorting and abrasion on a stable marine platform such as that making the floor of the epicon-tinental seas. The greywackes, unsorted sediments, are deposited in deep water by turbidity-currents operating on unstable sea-floors near to regions of high relief. The arkoses for the most part are ter-restrial piedmont-deposits. Sediments of these three types can be fitted into episodes of deformation of the adjacent crust, as we shall see later. The orthoquartzites are *platform*-deposits formed on the floors of shallow seas subjected to broad warping movements; the greywackes are deposits laid down when violent movements had begun to disturb elongated basins of great sedimentation, the *geosynclines*, and the adjacent land-areas; the *arkoses* are terrestrial deposits formed on the lands raised up as the final result of distur-bance in the geosyncline. The nature of a sediment thus ultimately depends on *tectonics*, that is on the deformation of the crust viewed in connection with the movements responsible (Chapter 8).

From our lithological descriptions given in the earlier part of this chapter we can illustrate other minor and more specialised environ-ments of sedimentation, such as the shallow tropical foreshores of oolite formation, the jerkily subsiding swamps of the coals and as-sociated rocks, the foul bottoms of partially enclosed basins in which accumulated the black shales, the turbulent margins of coral-reefs, the deserts of the salt lakes, and so forth.

By the combination of geographical environments, such as those just illustrated, with the genetic or tectonic controls, there can be constructed a second, rather mixed, classification of the sedimentary rocks.

A Second Classification of the Sedimentary Rocks

(1) *Deposits of Markedly Unstable Areas*, e.g. geosynclines in their later stages.

   Greywackes, polymict conglomerates, clays with graded bedding — the unstable deposits generally.

(2) *Deposits of Relatively Stable Areas*, e.g. platforms.

   (a) *Epicontinental Seas*

   Orthoquartzite, current-bedded sandstone, oligomict conglomerates and the stable deposits generally. Lime-stones and shales.

   (b) *Restricted Basins*

   Black shales of Black Sea type.

(c) *Marginal Platforms subjected to gentle subsidence*
'Paralic' sediments typified by those of the Coal
Measure Rhythm.

(d) *The Continental Areas*
Piedmont, e:g. arkoses formed at the end of the tectonic
upheaval.
Lacustrine, e.g. lake-clays, evaporates.
Ice-sheet, tillite.
Desert, eolian sandstone, loess.

FORMS OF SEDIMENTARY ROCKS

In dealing with the structure of sedimentary rocks on an earlier page, we stated that a bed or stratum of sediment was an almost horizontal sheet bounded top and bottom by more or less parallel bedding-planes. This is an idealisation not often attained by deposits of sediment in nature; but we can conveniently still call all deposits beds since their thickness is very much less than any other of their dimensions.

The shape of a stratum depends on a number of circumstances, some of which are now dealt with. The *nature of the constituent materials*, whether detrital or chemical-organic, exerts a great influence. Coarse conglomerates are lenticular in cross-section, scree-breccias almost triangular, whilst fine sandstones extend great distances compared with their thickness and fine-grained shales and clays may be still thinner and more extensive. The *manner of deposition* is likewise of importance. We can contrast a sand-dune deposit with a sand laid down on a marine foreshore. Salt deposits will have a primary discoid shape. Reef-limestones form knolls in the surrounding regularly bedded normal limestones.

The *stability of the area of deposition* exerts a fundamental influence on the deposit, especially with regard to its thickness. The thickness of a seam of coal, for example, depends on the gentle steady subsidence of the original coal-swamp; differential jerky subsidence produces a splitting of the seam as shown for the Barnsley Bed of the Yorkshire Coal-field in Fig. 170. Differential subsidence may take place across a fault (a fracture in the beds along which displacement occurs — p. 480) and vastly different thickness of the beds may be deposited on the two sides of the dislocation (Fig. 171). Uplift of an original coal-swamp promotes *erosion* of the vegetable matter by streams so that *wash-outs* are formed that appear in the coal-seam as sandstone casts of the stream-course (Fig. 172c). Sedimentation indeed is the resultant of deposition and erosion.

Compaction of a sediment may be irregular and may lead to the

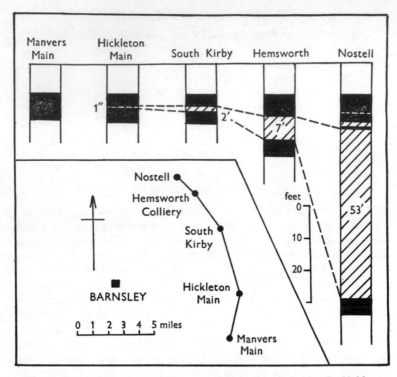

FIG. 170. Splitting of the Barnsley Bed in the Yorkshire Coalfield (based on Wray, H.M. Geological Survey).

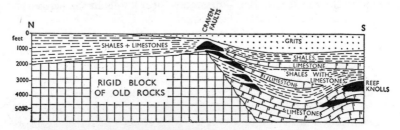

FIG. 171. Differential subsidence across an active fault line. Contrast in the Carboniferous sedimentation on the two sides of the Craven Fault belt in Yorkshire; length of section about 50 miles (based on Wray, H.M. Geological Survey).

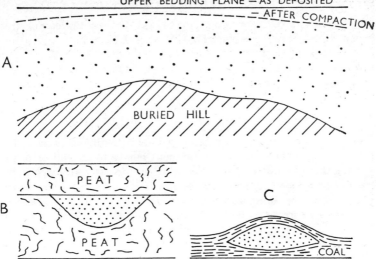

FIG. 172. *Compaction of Sediments.* A, compaction over a buried hill; B and C, differential compaction of peat beds over a sand-filled washout.

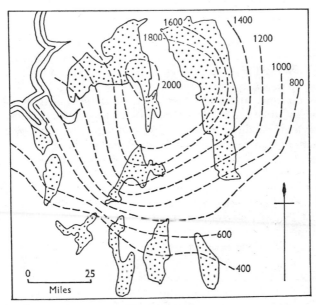

FIG. 173. Isopachytes (in feet) of a portion of the Coal Measures of Lancashire and Yorkshire: outcrops of the Coal Measures are dotted (after Trueman).

production of a *compaction-dip* (Fig. 172A). Differential compaction over a wash-out filling is illustrated in Fig. 172.

It is clear that beds may vary very considerably in shape. *Isopachytes* are lines joining points of equal thickness on a map of a particular bed and isopachyte maps are of value in coal-field studies (Fig. 173).

FACIES AND FACIES VARIATIONS

The area of deposition of a particular kind of sediment is limited in extent and sooner or later the sediment comes to an end or passes into another of a different lithological type. We can refer back to the passage from beach-gravel to foreshore-sand to deeper-water muds. The gravel, the sand and the mud each have their own special characters expressing their different conditions of formation; the nature, size and shape of their constituent particles, their structure and the remains of organisms occurring in them are determined by their environments of deposition and can therefore be used to deduce these environments. This sum total of the characters of a deposit, indicative of its depositional environment, is of course its *facies*.

The bed in our example changes from a shore-facies to an intertidal facies and this to a shallow marine facies. There are obviously a great number of facies, since there are a great number of different environments. We can illustrate this variety by reminding ourselves that a physiographic map is simply a map showing the distribution of the facies of today. Facies can therefore be classified on a geographic or physiographic basis, as we have already done (p. 241).

On uniformitarian lines, we can interpret the sedimentary rocks by their facies, directing our attention to such properties of the rocks as their style of bedding, their textures and structures, the sources of their materials, the possible habitats of their fossils and so on. On the assumption that any particular group of rocks took relatively little time to be laid down, we can construct a *palaeogeographical map* by plotting the distribution of their facies. We can illustrate such maps and the relevant facies changes by considering the facies of the sedimentary rocks belonging to the Lower Carboniferous as developed in Britain.

The deposits of the early part of Carboniferous (p. 293) time, which is of course a very lengthy time (p. 293), when considered as a whole present great differences in facies as they are traced from the English Midlands northwards through Yorkshire to Northumbria and thence to the Midland Valley of Scotland and again when they are followed northward through Ireland (Fig. 174). Early deposits of Carboniferous time are absent over an area of the Midlands which can be

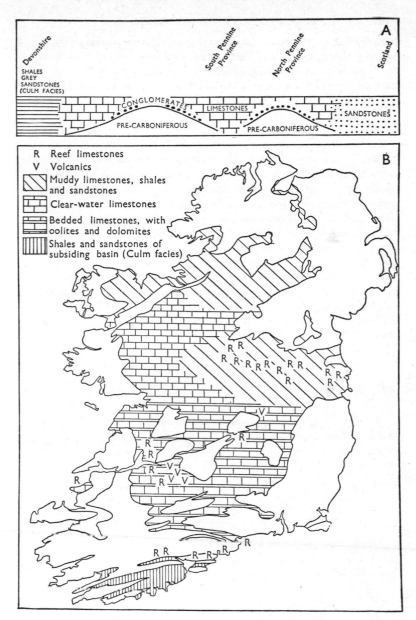

FIG. 174. *Facies Variations in Lower Carboniferous Sediments.* A, diagrammatic section from Devonshire northwards to the Midland Valley of Scotland; B, map of Ireland showing the distribution of the facies of the Lower Carboniferous (after Gill).

considered to have been an island in the early Carboniferous sea. Around the site of this island are found thick pure limestones, abounding in corals and shells and with oolitic bands; this pure limestone facies indicates that the island must have been low-lying so that it supplied little detritus to the surrounding sea. To the north in Yorkshire deposits of this age show a considerable admixture of shale-bands with the limestones, especially towards the top of the pile; goniatites, free swimmers, are characteristic fossils of the shales. Mud was obviously being delivered into the Carboniferous sea and that it came from the north is indicated by the deposits found in Durham and Northumberland. Here limestones no longer dominate in the sedimentary pile; sandstones and shales are the commonest sedimentary rocks and in the upper two-thirds coal-seams, thin but numerous, appear — the environment of the clean sea of the Midlands has changed to that of a land-margin subject to steady oscillations so that alternations of mud, sand, limy material and swamp material, were possible. In the Midland Valley of Scotland, the lower Carboniferous rocks are represented by sandstones, shales and oil-shales, fireclays, with very thin and few marine limestones but with thick and numerous coals. For most of the thick sediments, the facies is that of the coal-swamps liable to short-lived incursions of the sea. The map and section of Fig. 174 should be carefully studied as illustrating facies changes in a group of rocks.

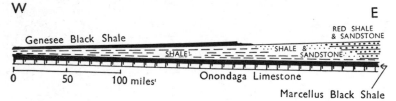

FIG. 175. *Facies Variation in a single Formation*, lying between two uniform continuous beds. The variations indicate, from left to right, the passage from marine through deltaic to terrestrial environments (Devonian strata of New York, based on Chadwick and Cooper).

Facies change in a more restricted formation is of common occurrence, but needs careful field-work for its demonstration. In Fig. 175 is given an example.

SEDIMENTARY ROCKS IN TIME: SUCCESSION AND ITS INTERPRETATION

The variation of one particular bed as it is followed laterally has just been dealt with — now the relations of a number of beds to one another have to be considered. We have to deal first with the order of deposition of a set of sedimentary rocks.

Succession. Now that we know how sedimentary rocks are formed it is obvious that in a pile of undisturbed sediments, the bottom layer is the oldest, the one on top of it is younger and the topmost bed of the pile is the youngest. This is a restatement of William Smith's First Law, '*of superposition*', mentioned in the first pages of this book — this law says that 'of any two strata the one that was originally the lower is the older'. The Second Law, '*of strata identified by fossils*', will be better appreciated when fossils have been dealt with in the next chapter. It too was mentioned early on and it follows naturally from the First Law immediately the evolution of organisms during the history of life on the earth is recognised. We may illustrate it once more, this time by using the fresh-water mussels found in the coal-bearing rocks of Great Britain (Fig. 176).

By the use of these two principles, a set of sedimentary rocks can be arranged in the order of their deposition, the oldest at the bottom of the list and the youngest at the top; a *succession* or *sequence* is established when the rocks are placed in their time order.

tenuis zone
Anthraconauta tenuis

phillipsii zone
Anthraconauta phillipsii

U. similis-pulchra zone
Anthracosia similis

L. similis-pulchra zone
Anthraiconaia pulchra

modiolaris zone
Anthraconaia modiolaris

communis zone
Carbonicola communis

lenisulcata zone
Anthraconaia lenisulcata

FIG. 176. Index Fossils of the Zones of the British Coal Measures (fossils are drawn to the same scale).

But there are occasions when William Smith's laws cannot be applied. Earth-movements may disturb the original order so that the first law is invalid; a great many very thick sequences of rocks contain no fossils and the second law cannot be used. It is in these circumstances that the methods of determining the 'way-up' of beds — their original order of deposition or their *stratigraphical succession* — already mentioned in connection with current-bedding and graded bedding become of great importance. Repeatedly folded and inverted beds are shown to be so by careful observations of these way-up structures — some examples are given in Fig. 257.

Interpretation of sedimentary successions. We have seen already

K2

that a sedimentary rock records the environment in which it was formed. Accordingly, a succession of sedimentary rocks records the succession of environments at one particular place. By interpretation of the successive facies we can reconstruct a sequence of geographies of the area and can go on to draw conclusions of importance in the history of the crustal segment involved.

A small-scale example of such interpretation has already been given in connection with the Coal-Measure rhythm (Fig. 169) wherein there is plainly revealed a jerky subsidence of wide expanses of the margins of bygone continents. Correct interpretation of any stratigraphical succession obviously depends on a thorough knowledge of the processes of sedimentation and of the ways in which the products of these processes may be subsequently modified. It is for this reason that Chapter 4 is so long.

When we come to study the history of the crust as revealed in the sedimentary rocks making the geological systems, we find that two recurrent events in that history are, first, the advance of the sea on the land and, second, the retreat of the sea — the first is called a *transgression*, the second a *regression*. We may now see how they are represented in a succession of sedimentary rocks.

A *transgression* requires that at any selected point a deepening of the sea takes place. The first deposit of the advancing sea will be of littoral facies, beach or intertidal, and will be followed by facies of deeper and deeper water as the transgression continues. The succession of the rocks indicating a transgression might therefore be conglomerates of oligomict character, sandstones with current-bedding, shales and possibly limestones (Fig. 177). On the other hand, a *regression* betokens a shallowing retreating sea and perhaps the emergence of land in a given area. It could accordingly be recorded by a succession beginning with deep-water deposits such as shales, followed by shallower-water sandstones, then maybe estuarine or lagoonal deposits and finally deposits of true terrestrial character (Fig. 177).

Breaks in the succession: diastems, disconformities, unconformities. An ideal complete stratigraphical succession would be one in which the whole time and every moment of the time taken to deposit the succession would be represented by sediment. This is clearly an impossibility — a bedding-plane itself records an interval of non-deposition, and breaks of greater magnitude are of common occurrence.

It must be remembered that any bed represents the balance between deposition and erosion over its particular area. A great deal of material deposited may be removed before the laying-down of the

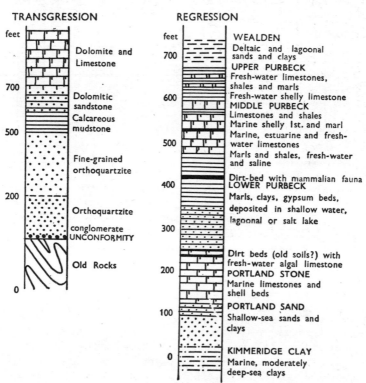

TRANSGRESSION		REGRESSION	
feet		feet	WEALDEN
	Dolomite and Limestone	700	Deltaic and lagoonal sands and clays
			UPPER PURBECK
700			Fresh-water limestones, shales and marls
	Dolomitic sandstone	600	Fresh-water shelly limestone MIDDLE PURBECK
500	Calcareous mudstone		Limestones and shales Marine shelly 1st. and marl
		500	Marine, estuarine and fresh-water limestones
	Fine-grained orthoquartzite		Marls and shales, fresh-water and saline
		400	Dirt-bed with mammalian fauna LOWER PURBECK
200			Marls, clays, gypsum beds, deposited in shallow water, lagoonal or salt lake
	Orthoquartzite		
	conglomerate UNCONFORMITY	300	
			Dirt beds (old soils?) with fresh-water algal limestone
	Old Rocks	200	PORTLAND STONE Marine limestones and shell beds
0		100	PORTLAND SAND Shallow-sea sands and clays
		0	KIMMERIDGE CLAY Marine, moderately deep-sea clays

FIG. 177. *Transgression and Regression.* (*Above*), diagrammatic section showing a transgressive sedimentary series, deposited in a sea advancing from right to left; the higher beds of the transgressive series *overlap* the lower beds of the series. (*Lower*), successions of actual examples of transgressive and regressive series: (*left*), the Cambro-Ordovician of the North-west Highlands of Scotland; (*right*), the Upper Jurassic of the South of England.

next bed seals it off from further erosion. In any area of swift currents, great wave-action, instability leading to gentle warping and all the other factors promoting erosion, minor breaks or *diastems* (Fig. 178) are likely to occur in the succession. Nothing violent has happened and the general conditions in the area as a whole have not changed.

Time-breaks of a much more fundamental character are recorded

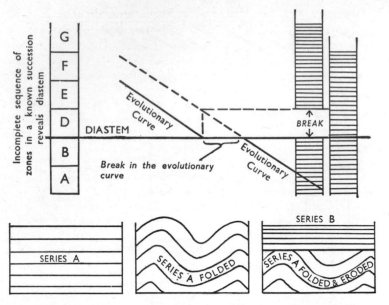

FIG. 178. *Breaks in the Succession.* (*Above*), a diastem, with Brinkmann's method of evaluating the break in fossiliferous strata, using steadily evolving characters in specific fossils (the *Evolutionary Curve*). (*Below*), unconformity.

by *unconformities*; an unconformity is shown by a discordant relationship between two sets of beds (Fig. 178). The older set has been folded, uplifted and eroded before the deposition of the younger set. The relationship records a violent act that has profoundly changed the style of geological happenings over a considerable area.

Where no physical discordance between the older and newer series is present, the break is referred to by some as a *disconformity*. The concordant bedding of the two series may be due to non-deposition for a considerable period of time. Accidental coincidence of the attitude of older folded beds with the stratification of a younger series is not regarded as a disconformity by us.

Correlation. Correlation is concerned with the time-relations between successions of strata exposed in separated localities. Two beds or two successions are *correlated* when it is established that they were formed at the same time. This can only be done with the help of fossils; but life has existed on the earth for only the last fifth of geological time and accordingly no fossils are available for the correlation of the earlier sedimentary rocks. In the correlation of these, and of course, of the fossiliferous rocks also, lithological similarity is employed; depending on the circumstances, such lithological correlations are not necessarily true time-correlations.

Lithological correlation can be achieved by 'walking-out' or tracing the mappable rock-unit, the *formation*, from one area to another. A succession of beds may be of so distinctive a kind that it can be recognised over considerable distances; particular styles of rhythmic sedimentation may be of use. *Key-beds* or *index-beds*, if possible of unique character, easily recognised and present over an extensive region, are of great value. But these methods are of course of restricted employment. Rhythmic or key beds may not be unique in a succession; the Coal-Measure rhythm, for example, is repeated hundreds of times. Further, facies changes sooner or later modify the lithological character of the formation; admittedly, if such changes take place slowly in well-exposed rocks it may be possible to make a valid correlation. Lenticular or wedging formations introduce another hazard. It can however be assumed that the rocks lying between two adjacent widespread key-beds are of about the same age, though their lithology may vary (see Fig. 175).

The relationships of a formation to major events in the geological history of the area may assist in correlation. The hiatus recorded by an unconformity may be significant in this connection, as may be the intrusion of an igneous rock or the onset of metamorphism.

When all is said and done, correlation in the non-fossiliferous rocks is not of a very high order, but it is different for the fossiliferous rocks. In these, William Smith's Second Law comes into operation and the evolution of organisms provides a continuous change with time. In the next chapter we shall examine the methods of *zoning* the fossiliferous rocks by the use of guide or *zone-fossils* of limited stratigraphical range and extensive geographical distribution.

It is considered that formations with the same faunas are of the same age. This conclusion was challenged by T. H. Huxley who held that the formations, if separated by any great distance, could not be contemporaneous since it would take time for the fauna to migrate from its place of origin to the distant regions where it is now found; the formations were, Huxley held, not contemporaneous but *homotaxial*. General opinion is against Huxley's views; the time taken for organisms to migrate even considerable distances is known to be trifling in comparison to that of the deposition of a series of rocks. For example, the European winkle has colonised great stretches of the Atlantic sea-board of the United States since its introduction there a century ago.

There may be, none-the-less, valid differences between lithological and true time correlations. This aspect can best be demonstrated by

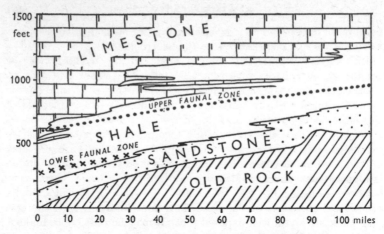

FIG. 179. Correlation by means of faunal zones in beds of varying sedimentary facies. Cambrian of the Grand Canyon of the Colorado (after McKee).

considering such a section of rocks as is illustrated in Fig. 179. This figure is based on one given by McKee in his investigation of the rocks perfectly exposed over great distances in the walls of the Grand Canyon of the Colorado. The time correlation is given by two extensive key-beds containing excellent zone fossils. It will be seen that the sandstone formation varies in age from left to right; on the left it is older than the older key-bed, on the right its upper part is much younger than this bed. The time-planes cross the rock-planes. The sandstone bed is said to be *diachronous*.

Dividing the geological record. The history of the earth's crust, like any other history, is a continuous affair so that any divisions that have to be made in the geological record are in some degree arbitrary. It has been the practice to view the sedimentary record of geological time as making a *geological* or *stratigraphical column*, with the oldest rocks at the bottom, the youngest at the top of the column. There are, as we shall see, a great many other events in the geological record besides sedimentation but, since the sedimentary rocks contain the records of evolving life, we have first to deal with the divisions of the stratigraphical column.

This division, whether of time or of rocks, is a difficult and contentious matter, because no world-wide event is recognisable. Unconformities were used for the major dividing lines in the mistaken belief that the disturbances recorded by them affected the whole of the crust. The sedimentary records of a transgression and a regression could supply a good unit of classification — but again the

292

THE STRATIGRAPHICAL TABLE

Eras	Periods			Time (in millions of years)
Quaternary	Pleistocene - - - - -			1·5
Tertiary	Pliocene Miocene	} Neogene -	- -	25
	Oligocene Eocene	} Palaeogene	- -	65
Mesozoic	Cretaceous -	- -	- -	135
	Jurassic -	- -	- -	190
	Triassic -	- -	- -	225
Upper	Permian -	- -	- -	280
	Carboniferous	- -	- -	345
Palaeozoic	Devonian -	- -	- -	400
	Silurian -	- -	- -	440
Lower	Ordovician -	- -	- -	500
	Cambrian -	- -	- -	570
Proterozoic and Archaeozoic	Pre-Cambrian	- -	- another 3000 or more	

record might be local; even though the oceans are connected the continental masses might move independently of one another. The best classification of the fossiliferous rocks will ultimately be based on the continuous and complete succession of the faunal and floral zones (p. 353); though there may be spurts in organic evolution there can be no breaks.

Until this complete succession is established, we will have to make do with a rough and ready classification of the sedimentary-rock record given here. The absolute ages are obtained by the methods described earlier (p. 48). The stratigraphical divisions of the immensely long span of Pre-Cambrian time are still not agreed on, since these Pre-Cambrian rocks are almost devoid of fossils.

FURTHER READING AND REFERENCE

Clarke, F. W., 1924, 'The Data of Geochemistry', Bull. 770, United States Geological Survey.

Pettijohn, F. J., 1956, Sedimentary Rocks, 2nd edit., Harper, New York.

Holmes, A., 1921, Petrographic Methods and Calculations, Murby.

Shrock, R. R., 1948, Sequence in Layered Rocks, McGraw-Hill.

Kuenen, P. H. and C. I. Migliorini, 1950, 'Turbidity currents as a cause of graded bedding', Journ. Geol. vol. 58, p. 91.

North, F. J., 1926, Coal and the Coalfields in Wales, Nat. Mus. of Wales

North, F. J., 1930, *Limestones, their origin, distribution and uses*, Murby London.

Bailey, E. B., 1930, 'New Light on Sedimentation and Tectonics', *Geol. Mag.*, vol. 67, p. 77.

Allen, P., 1959, 'The Wealden Environment: Anglo-Paris Basin', *Phil. Trans.*, B., vol. 242, p. 283.

Hatch, F. H., R. H. Rastall and M. Black, 1938, *The Petrology of the Sedimentary Rocks*, 3rd. edition, Allen and Unwin.

Harland, W. B., A. G. Smith and B. Wilcock (editors), 1964, 'The Phanerozoic Time-scale,' *Quart. J. Geol. Soc. Lond.*, 120s.

6

FOSSILS AND THEIR USES

THE FOSSIL-RECORD

Fossils. The surface of the solid earth or lithosphere is crowded with plants and animals which at the present day are often so numerous as to hide the rocks on which they live. The zone inhabited by these organisms extends for a few metres down into the crust and for a somewhat greater distance up into the air or water; it constitutes the *biosphere*, one of the characteristic features of our planet.

All organisms are geologically speaking ephemeral, but as a consequence of their power of reproduction their stock is continually renewed. The living organisms of today are merely the latest of an unbroken succession of generations reaching far back through geological time. Samples of earlier generations are available in the form of *fossils*, the remains of ancient organisms. Many fossils represent the actual body of a plant or animal more or less completely modified by changes after death. Others are simply *impressions* in sedimentary rocks representing the imprint of an organism which has decayed away. Still others, *trace-fossils*, are structures such as footprints or burrows produced by some activity of the living organism.

The most important thing about any fossil is that it was once a living organism. The animal or plant from which it was derived had a particular kind of anatomy and followed a particular way of life. It belonged to a natural community, such as that of a sea-beach, and was adapted to exploit the advantages of its environment. It lived at a definite moment of time and belonged to a distinctive line of descent or *lineage*. All these biological matters must be considered in the light of the evidence provided by the fossil itself and the rock containing it.

Fossils have an inherent importance as records of the history of life and, for the geologist, they are also of value as tools in the study of geological history. In the first place, as we have noted already, fossils may act as indices of the age of the rocks containing them. It was established long ago that strata of the same age contained fossils of the same types wherever they were found, this fact being expressed in William Smith's law of strata identified by fossils (p. 5). By this means, fossiliferous rocks of separated regions can be *correlated* and assigned to their correct places in the stratigraphical column (p. 293).

Secondly, fossils provide evidence of the mode of origin of the rocks in which they occur. The fossil-contents of sedimentary rocks vary according to the environment in which deposition took place; a marine clay, for example, may contain the remains of deep-sea animals, an estuarine clay such organisms as worms and mussels which live in the intertidal zone, and a lake-clay fresh-water fish and insects or pollen blown in from surrounding lands. The fossils thus establish the *faunal or floral facies* of the rocks.

Fossilisation of organisms. Complete animals or plants are seldom represented as fossils which, as a rule, consist simply of fragments such as empty shells, scraps of bone or isolated leaves or seeds. Their incompleteness is understandable when we come to consider how fossils are formed. In the ordinary way, the soft parts of animals and plants are quickly destroyed after death by bacterial decay, and the hard parts such as shells and bones are left exposed to the forces of weathering and erosion. They too are soon destroyed unless some accident puts them out of reach of the agents of decay. Freak circumstances may occasionally achieve this end at the surface of the earth but, far more often, organisms are preserved because they have been buried soon after death by a protective layer of sediment. They thus become incorporated in a growing pile of sedimentary rocks and may in favourable circumstances remain as fossils until they are once more exposed by erosion or human excavation.

When burial takes place soon after death, the soft tissues of an organism may leave an imprint on the enclosing sediment which on lithification hardens into a permanent impression. A black film of finely divided carbon may be deposited on the bedding-plane by the breakdown of organic compounds. Entirely soft-bodied creatures may be fossilised in this way and remarkably detailed impressions of such animals as worms and jelly-fish are known.

Many organisms possess protective or supporting structures which are harder and more durable than the rest of the body. Some of these structures are made of organic compounds like *chitin*, the horny material which is the basis of many shells and of the armour of crabs and insects, or the waxy substance *cutin* which covers many plant-spores and pollen-grains. Other hard parts are made of inorganic compounds. Shells, echinoderm-tests and coral-skeletons are largely made of *calcium carbonate* in the form of aragonite or calcite; many shells originally made of aragonite turn to calcite after fossilisation. Amorphous *silica* is used as a skeletal material by lowly animals such as sponges, and by many plants. Bone is a mixture of calcium carbonate and phosphate.

Long after burial has sealed them off from the surface-processes, fossils undergo further changes. They are often flattened by the weight of the overlying sediment and may be further distorted by earth-movements. Their substance may be dissolved by underground-water, leaving only a hollow *mould*, or replaced by new mineral matter carried in solution; thus wood, for example, may be *silicified* and a replica of the original structure preserved in a much more durable form.

From what has been said above, we can deduce that some kinds of organisms will stand a better chance of fossilisation than others. In the first place, creatures with a hard skeleton are more favourably situated than soft-bodied organisms. In the second place, organisms which live (or at least die) in regions where deposition is the dominant geological process are more likely to be preserved than those living in regions subjected to erosion. These probabilities are borne out by the actual fossil-record. Most fossiliferous rocks reveal a selection of animal- or plant-skeletons, but even prolonged search may fail to show up relics of the soft tissues that clothed them, or of wholly soft-bodied animals. Again, the marine faunas of most periods are far more abundantly represented by fossils than are the terrestrial faunas and this contrast is simply due to the fact that the sea is normally a region of deposition and the land a region of erosion. In studying the fossil-record we must of course concentrate on groups which are well represented, but we should remember that they do not necessarily provide a fair sample of the life of the past.

LIVING ORGANISMS AND THEIR CLASSIFICATION

The plant and animal kingdoms. The organisms of interest to the palaeontologist — the student of fossils — fall into two great categories. The *plants* are capable of using solar energy to synthesise from simple inorganic compounds the organic substances of which they are made. The *animals* lack this power of *photosynthesis* and require ready-made organic substances as food. Both groups obtain energy by a process of *respiration* which involves the absorption of oxygen, the breakdown of organic compounds and the liberation of carbon dioxide.

Bacteria are minute organisms differing in many ways from both plants and animals. They do not perform photosynthesis and live either as parasites or in environments where dead organic matter is available as food. Their methods of obtaining energy are varied and do not always involve the use of oxygen — some bacteria can therefore live in oxygen-poor or *anaerobic* environments, such as the Black Sea floor, which are closed to other organisms. Bacteria are the principal agents of decay in the biosphere, breaking down complex organic compounds to give water, carbon dioxide and simple salts. Without their activities life as we know it would be impossible, since the elements necessary to life would be locked up in accumulations of dead organic matter. It seems certain that bacteria have performed the same functions throughout much of geological history, but though their activities are everywhere apparent they are seldom preserved as recognisable fossils.

The fundamental contrast between the modes of subsistence of plants and animals is reflected in their structure. The basic requirements of *plants* are light, carbon dioxide and water for photosynthesis, oxygen for respiration, and simple compounds containing nitrogen, iron, sulphur and so on. All these substances can be found in the air, in water or in the interstices of the soil. They need not be sought, and plants are therefore normally fixed and immobile. The absorption of water, oxygen and carbon dioxide being facilitated by the increase of surface-area relative to volume, plants are generally diffuse and bushy.

Primitive aquatic plants such as the seaweeds draw their nourishment directly from the water surrounding them and show little differentiation of organs for special purposes. The more advanced land-plants, on the other hand, generally have a specialised *root-system* which serves for attachment and for absorbing matter from the soil, and an aerial part concerned with photosynthesis. A *vascular system* capable of transmitting food-material usually connects the two parts of the body. The *reproductive systems* of plants are designed to meet the special need for disseminating the offspring of fixed organisms; they commonly produce sealed *seeds* or *spores* capable of lying dormant till they reach a place suitable for germination.

The requirements of *animals* are very different. The organic substances needed for food can only be obtained from plants or other animals and must therefore be sought for. Hence, most animals are mobile, and stationary animals are provided with special food-catching devices. The habit of locomotion raises problems of its own. The body must be compact, its parts must be moveable and their activities must be co-ordinated; *muscular* and *nervous systems* serve these purposes and *sense-organs* put the animal in touch with the world it inhabits. Special *respiratory organs* supply the oxygen necessary for active locomotion. A *digestive system* converts the food into usable forms and a *vascular system* provides a means of transporting food, oxygen and waste-products from one part of the body to another.

The living substance of all organisms is a complex mixture of proteins, water and other compounds known as *protoplasm*; it is generally arranged in an extremely large number of minute units or *cells*. In primitive organisms the body-cells are all basically similar, but in more highly-organised creatures each cell becomes specialised to perform some particular function — muscle-cells are contractile, nerve-cells transmit impulses and so on. Thus are built up the complex bodies of the higher animals and plants.

The system of classification. The plant- and animal-kingdoms show an immense range of structural variation which reflects differences in the manner in which the essential activities of nutrition, respiration and reproduction are carried out. This variation is not unsystematic and it is expressed in a scheme of classification and nomenclature whose outlines were laid down in 1735 by the great Swedish naturalist Carl Linnaeus.

The organisms of each kingdom fall naturally into a relatively small number of groups or *phyla* which are distinguished by fundamental differences in construction. Within each phylum, the basic plan of construction is subjected to characteristic variations in each of the major subdivisions or *classes*. Each class is itself capable of further subdivision to give still smaller groups. There is thus produced a hierarchy of categories which provides the framework for a classificatory system covering all organisms whether living or fossil. This hierarchy is as follows:

KINGDOM
    PHYLUM
        CLASS
            ORDER
                FAMILY
                    GENUS
                        SPECIES

The smallest unit of the system is the *species* which represents a single kind of animal or plant recognisably different from all others. The members of one species are not all identical — the human species, for example, is very variable — but they interbreed freely and individual variations are thus woven into the common stock; there is seldom any interbreeding between the members of different species.

The nomenclature of animal- and plant-species is based on a binomial system established by Linnaeus. Each species has a name consisting of two words. The first or *generic name* is common to all species of a single *genus*. The second or *specific name*, denotes the *species* within the genus. By convention, the name is italicised in print and, in palaeontological literature, the name of the author who established the species should be added.

EVOLUTION

The diversity of animals and plants has been known and discussed since time immemorial, but it was not until the nineteenth century that the concept of evolution which offers an explanation of this diversity became widely accepted. This concept was the theme of Charles Darwin's *Origin of Species*, published in 1859. Darwin established that many species were variable and argued that in the struggle for existence individuals whose particular characters made them more efficient than the average would stand an unusually good chance of survival and reproduction. Their characters, if transmitted to their offspring, would in the course of generations spread through the population as a result of this *natural selection*; unfavourable variants would be suppressed because individuals showing them would be handicapped in the struggle to live and breed in competition with others of their race. Thus, with time, all lineages of living things underwent a gradual change or *evolution* and Darwin concluded that all organisms, living and extinct, constituted 'one grand natural system' formed by the gradual modification and diversification of ancestral stocks through the length of geological time.

In Darwin's view, the course of evolution was largely controlled by the effects of natural selection and of *adaptation to environment*. The mechanism of inheritance and change was then almost unknown, but more recent work has shown that the nuclei of the germ cells in each organism contain, as it were in coded form, the plan on which the structure of its offspring is based. Spontaneous changes, known as *mutations*, in the 'code' produce new, inheritable variations in the adult structure. These mutations become distributed through a population by interbreeding and so provide the material on which natural selection can work.

Once the concept of evolution was accepted, the Linnaean system of classification came to be seen as an expression of the relationships between organisms and a general indication of the lines of their descent. Species no longer figured as immutable units but as constantly changing populations of interbreeding organisms. The species of one genus were formed by the modification and splitting of a single *lineage* and could be traced back through time to a common ancestor; similarly the genera of a family spring from a common stock and so on through the categories of the classificatory system. In a genetic classification of this kind the place of fossil-organisms is of the greatest importance, since fossils supply the only direct evidence concerning the course of evolution.

The next sections of this chapter give brief accounts of the principal groups of the animal- and plant-kingdoms (see Tables I and II). An attempt is made to show how the structure of each group serves its needs and this involves describing the anatomy of the soft parts which are seldom preserved in fossils. No attempt is made to give the diagnostic features of individual fossil-species or genera. The student who wishes to identify the fossils he collects will in any case need to consult a more specialised book and the inclusion in this chapter of a restricted catalogue of names would serve no useful purpose.

TABLE I THE ANIMAL-KINGDOM

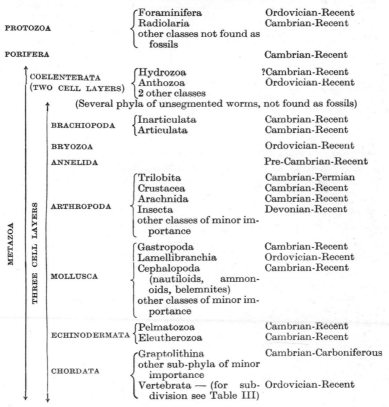

PROTOZOA	Foraminifera	Ordovician-Recent
	Radiolaria	Cambrian-Recent
	other classes not found as fossils	
PORIFERA		Cambrian-Recent
COELENTERATA (TWO CELL LAYERS)	Hydrozoa	?Cambrian-Recent
	Anthozoa	Ordovician-Recent
	2 other classes	
	(Several phyla of unsegmented worms, not found as fossils)	
BRACHIOPODA	Inarticulata	Cambrian-Recent
	Articulata	Cambrian-Recent
BRYOZOA		Ordovician-Recent
ANNELIDA		Pre-Cambrian-Recent
ARTHROPODA	Trilobita	Cambrian-Permian
	Crustacea	Cambrian-Recent
	Arachnida	Cambrian-Recent
	Insecta	Devonian-Recent
	other classes of minor importance	
MOLLUSCA	Gastropoda	Cambrian-Recent
	Lamellibranchia	Ordovician-Recent
	Cephalopoda	Cambrian-Recent
	(nautiloids, ammonoids, belemnites)	
	other classes of minor importance	
ECHINODERMATA	Pelmatozoa	Cambrian-Recent
	Eleutherozoa	Cambrian-Recent
CHORDATA	Graptolithina	Cambrian-Carboniferous
	other sub-phyla of minor importance	
	Vertebrata — (for subdivision see Table III)	Ordovician-Recent

METAZOA — THREE CELL LAYERS

NOTE: The time ranges given on the right are based on the fossil evidence and do not necessarily give the complete ranges of the groups.

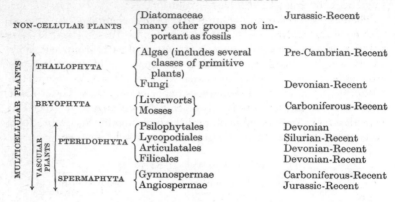

TABLE II THE PLANT-KINGDOM

NON-CELLULAR PLANTS		Diatomaceae many other groups not important as fossils	Jurassic-Recent
MULTICELLULAR PLANTS	THALLOPHYTA	Algae (includes several classes of primitive plants)	Pre-Cambrian-Recent
		Fungi	Devonian-Recent
	BRYOPHYTA	Liverworts Mosses	Carboniferous-Recent
	PTERIDOPHYTA (VASCULAR PLANTS)	Psilophytales Lycopodiales Articulatales Filicales	Devonian Silurian-Recent Devonian-Recent Devonian-Recent
	SPERMAPHYTA	Gymnospermae Angiospermae	Carboniferous-Recent Jurassic-Recent

NOTE: The time ranges given on the right are based on the fossil evidence and do not necessarily give the complete ranges of the groups.

THE ANIMAL-KINGDOM

PHYLUM PROTOZOA

The **Protozoa** are small creatures, the majority being microscopic and the giants of the phylum reaching a size of only a few centimetres. They differ from all other animals in being non-cellular; their protoplasm, though often quite elaborately organised, is not divided into cells comparable to those of the higher animals. Among numerous classes, only one, the *Rhizopoda*, is of palaeontological importance; this class is characterised by the ability to send out protoplasmic extensions or *pseudopodia* from the body.

The **Foraminifera** (Ordovician-Recent) are free-living marine rhizopods, most of them bottom-living but a few (e.g. *Globigerina*, Fig. 180) floating or *pelagic*. Their small shells or *tests* are abundant Mesozoic and Tertiary fossils which can be identified in thin slice or washed out of loose sediment even when they are too small to be seen in the field. They are much used as zone fossils in oil-fields, because they are small enough to be recovered from bore-hole samples.

In the simplest foraminifera, the protoplasm is housed in a single capsule with an opening through which the pseudopodia project. In more complex types, the test is made up of several *chambers* which are arranged in various ways according to species. These chambers are formed one after the other during growth; each opens out of the

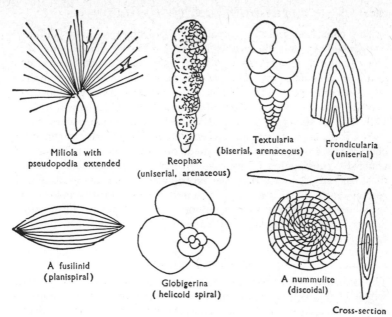

Miliola with
pseudopodia extended

Reophax
(uniserial, arenaceous)

Textularia
(biserial, arenaceous)

Frondicularia
(uniserial)

A fusilinid
(planispiral)

Globigerina
(helicoid spiral)

A nummulite
(discoidal)

Cross-section

Fig. 180. Foraminifera, all greatly enlarged.

preceding one and the protoplasm extends through them all and
envelops them in a film from which thread-like pseudopodia project.

Foraminifera (Fig. 180) are classified according to the composition
and structure of the test and the arrangement of the chambers. The
details of the scheme are very complex and we shall confine ourselves
to the major groupings, based on the character of the test:

1. *Chitinous or gelatinous tests* characterise some modern forms but
are not found as fossils.

2. *Arenaceous or agglutinated tests* are built of minute sand-grains
cemented together with chitin or lime secreted by the protoplasm.
Foraminifera with arenaceous tests (e.g. the Lituolids) appeared
early and were of little importance after the Palaeozoic.

3. *Calcareous tests* characterise most Mesozoic, Tertiary and modern
foraminifera. The structure of the test-wall varies from group to
group. In the Endothyroidea the test is made of minute calcite
granules and looks dark under the microscope. In *imperforate* forms
(e.g. the Miliolidea), calcite crystals are set parallel to the walls of the
test which appears milky in reflected light. In *perforate* forms (e.g.
the Lagenidae) the crystals are perpendicular to the walls and the
test appears glassy and is pierced by minute pores. Finally, a few
foraminiferal tests are made of single calcite crystals.

303

The chambers may be arranged according to many different patterns. They may lie serially in a single line or a double or triple line. They may be arranged concentrically or in a plane-spiral or a rising or helicoid spiral. The pattern may change during growth so that the oldest part of the shell is, say, triserial and the youngest part biserial or uniserial. The pattern of chambers, taken in conjunction with the test-structure, may be diagnostic of particular genera.

The **Radiolaria** (Cambrian-Recent) are a pelagic order of rhizopods characterised by a complex test made of silica (Fig. 207). This test is generally constructed of interwoven spines, or perforated spheres, discs and so on enclosed in the protoplasm. Being made of silica it remains insoluble in sea-water even under considerable pressure, and radiolarian skeletons may therefore accumulate to form *radiolarian ooze* in seas of such depth that calcareous shells are dissolved (p. 217).

PHYLUM PORIFERA

The Porifera (Cambrian-Recent), the *sponges*, are lowly animals which lead a sedentary life in fresh or salt water. Their bodies are made up of a large number of cells which show only a very low degree of specialisation. The simplest sponges are merely hollow cylinders pierced by many pores through which the water flows freely. The more elaborate types have a plant-like shape produced by branching and involution of the cylinder-wall. Many sponges secrete small supporting *spicules* of silica or calcium carbonate and these structures are common, though very inconspicuous, fossils. They form rods, hooks or rayed bodies which usually fall apart with the decay of the sponge, but occasionally remain linked into a coherent structure.

SUB-KINGDOM METAZOA

The two phyla so far dealt with have, as we have seen, very simple plans of construction. They may be contrasted with all the other phyla of the animal-kingdom which in varying degrees show specialisation of body-cells and organs for particular functions. All these phyla, together constituting the *Metazoa*, possess a *gut* or internal cavity lined by a special layer of cells adapted for the process of digestion. In the phylum Coelenterata, described immediately, the body is built on a simple two-layered plan: the inner cell-layer or *endoderm* lines the gut while the outer cell-layer or *ectoderm* serves as a cover and produces specialised cells acting as muscle-fibres, nerves, sensory organs and weapons of defence. In the remaining phyla of the Metazoa, the body is built on a three-layered plan, the ectoderm and endoderm being separated by cells derived from a third layer or *mesoderm*. The mesoderm proliferates to produce most of the body-organs, while the endoderm still supplies the gut-lining and the ecto-derm the skin, external skeleton and nervous system. The mesoderm usually contains a space known as the *body-cavity* or *coelom* in which the other organs are suspended. The basic variations in the arrangement of the body-cells in the animal-kingdom can be tabulated as follows:

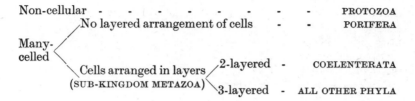

Non-cellular - - - - - - - - PROTOZOA

No layered arrangement of cells - - PORIFERA

Many-celled

Cells arranged in layers — 2-layered - COELENTERATA

(SUB-KINGDOM METAZOA) 3-layered - ALL OTHER PHYLA

PHYLUM COELENTERATA

Nomenclature. The coelenterates (Pre-Cambrian-Recent) are a group of aquatic, largely marine, animals which include sedentary forms such as sea-anemones and free-living forms such as jelly-fish. In these, the most primitive of the Metazoa, the body is essentially a hollow sac with a single opening or *mouth* which is generally fringed by tentacles. The rudimentary gut is lined by endoderm and the exterior surface by ectoderm. Coelenterates are able to react to outside stimuli and to co-ordinate their reactions by means of a loose network of nerve fibres, but have no central nervous system directing operations.

Most members of the phylum conform to one of two patterns (Fig. 181). In the types known as *polyps* the body is cylindrical and the mouth, surrounded by tentacles, appears at one end; polypoid forms are generally sedentary and are attached at the aboral end to a surface of rock or weed. The types known as *medusae* are generally free-living and float mouth-downwards in the water; the body is umbrella-shaped and is drawn out at right angles to the oral axis into a broad flange which serves as a floating or swimming organ. In both types the *symmetry* of the body is radial, the axis of symmetry passing through the mouth and making the oral axis.

Polypoid coelenterates reproduce by an asexual process of *budding* (Fig. 181). When detached from the parent, the buds set up as new individuals. In some groups, however, the buds may remain attached to the parent to produce a *colony* of many polyps united by a common stalk of living matter, the *coenosarc*. Medusae do not bud, but reproduce by sexual means; in some families an *alternation of generations*

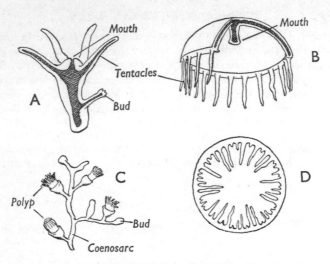

FIG. 181. *Coelenterata*. A, diagrammatic section of a polyp, showing the internal cavity (black); B, Medusa, cut open to show the internal cavity (black); C, colonial coelenterate; D, cross-section of sea-anenome, showing division of cavity by mesenteries.

takes place, a medusoid generation producing polyps which then give rise by budding to new medusae.

The phylum Coelenterata contains four classes, as follows:

(1) **Hydrozoa**: central cavity undivided, both polypoid and medusoid forms.

(2) **Anthozoa**: central cavity divided by radial partitions, exclusively polypoid, often colonial (corals, sea-anemones etc.).

(3) **Scyphozoa**: exclusively medusoid (jelly-fish).

(4) **Ctenophora**: aberrant forms not closely related to the remainder of the phylum.

Medusae, being adapted for a floating or pelagic existence, have no solid skeletons and are seldom found as fossils. The sedentary polyps of the Hydrozoa and Anthozoa, however, commonly secrete from the ectoderm a covering of chitin or calcium carbonate. Calcareous forms, which can be loosely termed *corals*, are among the commonest of fossils and act as rock-builders in coral-reefs (p. 212). The true corals are anthozoans, but we may mention along with them a group of rather similar hydrozoans.

Hydrozoa — Stromatoporoidea. The Stromatoporoids are an extinct Palaeozoic group of reef-building colonial organisms which are thought to be hydrozoans. Their colonies form rounded or lobate calcareous masses a foot or so across and are made up of close-set lamellae arranged parallel to the outer surface and supported by vertical pillars; the lamellae are pierced by branching canals which in life carried the coenosarc. The polyps themselves appear to have grown up from the surface of the colony and to have had no individual skeletons.

Anthozoa — the corals (Ordovician-Recent). The gut of the anthozoan polyp is partially divided by radial partitions or *mesenteries* which increase its surface and facilitate digestion (Fig. 181). The skeletons of calcareous forms range from a simple cup or *theca* housing a single polyp to a massive stony structure supporting an entire colony.

The theca of a single polyp is generally conical or tubular. Its lower part may be sealed off during growth by transverse partitions known as *tabulae* on which the polyp stands. Radially arranged *septa* alternating with the internal mesenteries are developed in some types and the theca wall is sometimes thickened by a spongy development of small tangential plates or *dissepiments*.

Three groups of fossil corals may be distinguished — the Tabulata (largely Palaeozoic), the Rugosa (Palaeozoic) and the Scleractinia (Mesozoic-Recent). The **Tabulata** have very simple thecae which are always united in colonies. Each theca is a simple tube, often very long relative to its diameter, and has no internal partitions other than tabulae. The colonies range from loosely-branched forms such as

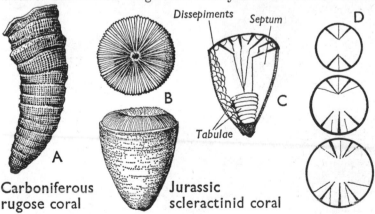

Carboniferous rugose coral

Jurassic scleractinid coral

Dissepiments Septum D

B C

Tabulae

A

FIG. 182. *Solitary Corals.* A and B, representative genera of the Rugosa and Scleractinia; C, structure of theca, diagrammatic; D cross-sections of *Zaphrentis* showing development of septa at three successive growth-stages.

Syringopora to compact bun-shaped masses such as *Favosites* (Fig. 183). *Tubipora*, the modern organ-pipe coral, may be related to the tabulates.

The **Rugosa** include both solitary and colonial corals in which the thecae are strongly built and show a horizontal ridging from which the group takes its name. The characteristic feature is the arrangement of the septa (Fig. 182) which is best understood by studying their mode of growth. The oldest part of each theca is the part near its point of attachment. By cutting serial sections from this base upwards we can therefore establish the structure of the coral at different stages of growth, as was shown in a classic study by Carruthers of the solitary rugose coral *Zaphrentis*. The first-formed part of the theca is a cone crossed by a single septum (Fig. 182). As growth proceeds, this partition divides into two parts which form the *cardinal* and *counter-cardinal septa*. Two new pairs of septa then arise symmetrically to make up a set of six *primary septa*, as shown in the figure. At later stages, new septa are added in four of the six spaces between the primary septa, but none appear in the spaces on either side of the counter-cardinal. The pattern of septa thus develops a gap and a bilateral symmetry is superimposed on the original radial symmetry of the theca.

The **Scleractinia** resemble the rugose corals in general structure and like them may be solitary or colonial. The theca shows a more perfect

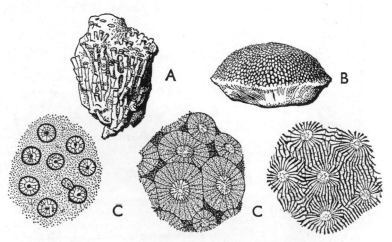

FIG. 183. *Colonial corals.* A and B tabulate corals, A, *Syringopora* and B, *Favosites*; C, three genera of rugose corals in cross-section, illustrating stages in the compaction of colonial forms.

radial symmetry than in the Rugosa; the septa appear throughout growth in multiples of six and are evenly spaced around the margin. *Colonial corals* belonging to the Rugosa and Scleractinia exhibit similar variations in habit which may be considered together (Fig. 183). Some forms build low encrustations on rock-surfaces. Others form loose bushy masses growing upwards from the point of attachment. Closer packing of the thecae leads to the development of *compound* domed or lobed colonies in which the walls of adjacent thecae touch; in the most compact types the thecae become polygonal in cross-section and may even lose their party walls (e.g. *Isastraea*). The compactness of the colonies depends on the species, and to some extent on the turbulence of the seas in which they live.

PHYLUM BRACHIOPODA

The first phylum of the more complex three-layered metazoans which we shall consider is the **Brachiopoda** (Cambrian-Recent). These are sedentary marine animals which, though now quite inconspicuous, were very numerous in Palaeozoic and Mesozoic times. They are a group which has long passed the peak of its evolution, their place as dominant shelled animals being now taken over by the Mollusca.

Brachiopods are generally an inch or so across and the largest are not much more than a foot in length. The body is completely enclosed in a horny or calcareous shell consisting of two *valves* placed dorsally and ventrally. A tough stalk or *pedicle* projecting through an aperture in the ventral valve, or between the valves, fixes the shell to the sea-floor. The valves are opened and closed by means of muscles, and in most groups they articulate along a toothed *hinge-line* near the pedicle-aperture (Fig. 184).

Since the adult brachiopod is boxed up in a fixed shell, it has no locomotory organs and only rudimentary sense-organs and nerves. Food is obtained in the form of minute particles in the water which are propelled towards the mouth by means of a special organ, the *lophophore*, bearing a pair of fringed arms or *brachiae* sometimes supported by calcareous loops or spirals fixed to the inside of the dorsal valve.

The *shell* is distinguished from that of bivalve molluscs (p. 319) by its form and symmetry. The two brachiopod valves differ from one another structurally, the ventral valve bearing the pedicle-opening and hinge-teeth and the dorsal valve the hinge-sockets and the lophophore-support, when present. But each valve is bilaterally symmetrical and the plane of symmetry for the whole animal bisects both valves. The major division of the phylum (Fig. 185) is based on

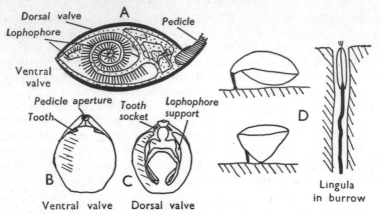

FIG. 184. *Brachiopoda.* A, cross-section of entire animal, showing position of body and lophophore in the shell; B, ventral valve; C, dorsal valve of a terebratuloid; D, positions in life of some attached and burrowing brachiopods.

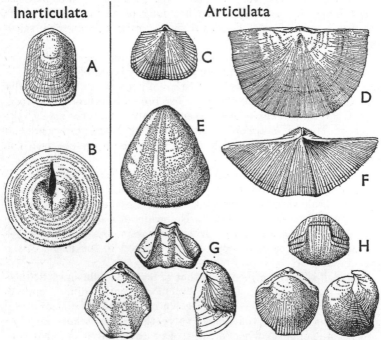

FIG. 185. Brachiopods (× ½ approx.). A, *Lingula*, an atrematous genus; B, a neotreme; C, an orthoid: D, a strophomenoid; E, *Pentamerus*; F, a spiriferoid; G, a terebratuloid; H, a rhynchonelloid.

the character of the hinge and brachial supports, while the shape and ornamentation of the shell are often characteristic of particular genera:

A. **Inarticulata**: primitive brachiopods with no hinge-structures or brachial supports. The valves are held together only by muscles.

(i) **Atremata**: the pedicle has no separate aperture, and emerges between the valves. The shell is chitinous, not calcareous. This group includes some of the earliest known brachiopods, and the genus *Lingula* has survived with little change from the Ordovician to the present day.

(ii) **Neotremata**: the pedicle projects through a hole near the centre of the ventral valve, or the valve is cemented directly to a rock.

B. **Articulata**: brachiopods in which the valves *articulate* along a toothed hinge-line. The shell is calcareous. This group includes all the more advanced forms.

(i) Brachiopods in which the pedicle emerges through a triangular slot (the *delthyrium*) notching the ventral valve at the hinge-line. The slot may be wholly or partly blocked off by a single plate called the *pseudodeltidium*.

(a) **Orthoids**: usually no pseudodeltidium. The hinge-line forms a straight margin to the shell, and the widest part of the shell is some distance from it (e.g. *Orthis*).

(b) **Strophomenoids**: a pseudodeltidium is present. The hinge-line is usually the widest part of the shell (e.g. *Strophomena*).

(c) **Pentameroids**: the shell-muscles are attached to a spoon-like outgrowth inside the ventral valve and the presence of this structure gives the internal cast a three-lobed shape (e.g. *Pentamerus*).

(ii) Brachiopods in which the delthyrium is more or less closed by a pair of *deltidial plates*. Calcareous lophophore-supports are generally present on the dorsal valve.

(a) **Spiriferoids**: the brachial supports form two spirally coiled ribbons (e.g. *Spirifer*).

(b) **Rhynchonelloids**: the brachial supports form two short hooks or *crura*. The shell is often rather globular and ornamented with strong radial ribs (e.g. *Rhynchonella*).

(c) **Terebratuloids**: the brachial supports form short or long loops. The shell is generally ovoid and is usually smooth, or ornamented with a few deep furrows (e.g. *Terebratula*).

L

Phylum Bryozoa

The Bryozoa or Polyzoa (Ordovician-Recent) are minute aquatic animals which form fixed colonies of many individuals, superficially resembling colonial coelenterates. The polyps are complex organisms possessing a fringed feeding organ not unlike the brachiopod-lophophore. The colonies are supported by a chitinous or calcareous skeleton and form encrustations on rocks, shells and weeds, or delicate fronds or bushy structures. They are very common fossils and contribute to the building of reef-limestones, but their identification is a matter for experts.

Phylum Annelida

The annelids (Pre-Cambrian-Recent) including the segmented worms and leeches, form a group which is both ancient and important, and includes some of the oldest known fossils. As the majority of its members are soft-bodied the fossil record is poor, but worm traces in the form of tracks on bedding-planes or burrows in sandy or muddy sediments are common, especially in shallow-water or intertidal sediments. Some marine worms (e.g. *Serpula*) make protective calcareous tubes which are also found as fossils.

Phylum Arthropoda

General anatomy. The arthropods (Cambrian-Recent) include the crabs, insects, spiders and so on and are distinguished by two features: the body is built of a series of *segments* arranged one behind the other, and it bears several pairs of jointed limbs or *appendages*. In the most primitive arthropods, all the segments are very much alike and each bears a pair of appendages. In the more advanced members of the phylum the front five or six segments are united into a definite *head*, and the remaining body-segments may also be specialised and may lose their appendages.

Arthropods are enclosed in a chitinous or calcified skeleton made up of a segmentally arranged series of rigid hoops united by flexible joints; fusion of the segments leads to the formation of a rigid armour, as in crabs. The appendages are covered by a similar jointed skeleton. During growth, the entire skeleton is periodically cast off and replaced by a newly-grown skeleton of a larger size.

The development of jointed armour enabled the arthropods to overcome the difficulties of active locomotion which confront all animals wearing their skeletons outside their bodies. The arrangement is both strong and flexible and allows the arthropods to adopt an active mode of life. Their anatomy is correspondingly highly organised; strong muscles serve the hinges of the skeleton, there is a controlling central nervous system with a brain and elaborate sense-organs, a blood vascular system and, in some groups, a complex respiratory system. The arthropods as a phylum are highly successful and flourish on land, and in the sea and air.

The classification of the arthropods is subject to some uncertainty, but for our purpose we may recognise five groups:

Trilobita (Palaeozoic): marine arthropods with many appendages (see below).

Crustacea (Cambrian-Recent): aquatic and terrestrial arthropods usually having many appendages — the shrimps, crabs, lobsters etc. Crustaceans are widely distributed, though not very common, as fossils; one specialised order, the *Ostracoda* in which the skeleton is modified into a minute bivalve shell, provides common fossils which are occasionally used in stratigraphical correlation.

Arachnida: aquatic and terrestrial arthropods which usually have four pairs of legs. They include the scorpions, the spiders and *Limulus* the king-crab. The extinct *Eurypterids* (Ordovician-Permian), which were perhaps arachnids, were fresh-water predators which reached the relatively enormous length of one or two metres.

Insecta: winged, air-breathing arthropods with six legs.

Myriapoda: many-legged air-breathing arthropods — the centipedes and millipedes.

TRILOBITA

The **Trilobita** (Cambrian-Permian) is the only arthropod group which we need consider in detail. The trilobites were marine animals, generally between an inch and a foot in length, which were among the most prominent inhabitants of shallow seas in the early Palaeozoic. The group reached its zenith about the middle of Lower Palaeozoic time, declined through Upper Palaeozoic and became extinct in the Permian. The trilobites have links with both the Crustacea and the Arachnida and all three groups may be descended from a common stock.

The majority of trilobites appear to have been bottom-dwellers. They are flattened and probably lived half buried in sand, protected by strong dorsal armour which is generally all that one sees in fossils. The armour is usually oval and is divided longitudinally into three lobes; the central axis is humped and contained most of the body-organs, while the lateral lobes form flaps protecting the appendages. The skeletons of the head-segments are fused into a single shield, the *cephalon*. Behind this follow a variable number of

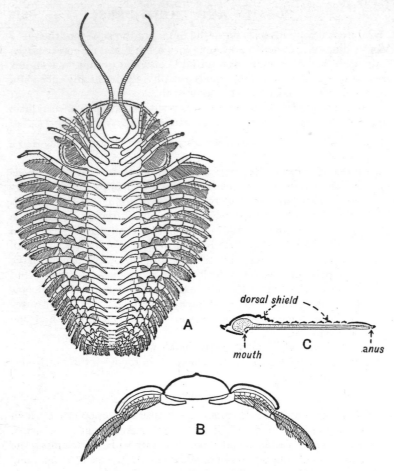

FIG. 186. *Trilobites.* A, ventral view of *Triarthrus*, showing
appendages; B, transverse section of thorax; C, longitudinal section.
(Bailey and Weir, *Introduction to Geology.*)

moveable segments forming the *thorax* and a group of fused segments
forming the tail or *pygidium* (Fig. 186).

Six originally independent segments are united in the *cephalon.*
The divisions between these segments are indicated in primitive
trilobites by grooves crossing the raised axial lobe or *glabella* of the
head; in more specialised trilobites, the glabella is smooth. The
lateral lobes of the head-shield form the *cheeks* which are in some
families crossed by a line dividing an inner portion or *fixed cheek* and
an outer portion or *free cheek*. This line of junction or *facial suture*,

314

with other sutures at the margin of the cephalon, was apparently a device to aid moulting, the cephalon splitting at the sutures to provide an exit for the trilobite; the cast skins of young trilobites are not uncommon as fossils.

Many trilobites possess paired *eyes* which appear on the free cheek, but which are seen in primitive forms to develop as outgrowths from the glabella. The eyes are compound structures made up of many small units, each with a hexagonal lens; they are in fact the characteristic arthropod type of eye and may represent the first efficient organ of sight ever to be evolved. The eyes are set on the upper surface of the head and the visual surfaces are generally raised and tilted forward and outward, an arrangement in accord with the needs of an animal living flat on a muddy or sandy sea-bottom.

The segments of the *thorax* vary in number from two to twenty-nine. They moved freely on one another and so allowed the trilobite to roll up like a woodlouse. The segments of the *pygidium* are united in a rigid plate which in primitive forms is small but in some advanced forms reaches about the same size as the cephalon.

The *appendages* lie on the soft under-surface of the body and are seldom preserved. Occasionally (e.g. in *Triarthrus*, Fig. 186) it can be seen that every segment except the first head-segment bears a pair of essentially similar appendages; each is biramous, the lower branch being leg-like and the upper branch being feathery and perhaps functioning as a gill. The appendages of the first head-segment are modified to form forwardly-directed antennae. There are no jaw-like head-appendages as in all modern classes of arthropods.

The classification of trilobites is not an easy matter. The genera fall readily into well-defined families but it is difficult to establish a genetic grouping into larger categories. The diagnostic feature most commonly used is the position of the facial suture. In the most primitive families (e.g. the *Mesonascidae*), this structure is not seen at all on the upper surface of the cephalon and the trilobites are said to be *hypoparian*. In *opisthoparian* trilobites the suture runs back from the front of the head to the inside of the eye and thence to the posterior margin of the cephalon. In *proparian* trilobites, the suture runs backward to the eye and then bends outward to the side of the cephalon (Fig. 187). Finally, certain highly specialised forms are also hypoparian. These include trilobites which are probably descended from opisthoparian or proparian ancestors; an example is the blind *Trinucleus* (Fig. 187) which is perhaps adapted for burrowing and seems to be related to the opisthoparian *Orometopus*. Other examples of specialised forms without facial sutures include the Cambrian fossil *Agnostus* which has only two thoracic segments and a pygidium

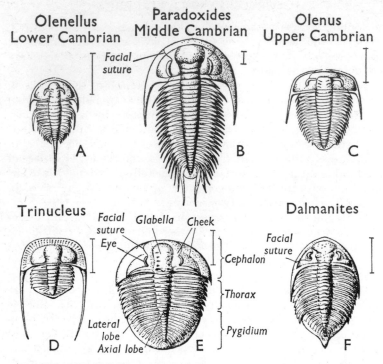

Olenellus
Lower Cambrian

Paradoxides
Middle Cambrian

Olenus
Upper Cambrian

Facial suture

A   B   C

Trinucleus

Dalmanites

Facial suture *Glabella* *Cheek*

Eye

Cephalon

Facial suture

Thorax

Lateral lobe

Pygidium

D *Axial lobe* E F

FIG. 187. Trilobites (vertical lines represent ½″). *Above*, three genera used as zone-fossils in Cambrian strata. *Below*, hypoparian (left), opisthoparian (centre) and proparian genera.

as large as its head; it may be only distantly related to other tri-lobites.

Summing up, we may recognise the following groups (Fig. 187).

(i) **The Mesonascidae and allied families**: these primitive families provide most of the earliest known trilobites in Lower Cambrias rocks, among them the zone-fossil *Olenellus*. Their characters suggest that they may be close to the ancestral stock. The thorax has many free segments while the pygidium is small. The glabella is marked by grooves indicating the divisions of the original head-segments. The eyes are joined to the glabella by a broad ridge. There is no facial suture.

(ii) **Opisthoparian trilobites** including the families Olenidae, Asaphidae and Illaenidae.

(iii) **Proparian trilobites** including the family Phacopidae.

(iv) Miscellaneous groups of specialised hypoparian trilobites, often of uncertain affinities (e.g. *Trinucleus*, *Agnostus*).

316

PHYLUM MOLLUSCA

Classification. The Mollusca (Cambrian-Recent) are a widespread group of shelled animals including the oysters, clams, snails and cuttlefish. They are among the commonest creatures of the sea-bottom and one class, the Cephalopoda, was of particular importance in the late Palaeozoic and Mesozoic. The molluscs are non-segmented animals with a basic bilateral symmetry and are generally characterised by a chitinous or calcareous shell. A muscular organ termed the *foot* generally projects from the shell and serves to assist locomotion; it is modified in a characteristic way in each class of the phylum. The general level of organisation in the molluscs is high, there is usually a circulatory system with a definite heart, a respiratory system and a central nervous system sometimes associated with a large brain and advanced sense organs. There are five principal classes:

Amphineura: primitive marine molluscs with shells made up of eight plates.

Scaphopoda (Silurian-Recent): aberrant marine molluscs with a single-valved tubular shell open at both ends. The elephant's tusk shell *Dentalium* is a modern representative of the group and similar forms are occasionally found fossil.

Gastropoda (Cambrian-Recent): marine, fresh-water and terrestrial molluscs with a univalve shell which is generally coiled into a spiral, e.g. whelks, snails etc.

Lamellibranchia (Ordovician-Recent): marine and fresh-water molluscs with bivalve shells, e.g. mussels, scallops, cockles etc.

Cephalopoda (Ordovician-Recent): advanced marine molluscs with a chambered univalve shell or no shell; the group includes the cuttlefish, octopus, nautiloids, ammonites and belemnites.

Class Gastropoda (Cambrian-Recent). The gastropods are unusual among the higher animals in being noticeably asymmetrical. Young gastropods are bilaterally symmetrical, but in the course of development one side of the animal grows more quickly than the other and imparts a spiral twist to the body. This torsion affects the internal organs in various ways; paired organs such as gills and kidneys may be suppressed on one side of the body and the gut and main nerves may be twisted into figures of eight. The shell acquires the characteristic form seen in the snails.

The majority of gastropods are crawling animals and the foot takes the form of a broad muscular structure with a flat base. There is a definite head equipped with sense-organs, which projects from the shell when the animal is in motion. The body wall is generally

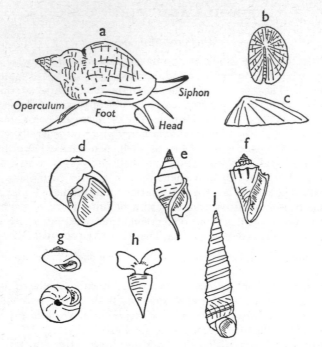

FIG. 188. *Gastropoda.* A, *Buccinum* (the whelk), showing head and foot extended; B, *Emarginula*; C, *Patella*; D, *Natica*; E, *Tibia*; F, *Volutospina*; G, *Cepolis*, lateral and ventral view showing umbilicus; H, a Pteropod, showing the animal with wing-like projections extending from the small shell; J, *Turritella.*

produced on one side into a flap or *mantle-lobe* enclosing a chamber known as the *mantle-cavity* which contains gills or, in terrestrial forms, acts as a lung. It communicates with the exterior by an aperture which may be a broad slit or a narrow hole, or may be prolonged into a spout-like *siphon* (Fig. 188).

The *shell* is made all in one piece and is essentially a cone open at the wide end. In the majority of gastropods it is wound on itself in a tight rising or *helicoid* spiral, a device which serves to make it more compact. The whorls of the spiral sometimes unite at the axis to form a central rod or *columella*; sometimes, instead, they enclose a small central cavity, the *umbilicus*. The mouth of the shell has a character-istic shape in many genera. Its rim may be thickened, and in forms with siphons it may be drawn out into a protective spout. The outer surface of the shell is often ornamented by growth-lines, ribs or colour patterns.

The strength and shape of the shell are largely dependent on the mode of life. Crawling marine gastropods tend to have heavy shells while fresh-water and terrestrial types often have lightly-constructed shells; in some of these types (e.g. the slugs) the shells are reduced to vestiges or entirely lost. The *Pteropoda*, an order adapted for a floating or pelagic marine life, have light, conical shells which are too small to contain the body; they are not uncommon fossils in open-sea deposits (p. 217).

The simplest form of shell (though not necessarily the most primitive) is a broad low cone exhibited by the limpet *Patella*. The shell-aperture is very wide and in the interests of security the limpet lives clamped down upon a rock-surface. Some genera have a small coil at the apex of the shell, some have a notch in the front of the shell-margin to allow for the entry of water into the mantle-cavity (e.g. *Emarginula*).

Coiled gastropod shells vary in shape according to the shape of the whorls and the *spiral angle*, that is, the angle between the tangents joining successive whorls. Where the spiral angle is large, the shell forms a broad low cone as in *Natica*; where it is small, the shell is elongated as in *Turritella*. A plane spiral, with a spiral angle of approximately 180°, is occasionally found (e.g. *Euomphalus*). Most spiral gastropods are *dextral*, the aperture appearing on the right when the shell is held apex uppermost, but a few genera, as well as occasional sports in normally dextral genera, are *sinistral*.

Class Lamellibranchia or Bivalvia (Ordovician-Recent). The majority of lamellibranchs are slow-moving or sedentary bottom-dwellers in salt or fresh waters. Some, like the oyster, are permanently fixed. Many, like the razor shell, are burrowers living half buried in sand or mud. Others plough their way along by contractions of the tongue-shaped foot which can be protruded from the shell. The majority are a few inches across, the largest reach a diameter of a few feet.

The *shell* consists of two *valves* placed laterally and articulating along a hinge-line. The plane of symmetry of the whole animal separates the two valves which are normally mirror-images of each other. The main part of the body occupies the hinge region of the shell and the foot projects downwards towards the free edges of the valves. Two *mantle-lobes* developed, as in gastropods, as flaps growing out from the body-wall, line the inside of the valves and are fixed to them by a band of *pallial muscle* a little distance within the rim of the shell. The *mantle-cavity* enclosed within the mantle-lobes forms a chamber containing the gills, and the mouth opens into this chamber, not directly on to the exterior. Food usually consists of small particles which are carried into the mantle-cavity in a current of water produced by the action of fine hairs or *cilia* on the mantle-lobes.

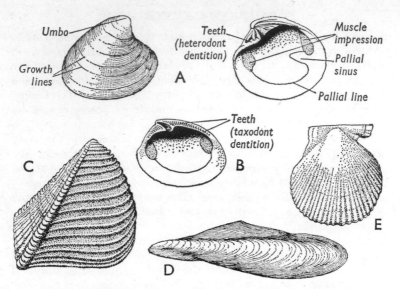

FIG. 189. Bivalves (× ½ approx.). A, outer and inner surfaces of one valve of an Eocene bivalve; B, a species of *Nucula*; C, D and E, three genera illustrating variations in the shape and ornamentation of the valves. C is allied to *Trigonia*, D is *Girvillella*, E is a scallop.

In some lamellibranchs, the mantle-cavity is partially enclosed by the fusion of the free edges of the mantle-lobes. An anterior opening provides an exit for the foot and two posterior openings or *siphons* serve as entrance and exit for the stream of water carrying food and oxygen. In burrowing forms, the siphons are often extended into long muscular tubes which can be protruded from the shell and so allow the animal to take in clear water. When retracted, the siphons occupy a space at the back of the mantle-cavity and the pallial muscles are shifted forward to make room for them (Fig. 189).

The *shell* begins as a largely chitinous structure which is reinforced with calcite or aragonite. The valves meet along a hinge-line, and near this line they are joined by a chitinous *ligament* so placed that its natural elasticity tends to open the shell. The effect of the ligament is counteracted in life by two transverse *adductor muscles* drawing the valves together; when the muscles relax, the ligament comes into play and hence dead shells always gape.

The structure of the *hinge* varies from group to group and is a useful diagnostic character (Fig. 189). The valves often articulate by means of *hinge-teeth* which fit into corresponding sockets. The most primitive arrangement consists of a row of similar teeth set perpendicular to the hinge-line; this *taxodont* type of dentition is exhibited by *Nucula*, a living genus which has survived with little change since the Silurian. In the *heterodont* type the teeth are few and their orientation is diverse. Finally, in many lamellibranchs, especially among fixed forms such as the mussels and oysters, the hinge is simplified and the teeth are rudimentary or absent; this is known as the *dysodont* condition and is related to environment rather than to lineage.

Each valve of the shell, when viewed from the outside, shows near the hinge a beak or *umbo* which represents the first-formed part. Growth-lines are concentrically arranged around the umbo. They show that growth did not take place evenly in all directions and the valve as a whole is often markedly asymmetrical. A few active forms like the scallop have nearly symmetrical valves but in the majority, and especially in the burrowers, the hinder part of the valve is elongated (e.g. *Pholas*). The ornament of the shell, provided by the growth-lines and by ribs, colour-patterns and spines, is very characteristic in some genera (e.g. *Trigonia*).

The inner surfaces of the valves show a number of markings which represent the attachments of muscles. The pallial muscles fixing the mantle leave a *pallial line* within the rim of the valve. A deep embayment or *pallial sinus* in the hind part of the shell records the displacement of the muscles in forms with large siphons. The adductor muscles leave circular impressions which are generally two in number and lie one in front of and one behind the hinge. *Pecten* and related genera have a single, centrally placed muscle-impression.

Variations in shell-shape and structure are often bound up with variations in way of life among the lamellibranchs. It is convenient to distinguish three groups — the *active forms*, in which the valves are generally similar and the shell not greatly elongated: the *burrowing forms*, in which the shell is sometimes elongated and generally provided with a pallial sinus: and the *fixed forms* in which there is often a difference between the two valves, reaching its maximum in *Hippurites*, where one valve forms a tube or cup and the other forms a lid to it; there is no pallial sinus and there may be only one adductor muscle. These features have only a limited genetic significance and we shall therefore not give a formal scheme of classification.

Class Cephalopoda (Cambrian-Recent). The cephalopods are bilaterally symmetrical marine molluscs typically possessing a univalve shell divided into several chambers. Unlike most other molluscs they may be strong swimmers and are often predatory in habit. They include the giant squids, the largest of all invertebrates. In keeping with their active mode of life, many cephalopods have a large brain and efficient sense-organs and their general level of bodily organisation is high. The foot is modified in two ways. Part of it is produced around the mouth into a ring of muscular tentacles, which are used for swimming and for catching prey. Part forms a muscular *funnel* leading to the mantle-cavity; water taken into the cavity through a valved slit can be violently expelled through the funnel to propel the animal swiftly through the water.

The cephalopods can be divided into the following sub-classes:

Nautiloidea: cephalopods with four gills in the mantle cavity, represented by a single living genus, *Nautilus*.

Ammonoidea: extinct cephalopods with a shell of many chambers.

Dibranchiata: cephalopods with two gills in the mantle-chamber. The shell is reduced or absent. The group includes the cuttlefish, octopus and the extinct belemnites.

Nautiloidea (Cambrian-Recent). The nautiloids are the oldest of the cephalopods and may have provided the ancestral stock from which the Ammonoidea and Dibranchiata were derived. Although they are now all but extinct, the survival of *Nautilus* gives us an opportunity to examine the anatomy of a primitive cephalopod.

Nautilus (Fig. 190) is housed in a univalve shell which is coiled in a plane spiral and is divided into numerous *chambers* by transverse partitions or *septa*. The body of the animal occupies only the final chamber and can be entirely withdrawn into this chamber, the

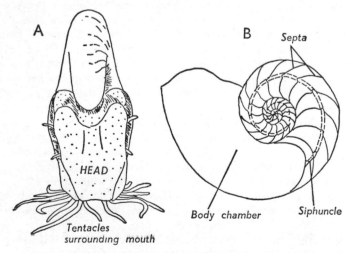

FIG. 190. *Nautiloids.* A, *Nautilus*; B, cross-section of Nautilus shell, × ⅓.

aperture then being blocked by a fold of tissue. When the animal is active a well-defined head, bearing many tentacles in a ring around the mouth, extends from the shell. The funnel lies against the outer side of the shell and the shell-mouth is notched by a *hyponomic sinus* to make room for it.

The nautiloid shell grows by the addition of new chambers at the mouth-end. The older chambers are vacated as each new septum is formed and are filled with gas so that they act as a buoyant apparatus bringing the average density of the animal down to somewhere near that of sea-water. This device of a gas-filled shell is shared by many cephalopods and helps to explain the contrast between their way of life and that of other shelled animals, most of which are permanent bottom-dwellers. A narrow tube, the *siphuncle*, filled with vascular tissue passes back from the body through the empty chambers of the shell. In *Nautilus* it pierces the centre of each septum, but in some fossil forms it is eccentric or marginal.

Fossil nautiloids agree with the living *Nautilus* in the essential structure of the shell but show different degrees of coiling. *Orthoceras* (Fig. 193), one of the earliest known cephalopods, has a straight conical shell in which the chambers lie serially one behind the other. *Phragmoceras* is curved but not coiled. Other genera have an older planispiral portion and a younger straight portion and may represent transitional stages connecting the straight and coiled types. Among the latter, forms in which the outer whorls do not overlap the sides of the

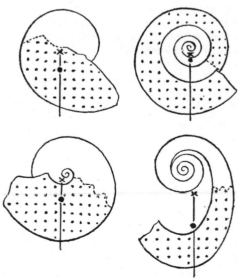

Fig. 191. Floating positions of Nautiloids and Ammonoids: body-chamber dotted, centre of gravity shown by a large dot, centre of buoyancy by a cross (after Trueman).

inner whorls are said to be *evolute*; those, like *Nautilus* itself, in which the inner whorls are hidden by succeeding whorls are said to be *involute*.

The uneven distribution of weight produced by the concentration of the body in a single chamber of the shell determines the natural attitude of the animal in the water. *Nautilus* floats with the buoyant empty chambers above the body-chamber and the shell-mouth facing upwards. *Orthoceras* may have balanced its shell with additional calcite to float horizontally and the partially coiled forms took up attitudes dictated by the position of their centres of gravity (Fig. 191).

Ammonoidea (Devonian-Cretaceous). The ammonoids became differentiated from a nautiloid stock in the Devonian and flourished in various forms throughout the Upper Palaeozoic and Mesozoic. While they lasted they were among the dominant marine animals of their day and they are the principal zone-fossils of the rocks in which they appear.

The chambered ammonoid shell is generally coiled in an evolute or involute plane-spiral. Curious forms in which the shell is partially uncoiled, or wound in a helicoid spiral appeared from time to time and may have been adapted for special modes of life (Fig. 191). In many early ammonoids the shell-mouth has a *hyponomic sinus* like that of *Nautilus*. Some later forms have instead a projecting beak or *rostrum* on the outer side of the shell-mouth, or a pair of laterally placed projections known as *lappets*. Two detached small plates borne on the body-wall closed the shell-mouth when the ammonoid withdrew into the body chamber; these *aptychi* are sometimes found as separate fossils. The *siphuncle* is marginal in position and generally lies on the outside of the shell-spiral; but in one group, the clymeniids, the siphuncle lies on the inside of the whorls.

The main distinguishing feature of the ammonoids is the form of the *sutures* joining the septa to the outer shell-wall. In nautiloids, the suture is a smooth line. In ammonoids it is sinuous because the outer parts of each septum are frilled or plicated, an arrangement which strengthens the junction between adjacent chambers. The suture-lines became more complicated during the evolution of the ammonoids and provide important diagnostic characters (Fig. 192).

Ammonoid sutures are conventionally represented in the manner shown in Fig. 192, where the arrow marks the mid-point on the outside of the shell-spiral. Simple *goniatitic* sutures show a zig-zag pattern; the forwardly-directed loops or *saddles* may be either angular or rounded, while the backwardly-projecting *lobes* are generally angular. With increasing complication, first the saddles and then the lobes are frilled by minor plications, the frilling appearing first near the centre-line.

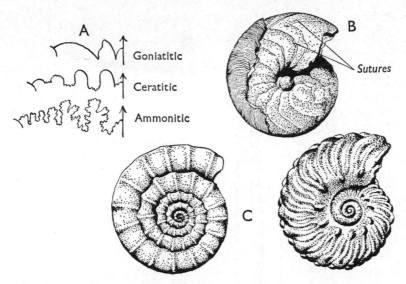

FIG 192. Ammonoids (× ½ approx.). A, diagrammatic representation of ammonoid sutures illustrating three stages of increasing complexity. The arrow marks the outer part of the whorl. B, an Upper Palaeozoic goniatite. C, two Mesozoic ammonites, *Arnioceras* (left) and *Euhoplites*, illustrating variations in coiling and ornamentation.

The details of ammonoid classification can only be appreciated by specialists. They are based on such characters as the form of the suture, the tightness of the coiling, the shapes of the whorls and the ornamentation of the shell (Fig. 192). For our purposes it is enough to distinguish three main divisions:

Goniatites (Upper Palaeozoic): siphuncle at outer margin of shell, simple sutures with lobes and saddles but little subsidiary frilling.

Clymeniids (Upper Palaeozoic): siphuncle at inner margin of shell, goniatitic sutures.

Ammonites (mainly Mesozoic): siphuncle at outer margin of shell, sutures elaborately frilled.

The goniatites were probably derived from nautiloid ancestors and were themselves the ancestors of the ammonites. The two groups are connected by types showing intermediate degrees of crenulation of the suture. The clymeniids may be regarded as a sideline.

Dibranchiata (Trias-Recent). The cuttlefish, squid and octopus, which are the living representatives of this sub-class, are distinguished from the cephalopods so far mentioned in that the shell is either entirely absent or reduced to a relatively small internal structure.

325

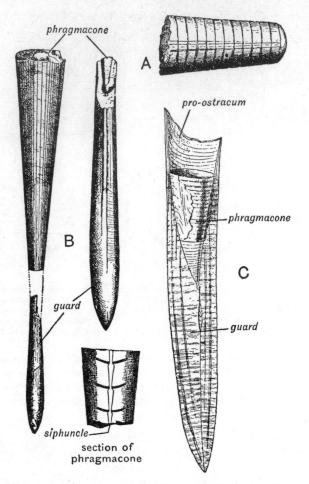

phragmacone

pro-ostracum

phragmacone

A

B

C

guard

guard

siphuncle

section of
phragmacone

FIG. 193. A, *Orthoceras*; B, a Belemnite; C, longitudinal section of a
Belemnite. (Bailey and Weir, *Introduction to Geology*.)

The reduction of the shell, however, may be a comparatively recent
event and the ancestral dibranchiates probably possessed a chambered shell; these ancestral forms are perhaps represented by the
Belemnites (Trias-Early Tertiary).

The earliest belemnites had a straight chambered shell distinguished by a thickening of the shell-wall at the apical end. In the more
typical members of the group (Fig. 193) the apex of the shell is produced into a solid rod known as the *guard* which is the only structure
commonly preserved in fossils. The chambered portion or *phragmacone*

326

is reduced in size and was probably too small to contain the body. The phragmacone is produced at its open end into an elongated plate, the *pro-ostracum* which may be analogous to the cuttlefish 'bone'.

PHYLUM ECHINODERMATA

Anatomy and classification. The echinoderms (Cambrian-Recent) are bottom-living marine animals generally only a few inches in size. At the present day the majority of echinoderms are free-living, but many fossil forms were fixed, and it is commonly supposed that the phylum is descended from sedentary ancestors. The echinoderms (starfish, sea-urchins etc.) are characterised by an imperfect five-rayed symmetry superimposed on a fundamental bilateral symmetry; radial symmetry in animals is generally associated with a sedentary mode of life and its presence strengthens the case for the derivation of the phylum from attached ancestors.

Echinoderms are unique among invertebrates in that the skeleton, though apparently external, is of mesodermal origin. It consists of a large number of plates or *ossicles* which are usually fitted together into a rigid or flexible *test*. Each ossicle is made of a single calcite crystal and shows the typical calcite cleavage when broken; echino-derm-plates are therefore very easily recognised in rocks.

The main part of the body is generally rounded, but in several groups it bears a ring of projecting *arms*, usually five in number. Fixed forms are often raised on a flexible *stalk* of many ossicles. Although there is no head, it is generally possible to distinguish an *oral surface* containing the mouth and an opposite *aboral surface*. In fixed forms the oral surface faces upwards; in free forms it faces downwards.

The distinctive feature of the internal anatomy is the presence of a *water vascular system*, a system of vessels in direct communication with the sea-water. This is concerned with respiration and is often connected with a large number of *tube feet* used as locomotor, tactile and respiratory organs. The principal channels of the water vascular system are a ring-vessel around the mouth and five radial vessels running longitudinally beneath the test and into the arms. The presence of these vessels defines five specialised radii or *ambulacra* which can generally be recognised in the living animal by the presence of a double line of tube feet projecting from the surface of the test. Fixed echinoderms show sunken *food-grooves* above the ambulacra; these are food-gathering devices in which the motion of cilia propels small particles in the water towards the mouth.

The Echinodermata can be classified into two sub-phyla, containing altogether seven classes, as shown below. From each sub-phylum we select a single large class for detailed description.

Pelmatozoa. Fixed forms generally mounted on a stalk with the oral surface uppermost. The body or *theca* often has projecting arms. Ambulacral food-grooves extend over the theca and along the arms.

(*a*) **Cystoidea** (Cambrian-Carboniferous): primitive stalked echinoderms with very imperfect radial symmetry. The ossicles of the theca are irregularly arranged and the number of arms varies from one to five.

(*b*) **Crinoidea** (Cambrian-Recent): stalked echinoderms with five simple or branching arms.

(*c*) **Blastoidea** (Silurian-Permian): small stalked echinoderms without arms.

(*d*) **Edrioasteroidea** (Ordovician-Carboniferous): echinoderms with food grooves but generally no stalk.

Eleutherozoa. Free-living forms with the oral surface facing downwards and the anus generally aboral. Tube feet are generally well-developed and there are no food grooves (Fig. 195).

(*a*) **Stelleroidea** (Ordovician-Recent): forms with five arms — the starfish.

(*b*) **Holothuroidea** (Cambrian-Recent): cylindrical forms with the mouth anterior (sea-cucumbers). The ossicles are not united into a solid test but are isolated in the skin.

(*c*) **Echinoidea** (Ordovician-Recent): globular or heart-shaped forms — the sea-urchins and heart-urchins.

Crinoidea (Cambrian-Recent). The Crinoidea, the most important division of the Pelmatozoa, is the only division represented by living forms. The present-day crinoids (sea-lilies) live in groves in clear, moderately deep water; the majority are raised on stalks which may be tens of metres long. In the Palaeozoic and early Mesozoic, crinoids were very numerous, and their loose stem ossicles occasionally piled up to form *crinoidal limestones*.

Crinoids have three main parts — the *stem*, the *theca* and the *arms* (Fig. 194). The *stem* is usually made of a line of single ossicles, each pierced by a central hole containing a strand of living tissue. Root-like branches near the base may anchor the animal to the sea-bottom, but in some crinoids the stem is tapering, coiled or even absent; these forms are not permanently fixed, but can attach themselves temporarily by twining the stem round other objects or by clinging with claw-like projections or *cirri*.

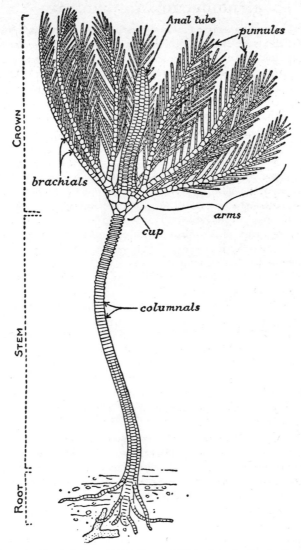

FIG. 194. *Typical Crinoid.* (Bailey and Weir, *Introduction to Geology.*)

The *theca* consists of a cup of regularly arranged plates rising from the stem and bearing the arms at its upper margin, and a cover or *tegmen* closing in the space above the level of the arms. The actual arrangement of the plates differs from one group to another. The cup always contains two circlets of ossicles, five being the normal number

329

in each circlet. The upper plates or *radials* are in contact with the bases of the arms. Beneath these come the *basals* which may fit directly against the top of the stalk (*monocyclic* crinoids) or may be separated from the stalk by a cycle of *infrabasals* (*dicyclic* crinoids). The cover or tegmen which completes the theca is in modern crinoids a flexible membrane containing many small plates. In some Palaeozoic genera the tegmen was a firm dome covering in the mouth and the bases of the food-grooves. The anus opens on the tegmen and its position may be marked by a special plate or tube.

The flexible *arms* are normally five in number and may remain unbranched (e.g. *Cupressocrinus*) or may bifurcate repeatedly; they are often fringed with small *pinnules*. Each arm contains a large number of *brachial plates*, the lowermost of which are sometimes incorporated in the theca (e.g. *Apiocrinus*). The food-grooves extend into each branch of the arms, and so provide an elaborate system of channels down which food-particles are passively swept to the mouth.

The **Echinoidea** (Ordovician-Recent) are, from a palaeontological point of view, the most important division of the Eleutherozoa. They are free-living bottom-dwellers found among rocks or on sandy shores. They are generally active feeders and do not possess the food-groove mechanism of the Pelmatozoa. Large numbers of *tube-feet* are arranged in double lines along the ambulacra; these tube-feet are mobile and in some forms are provided with terminal suckers by which the animal can cling to rock-surfaces and crawl along. The test is generally covered with *spines* which appear to be used for various purposes — as a defence mechanism, as buffers in rough water, as stilt-like organs of locomotion and even, in burrowing echinoids, as digging implements.

The structure of the *test* can be described by reference to the modern sea-urchin *Echinus*. The main part or *corona* forms a slightly flattened sphere with openings at the two poles (Fig. 195). The larger opening, covered in life by a membrane (the *peristome*) surrounding the mouth, faces downwards and marks the oral surface. The aboral opening is covered by a membrane with small plates (the *periproct*) which surrounds the anus and which is enclosed by two rings of polygonal plates, the whole constituting the *apical system*. The five plates of the inner ring (*genitals*), which are inter-ambulacral in position, are pierced by pores connected with the reproductive system; one of the genital plates, often rather large and rough, contains the inlet of the water vascular system and is known as the *madreporite*. The outer five plates or *oculars* are small and alternate with the genitals.

The *corona* is constructed on a regular pattern. Two columns of narrow plates, each pierced by two pores for the tube feet, mark each

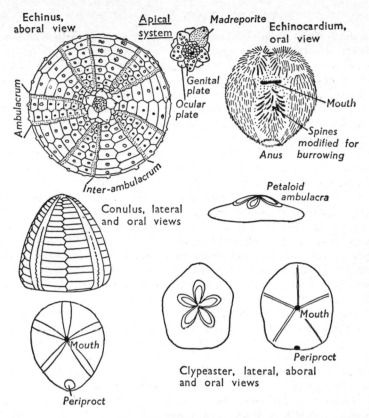

Echinus,
aboral view

Apical
system

Madreporite

Echinocardium,
oral view

Ambulacrum

Genital
plate
Ocular
plate

Mouth

Spines
modified for
Anus burrowing

Inter-ambulacrum

Conulus, lateral
and oral views

Petaloid
ambulacra

Mouth

Mouth

Periproct

Clypeaster, lateral, aboral
and oral views

Periproct

FIG. 195. *Echinoids* (× ½–⅓).

ambulacrum. Two columns of larger plates fill in each inter-ambulacrum, so that the whole test consists of twenty columns; the simple arrangement is modified by the grouping together and ultimate fusion of several plates. The plates of the corona bear rounded knobs which articulate in a ball-and-socket joint with the moveable spines.

Echinus shows an almost perfect pentamerous symmetry. No part of the body consistently takes the lead in locomotion and there is therefore, for practical purposes, no anterior-posterior axis. This arrangement is in accord with the sea-urchin's habits — living among shapeless and wave-washed rocks, it must be capable of adopting any attitude. The same general pattern characterises the majority of rock-dwelling sea-urchins (e.g. *Cidaris*) and these types are known as *regular* echinoids. A different arrangement is found in the *irregular* echinoids, the majority of which are adapted for life on sandy shores.

331

In these forms a new bilateral symmetry associated with a definite anterior-posterior axis is assumed.

In irregular sea-urchins, the periproct is no longer placed in the centre of the apical system. It migrates backward into one of the inter-ambulacral spaces and may reach a position at or near the circumference of the test. The mouth may remain central or may migrate forward in the ambulacrum diametrically opposite the periproct. The shape of the test is modified in various ways. The oral surface is generally flattened, to rest smoothly on the sea-bed as in *Conulus*; the entire test may be flattened, so that the animal is unlikely to be rolled over (e.g. *Clypeus*) or, in burrowing echinoids, it may become heart-shaped and develop a deep groove in the position of the anterior ambulacrum (e.g. *Micraster* and the modern heart-urchin). The tube-feet cease to act as locomotor-organs, having no hard surface to work on, and the ambulacra are partially suppressed; they may become confined to the aboral surface and exhibit a tapering *petaloid* form. The spines become slender and sometimes almost hair-like; in some burrowing urchins, spines on the front of the test are flattened into minute scoops for burrowing.

The Echinoidea remained inconspicuous throughout the Palaeozoic and differed from later regular echinoids in having a variable number — less or more than twenty — of columns in the test. All these variable forms disappeared at the end of the Palaeozoic and were replaced by a more standardised stock of regular echinoids with twenty columns of plates. The first irregular urchins — off-shoots of a regular group, distinguished at first only by the slightly eccentric position of the periproct — appeared during the Jurassic when migration into sandy habitats began. In the late Jurassic and Cretaceous numerous groups of irregular urchins appeared.

GRAPTOLITHINA

The **graptolites** (Cambrian-Carboniferous) are small colonial marine animals whose affinities have been much debated. They have in the past been compared with coelenterates and with bryozoa, but the balance of opinion now favours the view that they are related to a primitive chordate stock (see below). As they are utterly different from any of the other chordates we shall describe, and as they form an important group in their own right, it seems best to deal with them independently.

The colonies are delicate structures consisting of one, two, four or more stalks or *stipes* bearing the *thecae* which housed the individual animals. Each stipe is slender and is seldom more than an inch or so in length. The skeleton is chitinous and is generally preserved as a flattened film of carbon looking like a pencil mark (hence the name of the group). Graptolites entombed in limestones are occasionally preserved in a three-dimensional form and can be extracted by dissolving the matrix in acid.

The *thecae* are open cups a millimetre or so across, which when flattened appear as roughly triangular or rectangular shapes. They show internal markings which may represent muscle-impressions, but are otherwise uninformative as to the structure of the inhabitants. The grouping of individuals in the colony, on the other hand, provides a basis for classification and supplies a surprising amount of information about the evolution and way of life of the graptolites.

Two principal subdivisions may be distinguished:

Dendroidea (Cambrian-Carboniferous): bushy, many-branched colonies with thecae of more than one kind.

Graptoloidea (Ordovician-Devonian): colonies with restricted branching and only one kind of theca.

Dendroid graptolites appeared towards the end of the Cambrian. They became subordinate to the graptoloids soon after the appearance of the latter, but lingered as rather rare fossils until the end of the Palaeozoic. The graptoloids, among the commonest of Ordovician and Silurian fossils, evolved rapidly and provided many short-lived types which are used in stratigraphical correlations; by the middle of the Silurian they were declining and they became virtually extinct at the end of the period.

The Dendroid colonies are composed of a large number of branches springing from a common point of origin. The branches may be bound into a firm structure by connecting threads as in *Dictyonema* (Fig. 196). Some genera have a root-like base and seem to have grown

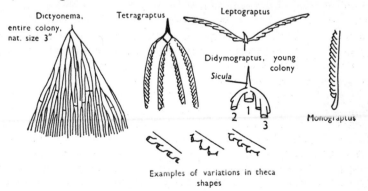

Examples of variations in theca
shapes

Fig. 196. *Graptolites* (about ⅔ natural size).

upright from a rock or weed. Others appear to have hung downward from drifting seaweed or to have developed a balloon-like float from which they were suspended. The thecae are arranged in threes along the stipes and the members of each group appear to have housed different kinds of individuals, some perhaps specialised for reproduction.

The earliest graptoloids were bushy and not unlike dendroid forms. The majority of the group were pelagic or floating. Some were attached to drifting seaweed, others had floats of their own, and most appear to have hung downwards from the point of origin at the beginning of their growth. This inversion of the colony, when compared with the usually upright dendroids, may have led to changes expressed in the evolution of the group.

The starting point of each graptoloid colony is a small conical structure, the *sicula*, which housed the first individual. This normally floated mouth-downwards and a thread or *nema* projected upward from its apex; a minute disc which served for attachment is sometimes present at the free end of the nema. The first ordinary theca of the colony is attached to the side of the sicula and appears to have been formed by budding. A second bud projects from the side of the first and, in most graptolites, both these buds give rise to branches of the colony, new individuals appearing successively beyond them.

The thecae of each colony are all identical and are generally borne on only one side of the stalk, so that when fossilised they appear like the teeth of a saw. Their shape varies (Fig. 196). In early graptoloids they are simple cylinders set at an oblique angle to the stipe. In later graptoloids they may be twisted to face along the stipe, elongated, hooked or even coiled.

The structure of graptoloid colonies as a whole changed progressively during the evolution of the group, similar changes taking place independently in several lineages (Fig. 197). The two principal trends were towards a reduction in the number of branches and towards a rotation of these branches from their original drooping attitude; both trends may reflect mechanical adjustments following the adoption of a pelagic habit.

Graptoloids in the lowest Ordovician strata have between sixty-four and four branches. Those of the rest of the Ordovician have two branches while those of the Silurian have typically only a single stipe. The earlier branched graptoloids were *pendent*, the branches hanging from the sicula to produce a 'tuning-fork' pattern. The trend of change from this condition leads to the appearance of colonies in which the stipes diverge more widely until they reach a horizontal position and begin to come together again, in a reversed attitude,

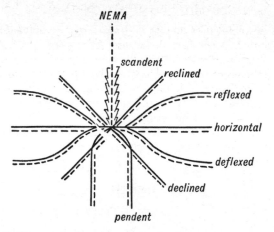

FIG. 197. Changes in direction of growth of graptolites, from pendent to scandent. (Bailey and Weir, FIG. 134, p. 261.)

about the sicula. Finally, in *scandent* graptoloids, the stipes are joined back to back with the thecae facing outward from them.

PHYLUM CHORDATA

The chordates (?Cambrian-Recent) are a large and very successful phylum which includes the fish, amphibia, reptiles, birds and mammals as well as some lesser-known creatures. The characteristic feature uniting the phylum is the occurrence of an internal skeleton produced by the mesoderm. This initially took the form of a single firm rod, the *notochord*, lying beneath the main nerve trunk. In higher chordates the notochord is largely replaced by a line of *vertebrae* which articulate to form a flexible *backbone*. We may thus recognise at once a fundamental division within the phylum:

(a) Several small sub-phyla in which the notochord is not replaced by a vertebral column; the **Graptolithina** (pp. 332-5) should perhaps be classified here.

(b) The sub-phylum **Vertebrata,** characterised by the possession of a vertebral column.

VERTEBRATA

In the **Vertebrata** (Ordovician-Recent) the skeleton is a complex structure made of bones or cartilages articulating with one another by means of moveable joints. The strength and flexibility supplied by the jointed internal skeleton make the vertebrates capable of rapid and powerful movements and are largely responsible for the high level of their general organisation.

The body is built on a bilaterally symmetrical, segmented plan, reflected in the repetition of vertebrae, ribs, nerves and muscles down the length of the body. Two pairs of limbs are generally present. The digestive, respiratory and blood vascular systems are all highly organised and the nervous system shows a remarkable degree of development. The main nerve is a dorsally placed tube which expands in the head to form a large brain connected with elaborate sense-organs.

TABLE III

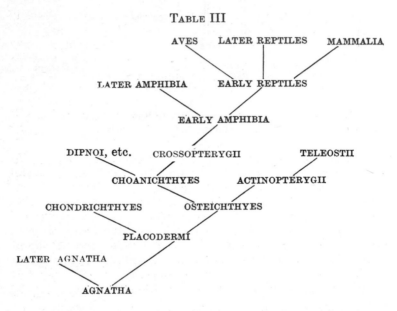

Vertebrate skeletons are far more complex than the shells or tests of any invertebrates, and we cannot give an adequate account of them in a book of this size. We shall, however, outline the history of the vertebrate classes (see Table III) and shall deal with certain evolutionary changes which are demonstrably related to the adoption of new ways of life and which provide particularly good illustrations of the working of the evolutionary process.

We may recognise seven classes among the vertebrates:

Agnatha (Ordovician-Recent): jaw-less fish-like organisms.
Placodermi (Silurian-Permian): fish-like organisms with primitive jaws.

Chondrichthyes (Devonian-Recent): true fish with a largely car-
tilaginous skeleton.
Osteichthyes (Devonian-Recent): true fish with a bony skeleton.
Amphibia (Devonian-Recent): tetrapods with an aquatic larval stage.
Reptilia (Carboniferous-Recent): egg-laying tetrapods.
Aves (the birds, Jurassic-Recent): egg-laying tetrapods adapted for
flying.
Mammalia (Triassic-Recent): warm-blooded viviparous tetrapods
and egg-laying Monotremes.

Primitive Vertebrates. Although the ancestral vertebrate stock was
probably marine, the early development of the sub-phylum appears
to have taken place principally in rivers and lakes. Aquatic vertebrates which can be loosely called 'fish' began with the group of the
Ostracodermi and allied forms which are placed with the modern
lampreys in the class **Agnatha.** The ostracoderms and their allies
were small fish-like creatures covered with an armour-plating of bony
plates which united over the head into a continuous shield (Fig. 198).
They were free-swimming and could maintain their position in
running water or propel themselves forward by sculling movements
of the flexible tail. There were no paired fins.

The ostracoderms were passive feeders, straining minute particles
from the water by a filtering mechanism. Water was taken in through

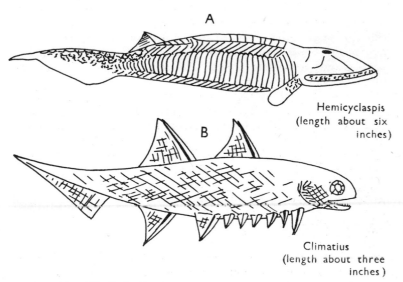

A

Hemicyclaspis
(length about six
inches)

B

Climatius
(length about three
inches)

Fig. 198. *Early Chordates.* A, Ostracoderm; B, Placoderm.

the small jaw-less mouth, passed through many pairs of segmentally arranged gill-pouches where food was collected and oxygen extracted, and expelled through paired *gill-slits* at the sides of the throat.

The **Placodermi,** the second vertebrate class to appear, included a number of groups of heavily armoured and often very grotesque animals, which might be regarded as early experiments with the vertebrate pattern (Fig. 198). They differ from the Agnatha in one significant feature, the structure of the head and jaw. The mouth in the Placodermi was supported by bony jaws hinged at the side of the head, capable of gaping widely, and often furnished with strong teeth. This jaw-apparatus would clearly have no function in animals which fed passively. Its development must be taken to indicate that the placoderms had gone over to an active mode of feeding; in so doing, they had taken the first step on the road which led to the evolution of the higher vertebrates. The placoderms themselves, however, were still very primitive. The tail was the main organ of propulsion, although a series of dorsal fins and spines, or rudimentary paired flaps ranging up to seven pairs, were present in some forms to act as balancing organs.

In the course of the Devonian period there arose from among the placoderm groups two lines whose general structure was more advanced than that of the earlier forms. These were the **Chondrichthyes** and the **Osteichthyes,** the two classes of true fish. With their appearance the vertebrate pattern became more stabilised; the number of limbs settled down at two pairs and the active mode of feeding was perfected by the development of a more efficient jaw-mechanism. The paired fins were for the first time supported by a strong skeleton and were so constructed that they could be used in locomotion as paddles and as steering organs. The muscular tail remained an essential organ of propulsion.

Since the skeletons of higher vertebrates are based fundamentally on the same pattern as that of the primitive groups, we must briefly consider the make-up of the primitive skeleton. In the ostracoderms, there are two sets of components — a set of bony plates which forms the *external armour*, and a cartilaginous *axial skeleton* protecting the nerve cord and brain. The axial skeleton consists of (*a*) the *notochord* associated with rudimentary vertebrae, (*b*) the *skull* enclosing the brain, (*c*) incomplete capsules protecting the eyes, ears and nasal organs, partly joined to the skull, and (*d*) up to ten pairs of *branchial arches*, slender rods supporting the partitions between the gill-pouches (Fig. 199).

In the placoderms, the skeleton shows an important modification connected with the adoption of the new mode of feeding. The enlargement of the mouth interfered with the functioning of the front

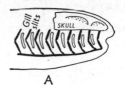 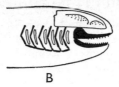 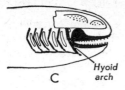

A   B   C

FIG. 199. *Development of Jaw Apparatus.* A, Agnatha, with un-modified gill arches; B, Placoderm with front gill-arches modified to produce jaws; C, true Fish, with hyoid arch incorporated in jaw (based on Romer).

gill-pouches and led to the suppression of the first two pairs of branchial arches. The third pair was modified into the *jaws* (Fig. 199). On each side, the jaw-arch now consists of two rods joined by a moveable hinge. The free ends of these rods project forward to meet those on the opposite side in the middle line above and below the mouth; bony *teeth* are set in each jaw. Behind the jaw-arch, the re-maining six branchial arches preserve their original function.

Fish. In the true fish, the skeleton shows further modifications. The *external armour* of the primitive vertebrates was retained by most early fish as a covering of strong bony plates. During evolution of the Osteichthyes, some of the plates covering the head became incorporated in the skull. The plates of the body became progressively smaller and lighter; they were reduced, in Chondrichthyes, to isolated tooth-like *denticles* and, in Osteichthyes, to delicate *scales*.

The *axial skeleton* shows as a rule a more complete replacement of the notochord by vertebrae. In the head, the jaw-suspension is improved by the incorporation of the fourth branchial arch or *hyoid arch* (Fig. 199). On each side, the upper bone of this arch is converted into a strut bracing the angle of the jaw against the side of the skull. The gill-chamber in front of the hyoid arch is crowded out of existence and its slit is suppressed entirely or reduced to a small hole, the *spiracle*. The number of pairs of functional gills is thus reduced in the true fish to five or less.

The evolution of *paired fins* in the two classes of fish led to the development of skeletal elements not represented in the earlier groups. The fins themselves are supported by groups of small bones or cartilages and by slender *fin rays*, arranged in various ways. The muscles moving the fins are given a firm base by two *limb-girdles* encircling the under side of the body; these girdles are essentially U-shaped structures within the body-wall.

Chondrichthyes. Both the classes of true fish have jaws, limbs and limb-girdles of the general types described above, though they differ in many details of their structure. The Chondrichthyes, which we

339

need not consider at length, are a compact, entirely marine group including the sharks, skates, chimeras and their ancestors. They are characterised by the cartilaginous composition of the skeleton and in this and many other features appear to lie off the main stream of vertebrate evolution.

Osteichthyes. The Osteichthyes or bony fish are a more numerous and varied class and include the stock from which all the higher vertebrates were derived. For our purposes, the class may be subdivided as follows:

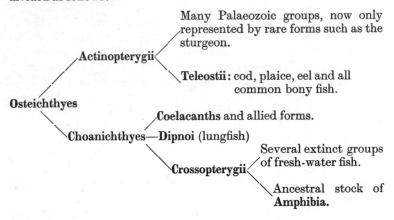

Actinopterygii

Many Palaeozoic groups, now only represented by rare forms such as the sturgeon.

Teleostii: cod, plaice, eel and all common bony fish.

Osteichthyes

Choanichthyes—Dipnoi (lungfish)

Coelacanths and allied forms.

Crossopterygii

Several extinct groups of fresh-water fish.

Ancestral stock of **Amphibia.**

The two main subdivisions of the Osteichthyes became differentiated soon after the first appearance of the class in the Devonian. The early actinopterygians retained in a somewhat reduced form the bony dermal plating characteristic of the ancestral stock, and the few surviving descendants of these groups such as the sturgeon show the same character. At about the beginning of the Mesozoic the important group of *teleost fish* arose in a marine environment from the actinopterygian stock; after an initial period of insignificance, this group multiplied in the late Mesozoic and Tertiary to become the dominant aquatic vertebrates of the present day. The Teleostii show a wide range of adaptation both in salt and fresh water and are anatomically very complex.

The *Choanichthyes* remained to a large extent in fresh-water environments and some of their groups, such as the *Dipnoi*, acquired the capacity to survive periods of drought buried in mud by the use of primitive lungs. The two surviving groups of fish belonging to the Choanichthyes, the Dipnoi and the coelacanths, can be traced back with remarkably little change to the Devonian; they are now very rare.

The *Crossopterygian fish*, now extinct, are of special importance as

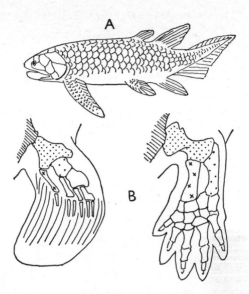

Fig. 200. *Development of Land Vertebrates.* A, Crossopterygian fish; B, fin-skeleton of crossopterygian fish (*left*) compared with pentadactyl limb of a land vertebrate; the homologous bones in the two skeletons are similarly ornamented, (based on Romer).

the stock from which the Amphibia and other land vertebrates were derived (Fig. 200). These fish, living often in waters subject to drought, possessed primitive lungs and had nostrils separated from the mouth to allow for the intake of air. The fins were supported by a column of short bones, instead of by spreading rays as in teleosts, and may have been strong enough to allow the fish to flounder along on land.

Adaptation to land-conditions. The migration of crossopterygian fish on to land precipitated a second revolution in vertebrate habits and structure and laid down the pattern of the skeleton for all succeeding classes. Four major changes took place — these changes were not completed in the earliest land-vertebrates and their progress can be traced through several groups. The *limbs* were elongated and provided with *feet* capable of taking the weight of the body. The *backbone* was strengthened by a firmer articulation of its vertebrae and was united more closely with the *limb-girdles*, both modifications being necessary to support the body in the less dense medium of air. Finally, the *tail*, losing much of its locomotor function, was commonly greatly reduced.

The land-vertebrates moved on four legs and are therefore known

341

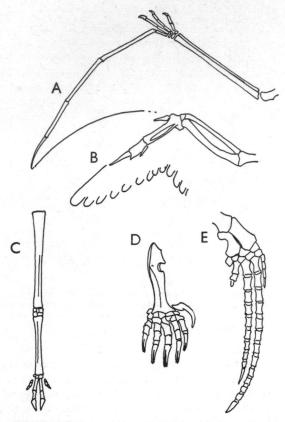

Fig. 201. *Adaptations of the Pentadactyl Limb.* A, for flight —
Pterodactyl, reduced in weight, finger elongated to support wing
membrane; B, for flight — bird, reduced in weight, fingers modified
to support wing feathers; C, for running — deer, hand lengthened,
bones fused, fingers reduced; D, for digging — mole, bones strengthened, hand broadened; E, for swimming — dolphin, fingers modified
to support paddle.

as *tetrapods*. Their feet were built on a five-fingered or *pentadactyl*
scheme which, though modified in creatures adapted for special ways
of life, was carried on through all the tetrapod groups. The skeleton
of the pentadactyl limb taken over from the fin-skeleton of the cros-
sopterygians (Fig. 200), was modified by the lengthening of the bones
nearer the body and by the development of a foot with spreading
toes which provided a surface for walking on. In the early amphibia
and reptiles the limbs generally sprawled out sideways and were too
weak to hold the body clear of the ground. They thus worked from a

342

position of mechanical disadvantage and in many of the more advanced reptiles and mammals the limbs were rotated into a vertical position and so the body was raised above the ground.

Among reptiles, birds and mammals, the standard pattern of the pentadactyl limb was modified in characteristic ways by forms which adopted unusual methods of locomotion. Some of the more extreme modifications are shown in Fig. 201. They illustrate well the irreversible character of evolutionary changes. The marine reptiles adapted for swimming have paddle-like limbs which are, in external form and in function, closely similar to the fins of fish, but their skeletons are obviously pentadactyl and are in essentials the same as those of land-reptiles. In the same way, the wing-supports derived from the fore limbs of pterodactyls, birds and bats are all forms of the pentadactyl limb producing a comparable mechanical effect, but they are structurally quite distinct.

Amphibia. The **Amphibia** which appeared at the end of the Devonian were, in their early days, a truly transitional class living near lakes and rivers and often spending much time in the water. The larvae, like the modern tadpole, were fish-like organisms which breathed by means of gills, fossil larvae with intact branchial arches being found in some rocks. During the Carboniferous, Permian and Triassic, amphibia were larger, more varied and more abundant than at any later period. The majority belonged to the group of **Labyrinthodonta** and showed a large, often grotesque, head with a strong heavy skull, and a low elongated body ending in a long tail.

Reptilia. The **reptiles** appeared in the late Carboniferous as offshoots of an unspecialised line of labyrinthodonts. They rapidly became dominant over the amphibia and throughout the Mesozoic era they remained the most abundant class of terrestrial vertebrates. Their emancipation from water, resulting from the development of a type of egg capable of hatching out on land, allowed the reptiles to spread far over the hitherto thinly-populated lands, where plants had now become available as a source of food. The primitive reptile stock gave rise within a short time to a large number of very diverse groups, specialised for different modes of life not only on land but also in the sea and the air (Fig. 202). This division of a group into many branches suited to different environments is termed *adaptive radiation.* At the end of the Mesozoic most of the specialised orders of reptiles died out, only the lizards, snakes, turtles, tortoises, crocodiles and a few other lines surviving to the present day.

The earliest reptiles or **cotylosaurs** closely resembled labyrinthodonts. They were stockily built, rather lizard-like creatures with strong but sprawling limbs. From them were derived the many

M

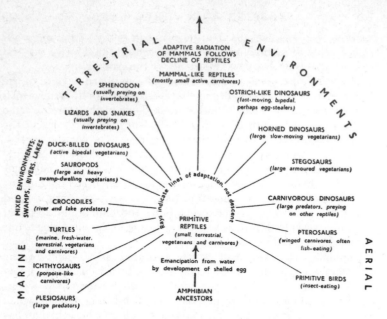

FIG. 202. *Adaptive Radiation of Reptiles.*

groups of Mesozoic and modern reptiles including those which still survive today. Among extinct lines were the **archosaurs** in which the lizard-like body was lifted off the ground by the lengthening and strengthening of the hind limbs; the archosaurs included swift runners moving on two legs. From these energetic bipeds arose the many kinds of **dinosaurs**, the flying **pterodactyls** and the **birds**.

The dinosaurs were abundant and varied. They included vegetarians standing on two legs to graze from trees (e.g. *Iguanodon*), four-footed vegetarians of enormous bulk (e.g. *Triceratops*) and predators such as *Tyrannosaurus* which stood nearly twenty feet high. Other reptiles, descended independently from the cotylosaurs, migrated back to the sea and were perhaps the largest marine animals of the Mesozoic. These included the grotesque long-necked **plesiosaurs** and the dolphin-like **ichthyosaurs**.

Mammalia. Early in the development of the reptiles there appeared a line of *mammal-like reptiles* including active carnivores whose body was held well clear of the ground. This line led by a transitional series to the true *mammals* which appeared at the end of the Triassic or early in the Jurassic. We have no means of telling at what exact point in the series the distinctive mammalian traits of warm-bloodedness, viviparous reproduction and care of the young were assumed; they may have arisen independently in more than one lineage. So far as the skeleton is concerned, an almost perfect transition between the reptilian and mammalian patterns can be traced.

The mammals remained small and inconspicuous during the Mesozoic, but with the extinction of the great reptiles they in turn underwent a phase of adaptive radiation and established themselves in almost every conceivable habitat. Specialised groups returned to the sea (whales, dolphins, sea-cows, etc.) or took to the air (bats) as the reptiles had done before them. The majority of mammalian orders are too well-known to need enumerating but we may mention a few lesser-known groups. The **pantotheres** were very small, somewhat shrew-like Jurassic mammals which are probably ancestral to most later groups. The **multituberculates**, a late Mesozoic and early Tertiary group of rodent-like creatures, and the egg-laying **monotremes** (the duck-billed platypus and spiny echidna), however, may be independent lines derived directly from reptilian ancestors.

The **marsupials** or pouched mammals such as the kangaroo and opossum are a living group distinct from all other mammals. Their fossil record is poor, but it is evident that they were once more widely distributed than they are at the present day. Among the more advanced groups of living mammals the first to appear were the unspecialised **insectivores** and from these were probably descended the **primates** including the monkeys, apes and man. Among many other orders, the vast groups of **ungulates** appeared early in the Tertiary. They are hoofed vegetarians and their evolution may have had some connection with the appearance of the flowering plants and especially the grasses.

THE PLANT-KINGDOM

NON-CELLULAR PLANTS

Plants, like animals, are generally built of very large numbers of protoplasmic cells but there are, as among the animals, a few groups of *non-cellular plants*. These are small or microscopic organisms which resemble plants in performing photosynthesis, but which are often free-living and mobile; they have much in common with the Protozoa and some authorities would unite all non-cellular organisms in a separate kingdom.

Diatomaceae. The diatoms are non-cellular free-living organisms which float in the surface-layers of the sea and of fresh-water lakes. They are enclosed in minute tests made of silica which are bilaterally symmetrical and show characteristic sculpturing (Fig. 207). Fossil diatoms go no further back than the Jurassic, but the group may actually be more ancient than this. Diatom-tests are the principal components of the rock *diatomite* (p. 268).

MULTICELLULAR PLANTS

Among the multicellular plants, we may make a first distinction between the *non-vascular plants*, which are primarily aquatic and which show little cell differentiation, and the *vascular plants* which are primarily terrestrial and which possess a vascular system of specially constructed cells capable of transmitting food-substances from one part of the body to another.

NON-VASCULAR PLANTS

Thallophyta (Pre-Cambrian-Recent). The thallophytes are non-vascular plants in which the body or *thallus* shows no differentiation into root, stem and leaves and is often little more than a disc or ribbon made up of many identical cells. This division of the plant-kingdom includes several groups of plants capable of undertaking photosynthesis, which are collectively known as *Algae*, and a group of degenerate plants, the *Fungi*, which have lost the power of photo-synthesis and live as parasites or in places where dead organic matter is available.

The *Algae*, which include the familiar seaweeds, belong to several groups characterised by distinctive colours. They range from a microscopic size up to a length of a few feet and may form simple branching filaments or more bulky and elaborate structures. Algal filaments have been identified in rocks as old as Devonian and when in sufficient bulk they occasionally give rise to a carbonaceous rock known as *boghead-coal*. Some algae reinforce the thallus with secretions of calcium carbonate and the nodular or branching masses which they produce are important fossils. *Calcareous algae* are some-times reef-builders and are common in coral-reefs (p. 212). They include the oldest known fossils and are in fact almost the only fossil organisms known in the Pre-Cambrian.

Bryophyta (liverworts and mosses). The liverworts and mosses are small non-vascular plants living in moist places on land. They are rather more highly organised than the algae but are so delicately constructed that they are seldom found as fossils. The first known bryophytes occur in Carboniferous rocks.

VASCULAR PLANTS

The migration of plants into terrestrial habitats was accompanied by numerous modifications of the simple thallus. Differentiation of a root-system concerned with the absorption of water and inorganic salts and of an aerial part concerned with respiration and photosynthesis led to the development of a vascular system through which exchange of material could take place. The structure of the vascular system varies, but in all groups the system consists essentially of bundles of elongated cells; the cell-contents are in some instances absorbed and the walls are pierced to provide continuous channels. The cell-walls are often thickened with organic compounds such as the woody substance *lignin* and the vascular system therefore helps to support the plant in the air.

The exposure of plants to air necessitated the development of devices to restrict water loss through evaporation. A waxy cuticle is commonly produced to form an impermeable covering and this is pierced by minute pores or *stomata* leading to microscopic air-chambers beneath the surface of the plant. The function of the stomata is to allow exchange of oxygen and carbon dioxide to take place without undue water-loss. They are guarded by two characteristically shaped cells and appear, in very much their modern form, in scraps of cuticle isolated from some of the oldest known rocks containing vascular plant-tissue.

Pteridophyta. The pteridophytes (Silurian-Recent) include several groups of vascular plants which are distinguished by the fact that they reproduce by means of *spores*. They were the earliest vascular plants to appear and enjoyed a brief dominance in the Upper Palaeozoic; they are now of little importance compared with the seed-plants.

The main divisions of the pteridophytes are as follow:

Psilophytales (Devonian):
Lycopodiales (Silurian-Recent): the club-mosses and their allies.
Articulatales (Devonian-Recent): the horse-tails and their allies.
Filicales (Devonian-Recent): the ferns.

The **Psilophytales** were a short-lived group of simple land-plants which may resemble the ancestral stock of the more advanced groups. They were first found in 1859 by J. W. Dawson in Nova Scotia and, fifty years later, were described by Kidston and Lang from a remarkable chert in the Old Red Sandstone of Rhynie, in Aberdeenshire. The chert was apparently deposited in a bog and the bog-plants and their debris were silicified in such a way as to preserve many details of their anatomy and cell-structure.

Most psilophytales have a prostrate stem or *rhizome*, anchored to the ground by bunches of root-like hairs. Slender, bifurcating upright stems spring from the rhizome and form the main part of the plant

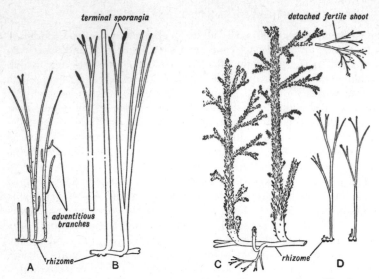

terminal sporangia   detached fertile shoot

adventitious branches

rhizome   B   C   rhizome

A   D

Fig. 203. *Fossil Plants from the Rhynie Chert.* A and B, *Rhynia*; C, *Asteroxylon*; D, *Hornea.* (Bailey and Weir, *Introduction to Geology.*)

(Fig. 203); in some genera they are bare, in others they are clothed in small sessile (i.e., stalk-less) leaves. Hollow capsules borne at the tips of the stems provide the organs of reproduction. These *sporangia* contain when ripe a crowd of microscopic unicellular *spores* each enclosed in a resistant skin.

The **Lycopodiales** are represented today only by the club-mosses *Lycopodium* and *Selaginella* which seldom reach a height of more than a few inches. Palaeozoic lycopods, however, included forest trees such as *Lepidodendron* (Fig. 204) and were among the dominant plants of the Coal-Measure swamps.

The living *Lycopodium* (Fig. 204) is a moss-like plant with a slender bifurcating stem clothed in small sessile leaves. Fibrous *roots* appear at several points along the stem. The fertile shoots on which the reproductive organs are borne show a close resemblance to the ordinary vegetative shoots and provide an insight into the derivation of the more complex structures of higher plants. Each fertile shoot terminates in a *cone* clothed in small *sporophylls* which differ from the foliage leaves only in bearing on their upper surface a single *sporangium*. The spores of each sporangium are commonly clustered in fours or *tetrads* and each tetrad of spores can be shown to be formed by the division of a spore mother-cell without the intervention at any stage of a sexual process.

The spores of Lycopodium are liberated by splitting of the

348

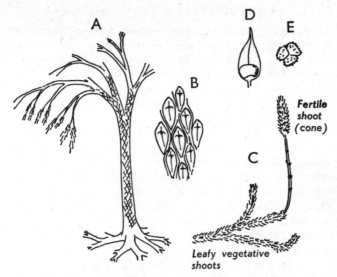

Fertile
shoot
(cone)

Leafy vegetative
shoots

FIG. 204. *Lycopods*. A, *Lepidodendron* (greatly reduced); B, fragment of bark of *Lepidodendron* showing leaf-bases; C, *Lycopodium*,
(× 1); D, sporophyll with sporangium; E, tetrad of spores.

sporangium and germinate to produce a new plant quite unlike the
parent; this *prothallus* is a small thalloid structure which lives an
independent life for a short time before reproducing sexually to give
rise to a fertilised egg from which a normal club-moss develops. The
life-cycle of *Lycopodium* thus involves an *alternation of generations*;
the sexually-produced generation consists of highly-organised individuals, while the generation derived from the asexually-produced
spores is small and simple. We shall note a progressive reduction in
the prothallus in the higher groups of plants.

The tree Lycopods of the Carboniferous forests (Fig. 204) reached
heights of at least a hundred feet. The main trunk divides at the base
in a characteristic way into four spreading roots which fork repeatedly and give off fine lateral rootlets. The trunk itself forks in the
upper part to produce a crown of branches. The leaves, as in
Lycopodium, are small and sessile and expand at their point of
attachment into broad cushions. The pattern of the leaf-scars on the
bark gives a distinctive sculpturing to the trunk and branches.

In the fertile cones the sporophylls are modified into scaly structures and no longer resemble the foliage-leaves. The sporangia are of
two kinds — *microsporangia* containing many tetrads of *microspores*,
and *megasporangia* containing one or a few tetrads of *megaspores*.
The spores develop into prothalli, which are occasionally found as

349

fossils; female organs are borne on prothalli derived from megaspores and male organs on those derived from microspores.

The nomenclature of fossil lycopods raises problems which illustrate some of the practical difficulties of palaeobotany. Most fossil-plants are fragments and not whole organisms, a fact which arises naturally from their mode of accumulation on forest-floors or in marshes or ponds. Twigs, leaves, roots, cones and spores all tend to occur as independent fossils and there is often no means of establishing that a particular type of cone, say, was borne on branches with a particular pattern of leaf-scars. For this reason, separate names have been proposed for different parts of the plant; *Lepidodendron*, for example, is largely a genus of trunks and branches, *Stigmaria* of roots and *Lepidophyllum* of leaves. Correlation depends on the occasional discovery of more complete fossils.

The **Articulatales**, like the lycopods, are an almost extinct group which is now only represented by the horsetails of the genus *Equisetum*. In the late Palaeozoic they formed sizable trees with a habit of growth not unlike a bamboo. They are characterised by a curious regular jointing of the hollow stems which makes them easily identifiable even in small fragments.

In *Equisetum* a branching rhizome gives off upright stems which show a strong vertical ribbing and are divided into segments by *nodes* at which the central cavity is crossed by horizontal partitions. Whorls of jointed branches and rings of minute leaves are borne at each node (Fig. 205). Reproductive cones are carried at the tips of the main stems; they are covered with umbrella-shaped structures each bearing several sporangia. The spores are all of one kind and germinate to produce minute prothalli. The fossil horsetails, of which

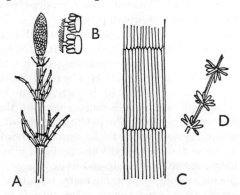

FIG. 205. *Articulatales*. A, *Equisetum* (× 1); B, sporophylls, enlarged, of *Equisetum*; C, stem of *Calamites*; D, leaves of *Calamites*.

Calamites (Fig. 205) is a common genus, resemble *Equisetum* in almost every respect except size.

The **Filicales** or ferns are the only pteridophytes which remain abundant at the present day. They differ from all the groups described above in that the stems are relatively inconspicuous and the leaves are very large, often forming deeply divided fronds which bear sporangia in clusters on their under surfaces. The sporangia and spores are all of one kind and the spores germinate to produce a small green prothallus.

Spermaphyta (Carboniferous-Recent). The Spermaphyta or *seed-bearing* plants include all the groups which dominate the modern land flora. They are probably derived from early spore-bearing ancestors and differ from the latter in the suppression of the alternation of generations in the life-cycle. Organs apparently corresponding with the megasporangia and microsporangia of pteridophytes are produced in the seed-bearing plants, but the spores formed in these organs never germinate to give independent prothalli. Instead, the megaspores are retained in the sporangia and give rise, by cell-division, to the *ovule*. The microspores are liberated as *pollen* and carried by wind or insects to fertilise the ovule and produce the *seed*. Germination of the seed gives rise directly to a plant of the same type as the parent. In primitive seed-plants the sporangia are borne on sporophylls resembling ordinary foliage leaves, but in the more advanced types the fertile shoots are modified into woody *cones* or elaborate *flowers*.

The main divisions of the spermaphytes are as follow:

A. **Gymnospermae** (Carboniferous-Recent). Seed not completely enclosed in an ovary.

   (i) **Pteridospermae** (Carboniferous-Jurassic). The Pteridosperms are herbaceous or scrambling fern-like plants bearing fruits slightly reminiscent of hazel nuts on the ordinary foliage-fronds. They are abundant members of the Coal-Measure flora and *Glossopteris* (Fig. 206), a genus with simple tongue-shaped leaves, is widely distributed in Permo-Carboniferous rocks of the southern hemisphere.

   (ii) **Cycadales** (Triassic-Recent). The cycads are stumpy palm-like trees with a crown of large pinnate leaves. The seeds are borne in distinct cones.

   (iii) **Bennettitales** (Triassic-Cretaceous). This group, which assumed considerable importance in the Mesozoic, resembled the cycads in general appearance but was distinguished by bearing its seeds in special flower-like shoots.

M2

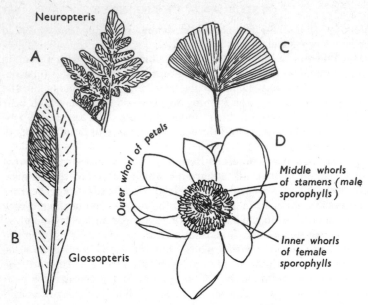

Neuropteris

A

C

Outer whorl of petals

D

Middle whorls
of stamens (male
sporophylls)

B

Glossopteris

Inner whorls
of female
sporophylls

FIG. 206. *Seed-bearing Plants.* A and B, Pteridosperms; C, *Ginkgo*;
D, flower of a primitive Angiosperm (*Magnolia*).

(iv) **Ginkgoales** (Triassic-Recent). The ginkgos were graceful trees characterised by leaves of a very distinctive form (Fig. 206). A single species, *Ginkgo biloba*, survives in cultivation.

(v) **Coniferales** (Carboniferous-Recent). The conifers are the only gymnosperms which are abundant at the present day and even this relatively successful group is now largely confined to the less favourable habitats where competition from the angiosperms is less intense. The conifers, the pines, cypresses, junipers, etc. are trees and shrubs characterised by very small needle- or scale-like leaves. The sporangia are carried in woody cones quite unlike the vegetative shoots.

B. **Angiospermae** (Jurassic-Recent): seed completely enclosed in an ovary — the **flowering plants.** The angiosperms are the most highly organised group of plants and show a greater differentiation of cells for special purposes than any other group. The fertile shoots are modified to form flowers of various kinds and elaborate devices ensure the fertilisation and dispersal of seeds. The flowering plants appeared in the Jurassic and by the beginning of the Tertiary era they had virtually ousted all other groups. The evolution of this group, and particularly the appearance of the grasses, had a profound effect on the food-supplies of the lands and may have influenced the development of the great Tertiary groups of grazing mammals. Also correlated with their evolution is the amazing complexity of the insects.

FOSSILS AS STRATIGRAPHICAL INDICES

William Smith's dictum (pp. 5–6) that strata could be identified by the fossils they contained was arrived at empirically as a result of observations in the field. Its meaning became apparent when the concept of evolution was established. Evolution is an irreversible process and every species evolved is unique — once a species has become extinct, its form is never precisely repeated.

The fossils of each geological system therefore represent the life of that period and of no other. Silurian rocks, for example, may contain trilobites, graptolites, rugose corals and characteristic genera of other groups such as brachiopods. Cretaceous rocks contain ammonites, belemnites, reptiles and different but equally characteristic species of brachiopods.

Fossils may be further used to establish chronological divisions within each geological period. A sequence of strata can be divided into small sections or *zones*, each of which is characterised by a particular association of fossils. One of these fossils gives its name to the zone and is termed the *zone-fossil* (see Fig. 176, for an example of zone sequences). The full sequence of zones for any system is only seen in regions where sedimentation went on without interruption. Pauses in sedimentation can be recognised palaeontologically by the absence of the fossils of a certain zone. *Correlation* of strata by means of their fossils involves the recognition and matching of zonal assemblages in rocks of separated localities (see p. 290).

The qualities which make fossils suitable for use as zonal indices are decided by the function these fossils fulfil. They must be reasonably common and distinctive. They should have a short time-range and are therefore most commonly supplied by rapidly-evolving groups. They should have as wide a geographical range as possible and they should appear in a variety of sedimentary facies. This last condition is more readily satisfied by free-swimming or pelagic animals like the ammonoids and graptolites, respectively, than by sedentary creatures such as corals or brachiopods. The most important fossil-groups, from a stratigraphical point of view, are the trilobites, graptolites, ammonoids and foraminifera, from which the zone-fossils of many standard sequences are drawn. Almost every conceivable type of fossil has at some time been used in zoning a succession of strata; the only test of a system of zoning is whether it can be made to work.

PALAEO-ECOLOGY: ORGANISMS IN RELATION TO THEIR ENVIRONMENT

Plants and animals live, not in isolation, but in mixed communities dependent for their livelihood on each other and on the inorganic world around them. The plants, which alone have the power of photosynthesis, are the basis of each community; the animals prey on plants or on each other, while scavengers, fungi and bacteria attack decaying organic matter. Every member of a community fills a slightly different role and its structure and physiology are adapted to fit it for this role.

The process of **adaptation to environment** is largely responsible for the astonishing diversity of living organisms and appears to have been one of the main factors in evolution. We can assume, on uniformitarian grounds, that the earth's surface has offered a comparable range of variety at least since the beginning of the fossil-record and we may therefore begin our study of organisms in relation to their environment by surveying the environments of life at the present day; we can compare these environments with those of deposition already noted in pp. 240–1.

Marine environments. Conditions in the sea vary both horizontally with distance from the land and vertically with depth. In the horizontal dimension we have distinguished three regions (p. 208): the *littoral zone* occupying the region between tide-marks; the shallow-sea or *neritic zone* extending roughly to the edge of the continental shelf and the *deep-sea zone* of the open ocean. In the vertical sense we may contrast the surface-waters lit by the sun with the sea-bottom and, in the deep oceans, with an intervening zone which lies in perpetual darkness.

The *littoral zone* is populated by seaweeds and animals which are capable of withstanding exposure during the periods of low tide. Typical littoral animals at the present day are molluscs such as mussels, limpets and winkles, crustaceans, sea-anemones and burrowing worms; they form characteristic associations and analogous assemblages of fossils are known.

The *neritic zone* is very variable. The sea-floor may be muddy, sandy or rocky, the water may be rough or smooth, clear or muddy, salt or brackish. The faunas are correspondingly diverse. A sandy sea-bed, for example, may harbour burrowing worms and molluscs, irregular echinoids and flatfish. A rocky floor may have lobsters, regular echinoids, bryozoa and corals. Coral-reefs are dominated by sedentary organisms — calcareous algae, and colonial corals and bryozoa. In most neritic environments, the sea-bottom is lit by the sun and aerated by waves or currents. It is therefore thickly populated by fixed and free-living organisms. Many of these are protected by heavy shells or skeletons and they therefore provide very suitable material for fossilisation.

In the *deep sea* a definite zoning of organisms is discernible. The surface-waters are occupied by communities of floating or *pelagic* organisms which drift more or less passively with wind and currents. These communities constitute the *plankton* which is the basis of all life in the open ocean (Fig. 207). The plants of the plankton are free-floating, often unicellular organisms such as the diatoms; since they depend on light for photosynthesis they are restricted to the surface-layer of water. Planktonic animals include radiolaria, jelly-fish and pteropods as well as hosts of crustacean, echinoderm and other

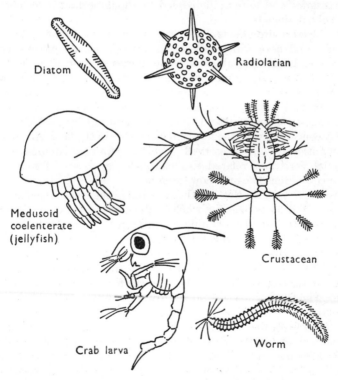

Diatom

Radiolarian

Medusoid
coelenterate
(jellyfish)

Crustacean

Crab larva

Worm

Fɪɢ. 207. *Planktonic Organisms* (greatly enlarged).

larvae. They are lightly-constructed, often nearly transparent creatures; many have no hard parts and those, like the pteropods, which have skeletons, show more delicate structures than related bottom-living forms.

The second open-sea community or *benthos* is made up of bottom-living organisms such as deep-water brachiopods, molluscs and crinoids. These forms are less abundant and varied than the bottom-dwellers of shallow seas. They live in perpetual darkness and are therefore not accompanied by an indigenous plant population. Organic debris raining down from the surface-layers of the sea provides the food-basis of the community.

Finally, the third open-sea association is the *nekton*, made up of free-swimming animals which are able to move at will through the whole depth of the ocean. At the present day, the majority of these animals are vertebrates such as fish, porpoises and seals. In the Mesozoic era, the vertebrates included marine reptiles such as the ichthyosaurs, and were accompanied by the important invertebrate group of ammonoids.

Terrestrial environments. Everybody is familiar with the variations in fauna and flora which reflect variations in environmental conditions on land. Special local communities appear in a host of restricted minor environments — for example, in the fissures of a limestone-surface, in a peat-bog, a river, lake or sea-cliff. On a somewhat larger scale, ecological variations are related to topography, soil-composition, rainfall and so on. We need not, as geologists, be greatly concerned with the local environments of the land, since their communities are only preserved in very exceptional circumstances. Regional variations related to climate, however, are of some importance and these we may now examine.

Climatic variations. Both on the land and in the sea, a broad zoning of faunas and floras over the whole of the globe reflects the influence of climatic factors. This zoning is illustrated, for example, by the distribution of the land-vegetation. The stunted tundras of the arctic regions give place successively to coniferous forests, to the deciduous woods of the temperate zones, the sparse and specialised plants of the great deserts and finally the tropical forests of the equatorial region. The smaller plants and the animals of each belt are equally distinctive.

In the oceans, there is a comparable zonal arrangement, modified to some extent by the effects of the great currents such as the Gulf Stream. An important dividing line marks out an equatorial zone extending for some thirty degrees north and south of the equator. Within this zone (Fig. 213), the temperature of the surface-waters seldom falls below 60° F. (15° C.) and reef-building corals, with the special communities that accompany them, are widespread (p. 212). Outside this zone coral-reefs are rare, although the more tolerant solitary corals have a wider distribution.

Fossils in relation to their environment. The aspect of the fossil-population in a rock determines its **faunal or floral facies.** In establishing this facies we must take into account not only the identity of the fossils, but their condition and mode of preservation, their relation to each other and the composition and structure of the enclosing rock. The first problem to be considered is whether the fossils which are associated with one another in the rock represent any single living community.

A *life-assemblage* of fossils is one which does in fact represent such a past community. The assemblage naturally does not include all the

Fig. 208. Trace-fossils preserved in their original position: vertical U-shaped worm-burrows in a bed of Devonian sandstone showing the relationship of the burrows to the bedding-plane at the top of the bed. (Photograph by P. Wallace).

FIG. 209. Mechanically produced assemblage of fossils: belemnites concentrated and aligned by current action (ex col. D. V. Ager).

members of the community — soft-bodied animals and plants, and bacteria are normally absent — but it is nonetheless an association which makes sense biologically. Examples may be supplied by certain reef-limestones, where colonial corals and bryozoa and calcareous algae may all be preserved upright in the position of growth, with their own debris and fragments of crinoids, gastropods and other creatures wedged between them. Similarly, a coal-seam may contain the stumps of forest-trees standing upright above an ancient soil still threaded by rootlets in the position of growth. The fossils of life-assemblages are commonly in a good state of preservation and, as in the examples mentioned above, there may be evidence that they were fossilised on the spot where they had lived (Fig. 208).

A *death-assemblage* of fossils is an association brought together mechanically by the activities of wind and water (Fig. 209). It may be recognisable by the jumbling together of diverse types, and by the worn and fragmental condition of the fossils. Common examples are shell-limestones, representing shell-banks washed up by waves. A special kind of death-assemblage is one containing *derived* fossils of

358

older geological formations; such fossils have been weathered out of older rocks and passively redeposited. The distinction between life-assemblages and death-assemblages is not of course an absolute one since the fossils of a rock may be derived from several sources. Estuarine or inshore deposits, for example, may contain a life-assemblage of brachiopods and worm-traces mixed with scraps of fossil-wood drifted out from the land, or pelagic fossils carried in from deeper water. Deeper-water deposits commonly contain remains of the benthos, nekton and plankton mixed together although, as we have seen, the three communities are distinct in life.

The faunal facies of a rock is thus determined by a combination of factors. It depends partly on the character of the organisms available for fossilisation and partly on the mode of accumulation of the sediment. The broad distinction between marine, fresh-water and terrestrial assemblages is generally fairly clear, although some mixing of populations is common; fresh-water deposits, for example, frequently contain fragments of terrestrial organisms such as vertebrates carried into them by flood-waters, and pollen or insects blown in by the wind. Among marine deposits, special shallow-water communities such as those of tidal mud-flats and coral-reefs can be preserved as life-assemblages, while mixed assemblages characterise the current-laid sediments, such as sandstones and clastic limestones. Sediments laid down beyond the reach of strong currents are usually dominated by the remains of planktonic and free-swimming animals.

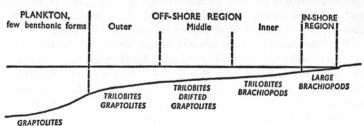

FIG. 210. Variation in faunal facies in the Lower Palaeozoic rocks of Wales (after Elles); diagrammatic section showing relation of fauna to distance from the shore line.

These contrasts are illustrated by the distribution of facies at many levels in the stratigraphical succession. In the Lower Palaeozoic rocks of Wales, for example, it is possible to distinguish a 'shelly facies' dominated by trilobites, brachiopods and corals and a 'graptolitic facies' dominated by the pelagic graptolites (Fig. 210). The two facies show a regular distribution, varying systematically with time, which

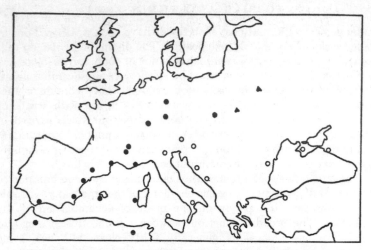

FIG. 211. Faunal facies of the European Trias. Triangles, terrestrial faunas: solid circles, mixed terrestrial and shallow sea faunas: open circles, open sea faunas with ammonites.

is related to changes in the shape of the sea in which the sediments were accumulating. Similarly, in European Mesozoic rocks shelly faunas of appropriate types again characterise inshore deposits while open-sea deposits contain fewer shelly fossils and are dominated by the free-swimming ammonites (Fig. 211).

The evidence of **climatic variations** supplied by fossils is naturally most reliable for recent geological periods, where fossils of still-living species provide points of reference whose climatic preferences are known. The fluctuations of climate during and after the Pleistocene ice-age are reflected in the succession of floras in Europe. Accumulations of peat formed during this period contain great quantities of pollen blown in from surrounding forests. Statistical analyses of samples collected from successive levels in the peat reveal variations in the proportions of different kinds of pollen, each species being distinguishable by the shape and ornamentation of the grains (Fig. 212). In East Anglia, *pollen analyses* show that the trees which first appeared after the withdrawal of the ice-sheet were birch and pine; they were superseded by hazel, oak, elm and lime, later joined by beech and hornbeam, which require warmer conditions and these in turn gave place to pine and birch, indicating a return to cooler weather.

The broad arrangement of climatic zones in earlier periods can often be deduced from the regional distribution of fossils, even where no modern species are available to act as points of reference. Regular

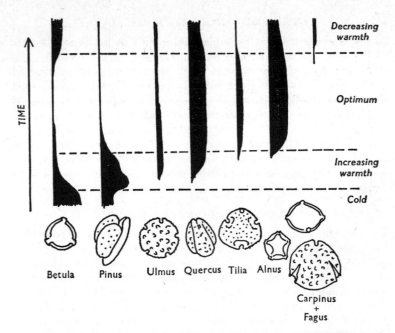

FIG. 212. *Pollen Analysis*. Schematic diagram showing variations in the post-Glacial forests of East Anglia: the pollen grains of genera dealt with are shown, greatly enlarged, below the appropriate columns (after Godwin).

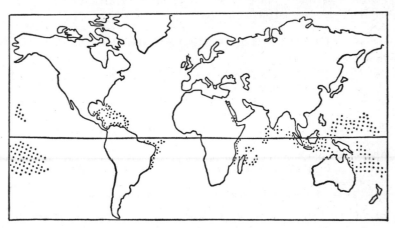

FIG. 213. Climatic control of faunas: the distribution of modern coral-reef faunas.

faunal changes towards an equatorial zone can reasonably be attributed to climatic variations. In Jurassic rocks, for example, reef-building corals, associated with distinctive brachiopods and lamellibranchs, occur in England as far north as Yorkshire and extend throughout a belt reaching 55° north of the equator and some 5° south. As we have seen, modern reef-corals only flourish in warm waters (Fig. 213) and it is probable that the Jurassic reef-builders, which belong to the same group, required similar conditions. The faunal evidence suggests that the Jurassic climatic belts were not symmetrically arranged about the present poles and, as we shall see, other lines of evidence lead to similar conclusions (pp. 644–7).

FAUNAL AND FLORAL PROVINCES

The climatic and other environmental factors discussed above play an important part in controlling the distribution of plants and animals. If they were the only factors involved, we should expect to find identical communities living in similar environments all over the world. In fact, however, almost every part of the globe has a distinctive population, and it is possible to delimit *faunal and floral provinces* characterised by particular associations of animals and plants. The origin of the faunal and floral provinces of the present day and of past ages cannot be discussed adequately in this book. It can only be understood in a historical context since it is bound up both with the evolution and migration of living organisms and with the geological processes controlling the distribution of land and sea at different times. Some of the problems that arise in these connections are touched on in Chapter 12.

FURTHER READING AND REFERENCE

Invertebrates

Davies, A. M., 1962, *An Introduction to Palaeontology*, 3rd edit., revised by C. J. Stubblefield, Murby.

Shrock, R. R., and W. H. Twenhofel, 1953, *Principles of Invertebrate Palaeontology*, McGraw-Hill.

Swinnerton, H. H., 1947, *Outlines of Palaeontology*, 3rd edit., Arnold.

Vertebrates

Romer, A. S., 1945, *Vertebrate Palaeontology*, 2nd edit., Univ. of Chicago Press.

——, 1954, *Man and the Vertebrates*, 2 volumes, Pelican Books.

Plants

Seward, A. C., 1936, *Plant Life through the Ages*, Cambridge Univ. Press.

Walton, J., 1940, *Introduction to the study of fossil plants*, Black.

History of life and fossils in relation to geology

Ager, D. V., 1963, *Principles of Palaeoecology*, McGraw-Hill.

Casanova, R., 1960, *Fossil collecting* (English edition prepared by E. Bryant), Faber.

Clarke, W. E. le Gros, 1949, *History of the Primates*, British Museum (Natural History), London.

Davies, A. M., 1937, *Evolution and its modern critics*, Murby.

George, T. N., 1951, *Evolution in Outline*, Thrift Books, No. I, Watts.

Moore, R. C., 1955, 'Invertebrates and geologic time-scale', *Crust of the Earth*, Geol. Soc. Amer., Special Paper, 62.

Simpson, G. G., 1953, *Life of the Past*, Yale Univ. Press.

——, 1953, *The Major Features of Evolution*, Columbia Univ. Press.

British Palaeozoic Fossils, British Museum (Natural History), London, 1964.

British Mesozoic Fossils, British Museum (Natural History), London, 1962.

British Cainozoic Fossils, British Museum (Natural History), London, 1963.

(Illustrated handbooks of value for the identification of fossils.)

7

VULCANICITY AND THE VOLCANIC ASSOCIATION

VOLCANIC eruptions are among the most spectacular forms of activity exhibited by the earth, and are of particular interest to geologists in that they provide evidence of processes taking place at levels in the crust which are not accessible to man. Vulcanicity is, in a narrow sense, a superficial phenomenon — its products are ejected at the surface and their mode of formation can often be established by direct observation. But the causes of vulcanicity are deep-seated; the molten substance by which volcanoes are fed is produced in the interior of the earth as a result of some disturbance of the normal equilibrium, and the surface-eruptions are merely symptoms of this internal disturbance. To understand the phenomenon of vulcanicity in the broad sense we have to take into account not only the superficial aspects but also the subterranean geological happenings connected with the development and migration of the molten rock-material or *magma*.

MAGMA AND ITS PRODUCTS

Magma is a fluid substance which is essentially a silicate melt carrying in solution considerable quantities of water-vapour and other volatile compounds. On cooling, magma solidifies to form **magmatic or igneous rocks** (ignis = fire) which are as a rule made up of silicate minerals such as feldspars, pyroxenes and amphiboles. The *volatile constituents* of the magma act as fluxes and reduce the freezing-point of the liquid; during cooling, some of these constituents are fixed in the igneous rocks and the remainder migrate outwards into the crust or the atmosphere.

Magma originates below the surface and is forced upwards through the crust by the pressure of the overlying rocks or as a result of earth-movements. It migrates along partings or planes of weakness and on reaching the surface flows out as *lava*, consolidating to form *extrusive or effusive igneous rocks*. Magma which remains within the crust ultimately solidifies in spaces and fissures; it is said to *intrude* the surrounding rock and its products are known as *intrusive igneous rocks*. Intrusive rocks can, naturally, only be seen at the earth's surface when the overlying *country-rocks* have been worn away by erosion; their formation can therefore never be observed directly, and our knowledge of their mode of origin is derived from their own structure and from laboratory experiments on artificial magmas. We are dealing here, for the first time, with rocks which are not easy to study by the uniformitarian method, because the modern equivalents are not accessible for comparison.

IGNEOUS ROCKS

The rocks which are formed as a result of the activity of magma can be united in an **igneous class**, equal in importance to that of the sedimentary rocks already described. With the extrusive and in-trusive igneous rocks may be mentioned the *pyroclastic rocks* which are by-products of volcanic action, representing the magma, rubble and dust blown out from volcanoes during explosive eruptions.

The rocks of the igneous class, like the sediments, assume certain characteristic primary shapes. The standard form of a sedimentary rock, it will be remembered, is a sub-horizontal layer or bed. The primary forms of the igneous rocks are much more varied and depend on the environment in which the parent magma came to rest. Extrusive lavas, and also the majority of pyroclastic rocks, form layers more or less analogous to sedimentary beds which are laid down successively at the earth's surface (Fig. 214).

The primary forms and geological relationships of intrusive igneous rocks are somewhat different. These rocks, as we have noted, are produced by the intrusion of magma into a framework of pre-existing solid rocks. It follows that the intrusive rock is always younger than the country-rock which it intrudes (Fig. 214). The age-relations of an intrusive body may be made apparent in a number of ways (Fig. 215). The contact of the body may cut across the primary stratification:

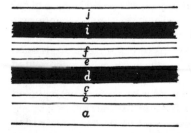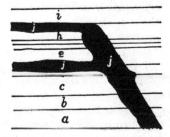

FIG. 214. Time-relations of effusive rocks (*left*) and intrusive rocks (*right*); letters are in order of age.

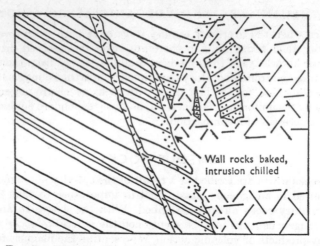

Wall rocks baked, intrusion chilled

FIG. 215. *Evidence of intrusion:* in the igneous rock, chilled edges, enclosure of unorientated inclusions of country-rock; in the country-rock, baking and veining.

the igneous rock may contain *inclusions* of material broken off from the walls or it may send offshoots or *veins* into the walls. The igneous rock may show signs of rapid cooling at its contact with the country-rocks, giving a *chilled edge* (p. 395), while the country-rock may be *baked* or *metamorphosed* at the contact by the heat of the intrusion. These last criteria help to distinguish sheet-like intrusions from lava-flows; a lava can only bake or chill against its floor, while an intrusion can also affect its roof.

The close *dating* of intrusive igneous rocks may be a difficult matter, since the country-rocks may be of any age greater than that of the intrusion. The youngest rock which is affected by the intrusion in the ways illustrated in Fig. 215 gives the lower limit for the possible age of the intrusion. The upper limit is given by the age of the oldest sedimentary rocks resting unconformably on an eroded surface of the intrusive body, or by the age of sedimentary rocks containing boulders of the igneous rock. It will be clear that sediments resting directly on intrusive rocks cannot be deposited until the intrusion has been unroofed by erosion and, especially with deep-seated intrusions, a long interval may elapse before the igneous rock is exposed. The age of the igneous rocks may be more closely pinned down by radiometric methods (pp. 49–50) and by their relation to certain geological structures of known age — for example, the intrusion may be later than certain folds, but displaced by dated faults.

The *primary forms* of bodies of intrusive igneous rock depend on

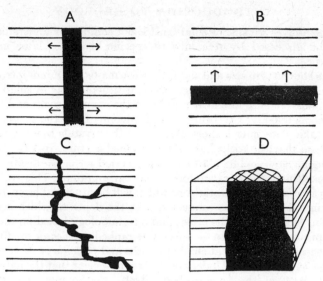

FIG. 216. *Minor Intrusions.* A, dyke; B, sill; C, veins; D, plug.

their size, their position in the crust, the local stress-conditions and the properties of the magma. These matters are discussed in more detail on a later page, and only a preliminary statement need be given here. *Minor intrusions* are small bodies formed as a rule by the consolidation of magma in opened partings such as bedding and joint-fractures or in other restricted spaces. Where they lie in bedding-planes they are said to be *concordant*; where they cut across the bedding they are *discordant* (Fig. 216). Since minor intrusions so frequently follow planes of weakness, the majority form sheet-like bodies which are seldom more than a few hundred feet in thickness but may be many tens of miles in their longer dimension. Sheets which have been intruded by overcoming a vertical pressure and are roughly horizontal are known as *sills*; those which have opened fractures against tangential pressure and are steeply inclined are known as *dykes* (Fig. 216). Other types of minor intrusions are irregular *veins* and roughly cylindrical *plugs* formed, as a rule, with their axes nearly vertical.

Major intrusions are igneous bodies of much larger dimensions having volumes of many cubic miles and making outcrops of the order of ten miles or more in diameter. Major intrusions are usually of a more compact form than minor intrusions and often have oval or circular outcrops at the surface; they may be either concordant or discordant. The problem of how large bodies of magma make space

367

for themselves within the solid crust is not completely understood; it will be discussed by reference to specific examples later in this chapter.

The contrasts in size and shape between major and minor intrusions are reflected in the characters of the constituent rocks. A small body of magma tends to lose heat rapidly to the country-rocks and therefore cools quickly. Crystallisation of minerals from the magma can only take place over a short period and the crystals tend to remain small, so that the rocks have a fine-grained texture. In large bodies of magma slow cooling allows a longer period for crystallisation and the resulting rocks are therefore often coarse-grained. This variation in texture, with other variations which will be discussed later, was at one time thought to be connected with the depth at which crystallisation took place in the crust, and a terminology based on the idea of depth-control grew up — rocks were ranked as *volcanic* or effusive, *hypabyssal* or intruded at shallow depths and *plutonic* or deep-seated (Pluto, the king of the Underworld). It is now clear that the habit and composition of the igneous body itself are the main controlling factors; the notion of depth-control and the term 'hypabyssal' are therefore best dropped. Nonetheless, it is useful to retain a term which expresses the contrast between the superficial volcanics and small intrusions connected with them on the one hand, and the large bodies of coarsely crystalline intrusive rocks, formed at whatever depth, on the other. The term *plutonic igneous rocks* is now generally used for the components of these large intrusive bodies.

But these two terms, volcanic and plutonic, can also be employed to express a more fundamental difference arising from facts connected with the primary origin of the rocks concerned. The rocks we deal with in this chapter, which we may, with Kennedy, call the **Volcanic Association,** comprise not only the effusive magmatic rocks but also such intrusive rocks as can reasonably be related to the volcanic activity and can be taken to originate in the same magmatic source. We thus regard the Volcanic Association as capable of including not only, say, a certain pile of lavas but also the dykes that fed them and the large bodies of the same magma which consolidated deeper in the crust. We shall deal in later chapters with a contrasted **Plutonic Series** made up of granites, gneisses and schists originating well below the surface. During the deep-seated processes leading to the formation of these rocks magmas may develop and may give rise to intrusive or even extrusive igneous rocks. It will be convenient to describe such igneous rocks along with their generators, the Plutonic Series. As research continues, we may find it possible to relate some of our volcanic rocks ultimately to a plutonic operation — obviously, the two groups must overlap, but these matters will sort themselves out in time.

Origin and properties of magma. At the present day, active volcanoes are confined to certain segments of the earth's surface and the intervening regions are free of volcanic activity (Fig. 255). In the active segments, the volcanic products show broad regional variations in chemical composition, and these may be traced back to variations in the character of the parent magma. It is therefore possible to distinguish a number of **volcanic** or **magmatic provinces** within which the vulcanicity is broadly all of one kind. If we trace the history of present-day magmatic provinces back through geological time we find that all have had a limited life. In pre-Tertiary times, the distribution of magmatic provinces was quite different, and it is clear that the centres of volcanic activity have shifted many times in the course of geological time. These facts suggest that vulcanism is a local and temporary, rather than a universal phenomenon.

We know from seismic evidence (p. 27) that the crust and mantle of the earth react to earthquake-waves as solid bodies, and it is therefore evident that there cannot be within these layers any world-wide reservoir of liquid magma. Magmas are believed to be generated by the local or partial melting of solid silicate material in the lower parts of the crust and the upper parts of the mantle; they may undergo many modifications during their upward migration and an originally more or less uniform *primary magma* may ultimately give rise to a diverse suite of igneous rocks; rocks derived from the same parent magma are said to be *co-magmatic*.

The mechanism of the development of magma-pockets in the solid crust or mantle is not yet understood. Near the base of the crust, the normal temperature is believed to be of the order of 5–600° C; basaltic material, which is probably the dominant substance at this level, melts at temperatures of over 1,000° C, and basaltic lava erupted at the surface generally has a temperature of 1,000–1,100° C. An abnormal accumulation of heat therefore seems to be needed to bring about fusion even in the presence of volatiles which might lower the melting-point. Several possible sources of heat have been suggested by physicists and geologists. Radioactive substances are relatively abundant in the granitic parts of the crust, and the heat produced by their breakdown may contribute to raising the temperature in depth; an influx of heat from the interior of the earth might be produced by the operation of convection currents in the lower part of the mantle; and finally, earth-movements and other geological changes in the crust might provide local sources of heat and thick accumulations of sediment might dam back the flow of heat from deeper levels.

When conditions favourable to the formation of magma have, by whatever means, been attained, the state of the overlying crust begins to exert an influence on magma-development. Deep fractures may appear in the crust under conditions of tension and these fractures not only provide paths for migrating magma but also, by relieving the pressure at deeper levels, facilitate the development of a fluid phase. Compressional earth-movements, which characterise the orogenic belts, disturb the whole structure of the crust affected by them and, as we shall see, are commonly associated with a regional heating of the crust; these changes make possible the development of magma from sialic rocks. It is evident that igneous activity must be closely related to other geological processes, and that particular kinds of crustal movements are likely to be associated with characteristic kinds of igneous activity.

The *chemical composition* of magmas is best dealt with at a later stage when the composition of the rocks derived from them is discussed. Nevertheless, we must give here some preliminary explanation of terms which are used in the next few pages; more exact definitions will follow later. The dominant lavas ejected at the surface are *basalts*. These rocks, already mentioned in Chapter 2, contain a relatively low percentage of silicon and a relatively high percentage of iron, magnesium and calcium, and are considered to be derived from a primary magma of approximately their own composition. They are said to be *basic* in composition and the parent magma is a *basic magma* which probably originates in the sima. *Acid lavas* are relatively rich in silicon, sodium and potassium and poor in iron, magnesium and calcium, and *alkaline lavas* contain an unusually high ratio of sodium and/or potassium to silicon. Lavas of these types are developed on a large scale principally in regions of crustal unrest.

The *temperatures* of magmas can sometimes be measured directly in newly-erupted lavas. Basic lavas emerge at temperatures of well over 1,000° C, whereas acid lavas are generally at temperatures of not more than 800° C. The presence of volatile substances in solution in magma lowers the melting-point, and deep-seated acid magmas which retain their volatiles may remain fluid at temperatures lower than those at which lavas solidify. Magma migrating towards the surface carries heat into relatively cool crustal levels. One effect of this migration is seen in the high temperature-gradients recorded in regions of active vulcanism.

A second effect is the transformation brought about in the surrounding country-rocks which may ultimately recrystallise to form metamorphic rocks; igneous intrusions may thus come to be surrounded by a *contact-aureole*.

The *viscosity* of a magma is controlled by its composition, its temperature and its content of volatiles. Basic magma is fairly fluid when it reaches the earth's surface, whereas acid and alkaline lavas are generally extremely viscous. Cooling of a magma increases its viscosity, and very rapid chilling due to contact with cold rock, or with water or air, results in the formation of a natural glass which is so viscous as to react like a solid. The presence of volatile substances in solution reduces the viscosity of magma. As magma nears the surface of the earth the pressure on it decreases and the volatile components therefore tend to come out of solution in the form of gas-bubbles, the process being analogous to the development of carbon-dioxide bubbles when pressure is released in a soda-water siphon. The escape of the volatiles brings about a sharp increase of viscosity and as a result of this physical change the gases may be trapped in the magma or beneath its cooling crust; such trapped gases build up powerful pressures in the roots of volcanoes and ultimately force their way to the surface with explosive violence. Gas-pressure is the driving force behind all explosive volcanic eruptions.

VULCANICITY

Volcanoes and volcanic eruptions. A volcano in its simplest form is merely an opening in the earth's surface through which magma escapes. As a result of repeated eruptions lavas, sometimes accompanied by pyroclastic rocks, are heaped up around the opening to produce a volcanic *cone* pierced by a central *crater*. Subsidiary *vents* opening on the flanks may give rise to *parasitic cones* and further modifications of the original structure may result from explosions within the volcano and erosion of its surface. We shall begin by considering the variations in *volcanic forms* resulting from different kinds of activity, and pass from these to a discussion of the processes by which they are constructed.

The first distinction we must draw is that between *volcanoes of fissure type* and those of *central type*. In *fissure eruptions*, magma issues from a linear crack which represents the outcrop of a plane of fracture. Between eruptions, the crack tends to become blocked by congealed lava and debris, and the later eruptions then take place only at a restricted number of points; the continuous fissure is replaced by a string of small cones. *Volcanoes of central type* are roughly circular in plan and connect with a pipe-like feeding-duct or *neck*. Central volcanoes are often arranged in linear series (Fig. 217) and are probably connected at depth with extensive fractures.

Most volcanoes of fissure type are fed by magmas of low viscosity,

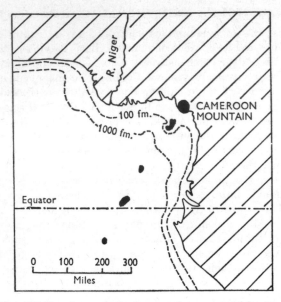

FIG. 217. Development of volcanoes along a crustal fracture.

since the fissures are easily choked by the solidification of viscous magma. They are found predominantly in basic volcanic provinces where they are associated with the outpouring of basalts. Magma wells up quietly and flows out in sheets or tongues over the surrounding land, building up small spatter-cones and cinder-cones at points of special activity. Individual flows may be of the order of twenty feet in thickness and many square miles in area.

Repeated eruptions from a number of fissures build up lava-piles covering hundreds of square miles and totalling thousands of feet in thickness. Such great accumulations of basic lavas are known as *plateau-basalts*. They are exemplified in the early Tertiary *Deccan Traps* of India which cover some 200,000 square miles. Similar plateau-basalts of Tertiary age occur in Greenland, Iceland, the Faeroes and north-west Britain, where they form parts of a very extensive *North Atlantic Tertiary Igneous Province*; in Iceland, fissure-eruptions have continued until the present day. Plateau-basalt flows are frequently piled up with little admixture of other material. Thin beds of sediment or flows of different composition may however be intercalated in the sequence, and sub-aerial weathering may affect the top of one flow before the arrival of the next. The Tertiary basalts of Antrim and the Inner Hebrides show locally bright red lateritic tops formed by weathering in a hot climate, and contain a few intercalated plant-beds. The lava-flows are often traversed by numerous dyke-intrusions of basaltic composition. Some of these undoubtedly fill fissures which opened at the surface and thus constitute *feeders* of the flows.

Volcanoes of central type make cones varying in shape, size and complexity. They may incorporate volcanic forms of three different origins:

        (*a*) Effusive forms
        (*b*) Explosive forms
        (*c*) Collapse forms.

(*a*) **Effusive forms** are dominant in volcanoes supplied by magmas of low viscosity, where the eruption of magma is not accompanied by violent explosions. In volcanoes fed by more viscous magmas the effusive forms are shattered and modified by explosive action.

Broad low cones or *shield-volcanoes* are built up around vents supplied by magma of low viscosity and are characteristically developed in basic volcanic provinces. With each eruption, the relatively fluid lava flows for some distance before congealing, and spreads out into a thin sheet or tongue; the volcanoes therefore have wide bases and their sides slope at angles of little more than 10°. Some of the largest examples of shield-volcanoes are provided by the Hawaiian islands of the mid-Pacific volcanic province (Fig. 218). These volcanoes are enormous mounds rising directly from the

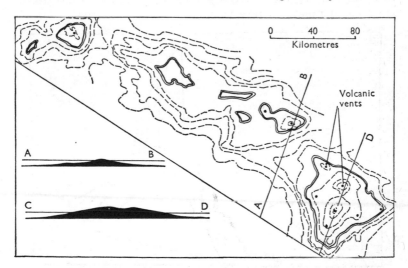

FIG. 218. Shield Volcanoes of the Hawaiian Islands. Sea and land contours in thousands of metres: cross-sections drawn to same horizontal and vertical scales.

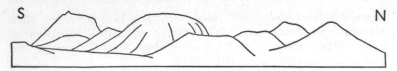

FIG. 219. Puy Topography of the Central Plateau of France (length of view about 10 kilometres).

Pacific floor some 12,000 feet below sea-level and culminating in peaks more than 13,000 feet above the sea. They are made almost entirely of basalts and lavas genetically connected with basalt.

Where viscous magmas are active, the effusive forms built up are small, steep-sided *volcanic domes* produced by the heaping-up of short thick flows around the vent, or by the solidification of lava within the vent itself. Since the vents are readily blocked, individual domes do not grow to a great size, and the effusive forms are modified by frequent explosions of trapped gases. The strange topographical forms produced by the clustering of small domes are well seen in the Puys of the Auvergne (Fig. 219). Still more remarkable structures may be developed during the eruptive phase itself, when a solidified lava-plug may be pushed bodily up out of the neck by the pressure of magma and volatiles trapped beneath it, or when magma is forced up beneath a confining skin of lava; cracking of the skin may lead to the protrusion of vertical lava-*spines* standing hundreds of feet above the summit of the dome (Fig. 220).

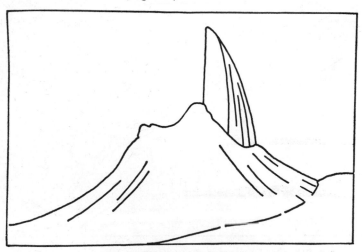

FIG. 220. Mont Pelée, Martinique, West Indies. Dome and spine formed during the eruption of 1903; height of spine about 800 feet.

374

(b) **Explosive volcanic forms** result from explosive eruptions in volcanoes fed by somewhat viscous magmas; the explosive action is due to the pressure of volatile components of the magma which, on coming out of solution, are unable to escape readily. *Explosive vents* are perforations of the surface formed by these gases; they may appear at random over a volcanic district but are often located along the line of plane or arcuate fractures. Around these vents the wall-rocks are shattered and the uprush of gas carries with it dust and debris from these rocks as well as fragments of solidified lava and clots of still-liquid magma. All this pyroclastic material falls back to earth to make a *cinder-* or *ash-cone* whose sides slope 30–40° at the angle of rest. The magma-clots are moulded in flight to a stream-lined shape and fall as *volcanic bombs* often showing a solid crust and a spongy centre inflated by trapped gas-bubbles. The finest ash is blown far away and settles out over the surrounding country.

Explosions of catastrophic violence take place in some volcanoes as a result of the simultaneous exsolution of gas-bubbles throughout the mass of magma beneath. The enormous increase in volume effectively disrupts the magma and sweeps it upwards as an intensely hot cloud of droplets lubricated by the released gases. Such explosions may shatter and partially destroy the cone, while the resultant emptying of the magma-chamber may lead to foundering of the unsupported roof and development of a caldera (see below). The cloud of incandescent magma-froth expelled from the volcano forms a fast-moving glowing avalanche or *nuée ardente* which may flow for many miles, causing great destruction before it comes to rest. Finally, it consolidates as a mass of broken glass shards, crystal-fragments and scraps of spongy lava, which are often welded into a coherent rock by the residual heat. Such *welded tuffs* or *ignimbrites*, though of pyroclastic origin, are made almost exclusively of magmatic material.

(c) **Collapse forms** in volcanoes are produced by the foundering of the roof of the underlying magma chamber along arcuate fractures. A circular depression or *caldera* is left in the centre of the original cone, and the magma may be exposed in a *lava-lake* within it. The caldera is usually of the order of five miles in diameter and is thus readily distinguished from a normal vent or crater which is seldom more than a mile across. The development of collapse calderas at the surface is often associated with the development of specialised intrusion forms (*ring-complexes* and *cauldron-subsidences*, pp. 397–9) at depth.

Calderas may be formed in association with both effusive and explosive volcanic forms. In shield-volcanoes such as those of Hawaii, the escape of magma through fissures low down on the flanks may partially drain the magma-chamber and lead to collapse of the unsupported roof. On Hawaii itself, a caldera formed in this manner is seen in the volcano Kilauea. Within it, the magma-chamber is now roofed over by solid lava, but liquid magma can be seen in an open pit in the floor. When the magma-level in this pit is low, the ground-surface can be shown by geophysical measurements to sag gently towards the caldera over a radius of twenty miles. In the early part of 1924, the magma-level fell to about 3600 feet below the mouth of the pit, apparently as a result of the submarine eruption of lava. The walls of the pit then caved in and an estimated seven billion cubic feet of rock were engulfed by magma.

Collapse calderas associated with explosive volcanoes owe their origin to the sudden emptying of the magma-chamber as a result of the emission of *nuées ardentes*. There has been considerable discussion as to the origin of these calderas, and it is sometimes suggested that they are simply the result of the explosive disruption of the top of the volcano. This explanation, however, is at variance with the evidence of the pyroclastic deposits associated with the calderas. If the whole top of the volcano had been blown off, one would expect to find enormous beds of debris derived from the missing material, but in fact almost the only pyroclastic deposits found are welded tuffs composed of newly-erupted magmatic material. It is therefore more reasonable to assume that the missing parts of the volcano sank downwards to fill the space left by the ejected magma.

Volcanic eruptions. The morphology of a volcano is, as we have seen, related to its mode of activity which in turn is controlled to a large extent by the properties of the magma supplying it. The early stages in the evolution of a new volcano are often marked by great activity. Subsequently, a definite rhythm may be established and phases of explosion or eruption may begin to alternate with phases of relative quiescence; the pattern and timing of events vary according to the style of igneous activity. Modifications of the rhythm are induced from time to time by changes in the composition of the magma, by the development of a caldera, or the opening of a new volcanic centre or other similar changes in environment. Finally, the volcano reaches a condition of old age, its activity is reduced to the emission of steam and other volatiles and it ultimately becomes extinct. The extinction of all the volcanoes of a magmatic province suggests the cessation of igneous activity in that province.

Several new volcanoes have established themselves in historic times, some appearing suddenly as islands from beneath the sea. One example is Paricutin in Mexico, which began its career in 1943. On February 20, after a fortnight of minor earth-tremors, a crack eighteen inches deep appeared in a field being ploughed; the earth around this crack heaved up, vapour appeared and hot stones were ejected. By next morning, the pile of debris had reached a height of thirty feet and within a week it was built up into a 550-foot volcanic cone. Lava flowed out of the vent within a few days of its first appearance and clouds of ash were blown 20,000 feet into the air. By 1946 Paricutin stood 1,500 feet high and had become a composite structure containing both pyroclastic rocks and lavas ejected from several vents. This rapid evolution emphasises the catastrophic speed of some volcanic activities, as compared with the slow rate of most other geological processes.

The patterns of activity in established volcanoes are of various kinds, and can be classified into six groups named after active volcanoes now behaving in the specified manner. The first five groups form a connected series characterised by the increasing violence of the eruptions, which is in turn related to the increasing viscosity of the magma.

(a) The **hawaiian type** of eruption is dominated by the frequent and quiet effusion of lava without notable explosive activity. The fluidity of the magma allows the volatile components to escape readily, and the repetition of small eruptions prevents the passages from becoming blocked by a thick layer of congealed lava.

(b) The **strombolian type** of eruption is associated with a slightly less fluid lava and is characterised by a succession of frequent but small explosions. The pent-up gases spurt out repeatedly, carrying with them clouds of dust and clots of magma. In Stromboli itself, to the north of Sicily, small outbursts take place several times a day, although lavas are not ejected at such frequent intervals.

(c) The **vulcanian type** of eruption, named from Vulcano near Stromboli, is characterised by less frequent and correspondingly more violent explosions due to the trapping of gas beneath a crust of solidified lava. Dust clouds blown out during eruptions rise into a cauliflower shape resembling that produced by an atomic bomb, and deposit layers of ash over the surrounding country. Vulcanian eruptions are often the first signs of renewed activity after a period of dormancy, and have the effect of clearing the vents blocked by lava and slumped debris.

(d) **The vesuvian type** of eruption carries the trend towards increasing violence of explosion a stage further and is exemplified by the major eruptions of Vesuvius. These eruptions follow periods of relative quiet, and are generally heralded by moderate vulcanian explosions which clear the old conduits. The pressure on the magma is reduced by the freeing of the vents, a rapid exsolution of gases takes place and the magma is converted into a mobile froth which rises in clouds and pours down the mountain to solidify as spongy *pumice*. At the climax of the eruption, blasts of gas and debris shoot up many miles into the sky. The distinctive feature of the vesuvian eruption is the explosive ejection of mobile lava-froth.

The first eruption of Vesuvius recorded by man was that of A.D. 79, witnessed and described by Pliny. In this eruption, the towns of Pompeii and Herculaneum, both some ten miles from the volcanic vent, were overwhelmed and smothered by pyroclastic material, the first by ash and the second by hot mud. In the next sixteen centuries, ten major eruptions are known to have occurred, and long periods of quiescence intervened between these eruptions. From 1631 onwards, minor explosions and emissions of lava became more frequent, and major eruptions of vesuvian type have taken place at intervals of less than fifty years, the latest in the series being those of 1872, 1906 and 1944.

(e) The **peléan type** of eruption represents the final stage in the series controlled by increasing violence of explosive activity. It is characterised by the emission of gas-fluxed clouds of magma-droplets or *nuées ardentes* and is exemplified by the eruption of Mont Pelée in 1902. This volcano, on the island of Martinique in the West Indies, had for long been quiescent or subject only to minor eruptions. In the early part of 1902 it resumed activity with a succession of vulcanian eruptions which cleared out the old neck. A lava-dome then began to swell up within a solid crust, and continued to grow for sixteen months, finally reaching a height of a thousand feet above the crater-rim (Fig. 220). During growth, the skin of the dome was repeatedly cracked by explosions from within, and a succession of *nuées ardentes* was discharged through the cracks. Most of the *nuées* flowed harmlessly down the volcano to the west, but a single one flowing southward obliterated the town of St. Pierre with its 30,000 inhabitants. This one eruption deposited in four minutes a layer of ash forty centimetres in thickness. The explosive outrush of the clouds of magma and gas continued at intervals for a few months, until the pressure within the volcano was finally relieved. The upper parts of the lava-dome, shattered and laid open to the weather, rapidly disintegrated and the volcano passed back into quiescence.

The volcano of Krakatao, which forms a group of islands between Sumatra and Java in the East Indies, underwent an eruption of peléan type in 1883 and in the course of this eruption a new caldera was formed. The volcano had a long history of complex eruptions and had apparently possessed an earlier caldera. Before 1883, its visible parts consisted of a cluster of small islands representing conelets built up within this caldera. From May to August, a number of vulcanian and vesuvian eruptions of increasing violence took place from the vents of these cones and from several newly-formed vents. In the last week of August the eruption reached its climax in a series of tremendous explosions, the loudest of which was heard three thousand miles away in Australia. Nearly five cubic miles of magmatic material were expelled in the form of incandescent clouds which mounted fifty miles into the air. Most of the material settled to form thick beds of tuff, but the finest dust remained for long in suspension and coloured the sunsets of the world for many months. The expulsion of the magma was followed by collapse of the magma-chamber roof, carrying parts of the old conelets with it. The geography of the volcanic islands was completely changed, and nearly fifty years later a new minor cone built up into an island within the circle of the caldera.

(*f*) The quiescent periods of active volcanoes and the dying phases of old volcanoes are often marked by a **solfataric type** of activity. This type, named from Solfatara, a steam-and-gas vent near Naples, is characterised by the emission of volcanic gases rather than by the ejection of solid matter. The gas-vents or *fumeroles* build up small cones or encrustations of substances deposited from the escaping gases, as they are cooled by contact with the air.

Pyroclastic rocks. Pyroclastic rocks are accumulations of fragmentary rocks and minerals brought to the surface by the explosive escape of volcanic gases. They include blocks and chips of already solidified volcanic material, accidental fragments of non-volcanic rocks disrupted by the explosions, and contributions thrown up from the active magma itself. Some pyroclastic material remains lodged in

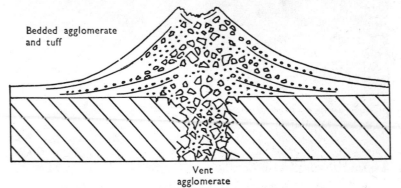

Bedded agglomerate and tuff

Vent agglomerate

FIG. 221. *Pyroclastic Rocks*. Diagrammatic section showing vent agglomerate passing outwards into bedded agglomerate and ash.

vents or fissures to form bodies of *vent agglomerate* with intrusive relationships. The greater part, however, is thrown out at the surface and settles again under the influence of gravity. A rough sorting according to size and density takes place during the settling process. Large fragments pile up near the vents to form roughly bedded *agglomerate* or *volcanic breccia.* The finer *ash* spreads further from the vent and forms *tuff.* A bed formed by a single eruption may thus show a lateral gradation from coarse to fine (Fig. 221); light fragments of pumice and glassy fragments containing gas-bubbles settle out with the finer material, and the finest dust is blown far from the site of the eruption. A vertical grading shown by the concentration of coarse or dense components at the base of the bed may also be apparent.

Pyroclastic rocks are characterised by their high content of igneous material. Much of this material is unstable under surface-conditions, especially in the presence of the active volcanic gases, and the original glass and mineral fragments are often decomposed into masses of soft hydrated compounds. Texturally, the rocks are characterised by the poor sorting resulting from rapid deposition and by the angular shapes of the fragments of all sizes (Fig. 222). Some varieties (*crystal-tuffs*) are made up largely of broken crystals thrown up from a partly solidified magma. *Lithic tuffs* are characterised by abundance of rock-fragments. *Vitric tuffs* contain a high proportion of volcanic glass and

A

B

FIG. 222. Textures of pyroclastic rocks. A, Broken fragments of crystals in a crystal-tuff, × 20. B, Broken fragments of rocks in a lithic tuff, × 40.

are produced by vesuvian or peléan eruptions. The clouds of magma-droplets discharged during these eruptions solidify in flight to form a friable spongy substance which shatters into a multitude of curved or splintery glass shards. *Welded tuffs*, formed by the almost instantaneous accumulation of hot magmatic material carried by a *nuée ardente*, show relics of fragmental textures like those of vitric tuffs, but the glass-shards and scraps of glassy froth are flattened and annealed by the residual heat of the material, aided by the pressure of the overlying tuff. Welded tuffs form coherent beds, often tens of feet in thickness, which may be difficult to distinguish from ordinary lava-flows (Fig. 223A).

Pyroclastic rocks naturally vary in composition according to the composition of the wall-rocks and of the magma supplying the volcano; basic tuffs are found in basic provinces and so on. The proportions of old volcanic fragments and new magmatic material depend on the kind of eruption. Quiet eruptions of the hawaiian or strombolian types do not throw out large quantities of fluid material, whereas vesuvian and peléan eruptions eject great volumes of magma, and the bulky pyroclastic rocks produced by these eruptions are largely vitric tuffs and welded tuffs. Variations of another type are produced by the mixing of pyroclastic and sedimentary components. Ash falling in the sea may be laid down along with ordinary sediments to produce *tuffaceous sandstones* and similar rocks. Loose pyroclastic accumulations are always liable to be reworked by wind, streams and other surface-agents and may then be redeposited along with appropriate kinds of sedimentary rocks.

Volcanic gases. The volatile constituents expelled from a magma may behave in various ways as they migrate towards the surface. Volatiles escaping at depth may react with the country-rocks or may deposit substances carried in solution in veins or replacement bodies within the crust. This process of *pneumatolysis* is responsible for the formation of metallic ores such as those of tin and silver as well as of various gemstones (Chapters 10 and 11). Volatiles released nearer the surface may escape into the atmosphere during eruptions and through gas-vents or *fumeroles* during the stages of solfataric volcanic activity. They reach the surface at temperatures ranging from not much over 100° C to about 500° C and the sudden cooling caused by contact with the air and the cold surface-rocks leads to the precipitation of various compounds around the walls and mouth of the vent. Among the common *sublimates* so deposited are sulphur, chlorides of potassium, magnesium, calcium, iron and lead and sulphides of arsenic (e.g. realgar, As_2S_2, and orpiment, As_2S_3).

The gases escaping from fumeroles vary in composition from place to place. Water-vapour is universally present and there may be in addition carbon dioxide, CO_2, carbon monoxide, CO, sulphur dioxide, SO_2, chlorine, hydrochloric and hydrofluoric acids, HCl and HF, sulphuretted hydrogen, H_2S, hydrogen and methane, CH_4. In Iceland, the most important gases of magmatic origin seem to be CO_2, H_2S and H_2. In one of the Hawaiian volcanoes tested, CO_2, N_2, and SO_2 predominated.

Water vapour of magmatic origin condenses to give *juvenile water* which may take into solution other volatile magmatic components; this juvenile water mixes with the ordinary groundwater and ultimately issues at the surface in *hot springs, geysers* or *mineral springs*. The waters of volcanic districts tend to be more reactive than unmixed groundwater and often precipitate thick deposits around the mouths of springs. *Travertine* is made of calcium carbonate and may show very beautiful terraced structures built up around the outlet (p. 266). *Siliceous sinter* is a similar deposit made of silica (p. 268). *Geysers* are hot springs which erupt periodically as a result of the spontaneous transformation of water into steam. The mechanism is controlled by the fact that the boiling-point of water is raised by pressure; water in channels below the surface is continually heated by the addition of volcanic water until it is superheated and reaches a temperature at which the pressure of expanding steam is sufficient to throw out the column of water in the channel leading to the surface. The eruption reduces pressure and a period of quiescence follows till the rise in temperature causes a repetition of the cycle. Many geysers, such as Old Faithful in Yellowstone Park, erupt with great regularity.

GENERAL CHARACTERS OF IGNEOUS ROCKS

The igneous rocks, according to the definition given at the beginning of this chapter, are formed by the consolidation of magma. Their chemical and mineralogical composition and their texture vary according to the character of the parent magma and the environment in which consolidation takes place. The adoption of a system of classification to express these variations brings to light a number of difficulties. In the first place, the uniformitarian method which allows geologists to link the characters of a rock with its mode of formation cannot be applied to the plutonic igneous rocks. In the second place, the most conspicuous variations are not always those of most genetic significance. We may recall that variations in grain-size are often related to the cooling history of the rock; to use this as a basis for classification would actually obscure genetic relationships, since it would place in different categories the plutonic and volcanic derivatives of a single magma.

An ideal classification would group together all the derivatives of each magma-type, secondary divisions being then made according to the lines of magmatic descent and the environment of formation. Such a classification cannot be derived from a study of rock-specimens as such, but must be built up by considering the igneous rocks in relation to their whole geological setting. Nevertheless, rock-species must be named and grouped according to their own inherent characters, and for this reason two rather different schemes of classification are simultaneously in existence. The first, non-genetic and primarily descriptive or *petrographic scheme*, pigeon-holes rocks according to their composition, mineralogy and texture. This scheme can accommodate rocks of many different origins, some not even magmatic, and in tabulating it we shall include for completeness all the types which fall within its scope, although the types which belong to the Plutonic Series are not dealt with in detail until Chapter 10. The second, *petrogenetic scheme* of classification provides a broad grouping developed from the idea of *magmatic provinces* mentioned on p. 369. It attempts to bring together rocks derived from a single parent magma and to express their lines of descent.

For petrographic purposes, the most important characters of igneous and plutonic rocks are the *chemical composition*, the *mineral composition* and the *texture*. We shall gain a general idea of the igneous rocks by examining the ranges of variation in these characters.

Chemical composition. In the majority of igneous rocks, something like 99 per cent of the total bulk is made up of only eight elements — oxygen, silicon, aluminium, iron, calcium, sodium, potassium and magnesium — the remaining fraction being made up by a very large number of *trace-elements* among which titanium, phosphorus and hydrogen are some of the more important. It will be remembered that a similar distribution of major elements and trace-elements is found in the crust as a whole (Chapter 2, p. 43). Most of the elements present in igneous rocks enter into the lattices of the rock-forming silicates, and we may now consider briefly how they are distributed between the common mineral species; for this purpose we refer to quantities in terms of the percentages of oxides of each element, this being the form in which rock analyses are conventionally presented.

Silica (SiO_2) is usually by far the most abundant oxide, making from 40 to 75 per cent of the total. The SiO_4-tetrahedron, as we have seen, is the fundamental unit of all silicate lattices, and excess silica appears in the form of quartz. The *silica-percentage* is an important

N2

INTRODUCTION TO GEOLOGY

diagnostic character of igneous rocks and provides the basis of a four-fold chemical subdivision:

CLASSIFICATION BASED ON SILICA-PERCENTAGE

over 66 per cent —— ACID
52–66 per cent —— INTERMEDIATE
45–52 per cent —— BASIC
under 45 per cent —— ULTRABASIC

Alumina (Al_2O_3), often the most abundant oxide after silica, reaches a maximum of about 18 per cent. As we have seen, it can substitute for silicon in the lattices of such minerals as feldspars, feldspathoids, monoclinic pyroxenes, amphiboles and micas; its most important role is as an essential constituent of the feldspars.

Iron oxides (FeO and Fe_2O_3) and **magnesia** (MgO) are present in the olivines, pyroxenes, amphiboles and dark micas, which are therefore collectively known as *ferromagnesian minerals*, and the iron oxides also form a number of non-silicate compounds such as the opaque iron oxides magnetite, hematite and ilmenite. Ferromagnesian minerals are generally most abundant in basic and ultrabasic rocks.

Lime (CaO) is a component of many ferromagnesian minerals and also of the plagioclase-feldspars. It reaches a maximum, seldom exceeding 10 per cent, in basic and ultrabasic rocks and falls to only a few per cent in acid rocks. Rarely, calcium appears also as the carbonate, calcite.

Potash (K_2O) and **soda** (Na_2O), collectively known as the *alkalies*, are essential components of orthoclase and albite, the alkali-feldspars, and reach maximum concentrations of around 6 per cent in rocks rich in these minerals. The percentage of total alkalies increases in a general way with increase in silica; but for every value for silica there is a considerable range of values for alkalies and rocks which are, for their silica-percentage, rich in alkalies are said themselves to be *alkaline*.

Water (H_2O) is an important component of many igneous rocks — as we have seen, considerable quantities of water are dissolved in the parent magma, but much of this magmatic water escapes during cooling; the residue enters the lattices of amphiboles, micas and other minerals in the form of the hydroxyl (OH) radicle. In addition, igneous rocks may contain *secondary* hydrous minerals such as zeolites formed after consolidation by reaction with circulating waters.

Many of the **trace-elements** of igneous rocks find accommodation in the lattices of the common silicate minerals; titanium, for example, can substitute for aluminium in augite, fluorine for (OH) in muscovite and so on. Some trace-elements build independent minerals of which common examples are apatite $(Ca_5(F,Cl)P_3O_{12})$, sphene $(CaTiSiO_5)$ and zircon $(ZrSiO_4)$. The abundance and distribution of the trace-elements are closely related to the evolution of the parent magma, and in recent years the use of spectroscopic and other techniques to determine trace-elements has played an important part in petrology. Certain trace-elements such as nickel, chromium and tin are of great economic value.

Mineral composition. The minerals present in volcanic and plutonic rocks vary according to the composition of the rocks and the environment of cooling. In the volcanic environment, most of the volatile components of the magma are lost and minerals incorporating such components are rather restricted. In a plutonic environment, the volatiles may escape less easily and may enter more freely into the crystal-lattices, producing minerals bearing (OH) or other volatile components (e.g. topaz, the aluminium fluo-silicate, tourmaline, the complex borosilicate, or fluorite, CaF_2).

The percentage mineral composition of a rock is given by its *mode* (p. 386). The *essential minerals* are those on whose presence a rock-species is defined; for example, the basic rock dolerite has as essential minerals monoclinic pyroxene and labradorite-feldspar, and a rock lacking one of these components cannot be called a dolerite. In addition, most rocks contain *accessory minerals* which are not essential to the definition of the species. They may include members of the main rock-forming groups as well as minor components such as zircon, sphene and iron oxides. Common accessory minerals in dolerites are olivine, ilmenite, magnetite or quartz — when present in notable quantities, their name can be tacked on to that of the rock-species, so that we speak of olivine-dolerite, quartz-dolerite and so on. The essential and accessory minerals together make the *primary minerals* formed directly from the magma. *Secondary minerals* such as chlorite, serpentine, zoisite, calcite and sericite may be formed after consolidation by reactions in the cooling rock.

Three chief *mineralogical criteria* are used in the subdivision of igneous and plutonic rocks:

(i) The presence or absence of *quartz*: quartz is an essential mineral of acid rocks and occurs only as an accessory in intermediate, alkaline and basic rocks.

(ii) The composition of the *feldspars*: feldspars relatively rich in alkalies — *orthoclase, albite* or *oligoclase* — are essential minerals of acid and of many alkaline rocks but are rare or absent in intermediate, basic or ultrabasic rocks. *Andesine* is characteristic of intermediate rocks and basic plagioclase — *labradorite, bytownite* or *anorthite* — of basic rocks. Many ultrabasic rocks contain no feldspar. *Feldspathoids*, which are chemically like the feldspars but poorer in silica, are confined to the alkaline rocks.

(iii) The proportion and kinds of *ferromagnesian minerals*: in broad terms, basic and ultrabasic rocks are rich in ferromagnesian minerals or *mafic*, while acid rocks are rich in quartz and feldspar or *felsic*. Olivine is generally confined to basic and ultrabasic rocks, pyroxenes and amphiboles range through ultrabasic, basic, intermediate and alkaline rocks while biotite, though widely distributed as an accessory, is most common in intermediate and acid rocks. Alkaline rocks frequently contain rare species of ferromagnesian minerals such as the sodic amphibole riebeckite or the sodic pyroxene acmite.

Total Percentage of Ferromagnesian Minerals	Ultrabasic >90%	Basic 70–40%	Intermediate 40–20%	Acid <20%
OLIVINE	Common	Common	Very rare	Very rare
ORTHORHOMBIC PYROXENE	Common	Common	Very rare	Very rare
MONOCLINIC PYROXENE	Common	Common	Common	Very rare
HORNBLENDE	Accessory	Accessory	Common	Accessory
BIOTITE	Accessory	Accessory	Common	Common
PLAGIOCLASE	<10% Anorthite-Labradorite	Anorthite-Labradorite	Andesine	Oligoclase-Albite
ORTHOCLASE	—	[only present in alkaline varieties]	[only present in alkaline varieties]	Usually abundant
QUARTZ	—	Accessory	Accessory	Essential, usually more than 10%

(The first two columns of rows OLIVINE–BIOTITE are grouped under *Ferromagnesian Minerals*; PLAGIOCLASE, ORTHOCLASE and QUARTZ under *Feldspar*.)

SAMPLE MODES OF PLUTONIC ROCKS

Granite

(Rosses Ring-Complex, Co. Donegal, Ireland: W. S. Pitcher)

Quartz	34 per cent
Potash-feldspar	24
Plagioclase	37
Biotite + oxides + secondary minerals	4
Muscovite	0·2

Granodiorite

(Thorr Older Granodiorite, Co. Donegal, Ireland: W. S. Pitcher)

Quartz	16 per cent
Potash-feldspar	17
Plagioclase	52
Biotite + epidote	13
Hornblende	2
Sphene	0·2

Syenite

(pulaskite: Ben Loyal Complex, Sutherland: B. C. King)

Potash-feldspar	52 per cent
Plagioclase (albite)	28
Clinopyroxene	17
Opaque minerals, etc.	3
Apatite	1

Hypersthene-gabbro

(Ardnamurchan, Inverness-shire: M. K. Wells)

Plagioclase	60 per cent
Pyroxene	30
(>20 per cent augite, <10 per cent hypersthene)	
Olivine	8
Opaque minerals	<2

These mineralogical variations are summarised in the Table opposite. It should be emphasised, firstly, that there are no hard and fast natural boundaries between rock-species, and divisions are therefore arbitrary; and, secondly, that the 'rules' set out above are no more than general guides, and the student must be prepared to meet with exceptions to most of them.

Textures. The arrangement of minerals, and the relation of a mineral to its neighbours, give each rock its characteristic texture, which is an important diagnostic feature. The general appearance of igneous rocks is broadly related to the conditions under which they consolidated; as a rule, fine-grained or glassy rocks are produced by rapid cooling and coarse-grained rocks by slow cooling in a plutonic environment. Abnormally coarse-grained rocks are often formed when crystallisation takes place in the presence of abundant volatiles.

Volcanic glass — really a supercooled liquid — is a non-crystalline rock produced by the rapid chilling of magma (Fig. 223). It is usually black or greenish in colour and breaks with a conchoidal or splintery fracture to give a lustrous surface. Under the microscope, the glass appears as a transparent, isotropic substance with a refractive index varying from about 1·5 to 1·6 and decreasing with increase of silica-percentage. The glass often carries incipient crystals in the form of

 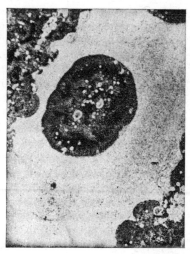

A B

FIG. 223. Textures in welded tuffs and lavas. A, Flattened glass fragments in a welded tuff, × 40. B, Spherulitic texture in obsidian, × 15.

minute globular or hair-like *crystallites* or small birefringent rods termed *microlites*. Volcanic glasses of early geological periods are *devitrified* by very slow crystallisation.

In some lavas and minor intrusions the texture is partially crystalline or *hypocrystalline*, recognisable crystals being set in a glassy matrix. Such rocks are formed by rapid consolidation after the start of crystallisation. *Holocrystalline rocks* are crystalline throughout and contain no glass; they include many lavas and minor intrusions and all plutonic rocks. The *grain-size* of holocrystalline rocks is defined by reference to the diameter of the largest common grains in the body of the rock, approximate divisions being as follow:

> Fine-grained <1 mm.
> Medium-grained 1–5 mms.
> Coarse-grained >5 mms.

Where the crystals are too small to be separable with a low-power microscope, the rock is said to be *cryptocrystalline*. Where they are too small to be distinguished with the naked eye, the rock is *aphanitic*. Where the crystals reach dimensions of several centimetres the rock becomes *pegmatitic*; these very coarse rocks are almost invariably derived from volatile-rich fractions of a magma and generally form veins or patches in which crystals may reach sizes of as much as a metre.

A distinctive *porphyritic* texture is produced by the occurrence of crystals of two sizes in the same rock (Fig. 227). Large *phenocrysts*, often displaying good crystal faces, are scattered through a *groundmass* of medium- or fine-grained rock. This texture is widely developed in lavas and minor intrusions and appears often to be produced as a result of changes in the physical or chemical environment during crystallisation following the transference of magma to higher levels; the migrating magma carries phenocrysts formed at depth and on reaching its destination completes its crystallisation to give the finer-grained groundmass.

In addition to the variations in grain-size and degree of crystallinity already discussed, igneous rocks show variations in the shapes of grains and in their marginal relations; many of these variations are related to the order of crystallisation in the cooling magma (pp. 402–7). Minerals which crystallise while the bulk of the magma is still fluid are free to develop without hindrance from their neighbours, and often build good crystals; such minerals are said to be *euhedral* or *idiomorphic* (Fig. 237A). Minerals which grow in a magma already crowded with crystals have to accommodate themselves to the shapes of the spaces still remaining; they are generally *hypidiomorphic*, exhibiting imperfect crystal form, or entirely *anhedral*. Minerals

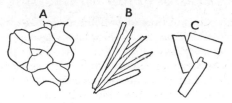

FIG. 224. *Grain shapes in crystalline rocks.* A, granular; B, acicular; C, tabular.

formed from the last magma held in the mesh of crystals occupy irregular or angular spaces and are said to be *interstitial*. Hypidiomorphic and anhedral minerals may be roughly equidimensional or *granular*, book-shaped or *tabular* or elongated and *acicular* (Fig. 224). Still other variations are produced by the inclusion of early-formed minerals by later crystals; random inclusions are widespread, and call for no special description, but distinctive effects are produced by the growth of concentric rims of later minerals around an early-formed core (*corona-structure*, p. 404, Figs. 239, 246); by the growth of large pyroxene grains partially engulfing tabular plagioclases (*ophitic* texture, Fig. 225); and by the development of large spongy or *poikilitic* grains enclosing a host of smaller crystals (Fig. 225). Finally,

A
B

FIG. 225. A, Poikilitic texture: olivine and pyroxene crystals enclosed in a single plate of biotite which fills the field, × 15. B, Ophitic texture: well-shaped laths of feldspar enclosed in plates of pyroxene, × 15.

simultaneous crystallisation of two minerals may produce curious intergrowths in which one mineral forms wedge-shaped or cuneiform patches in the other (Figs. 1, 352B). This texture is most commonly seen in mixtures of quartz and feldspar and is termed *graphic* or *granophyric* when the inclusions of quartz have angular outlines; *myrmekite* is a quartz-plagioclase intergrowth in which the quartz inclusions are curved and vermicular (Fig. 345B).

The arrangement of the minerals in space, and their orientation in relation to the broad structure of the igneous body, determine the *fabric* of the igneous rock. In many rocks the minerals show an entirely random orientation and the fabric is *isotropic*; such rocks are said to be *massive* and present the same appearance on any surface of a rectangular block. In some circumstances, however, certain minerals show a tendency towards a parallel alignment, and so produce an *anisotropic fabric*; rocks with such a fabric present a different appearance when viewed on each of three mutually perpendicular planes. Parallel structures may be due to several causes. *Flow-structures* are produced by the alignment of crystals carried along in a moving magma (p. 394, Fig. 227). *Growth-fabrics* result from the parallel growth of minerals springing from a common base; these fabrics are occasionally seen in veins where minerals grow outwards from the vein-wall, but are of little importance in igneous rocks. Finally, *protoclastic* textures are produced by the continued flow of an almost solid igneous body; the original minerals may be realigned and often partly crushed during this process.

SUMMARY OF A PETROGRAPHIC CLASSIFICATION

By assembling the criteria discussed in the last few pages, we can now adopt a system of igneous rock-classification which is tabulated on p. 391. The horizontal divisions are made according to grain-size, fine-grained or glassy volcanic rocks appearing in the uppermost row and medium to coarse-grained plutonic rocks in the lowest row. The vertical divisions correspond to variations in silica-percentage, the separate columns representing ultrabasic, basic, intermediate and acid rocks. Each rectangular pigeon-hole is divided diagonally; rocks with normal percentages of alkalies, which can be collectively referred to as *calc-alkaline rocks* are placed above the diagonals and alkaline rocks of comparable silica-percentages below the diagonals. Names printed in *italics* refer to rocks which are described in Chapter 8. It should be made clear that the names occupying each space represent rock-*families* which are called after one prominent variety. The names of individual *species* are introduced and defined in the paragraphs describing each family.

| | Volcanic Rocks and Minor Intrusions | | Plutonic Rocks |
	Fine-grained or glassy	Medium or fine-grained	Coarse or Medium-grained
Acid	RHYOLITES FELSITES / ALKALI-RHYOLITES	GRANITE-PORPHYRIES MICRO-GRANITES / ALKALI MICROGRANITES	GRANODIORITES GRANITES / ALKALI-GRANITES
Intermediate	ANDESITES / TRACHYTES	PORPHYRITES MICRO-DIORITES / [INTERMEDIATE LAMPROPHYRES]	DIORITES / SYENITES
Basic	BASALTS / ALKALI-BASALTS	DOLERITES / [BASIC LAMPROPHYRES]	GABBROS / ALKALI-GABBROS
Ultrabasic	(Ultrabasic lavas very rare)		PERIDOTITES SERPENTINES / MICA-PERIDOTITES

FORMS AND STRUCTURES OF IGNEOUS ROCKS

Lavas. The primary shapes of lava-flows have already been discussed, and it has been noted that fluid lavas tend to form thin sheets or tongues while viscous lavas form short thick flows or domes. Under some circumstances, especially when erupted under water, lava consolidates as a pile of tightly-packed rounded masses a foot or so in diameter. These *pillow-lavas* (Fig. 226) are formed by the rapid chilling of the lava as it oozes from the vent; details of the shapes of the pillow enable the stratigraphical order of the flows — their 'way-up' (p. 435) — to be determined as shown in Fig. 226. The interstices of submarine pillow-lavas are often filled with *chert* made of amorphous silica deposited from volcanic or organic (radiolarian) sources.

The surfaces of lava-flows assume characteristic forms as a result of the flow of the still-liquid interior. The outer layer may be pulled into a *ropy* pattern or fragmented to give a *blocky* structure; some lavas carry on their backs a jumble of cindery fragments distorted by gas-bubbles, and consolidate with a *slaggy* top. Gas-bubbles released during consolidation are often frozen in as hollow vesicles which may be scattered through the flow or concentrated near the top; *pipe-amygdales* are open tubes formed by bubbles rising through the flow. *Pumice* is a spongy or *vesicular* lava formed from magma charged with small gas-bubbles. The vesicles of lavas are often filled in after consolidation by secondary minerals such as calcite and zeolites to give *amygdales* (see Fig. 66).

The movements of lava or of intrusive magma tend to rotate solid particles such as phenocrysts, small crystals or accidental inclusions into a parallel alignment, and the rock-fabric so produced is termed a *flow-structure*. *Flow-lines* are formed by the alignment of needle-

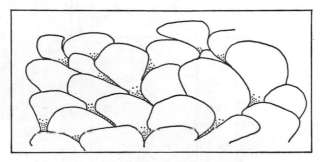

FIG. 226. Pillow-structure in lavas.

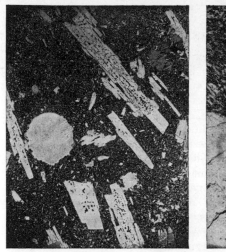

A   B

FIG. 227. Flow textures. A, alignment of elongated feldspar crystals
to give a flow pattern in a basaltic lava, × 6; B, flow pattern produced
by small feldspar laths in a porphyritic trachyte, × 40.

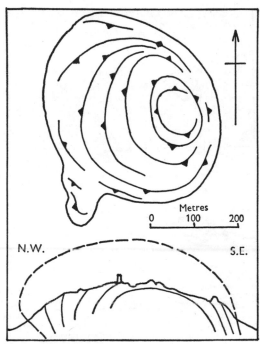

FIG. 228. Flow structure in the Drachenfels Trachyte Dome,
Rhineland, map and section; triangles point in the direction of
inclination of the flow bands.

shaped crystals and elongated inclusions, *flow-planes* by flat crystals and inclusions and *flow-banding* by the streaking-out of inhomogeneous material (Fig. 227); the arrangement of the flow-structures gives an indication of the direction of movement of the magma (Fig. 228).

Lavas, and also all kinds of intrusive igneous rocks, may carry foreign bodies which are known as *xenoliths*, or *xenocrysts* when they consist of single crystals (*xenos* = a stranger). Many xenoliths are of sedimentary origin and represent fragments picked up from the country-rocks through which the parent magma migrated. Others are derived from already solidified portions of the magma; *cognate inclusions* are bodies, such as clots of early-formed crystals, which are genetically related to the rocks in which they occur. Xenoliths picked up early in the history of the magma are usually recrystallised, and may begin to show signs of reaction with the magma (Fig. 229), whereas xenoliths acquired as the activity of the magma was waning, may be sharp-edged and unaltered. Magma which has absorbed xenolithic material is said to be *contaminated* and the rocks derived from it are often patchy and inhomogeneous (see p. 420).

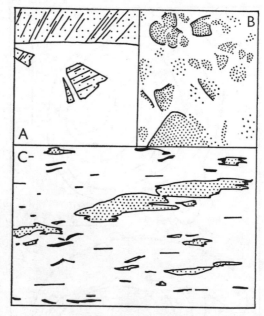

Fig. 229. *Xenoliths*. A, sharp-edged and disorientated; B, partly digested; C, flattened in flow-planes.

As lavas cool and consolidate, they shrink, and develop fractures or *joints*, which are often arranged in regular systems geometrically related to the surface of the flow. Even-grained lavas such as basalts may show a honeycomb pattern of *columnar jointing* in which the lava is divided into vertical hexagonal columns. Columnar jointing is well displayed in the basalts of the Giant's Causeway, Antrim (p. 494).

Intrusive rocks. Minor intrusions, as we have seen, form flat-lying *sills*, steeply-inclined *dykes*, irregular *veins* and cylindrical *plugs*. Small bodies of these kinds are usually associated in clusters which may be geometrically related to a larger igneous centre or to large-scale structures (Fig. 230). *Dyke-swarms* fill a number of parallel or radiating fractures whose patterns are determined by magmatic pressures or by earth-movements. *Cone-sheets* fill conical fractures inclined towards a central point and are usually arranged concentrically about an igneous centre (Fig. 233); the fractures are thought to be produced at moments when the magma exerted a strong pressure against its roof. *Sills* may be intruded in great numbers at shallow depths, following flat-lying bedding-planes, but are seldom formed at deep levels where magmatic pressures are usually insufficient to open up partings against the weight of the overlying rocks.

Minor intrusions commonly show glassy or fine-grained *chilled edges* formed from magma rapidly cooled by contact with the wall-rocks. Their inner parts are usually fine to medium-grained and may

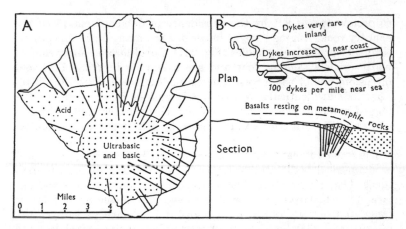

FIG. 230. *Dyke-swarms.* A, radial swarm centred on a plutonic intrusion, Rhum, Scotland; B, parallel swarm in fracture belt related to crustal flexure, east Greenland (after Wager).

carry xenoliths and exhibit flow-structures. Joint-systems formed on cooling are regularly arranged with respect to the walls of the intrusion and represent shrinkage-fractures (p. 494).

Major intrusions are formed by the accumulation of many cubic miles of magma within the crust, and it is obvious that this magma must make room for itself against the pressures prevailing at depth by special mechanisms. The *emplacement of intrusive magma* involves *displacement* of the country-rocks — this is of course no less true of minor intrusions, but the displacements involved are there much smaller. Among large intrusive bodies we may distinguish two types: those which forcibly made room for themselves by shouldering aside the country-rocks, and those formed more passively by magma rising

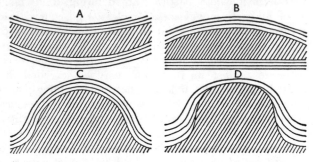

Fig. 231. *Major Intrusions.* A, lopolith; B, laccolith; C, dome; D, diapir.

to occupy spaces left by the subsidence of detached masses of the country-rock. Among *forceful intrusions* are many large concordant sheet-like or lenticular bodies (Fig. 231). *Lopoliths* are saucer-shaped bodies with a sagging floor and are exemplified by the Bushveld intrusion, one of the largest igneous bodies in existence (Fig. 250). *Laccoliths* are lenticular concordant intrusions in which the roof is bulged upwards. *Domes* have strongly arched surfaces and their roof-rocks are tilted, fractured and wrinkled by pressure of the accumulating magma.

Discordant forceful intrusions most usually form roughly conical or cylindrical bodies breaking across the bedding of the country-rocks. They may disturb the structure of the country-rocks and impose on their envelopes new structures such as concentric folds or tangential thrusts formed by upward and outward pressure of the magma (Fig. 232). Small compact intrusions, say five to twenty miles in diameter, are given the general name of *plutons*; if roughly circular in plan they are termed *stocks* or *bosses*. *Diapirs* are developed from

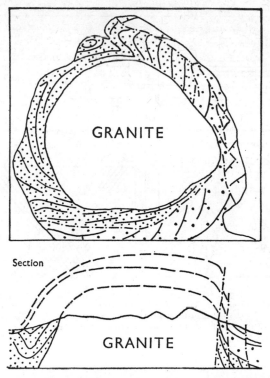

GRANITE

Section

GRANITE

FIG. 232. Structures produced in the envelope rocks by the intrusion of the Arran granite dome.

domes when the roof-rocks are ruptured and the intrusive body forced upwards in the manner of a diapiric salt dome (Fig. 231). *Batholiths* are plutonic bodies of quite a different order of size from the plutons already mentioned, their largest diameter being many tens or even hundreds of miles in length; these bodies are developed in connection with the Plutonic Series and will be discussed in Chapter 10.

Passively formed or *permitted intrusions* which enter spaces left by subsidence of crustal masses are, naturally, associated with faults and fractures. On a relatively small scale, the foundering of irregular blocks from the roof of a magma-chamber allows the magma to eat its way upwards by a process known as *stoping*, becoming charged with xenoliths in the process. On a larger scale, *ring-intrusions* are formed by the subsidence of a plug of country-rock detached from its surroundings by a cylindrical or conical ring-fracture (Fig. 233). *Ring-dykes* are annular intrusions along the ring-fracture itself;

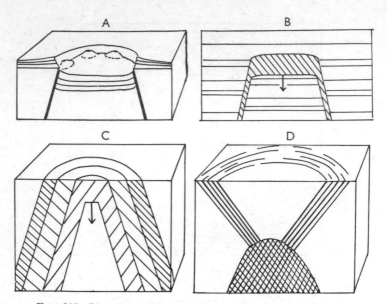

FIG. 233. *Ring Intrusions.* A, caldera formed at the surface by cauldron subsidence; B, space provided for intrusion by cauldron subsidence (permitted intrusion); C, ring complex of three ring dykes resulting from repeated cauldron subsidences; D, cone sheets.

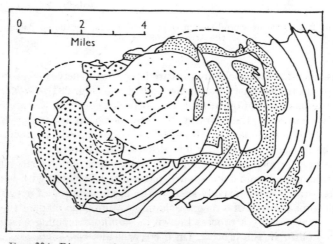

FIG. 234. Ring complexes of Ardnamurchan, Scotland, showing positions of successive centres, 1, 2 and 3, and the intrusions related to each (after Richey, H.M. Geological Survey). Ring-intrusions dotted, cone-sheets lines.

repeated subsidence of the central plug allows the intrusion of a sequence of ring-dykes about a common centre, as is seen in the Tertiary centre of Ardnamurchan (Fig. 234). The process of *cauldron subsidence*, by which *ring-complexes* are formed, is often closely linked with surface vulcanicity; ring-complexes are formed at the root of the volcano while calderas may develop by a similar mechanism at the surface.

The mechanisms of intrusion so far considered are concerned, in one way or another, with the displacement of country-rocks to make room for an invading magma. In theory magmatic bodies could also be formed by an entirely different mechanism — that is, by the conversion *in situ* of crustal rocks into magma, involving replacement rather than displacement of the country-rocks. It is a matter for debate how far this process of magma-formation has operated at levels made accessible by erosion, but many geologists agree that the enormous batholiths of the Plutonic Series must have been manufactured largely *in situ*, although the mechanism remains in doubt; this matter is further discussed in Chapter 10.

Large bodies of igneous rock are frequently associated with families of minor intrusions. These may take the form of small satellite bosses or of irregular systems of veins. They may also fill regular fracture-systems produced by the stresses set up by magmatic activity. Dyke-swarms and sets of cone-sheets are often centred about larger intrusions, especially about ring-complexes (Figs. 230, 234). Other minor intrusions may fill joints developed during the cooling of the igneous body itself; these veins often represent a volatile-rich fraction of the magma which is the last part to solidify.

The structure of an igneous intrusion and its envelope of country-rocks reflects the history of the invasion and cooling of the magma. The earliest recognisable structures in the igneous body itself are those formed during the period of crystallisation. These include planar and linear *flow-structures* produced by the alignment of minerals and xenoliths. As a rule, these structures are arranged more or less parallel to the roof and walls of the intrusion (Fig. 235); they are believed to lie roughly at right angles to the direction of upward and outward movement of magma, the flow-lines marking the direction of extension due to this magmatic pressure. Structures of quite different origin are seen in many basic intrusions where early-formed crystals sank in the magma to accumulate on the floor of the magma-chamber. These *layering-structures*, analogous to the bedding of detrital sediments, are described later (pp. 417–19).

Xenoliths picked up at depth or provided by stoping are common in many large intrusions. They are often rounded, flattened or elongated,

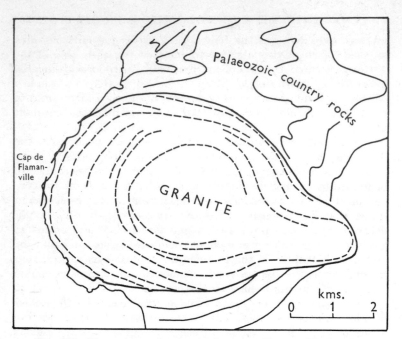

FIG. 235. *Flow structure in a major intrusion.* Flamanville Granite,
Cotentin, France (after Martin).

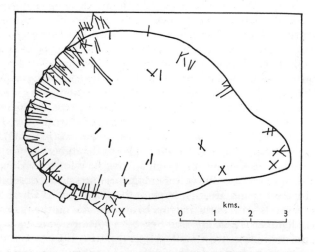

FIG. 236. Joint directions in a major intrusion, Flamanville Granite
(after Martin).

and may have hazy margins. Igneous rocks with such partly digested xenoliths pass into blotchy contaminated varieties (Fig. 252), reaction between xenolith and magma having taken place during the long period of cooling.

The magmatic pressures which drove an igneous intrusion into place often continue in force after the bulk of the intrusion solidified, and these residual pressures impose new structures on the intrusion and its country-rock envelope. Such structures may include enhanced planar and linear structures, zones of crushing and faults. When the cooling body reaches a certain stage of rigidity, *joints* are formed in definite patterns related to the form of the intrusion. *Cross-joints* or *Q-joints* are steep planes formed at right angles to the flow-lines in response to the extension which had earlier produced these lines; in many circular intrusions, the cross-joints are radially arranged (Fig. 236). *Longitudinal* or *S-joints* are steep joints parallel to the flow-lines. With the Q-joints, and a further common set of flat-lying joints, they divide the igneous rock into roughly rectangular blocks, whose shape is taken advantage of in quarrying for building-stones. All the *primary joints* formed during the cooling period may be filled by veins derived from the still-liquid interior of the intrusion.

BASIC IGNEOUS ROCKS

Crystallisation of basic magma. Basic rocks, which include the superficial *basalts* and *dolerites* and the plutonic *gabbros*, have been the predominant members of the Volcanic Association throughout geological time. Daly estimated that basalts made 80 per cent of all lavas, and if we add to these the percentage of lavas which are generally considered to be closely related to the basalts, the figure becomes even higher. The abundance of basic rocks and their uniformity through geological time have led to the view that these rocks are derived from a *primary basic magma* formed by partial or complete melting of silicate material in the upper mantle.

In basic igneous provinces, basalts or gabbros are usually associated with small quantities of ultrabasic, alkaline, intermediate or acid rocks. These chemically more diverse rocks are related to the dominant basic types and appear to have been formed indirectly from the primary magma as a result of changes brought about in two ways. The first is a chemical *differentiation* of the magma which results in the segregation of fractions of magma or accumulations of crystals differing in composition from the parent liquor. The second type of change is due to *contamination* of the magma following on the digestion or *assimilation* of xenolithic material. To appreciate the

Fig. 237. *Order of Crystallisation.* A, early idiomorphic crystals in a fine-grained groundmass; B, late hornblende filling interstices between early olivine crystals; C, early apatite crystals enclosed in a later biotite crystal.

workings of these processes, we must first consider the way in which crystallisation takes place in a cooling magma.

In the initial stages of cooling, the first-formed crystals float freely in the liquid, then, as crystals multiply, they form a loose mesh filled with the remaining liquid; finally, the magma in the interstices of the mesh crystallises out and the rock becomes entirely solid. The order in which individual minerals made their appearance may be revealed by the texture of the igneous rock — early minerals are often euhedral, later minerals enclose earlier crystals, and the last-formed minerals are interstitial (Fig. 237). The comparison of large numbers of igneous rocks shows that there is a certain regularity — by no means rigid — about the order in which the common minerals make their appearance, and the significance of this regular order of crystallisation has been made clear as a result of experimental work on artificial melts. This work, perhaps the most fruitful application of experimental methods to geological problems yet achieved, was largely due to N. L. Bowen whose book *The Evolution of the Igneous Rocks* is one of the landmarks of petrology.

Since magmas, whether natural or artificial, are complex melts containing many components, the temperature at which a given mineral begins to crystallise depends upon its relative solubility under the prevailing physical and chemical conditions, and not directly upon its freezing-point. A mineral crystallises when the magma, under the prevailing conditions, is saturated for its components; an example of this control is supplied by the behaviour of

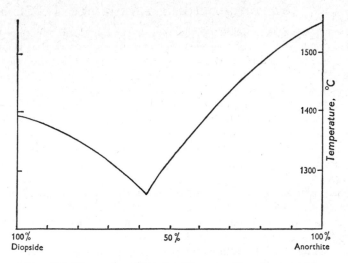

Fig. 238. Binary Crystallisation Diagram: Diopside-Anorthite.

melts containing the components of plagioclase-feldspar and diopside. Where pyroxene forms more than 42 per cent of the total, it is the first mineral to crystallise, and the greater its concentration the higher is the temperature at which it first appears (Fig. 238). When plagioclase forms more than 58 per cent of the melt, it appears before pyroxene and the temperature at which it begins to crystallise varies according to its concentration as shown in Fig. 238. As cooling proceeds, the mineral which is present in excess is gradually abstracted by crystallisation and the residual melt therefore becomes progressively richer in the other component. As the temperature falls, the composition of the melt changes in the manner shown by the curves on Fig. 238 until pyroxene and plagioclase reach proportions of 42 and 58 per cent respectively. These are the *eutectic proportions* for the two minerals and provide a mixture with the lowest possible temperature of crystallisation, marked by the meeting-point of the two curves in the figure. At the *eutectic point*, both minerals begin to crystallise together and there is no further change in the composition of the melt.

A natural magma is of course more complicated than the two-component melt considered above and the course of crystallisation may show many variations. The first minerals to separate are again those for which the magma is first saturated. When these minerals crystallise they are in chemical and physical equilibrium with the surrounding magma and are therefore *stable*. As the temperature falls, however, the composition of the magma changes for the reasons already mentioned, and the early-formed minerals may find themselves out of equilibrium in the new chemical and physical environment. They react with the residual magma to precipitate minerals stable in the prevailing conditions and, as the temperature continues to fall, still further species are formed in turn. We may therefore consider the minerals developing from the magma as members of a number of *reaction-series*; the highest members of each series are normally the first to appear and the lower members represent species in equilibrium at successively later stages in the evolution of the magma.

The common ferromagnesian minerals of igneous rocks form a *discontinuous reaction-series*. *Olivine* is the first mafic mineral to crystallise from a basic magma. It is followed in turn by the orthorhombic pyroxene *enstatite*, by *monoclinic pyroxene, hornblende* and finally *biotite*. With falling temperature, minerals of increasing structural complexity become stable (p. 98). If the reaction between early-formed crystals and magma is complete, these crystals are entirely replaced and only the lower members of the reaction-series appear in the final rock. If reaction is not completed, the later members of the reaction-series form *reaction-rims* around cores of the earlier members and a *corona structure* is produced (Fig. 239). If cooling is too rapid to allow time for reaction, the early members of the series may survive as euhedral grains or as phenocrysts set in a groundmass containing later members of the series.

A second important reaction-series in basic magmas is made by the

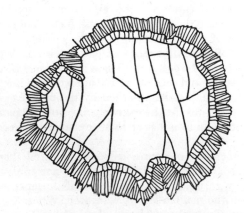

FIG. 239. *Corona Structure.* Early olivine crystal surrounded by rims of enstatite (inner) and actinolite (outer).

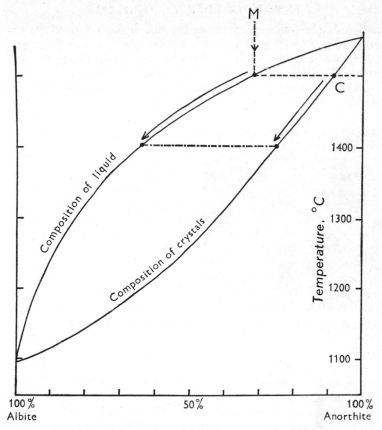

FIG. 240. Crystallisation Diagram of plagioclase feldspars.

plagioclase-feldspars. In a melt of plagioclase composition, the temperature at which crystallisation begins varies according to composition in the manner shown in Fig. 240; pure anorthite appears at the highest temperature and pure albite at the lowest temperature. When a melt of mixed composition cools to such a temperature that crystallisation begins, the plagioclase which separates from it is more basic than the parent liquor; for example, a melt M on reaching the temperature T, deposits crystals of composition C (Fig. 240). As crystallisation proceeds, the composition of the magma changes along the upper curve shown in the figure while the composition of the plagioclase deposited from it changes continuously along the lower curve; at each stage, the melt is in equilibrium with crystals more basic than itself, the links between liquid and crystals being

405

shown by the horizontal lines on the figure. Early-formed crystals react with the melt and are progressively made over to more sodic varieties in equilibrium under the new conditions. The plagioclase-feldspars therefore make a *continuous reaction-series*.

In natural magmas, the feldspars behave in a similar way. The first-formed crystals are rich in anorthite and later-formed crystals become progressively more albitic. Incomplete reaction between the plagioclase and magma leads to the formation of *zoned feldspars* (Fig. 241) in which an anorthitic core is rimmed by shells of more acid plagioclase. Continuous reaction-series of similar kinds are formed by the members of other solid solution series of minerals such as the forsterite-fayalite olivine-series, and the enstatite-hypersthene and diopside-hedenbergite series of pyroxenes. In all these series magnesian varieties appear at high temperatures and iron-rich varieties are formed as the temperature falls.

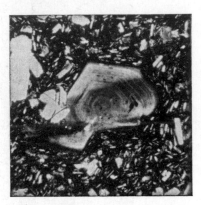

FIG. 241. Zoned plagioclase feldspars; polars crossed, × 35.

We are now in a position to interpret the sequence of crystallisation revealed in igneous rocks. The first minerals to crystallise are those high in the two main reaction-series — basic plagioclases and magnesian olivines or pyroxenes. With them, or before them, there often separate some of the minor components such as zircon, apatite and the iron oxides which have a limited solubility. At later stages more sodic plagioclase appears, together with iron-rich olivines or pyroxenes, hornblende and biotite. Finally, quartz, potash-feldspar and muscovite may be formed, and the full sequence, never seen in a single rock, is therefore as opposite.

Because basic magma is rich in the components of minerals high in the reaction-series it begins to crystallise at high temperatures. The olivines, pyroxenes and basic plagioclases form the greater part of the rock and minerals lower in the reaction-series are usually restricted to reaction-rims or to interstitial spaces, or completely absent. More acid magmas begin to crystallise at considerably lower temperatures, because the minerals in equilibrium with them are those, such as monoclinic pyroxene, hornblende and andesine, which are lower in the reaction-series. The most acid rocks such as granites are made up entirely of the relatively low-temperature components

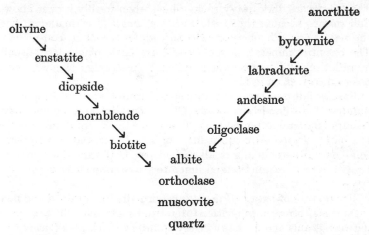

quartz, alkali-feldspar and mica; the composition of many granites approaches a eutectic mixture of quartz and feldspar. Whatever portions of the reaction-series are represented in a particular rock, however, we may expect the minerals to appear in regular sequence if crystallisation has followed an undisturbed course. Reversals of the normal order of crystallisation — *reversed zoning* in plagioclase, or the replacement of hornblende by pyroxene, for example — are generally connected with geological changes which have interrupted the simple routine of cooling; they may for example follow changes of composition due to the mixing of magmas or to contamination by sedimentary material.

As the components of the early-formed minerals are withdrawn from the magma the remaining liquid is enriched in the elements not taken up by these minerals and its composition changes in a way analogous to that of the artificial melts discussed above. *Crystallisation-differentiation* thus takes place and if by some means the residual magma is drawn off from the early-formed crystals it may ultimately consolidate as an independent body which is chemically distinct from the parent magma. As the higher members of the reaction-series are relatively rich in calcium, aluminium and magnesium, the residual liquors tend to be enriched in iron, silica and alkalies. As we shall see below, rocks which appear to be the derivatives of secondary magmas formed by differentiation are found in most basic igneous provinces; they form only a small percentage of the total volume of igneous rock and are *co-magmatic* with the more abundant basic types.

Basalts and related rocks. The first group of basic igneous rocks we shall consider is that of the lavas and small superficial intrusions.

The *basalts* are dark heavy rocks which when freshly broken show a dull surface because the crystals are too small to be made out with the naked eye. Phenocrysts and amygdales are often conspicuous. The essential minerals of true basalt are basic plagioclase, usually labradorite, and monoclinic pyroxene; an average chemical composition is given on p. 42.

Basalts fall into two main divisions, around which are grouped a number of less important species. *Olivine-basalts* contain olivine as an essential mineral, often making 20 per cent of the total, and are free of quartz. *Tholeiites* contain little or no olivine and usually carry small quantities of quartz or alkali-feldspar. Orthorhombic pyroxene, apatite, zircon, magnetite and ilmenite are common accessories in all types.

The texture of basalts (Fig. 242) is normally fine-grained and holocrystalline, often porphyritic. Interstitial glass may fill the spaces between grains and a wholly glassy splintery black rock (*tachylyte*) is formed by rapid cooling at the chilled edges of small intrusions. Phenocrysts, when present, may be of olivine, augite or plagioclase. They are generally idiomorphic or hypidiomorphic, but may be corroded by reaction with the magma; plagioclase phenocrysts may be zoned, with the more calcic variety at the centre. In the ground-

A   B

FIG. 242. Basalts. A, Olivine-basalt, composed of olivine and pyroxene grains (dark) and feldspar crystals (light), × 40. B, Basalt, composed of pyroxene grains (dark), feldspar crystals (light) and interstitial glass (black), × 40.

mass, plagioclase, usually rather more sodic than that of the pheno-crysts, and augite or pigeonite are the principal minerals. The feld-spar generally forms a swarm of minute laths arranged at random, or in a parallel fashion resulting from magmatic flow. The pyroxene, with the minor constituents, forms small granules packed between the feldspar-laths. In tholeiitic varieties the final interstices of the crystal mesh are occupied by quartz, alkali-feldspar or an acid glass, these representing the residual liquor resulting from differentiation and consisting of minerals low in the reaction-series.

Basaltic lavas and related types, with minor intrusions of similar composition, are found in a great variety of geological environments. All are probably derived from the same ultimate source, but there are certain constant differences between the basaltic associations found in different environments. We may distinguish three asso-ciations characteristic of distinct types of volcanic province.

In *oceanic regions* an *olivine-basalt* association predominates, and the minor members of the association appear to have been formed by crystallisation-differentiation of the basaltic magma. These minor varieties include lavas which are enriched in the early-formed crystals of the magma, such as *oceanites* containing as much as 50 per cent of olivine phenocrysts. Other associates of the olivine-basalts appear to represent residual fractions of the differentiated magma and are richer in alkalies or in silica than the olivine-basalts. These include lavas containing oligoclase in place of labradorite (*mugearites*), alkaline *trachytes* (p. 426) and other alkaline lavas, such as the nepheline-bearing *phonolites* (p. 426), which are feldspathoidal and notably poor in silica.

Olivine-basalt and its associates make the great shield volcanoes of the Hawaiian Islands, the other island groups of the central Pacific, and are in fact the typical association in regions where the crust is of the thin oceanic type. In many of the volcanoes, long periods of eruption of basaltic lavas, building up the main parts of the cones, have been followed by the explosive discharge of small volumes of trachytes, phonolites and other alkaline lavas; erosion reveals in some volcanoes, such as those of Tahiti, plugs of alkaline rocks filling volcanic necks. The sequence of lavas and the proportions of the various types accord well with the view that the entire suite is produced by differentiation of primary basic magma.

In *stable continental regions* — that is, regions outside the mobile belts — an olivine-basalt-trachyte association like that of the oceanic regions is widely distributed and is seen for example in the Permian lavas of the Midland Valley of Scotland. A second as-sociation, sometimes occurring independently and sometimes in connection with olivine-basalts, has tholeiitic basalts as its principal type. These constitute a great part of the piles of *plateau-basalts* in the Deccan Traps, the Columbia-Snake River plains of Washington and many other areas. The plateau-basalts of the North Atlantic Tertiary province include both olivine-basalts and tholeiites in close association. The tholeiitic association does not as a rule include the highly alkaline feldspathoidal lavas found in olivine-basalt provinces, but is characterised instead by rather more siliceous minor members such as *andesites* (p. 422) *rhyolites* (p. 425) and more rarely *trachytes*. These lavas form only a small percentage of the total volume erupted and may well represent siliceous residues of differentiated tholeiitic magma.

In the *geosynclinal mobile regions*, basalts comparable to those already mentioned are interbedded with the thick sedimentary piles. They are often associated with *spilites* which differ from normal basalts in containing albite in place of basic plagioclase. These geosynclinal basic rocks together with associated ultrabasic types (see p. 422) are collectively known as *ophiolites* (Chapter 12). Spilites often take the form of pillow-lavas and their interbanding with marine sediments indicates that they were generally erupted beneath the sea; their characteristic associates are soda-rich acid lavas or minor intrusions known as *keratophyres*.

FIG. 243. Spilite showing alteration of the groundmass feldspars and ferromagnesian minerals; the white patches are chlorite-filled vesicles flattened after consolidation, × 15.

Spilites generally show evidence of considerable secondary alteration, affecting the primary magmatic minerals (Fig. 243). Chlorite, actinolite and calcite replace pyroxenes and in many specimens it is evident that the distinctive mineral albite is itself formed by replacement of original basic plagioclase. The characteristic features of the spilite association may be due to late reactions in originally basaltic rocks taking place in the presence of sodic solutions. The origin of the transforming fluids is not known, but it is possible that these fluids are derived from sea-water trapped in the geosynclinal sediments.

Dolerites and related rocks. The *dolerites* (Fig. 244) are closely related to basalts in origin and occurrence and form dykes and sills in basaltic provinces. They are dark, heavy, medium-grained rocks in which the individual components can generally be distinguished with the naked eye. The essential and accessory minerals are the same as those of basalts and the range of variation is comparable. *Olivine-dolerites* and *quartz-dolerites* may be distinguished.

In texture, the rocks are holocrystalline and may be porphyritic or non-porphyritic. Phenocrysts when present may include olivine, monoclinic pyroxene and basic plagioclase. In the groundmass, plagioclase forms lath-like crystals, of a somewhat larger size than those of basalts, which generally interlock to form a loose mesh.

FIG. 244. Dolerite, composed of pyroxene grains (dark) and labradorite feldspar laths and plates (light), × 15.

Pyroxenes often include both augite and pigeonite; they occupy the spaces between the feldspars and are sometimes granular giving the *intersertal* texture, but may also form crystals much larger than the feldspar which spread between and enclose the laths; this arrangement gives the rock an *ophitic* texture (Fig. 225B). In quartz-dolerites, the final interstices of the crystal mesh are filled by shapeless pools of quartz, or of an intimate intergrowth of quartz and alkali-feldspar representing the last part of the rock to consolidate. Small amounts of hornblende and biotite may appear as interstitial minerals or as reaction-rims around pyroxenes. Quartz-dolerites often contain streaks and veins of coarse-grained rock rich in feldspar, which are *segregations* of the residual fluid portions of the magma.

In basic volcanic provinces, dolerite dykes and sills occur in great numbers, and their total volume often runs to many thousands of cubic miles. These minor intrusions may account for a substantial proportion of the igneous rocks of the province and in some regions they are the principal igneous forms; the Mesozoic Karroo System of South Africa, for example, contains an enormous volume of dolerites which are not associated with comparable volumes of lavas.

Some large dolerite-sills show petrological variations from bottom to top which appear to have resulted from differentiation *in situ* during the relatively slow cooling-period. The great Palisade Sill of New Jersey provides an example of such variation (Fig. 245). This doleritic sheet is more than 1000 feet thick and shows chilled marginal zones, of the order of fifty feet in thickness, made of basalt. Above the lower marginal zone comes a layer of olivine-dolerite rich in ferromagnesian minerals. Olivine is almost confined to the lower third of the sill and it appears that early-formed crystals of this mineral, being heavier than the magma, sank and accumulated on the floor of the intrusion. Gravity is a principal control in the formation of these rocks. In a similar way, the early-formed species of pyroxene (magnesium-rich augite and hypersthene) are concentrated in the lower layers of the intrusion; pyroxenes in the upper parts of the sill are more iron-rich species of clinopyroxene and represent crystals which grew at later stages in the cooling-history. Plagioclase is relatively scarce in the lower part of the intrusion, making some 40 per cent of the rock, and forms zoned crystals with cores of labradorite or even bytownite. It increases upward to form about 65 per cent of the rock, and becomes more sodic in composition. Intergrowths of quartz and alkali-feldspar form interstitial patches which increase in size upwards. With these mineralogical variations go changes in texture. The olivine-dolerites are moderately fine-grained and the grain-size increases upwards as far as the upper

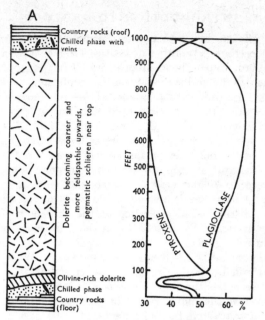

FIG. 245. Differentiation in the Palisade Dolerite Sill, New Jersey. A, diagrammatic vertical section of the sill; B, vertical variation in pyroxene and plagioclase.

chilled zone; the higher layers contain very coarse-grained patches, and coarse acid veins from these layers invade the chilled roof-zone. All the features described above seem to be compatible with an origin by crystallisation-differentiation in the course of which early-formed crystals were segregated under the influence of gravity to produce *accumulative* rocks, or *cumulates*, formed by the piling-up of crystals. Minerals high in the various reaction-series are concentrated at the bottom of the sill and those lower in these series at the top; the upward increase in grain-size may be correlated with increasing concentration of volatile components in the residual portion of the magma.

Gabbros and related rocks. The *gabbros*, the plutonic equivalents of the basalts and dolerites, are distinguished by their coarseness of grain. Seen in hand-specimen a gabbro generally displays a mottling due to the scattering of pale feldspars through the dark ferromagnesian minerals; in fresh rocks, the cleavage-surfaces of the components are large enough to catch the eye and give the rock a clean sparkling appearance.

The essential minerals of gabbro proper are labradorite and augite.

413

Accessory olivine, hypersthene, hornblende or quartz are common and when present in notable quantities produce varieties such as olivine-gabbro, hypersthene-gabbro and so on. Pigeonite is never present, as this mineral is unstable under conditions of slow cooling. The customary minor accessories of basic rocks — magnetite, ilmenite and apatite — are almost universal and other minerals such as biotite, chromite ($FeCr_2O_4$) and spinel ($MgFeAl_2O_4$) may be present. In related rock-species, olivine or hypersthene appear as the dominant, or the only, ferromagnesian minerals, and bytownite or anorthite instead of labradorite. The ferromagnesian minerals usually total 40–70 per cent of the rock. By an increase in this proportion, gabbros grade into *ultrabasic rocks*, among which several species are distinguished according to the character of the ferromagnesian minerals. By a decrease in the proportion of ferromagnesian minerals, gabbros pass into *leucogabbros* and, when feldspar reaches 90 per cent of the total, into *anorthosites*. Where the ferromagnesian minerals are near the iron-rich end of their respective solid solution series the term *ferrogabbro* is used. The mineralogical compositions of the main species of basic and ultrabasic plutonic rocks are summarised in the following table:

BASIC AND ULTRABASIC PLUTONIC ROCKS

	Augite	*Hypersthene*	*Olivine*	*Olivine +* *Pyroxenes*	*Total ferromag-* *nesians 10% or less*
Labradorite	GABBRO	NORITE	TROCTOLITE (Labradorite or bytownite)	OLIVINE-GABBRO	
Bytownite or Anorthite	EUCRITE		ALLIVALITE (anorthite)		
Feldspar forms 90% of rock					ANORTHOSITE
			ULTRABASIC		
Feldspar forms 10% or less	PYROXENITE		DUNITE (serpentine)	PERIDOTITE (serpentine)	

The textures of gabbros (Fig. 246) differ from those of basalts and dolerites in a number of ways which are clearly related to the environment of consolidation. The larger grain-size has already been mentioned, and it should also be noted that gabbros are never porphyritic; the absence of two separate generations of crystals is of course due to the fact that the crystallisation of the plutonic rocks was not interrupted by transference of the magma to higher levels. The long slow cooling resulted in the continuous growth of minerals in competition with one another; the texture is therefore hypidiomorphic and well-formed crystals are rare. Zoning of plagioclase is less common than in volcanic rocks, presumably because more time was available for reaction between the early-formed feldspars and

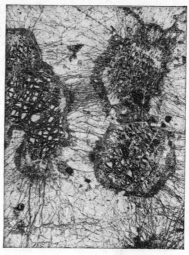

A

B

FIG. 246. Gabbros. A, Olivine-gabbro, showing a large olivine
(centre) with pyroxene (grey) and labradorite feldspar (white), × 15.
B, Troctolite, partly serpentinised olivine in cracked labradorite; the
olivine is surrounded by a narrow corona or reaction-rim of pyroxene
and amphibole, × 15.

the magma. Minerals such as olivine which are high in the reaction-
series are often partially enclosed in later species. The reaction-rims
which make *coronas* around olivines and pyroxenes are so arranged
that the later minerals follow each other outward in the order of their
position in the reaction-series. Olivine may be rimmed by enstatite
which is in turn surrounded by augite, all three minerals being
primary (Figs. 239, 246). Augite may be surrounded by primary hornblende or by a fringe of secondary fibrous amphibole and then by
minute flakes of biotite.

The slow cooling of gabbros facilitates chemical reactions taking
place during the final stages of consolidation and immediately after
consolidation is completed. These reactions are also favoured by the
presence of watery fluids derived from the volatile components of the
magma which find it less easy to escape than in superficial bodies of
magma; evidence of the presence of such volatiles is provided by the
occurrence of very coarse-grained patches and veins of *gabbro-
pegmatite*. The *late-stage* or *deuteric reactions* leading on to *autometamorphism* result in the partial or complete replacement of primary
species by secondary minerals. The changes lead to the production of
minerals stable at temperatures lower than those at which the magma
crystallised, and may therefore be regarded as attempts to bring the

rock into equilibrium under the conditions of cooling. Basic feldspar is often replaced by granular associations of zoisite and albite known as *saussurite*. Olivine and hypersthene may be replaced by hydrous *serpentine*; this reaction involves an increase of volume which in olivine-rich rocks like troctolites often results in the cracking of the adjacent feldspars (Fig. 246). All these secondary changes dull the clear crystalline appearance of the gabbros in hand-specimen.

From what has been said above, it is evident that gabbros show considerable variation in primary mineralogical composition. Many gabbroic intrusions contain a number of different rock-species and from the arrangement and mutual relations of these species it is possible to gain some idea of the way in which the variations originated. This purely geological evidence proves to be in remarkably close harmony with the chemical evidence on the crystallisation of melts supplied by experimental work (p. 402). Crystallisation-differentiation and contamination are found to be the processes determining the characters of the igneous rocks. The workings of these processes in plutonic basic magma can be illustrated by a number of examples.

The *Skaergaard intrusion* is a discordant gabbro body exposed on the ice-scoured coast of east Greenland. As a result of the work of Wager and Deer (1939) it has become a classic example of the effects of crystallisation-differentiation. The Skaergaard intrusion (Fig. 247) is one of the plutonic masses belonging to the North Atlantic Tertiary igneous province. It is shaped like a tilted inverted cone and at the present level of erosion a vertical thickness of about 2500 metres, believed to represent the upper half of the intrusion, is exposed. The walls of the cone are lined by *marginal*

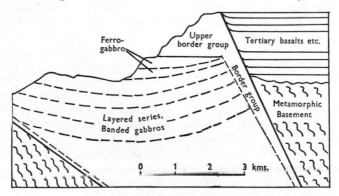

Fig. 247. Skaergaard Intrusion, Greenland: diagrammatic cross-section (after Wager and Deer).

gabbros which are considered to have been formed at an early stage by chilling of the magma; a similar chilled phase spreads over the top of the exposed gabbros and suggests that the roof lay only a short distance above the present land-surface. The gabbros enclosed within the marginal facies show a near-horizontal *layering* which is due to the fact that they were built up from bottom to top by the settling of crystals under the influence of gravity. The oldest layered gabbros seen are those at the base of the exposed section.

The marginal gabbros, whose composition can be taken to be not far from that of the original magma, are olivine-gabbros chemically similar to the widespread olivine-basalts of many basic volcanic provinces. The lowest rocks of the layered gabbros are olivine-gabbros whose constituent minerals — plagioclase, augite, hypersthene and olivine — are all high in their respective continuous reaction-series. The plagioclase is a basic labradorite, the augite is rich in calcium and magnesium and the hypersthene and olivine are magnesian varieties; the composition of these minerals is consistent with the view that they crystallised at a fairly early stage in the cooling of the magma. At successively higher levels in the intrusion the plagioclase becomes increasingly sodic and the ferromagnesian minerals become more iron-rich. The olivine-gabbros pass upwards to gabbros containing no olivine and then to fayalite-bearing *ferrogabbros* made of andesine, iron-rich augite and the iron-rich olivine fayalite. The highest parts of the layered gabbros are

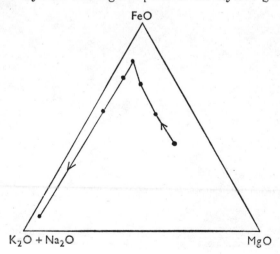

FIG. 248. Skaergaard Intrusion, the course of the differentiation shown in an alkali: MgO: FeO diagram.

quartz-ferrogabbros containing lenses of acid *granophyre* (p. 572) made largely of oligoclase, potash-feldspar and quartz. The ferrogabbros and granophyres represent the final residues of the differentiated magma; the former are very rich in iron, somewhat rich in alkalies, and correspondingly poor in magnesium and lime when compared with the marginal gabbros (Fig. 248).

The layered gabbros of Skaergaard show, in addition to the vertical chemical changes discussed above, a small-scale *rhythmic banding* (cf. Fig. 249) produced by the repetition of layers which grade over a few inches from ferromagnesian-rich rock at the base to rock rich in plagioclase at the top. The tabular feldspars in these layers are arranged with their largest dimensions parallel to the banding and so give the rock an anisotropic fabric. The rhythmic banding lies almost horizontally and is tilted up a little towards the contact with the marginal gabbros. It is regarded as a sedimentation-structure produced by the deposition of crystals layer by layer as they were brought down through the magma by convection-currents. The grading of each layer is the result of sorting by gravity, the heavy components being concentrated at the base, as in a sedimentary graded bed; the parallel orientation of minerals is due to the effects

FIG. 249. Banded gabbro from Somalia showing igneous layering attributed to gravitational differentiation. (Photograph by W. Skiba.)

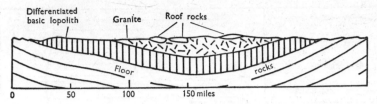

FIG. 250. Bushveld, section across the lopolith.

of settling and to the influence of the convection-currents flowing over the pile of crystals on the magma-chamber floor.

The *Bushveld Complex* provides a second example of a layered basic intrusion in which differentiation and gravity-settling of early-formed crystals played a dominant part. The complex forms one or more concordant lopoliths, far larger than the Skaergaard intrusion (Fig. 250). It shows, in broad terms, an upward transition from accumulative gabbros and ultrabasic rocks through banded gabbros to syenitic and dioritic rocks. The feldspars become more sodic and the ferromagnesian minerals more iron-rich upwards (although there are local reversals of these trends); the final products of differentiation are not ferrogabbros, as at Skaergaard, but alkaline or intermediate rocks. Four zones can be distinguished from bottom to top:

(a) *Basal zone* of hypersthene-gabbro representing material chilled against the floor.

(b) *'Critical zone'* up to a mile thick in which norites alternate with bands of pyroxenite, anorthosite and chromite-rich rock; these basic and ultrabasic rocks are mostly of accumulative origin.

(c) *'Main zone'*, more than three miles thick, of hypersthene-gabbros. These rocks sometimes show rhythmic banding and contain towards the top bands of titaniferous iron ore.

(d) *Upper zone* consisting of 'red rocks' which include syenites, diorites and granodiorites with feldspars as sodic as andesine. The upper zone, which may be nearly two miles in thickness, probably includes the final products of differentiation, but its volume may have been increased by the assimilation of acid volcanic rocks making the roof of the lopolith.

The *gabbros of north-east Scotland* form a group of closely related bodies whose petrological variations are attributed not only to the effects of differentiation but also to those of contamination. Several of the intrusions (Fig. 251) show a layered structure and pass upward from accumulative dunites, troctolites and peridotites to gabbros and, in one body, to syenitic rocks; these variations are comparable to those already discussed. In addition, the Huntly, Arnage, Haddo

419

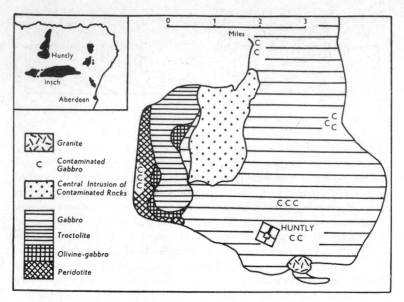

Legend:
Granite
C — Contaminated Gabbro
Central Intrusion of Contaminated Rocks
Gabbro
Troctolite
Olivine-gabbro
Peridotite

FIG. 251. The southern part of the Huntly Gabbro Complex, Aberdeenshire; inset, the Gabbro Province of north-east Scotland (after Read, H.M. Geological Survey).

House and Insch masses show considerable developments of *norites* in which hypersthene is the only pyroxene present. These were considered by Read to have been produced by the contamination of gabbroic magma by argillaceous material. Many of the *contaminated norites* (Fig. 252) hold partly digested xenoliths; they are patchy rocks and may contain minerals such as biotite, cordierite and garnet which are not normally found in basic igneous rocks. According to the reaction-principle, the magma is capable of absorbing from xenoliths substances for which it is not yet saturated, and the chemical changes so produced have influenced the course of crystallisation and led to the development of hypersthene in preference to monoclinic pyroxene. Material not readily digested by the magma is concentrated in the xenoliths which are thus modified in another direction; they develop aluminous and magnesium-rich minerals such as corundum (Al_2O_3), cordierite and spinel.

One final, rather isolated type of basic rock must be mentioned, the group of *anorthosites*. Anorthosite, a somewhat misleading name, denotes a plutonic rock made up of 90–100 per cent of labradorite or bytownite; it passes by transitions into *leucogabbro* with more than 10 per cent of ferromagnesian minerals. Anorthosites are gener-

420

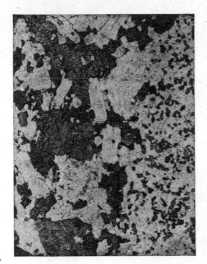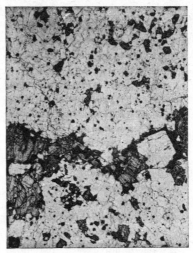

A   B

Fig. 252. Contaminated Gabbros, Aberdeenshire. A, Norite (hypersthene and labradorite) with a micronoritic patch of the same composition produced by the modification of a pelitic xenolith, × 15. B, Hypersthene-labradorite-spinel xenoliths with a noritic streak between them, × 15.

ally coarse-grained hypidiomorphic granular rocks of pale colour containing in addition to the dominant plagioclase, accessories which may include hypersthene, augite, olivine, iron oxides and garnet. Rocks of this type occur in two different settings — some form minor members of differentiated basic plutonic bodies, as in the Bushveld complex already discussed, while others make large independent masses usually emplaced in strongly-metamorphosed country-rocks. These anorthosites may be derived from near the base of the crust.

ULTRABASIC IGNEOUS ROCKS

The ultrabasic igneous rocks are feldspar-poor or *ultramafic* rocks composed of combinations of the minerals olivine, orthorhombic pyroxene, monoclinic pyroxene and hornblende, or the secondary alteration products of these minerals. Iron oxide, chromite, spinel and biotite are common accessory minerals. The rocks falling within this definition are the *peridotites, pyroxenites* and *dunites* (Table, p. 414); *hornblendites* in which hornblende is the dominant mineral; and *serpentines* produced from the three first-mentioned species by the partial or complete replacement of the magmatic minerals by secondary products.

Dunites, peridotites and pyroxenites commonly show a more or less equigranular texture. Hornblende and biotite, when present, often build large poikilitic crystals enclosing the other constituents (Fig. 225) and were probably formed as late-magmatic or secondary minerals. Other widespread secondary changes are the conversion of olivine and hypersthene to serpentine and the development of pale fibrous amphiboles, talc and calcite. These changes may be largely autometamorphic and take place during the cooling of the igneous rocks. They give the rocks a dull, non-crystalline appearance. Many serpentines are streaked with vivid red and green, and are used as ornamental stones.

Ultrabasic rocks appear in two quite distinct environments. As we have already seen, relatively small volumes of ultrabasic rock are formed as *cumulates* during the differentiation of basic magmas. They are of economic importance because they occasionally contain ore minerals of chromium, platinum and nickel which are segregated with the early-formed minerals from basic magma (p. 597).

Much more extensive masses of ultrabasic rock are found in geosynclinal and orogenic belts. In this environment serpentines are the commonest ultrabasic types and belong to the ophiolite assemblage. The clue to the parentage of these rocks probably lies in the fact that they are restricted to zones in which the crust has suffered extreme disturbance. It is possible that disturbance reaches down to the Mohorovičić discontinuity and taps ultrabasic material in the mantle beneath. The manner in which the material migrates upward presents another problem; ultrabasic magma should theoretically have a higher melting-point even than basic magma, but there is much evidence that ultrabasic intrusions are emplaced at quite low temperatures, since their country-rocks are rarely strongly metamorphosed. The ultrabasic material is therefore believed to migrate as a mush of crystals lubricated by small amounts of liquid, rather than as a true magma. This proposition is supported by the fact that the minerals of dunites and peridotites are often crushed and the contacts of ultrabasic bodies generally show evidence of movement; and also by the fact that ultrabasic lavas are almost non-existent. These characters could also be accounted for by the emplacement of solid ultrabasic masses by mechanical means during crustal deformation.

ANDESITES AND RELATED ROCKS

Andesites are intermediate lavas characterised by a plagioclase whose average composition is that of andesine. At least one ferromagnesian mineral is always present and the dominant species may be orthorhombic or monoclinic pyroxene or hornblende (Fig. 253). Basic andesites, verging on basalts, may contain olivine, and the more acid varieties may contain biotite. In addition, quartz and orthoclase or the high-temperature potash-feldspar sanidine may be present in small amounts, and magnetite, hematite and apatite are widespread as accessory minerals. Chlorite, calcite and sphene are common secondary minerals.

Andesites pass into basalts by increase in the anorthite content of the plagioclase. With increase in quartz they pass into the acid lavas *dacites* (Table below). When orthoclase or sanidine increases to make a third of the total feldspar the rock becomes a *trachyandesite* and when potash-feldspar is dominant it becomes the alkaline lava *trachyte*. Medium-grained rocks resembling andesites in texture and composition, and generally forming minor intrusions, are given the general name of *porphyrites*.

INTERMEDIATE, ALKALINE AND ACID LAVAS

Potash feldspar less than ⅓ of total feldspar	Potash-feldspar and plagioclase approximately equal	Potash-feldspar more than ⅔ of total feldspar
INTERMEDIATE AND ALKALINE		
ANDESITE	TRACHYANDESITE	TRACHYTE
ACID		
DACITE	RHYODACITE	RHYOLITE

Most andesites are dark, dull-looking rocks carrying hypidiomorphic phenocrysts of plagioclase and/or pyroxene or hornblende. The groundmass is usually very fine-grained and often partially cryptocrystalline or glassy. As a rule, minute laths or microlites of plagioclase are locked in a felted mass or aligned to produce a flow-structure (Fig. 253). Between them may be scattered granules of pyroxene and iron oxides with interstitial patches of quartz-potash-feldspar intergrowth, or an unresolvable matrix of greenish or brownish material often dusty with iron oxides. The plagioclase-phenocrysts are usually strongly zoned. Their cores may be as basic as bytownite and they may be surrounded by rims of oligoclase or even of potash-feldspar. Zoning within the crystals is often *oscillatory* and results from the repeated alternation of more and less albitic zones; such zoning is uncommon in basalts and its wide development in andesites suggests disturbance of the simple routine of crystallisation. The plagioclase of the groundmass is invariably more acid than

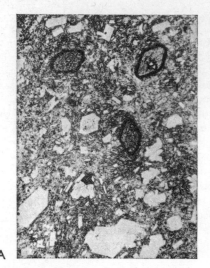
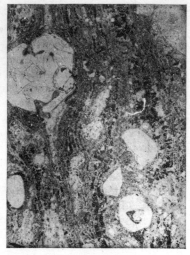

A
B

Fig. 253. A. Andesite, composed of hornblende and plagioclase phenocrysts in a fine-grained groundmass, × 15. B, Rhyolite, embayed quartz phenocrysts in a glassy matrix showing flow texture, × 15.

that of the phenocrysts. Potash-feldspar, when present, is generally associated with quartz in interstitial spaces but may grow at a late stage around phenocrysts, especially in the trachyandesites. The pyroxene phenocrysts include hypersthene and augite, while augite and pigeonite appear in the groundmass. The hornblende forms prismatic phenocrysts which usually undergo partial alteration to a bright red-brown variety. Many andesites show a development of secondary minerals, such as chlorite, zoisite and calcite, that are assigned to a post-consolidation stage — such altered andesites are known as *propylites*.

Andesitic lavas are second only to basalts among the extrusive rocks. Unlike the basalts, they are confined to continental areas and are most abundantly produced in orogenic belts during periods of mountain-building. At the present day andesites are common among the volcanic products of the great circum-Pacific belt of vulcanism extending through the Andes and the Rockies westward to the archipelagoes of eastern and south-eastern Asia. The central Pacific volcanic province, as we have seen, is dominated by olivine-basalts and the junction of the oceanic and circum-Pacific provinces is termed the *andesite line*.

The andesites of orogenic regions are associated with both basalts and rhyolites, the three types apparently alternating in a rather

424

haphazard manner. The combined volume of intermediate and acid lavas generally exceeds that of the basalts in the province and it therefore seems unlikely that the more acid lavas are simple residual products of differentiation of basic magma. In tholeiitic provinces where andesites and rhyolites do appear to be formed by such a process, these lavas make only a small percentage of the total volume of extrusive rock. It seems probable that in the andesitic provinces, basic magma is contaminated on a large scale by acidic material derived from the higher or sialic layer of the continental crust. This conception is in harmony with the fact that andesites are absent from oceanic provinces and, as we shall see, there is independent evidence that the sial reaches a state of unusual hotness and mobility in orogenic belts.

RHYOLITES AND RELATED ROCKS

The **rhyolites** and their allies are the most acid of the common extrusive rocks. They are derived from relatively cool and viscous magmas and are therefore generally glassy, sometimes pumiceous and often associated with vitric tuffs or welded tuffs. Quartz, oligoclase and potash-feldspar (sanidine or orthoclase) are the main minerals; one or other of the ferromagnesian minerals pyroxene, hornblende or biotite is generally present in minor amounts. Since the groundmass is either very fine-grained or glassy, it is impossible to establish the true character of the rock without a chemical analysis. The three main varieties are distinguished in the Table on p. 423.

Any of the minerals mentioned above may be found as phenocrysts (Fig. 253). The ferromagnesian minerals are often partially altered to chlorite, the feldspars tend to be sericitised. Quartz forms idiomorphic bipyramidal crystals, and often shows deep embayments due to partial resorption by the magma. The groundmass, when entirely glassy, forms a shiny black rock known as *obsidian* or a resinous-looking water-rich glass termed *pitchstone*. When crystalline, the groundmass generally consists of a very fine or cryptocrystalline mosaic of quartz and feldspar which gives a dull, pale-coloured surface when broken. This fine mosaic is said to have a *felsitic* texture and rocks with a groundmass of this type are given the general name of *felsites*; they include minor acid intrusions and devitrified acid lavas. Acid lavas commonly show swirling flow-structures produced by colour-banding in the glass or by the alignment of trails of incipient crystals (Fig. 253). Under the microscope, they often display arcuate cracks (*perlitic* structure) and contain swarms of crystallites or microlites. Minute crystals sometimes radiate from a central base to give a *spherulitic texture* (Fig. 223).

Rhyolites and related rocks are found in small volumes in many volcanic provinces; like andesites, they are restricted to continental environments. The composition of many acid lavas approaches that of a eutectic mixture of quartz, plagioclase and potash-feldspar; these rocks therefore consist of the most easily-fused mixture of common silicate minerals and it is reasonable to suppose that acid magma might be formed by heating at quite shallow depths in the crust. Rhyolites occur on a large scale in andesitic provinces where they may result from the reaction of basic magma with sialic material. They also appear in tholeiitic provinces as minor associates of basic rocks, and are among the possible end-products of differentiation of basic magma.

ALKALINE IGNEOUS ROCKS

Under the heading of **alkaline rocks** we unite for the purposes of description a variety of types formed by several independent processes. The common feature linking members of this group is the possession of a higher ratio of alkalies to silica than that characterising the series basalt-andesite-rhyolite already described. This peculiarity finds expression in the development of alkali-feldspars, feldspathoids and sodium- or potassium-bearing ferromagnesian minerals. The alkaline rocks contain a great range of mineral species, and for this reason they have been subjected to much study and detailed subdivision. For our purposes it is sufficient to recognise four broad groups — the alkali-basalts and their plutonic equivalents the alkali-gabbros, the trachytes and their plutonic equivalents the syenites.

The **alkali-basalts** differ from normal basalts principally in the presence of one or more feldspathoidal minerals such as nepheline, leucite, hauyne or nosean. These minerals generally appear as conspicuous phenocrysts in a groundmass texturally not very different from that of basalts (Fig. 254). With the appearance of noticeable quantities of alkali-feldspar the alkali-basalts pass into *trachybasalt* and *phonolite*.

Trachytes are light-coloured alkaline lavas richer in silica and poorer in ferromagnesian minerals than the alkali-basalts. They contain as essential minerals an alkali-feldspar — either orthoclase, sanidine or very sodic plagioclase — and a ferromagnesian mineral which may be a pyroxene, amphibole or dark mica. The ferromagnesian components often show vivid tints of blue, green or red-brown, which reflect the fact that they are often sodic species of

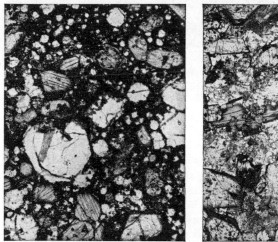

A   B

FIG. 254. Alkaline Igneous Rocks; A, Leucite basalt, phenocrysts of
leucite and pyroxene in a glassy groundmass, × 15. B, Nepheline-
syenite, composed of pyroxene, biotite and nepheline (cloudy), × 6.

somewhat unusual composition. Feldspathoids appear in silica-poor
trachytes where the silica-content is not adequate to convert all the
alkalies to feldspar. *Quartz-trachytes* are relatively rich in silica and
provide a link with rhyolites.

Trachytic lavas are commonly porphyritic and, like acid lavas,
generally have a wholly or partly glassy groundmass. Feldspar
microliths in the groundmass tend to show a strong parallel orientation which is due to the drag of the pasty magma. This flow-orienta-
tion of minute laths is so characteristic of the trachytes that it is
often called *trachytic texture* (Fig. 227).

Plutonic rocks are frequently associated with alkaline lavas in the
form of small plugs and ring-intrusions. They include a great number
of species, and show very irregular textures, extreme variability
being one of the characteristic features of the whole alkaline group.
Feldspathoids are generally absent, with the exception of nepheline,
since they are unstable in a plutonic environment. The characteristic
features are therefore the presence of alkali-feldspars in mafic rocks,
or the presence of nepheline and the occurrence of alkali-pyroxenes,
amphiboles, micas and other species of ferromagnesian minerals. An
unusually wide range of accessory minerals is also found in alkaline
rocks; many of them incorporate rare elements including radioactive
elements and, where they are gathered in local concentrations, they
provide important economic deposits.

427

Alkali-gabbros are mafic rocks containing olivine, pyroxenes, amphiboles or dark micas in association with orthoclase, sodic plagioclase and/or nepheline. They pass into *nepheline-syenites* (Fig. 254) and *syenites* by reduction in the proportion of ferromagnesian minerals. The essential minerals of *syenites* are alkali-feldspars and a pyroxene, amphibole or dark mica. They grade into granitic rocks — the *alkali-granites*, characterised by alkali-feldspars — with the appearance of quartz.

A final rock-type which may be mentioned in connection with alkaline plutonic rocks is **carbonatite**, composed essentially of calcite, $CaCO_3$, and frequently carrying rare accessory minerals, including minerals with radioactive components, similar to those found in the alkaline rocks themselves. Carbonatites are, of course, strongly contrasted with the alkaline rocks in composition, but they are closely associated with certain alkaline types in the field (see below). They generally form small intrusive bodies and may have been emplaced by volatile-rich fluids.

It is evident, from what has been said already, that many quite separate processes may lead to the production of alkaline rocks of particular kinds. We may distinguish, first of all, certain occurrences of alkaline rocks found in provinces where the parent magma is not itself very strongly alkaline, or is a normal calc-alkaline magma. Firstly, *alkali-basalts, trachybasalts and trachytes* are, as we have already seen, developed by magmatic differentiation of olivine-basalt magma. Secondly, local developments of highly alkaline plutonic or volcanic rocks sometimes result from *contamination* of magmas, and especially from the addition of *limestone*. Calcium carbonate dissociates in contact with the magma, the carbon dioxide escapes and the calcium combines with magmatic silica to produce lime-silicate minerals. The resulting *desilication* of the magma leads to the production of feldspathoids instead of feldspars. Such a mode of origin has been suggested for certain nepheline-syenites, and for the leucite-rich lavas erupted by Vesuvius — in the latter instance, the parent magma was already somewhat alkaline. Thirdly, local, and even extensive, bodies of syenitic plutonic rocks appear as a result of the granite-forming processes discussed in Chapter 10, when for some reason the supply of silica is limited; for example certain migmatites derived from basic hosts develop a syenitic character.

Localised occurrences of alkaline rocks can be ascribed to accidents of the types mentioned in the previous paragraph; but there still remain to be explained the origin of *magmatic provinces which are alkaline throughout*. At the present day, the most important alkaline province is that of the East African Rift-valleys (p. 491, Fig. 305).

Here, the dominant rocks are lavas ranging from types related to alkali-basalts to very highly feldspathoidal types; soda-rich lavas are characterised by nepheline and potassic lavas by leucite. Plutonic rocks, alkali-gabbros, syenitic types and carbonatites, occur in ring-complexes at the roots of the volcanoes. The igneous activity as a whole is clearly related to the peculiar tectonic environment of the rift-valleys, but the way in which the two phenomena are connected is still not clear.

In some alkaline ring-complexes, material from the magma appears to have migrated into the adjacent country-rocks and reacted with them by a process of *metasomatism* (Chapter 9). As a result of this introduction of material, the country-rocks themselves are enriched in alkalies and recrystallised to form alkaline rocks resembling those of the plutonic bodies themselves. This transformation gives rise to *fenites* or metasomatic alkaline rocks, named from the Fen ring-complex of the Oslo district of Norway, where concentric zones of fenites surround a core of intrusive alkaline rocks and carbonatite.

MAGMATIC PROVINCES

The arrangement of magmatic provinces in the earth and the history of igneous activity through geological time are bound up with the whole history of the crust, and will be considered again in later pages. It may be useful however to close this chapter with a brief summary of the characters of the great igneous provinces which have developed in the recent geological past and are still active at the present day. The map (Fig. 255) shows the distribution of active volcanoes and

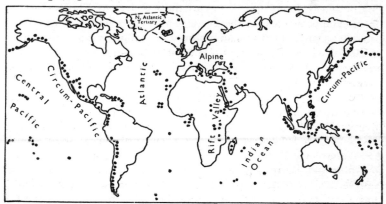

Fig. 255. Distribution of Recent Volcanic Centres and the Tertiary North Atlantic Province.

the extent of areas where igneous activity has been widespread since the early Tertiary. Ignoring minor variations, we may recognise five great divisions:

(i) In the *oceanic basins* proper, most islands and seamounts are volcanic. In the Pacific we may mention the Hawaiian, Samoan and Society Islands, Easter Island and Tahiti; in the Indian Ocean, Reunion and St. Paul, in the Atlantic, St. Helena and Tristan da Cunha. In all these groups, basalts are the dominant rocks and their associates appear to be derived from basaltic magma. The oceanic provinces display a type of vulcanicity in which sialic material plays no part. Much of the igneous activity is related to the mid-oceanic ridge systems which may mark the site of rising convection-currents in the mantle (see pp. 644–8).

(ii) In the *North Atlantic* a distinctive, now almost extinct, igneous province extends from east Greenland to Iceland, Jan Mayen, the Faeroes, western Scotland and northern Ireland. In all these areas plateau-basalts are the predominant igneous rocks and in Iceland fissure-eruptions of basalt have taken place in historic times. Volcanoes of central type were also widely developed in the Tertiary periods, and plugs and ring-intrusions of plutonic rocks were formed in their roots. Throughout the province olivine-basalts and tholeiites are associated in the lava piles, which in places reach totals of more than 5 kms. in thickness. Their minor associates include trachybasalts and trachytes on the one hand and rhyolites on the other. The plutonic intrusions of the province include gabbros and their differentiation products (e.g. at Skaergaard, p. 416) and a number of conspicuous bodies of granite or granophyre; intermediate rocks linking the acid and basic types are quite restricted. The association of acid and basic rocks in the Tertiary plutonic complexes has always provided a problem; the acid material may represent a differentiate of the basic magma, but it is also possible that the acid fraction was augmented by contributions from sialic material mobilised by the basic magma.

In the British section of the province, relics of Tertiary plateau-basalts are found in Skye, Mull and the adjacent parts of the Scottish mainland, and in Antrim. Plutonic complexes, many of which occupy the roots of eroded central volcanoes, occur in St. Kilda, Skye, Rhum, Ardnamurchan, Mull, Arran, the Mourne Mountains, the Carlingford hills and Slieve Gullion; with the exception of St. Kilda, these centres lie close to a single north-south line, and there is little doubt that they were built up along the line of a far-reaching crustal fracture (Fig. 256). Swarms of doleritic dykes run north-west and south-east across the volcanic region and are concentrated about the

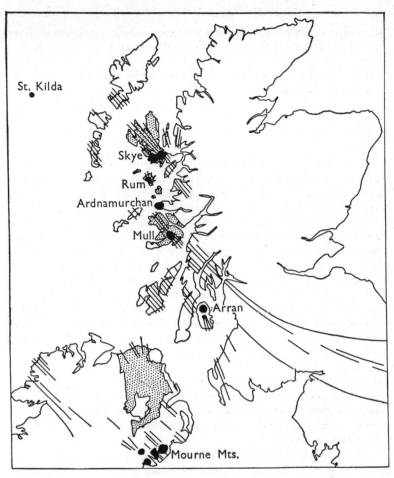

Fig. 256. Tertiary Igneous Province of the British Isles; plutonic centres, black: plateau lavas, dotted: dyke swarms, lines (after Richey, H.M. Geological Survey).

plutonic centres. The formation of the plutonic bodies was at most centres bound up with the development of ring-fractures; in at least one centre (Mull) calderas developed at the surface in association with the ring-structures. Igneous activity at each volcanic centre was highly diversified. At Ardnamurchan (Fig. 234), for example, activity began with the formation of explosive vents with which were associated some early intrusions of dolerite and a set of basaltic

431

cone-sheets. A new centre further west gave rise to a concentric series of ring-dykes, largely gabbroic in composition, and a set of cone-sheets. Both these early centres were then broken through by a third ring-complex whose ring-dykes produce at the present day a remarkable concentric topography.

(iii) A *circum-Pacific belt* which extends northward up the Cordilleran systems of America, through the Aleutian Islands and southward through Japan, the Philippines and the East Indies to New Zealand: and

(iv) A *Mediterranean-Himalayan belt* where vulcanicity is sporadically developed from the Canary Islands eastward through the Mediterranean and the Middle East and recurs again in Burma, Sumatra and Java, finally linking up with the circum-Pacific belt.

These two great belts of vulcanicity follow the *active orogenic zones* of the earth where many other signs of crustal unrest are visible, and there is no doubt that the vulcanicity is a byproduct of the orogenic processes. Many of the volcanoes are arranged in linear or arcuate series related to fractures or zones of deformation at depth.

The volcanic products and volcanic forms of the circum-Pacific and Mediterranean belts show so much variation that it is hardly possible to generalise. Basalts are widespread, but do not show the overwhelming dominance of the basalts of the oceanic and north Atlantic regions. Andesites and rhyolites are conspicuous in the Andes and the North American cordilleras, and alkaline rocks are developed in the Mediterranean. In addition to the superficial igneous products, a variety of plutonic bodies, formed well below the surface, are now being exposed where the mountain-belts are dissected by erosion. These bodies are largely granitic and belong to the Plutonic Series considered in Chapter 10.

(v) A *Rift-valley belt* following the rift-valley systems of Africa and the Middle East. In this belt alkaline rocks are, as we have already noted, very conspicuous. Recent igneous activity is more or less confined to the line of the rift-valleys and associated earth-fractures, and the distinctive alkaline cast of the igneous rocks must be in some way connected with the tectonic setting; the controlling factors, and the origin of the alkaline magmas, remain uncertain.

FURTHER READING AND REFERENCE
General

Bowen, N. L., 1956, *Evolution of the igneous rocks*, Dover Publications. A new edition of a classic embodying results of a long study of the physical chemistry of silicate melts.

Daly, R. A., 1914, *Igneous rocks and their origin*, McGraw-Hill. A classic for the geological interpretation of igneous rocks.

Mason, B., 1958, *Principles of geochemistry*, 2nd edit., Wiley, New York.

Williams, H., F. J. Turner and C. M. Gilbert, 1954, *Petrography: an introduction to the study of rocks in thin sections*, Freeman, San Francisco.

Special topics

Cotton, C. A., 1944, *Volcanoes as landscape forms*, Whitcombe and Tombes.

Williams, H., 1942, 'The geology of Crater Lake National Park, Oregon', *Carnegie Inst. Washington*, Publn. 540.

Kennedy, W. Q. and E. M. Anderson, 1938, 'Crustal layers and the origin of magmas', *Bull. Volc.*, Ser. ii, t. 3, p. 24.

MacDonald, G. A., 1949, 'Hawaiian petrographic province', *Bull. Geol. Soc. Amer.*, vol. 60, p. 1541.

Walker, G. P. L., 1960, 'Zeolite zones and dyke distribution in relation to the structure of the basalts of Eastern Iceland', *Journ. Geol.*, vol. 68, p. 515.

Wager, L. R. and W. A. Deer, 1939, 'The petrology of the Skaergaard intrusion, Kangerdlugssuaq, East Greenland', *Med. om Grönland*, vol. 105, no. 4.

Read, H. H., 1935, 'The gabbros and associated xenolithic complexes of the Haddo House district, Aberdeenshire', *Quart. Journ. Geol. Soc.*, vol. 91, p. 591.

——, M. S. Sadashivaiah and B. T. Haq, 1961, 'Differentiation in the olivine-gabbro of the Insch mass, Aberdeenshire', *Proc. Geol. Assoc.*, 72, 391.

King, B. C. and D. S. Sutherland, 1960, 'Alkaline rocks of eastern and southern Africa, Part I: distribution, ages and structures', *Sci. Prog.*, vol. 48, p. 298. 'Part II: Petrology', *ibid.*, vol. 48, p. 504.

Stewart, F. H., 1965, Tertiary igneous activity. In *The Geology of Scotland*, Oliver and Boyd.

Yoder, H. S. and C. E. Tilley, 1962, 'Origin of basalt magmas: an experimental study of natural and synthetic rock-systems', *Journ. Petrology*, vol. 3, 342–532.

8

GEOLOGICAL STRUCTURES

INTRODUCTION

IN the foregoing chapters we have dealt with the primary or original characters of rocks. We saw that when a rock is formed it acquires a certain shape and shows certain relations to the rocks associated with it. But the history of a rock does not end with its original production — the mere fact that we can examine on dry land rocks formed in the depths of the ocean reminds us that rocks are liable to assume new positions in the crust and, in doing so, to acquire new and secondary shapes and relationships. We now take up the subject of *structural geology*, the elucidation of the history of a rock as it is recorded in its geometry. This subject is a necessary preliminary to the wider matter of *tectonics*, dealt with in a later chapter, which concerns the deformation of the earth's crust viewed in connection with the movements and forces responsible, and with the other contemporary geological processes. As always in our science, the timing of events becomes of fundamental importance in tectonics and the final aim is to relate the architecture of the crust to the complete geological history of the segment concerned — here we must observe the interplay in time of sedimentation, deformation and volcanic and plutonic activity. On a more utilitarian level, the location of a large number of mineral deposits is controlled by the structure of the country-rocks. The workability of a coal-series often depends on its structural condition, and the concentration of oil into pools of a size suitable for exploitation is largely controlled by geological structures. The methods and results of structural geology are therefore of importance to both academic and economic geologists.

The methods employed are largely observational; data concerning the shape and orientation of all visible structures are collected in the field and presented in maps, sections and projections. The mass of information so collected must be analysed to determine the style of movements and the pattern of forces which were responsible for producing the observed structures. In this study experimental evidence can be of value provided that the principle of *scale-models* is observed; by this principle, all physical properties must be reduced in magnitude in accordance with the size of the model and the duration of time of

434

the experiment, the strength of the material simulating rock-masses being often reduced to that of butter or molten wax.

THE PRIMARY SURFACES AND SEQUENCES OF REFERENCE

As we have stated, structural geology is concerned with the present attitudes and forms of primary surfaces, layers and successions of layers which have been disturbed in some way. The chief of these primary surfaces is the *bedding-plane* of sedimentary rocks (p. 252), originally approximately horizontal. Other types of original surface are the tops and bottoms of lava-flows and the contacts of igneous intrusions, especially the planar margins of dykes and sills.

The recognition of true *original bedding*, however it may have been subsequently deformed, is a prime object of enquiry in structural geology. Unless bedding can be determined, there is no way of establishing the *stratigraphy* in the area under study. If bedding is recognisable, then the next requirement is to determine the *stratigraphical succession*, the order in which the beds were deposited, so that a pattern of beds becomes available against which to refer subsequent deformation. Where the rocks are fossiliferous, their relative ages may be given by the presence of zone-fossils which allow William Smith's second law, of strata identified by fossils, to be applied. Where the rocks are unfossiliferous, or where no distinctive organisms are present, other evidence must be sought. It may be possible to trace a rock-sequence, distinguished perhaps by the presence of easily recognisable key-beds, from an area where it is undisturbed and demonstrably right way up into an area where the stratigraphical order is suspect. The presence of an *unconformity*, which may be regarded as a special kind of primary surface, gives unequivocal evidence of the order of succession, since the bed originally above the unconformity cuts at an angle across the eroded edges of the older series of rocks.

Where large-scale evidence of the kinds mentioned above is not available, it becomes necessary to determine the order of succession from evidence provided by the make-up of the local rocks themselves. We have already examined the principal methods by which '*way-up*' can be found in sedimentary rocks. For our purposes, the examination of *current-bedding* (Figs. 93, 153) and *graded bedding* (Fig. 129) are the most valuable, but we may mention also certain other structures which are occasionally useful. Symmetrical *ripple-marks* (p. 254), but not current-ripples, show upward-pointing cusps separated by rounded hollows. *Rain-pits*, formed by rain falling on soft sediment, are rounded depressions, sometimes with a small raised rim, which appear on the upper surfaces of beds. *Suncracks* developed in drying mud taper downwards and may be filled with sediment from the bed next deposited. *Tracks* or *footprints* of organisms appear as depressions on the upper surfaces of beds, while *burrows* project downwards from these surfaces. Pebbles or volcanic bombs falling into soft material may produce a *pebble-dint* in the upper surface of a bed and a downward deflection of the stratification beneath. All the structures formed on the upper surfaces of beds may, of course, be represented also by casts attached to the base of the bed above. Erosion contemporaneous with deposition produces distinctive structures. *Rill-marks* and *wash-outs* are small channels cut in beds already laid down, and are generally filled by sediment continuous with the bed above. *Slumped beds* show strong internal contortions which are often planed off at the top by erosion, so that the next bed rests discordantly on the edges of the contorted structure. Contemporaneous erosion may also produce *derived fragments* of older beds which are incorporated in later beds.

We have mentioned the tops and bottoms of *lava-flows* as providing possible reference-planes. The tops of many flows are ropy, scoriaceous or reddened by subaerial weathering, and they or their casts may be identifiable. The bases of lavas chilled against the cold ground tend to be very fine-grained. From top to bottom of many flows the grain-size increases to a point below the centre and then decreases — a consequence of the rapid basal cooling. In the interior of flows, the shapes of *pillow-structures* may indicate the way-up (p. 392). *Vesicles* arising from the escape of gas are generally more abundant in the upper parts of flows. *Pipe-amygdales*, on the other hand are found preferentially near the bases of flows; they are the paths of gas-bubbles rising through the lava — if two bubbles join they do not part again, so that forked pipe-amygdales always branch downwards. Minerals in amygdales normally crystallise from solution; if therefore the bubble was only partly filled, the crystalline deposit may appear only in the lower part.

The original position of most beds and lavas is, as we have seen, roughly horizontal and their original order of succession is, as stated in William Smith's first law, from oldest at the bottom to youngest at the top. As a result of earth-movements, such a succession may be tilted, made vertical or overturned. It therefore becomes useful to have a term indicating the direction in which a series of beds becomes stratigraphically younger, and the verb *to young* was introduced by Bailey to serve this need. An equivalent term introduced by Shrock is *to face*, a bed being said to face towards its younger side. Horizontal beds may obviously young either vertically upwards or

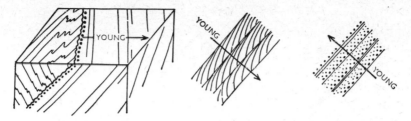

FIG. 257. Criteria for the determination of order of succession ('way-up') in disturbed sedimentary series.

vertically downwards, and beds in other attitudes in one of two possible directions — which is correct, must be determined by use of the criteria already described.

All the primary surfaces, and the geometrical relations between them, may be disturbed and modified during a tectonic episode — but this episode may not complete the tectonic development. The same rocks, in their disturbed state, may become involved in later phases of deformation, with the result that early folds are faulted or refolded on a new pattern. The later patterns can only be determined by treating the results of the first deformation as primary for the second. In Fig. 257, are presented examples of primary reference planes subjected to a variety of secondary disturbances, with illustrations of some of the 'way-up' criteria used in their interpretation.

DIP AND STRIKE

The two fundamental geometrical observations about any plane that the structural geologist has to make are the *dip* or inclination of the plane, and the *strike*, its horizontal direction (Fig. 258). These two measurements together define the attitude of the plane in space, and structural mapping is largely an affair of recording dips and strikes.

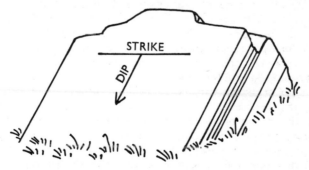

FIG. 258. Dip and Strike.

437

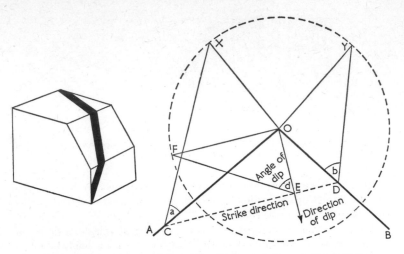

Fig. 259. Apparent and True Dip. (*Left*), variation of apparent dip with position of surface of exposure. (*Right*), construction for obtaining the true dip from two directions of apparent dip.

Where used without qualification, the terms refer to bedding-planes.

Dip is defined as the angle and direction of the maximum inclination, measured from the horizontal, of the bedding or other geological plane. *Strike* is the bearing of a horizontal line drawn on the plane; it is at right angles to the dip and can loosely be described as the general run of the beds on level ground — our word strike is cognate with the German *strecken*, to stretch, reach or extend.

It is important to realise that the dip of a plane is its *maximum* inclination. An *apparent dip* is given by some direction other than the steepest slope, and is often revealed in cliffs or quarry-walls that are oblique to the true dip direction (Fig. 259). Where three-dimensional exposures are available, the true dip can be obtained from measurements of apparent dip by a simple geometrical construction shown in Fig. 259. Two faces, OA and OB, of a quarry cut through the bed whose dip is to be found. OX is drawn perpendicular to OA and OY, of equal length to OX, perpendicular to OB. The apparent dip a observed on the wall OA is represented as the angle OCX and the apparent dip b on OB as the angle ODY. The strike is then given by the line CD and the true dip direction by the line OE perpendicular to it. The angle of true dip, d, is obtained by drawing $OF = OX$ perpendicular to OE and measuring the angle OEF. Since the bearings of the quarry walls can be measured, the direction of dip can be got by measuring either the angle AOE or BOE. If a quarry-wall or cliff runs in the strike-direction, the beds emerging on it will necessarily appear horizontal.

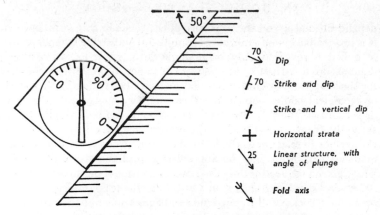

FIG. 260. Use of the Clinometer. Structural symbols.

The *directions of dip and strike* are determined in the field by compass and are best recorded in terms of a 360° bearing from true north (allowance for the magnetic declination must of course be made). The *angle of dip* is measured by *clinometers* of which there are various types (Fig. 260).

Various symbols are employed to represent the attitude of bedding-planes on geological maps (Fig. 260). A short arrow may be drawn in the true dip-direction with the amount of dip entered in figures alongside, or a short line may be drawn in the strike-direction with a tick on the dip-side and the amount of dip entered in figures. The use of a strike-symbol helps to bring out the run of the beds and is therefore often preferable to the use of dip-arrows. Whatever symbol is chosen, it should be plotted accurately on the field-map, or at least on a clean-copy of this map, by means of a protractor; the actual bearings and dips obtained should be recorded and, as with all geological symbols, a key should be provided.

GEOLOGICAL STRUCTURE IN RELATION TO TOPOGRAPHY: THE GEOLOGICAL MAP

The structure of the rocks making up the crust is naturally three-dimensional — the rocks extend in depth into the crust, while man's observations of them are as a rule confined to the parts revealed at the surface. It is therefore important for the geologist to be able to deduce from the surface-evidence the solid geometry of the structures he examines. He is able to do this very largely because the land-surface is dissected by erosion and so provides sections in the vertical as well as in the horizontal dimensions. All structural observations

P   439

depend ultimately on the exposure of the rocks in three dimensions; it is impossible even to measure a simple dip and strike when the edge of a bed is revealed only on a single flat surface, as can easily be demonstrated with the aid of sheets of paper. Geometrical evidence for the shape and orientation of sedimentary beds and all other kinds of geological bodies comes therefore from two sources: firstly, from direct measurement of dips, strikes and so on made in the field; and secondly, from observations of the pattern made by beds emerging at the surface in relation to the form of the topography. This large-scale evidence can often only be appreciated from the study of a map, which gives a reduced and stylised two-dimensional picture of the land.

The *geological map* shows, in addition to the topography, the areas over which rocks of different kinds and ages appear at the surface. In practice, the bedrock is never perfectly exposed, but appears through the superficial cover of vegetation, soil and the like in detached *outcrops* in which it is said to *crop out* (not to outcrop). For the purposes of understanding geological structures, however, we can treat beds and formations as if their outcrops were continuous and may proceed to consider the patterns of outcrops which result from various common combinations of geological structure and topographical form.

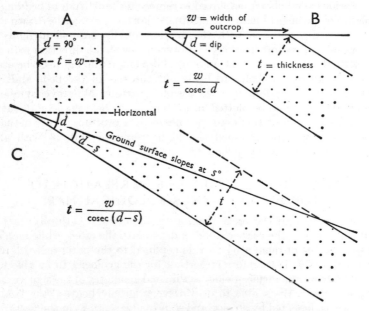

FIG. 261. Width of outcrop in relation to dip and to slope of ground. A, vertical dip; B, inclined dip; C, inclined dip and sloping ground.

We may deal first with the *width of outcrop* of a bed, which in certain circumstances provides a clue to the true thickness of that bed (Fig. 261). A horizontal bed exposed on a horizontal surface would have an outcrop equal to the original area of the bed. A vertical bed cropping out on a horizontal surface has a width equal to its real thickness. An inclined bed has an outcrop-width greater than its thickness and given by the equation:

width of outcrop = thickness × *cosec* of angle of dip

The true thickness can be obtained by the geometrical construction shown in Fig. 261. On sloping ground, the width of outcrop is affected by the direction of slope in relation to the dip, as shown in the figure.

We may next consider the relations between the *shapes of outcrops,*

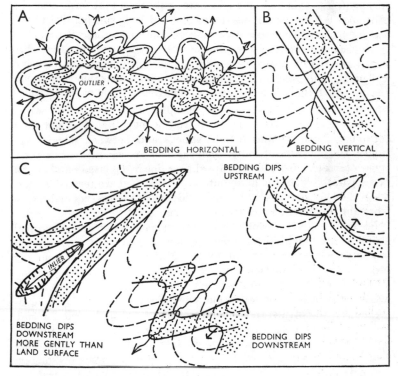

FIG. 262. Shape of outcrop controlled by dip and topography. A, horizontal beds; B, vertical beds; C, inclined beds; topographic contours shown by broken lines.

the dip and the topography, limiting ourselves at this stage to beds which are parallel-sided and either horizontal, vertical or *homoclinal*, which is to say, tilted at a constant angle; the outcrops of folded beds are dealt with later. Where the beds are flat and the topography is undulating, the geological boundaries are parallel to the contours and each bed crops out over irregular areas — a high bed may form cappings on hills, a low bed appears in valley-bottoms and so on (Fig. 262). Where the beds are vertical, geological boundaries run in straight lines across hills and valleys, showing no deflections related to the topography. When an inclined bed crossing a valley dips upstream, its outcrop forms a V pointing upstream; the steeper the dip the less is the deflection of the outcrop and the more obtuse the angle of the V. A bed dipping downstream at an angle greater than the slope of the valley-floor presents a V downstream; but if the dip is less than the valley-gradient, then the outcrop forms a narrow V closing up the valley at an angle more acute than that formed by the contours. Where the boundaries of inclined beds run parallel to the contours, their direction is, by definition, the strike-direction.

The curving of outcrops as they cross over high ground can readily be interpreted by regarding a ridge as, for this purpose, an inverted valley. Beds crossing a ridge thus form a V in a direction opposite to that in which the V faces across a valley. Recognition of the relations between outcrop-form, dip and topography allows one to reconstruct the local geological structure even from a map that does not show contours. Thus, streams denote valleys and between streams are ridges; the outcrops of gently-inclined beds are irregular or sinuous, those of steeply-inclined beds are almost linear. Isolated patches of a bed separated from the main outcrop of that bed are termed *outliers* when they are surrounded by rocks older than themselves and *inliers* when the surrounding rocks are the younger.

So far, we have assumed that the surface-relief and geological structure are independent of one another. But in many areas erosion is controlled to some extent by the geological structure, and the form of the land-surface thus provides a clue to the underlying structure. *Differential erosion* wears down soft beds into valleys and leaves hard beds as ridges, while the drainage-pattern may be controlled by the strike and dip directions or by fault and fracture systems (Chapter 4). In particular, many parallel ridges represent *strike-features* marking the exposed edges of tilted hard beds. Such ridges show a gentle *dip-slope*, roughly parallel with the bedding on one side and a steep *escarpment* on the other, the two features together forming a *cuesta* (Fig. 109).

The close relation between structure and topography extends from the great features of hill and valley to the fine details governing the shapes of individual outcrops. *Aerial photographs* (Fig. 264), on which the whole pattern of the landscape is of course accurately recorded, are, for this reason, valuable sources of evidence concerning geological structure. In recent years there has grown up a new subject of *photogeology*, dealing with the geological interpretation of aerial photographs. These studies are proving of great value in the reconnaissance of little-known terrains where the progress of mapping can be guided and much time saved by preliminary examination of aerial photographs. Geological structures giving rise to very distinctive topographical forms, such as ring-intrusions (p. 397), have in some areas been located on photographs before they were visited by geologists on the ground.

STRATUM-CONTOURS

The dip of a bed over a considerable area can be calculated in regions of moderate topographical relief by the construction of *stratum-contours* on the geological map. The strike of a bed is, by definition, the bearing of a horizontal line in the plane of the bed. If therefore a geological boundary crosses the same contour-line on opposite sides of a valley or ridge, a line joining the two points is horizontal and a strike line. Such a line drawn at a known elevation above or below a given datum is a stratum-contour for the particular geological horizon. A series of stratum-contours can be constructed where the same geological boundary intersects several topographical contours. In a homoclinal set of beds, all the stratum-contours will be parallel; the dip-direction is perpendicular to them and the amount of dip can be found by construction, or from the formula:

$$Cot \text{ angle of dip} = \frac{HE}{VI}$$

where VI is the vertical interval between adjacent stratum-contours and HE the horizontal equivalent, or distance measured on the map between adjacent stratum-contours. The steeper the dip, the smaller is the horizontal equivalent and the more crowded the stratum-contours.

Stratum-contours drawn on homoclinal beds are straight lines, and are all parallel to one another. Stratum-contours of folded beds are curved, and cannot be accurately constructed unless a geological boundary intersects the same topographical contour a number of times. *Stratum-contour maps* provide convenient and easily-comprehended pictures of the form of any kind of geological surface, and

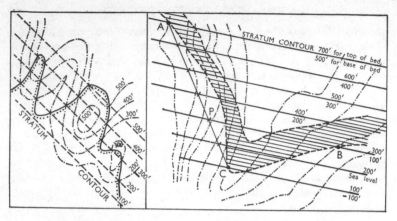

FIG. 263. Stratum-contours. (*Left*), stratum-contours drawn on a homoclinal bed. (*Right*), use of stratum-contours to determine the outcrop of a bed.

may be of special value in coal-fields or oil-fields where attention is centred on a particular productive bed, and where data from bore-holes and mines are available. Before leaving the subject of stratum-contours we may examine some further points about their construction.

In Fig. 263, the upper surface of a bed in a homoclinal series crops out at *A*, *B* and *C*, situated on the 700 feet, 300 feet and 100 feet topographical contours. From *C* to *A*, the bed rises 600 feet, and by dividing the line *AC* into six equal parts we can obtain points on the stratum-contours at 100 foot intervals. Point *P* on *AC* is at 300 feet, and the line *PB* therefore represents the stratum-contour at 300 feet O.D. Since the beds are homoclinal, other stratum-contours can be drawn parallel to *PB* through the points of division on *AC*, and can be produced in both directions to give a picture of the extension of the bedding-plane. The angle of dip can be determined by the formula already given, or from measurements on the figure. From the information now available, the outcrop of the geological horizon can be extended by joining the points of intersection of equal topographical and stratum-contours. If the thickness of the bed is known, the outcrop of its lower surface can be plotted by adjusting the values of the stratum-contours and joining up their intersections with the appropriate topographical contours — in the example given, the thickness is taken as 200 feet. Conversely, where the outcrops of both sides of the bed have been mapped, its thickness can be found by stratum-contouring both surfaces and comparing the values at a given point.

444

THE MAIN STRUCTURAL TYPES

Division of structural types. When the rocks of the earth's crust are subjected to appropriate pressures they will, like other materials, either bend or break. *Folds* or *fractures* result, the type of the structure depending on the physical properties of the rocks and on the environment in which deformation takes place. In this chapter, we are concerned almost wholly with the results of crustal deformation as they can be established by direct observation and geometrical study. Our aim is to establish the *structural pattern* — the arrangement in space and mutual relations of the systems of folds, fractures and so on exhibited by the rocks of a given area — and the *structural style*, as shown for example by the dominance of particular kinds of structures related to particular conditions of deformation. Only when information along these lines is assembled does it become useful to speculate on the regional distribution of the crustal stresses responsible for the structures.

For this geometrical approach, it is convenient to consider folding and fracturing as separate topics, although by doing so we make a somewhat artificial division in a series of closely related phenomena. In nature, fracturing of rocks is often accompanied by preliminary bending, while folding is sometimes accomplished largely by small displacements along large numbers of fractures. Nevertheless, since the geometrical results are fairly distinct, we may make a temporary list of structural types as follows:

(i) **Folds** are structures in which the primary surfaces of reference are bent or distorted without loss of essential continuity.

(ii) **Cleavages** are sets of closely spaced parting-planes; their development is essential to the formation of certain types of folds.

(iii) **Linear structures** — that is, structures in which one dimension is very much greater than the other two — may be associated with the development of folds, cleavages and fractures; they are grouped together purely for convenience of description.

(iv) **Slides, lags** and **thrusts** are fractures formed in close connection with folding, often by a continuation of folding movements.

(v) **Faults** are fractures by which the primary surfaces are broken and displaced, so that they lose their continuity. Thrusts are merely special kinds of faults classified separately on account of their connection with folding.

(vi) **Joints** are fractures by which the primary surfaces are broken but not displaced.

Controls of rock-deformation. Some idea of the factors controlling the development of different structural types can be gained from a consideration of the mechanical properties of rocks. It is necessary, in this connection, to make sure that certain ordinary words much in use are employed in their technical sense. Two such words are stress and strain. *Stress* is the force acting on a body, its magnitude being that exerted on a unit area of a given plane within the body. *Strain* is the change of shape or of volume resulting from the application of the stress.

When the stress acting on a body is progressively increased, the body at first suffers strain either by change of volume or shape, but when the stress is removed, the strain becomes neutralised and the body returns to its original size and shape. It is then said to be *elastic* and obeys Hooke's Law that strain is proportional to stress. With the increase of stress, the strain becomes *permanent* and the body does not return to its original form on the removal of the stress. The stress at which the body ceases to be elastic is its *elastic limit*. Above the elastic limit, the body yields to stress by *plastic flow* and strain is no longer proportional to stress. Finally, at a certain stress, which gives the *ultimate strength* of the body, fracture takes place. The properties which control the reactions of rocks are therefore the values of the elastic limit and the ultimate strength. Rocks whose elastic limit and ultimate strength are not very different are *brittle* and tend to yield by fracture. Rocks which have a wider interval between the two values are *ductile* and yield more readily by plastic flow.

Plastic flow in rocks takes place in several different ways. Rocks may be deformed by the movement past one another of their constituent grains, lubricated in some instances by water or other fluids. Flow may take place by rotation of the mineral grains, or by translation on twin-planes and glide-planes within these grains; or by continuous solution and recrystallisation of the constituents. Finally, movement on a large number of closely-spaced shear-planes may produce the effect of continuous flow, since only a minute displacement takes place on each individual shear-plane. It will be seen that the rocks which most easily undergo plastic flow are likely to be incompletely consolidated sediments holding much water (e.g., clays, and sheets of sediment slumping on the sea-floor), rocks whose minerals are readily recrystallised at low temperatures (e.g. evaporates such as rock-salt and gypsum) and rocks undergoing metamorphism.

The reaction to a given stress depends on the conditions under which it is applied. Many rocks which are brittle at low temperatures and pressures become more ductile at high temperatures and pressures, and may therefore yield by plastic flow when deeply buried. Furthermore, the rate at which the stress is applied, and its duration, are of importance; rocks may yield plastically to slow pressures whereas they yield by fracture to sudden stresses.

With all these variables to consider, it is not surprising that a single phase of deformation, acting on a mixed series of rocks, may give rise to structures formed both by flow and by fracture. Within a given series at a given time, we can draw an antithesis between *competent* rocks and *incompetent* rocks; however these terms were first defined, we may simply say that competent rocks are, in the prevailing circumstances, strong, and incompetent rocks are weak. The style of deformation is to a large extent determined by the behaviour of the competent rocks, to which the incompetent rocks more passively accommodate themselves.

FOLDS

Geometry of folds. That rocks can be folded is a matter of observation — visible crumpling and buckling of primary layers is seen in many outcrops. Folding on a scale too large to be recognised in single outcrops is demonstrated by the curvature of strike-direction (Fig. 264) or stratum-contours, by the association of beds dipping in opposite directions or by the orderly repetition of the same beds along a line of traverse.

We can conveniently begin by examining the geometry of folds as they would appear if the surface of a single bedding-plane were stripped bare, leaving till later the consideration of families of folds and the details of the outcrop-patterns made by folded rocks.

Three geometrical varieties of folds can be distinguished, *anticlines*, *synclines* and *monoclines* (Fig. 265). An **anticline** is, in its simplest form, an arch in which the two sides or *limbs* dip outwards away from one another. Put in another way, the anticline has a *core* or central part which is older than the *envelope* wrapped round the core. A **syncline** is a fold in which the limbs dip towards one another, or in which the core is younger than the envelope. A **monocline** is a simple step-like flexure in which more or less horizontal beds locally assume a dip in one direction and then flatten out again. These three structures are illustrated in Fig. 265 both in *plan*, as they would appear on level ground and in *cross-section*, as they would appear on a vertical plane perpendicular to their trend.

The elements making up a fold are illustrated in Fig. 266. In a single bed, the two sides or *limbs* meet at the *fold-axis* or *hinge-line* which is the line of maximum curvature. The *axial plane* is the locus of the fold-axes of successive layers, that is, it is the plane at which

FIG. 264. Aerial photograph of folded beds, Bahktiari Mountains, Iran. Anticline on the left, tight isoclinal syncline in centre. (Aerofilms).

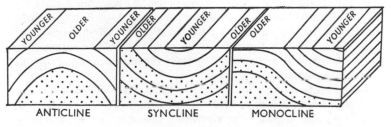

FIG. 265. Anticline, syncline and monocline.

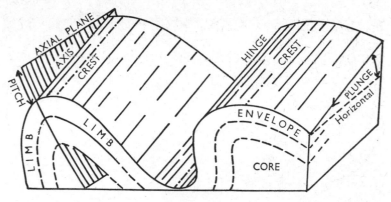

FIG. 266. Elements of a fold.

the two limbs meet. The *crest* of an anticline is the highest point of the fold with reference to any particular bed; it is parallel to, but does not necessarily coincide with, the fold-axis. Similarly the *trough* of a syncline is the bottom of the fold with reference to a given bed.

The orientation of a fold in space is given by the orientation of its axial plane, defined by the strike and dip of this plane, and of its axis. The fold-axis may be horizontal, like the top of a railway tunnel, or it may be inclined, in which case the axis and the fold are said to *plunge* or to *pitch*. The *plunge* is measured in degrees from the horizontal in a vertical plane (Fig. 266), while the *pitch* is given by the angle between the fold-axis and the strike of the axial plane, measured in the axial plane. The *direction of plunge* is given as a bearing on a 360° scale and is often represented on maps by some form of long arrow pointing down the plunge (Fig. 260). The main elements of a fold — the two limbs, axial plane and axis — can be represented in their true geometrical relations on a *stereographic projection* (Fig. 267, for details of projections see Chapter 3, p. 66). As used in structural geology, the projection is taken to represent the *lower* hemisphere of an imaginary sphere enclosing the structures. Since geometrical relationships are preserved, the great circles representing the limbs and axial plane of any fold intersect in a single point which is the fold-axis (Fig. 267); it is therefore possible by the use of a stereographic net to determine the axis of a fold where this cannot be measured directly in the field, by plotting a large number of measurements of strike and dip on the fold-limbs.

The *profile* of a fold is its form as seen in a plane perpendicular to the axis — in a fold with a horizontal axis, the profile corresponds to a vertical cross-section. The shape of the fold in profile depends on

449

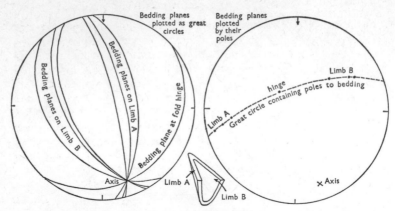

FIG. 267. Stereographic projection of fold limbs intersecting in the
direction of the fold axis.

the attitude of the axial plane, the angle between the limbs and the
degree of curvature of the limbs (Fig. 268). The fold is *upright* and
symmetrical when the axial plane is vertical and the two limbs dip
at similar angles. Where one limb dips more steeply than the other,
the axial plane is inclined and the fold is *asymmetrical*. With increasing asymmetry, the *middle limb* connecting an anticline with its
adjacent syncline becomes inverted and the fold is said to be
overturned. Where the axial plane is roughly horizontal, the fold is
said to be *recumbent*. According to the degree of compression, a fold
may be *open*, with a wide angle between the limbs, *tight*, or so compressed that the limbs are approximately parallel, when the fold is
said to be *isoclinal*. A further variation in profile is produced by

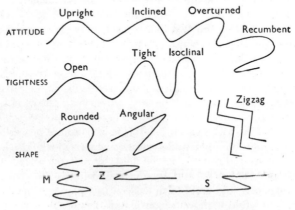

FIG. 268. Shapes of folds in profile.

450

variations in the relative lengths of the fold-limbs. Where the two limbs are approximately equal in length, a connected sequence of folds appears symmetrical and can be conventionally represented by the letters M or W. Where the middle limb joining a syncline-anticline pair is much shorter than that linking adjacent pairs, the series of folds is asymmetrical and can be represented by the letters S or Z, according to the form of the profile when viewed looking down the plunge. Finally, the profiles of folds may be *rounded*, where the limbs are continuously curved, *angular* where the hinges are sharply curved, *chevron* where the limbs are straight and the folds open, and *zigzag* when the fold is straight-limbed and tight (Fig. 268).

So far, we have considered folds simply in terms of their shape; but to complete our knowledge of any fold we must consider also the *order of succession* of the beds within it. In an upright or slightly asymmetrical anticline folding a normal sedimentary sequence, the order of succession is self-evident. The fold may be said to *face* in the direction in which progressively younger beds are encountered at the hinge, and an upright anticline therefore faces upwards. A recumbent anticline, however, faces laterally and a recumbent anticline in which the hinge region sags or *droops* faces downwards (Fig. 269). Under these circumstances, the simple definition of an anticline as a fold in which the limbs dip outward away from the hinge fails entirely. The alternative definition — that an anticline is a fold in which the core is older than the envelope — still holds, and we can therefore continue to distinguish anticlines from synclines so long as we can establish the order of succession. When the order of succession is unknown, it is necessary to refer to folds by more non-committal terms, and for this purpose the words *antiform* and *synform* are used. An antiform is simply a fold which *closes* upwards — that is, the

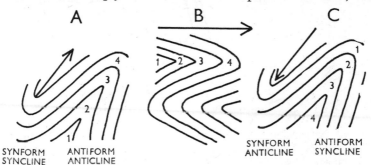

FIG. 269. The direction in which folds face. A, facing upwards; B, facing to the right; C, facing downwards. Order of succession of beds is shown by numbers.

limbs meet upwards — and a synform is a fold which closes downwards. If an antiform can be proved by 'way-up' evidence to face
upwards, then it is a true anticline, but if it faces downwards then it
must be regarded as a syncline (Fig. 269).

The two-dimensional picture of a fold given by its profile has to be
completed by considering the shape of the structure in the longitudinal direction. Where the axes of a series of folds plunge at a
constant angle, the folds are said to be *homoaxial* and the folding is of
cylindrical type (see below). Where the axis of any given fold is
undulating, the fold as a whole becomes canoe-shaped. The high
points on the axes of such folds are termed *culminations*, the low
points are *depressions*. Where the axes are strongly undulating, the
folds become *periclines* showing radial dips inwards or outwards;
domes are upfolds which are almost as broad as they are long, and
basins are downfolds of similar proportions (Fig. 270).

Folding of cylindrical type gives rise to homoaxial folds which show
remarkable continuity in the axial direction. Geometrically, their
shape can be produced by a single straight line moving parallel to
itself, the straight line being of course in the axial direction.
Cylindrical folds often maintain the same profile for distances of
many miles along the axis and it is therefore possible to make a close
approximation to the structure at depth by projecting evidence seen
at the surface downwards parallel to the plunge. This technique is
used in the construction of cross-sections and profiles showing the
structures deep in the heart of a mountain-chain such as the Alps. In
nature, fold-axes are seldom perfectly straight and the folds are

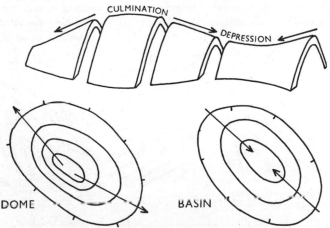

FIG. 270. Culmination and depression, dome and basin.

therefore not strictly cylindrical; the further they depart from the cylindrical form the more rapidly does their profile vary and the more difficult does it become to predict their continuation in depth.

Folds cropping out at the surface: folds on maps. The land-surface commonly provides an oblique cross-section of the underlying fold-structures, and the form of these structures can often be deduced from the shapes of the outcrops and their relation to topography. Where the folding is not too tight, its effects are revealed by the way in which the beds curve, zigzag or change direction irrespective of the topography. The common strike directions are usually parallel to the strike of the fold-limbs and rapid changes of strike are seen at the fold-hinges. Individual beds may be repeated in orderly sequence on the limbs of successive folds; and opposed dips, or opposed 'youngings' recorded by way-up criteria, may be seen on alternate limbs. Thus, a traverse from north to south across the dome of the Weald in southern England yields a sequence of Chalk of the North Downs, Gault Clay, Lower Greensand and Wealden Clay, all dipping north-ward on the north limb, followed by Hastings Sands in the centre of the structure and then by Wealden, Lower Greensand, Gault Clay and Chalk of the South Downs all dipping south. Each horizon on the north limb can be traced continuously westward till it swings rapidly round the hinge of the fold and turns back with opposite dip on to the southern limb (Fig. 271).

The outcrops of folded strata respond to variations in topography

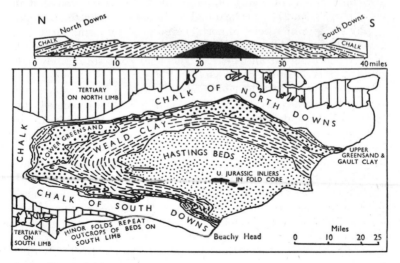

Fig. 271. Map and Section of the Weald of south-east England.

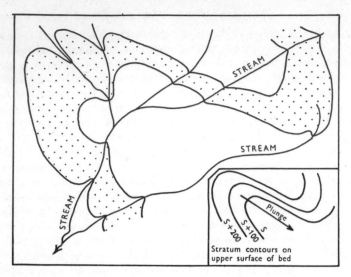

Stratum contours on
upper surface of bed

FIG. 272. Effect of topography on the outcrop of an inclined anticline
and syncline with south-easterly plunge.

according to the local values of the strike and dip. Thus, beds on
opposite limbs of an open syncline form V's pointing towards each
other as they cross valleys, while anticlines form outwardly-directed
V's (Fig. 272). In asymmetrical folds, outcrops are narrow on the
steep limbs, broad on gently-dipping limbs, and often broadest of all
at the hinge (Fig. 271). Vertical fold-limbs are not deflected by topography and are of special importance because they run parallel to
the trend of the fold-axis. *Fold-inliers* or *fold-outliers* appear where
the beds forming an anticlinal or synclinal core are entirely surrounded by rocks of the envelope (Fig. 271).

Stratum-contours can be constructed for folded beds according to
the method already given, provided certain pitfalls are avoided. It is
necessary first to determine the general run of the fold-limbs and to
draw the contours in accordance with this information: alternative
directions are presented when the same horizon crops out at the same
height on both limbs of a fold, and lines drawn in these directions are
obviously not stratum-contours. Where the fold-axis is horizontal,
stratum-contours on opposite limbs are parallel. If the fold plunges,
the stratum-contours converge towards the hinge, closing in the
direction of plunge if the fold is an anticline and in the opposite
direction if the fold is a syncline. The angle of plunge can be estimated by calculating the dip at the hinge according to the formula
already given (p. 443).

454

We have noted that the land-surface normally provides an oblique cross-section of the fold-structures. Where homoaxial structures of gentle plunge crop out, a rough and ready idea of their form in profile may be obtained by looking at the map obliquely along the projected direction of the fold-axis, so that foreshortening counteracts the distortion due to the obliquity of the section; this method of 'looking down the plunge' may reveal the general pattern of structures which can then be checked by accurately constructed cross-sections.

Cross-sections of fold-structures. The production of *vertical cross-sections*, accurately drawn from data supplied by geological and topographical maps and field-measurements, provides a useful means of illustrating the shapes of folds and other geological structures. *Profiles* projected on to a plane perpendicular to the fold-axis, and *block diagrams* give even better pictures, but are more tedious to construct.

The line of a cross-section is usually drawn as nearly as possible at right angles to the axial direction, or to the average strike. Where practicable, the vertical and horizontal scales should be the same, since exaggeration of the vertical scale distorts the picture of the structure. The *construction of the cross-section* is carried out in the following manner:

Mark off on a strip of paper, laid along the line of section on the map, the points where the line crosses or touches a topographical contour or a known altitude; at the same time, the points at which the line crosses a geological boundary should be marked. Transfer the measurements to the base-line of the section, noting the altitude of each topographical point marked. For every point thus plotted, draw a vertical line and measure up it the appropriate height to scale. The points so obtained can then be joined by a smooth curve representing the land-surface, care being taken that wherever the line of section crosses a stream the profile shows a valley-bottom.

The points where geological boundaries cross the line of section are then transferred to the topographical profile. These boundaries can be projected downwards, provided one of three sets of data is known.

(i) *If the dips are known*, they are marked off on the profile by lines drawn at the angle of dip in the plane of section. Where the dips are not constant, projection of the boundaries can be continued by constructing rays perpendicular to each line of dip and extending the boundaries in smooth curves drawn to cut all the rays at right angles (Fig. 273A). If the vertical scale is exaggerated, the angles of dip must be increased according to the formula $tan\ E = r\ tan\ D$, where D is the true dip, r the ratio of vertical and horizontal scales and E the exaggerated dip. The section must then be sketched in by eye as the construction given above works only when r is unity.

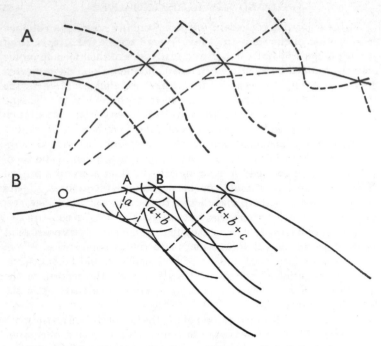

FIG. 273. Plotting a cross-section. A, where the dips of the beds are known; B, where the thicknesses of the beds are known.

(ii) If *stratum-contours* for different horizons have been drawn, their points of intersection with the line of cross-section can be plotted as for the topographical contours and the boundaries drawn in accordingly. This method is not affected by exaggeration of the vertical scale, and can be used where the plane of section is not parallel to the true dip.

(iii) Lastly, if the *thicknesses of the beds* are known and are constant, the geological boundaries can be drawn on a true-scale section by the method illustrated in Fig. 273B. OA, AB and BC are the outcrops of beds whose thicknesses are a, b and c respectively. With A as centre, an arc of radius a is drawn; with B as centre, arcs of radii b and $a + b$ are drawn, from C arcs of radii c, $b + c$ and $a + b + c$ and so on. The boundaries can then be drawn as smooth curves tangential to the appropriate arcs.

When the beds cut by the plane of section itself have been dealt with, attention must be turned to the outcrops on either side, since beds cropping out close at hand may continue across the line of section below ground-level. Thus, the core of an anticline plunging

456

towards the plane of section and cropping out some distance away can be projected down the plunge and entered in its appropriate position. It is obvious that the further the structures are produced below the surface the more speculative they become, unless they can be controlled by evidence from mines, boreholes or geophysical surveys.

Mechanism of folding. Folds showing the forms described in the previous sections are produced in the crust by a number of different mechanisms. In *true folding*, the beds are actually bent and slip takes place on the bedding-planes, in a way that can be illustrated by bending a pack of cards (Fig. 274). In both anticlines and synclines, the beds nearer the core are squeezed and tend to move outwards from it; the higher beds move upwards towards the anticlinal crests and away from the synclinal cores as shown in the figure. The bending of thick beds causes compression, which may be expressed by small-scale puckering, on the inner side of the curve, and stretching, which may give rise to tension cracks on the outer side. The differential movement between beds on the limb of a large fold may cause a rucking-up of thin incompetent layers sandwiched between more competent beds. Small asymmetrical S or Z-shaped folds produced in this way are termed *drag-folds*; their shape in profile reflects the direction of the movements which formed them (later, p. 468).

Secondly, a set of beds may be folded by means of an infinite number of small displacements on parallel shear-planes to give *shear folds* (Fig. 275). The shear-planes or *cleavage-planes* cut through the

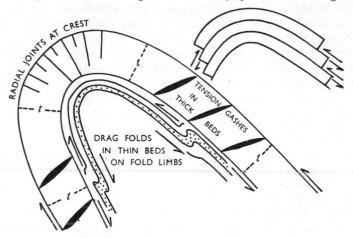

FIG. 274. True Folds, Drag Folds, Tension Cracks. The thicknesses of the beds remain constant perpendicular to the bedding.

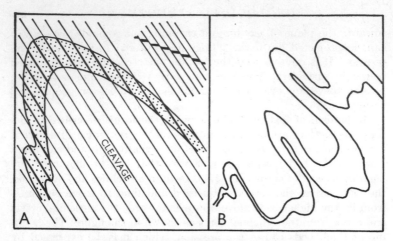

FIG. 275. A, Shear Folds; B, Flow Folds.

beds at an angle; movement takes place on these planes and not on the bedding, which remains passive during shear-folding. The production and significance of cleavage are dealt with in a later page. The third mechanism of rock-folding which may be mentioned is *flow-folding* produced by the contortion of incompetent beds between more competent ones, or by the plastic flow of mobile rock-materials (Fig. 275). It is illustrated by the folds of many salt bodies, of slumped unconsolidated sediments, and of migmatitic and metamorphic rocks in the deep crustal zones. Again, the folded surface is passive.

The *style of folding* in a given series of rocks depends partly on the environmental conditions, and partly on the make-up of the rock-series. Strong *competent beds*, such as thick-bedded sandstones, grits, limestones or lavas, resist stresses and usually control the structural style. A series of competent beds tends to bend into large, rounded or sweeping curves. The beds are not readily distorted, and therefore retain their original thicknesses, so that successive bedding-planes remain parallel to one another. Structures of this type are referred to as *parallel folds*; the term 'concentric folds' is sometimes applied to them, but is not necessarily geometrically correct. In parallel folds, the curvature of the strata decreases away from the fold-cores and the folds themselves die out upwards and downwards in consequence (Fig. 276). The folding of thick competent sequences is often accompanied by thrusting and fracturing.

Incompetent beds composed of soft rocks, or of thinly-bedded series containing such rocks as shales or marls with thin limestones or sandstones, are usually crumpled into a mass of small folds. They

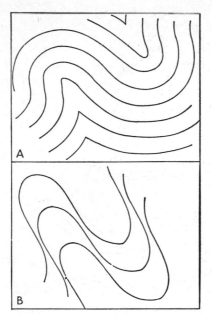

FIG. 276. A, Parallel Folds; B, Similar Folds.

yield, as a rule, by flow-folding or by shear-folding, and may be
strongly distorted, so that individual beds show rapid changes in
thickness. Where an incompetent series is sandwiched between more
competent beds, it accommodates itself passively to the folding of
these beds. The incompetent series then tends to be compressed and
thinned on the flanks of the folds where pressures are greatest, and
forced into thick masses in the relatively low-pressure hinge-regions.
In consequence, the curvature of the successive competent beds
remains more or less constant; the folds tend to persist upwards and
downwards, and are said to be *similar* (Fig. 276). Shear-folding, due
to movement along cleavage-planes produces the effect of thinning
on the limbs and thickening in the hinges without any lateral flowage
of material; in shear-folding, the thickness of a bed remains constant
when measured in the plane of the cleavage, but varies when measured
perpendicular to the bedding (Fig. 275).

Extreme differences in the competence of different members of a
succession lead to the production of *disharmonic structures* in which
individual beds react independently to stress, so that the structure
has no continuity in depth (Fig. 277). In some circumstances a strong
bed may become separated into pieces still outlining the pattern of

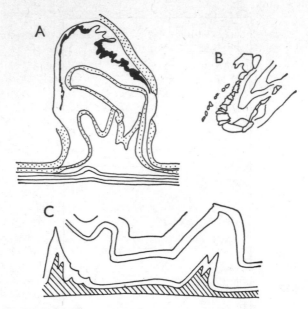

FIG. 277. A, Disharmonic fold, produced experimentally; B, disjunctive fold; C, Jura-type folding, disharmonic structure, with decollement at a salt horizon (lined), in the Jura Mountains.

the fold, while the weak rocks flow round them (*disjunctive folding*, compare boudinage, p. 464); or a strong bed may yield by thrusting while the weak beds are folded. *Decollement*, or ungluing, takes place where one portion of a succession parts company with that below and folds independently. In the Jura Mountains, decollement takes place at a slippery evaporate-bearing horizon lying near the base of a sequence of competent rocks (Fig. 277). *Diapiric or piercement-folds* are produced where highly mobile material such as evaporates breaks through overlying beds and rises as intrusive bodies. *Salt plugs* and *salt domes* of this type are formed where the weight of overlying rocks is great enough to force the salt up into its cover at points of special weakness (Fig. 165).

MINOR STRUCTURES ASSOCIATED WITH FOLDS

Cleavage. The development of certain kinds of small-scale structures is so closely bound up with folding that it seems logical to describe these structures along with the folds. Having done so, we can then proceed to a more general consideration of the structural patterns produced by folding.

The first of the small-scale structures is *cleavage* already referred to

460

in connection with shear-folding. Many rocks now possess a secondary direction of easy splitting, developed by mechanical or chemical reconstruction under the influence of pressure and movement in the crust. This rock-cleavage is of several different types formed under different conditions.

We can distinguish three types of cleavage, *flow-cleavage*, *fracture-cleavage* and *strain-slip cleavage*. *Flow-cleavage*, or *slaty cleavage*, results from the reorientation of pre-existing minerals and the growth of new minerals with a *preferred orientation* during tectonic deformation. Flow-cleavage is not developed near the surface of the earth, as the necessary recrystallisation requires somewhat elevated temperatures and pressures. *Slates*, in fact, are metamorphic rocks of very low grade and the processes by which they are formed give rise with increasing metamorphism to phyllites and schists (Chapter 9). Flow-cleavage results from the parallel orientation of an infinite number of minute minerals making up the bulk of the rock and is thus inherent in the *microfabric* or arrangement in space of the mineral components. There are theoretically an infinite number of possible parting-planes in a slate, and the rock is therefore capable of being split into very thin even sheets which can be used as roofing material.

Fracture-cleavage is a mechanically-formed rock-structure in which the rock is split by closely-spaced partings on each of which there has been a small amount of movement. There is a finite number of cleavage-planes and the rock between them remains, under the simplest conditions, unmodified; the rock therefore splits less finely and regularly than a slate. Planes of fracture-cleavage may in suitable circumstances provide channels along which active fluids can migrate, and these fluids may promote the growth of metamorphic minerals, with parallel orientation, along the cleavage.

Strain-slip cleavage is a distinctive structure most commonly developed in rocks already possessing a fine lamination either along the bedding or along an earlier cleavage. The strain-slip cleavage is associated with a regular small-scale crenulation of the lamination and is produced by fracturing at the sharp hinges or by thinning out of the middle limbs of the crenulations (Fig. 279).

The relationship of *flow-cleavage* to the deformation that the rocks have undergone has been demonstrated in the field and with artificially produced cleavages in the laboratory. From observations on slaty rocks it is found that fossils, concretions, pebbles, oolite grains and other objects with recognisable primary shapes have been extended in the plane of the cleavage and compressed in a direction at right angles to it (Fig. 278). Frequently, extension in the

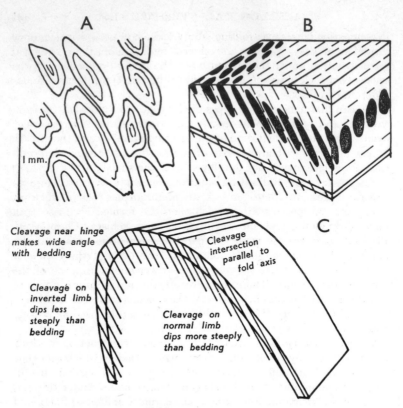

Cleavage near hinge
makes wide angle
with bedding

Cleavage on
inverted limb
dips less
steeply than
bedding

Cleavage
intersection
parallel to
fold axis

Cleavage on
normal limb
dips more steeply
than bedding

FIG. 278. *Flow Cleavage.* A, distortion of oolitic grains; B, distortion of pebbles, showing flattening and elongation in the cleavage planes; C, relation of cleavage to bedding.

cleavage-plane is greatest in one direction which is considered to correspond to the direction of slip on the cleavage during folding.

In folded rocks, the cleavage-planes are observed to lie parallel to the axial planes of the folds associated with them, and slaty or flow-cleavage is therefore often referred to as *axial-plane cleavage*. Consideration of the mechanism of shear-folding already discussed (p. 457, Fig. 275), shows that the cleavage-planes are the active surfaces in shear-folding and must of necessity lie in the axial-plane direction. The direction of slip on the cleavage is, in straightforward circumstances, perpendicular to the axes of the folds produced by this slip. A very close connection therefore exists between the orientation of slaty cleavage and the geometry of folds produced in connection with it (Fig. 278). Field-observations of cleavage can accordingly be used in the interpretation of geological structure; its strike corresponds to the horizontal trend of the folding (Fig. 284) and its dip reveals the asymmetry of the structure, while the intersections of cleavage- and bedding-planes are parallel to the local fold-axes as shown in Figure 278.

Flow-cleavage is, as we have seen, normally oblique to the bedding-planes. At fold-hinges, the cleavage cuts the bedding almost at right angles. On the fold-limbs, the angle between bedding and cleavage varies according to the tightness of the folding; in open folds, there is a wide angle between bedding and cleavage, but in isoclinal folds the angle is only a few degrees. The relative dips of cleavage and bedding differ on the two limbs of a fold and this fact can, with some precautions, be used to provide 'way-up' evidence (Fig. 278). In an overturned fold, it will be seen that the cleavage must dip less steeply than the overturned limb and more steeply than the normal limb. So long as we are dealing with true anticlines and synclines formed contemporaneously with the cleavage, we may therefore deduce that rocks in which the cleavage dips less steeply than the bedding are inverted, and that rocks in which the relative dips are

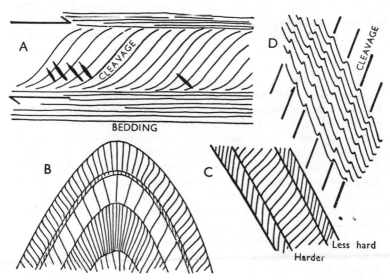

FIG. 279. *Fracture Cleavage and Strain-slip Cleavage.* A, Fracture cleavage related to a thrust; production of fracture cleavage and tension gashes (black) in a thrust zone. B, fracture cleavage related to a fold; variation in the attitude of the cleavage in different lithological beds. C, differential fracture cleavage; D, development of strain-slip cleavage.

reversed are right-way-up. Where the structural pattern is complex, this deduction must be checked by evidence of way-up given by primary structures.

Fracture-cleavage results either from slip connected with shear-folding (Fig. 279B) or from rocks slipping past one another along thrusts and in other fault-zones (Fig. 279A). In folds, fracture-cleavage can be used in the same way as flow-cleavage to indicate the order of succession. It is not, however, so closely parallel to the axial planes and may fan out somewhat on the limbs of the folds. Its orientation largely depends on the lithology of the rocks involved, the cleavage-planes forming a larger angle with the bedding in competent rocks such as sandstones than in incompetent mudstones or shales. In consequence, the fracture-cleavage in beds of mixed lithology is undulating and is referred to as *differential* or *ripple-cleavage* (Fig. 279c). At levels in the crust where flow-cleavage is just beginning to develop, fracture-cleavage in competent beds may pass into flow-cleavage in incompetent layers and, at depth, the two types of cleavage become more or less indistinguishable. Strain-slip cleavage, when associated with larger folds, shows much the same relationships as the other types. Sometimes, with continued movement, cleavages of more than one type may be formed successively. Thus slates may be cut, and for economic purposes ruined, by a later fracture or strain-slip cleavage formed after free recrystallisation had ceased.

Boudinage and tension-gashes. A structure associated with the folding of mixed series of competent and incompetent beds is *boudinage* (Fig. 280). During the folding of, say, interbedded sandstones and shales, the more brittle sandstone beds become fractured over the crests of the folds into long 'telegraph-pole-shaped' pieces slightly separated from each other. The lengths of the boudins ('sausages') are usually parallel to the fold-axes. The spaces between adjacent boudins may be filled in by quartz partitions, and the incompetent material above and below may also flow into these spaces. The folding of the competent layer is achieved by breaking and movement of short segments; such folding passes into disjunctive folding already discussed (Fig. 277).

During the distortion of brittle rocks, *tension-gashes* may be opened up as a result of stretching over the crest of a fold, or of local extension due to the drag exerted by beds slipping past one another. Tension-gashes due to the bending of competent rocks generally appear as radial fractures concentrated at the crests of anticlines (Fig. 274). Tension-gashes formed by differential slip appear on the limbs of the folds and in thrust- and fault-zones, and are roughly perpendicular to the local direction of extension or of least pressure.

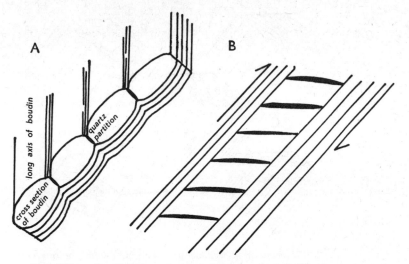

long axis of boudin

quartz partition

cross section of boudin

Fig. 280. A, boudinage; B, tension-gashes producing a ladder vein system.

Tension-gashes are distinguished from fracture-cleavage and other kinds of fractures by the fact that their sides tend to gape, and they frequently contain lenticular bodies of vein-quartz or calcite. *Ladder veins* are series of quartz-filled tension-gashes arranged *en echelon*.

Lineation. We have already seen that the folding of rocks may produce structures on various scales that have one dimension much greater than the others. The folds themselves are usually elongated parallel to the axis, boudins are longest in a direction often parallel to the fold-axis, fossils and oolites may be drawn out in a preferred direction within the cleavage. All these are examples of *linear structures* which produce a *lineation* in the rocks containing them. Linear structures may be of many kinds and origins, some connected with folding and some with other tectonic events, and we give here a purely descriptive, non-genetic, terminology.

Fold-axis lineations are expressed by the alignment of the axes of folds of many sizes. Small-scale crinkling may produce a regular lineation resembling that shown by corrugated iron. In mixed successions, competent layers may be divided into *boudins* (Fig. 280), or the fold-hinges may be separated from the limbs to produce *rods* (Fig. 281). Pebbles, oolites, fossils and other objects of known primary shape may be distorted to produce a *distortion-lineation* in their longest dimension. When plastic flow is accompanied by solution

465

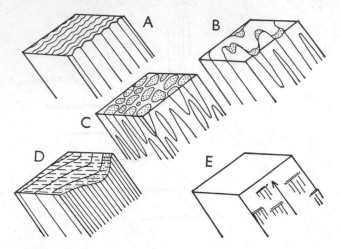

FIG. 281. *Lineations.* A, crinkle lineation; B, rodding of quartz segregations; C, distortion-lineation in pebbles; D, intersection-lineation, produced by the intersections of cleavage and bedding; E, slickensides, arrow shows the direction of movement of the creative block, now removed.

and recrystallisation, as in many metamorphic rocks, new minerals such as hornblende, sillimanite, tremolite or andalusite may grow with a parallel orientation to give a *crysiallisation-lineation* (Fig. 309). An *intersection-lineation* is produced as a series of fine striations or grooves by the intersection of two sets of planes of different orientation; the most common lineation of this type is formed by the intersection of flow-cleavage and bedding. Finally, *slickensides* are fine scratches, grooves or striations developed on rock-surfaces where adjacent masses have slipped past one another. Slickensides are formed on bedding-planes as a result of slip during true folding and are also common on the surfaces of faults.

Linear structures may be related in various definite ways to larger-scale structures such as folds, and so to the forces responsible for the structural pattern; and the mapping of such structures may therefore contribute to the understanding of the regional pattern, provided that their geometrical relations can be established. Lineations are generally represented on maps by long arrows pointing in the direction of plunge; suitable variants with double heads, cross-bars and so on can be devised as required for the different types.

The connection between fold-axis lineations and the related folds is self-evident; likewise, intersection-lineations produced by the intersection of axial-plane cleavage and bedding, and rods, are of

466

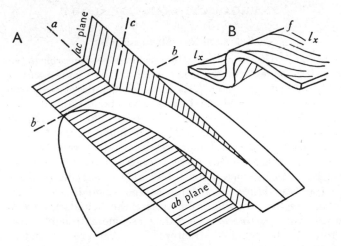

FIG. 282. A, structural co-ordinates, a, b and c, in relation to a fold. B, lineation, l_x, distorted by a later fold, f; the lineation is incongruous with respect to the fold.

necessity parallel to the axes of the associated folds. Commonly, but not invariably, boudins and crystallisation-lineations follow the same direction. Distortion-lineations may do so also, but such lineations may instead be at right angles to the fold-axis; distortion in cleavage-planes commonly leads to elongation perpendicular to the axis and in the direction of slip (Fig. 278). Slickensides produced by differential slip during true folding are generally perpendicular to the axial direction. These simple geometrical relationships naturally refer only to examples where lineation and folding are related to the same tectonic act — in many areas, several lineations of different types and ages may be seen criss-crossing on a single bedding-plane, and most of these will bear little relation to the orientation of a given fold (Fig. 282).

In the discussion of lineations, their origins and relations to folds, it is customary to use three co-ordinates, a, b and c at right angles. The co-ordinate b is in the direction of the fold-axis, and lineations in this direction are sometimes referred to as b-lineations. The plane ab is the movement plane, c is perpendicular to ab, and ac is a plane of symmetry for the fold, at right angles to the axis (Fig. 282). Since many lineations are so closely connected with folds, there is a temptation to regard observable lineations, which are very easily measured and mapped in the field, as indicating the direction of regional movement or its perpendicular; the complexity of most fold-systems makes this an unsafe procedure.

467

MAJOR AND MINOR FOLDS

The largest folds seen in the earth's crust are measureable in tens and hundreds of miles. The wide flat dome of the Chalk enclosing the Weald, for example, (Fig. 271) is some 40 miles across, from the North Downs to the South Downs, and about 120 miles from its western closure in Hampshire to the eastern closure in the Boulonnais. Tight recumbent folds such as are found in the Alps and the Scottish Highlands are still more extensive. Many very large flexures of low amplitude are made up of a series of moderate-sized folds so arranged as to produce a general arching or sagging of the stratigraphical boundaries. Such large composite folds are called *anticlinoria* (singular, anticlinorium) where the boundaries are arched upwards and *synclinoria* where they assume a trough shape.

From the largest fold-structures, we can proceed indefinitely downwards to folds which can be seen in a mountain-side, a single outcrop, a hand-specimen or a thin slice. Structures on many scales are usually formed in response to a single act of deformation (Fig. 283), and it is often useful to think of these in terms of the *major folds* which control the pattern of outcrops revealed on the map, and the *minor folds* which are too small to show up on a map but which determine the structural style as seen in the outcrop. The minor structures commonly reproduce on a small scale the style and orientation of the major folds and are then said to be *congruous* with these folds. The axis and axial plane of a congruous minor fold are parallel to those of the associated major fold, and the crest normally faces in the same direction. Since the orientations of large numbers of minor folds and cleavages can be measured in the field, they provide a valuable guide to the structural pattern; the measurements can be plotted on a map to bring out regional variations in direction (Fig. 284), or they may be plotted on a stereographic net, by which means their geometrical relationships can be made apparent. In the form of the profile, the minor folds often reflect the style of the major folds — small recumbent folds appear on the limbs of large recumbent folds, and so on — but details tend to vary according to the position of the minor structure with relation to the limbs and hinge of the local major structure (Fig. 283). Thus, symmetrical M-shaped folds may appear in the hinge region, asymmetrical S-shaped folds on one limb and Z-shaped folds on the other. Since the axial planes of the S- and Z-folds are parallel to the major axial plane, their dip relative to that of the long limbs of the minor folds can be used to determine the 'way-up' in exactly the same way as can the dip of axial-plane cleavage (Fig. 283, compare Fig. 278). *Drag-folds* (p. 457) represent a

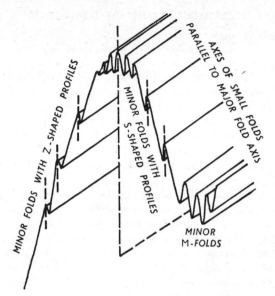

FIG. 283. Congruous minor folds on larger folds.

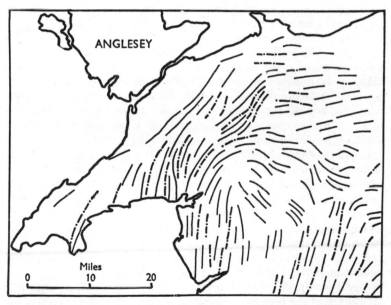

FIG. 284. Regional variation in cleavage directions in north Wales. Strike of the cleavage is shown by short lines, the axial planes of the related major folds by dot-dash lines (after Shackleton).

special type of minor structure and, though formed by a separate mechanism, provide way-up criteria in the same way.

TYPES OF FOLDING AND FOLD PATTERNS

A fold seldom occurs in isolation and most folds contribute to build up a *fold-system* whose pattern depends on that of the controlling forces. The most extensive and spectacular fold-systems are developed in the *orogenic belts* as direct or indirect products of tangential pressures in the crust. Before considering these systems, we may briefly review some other types of folding and the kinds of forces which produce them.

Folding connected with faulting may be developed especially where rocks of differing competence are involved. On a small scale, the rocks may be rucked and dragged by movement along the fault (Fig. 302). On a larger scale, a great monoclinal fold may develop in a sedimentary sequence overlying a rigid basement subjected to faulting (Fig. 299), and shallow troughs or basins may be formed above a subsiding block bounded by two faults. **Folding connected with intrusions** is seen in the vicinity of forcefully-intruded igneous bodies and of salt domes. Domes, concentric ridges and folds with axial planes parallel to the sides of the intrusion are common structures produced by forceful intrusion (Figs. 165, 232).

Folding of superficial deposits at the earth's surface may be due to a variety of causes. The drag of a moving ice-body may wrinkle the underlying rocks, and in regions of permafrost (p. 149), slow movements of saturated material may produce chaotic folds. Erosion, by unevenly reducing the load on plastic rocks, and by severing the continuity of competent horizons may induce superficial movements of material under the influence of gravity. Examples of structures resulting from such movements are shown in Fig. 285.

Gravity-controlled folding of other kinds takes place where rock-masses slide down a slope under gravity. *Slump-structures* (p. 255) are small-scale examples of this kind of folding. More important examples are seen in the orogenic belts where the upheaval of a large region may cause the covering succession to slide off the newly formed slope, like a cloth sliding off a tilted table, and to pile up in recumbent *cascade folds* at the foot of the slope (Fig. 285).

In the formation of the structures mentioned above, **tangential compression** plays little part. In most other kinds of folding, however, compression appears to be a motive force, and its effects are seen in a shortening of the beds in a direction at right angles to the trend of the folds. Except at considerable depths, the direction of least pressure and easiest relief is upwards; the folds are therefore formed with axes

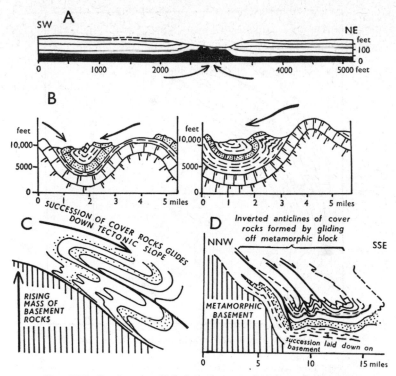

FIG. 285. *Gravity-controlled Structures.* A, bulging of clay below valley bottom (after Hollingworth and others); B, collapse structures in alternating limestones and marls on the flanks of an eroded anticline, Iran (after Harrison and Falcon); C, cascade folds on the flank of a rising mass; D, cascade folds from the Montagne Noire, Central France (after de Sitter and Trumpy).

on average more or less horizontal and the crests of the anticlines rise as they grow. The axes of the main folds of any system are generally roughly parallel, and it is usually considered that they lie perpendicular to the direction of the compressive stress. On a large scale, the fold-trends are often arcuate, and the main stress is then thought to operate from the concave side of the arc (Fig. 286).

Simple squeezing of the rocks in an orogenic belt might be expected to produce upright folds with vertical axial planes: in fact, however, conditions are never as simple as this. The rocks of the compressed belt tend to move outwards as well as upwards, the applied stress forms a couple with the resisting pressure of the strata, and a rotational deformation takes place. Under such stress conditions as these, the folds become asymmetrical, overturned or even recumbent, and

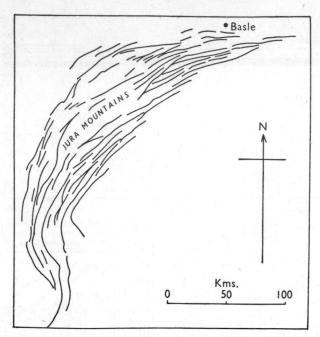

FIG. 286. Pattern of folds in the Jura Mountains.

their crests face away from the direction of the applied stress. The *sense of movement* of a fold is generally expressed in terms of the movement shown by high levels in the structure relative to those below; thus, a fold overturned towards the west is said to be formed by westerly movement although in theory a structure of the same pattern could be formed by relative easterly movement of an underlying basement.

TIMING OF FOLDING

Episodes of folding are important events in the geological history of a crustal segment and accordingly have to be dated as closely as possible. Folding is obviously later than the deposition of the youngest rock seen to be folded and earlier than that of the oldest rock seen to rest unconformably on folded rocks. The limits thus set may be very wide, and they can sometimes be narrowed by indirect evidence. Fragments of rocks showing minor structures (e.g., cleavage or small folds) developed during folding may be included in conglomerates of known age; igneous intrusions which can be dated by evidence available elsewhere may cut across the folds, and later structures such as faults whose age is known may disrupt them.

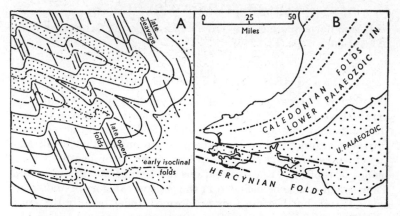

Among minor structures such as small folds, cleavages and lineations a sequence of events may often be established. In the field, structures of early generations are seen to be folded, distorted or cut through by later structures *superimposed* on them (Fig. 287). Structures which are older or younger than a particular major fold are naturally *incongruous* with respect to it, and it is therefore important in regions of multiple folding to sort out the age-relations of the various structures before attempting to establish the structural pattern. The geometry of superimposed folds is often very complex and the relations between the orientation of the structures and the controlling forces may be obscure.

When a sequence of folding-episodes can be established, the local geological evidence will have to be assembled to determine whether the later folding is merely one of a connected series of episodes, or whether it belongs to an entirely separate period of earth-history. In the development of many structures, several phases follow one another with no essential change in the stress-field; true folding, with bedding-plane slip, may be followed by shear-folding with the development of flow-cleavage and this by the appearance of fracture-cleavage, all the structures building up a consistent pattern. On the other hand, the earlier and later structures may bear no relation to one another and may result from earth-movements of entirely different kinds and ages. Superimposed structures of this kind are naturally best displayed at the crossing of great fold-systems, as for example in Pembrokeshire where Hercynian folds

473

of Permo-Carboniferous date cross at an angle the Caledonian folds
of late Silurian age (Fig. 287).

THRUSTS, LAGS AND SLIDES

The folding of rocks implies a gradual yielding of the strata to an
external, usually tangential, force. If deformation is driven beyond
the limits that can be accommodated by folding, or if the rocks are
brittle and cannot fold in their present environment, they break, and
the crustal shortening is taken up by movement on gently-inclined
planes of rupture. These dislocations are termed *thrusts* and *slides*.
They can of course be included in the general category of *faults* considered later, but because they are formed under broadly the same
conditions as folds and are often genetically connected with folds,
their treatment here seems more reasonable. Slides have indeed been
defined as *fold-faults*.

The planes of break on which movement takes place are termed
thrust-planes. Where several such planes occur close together as
products of one act of deformation, they make up a *thrust-zone*. We
here deal separately with two rather different kinds of structures:
firstly, the slides formed by continued evolution of folds already in
existence, and secondly, clean-cut thrusts and thrust-zones formed
where deformation leads directly to fracturing.

Development of thrusts in folding. Folds develop into thrusts either
by breaking at the hinge-line where the bending-moment is greatest,
or by thinning and shearing of their middle limbs as illustrated in
Fig. 288. Such structures are of common occurrence in areas of simple
folding, especially where brittle or competent beds are involved.
They are well seen in parts of the Appalachians (Fig. 381) and in the
more compressed part of the South Wales Coal-field in Pembrokeshire.

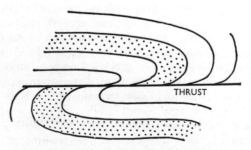

Fig. 288. Fold developing into a Thrust.

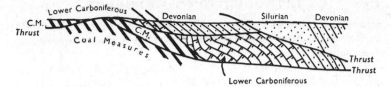

FIG. 289. Reduplication of strata by thrusts, Belgian Coal-field (after Fourmarier).

Thrusts developed in the manner described above strike sub-parallel to the general fold trend. Their effect as seen on a map is to cut out some beds that would normally appear at the surface. Thrusting may thus lead to the non-appearance of the full strati-graphical sequence, a hiatus being found at the thrust-plane. On the

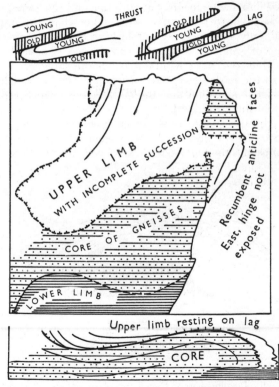

FIG. 290. (*Upper*), thrust and lag. (*Middle and lower*), diagrammatic map and section of the Banff Nappe or Recumbent Fold in north-east Scotland showing the development of a lag in the normal limb.

475

other hand, thrusting often duplicates strata in depth, as is illustrated by a section across the Belgian Coal-field where thrusting was first really well demonstrated (Fig. 289).

In the great *recumbent flow-folds* seen in highly disturbed regions such as the Alps and the Scottish Highlands, the middle limbs of the folds are often thinned and partially replaced by slides. We show in Fig. 290 an interpretation proposed for the structure of north-east Scotland. The great recumbent anticline there shown is sliced by a flat plane of movement which thins out the upper, uninverted, limb of this fold. The slide-plane is itself folded along with the rocks above and below it, a feature which is commonly displayed by fold-faults.

The example of north-east Scotland illustrated in Fig. 290 provides us with some data on which we can effect a subdivision of fold-faults. In this example, as already mentioned, the slide partially replaces the uninverted limb of the recumbent anticline and the *lower* limb of the anticline appears to have advanced further than the upper limb. More commonly, it is the inverted fold-limb which is thinned, and the *upper* limb of an anticline appears to advance over the lower limb. We may thus recognise within the general category of *slides* or 'thrusts' in the loose sense, two varieties — the *lag* which replaces the uninverted fold-limb and the *thrust proper* which replaces the inverted fold-limb (Fig. 290).

In the Alps, piles of great recumbent folds were driven northward over their basement, and where the movement was most intense the middle limbs of these folds were sheared away and replaced by flat or

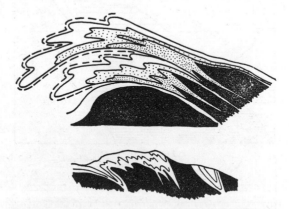

FIG. 291. Development of Nappe Structure. (*Above*), diagrammatic section across the Helvetic nappes of the Alps (after Collet); (*below*), thrust wedges of basement (black) rising into the deformed cover, western end of the Aar massif (after Lugeon and Goguel).

undulating thrust-planes. The thrust-sheets so formed — really the torn-off upper limbs of recumbent anticlines — lie one above the other and are folded together by continued deformation (Fig. 291). Thrust-sheets of this type are known as *nappes* from the French term *nappe de charriage* (= transported sheet); the German equivalent is *Decken*. The hinge-regions of the Alpine nappes — the *brow-folds* — face northward in the direction of transport. Their *roots*, the regions from which the nappes rose and to which they may be still connected, lie to the south. Portions of nappes isolated by erosion form structural outliers or *klippes* in which a detached outcrop of a higher nappe rests with a tectonic junction on a lower nappe whose outcrop entirely surrounds it. The reverse form, the structural inlier or *window*, in which an exposure of a lower nappe is framed by a continuous outcrop of the overlying nappe, is seen where streams cut down through the nappe pile or where subsequent folding has brought lower nappes within reach of erosion.

CLEAN-CUT FRACTURE-THRUSTS

Dislocations of our second type cannot be directly related to the development of specific folds and appear as clean-cut fractures carrying apparently brittle wedges of rock; it is of course possible that these fractures began as fold-faults and later passed out of their generative area. The effects of the dislocations correspond to those of the *thrusts proper* as defined in the last section, in that rocks above the dislocation appear to have advanced relative to those below. The term *overthrust* implies that the upper rocks were actively moved over a static basement, and the term *underthrust* that the basement moved beneath a passive cover; unless definite evidence is available, these terms are best avoided.

Clean-cut thrusts and thrust-zones are most commonly developed along the margins or *fronts* of mountain-belts where the mobile orogenic belt joins the more stable regions or *forelands* on either side. These fractures are often of great magnitude, running for hundreds of miles and carrying rocks over horizontal distances of many tens of miles. Marginal thrusts of this type are found along the edge of the Rocky Mountain system, on the south side of the Himalayas, and on the western side of the Appalachians. The classic example is provided by the *Moine Thrust-Zone* at the north-western margin of the ancient Caledonian mountain-belt which at the end of the Lower Palaeozoic era extended from Scandinavia through north-west Britain.

The Moine Thrust-Zone can be traced from the north coast of Sutherland to Skye, Iona and Islay, its length in Scotland approaching 200 miles (Fig. 292). To the west of the zone in the foreland of the

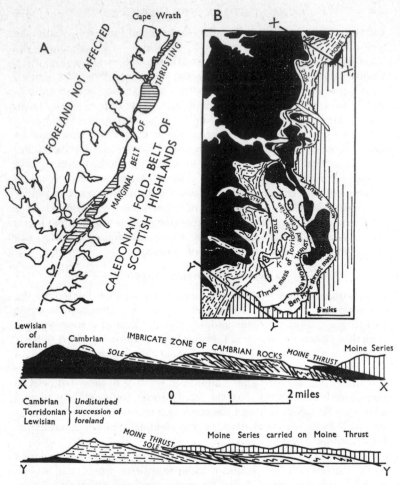

FIG. 292. The Moine Thrust Zone in the north-west Highlands of Scotland. A, the belt of complication (lined); B, map and section of the Assynt area, Sutherland; explanation of the ornament used is given in the sections below: thrusts indicated by lines with ticks on the map, klippen, outliers of the thrust sheets, by K.

Caledonian belt lies an undisturbed succession of ancient Pre-Cambrian crystalline rocks (Lewisian) covered unconformably by younger Pre-Cambrian arkoses (Torridonian) and then by shallow-water Cambro-Ordovician sandstones and limestones. To the east lie strongly folded and metamorphosed sedimentary rocks (the Moine Series) resting on intensely disturbed Lewisian. The zone contains a

478

number of large and many small thrusts, all running roughly north-north-east/south-south-west and dipping gently eastward. The lower and more westerly thrusts carry slices of the western succession which is thus piled up and reduplicated in the thrust-zone. The highest and most easterly thrust — the *Moine Thrust* itself — carries the Moine Series to rest with complete discordance on the piled-up slices below or even on the undisturbed rocks of the foreland. Along and near the thrust-planes, the rocks are broken down — a process known as *cataclasis* — or milled out into very fine-grained *mylonites*. These changes are examples of *dislocation-metamorphism* dealt with in Chapter 9.

The deformation in the Moine Thrust-Zone may have begun with simple folding of the bedded rocks, but with further compression, these rocks broke along a swarm of small fractures and piled up in slices like tiles on a roof to give *imbricate structure* or *schuppen-structure*. The orientation of these minor thrusts corresponds closely with that of the theoretical planes of shear produced by horizontal compression, and the structure can easily be reproduced experimentally. As the strata piled up, resistance to further movement on these planes increased and the whole pile was then driven forward on a series of major thrust-planes reaching down into the crystalline Lewisian basement (Fig. 292). The Moine Thrust is the highest and latest of the large thrusts.

The distance travelled by the rock-mass resting on the Moine Thrust is known to exceed ten miles at one locality and is probably very much more. The direction of travel can be deduced from small-scale phenomena — the dip-directions of minor imbricate structures, the stretching of conglomerate pebbles, and the bending over or 'candle-flaming' of worm-tubes originally perpendicular to the bedding. This direction is towards the west or west-north-west, at right angles to the strike of the thrust-zone and outward from the orogenic belt towards the stable region on the west. On the south-east side of the Caledonian mountain-belt, a similar thrust-zone is seen in Scandinavia. The movement in this zone is towards the south-east, and the two thrust-zones together therefore present a picture of the outward expulsion of material from the orogenic belt as a result of horizontal compression.

Clean-cut thrusting, as we have noted, takes place in response to tangential compression in circumstances where this compression cannot readily be accommodated by folding. Such circumstances arise particularly where very massive and rigid crystalline rocks are deformed. Such rocks are brittle when cold, they often have no regularly arranged bedding-planes to make flexuring possible, and

Q2

consequently they yield mainly by fracturing. In many orogenic belts a *basement* of crystalline rocks underlies the sedimentary succession making the *cover*. During compression, the basement is at first warped and later broken into *thrust-wedges* while the cover is folded and pinched between the wedges (Fig. 291). Folding and thrusting are in such regions clearly alternative responses to the same set of stresses.

FAULTS

Definitions. A *fault* is a fracture or dislocation in the earth's crust along which there has been displacement of the rocks on one side relative to those on the other. The movement of the rocks on a fault may have been in any direction, vertical or horizontal or some combination of these. It must be remembered that the slip between the two sides is relative and it cannot be said that one rock-mass moved while the other remained stationary.

The surface of the break along which the movement has taken place is the *fault-plane* (Fig. 293); a *fault-zone* comprises a group of such surfaces. The fault-plane may be vertical, inclined or gently undulating and its inclination is recorded as a *dip*, the angle between the fault-plane and the horizontal. The old term *hade* is the angle between the fault-plane and the vertical; this term is now rarely used and it would simplify matters if it were dropped completely. The horizontal trend of a fault is its *strike*. If the fault-plane is inclined, the upper side and the rocks which lie above it are referred to as the *hanging-wall*; those below it are the *foot-wall*. The intersection of a

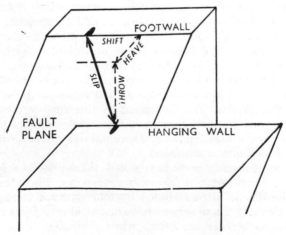

FIG. 293. Elements of a Fault.

fault-plane with the ground-surface — its outcrop — is known as the *fault-line* or *fault-trace*.

As with any other plane, the shape of a fault-line reveals the attitude of the fault-plane. If the fault-line is straight, no matter how diversified the topography, then the fault-plane is vertical. If the fault-line is curved in accord with the topography it is probably inclined, and its strike and dip can be found in the same way as those of any other surface. If a fault-line winds in and out of valleys in a manner akin to topographic contours, the fault may be flat or gently dipping and is most likely a thrust.

Faults can be classified in various ways depending on such factors as their geometry, the movements that have taken place on them, or the forces responsible for their formation. By surveying these three classifications we shall obtain a complete picture of faulting.

Geometrical classification of faults. First of all we may view faults in relation to the attitude of the rocks affected by them (Fig. 300). *Dip-faults* run parallel to the direction of the local dip; *strike-faults* are parallel to the local strike, and *oblique faults* cut obliquely across the strike of the beds. *Bedding-plane faults* coincide with the local stratification. Secondly, faults may be *high-angle* or *low-angle faults* depending on their dips. Lastly, the geometrical pattern of a group of faults may comprise *parallel, en echelon* or *radial faults*. *Ring-fractures* form a special group associated with the emplacement of certain igneous bodies and already considered with these in Chapter 7.

Classification of faults by movements. Faults may be divided into several categories in relation to the movements that have taken place on them (Fig. 294). A first group is the *normal faults*, the type commonly or normally met with in the British Coal-fields, in which the hanging-wall rocks moved *down the dip* of the fault-plane relative to the rocks of the foot-wall. *Reverse faults* are those in which the hanging-wall rocks moved *up the dip* of the fault-plane relative to the rocks of the foot-wall. *Tear-faults* or *wrench-faults* are formed where the movement was dominantly horizontal and are often called *transcurrent or strike-slip faults*. They may be *dextral* or *sinistral*, depending on whether the movement of the block on the far side of the fault-plane from the observer is towards his right or left hand. *Left-handed* or *right-handed faults* are faults in which dipping structures have been displaced left- or right-handedly when seen beyond the fault-plane, but not necessarily by a horizontal movement. *Hinge-* or *pivotal faults* are those in which the rocks on one side of the fault apparently rotated about a pivot, perpendicular to the fault-plane, relative to those on the other side.

Relation of faults to the forces that caused them. Although it is

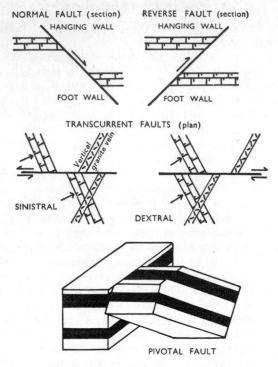

FIG. 294. Faults classified by movements.

rarely possible to define the actual system of forces that was responsible for the production of a certain fault, many dislocations have been somewhat arbitrarily classified on this basis. Normal faults, because they result in a lengthening across the fault of the portion of the crust affected (Fig. 294), are commonly referred to as *tension-faults*; because their hanging-wall rocks have apparently moved downwards, they are sometimes called *gravity-faults*. There is much more justification for referring to reverse faults, which involved a shortening of the crust, as *compressional faults*, though even here the effect may not point directly to the true cause.

Nevertheless, the presence of faults is itself proof that forces have acted on the crust and that the stresses operating have been greater than the strengths of the rocks. Hence, given a known distribution of forces, it is possible to deduce the style of faulting which would probably result — it is found that the naturally occurring fault-planes commonly conform to certain definite patterns which might be expected from theoretical considerations.

By choosing the correct co-ordinates, we may resolve any system of forces into three unequal pairs of *principal stresses* which are mutually at right angles to each other. If one pair of stresses is sufficiently great the strength of the rocks will be overcome and rupture will take place. Theoretically, and in the laboratory where conditions can be closely controlled, rupture will occur along two *shear-planes*, which lie a few degrees less than 45° to the direction of the maximum stress, P_{MAX}, and a few degrees more than 45° to the minimum stress P_{MIN}. The shear-planes intersect in the direction of the intermediate stress P_{INT}. The same pattern of shear-planes is obtained whether the stress applied is one of tension or of compression.

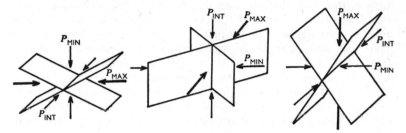

FIG. 295. Orientations of the stress-fields; production of shear-planes for different orientations of the principal stresses.

In the crust, the orientation of the stress-field is of course influenced by the effect of gravity and one of the three principal stresses normally lies roughly vertical, parallel to the direction in which gravity works. Three alternative arrangements are possible (Fig. 295).

(a) The maximum and intermediate stresses are both horizontal and the minimum stress is vertical.

(b) The maximum and minimum stresses are horizontal and the intermediate stress is vertical.

(c) The maximum stress is vertical and the intermediate and minimum stresses are horizontal.

Many known tectonic patterns would be consistent with development under the influence of one or other of these arrangements. Such patterns are produced not only by faults but also by folds, minor structures associated with folds, and by joints; but as fracture-patterns are on the whole easier to interpret than fold-patterns it seems most reasonable to deal with them at this point.

Stress-distribution a (P_{MAX} and P_{INT} horizontal and P_{MIN} vertical) is developed during tangential compression, especially in the orogenic

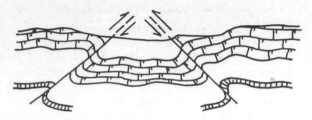

FIG. 296. Opposed thrusts in the Jura.

belts, where the direction of easiest relief is upwards. Folds with roughly horizontal axes lying at right angles to P_{MAX} might be expected to form and, as would be expected from their close connection in the field, thrust-planes dipping at angles of less than 45° could also be developed. If the compression were a truly vice-like squeeze, two sets of thrusts dipping in opposite directions should be produced; and examples of equally-developed opposed or *counterthrusts* have in fact occasionally been recognised. They result in the uplifting or depression of wedge-shaped blocks between two inclined thrusts as illustrated in the Jura (Fig. 296). More commonly, however, one set of thrusts is developed to the exclusion of the other. Conditions are rarely symmetrical, as we have seen in connection with folding; rupture occurs first on the most favourably-placed set of shear-planes and the internal stresses immediately diminish so that the second set is suppressed.

The *stress-distribution of type b* (P_{MAX} and P_{MIN} horizontal and P_{INT} vertical) may also result from horizontal compression, where the direction of easiest relief is not vertical. It explains the formation of tear- or wrench-faults which often cut obliquely across belts of folding. The faults are steep and often form two sets corresponding to the two planes of maximum shear; the two sets intersect in a roughly vertical line giving the orientation of P_{INT} and movement on them is such that one set is sinistral and the other dextral. The fault-sets are commonly more or less symmetrical with respect to the axes of the related fold-system and may then be presumed to have resulted from a continuation of the same act of compression. A good example is seen in south Pembrokeshire where folds and faults were formed by Hercynian orogenic movements at about the end of the Upper Palaeozoic (Fig. 297).

Transcurrent faults are important structures in the Scottish Highlands where one predominant set strikes north-east or north-north east and a second, more restricted, set strikes north-west. These faults are considered to have resulted from a roughly north and south compression which was later than and independent of the more

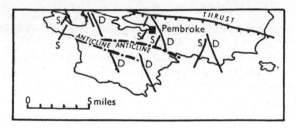

FIG. 297. Folding and faulting in south Pembrokeshire, Wales; s, indicates sinistral transcurrent fault, D, dextral transcurrent fault.

nearly north-west/south-east compression responsible for the formation of the Highland fold-systems. By far the most important of the tear-faults is the *Great Glen Fault* forming the long depression in which lie Loch Ness and the Caledonian Canal (Fig. 298). The strike-length of the fault in Scotland is nearly 100 miles. The movement along it is sinistral and its extent can be suggested from the displacement of a zoned granite mass which it traverses. The two portions of this granite, the Strontian granite on the north-west side and the Foyers granite on the south-east, are now some 64 miles apart and it has accordingly been suggested that the lateral displacement on the Great Glen Fault is over 60 miles (100 kms.). The main movement was Palaeozoic, but even at the present day the

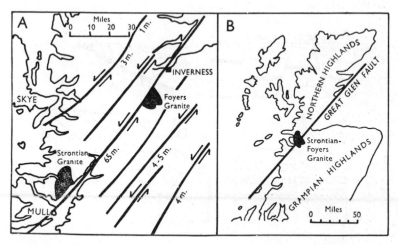

FIG. 298. Transcurrent faults of the Scottish Highlands. Black, Strontian and Foyers granites. A, main transcurrent faults, with displacements indicated; B, proposed original positions before the production of the Great Glen Fault (based on W. Q. Kennedy).

485

Great Glen still suffers occasional small earthquakes; faults, once initiated, have very long lives.

Stress distribution c, in which the maximum stress acts more or less vertically, is that generally associated with normal faulting. It may result from a stretching of the crust as a result of which one of the horizontal stress components is reduced and the rocks fail under their own weight. Alternatively, it may result from dominantly vertical crustal movements by which a crustal block is bodily raised or lowered relative to the adjacent regions. As we shall see in Chapter 12, stress-conditions of these kinds may develop in the relatively stable parts of the crust outside the active orogenic belts; they may also follow the periods of strong compression in orogenic belts, so that the fold-belt is disturbed by block-faulting.

Groups of normal faults commonly occur with their fault-planes dipping in opposite directions at angles which agree closely with those postulated on theoretical grounds (Fig. 299). In other groups, referred to as *step-faults,* the faults are more or less parallel and the beds affected are all dropped down in the same direction (Fig. 302B). In both types, it will be noticed that the fault-movements result in an elongation of the crust in a line at right angles to the strike of the faults. A similar tangential elongation of the crust is indicated in some areas by the occurrence of *dyke-swarms* (p. 395), filling parallel fractures at right angles to the direction of extension. In parts of the North Atlantic Tertiary Volcanic Province it has been estimated that

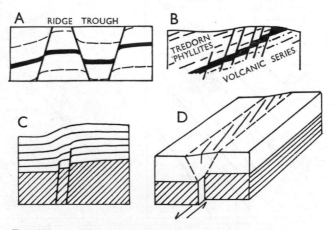

Fig. 299. A, ridge and trough faults, in section; B, normal step-faults, Tintagel, Cornwall (after Gilbert Wilson); C, fault in basement passing up into a monocline in the cover; D, transcurrent fault in basement giving rise to en echelon faults in the cover.

the crust over distances of 20–50 miles has been extended by amounts of the order of 5–10 per cent as a result of the intrusion of dyke-swarms.

Normal faults resulting from uplift or lowering of crustal blocks may be present in regions that otherwise show little tectonic activity. Thus, flat-lying beds resting on a foundation of ancient rocks may be warped or broken by radial movements in the basement. In this way monoclines may be formed and may grade into zones of normal faulting (Fig. 299c) as in the central plains of the United States. *En echelon* zones of faulting which possibly result from lateral (tear-fault) movements of the basement below the overlying sediments also occur in the same region (Fig. 299D).

Fault-movements. In the theoretical discussion of faults and the forces that caused them, only the simplest relationships have been considered. It is seldom that the forces have acted truly vertically or horizontally; usually the sum of the movements on the fault-planes have had both horizontal and vertical components (Fig. 293). The total movement on one side of a fault relative to that on the other, in the fault-plane, is termed the *slip* or *displacement*; the vertical component of the slip is the *throw*; the horizontal component in the strike direction of the fault-plane is usually referred to as the *shift* and the other horizontal component of the slip, at right angles to the strike, is the *heave*. There is, however, some ambiguity in the use of these two last terms and, when they are used, it is best to define them so as to avoid confusion.

The displacement on a fault is obtained by matching up the geometry of the rocks on either side of the dislocation (Fig. 300). If however the strata are evenly dipping or homoclinal it is impossible to say, without some additional information, what the true direction of movement actually was. In a homoclinal series, the *downthrown* side of a dip-fault is shown by younger strata abutting against older on the upthrown side. Strike-faults result in the cutting out or the repetition of beds, depending on whether the side that was dropped moved in the same direction as or against the dip of the bedding.

The absolute movement on a fault can be obtained if the beds on opposite sides of the dislocation are folded, or if two or more recognisable structures having different dips have been faulted. Thus in Fig. 300c, the sudden but symmetrical broadening of the syncline, combined with the parallelism of its limbs on either side of the fault, shows that the movement must have been directly downwards. It should be noted that the width of a faulted syncline is greater on the downthrown side of the fault, while that of an anticline is reduced. Structures which dip in opposite directions are displaced horizontally

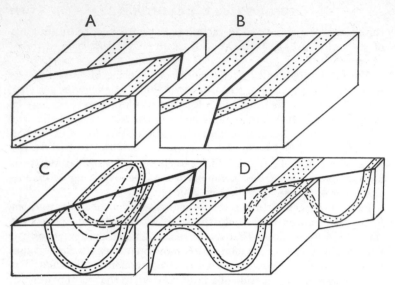

Fig. 300. Shifting of outcrops by faulting. A, dip fault, downthrow on near side; B, strike fault, downthrow on right; C, faulted syncline, downthrow on near side; D, transcurrent fault affecting folded beds.

in the same sense by tear- or wrench-faults so that, for example, anticlines may be brought into juxtaposition with synclines. Pivotal or hinge faulting is recognisable by abrupt changes in the dips of the beds or other structures on opposite sides of the faults or by changes in the amount of throw of the fault as it is traced along its strike; a simple non-rotational fault may grade into a pivotal fault as it dies out at either end.

One of the most satisfactory methods of elucidating fault-movements is to draw a *composite cross-section* of the structures on either side, using the fault-plane as the plane of section: in this way the same diagram shows two superposed cross-sections and the displacement between the two. We may illustrate this operation by reference to the three diagrams of Fig. 301. It has been seen that the possible movement on a fault cutting a homoclinal series of strata is indeterminate without further evidence, such as slickensides or drag, etc. (p. 489). It is customary under these circumstances to give the movement in terms of vertical displacement or throw. The true displacement can be determined if one can fix two or more *points*, as distinct from two linear structures, on opposite sides of the fault. Such points are provided by the fault-plane cutting fold-axes, or offsetting the lines of intersection of other types of geological

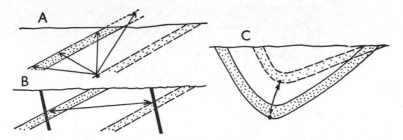

Fig. 301. Composite cross-sections on fault planes. A, in homoclinal beds, direction of movement not determinable; B, displacement fixed by intersections of a bed and a dyke; C, displacement fixed by displacement of the trough of the fold.

structures, e.g. a marker horizon in evenly dipping strata cut by a dyke (Fig. 301B). This method of solving fault-problems is simple to carry out and is accurate if the fault-plane is steeply dipping. It can also be used to elucidate fault-movements in which rotary as well as rectilinear slip has occurred on the fault-plane as shown in Fig. 301C.

Structures on the fault-plane. Some faults appear in the field as simple planes showing little local evidence of disturbance apart from that provided by the abrupt cutting-off of strata. Often, however, the fault-plane is polished, scratched or grooved by the movement. The scratches, known as *slickensides*, may vary in depth from grooves like those on a gramophone record to coarse *flutings* several inches deep. They are generally parallel to the direction of slip, but as a rule they only record the last movement to take place on the fault-plane. Movement in a fault-zone is not always confined to a single surface. Slip may take place on a number of sub-parallel surfaces which together make a *sheeted fault-zone*.

The strata on either side of a fault may also be bent by the frictional drag of the fault-movement. The orientation of the flexure is commonly accordant with the movement and can be used in assessing its sense, as shown in Fig. 302. Minor drag-folds, fracture-cleavages and tension-gashes are also frequently developed in rocks adjacent to faults, while small faults oblique to the main plane and representing the other direction of maximum shear may also appear. The orientations of the small folds, cleavages and tension-gashes are controlled by the couple set up by the fault-movement and may therefore be used as indications of the direction of slip as illustrated by the examples shown in Fig. 302.

The breaking of rocks in a fault-zone produces *fault-breccia*, a mass of angular fragments lying between smooth or shattered walls, the whole zone often being made conspicuous at the surface by reddening

489

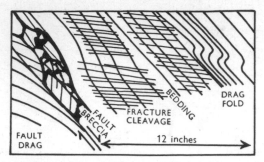

FIG. 302. Minor structures connected with normal faulting (after Gilbert Wilson).

due to weathering. Intense movement breaks the rocks down to a fine clayey material known as *gouge*. Fault-breccias may be partly or wholly cemented by mineral matter such as quartz or calcite, possibly carrying metallic ores.

Broken fragments of rock or mineralised material from some identifiable bed or lode may be wrenched from the wall of a fault and carried along in the breccia or gouge during movement ('*drag of ore*'). Such fragments can be used to indicate the direction of movement; the continuation of a faulted mineral lode has often been picked up underground by following along the fault-plane the trail of dragged fragments.

Dating of faults. Faulting is dated in the same ways as other types of crustal disturbance. The latest rock found affected by the fault gives the early limit and the oldest rock unaffected gives the later limit. Intrusions of known age may be displaced by the fault or, if younger than the faulting, may traverse the fault without deviation or may invade the fault-plane and chill against it. All these and other similar criteria must be considered when assigning an age to a fault.

It must also be remembered that many faults have moved repeatedly since their first inception, the kind of movement changing according to variations in the stress-field. The reason for the longevity of faults is fairly obvious. A fracture, especially a deep fracture, remains a surface of weakness in the crust and later stresses may be more readily relieved by movement along it than by the initiation of new structures. It is believed by some geologists that many great faults active at the present day, such as those of the African Rift-Valleys, follow very ancient lines of fracturing.

Faulting and land-forms. Where faulting is still in progress, the present-day land-surface is displaced by the movements. Small-scale

490

FIG. 303. Basin and Range Structure.

examples of such displacements are seen after earthquakes when roads, fences and streams may be severed (p. 16). On a larger scale, vertical movements elevate the land-surface on the upthrow side or depress it on the downthrow side, the cumulative difference in level resulting from repeated movements running up to several thousands of feet. The junction of two recently-moved fault-blocks is marked by a step or cliff known as the *fault-scarp*, which is rapidly gullied and worn back by erosion to a normal angle of rest.

Recently faulted regions show distinctive topographical forms. Uplifted blocks bounded on either side by fault-scarps are known as *horsts* (Fig. 304) and can be exemplified by Ruwenzori in East Africa (later, p. 624) and the Sierra Nevada in the United States. The 'Basin and Range' Province of the Western United States shows a series of mountain ridges marking recently uplifted and tilted fault-blocks (Fig. 303). Topographical depressions or valleys resulting directly from fault-action are known as *graben* or *rift-valleys* (Figs. 304, 305).

Of present-day graben the Rhine Valley is probably the best known. This valley is bounded by faults and its floor lies about a thousand feet below the level of the land on either side. The bounding faults are considered to be normal faults and experimental reproduction of the structure points to a collapse under gravity of a central strip during stretching of the crust. The Rift-valleys of Africa (Fig.

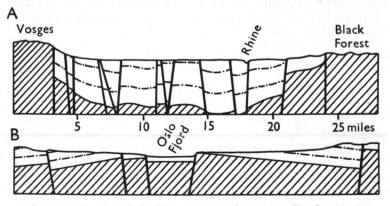

FIG. 304. Cross-sections of horsts and graben; crystalline basement lined. A, the Rhine graben; B, the Oslo graben.

491

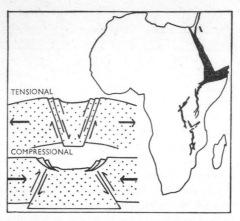

FIG. 305. The African Rift-valleys, with alternative explanations.

305), the Red Sea and the Jordan Valley also owe their origin to the depression of long narrow strips along faults. Opinion is divided as to whether these rift-valleys are due to normal faulting, or to the forcing-down of the central tract by overthrusting along opposed reverse or *ramp*-faults due to compression, followed by marginal collapse of the upthrust blocks along normal faults; some further discussion of rift-valley problems will be found in Chapter 12.

In the more stable parts of the earth's surface, where there are no large-scale movements at the present day, old faults have an indirect effect on the topography. The weakened *fault-lines* are picked out by erosion to form *fault-valleys* such as the Great Glen, coastal gullies, caves and so on. Differential erosion of hard and soft rocks brought together by faulting may produce *fault-line scarps* and contrasts of level on the two sides.

JOINTS

Effects of jointing. A *joint* is a parting-plane which separates or tends to separate a once continuous mass of rock into two parts. Joints differ from faults in that no appreciable movement has taken place along them. They result from fracture due to stresses within the rock-mass and few rock-exposures are devoid of them. Groups of parallel joints are termed *joint-sets*. Intersecting sets produce a *joint-system* and, if the two sets are at right angles, the system is said to be a *conjugate* one.

Jointing is important in the geomorphological field where it may control the shape of a coast-line or the drainage-pattern of a district

492

(see ante, pp. 205-6) and has also considerable economic significance. Joints form passages in otherwise impermeable rocks for water, oil or mineral-bearing solutions. London draws its artesian water supply from the strongly jointed beds of the Chalk (p. 144). The main reservoir rocks of the Iranian oil-field belong to the jointed Asmari Limestone. The distribution of joints has to be carefully considered in areas where it is proposed to construct reservoirs or dam-sites, because of the possibility of leakage once the impounded water accumulates. Well-jointed rocks or mineral deposits are more easily excavated, and considerable saving in explosives may be effected since they are already partly broken up. *Master joints* are persistent joints which can be followed for long distances and which cut through several beds. They may control the style and shape of a quarry, while the spacing between smaller joints and their directions control the size and shape of blocks that can be quarried. Conjugate joint-systems normal to the bedding yield rectangular blocks and so cut down the amount of waste where building-stones are being quarried. Jointing in a coal-seam may determine the lay-out and method of working of a mine and will control the average size, and hence the utility, of the mined coal.

Joints, being planes of weakness in the rocks, are picked out by weathering agents. *Latent* or *blind joints* only appear near the surface, and the upper part of a weathered quarry-face is commonly seen to be more strongly jointed than the lower. As we have seen (p. 132) joints in limestones become widened by solution to form *grikes* and many *pots* are located at joint-intersections. Weathering and decomposition of the rocks down joint-planes may penetrate tens of feet below the normal weathering depth. In construction work, this may necessitate extra and often awkward excavations for foundations.

Classification of joints. Joints are the result of different processes, some tectonic, some not, and it will be convenient to note here joints of many different origins. A first category is produced by *shrinking* of the rock and is not related directly to any tectonic event. Other joints are connected with folds and are manifestations of crustal stresses, either *tensional* or *compressional*.

Shrinkage-joints. Shrinkage-joints, analogous to sun cracks, may develop from the slow drying and lateral shrinkage of sedimentary beds after their deposition. Such joints are normally limited by the bedding-planes and form an irregular pattern when seen in plan. It is possible that the development of such *desiccation-joints* may also control the distribution of similar partings in the beds above when they too reach the stage of joint-production.

Jointing is strongly developed in loess (p. 157) and the formation of vertical columns bounded by joint-planes is characteristic of this fine-grained eolian deposit. This loess-jointing may possibly be encouraged by the presence of vertical tubes once occupied by rootlets or stems of grasses which were buried when the next wind-blown layer was deposited.

Contraction-joints are especially well seen as *columnar jointing* in fine-grained homogeneous igneous rocks occurring as lava-flows or as dykes. Cooling of the sheet of igneous rock results in contraction. This cannot be accommodated by shrinkage of the sheet as a whole because of frictional resistance to movement at the base or sides of the body. The contraction is therefore taken up by the development of tension-joints, formed when the internal stresses due to shrinkage exceed the strength of the rock. As conditions within the sheet are uniform, the shrinkage-cracks tend to develop around equidistantly spaced centres towards which the tensional stresses converge. Interference between centres leads to the production of a honeycomb pattern of joints, in columns having theoretically six sides. This columnar jointing is well seen in the Giant's Causeway in Northern Ireland and in Staffa in the Western Islands of Scotland.

The columns are perpendicular to the cooling surfaces. In flat-lying lavas they are thus vertical, as in Staffa; in vertical dykes they are horizontal, perpendicular to the walls. Curved or radiating columns may develop where conditions are not uniform, or around some nucleus such as the famous McCulloch's Tree embedded in a Mull lava-flow. Columnar jointing may be propagated downwards into baked underlying sediment which will then also tend to break into polygonal prisms.

Sheet-jointing. We may here mention the *sheeted structure* shown by many granite outcrops. This may not be the direct result of shrinkage, but is possibly due to stresses developed by unloading or to the expansion of the near-surface rock by weathering (p. 129). These are tension joints and the relief is upwards. The conformity of the jointing to the hillsides in many parts of the northern granite of Arran is remarkable. Similar relations have also been observed in the granite masses of Devon and Cornwall.

Jointing in igneous intrusions. Complex joint-systems may develop during the emplacement and cooling down of masses or plutons of igneous rocks, as mentioned already (p. 401, Fig. 236). Some of the fractures are caused by contraction on cooling, others result from stresses connected with the emplacement of the mass itself. Many of these were formed while the magma at depth was still mobile and they acted as passages for minor intrusions, such as aplite and pegmatite dykes (p. 574). Other joints developed later and may be lined with hydrothermal minerals (p. 577) or they may show wall-rock alterations effected by hot gases or solutions. Still later joints are barren and it is with difficulty that they can be distinguished from sheet-joints or joints resulting from external stresses.

Conjugate joint-systems together with oblique or gently inclined sets are common in large igneous masses. Erosion guided by these fractures and helped by sheet-joints leads to the formation of wall-like exposures composed of rectangular blocks and showing *mural jointing*. The granite *tors* of Dartmoor and Cornwall present excellent examples of this structure.

Tectonic joints. The orientation of many joint-sets shows a direct relationship to folding and thrusting caused by tectonic movements. Such *tectonic joints* appear to be the visible expression of residual stresses remaining in the rocks after the deformation had ceased. Three sets may be developed (Fig. 306): (i) *longitudinal joints* parallel to the fold-trends and resulting from the flexure of competent beds (ii) *cross-joints* perpendicular to the fold-axes or plunge-directions and (iii) *oblique joints* lying about 45° or less to the direction of tectonic movement; these oblique joints correspond to the theoretical directions of maximum shear, though the two sets are not necessarily equally developed.

Irregular folding or torsion of strata will set up a complex stress-system which may result in the development of conjugate jointing. The pattern can be easily produced experimentally by torsion of a piece of glass but the amount of twist required, even in this brittle substance, is greatly in excess of that seen in bedding in many areas where a clear rectangular joint-pattern exists.

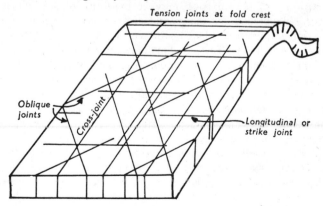

FIG. 306. Jointing in a folded bed.

The control by jointing of the layout of a coal-mine and the utilisation of the coal has already been mentioned. The closely spaced vertical jointing found in coal is called *cleat*; a less well-developed joint set at right angles to the cleat is called the *end*. As mentioned in Chapter 5, the cleat, end and the fusain layers present in bituminous coal determine the cuboidal shape of a piece of coal (Fig. 167). Cleat does not appear in anthracite which breaks irregularly along *slips* directly related to tectonic movements: these slips are a form of fracture-cleavage. Cleat has been the subject of much rather inconclusive research. It appears to be remarkably constant in direction throughout the northern hemisphere, striking north-west or north-north-west. This direction does not vary even when the coal-measures are folded. The strike of the cleat does not always coincide with that of the jointing in the beds above and below the coal-seam, but on the other hand it appears to be constant in seams separated by some thickness of other sediments. Some authorities regard cleat as of tectonic origin, others suggest that it is due to contraction of the coal on loss of volatiles; its extraordinary regularity is difficult to explain by either hypothesis. In despair, other authorities have appealed to tidal movements in the crust.

STRUCTURAL UNITY

Earlier in this chapter we stated that the separation of the structural types into folds, thrusts, faults and joints, with their associated minor structures, was merely a matter of convenience. We have already seen this separation break down at many points, and it is hardly necessary to emphasise the fact that the **structural pattern** resulting from any act of deformation may be made up of many types of structures developed on many scales. We may quote by way of illustration an example already referred to, that of the Hercynian fold-belt of south-west Britain. This belt, only a small part of which enters the British Isles, runs roughly east and west through South Wales, Devon and Cornwall into Southern Ireland (Fig. 307); the local sense of movement is northward towards a stable foreland occupying the northern part of Britain. A system of great asymmetrical folds, facing towards the foreland, corrugates the Palaeozoic strata; it is well revealed in Ireland by large fold inliers of Devonian and Silurian exposed in the anticlinal cores, and in South Wales by the horse-shoe shaped outcrop of Lower Carboniferous framing the synclinal coal-field. Strong marginal thrusts dipping southward are seen in Ireland, and thrusts developing from folds in the South Wales and Bristol Coal-fields (p. 485). Transcurrent faults, formed by

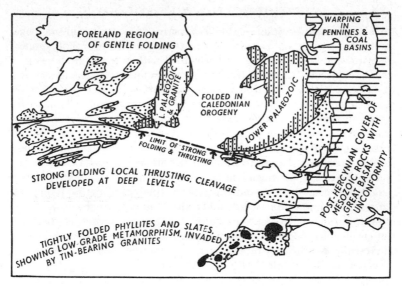

Fig. 307. The Hercynian Orogenic Belt in Britain. Devonian dotted, Carboniferous blank, granite black.

pressure in the same direction as that producing the folds, traverse the South Wales Coal-field (Fig. 373). Towards the interior of the fold-belt, in Devon and Cornwall, the rocks are slightly metamorphosed and show structures of rather different types. In some regions recumbent folds are developed and great inversions of strata are seen. Minor structures such as slaty cleavage, boudinage, intersection- and crystallisation-lineations are widely distributed; these minor structures can often be shown to be congruous with larger folds or genetically related to thrusts. All these various structures, great and small, were formed during the same general period in the late Palaeozoic and all can reasonably be related to the same general pattern of forces.

On a large scale, the orientation of structural elements builds up the structural pattern which can be depicted on maps and stereographic projections. On a small scale, it determines the *fabric* of a rock as seen in a small outcrop, a hand-specimen or a thin slice. *Petrofabric analysis*, or the study of rock fabrics, deals with the orientation and mutual relations of primary surfaces and of tectonically produced structures such as cleavages and lineations; and with the shapes and orientations of the mineral grains making up the rock. Where the individual grains are rotated or deformed during movement, or where they recrystallise under stress, they commonly take

497

up a *preferred orientation* related to the stress direction, and the rocks are then said to be *tectonites*. Such tectonites are normally metamorphic and are more appropriately dealt with in the next chapter.

The **style of structures** resulting from deformation varies, as we have seen, with the distribution and strength of the stresses and with the properties of the rocks and their position in the crust. To take an extreme example, it is obvious that great recumbent folds and rift-valleys are formed in totally different circumstances, the one by plastic deformation associated with compression or gravity sliding, and the other by failure of brittle rocks under tension. On a smaller scale, sharp-angled zigzag folds with fractures at the hinges, for example, reflect an environment notably different from that indicated by irregular and rounded flow-folds, although both might result from the same act of deformation. These variations in structural pattern and style must be interpreted in the light of all the available evidence concerning the history of the crust, and will be referred to again in the last chapter of this book.

FURTHER READING AND REFERENCE

General

Blyth, F. G. H., 1965, *Geological maps and their interpretation*, Arnold.

Hills, E. S., 1963, *Elements of Structural Geology*, Methuen.

Phillips, F. C., 1960, *The use of Stereographic Projection in Structural Geology*, 2nd edit., Arnold, London.

Sitter, L. U. de, 1964, *Structural Geology*, 2nd Edit., McGraw-Hill.

Stoces, B. and C. H. White, 1935, *Structural Geology*, Macmillan.

Folding and associated phenomena

Cloos, E., 1947, 'Oolite deformation in the South Mountain Fold, Maryland', *Bull. Geol. Soc. Amer.*, vol. 58, p. 843.

——, 1947, 'Boudinage', *Trans. Amer. Geophys. Union*, vol. 28, p. 626.

Harrison, J. V. and N. L. Falcon, 1936, 'Gravity collapse structures and mountain ranges as exemplified in South-western Iran', *Quart. Journ. Geol. Soc.*, vol. 92, p. 91.

Hollingworth, S. E., J. H. Taylor and G. A. Kellaway, 1944, 'Large-scale superficial structures in the Northamptonshire Ironstone field', *Quart. Journ. Geol. Soc.*, vol. 100, p. 1.

King, B. C. and N. Rast, 1955, 'Tectonic styles in the Dalradians and Moines of part of the central Highlands of Scotland', *Proc. Geol. Assoc.*, vol. 66, p. 243.

Ramsay, J. G., 1958, 'Superposed folding at Loch Monar, Inverness-shire and Ross-shire', *Quart. Journ. Geol. Soc.*, vol. 113, p. 271.

Shackleton, R. M., 1958, 'Downward-facing structures of the Highland Border', *Quart. Journ. Geol. Soc.*, vol. 113, p. 361.

Wilson, G., 1946, 'The relationship of slaty cleavage and kindred structures to tectonics', *Proc. Geol. Assoc.*, vol. 57, p. 263.

Wilson, G., 1961, 'The tectonic significance of small-scale structures, and their importance to the geologist in the field'. *Ann. Soc. Géol. Belgique*, 84, 423–548.

Faulting

Anderson, E. M., 1951, *Dynamics of faulting and dyke formation*, 2nd edit., Oliver and Boyd, Edinburgh.

Kennedy, W. Q., 1946, 'The Great Glen Fault', *Quart. Journ. Geol. Soc.*, vol. 102, p. 41.

Peach, B. N. and J. Horne, 1914, 'Guide to the Geological Model of the Assynt Mountains', *Geol. Surv. and Museum.*

Price, N. J., 1966, *Fault and joint development in brittle and semi-brittle rock*, Pergamon Press.

Wilson, G., 1951, 'The tectonics of the Tintagel area, N. Cornwall', *Quart. Journ. Geol. Soc.*, vol. 106, p. 393.

9

THE METAMORPHIC ROCKS

INTRODUCTION: THE PLUTONIC SERIES

In earlier chapters we have dealt with two of the three great classes of rocks which together make the earth's crust — firstly the sediments formed by surface-processes and secondly the igneous and pyroclastic rocks produced by magmatic action. In this chapter we begin the study of the third class, the *plutonic series*, which includes those rocks formed in the interior of the crust under the influence of heat and pressure. The raw materials from which rocks of the plutonic series are produced can include every kind of pre-existing sedimentary, igneous and metamorphic rock. The final products are crystalline rocks whose textures and mineral assemblages vary according to the conditions under which they were made.

The plutonic series includes three divisions — the metamorphic rocks, which are the subject of this chapter; and the granites and migmatites which are dealt with in Chapter 10. The **metamorphic rocks** are produced by mineralogical reactions and structural and textural readjustments, which take place while the matrix remains essentially solid. The coherence of the parent rocks is not entirely lost and some of their original structural and chemical characteristics are retained by their metamorphic derivatives.

The **granitic rocks** (using the term in a wide sense) are acid plutonic rocks showing a fairly limited range of composition. Their relations to the surrounding rocks are variable. At one extreme they pass gradually into the country-rocks and their structure appears to be a continuation of that of these rocks; such granites are always associated with broad zones of metamorphic rocks and are considered to have been formed more or less *in situ* by the transformation of pre-existing rocks. They may be said to be products of ultrametamorphism. At the other extreme are granitic bodies showing intrusive relations with their country-rocks in which they appear to have been forcibly emplaced; the granitic material of these bodies has clearly migrated from its place of origin as magma, and sometimes shows obviously igneous structures or is associated with sets of minor intrusions and lavas.

Migmatites are mixed rocks in which two components are intimately mingled, a *host* material representing pre-existing rocks and a *granitic component* which is at least in part derived from an outside source. Migmatites pass insensibly into metamorphic rocks on the one hand and into more or less homogeneous granites on the other and thus link the two great divisions of the plutonic series into a connected whole. At one end of this series are the metamorphic rocks which represent modified and recrystallised assemblages of pre-existing country-rocks. They pass into migmatites or into granites formed *in situ* which are chemically and mineralogically different from the country-rocks, but which may still retain the broad outlines of an inherited structure. These in turn are connected with intrusive granites and their associates, formed by the bodily migration of material in which all structural coherence has been lost.

METAMORPHISM AND ITS CONTROLS

Metamorphism is the process by which rocks within the crust are modified under the influence of heat, pressure and chemical change; the field of metamorphism excludes, on the one hand, the processes of weathering, cementation and the like which are due to superficial agents and, on the other, the related plutonic processes of migmatisation and granite formation. Rocks remain essentially solid during metamorphism and therefore retain some *primary characteristics* inherited from the parent materials; their final structure, texture and composition are controlled partly by the characters of the parent and partly by the conditions of metamorphism.

Metamorphic changes are always concerned with the restoration of equilibrium in rocks subjected to a new environment. The parent materials may include rocks formed under very varied conditions — they might, for example, consist of marine sediments formed at surface temperatures and pressures interbedded with basic lavas which crystallised at very high temperatures — and their original components are likely to be unstable at the temperatures and pressures prevailing in the interior of the crust. Given time, they react in such a way as to produce a new assemblage of minerals stable under the new conditions. But environmental conditions seldom remain constant over large areas or for long periods of time, and the metamorphic reactions may not keep pace with their changes. The rocks may therefore fail to reach a state of equilibrium and may retain *relict* textures, structures and minerals which survive from earlier periods in their development (Fig. 308). As documents of earth-history, metamorphic rocks have a special value because a single rock may retain a record of events spanning long periods of

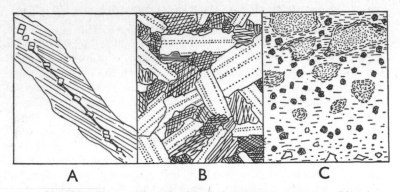

A   B   C

FIG. 308. Preservation of original characters on metamorphism. A, fragments of a belemnite drawn apart during movement and metamorphism; B, preservation of ophitic texture in a metamorphosed dolerite now composed of new hornblende and original plagioclase; C, preservation of graded bedding in a recrystallised greywacke, indicated by the distribution of the new andalusite (dotted) which represents the clay fraction of the graded bed.

geological time, from the original moment of formation of the parent rock to the ending of the last phase of metamorphic change.

Pore-fluids. Although the bulk of each rock remains solid during metamorphism, the interstices between minerals and the parting planes in the rock are generally occupied by aqueous fluids derived largely from the rock itself. There is a constant interchange of material between these *pore-fluids* and the crystal-lattices with which they are in contact, this interchange providing the chief means by which new crystals are formed and old ones broken down. The pore-fluids also provide a medium in which material in solution can diffuse through metamorphic rocks and they thus assist in the rearrangement of substances already present, the introduction of new material and the escape of surplus elements.

Temperature. The physical factors controlling the environment of metamorphism are the temperature, the confining pressure and the stress-conditions. *Temperature* is perhaps the most important variable, and metamorphism depending simply on high temperatures is known as *thermal metamorphism*. At temperatures below 100–200° C, minerals may remain out of equilibrium with their surroundings over millions of years, because reactions at these temperatures are too sluggish to have any appreciable effect; the survival of high-temperature minerals in igneous rocks exposed at the surface illustrates this state of affairs. With rise in temperature, reactions become more vigorous, and new mineral assemblages appear. At temperatures over 700° C, the more fusible components of the rocks become fluid, and metamorphism passes into other processes. In rocks of a particular composition different minerals come into equilibrium at successively higher temperatures and the mineral composition of the rock therefore provides a rough guide to the temperature at which reaction took place. It is found that such temperature-assemblages often show a zonal arrangement in the field which expresses a thermal gradient existing at the time of metamorphism. Such an arrangement is sometimes taken to indicate a *progressive metamorphism*, but it should be realised that the demonstrable progression is one in space and that a time-sequence is not necessarily implied. When the peak of metamorphism is passed and the rocks begin to cool again, lower-temperature minerals may appear once more, but as the energy of the system is now diminishing, they do not as a rule entirely replace the earlier-formed assemblages. Metamorphism which takes place on a falling temperature-scale, or in other circumstances where high-temperature minerals are replaced by lower-temperature minerals, is known as *retrogressive metamorphism.*

Pressure. The confining or *hydrostatic pressure* in the crust increases with the load and therefore with the thickness of the cover; at depths of 20 kms., the pressure is of the order of 6,000 atmospheres. High pressures change the physical properties of many rocks, rendering them ductile and capable of flow. They tend to inhibit reactions which involve a volume increase by liberating gas, such as the breakdown of calcite with the release of carbon dioxide. Conversely, pressure may favour the development of dense minerals with closely-packed atomic lattices, such as garnet and kyanite.

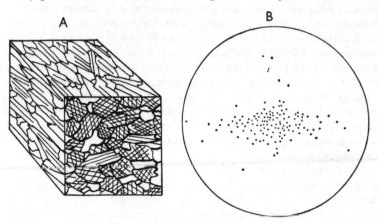

Fig. 309. Preferred orientation in a tectonite. A, block of hornblende-schist; B, stereographic projection of the c-axes of the hornblendes.

Many rocks undergoing metamorphism are subjected also to *directed pressures* or *stress* due to earth-movements connected with folding, faulting and similar structural changes. Stress acting on cool rocks results in a mechanical break-down or *cataclasis* (p. 528). At higher temperatures, or in the presence of active pore-fluids, stress may speed up crystal-growth by providing new surfaces at which reaction can take place and so may lead to a constructive metamorphism. Rocks in which crystallisation took place under the influence of stress are known as *tectonites*. Their minerals often show a *preferred orientation* (Fig. 309) and their *fabric-pattern* is related to the stress-field (p. 515).

Chemical factors. Metamorphism due solely to heat and pressure leaves the total composition of the rocks unchanged and is said to be *isochemical*. *Metasomatic metamorphism* or *metasomatism*, on the other hand, involves a change in the bulk composition of the rock and is generally connected with the migration of alien material through the pore-fluids. Metasomatism on a local scale often results from the exchange of material within the metamorphic complex itself; on a regional scale, it may be connected with the introduction of material expelled from a solidifying magma, or of material rising from deep in the crust.

The Geological Setting of Metamorphism

Before metamorphism can take place, rocks must be subjected to elevated temperatures and, as a rule, reactions must be facilitated by the effects of stress or the presence of active pore-fluids or both. In stable parts of the crust where the thermal gradients are low, conditions appropriate for metamorphism are only attained near the base of the crust. Even in many unstable regions, it can be shown that certain rocks have been buried to depths of 5–10 kms. without undergoing effective metamorphism; such rocks are seen, for example, in the Lower Palaeozoic of Wales where the basal members of a very thick sedimentary succession, brought to the surface by folding, show only a very low grade of metamorphism. We may conclude that metamorphism takes place at moderate depths in the crust only in special geological circumstances; four such geological environments can be recognised, connected with four types of metamorphism, as follow:

(1) **Contact-metamorphism** is caused by the heat of magmatic intrusions and is seen in the *metamorphic aureoles* which surround large igneous bodies. Contact-metamorphism is predominantly thermal in type, but its products may be modified by the stresses set up during the intrusion and by the metasomatic effects of volatiles escaping from the magma.

(2) **Autometamorphism** takes place within igneous bodies during the period of cooling; this type of metamorphism was briefly dealt with in Chapter 7 and will not be referred to again in the present chapter.

(3) **Dislocation-metamorphism** takes place in zones subjected to strong earth-movements, such as the Moine Thrust-Zone already described (p. 477). Stress is here the principal control and many of the products are cataclastic rocks; but heat supplied by friction or regional high temperatures may bring about recrystallisation and the development of tectonites.

(4) **Regional metamorphism** is related to geological processes operating on a far larger scale. It takes place in active segments of the crust where high temperatures and strong stresses prevail at unusually shallow depths and is primarily a phenomenon of the *mobile belts* or *orogenic belts*. Rocks formed by regional metamorphism are thus found in the great fold-belts of the world where they are often associated with granites and migmatites, the other members of the Plutonic Series. Regionally metamorphosed rocks make tracts of country often a hundred miles broad and many hundreds of miles in length; by comparison with these great outcrops, the products of contact- and dislocation-metamorphism fall into place as local and accidental developments, mainly of interest in supplying relatively simple and small-scale examples of metamorphic phenomena.

In regional metamorphism, all the metamorphic agents tend to work together. The period of folding often overlaps with the period of metamorphism, and many of the products are therefore tectonites. The deep disturbance of the crust produced by orogeny favours the migration of material and so leads to changes in the chemical environment and to widespread metasomatism. The scale of the metamorphism is matched by the length of time over which it continues, and the effects of late phases are often found superimposed on those of earlier phases.

GENERAL CHARACTERS OF METAMORPHIC ROCKS

The parent rocks. Although any kind of crustal rock may suffer metamorphism and produce a distinctive metamorphic derivative, most of the metamorphic rocks are naturally derived from a small number of common sedimentary and igneous parents. The common metamorphic types can be classified as follows:

A. **Of sedimentary origin:**
  (1) **Pelitic rocks** derived from argillaceous sediments
  (2) **Psammitic rocks** derived from sandstones

(3) **Semi-pelitic rocks** derived from impure sandstones
(4) **Metamorphosed greywackes**
(5) **Calcareous rocks,** including **marbles** derived from pure lime-stones and **calc-silicate rocks** derived from impure limestones or other limy sediments.

B. **Of igneous origin:**
(1) **Basic rocks** derived from dolerites and basalts
(2) **Acid rocks** derived from granites and allied rocks.

The parentage of a metamorphic rock may be revealed by various lines of evidence. Diagnostic primary structures or textures are often preserved. Relics of pillow-structure, for example, may serve to identify a lava, while original bedding-structures such as current-bedding, graded bedding and slumping-structures, and the outlines of the larger grains, pebbles and fossils may remain visible in meta-morphosed sedimentary rocks. Where primary structures and textures have been entirely destroyed by recrystallisation or by deformation, the chemical composition of a metamorphic rock still serves as a guide to its origin; but it must be remembered that considerable chemical change may have taken place during meta-somatism.

The *primary characters* of metamorphic rocks have a two-fold importance. They provide a key to the pre-metamorphic history of the rocks, and at the same time they provide a standard of reference by which the metamorphic changes themselves may be assessed. The determination of the parentage and primary characters of metamorphic rocks generally rests on field-evidence, and careful search should be made for such evidence while mapping is in progress.

METAMORPHIC TEXTURES

Metamorphic minerals grow in rocks that are already solid, and compete for space with their neighbours throughout their develop-ment. Their characteristic growth-textures or *crystalloblastic textures* differ in a number of ways from the textures resulting from crystal-lisation from magma. The minerals are generally *anhedral* (p. 388) and grain boundaries are often sinuous or interlocking. Haphazard inclusions of one mineral in another are common and, as the majority of minerals crystallise over the same period of time, a mineral may both enclose and be enclosed by grains of a single species (Fig. 310).

Good crystal faces may be shown by one or a few minerals in a metamorphic rock when the remainder are anhedral. These *eu-hedral* minerals are not necessarily of early crystallisation —

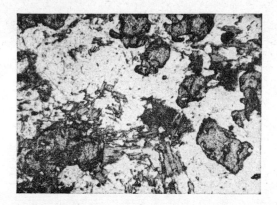

FIG. 310. Metamorphic Texture, as illustrated by a contact-metamorphosed pelitic rock; the constituents are garnet, biotite, quartz and feldspar, × 35.

sometimes they are demonstrably late — but they are for some reason able to establish their own crystal form against the competition of their growing neighbours. Minerals such as garnet, staurolite and tourmaline, which most commonly show euhedral outlines, are for the most part those in which the space-lattice shows a dense packing of ions, as in the nesosilicates. Minerals with lattices made up of chains or bands, such as the amphiboles, often form needle-like or *acicular* grains, since growth takes place most readily along the length of the bands, but they seldom show well-developed crystal faces. Similarly, the phyllosilicates such as the micas generally have a flaky habit. Minerals such as quartz and feldspar which have an open continuous lattice make rounded, flattened or entirely irregular grains.

The *grain-size* of a metamorphic rock is influenced by so many factors that few general rules can be stated. In the finest-grained rocks such as the slates, the individual minerals can hardly be distinguished even with the aid of a microscope; in the coarsest-grained, the larger minerals may be many centimetres across. Low-temperature metamorphism generally produces fine-grained rocks, and strong stress, by promoting mechanical breakdown, also tends to limit the grain-size. Prolonged metamorphism tends to produce coarse textures, while the coarsest rocks are generally those formed under the influence of active pore-fluids — marbles and calc-silicate rocks whose crystallisation may be aided by the presence of abundant carbon dioxide are often very coarse-grained.

Many metamorphic rocks contain large grains or *porphyroblasts* of a different order of size from the minerals in the body of the rock.

507

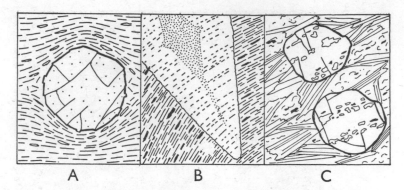

A   B   C

FIG. 311. Porphyroblasts. A, garnet porphyroblast distorting the pattern of the groundmass; B, andalusite (chiastolite) porphyroblast enclosing undisturbed trails of groundmass material; C, garnet porphyroblasts in mica-schist, revealing the original lamination by the arrangement of their quartz inclusions.

These large minerals may push aside the smaller minerals surrounding them as they grow (Fig. 311). Porphyroblastic minerals growing in a finer-grained rock must draw material which they require from the rock surrounding them and must expel from the area that they occupy elements not needed to form their crystal lattices.

Porphyroblastic growth demonstrates the mobility of material in metamorphic environments and provides a small-scale example of the phenomenon of *metamorphic differentiation* which we shall consider later in another connection.

Porphyroblastic minerals often contain many inclusions and when crowded with such inclusions are said to be *poikiloblastic* or to exhibit *sieve-structure*. Some inclusions represent by-products of reactions producing the porphyroblasts and may be arranged in a regular pattern related to the lattice-structure of the host mineral; in chiastolite, a variety of the mineral andalusite, dark dusty inclusions accumulate in two planes diagonal to the prism faces and form a cross when seen in basal section (Fig. 311). Other inclusions represent accidental grains engulfed during growth, and these often keep their original positions; *trails* of such inclusions preserve relict structures within the porphyroblasts which are often of value in deciphering the metamorphic history of the containing rock (Fig. 311, see later, pp. 510–12).

Age relations in metamorphic minerals. From what has already been said, it will be clear that the *order of growth* of metamorphic minerals must be established by means of criteria very different from those used to determine the order of crystallisation in magmatic

A

B

FIG. 312. Timing in metamorphic crystallisation. A, A large, originally single, grain of garnet is being split up and replaced by fine-grained hornblende, in a garnet-amphibolite, × 4. B, Late muscovite plates, orientated diagonally across the slide, oblique to the dominant texture, × 40.

rocks. In rocks which reached equilibrium, no relict textures or minerals may remain, and the minerals of these rocks must be regarded as effectively contemporaneous. In rocks which failed to reach equilibrium (Fig. 312), early minerals may survive as cores rimmed round or partly replaced by later species. The new mineral may preserve unchanged the outline of the original grain, and is then said to form a *pseudomorph* of the mineral it replaces. Minerals which develop late in the history of the rock may grow along grain-boundaries, or in cracks and cleavages in earlier minerals or may form ragged poikiloblastic grains which either distort the fabric of the rock or are obviously superimposed upon it.

Crystallisation in relation to movement. Another means of establishing age-relations among metamorphic minerals is available where the rocks have suffered deformation. The effects of earth-movements are recorded by the presence of minor structures such as cleavages, lineations and small folds (Chapter 8), and it is often possible to determine the age of particular minerals relative to these structures. Some simple examples will illustrate the possibilities. Let us suppose that a mica-rich metamorphic rock is crumpled by a series of minute folds. The crumpling may be entirely *post-crystalline*, in which case the minerals suffer mechanical deformation; tough

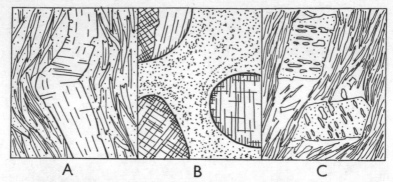

A   B   C

FIG. 313. Post-crystalline Movements. A, kyanite porphyroblast fractured, bent and traversed by glide planes, Donegal Main Granite aureole; B, early pyroxene grains, later rounded, set in a fine-grained calcite matrix of later crystallisation, Tiree Marble; C, rotated staurolite porphyroblasts with trails divergent from the schistosity of the groundmass, Donegal Granite Aureole.

minerals are fractured, the flexible micas are bent over the crests of the folds and porphyroblasts are bodily rotated so that their trails are no longer in continuity with the structure of the groundmass (Fig. 313). When the movement is *para-crystalline*, the minerals continue to recrystallise during the development of the folds. Deformed and undeformed minerals may be seen together and the new minerals may show a strong *preferred orientation* related to the pattern of the stresses; porphyroblasts continue to grow as they are rotated and their trails of inclusions may show S-shaped or even spiral twists (Fig. 314). Finally, when movement is *pre-crystalline*,

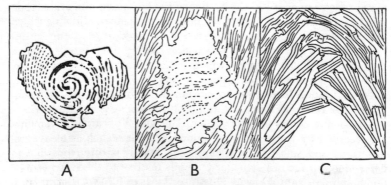

A   B   C

FIG. 314. Para-crystalline Movements. A, snowball garnet with spirally arranged inclusions; B, albite porphyroblast with curved trails continuous with the groundmass texture; C, distorted and undistorted mica-plates in a fold crest.

510

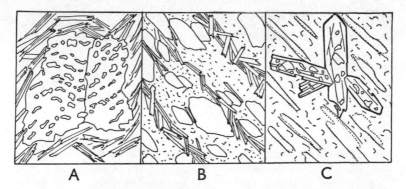

A   B   C

FIG. 315. Pre-crystalline Movements. A, two differently orientated
staurolite porphyroblasts enclosing quartz grains arranged in a
continuous fold-pattern, Unst, Shetland; B, crystallisation of unorientated micas along planes of fracture-cleavage in greywacke,
Collieston, Aberdeenshire; C, unorientated hornblende porphyroblasts in a groundmass of highly deformed quartz and feldspar, Sleat,
Skye.

mineral growth takes place in static conditions. The new minerals
may show a *mimetic* orientation parallel to some pre-existing
structure, or they may lie at random. Mica-flakes at the crest of a
fold form a polygonal arch in which each crystal is undeformed.
Porphyroblasts are superimposed on the folded structure and their
trails are continuous with the pattern of the groundmass (Fig. 315);

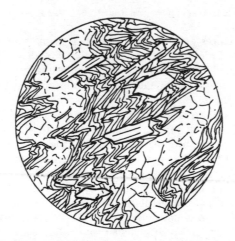

FIG. 316. Two phases of crystallisation. Late mica porphyroblasts
growing along a strain-slip cleavage which distorts the schistosity
formed by the early micas.

R2   511

this arrangement of the trails gives the *helicitic* texture. In rocks with a complex history, more than one generation of structures may be present — an early cleavage, for example, may be crossed by a later strain-slip cleavage (Fig. 316) — and by determining the relation of each mineral to the appropriate phase of deformation it becomes possible to build up the history of a long sequence of crystallisation and deformation.

Texture types. The general aspect of the texture of a metamorphic rock depends to some extent on its mineral composition — a rock rich in flaky micas has inevitably a different appearance from a rock composed of granular carbonates, even when both were metamorphosed in the same environment. But in spite of the modifications induced by composition, however, the principal factors determining the texture are those which control the conditions of metamorphism. For our purposes, we may recognise seven types of texture, as follow:

(1) **Cataclastic textures** result from the mechanical breakdown of rocks under stress. They are characterised by the presence of bent and fractured minerals in mechanical contact with one another, and are the only metamorphic textures in which mineral growth is not a dominant factor.

(2) **Hornfelsic textures** are characteristic of rocks formed in an environment free from directed stress. The majority of minerals occur as equidimensional grains welded into a regular mosaic, while inequidimensional minerals such as micas have a random orientation (Fig. 310). *Hornfelses* are massive, tough rocks with a more or less isotropic fabric.

(3) **Slaty textures** are characterised by a strong parallel structure produced by the alignment of minute flaky minerals (Fig. 317). The *slates* are very fine-grained and part readily along the cleavage to yield smooth platy fragments made somewhat lustrous by the abundance of micas.

(4) **Phyllitic textures** are again characterised by a very strong parallel orientation of minerals and give rise to silky-looking leaf-shaped or lenticular fragments. *Phyllites* (Fig. 317) are somewhat coarser-grained than slates, but the constituent minerals are not as a rule distinguishable with the naked eye.

(5) **Schistose textures** are exhibited by moderately coarse-grained rocks in which a parallel structure or *schistosity* is produced by the orientation of inequidimensional minerals. *Schists* are normally rich in micas or other flaky or acicular minerals; they are generally coarse enough for the grains to be distinguished with the naked eye and have a clean crystalline appearance. They may be pelitic, calcareous or basic in character.

A

B

Fig. 317. A, Slate. Thin section showing the fine-grained slaty groundmass and a pyrite porphyroblast (black) with a 'pressure-shadow' of quartz, × 15. B, Phyllite. A groundmass of sericite and chlorite showing schistosity and strain-slip cleavage, and containing chloritoid porphyroblasts that were formed during the production of these textures, × 15.

Slates, phyllites and schists are normally produced by metamorphism in the presence of directed stress and are therefore tectonites. The characteristic feature in each class is the preferred orientation of minerals to which the cleavage or schistosity is due. The alignment of micas and other similar minerals can be readily observed under the microscope because it involves a *dimensional* orientation of the grains. Granular minerals, such as quartz, cannot show a strong dimensional orientation, but in many tectonites they have a preferred orientation *of the crystal lattice* which can be established by the use of special microscopic techniques (p. 515). The whole internal fabric of the rock is thus bound up with the conditions of stress prevailing during its metamorphism.

(6) **Granular textures** are shown by a wide variety of rocks rich in minerals which have a roughly equidimensional habit. Marbles and quartzites, for example, are generally more or less granular, though the details of their textures vary according to the conditions of their metamorphism. Granular rocks formed in the absence of stress have isotropic fabrics.

In tectonites, any inequidimensional minerals, such as micas, scattered through the rock may assume a parallel orientation which produces a rough parting or schistosity. Minerals like quartz which are normally equidimensional may be flattened or elongated and may show a preferred orientation of the lattice-structure; the term *granulitic texture* is sometimes used to describe textures of this kind. The name *granulite* is applied by some geologists to a variety of granular or granulitic rocks; by others, it is restricted to rocks containing certain specific minerals (p. 539) and in view of this confusion it is as well to avoid the term or to define clearly the sense in which it is being used.

(7) **Gneissose textures** are characterised by a rough banding or streaking of the minerals or by the presence of an irregular parting or *foliation*. *Gneisses* are coarse rocks in which the majority of minerals are upwards of 2 mms. in diameter; the name is usually restricted to rocks showing visible feldspar. *Augen-gneisses* show large eye-shaped feldspars or clusters of feldspar grains in a darker groundmass.

METAMORPHIC STRUCTURES

The structural forms of bodies of metamorphic rocks depend, in the first place, on those of the parent rocks. A sequence of metamorphosed sediments maps out as a succession of parallel bands of different composition, a pre-existing dyke maps as a discordant band, a large gabbro intrusion as a homogeneous lenticular or rounded body, and so on. Examination of well-exposed areas of metamorphic rocks in glaciated hills or sea-coasts shows, however, that these rocks exhibit distinctive styles of architecture unlike any shown by assemblages of unmetamorphosed sedimentary or igneous rocks. The final pattern is the result of structural changes imposed on the original forms during the metamorphic period itself.

The structural changes accompanying metamorphism are of two kinds: the first kind is due to the bodily movement and distortion of material under the influence of external stresses: and the second to the chemical activity of material migrating piecemeal through an unmoving framework of solid rock. Structural changes due to stress are of tectonic origin, and we have dealt with many aspects of these changes already; it is only necessary to add a few points concerned specifically with the tectonics of metamorphic rocks. Heat and high pressure increase plasticity, and rocks undergoing metamorphism therefore tend to yield by flow rather than by rupture and to develop folds rather than faults. When a series of mixed rocks is deformed together, the more rigid types tend to be broken up and enclosed in the more mobile; since recrystallisation accompanies movement, fractures are healed and new contacts welded, so that the final product shows no sign of mechanical disruption. *Tectonic inclusions* produced by differential movements in metamorphic rocks tend to form stream-lined fish-shaped bodies, ranging from many miles to an inch or so in size (Fig. 330).

Metamorphic rocks react to stress by continuous adjustments of their microscopic fabric and thereby differ from non-metamorphic rocks in which stress is largely relieved by movement along bedding, fracture-cleavage and other parting-planes. The structural pattern of the deformed rocks is therefore revealed not only by the orientation of folds, cleavages and other structures which can be examined in the field, but also by the *microfabric*, or the arrangement of individual grains of microscopic dimensions; very often, the same general pattern is carried through from the scale of the largest folds to that of the microfabric. We can illustrate the connection between major structures and microfabric by reference to slates. The cleavage of these rocks is generally orientated parallel to the axial planes of folds which may be many miles in width; but the cleavage is itself produced by the parallel orientation of the minute micaceous minerals in the rock, and there is therefore a direct link between the microfabric and the largest structures of the area (Fig. 284).

Other kinds of microfabric are most readily revealed by statistical analysis. A thin section of the rock to be investigated is cut so that the plane of the section bears a known geometrical relationship to the geographical co-ordinates or to a measured megascopic structure such as a lineation. This section is mounted under a microscope on a *universal stage*, a device by means of which it can be tilted into any position, and by suitable methods the orientation of a particular crystallographic direction in the mineral chosen for study is determined. The orientation of the same direction in a large number of grains within the slide is measured and plotted on a stereographic projection; the plane of the projection coincides with the plane of the thin section and the conventional assumption that the viewer looks down into the lower half of a spherical projection is adopted. An example of a *fabric diagram* constructed in this manner is given in Fig. 309 where the crystallographic c-axes of hornblendes in a hornblende-schist are seen to form a pronounced *maximum* indicating the preferred orientation of the crystals; in this instance, the oriented hornblendes produce a crystallisation lineation visible in the field, and the microfabric can therefore be linked to the regional structural pattern.

A common fabric-pattern revealed by quartz is shown in Fig. 318. The orientations of several hundred crystallographic c-axes of quartz-grains from a single specimen are plotted on a projection

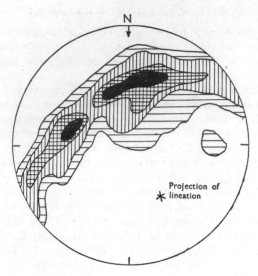

FIG. 318. Petrofabric diagram of quartz c-axes in a metamorphosed psammite. Diagram shows a girdle-fabric, c-axes lying in a plane dipping north-westwards, almost perpendicular to the direction of the lineation. See Fig. 151 for explanation of contouring.

oriented so that the points of the compass fall as shown in the figure. The quartz shows a *girdle-fabric*, the points falling on a great circle about a line plunging south-eastward. A striation-lineation visible in the field has roughly the same direction. Its relation to the girdle of c-axes can be visualised by thinking of these axes as spokes of a wheel radiating from the lineation-direction.

Metamorphic differentiation. Metamorphic structures of a different kind are produced as a result of the migration of material through the pore-fluids. We have already seen a small-scale example of such structures in the growth of porphyroblasts; large grains of a particular mineral, say garnet, are built up in a hitherto homogeneous rock by the migration of ions towards and away from certain centres of crystallisation. When the process is brought about by a rearrangement of material already in the rock, it is known as *metamorphic differentiation*. On a larger scale, metamorphic differentiation may lead to conspicuous structural changes. A pre-existing banding may be accentuated or a new banding produced by the segregation of certain minerals along parallel planes; differentiation taking place during movement commonly produces a secondary banding parallel to a cleavage or schistosity. Material which readily enters into the pore-fluids and is easily mobilised may migrate to fractures or planes

516

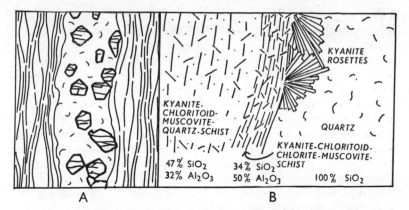

FIG. 319. Metamorphic differentiation. A, garnet-quartz segregation in mica-schist, Main Granite aureole, Donegal; B, diagrammatic representation of quartz-kyanite veins, Unst; SiO_2 and Al_2O_3 percentages of the country-rock and the selvage near the quartz-kyanite veins are given and demonstrate the impoverishment in silica of the selvages.

of weakness and consolidate again as *segregation-veins, exudates* or *sweat-outs* (Fig. 319). The composition of these veins varies according to that of the rocks from which they are derived. *Quartz-veins* are by far the most widespread types, being found especially in pelitic and psammitic rocks. They often carry minor amounts of other minerals present in the parent rock — chlorite-schists have been found to contain quartz-chlorite veins, kyanite-schists may contain quartz-kyanite veins and so on (Fig. 319). *Calcite veins* are abundant in limestones and *quartzo-feldspathic veins*, some of which are coarse enough

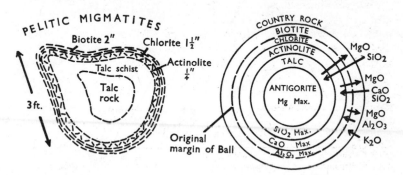

FIG. 320. Metamorphic differentiation in the zoned balls of Unst. A, an example; B, diagram showing the ideal arrangement of the zones and the suggested movements of material in their production.

517

to be called *pegmatites*, appear as segregation products of high-grade gneisses.

Further effects of metamorphic differentiation are commonly shown at the contacts of two rocks of different composition. Migration of material across the border often leads to the development of a *reaction-zone* which may be seen, for example, surrounding a pebble in a metamorphosed conglomerate or a chert nodule in a limestone. Spectacular reaction-zones sometimes appear at the contacts of serpentine intrusions, where there is a strong chemical difference between the serpentine and its pelitic or psammitic country-rock. Examples of *zoned balls* derived from serpentine from Unst in the Shetland Islands are shown in Fig. 320; each serpentine core is sheathed in concentric zones of talc, chlorite, actinolite and biotite, the migrations involved in the formation of these monomineralic zones being indicated in the figure.

MINERAL ASSEMBLAGES

Since metamorphic rocks are formed under variable conditions, and from many kinds of parent rocks, they contain altogether a very large number of minerals, many of which do not occur at all in igneous rocks. The derivatives of each type of parent rock naturally contain a more limited suite of minerals and we may illustrate this point by

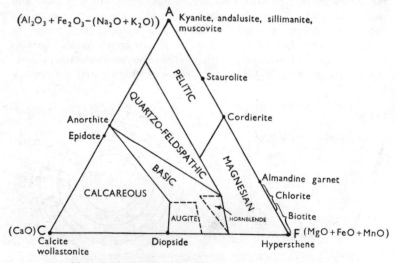

FIG. 321. ACF-diagram, showing the fields of the original raw materials for metamorphism and the composition of some metamorphic minerals. The ACF triangular plot shows variations of major components other than SiO_2 which is assumed to be present in excess.

the diagram showing the relation between mineral- and rock-compositions (Fig. 321). Pelitic rocks are characterised by aluminous silicates such as micas, the Al_2SiO_5-minerals — andalusite, kyanite and sillimanite —, garnet, cordierite, chloritoid and staurolite. Calcareous rocks contain carbonates and lime-silicates, formed by reaction between the carbonates and the impurities present in the original limestone. Basic rocks are rich in ferromagnesian minerals such as chlorite, hornblende or pyroxene. Within a single rock, the *mineral assemblage* generally includes no more than 6–8 major components, with a number of accessory minerals such as apatite, sphene, zircon and iron oxides. In rocks which reached equilibrium, the number of minerals is controlled by definite chemical laws derivable from the Phase Rule. In rocks which failed to reach equilibrium, a larger number of species may be present and signs of reaction such as those already discussed may be visible.

Variations in mineral composition from one rock to another may be due to two causes, working independently or in conjunction:

(1) *When the physical conditions of metamorphism are uniform* variations in stable mineral assemblages are related solely to chemical variations. Pelites contain one set of minerals, basic rocks another and so on. Rocks of every composition which reached equilibrium under the same general conditions of metamorphism are said to be of the same **metamorphic facies** (p. 548) or **isophysical.**

(2) *When the physical conditions of metamorphism change*, rocks of the same composition or **isochemical rocks** develop different mineral assemblages according to the temperature and pressure. The minerals formed depend on the **grade** of metamorphism, *low-grade* rocks being produced at low temperatures and *high-grade* rocks at high temperatures. In any terrain undergoing metamorphism, there is likely to be a broad zoning of environments controlled largely by the temperature gradient. We may therefore recognise in the products a number of *zones of metamorphism* each of which shows mineral assemblages appropriate to the environment (pp. 541–5). The zone-boundaries are surfaces of equal metamorphic grade or *isograds*. All the rocks within each zone were metamorphosed under approximately the same conditions and are therefore of the same facies.

The concepts of metamorphic facies and of metamorphic zoning are of great value when it comes to interpreting the history of an association of metamorphic rocks. Both concepts rest on the same fundamental observations and they differ only in the line of approach. The facies principle is concerned chiefly with rocks in equilibrium, and is most useful in studies of metamorphic environments.

CLASSIFICATION AND NOMENCLATURE

Most metamorphic rocks are named first of all according to their texture, and specific varieties are then distinguished by prefixing the names of conspicuous mineral components; examples of such names are pyroxene-hornfels, garnet-mica-schist, hornblende-augen-gneiss and so on. A few rock-names such as amphibolite, denoting a rock composed of hornblende and plagioclase, are strictly defined in terms of mineral components, but on the whole the nomenclature of metamorphic rocks is more flexible than that of igneous rocks.

No single system of grouping and classification is available and geologists tend to adopt whatever scheme best suits the purpose of their investigation. Rocks can be grouped according to the *nature of the parent* (p. 505), according to *facies* (p. 548) or according to the *process* by which they were metamorphosed. The final interpretation of any metamorphic rock must always take into account its geological setting as well as its mineralogical and textural characteristics. In the remainder of this chapter, we deal separately with the processes of contact-, dislocation- and regional metamorphism, considering in turn the products of each of the main types of parent rock.

CONTACT-METAMORPHISM

When a body of magma is intruded, heat flows out from it into the country-rocks and sets up a temperature gradient declining away from the contact. A minor intrusion such as a dyke may harden and discolour the rocks within a few inches of its margin, while a large plutonic intrusion may produce a coarsely crystalline aureole a mile or more in width of outcrop. The aureole is generally zoned, the highest-grade rock appearing nearest to the contact.

Hornfelses are the most common products of contact-metamorphism. They show granoblastic textures reflecting the tranquil conditions of metamorphism in an environment where heat is the dominating influence, and frequently carry ragged and sieved porphyroblasts of one or more minerals. The hornfelses often fade out away from the intrusion into *spotted rocks* which are only partially recrystallised. Towards the igneous contact, the hornfelses may become coarser and pass into granular rocks or gneisses. Their characteristic textures may be modified to schistose textures by movements connected with the emplacement of the intrusion, resulting in the production of *contact-schists*. Xenoliths picked up in lavas or small intrusions are occasionally melted as a result of rapid heating; they consolidate to form *buchites* in which corroded grains of the original minerals are set in a glassy or cryptocrystalline groundmass containing minute rod-like new crystals.

Metasomatic changes are brought about in many contact-aureoles as a result of the activity of substances emanating from the magmatic intrusion. Parts of the volatile fraction, and the more mobile residue of the magma, may diffuse into the country-rocks and there react with material already present. At the same time, discrete bodies of fluid derived from the magma penetrate the aureole in the form of dykes, veins and other small intrusions. A very widespread chemical change, not usually classified as metasomatic, is the progressive *loss of water* during the heating of the aureole. It is made evident by the disappearance of (OH)-bearing minerals and the appearance of anhydrous high-temperature minerals such as pyroxenes.

The effects of contact-metamorphism in **pelitic rocks** can be best dealt with by considering the evolution of pelites in certain contact aureoles. The *Insch Gabbro* of north-east Scotland (Fig. 322) intrudes late Pre-Cambrian greywackes and pelites of the Dalradian Series, and produces a contact-aureole some two miles wide at its northern margin; its southern margin is dislocated and shows no metamorphism. The pelitic country-rocks which form the starting-point for the series are *slates* which had already suffered a low-grade regional metamorphism. They are strongly cleaved rocks made up of very minute flakes of white mica and chlorite, with interstitial grains of quartz and specks of iron oxide and graphite. When traced towards the gabbro (Fig. 322), the slates pass into *spotted slates* containing rounded nodules and prisms a few millimetres across. Under the microscope, the main part of the rock appears almost unchanged. The spots growing in this matrix are vague structures so clouded with dusty inclusions that they can hardly be identified. Some show rectangular outlines in cross-section and represent chiastolite crystals choked with undigested material from the groundmass;

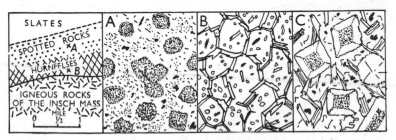

Fig. 322. Contact-metamorphism, the Insch aureole, Aberdeenshire.
A, spotted rock; B, cordierite-hornfels; C, andalusite-hornfels.
The positions of A and B are shown in the index map.

others appear to be cordierite. Towards the contact, the spots become better defined and begin to clear themselves of inclusions and display the characteristic optical properties of *andalusite* and *cordierite*. Pale *biotite* appears as large, very ragged flakes sieved with droplets of quartz and specks of dust.

In the inner parts of the aureole the pelitic rocks recrystallise entirely to form *cordierite-andalusite hornfelses*. The original chlorite disappears and its place is taken by biotite which, with muscovite, quartz and minor amounts of feldspar, forms a granular mosaic. Cordierite occurs as large, shapeless grains, now fairly free from inclusions, while andalusite appears in hypidiomorphic prisms; the large biotites remain ragged and sieved.

The *Ardara intrusion* of north-west Donegal is a granitic body which is in contact on its northern side with a mixed sequence of pelitic, semi-pelitic and calcareous rocks of the Dalradian Series. In the pelitic rocks a number of metamorphic zones can be distinguished from the margin of the aureole inwards:

(i) A zone of incomplete recrystallisation in which the bulk of the rock retains minerals and textures formed during an earlier phase of regional metamorphism. Chlorite-porphyroblasts characterise the outermost parts of the zone and inwards biotite appears in its stead.

(ii) An *andalusite-zone* of completely recrystallised hornfelses and schists. The rocks contain hypidiomorphic andalusites up to six inches in length set in a groundmass of biotite, muscovite, quartz, feldspar, garnet and staurolite.

(iii) A narrow *sillimanite-zone* of coarse hornfelses containing tufts of small sillimanite needles which appear to grow by the replacement of biotite (Fig. 323). Andalusite is not present, and at the border of the andalusite and sillimanite zones sillimanite fibres can be seen growing on the andalusite porphyroblasts. At the granite contact itself, *cordierite* appears in association with sillimanite in some parts of the aureole.

The contact-rocks of the Ardara aureole are strongly folded by stresses related to the emplacement of the granite, and under the microscope it is evident that para-crystalline movements accompanied the growth of many of the minerals; porphyroblasts are locally rotated and micas may show a preferred orientation. Some rocks also show evidence of a phase of post-crystalline movement accompanied by a retrogressive metamorphism. The andalusites are broken and partially replaced by mats of white mica known as *shimmer aggregate*, while the groundmass is traversed by shear-planes along which grow flakes of late muscovite.

A   B

Fig. 323. Contact Metamorphism, the Ardara Complex, Donegal. A, Andalusite-hornfels. A large porphyroblast of andalusite in a schistose groundmass, ×15. B, Sillimanite-hornfels. A cluster of sillimanite needles (fibrolite) runs obliquely through the centre of the field; garnet seen at the bottom of the slide, ×45.

In both the aureoles described, the characteristic features of metamorphism in the pelites are the reconstruction and coarsening of the texture, the appearance of biotite and of alumino-silicates such as andalusite, cordierite and sillimanite. These three minerals are among the commonest products of contact-metamorphism, andalusite being usually found at medium grades and sillimanite at high grades. In aureoles where movements of the magma against the wall-rocks set up directed stresses, *contact-schists* rather than hornfelses are produced. Around the Main Granite of Donegal, for example, contact-schists bearing one or more of the minerals garnet, kyanite, staurolite and andalusite are developed: clearly, the conditions in the aureole influence the course of metamorphism.

Metasomatism is an important process in the contact-metamorphism of pelites in many aureoles, being of especial significance at the contacts of certain granites. Here, *feldspathisation* or the growth of metasomatic feldspar may result from the transfer of alkalies from the granite; this feldspathisation is connected with the formation of *contact-migmatites* and is discussed in more detail in Chapter 10. Another common indication of metasomatism in granitic aureoles is the development of tourmaline as a result of the introduction of boron by volatiles from the magma.

At the contacts of basic magmas, metasomatic changes of other kinds are sometimes observed in pelites. Reaction between the magma and pelitic xenoliths or contact-rocks may lead to the subtraction

523

from the country-rock of silica and other components in which the magma is not yet saturated. The residual material of the xenoliths is enriched in alumina and magnesia and produces *silica-poor horn-felses* containing as well as biotite and cordierite, such minerals as corundum (Al_2O_3) and spinel, which are not stable in the presence of excess silica. A very different type of metasomatism associated with basic magmas invading shales or slates in minor intrusions, is a soda-metasomatism resulting in the development of large amounts of albite. The fine-grained contact-rocks with pale albitic spots formed by this process are known as *adinoles*.

Among **calcareous rocks**, the course of metamorphism is strongly influenced by the amount and kind of impurities present. Pure limestones recrystallise without mineral changes to give sugary-looking *marbles*, which may be streaked with decorative red or green markings. Dolomitic limestones are *dedolomitised* by the breakdown of the double carbonate with the formation of calcite, periclase (MgO) or brucite ($Mg(OH)_2$) and carbon dioxide. Impure limestones containing sandy, cherty or clayey material give *calc-silicate rocks* in which silicates of Ca, together with Al, Mg or Fe according to the nature of the impurities, are scattered through a matrix of calcite. The calc-silicate minerals often grow into large, idiomorphic crystals, which are commonly clustered in bands, nodules or radiating sprays based on original patches of silica in the limestone (Fig. 324).

The most common minerals formed by simple contact-metamorphism of impure calcareous rocks are periclase, the magnesian olivine forsterite (both formed only in silica-poor rocks), tremolite, diopside and wollastonite, where the supply of alumina is limited; and, in addition, anorthite, idocrase and the lime-garnet grossular, where alumina is present in larger quantities. Which of these minerals appears depends very largely on the temperature of metamorphism, and Bowen has shown that it is possible to recognise a succession of 'steps' marked by the disappearance of minerals which have ceased to be stable in the given chemical environment at particular temperatures (Table I). The large number of reactions possible in impure calcareous rocks makes them delicate indicators of grade of metamorphism. We may note here that since the formation of calc-silicate rocks involves the release of carbon dioxide, it goes on more readily at shallow depths where the hydrostatic pressure is low; at the depths where most regional metamorphism takes place, the temperature of formation of the various minerals is increased, and the higher-temperature minerals such as wollastonite are not found at all.

Fig. 324. Contact-metamorphism of calcareous rocks: skarns; A, garnet crystals; B, idocrase rosettes.

TABLE I. BOWEN'S STEPS IN THE METAMORPHISM OF IMPURE
CALCAREOUS ROCKS

*Minerals stable in association with one another at temperatures below those
of the appropriate step.*

Below step 1   dolomite-quartz
             2   dolomite-tremolite
             3   calcite-tremolite-quartz
             4   calcite-tremolite
             5   dolomite
             6   calcite-quartz
             7   calcite-forsterite-diopside
             8   calcite-diopside
             9   calcite-forsterite
           10   calcite-wollastonite

(Above step 10, there appear a number of rare lime-silicates formed
only at very high temperatures, which need not be listed here.)

Metasomatic alteration of limestones is of great importance in the
aureoles of certain acid and intermediate intrusions. Silica, iron and
magnesia are introduced into the calcareous rocks with the production
of metasomatic calc-silicate assemblages known as *skarns* (Fig. 324).
In addition to the minerals already mentioned, andradite (iron-rich
garnet), iron-rich pyroxene and scapolite (which chemically resembles
plagioclase but contains CO_3 or Cl) may be present. Associated with
the skarns are deposits of metallic sulphides forming contact ore
deposits of the type described in pp. 602–3.

In psammitic rocks, contact-metamorphism may lead to little
more than recrystallisation. Pure sandstones are converted to
quartzites in which the quartz-grains form an interlocking mosaic;
the original boundaries of the clastic grains are lost, but primary
structures such as ripple-marks or current-bedding are often preserved by mimetic crystallisation. Lines of micas or of heavy minerals
still mark the bedding. In impure sandstones or greywackes, feldspars recrystallise, aluminous material gives rise to micas or garnets,
while calcareous impurities may produce minerals such as calcite,
epidote, hornblende or diopside.

Basic rocks often show, in the lower grades of contact-metamorphism, a partial recrystallisation which leads to the formation of
a fibrous amphibole or of hornblende on the site of original pyroxenes;
they may subsequently recrystallise to form *hornblende-plagioclase
hornfelses*, often containing minor amounts of biotite, quartz and
sphene (Fig. 325). The outlines of the igneous textures — the ophitic

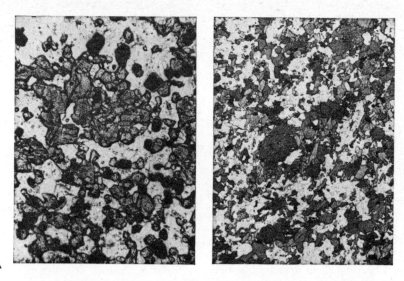

A   B

Fig. 325. Contact-metamorphism of basic rocks. A, pyroxene-horn-fels, a granular association of pyroxene, magnetite and plagioclase, a contact-metamorphosed dolerite, × 45. B, hornblende-hornfels, a granular association of hornblende and plagioclase, a contact-metamorphosed dolerite xenolith in a granite, × 15.

grouping of minerals in a dolerite, the phenocrysts of a porphyritic lava, or the nodules of amygdale minerals — are often preserved mimetically. At high grades of metamorphism, basic rocks recrystallise to produce pyroxene-hornfelses made up largely of equigranular labradorite, hypersthene and diopside (Fig. 325). It will be noticed that these hornfelses have approximately the same mineralogical constitution as the parent dolerite or basalt; since the temperature in the inner part of the aureole approaches that of the intrusion itself, this convergence of mineral assemblages is to be expected.

The inner zones of many contact-aureoles provide a constant and characteristic environment of metamorphism in which the temperatures are high, the pressures relatively low and directed stress slight. The rocks formed in this environment are united in a single metamorphic facies, the **pyroxene-hornfels facies**, named after the characteristic type of basic rock. Some of the typical minerals of this facies are given on the next page in Table II; they may be compared with those of other facies discussed later.

TABLE II. PYROXENE-HORNFELS FACIES

PELITES	PSAMMITES	CALCAREOUS ROCKS	BASIC ROCKS
quartz	quartz	calcite	**plagioclase**
biotite	potash feldspar	*plus*:	**diopside**
potash feldspar	plagioclase	basic plagioclase	**hypersthene**
plus:	biotite	wollastonite	
andalusite or		grossular	
sillimanite		idocrase	
cordierite		forsterite	

Notes on Tables II–V

(1) Only the minerals of common rock-types are listed in the tables. Rocks of other compositions may contain minerals not mentioned in the lists.

(2) The minerals listed are *possible* components of each group — they are not essential minerals, and not all the species mentioned are likely to appear in a single rock.

(3) Rare and accessory minerals are omitted from the lists.

(4) Many minerals such as quartz and biotite have a wide range of stability and appear in more than one facies. It is the presence of a distinctive *assemblage* of minerals in a particular rock-type rather than the occurrence of a particular index mineral which is used to define the facies. The diagnostic assemblages of basic rocks are shown in bold type.

(5) It must be remembered that rocks which did not reach equilibrium may contain minerals characteristic of more than one facies.

DISLOCATION-METAMORPHISM

The factor controlling the process of dislocation-metamorphism is stress connected with earth-movements. Metamorphism of this type may take place along thrusts or shear-zones in regions where no other kind of metamorphic activity is in progress, or it may occur along lines of disturbance in contact-aureoles and regionally meta-morphosed terrains, where it constitutes only one phase of a complex process; for simplicity, the term dislocation-metamorphism is confined to changes taking place in restricted belts of concentrated movement.

In areas of low regional temperatures and pressures, dislocation-metamorphism leads to mechanical breakdown or *cataclasis*. Simple shattering produces a *breccia* in which angular rock-fragments are jumbled together in a clayey gouge; such a breccia suffers only limited internal rearrangement and is not strictly a metamorphic rock. More thoroughgoing deformation disrupts the entire fabric of the rock and produces a micro-breccia or *mylonite* composed of

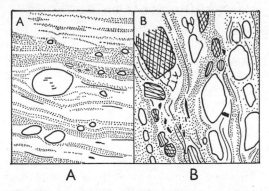

A   B

FIG. 326. Mylonites, Insch, Aberdeenshire. A, banded mylonite produced by the mechanical mixture of pegmatite and hornfels, feldspar porphyroclasts in the former and garnet relics in the latter; B, mylonitised gabbro with hornblende and plagioclase porphyroclasts.

microscopic angular particles bound together by fine dust. Mylonites are exceedingly fine-grained, compact rocks which often show a striping due to the rolling-out of components of different composition. Since much of the constituent material is reduced to indeterminable dust, mylonites tend to look much the same whatever the composition of the parent rock. Large grains in the original rock, and minerals which resist granulitisation, often remain as stream-lined *porphyroclasts* which form eyes distorting the striping of the matrix (Fig. 326). The edges of these relict grains may be granulitised and coated with minute wisps of chlorite; the grains themselves are often fractured or bent. *Ultra-mylonites, pseudo-tachylytes* or *flinty crush-rocks* are opaque compact rocks, often black or red, in which only occasional mineral particles can still be distinguished. The comminuted paste from which they are formed is sufficiently mobile to be injected along fractures as small veins. In some circumstances, the heat of friction appears to have melted rocks along a dislocation to produce flinty crush-rock containing minute, newly-formed crystals; such rocks appear in a zone an inch or so wide along the ring-fracture surrounding the subsided plug of the Glencoe cauldron subsidence (p. 641).

In *mylonites*, the texture results almost exclusively from the mechanical breakdown of larger grains. New crystallisation is very limited but, nevertheless, granules of quartz and calcite may recrystallise and wisps of chlorite and sericite frequently appear. Under conditions where more recrystallisation is possible — at slightly higher temperatures, or in the presence of active pore-fluids — the granules of cataclastic rocks are welded together by new growth, the indeterminable powder disappears and a more extensive assemblage of new minerals is developed. Where the parent rocks were coarse-grained, granulitisation is still the dominant process. Granites or gneisses are converted into *flaser-gneisses* in which the more easily-deformed minerals such as quartz and micas are reduced to trails of granules winding between stream-lined porphyroclasts of feldspar and other resistant minerals. Where the feldspars make prominent eyes, the rocks become *cataclastic augen-gneisses*. With further cataclasis, all these rocks pass into *mylonite-gneisses* and mylonites. At every stage in the process, the original minerals are broken and fractured. Micas are twisted, the twin-planes of feldspars bent, calcite crystals show strong twinning and bending and so on. The new minerals, themselves often distorted, commonly include chlorite, sericite, albite, epidote or zoisite and calcite.

Chlorite, sericite and muscovite, the most widespread products of dislocation-metamorphism, are formed at low temperatures by the breakdown of many kinds of silicates including feldspars, biotite, garnet, amphiboles and the aluminium-silicates, and are therefore abundant in rocks of a wide range of composition. They form microscopic flakes generally orientated to produce a phyllitic parting. *Phyllonites* are phyllitic rocks formed by extreme deformation of originally coarser-grained rocks. They may be indistinguishable in the field and under the microscope from phyllites produced by the further metamorphism of slates, and the two types of rock provide an example of the phenomenon of *metamorphic convergence*; similar mineral assemblages and textures appear in rocks of totally different geological history when they are subjected to metamorphism under the same conditions.

So far, in considering the products of dislocation-metamorphism, we have dealt with rocks formed at low temperatures, in which the characteristic minerals are chlorite, muscovite, epidotes, albite and calcite. These rocks belong to the **greenschist facies** (p. 534 and Table III), which takes its name from the chlorite-rich *greenschists* derived from basic rocks. Dislocation-metamorphism may take place also in the environments of other facies but, since at higher temperatures movement is more often distributed through a rock than concentrated in a narrow zone, the products are less widespread. A classic example described long ago by Teall is seen in the Lewisian of north-west Scotland where a swarm of Pre-Cambrian dolerite dykes is crossed by narrow vertical shear-belts; in these shear-belts, the dolerites are converted to *hornblende-schists* which are both coarser-grained and less granulated than the cataclastic rocks of the greenschist facies (Fig. 327); the mineral assemblage is that of the amphibolite facies (p. 535).

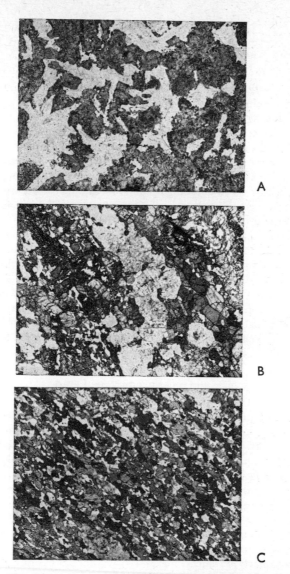

Fig. 327. Dislocation-metamorphism, illustrated by the transformation of dolerite to hornblende-schist, Scourie, Sutherland, × 15. A, slightly altered dolerite showing the original igneous texture, pyroxene mostly gone over to hornblende; B, more advanced stage of metamorphism, showing the production of foliation in a granular association of hornblende, quartz and oligoclase, the last in groups derived from original large plates of feldspar; C, final stage of metamorphism, giving a hornblende-schist with evenly distributed feldspar and hornblende in a schistose association.

REGIONAL METAMORPHISM

Regional metamorphism is defined, for our purposes, simply as the type of metamorphism which takes place over extensive areas and is not related to specific local causes. The controlling factors are high temperatures and pressures which may be accompanied by strong stresses; there is often a close connection between high-grade regional metamorphism and migmatisation. Regional metamorphism seems to have been confined, since early Pre-Cambrian times, to areas which were undergoing orogenesis, and its causes are bound up with the process of mountain-building which will be discussed in a later chapter.

The products of regional metamorphism are very varied both in texture and in mineralogical composition. Slates, phyllites, schists, gneisses and granular rocks are the most common types; the majority of the rocks are tectonites, but in regions where stress was low, or crystallisation was post-tectonic, the fabrics of the rocks may be totally isotropic. For the purposes of description, we may group the regionally metamorphosed rocks into three categories which can be thought of loosely as products of low-grade, medium-grade and high-grade metamorphism respectively:

(1) Slates, phyllites and rocks of equivalent grade
(2) Schists and rocks of equivalent grade
(3) Gneisses.

Slates, Phyllites and rocks of equivalent grade. The rocks to be considered first are those formed, generally under conditions of strong stress, at fairly low temperatures. The majority belong to the **green-schist facies** and their characteristic minerals are albite, epidote, chlorite, muscovite and calcite (Table III, p. 534). Pelitic rocks, and certain other fine-grained types such as marls and volcanic ashes, generally show a strong axial-plane cleavage, while fossils, pebbles and other primary structures contained in them tend to be strongly distorted. Rocks which are hard and brittle, such as sandstones or lava-flows, are often shattered or traversed by fracture-cleavages. Segregation veins of quartz or calcite may be very abundant, especially in competent beds whose fractures provide space for the migrating material.

Pelitic rocks consist before metamorphism of very fine clay-minerals and clastic fragments, and since this finely-divided mixture reacts readily, they are completely recrystallised to form *slates* (Fig. 317) or *phyllites*. The original clay-minerals are reconstituted to make new flaky minerals of which chlorite and white mica are the most abundant; other minerals recrystallise to produce granules of quartz and iron oxides, while organic matter reacts to give dusty specks of graphite and conspicuous idiomorphic cubes of pyrite (FeS_2). The alignment of the flaky minerals produces an almost perfect flow-cleavage which is often wrinkled or distorted by later strain-slip cleavages.

Psammitic rocks consist before metamorphism of moderately large grains of quartz and of other minerals such as feldspars and micas. They do not react so readily as do the finely-divided pelites, and are moreover protected to some extent from deformation by their greater rigidity. They may therefore retain relics of primary structures and textures (Fig. 328a). As metamorphism proceeds, large grains are granulitised and recrystallised and the new grains form a complex mosaic with interlocking boundaries. Plagioclase in a feldspathic sandstone is often replaced by aggregates of zoisite and albite (known as *saussurite*), orthoclase is sericitised and biotite chloritised.

In **calcareous rocks,** the carbonates recrystallise to give fine-grained *marbles*; under strong stress calcite is twinned, bent and granulated and the marble develops a rough schistosity. Impurities in the original limestone produce minerals such as quartz, albite, epidote or muscovite. At low temperatures, reaction between these impurities and the carbonate does not take place, but as metamorphism increases, needles of colourless tremolite (the first calc-silicate mineral to appear) may form long spears penetrating the granular mosaic.

Basic rocks such as dolerites or basalts may resist deformation by reason of their rigidity, and in these circumstances may retain their primary textures; their feldspars are saussuritised and their ferro-

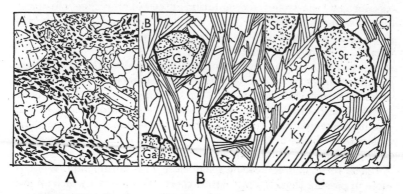

A   B   C

Fig. 328. Regional Metamorphism. A, low-grade psammite. A greywacke showing relics of large clastic grains in a recrystallised matrix of quartz, biotite and feldspar. B and C, medium-grade pelites; B, garnet-mica-schist; C, staurolite-kyanite-mica-schist; Ga, garnet; St, staurolite; Ky, kyanite.

magnesian minerals replaced by serpentine, chlorite or a pale fibrous amphibole known as *uralite*. With strong deformation, basic rocks go over to *greenschists*, the typical rocks of the greenschist facies, made up of chlorite, albite and epidote, often accompanied by actinolite or calcite.

TABLE III. GREENSCHIST FACIES

PELITES	PSAMMITES	CALCAREOUS ROCKS	BASIC ROCKS
quartz	quartz	calcite	**albite + epidote**
chlorite	albite	*plus*:	**chlorite**
muscovite	epidote	dolomite	*plus*:
albite	muscovite	quartz	calcite
plus:	chlorite	epidote	actinolite
chloritoid		tremolite	

Schists and rocks of equivalent grade. At higher temperatures, the products of regional metamorphism are coarser-grained. Relics of primary textures and indications of cataclasis accompanying metamorphism are rare, but primary structures such as pebbles, concretions, current-bedding or graded bedding are often still visible. Primary graded bedding may be reflected by the distribution of the metamorphic minerals; in the example shown in Fig. 308, andalusites are seen growing in the upper, more argillaceous part of a graded bed but are almost absent in the lower sandy part. The schists and their associates show as a rule a more plastic style of tectonics than do lower-grade rocks. They often show evidence of para-crystalline deformation and exhibit well-marked schistosities and lineations produced by the preferred orientation of the minerals. The schistosity may be an axial-plane structure like slaty cleavage, or it may be a *bedding-schistosity* which is perhaps largely mimetic. Segregation quartz-veins may be abundant.

In the medium grades of regional metamorphism, the assemblages of minerals characteristic of the greenschist facies are absent, and biotite, garnet, hornblende and lime-bearing plagioclase are commonly found. Two metamorphic facies are represented (Table IV). In the lower-temperature **albite-epidote-amphibolite facies,** the diagnostic assemblage in basic rocks is albite and epidote in association with hornblende. In the **amphibolite facies** the critical assemblage of basic rocks is lime-bearing plagioclase with hornblende. We may note in passing that, as one might expect, the minerals which appear with increasing temperature in basic rocks do so in inverse order of their position in the reaction-series (p. 407); thus albite appears at lower temperatures than lime-bearing plagioclase, hornblende appears at lower temperatures than pyroxene and so on.

Pelitic rocks form *mica-schists* rich in biotite or muscovite or both and in quartz. Mica-rich and mica-poor layers may alternate to produce a banding which may reflect the bedding or may be the result of metamorphic differentiation. With increasing metamorphism, a number of new alumino-silicate minerals appear which often, though not invariably, form conspicuous porphyroblasts (Fig. 328). The successive appearance of the new species can be used in some areas to delimit zones of increasing metamorphism (p. 542). *Garnet-mica schists* contain the pink (FeMg)-garnet almandine, which may appear in idiomorphic crystals up to about a centimetre in size, or may form irregular grains commonly sieved with inclusions whose twisted trails record para-crystalline rotation; *snowball-garnets* show trails wound in a spiral form by continuous rotation. Staurolite and kyanite are other common species which may form large porphyroblasts in pelitic schists; the kyanite is sometimes segregated in clusters or knots of long blue blades. At higher grades sillimanite may appear as large prisms or as tufts of fibres replacing biotite. Cordierite and andalusite, the alumino-silicates most commonly formed by contact-metamorphism, are rare.

TABLE IV. ALBITE-EPIDOTE AMPHIBOLITE AND AMPHIBOLITE FACIES

	PELITES	PSAMMITES	CALCAREOUS ROCKS	BASIC ROCKS
ALBITE-EPIDOTE AMPHIBOLITE FACIES	quartz muscovite biotite *plus*: chloritoid garnet	quartz muscovite biotite albite epidote	calcite *plus*: quartz epidote tremolite diopside idocrase forsterite	albite + epidote hornblende
AMPHIBOLITE FACIES	quartz biotite muscovite *plus*: plagioclase potash-feldspar garnet kyanite staurolite sillimanite cordierite andalusite	quartz plagioclase muscovite potash-feldspar biotite	calcite *plus*: quartz epidote diopside grossular idocrase forsterite	plagioclase hornblende *plus*: garnet

S

Psammitic rocks develop granulitic textures and often show a rough schistosity due to the flattening or elongation of quartz grains and to the orientation of micas scattered through the mosaic. Fabric analysis reveals that the quartz frequently has a strong preferred orientation and girdle-fabrics are widely developed (p. 515). Feldspars are now generally represented by oligoclase and orthoclase or microcline. Muscovite and biotite are almost universal, and when present in large amounts give rise to speckled *semi-pelitic schists* which pass into true mica-schists. *Calcareous psammites* are often studded with grains of garnet, epidote or hornblende.

Among **calcareous rocks,** pure marbles are coarser-grained than those of lower grade; dolomite is not present and the calcite forms twinned and often somewhat flattened grains which may show a preferred orientation of the crystallographic *c*-axis. In impure limestones, diopside, epidote and hornblende are common minerals, together with plagioclase ranging from oligoclase to labradorite, quartz and grossular. Highly metamorphosed limestones often show remarkable flowing contortions of the bedding (Fig. 329) and appear to have reached a state of considerable plasticity.

In **basic rocks** the two characteristic assemblages formed with increased temperature are, as we have seen, epidote-albite-hornblende and plagioclase-hornblende; the rocks containing these assemblages are respectively *albite-epidote-amphibolites* and *amphibolites*. Small amounts of quartz, biotite and sphene, the latter derived from ilmenite in the original igneous rock, are common, while *garnet-amphibolites* containing red almandines may be formed at higher grades. Undeformed amphibolites may still preserve relics of primary textures and generally form massive granular rocks. Deformed varieties are foliated and pass into *hornblende-schists* (Fig. 309). Since amphibolites tend to resist shearing, it is common to find that amphibolite bands in metamorphosed sediments are dismembered into lenticles, or that a massive amphibolite core passes at

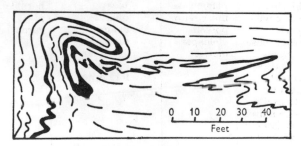

Fig. 329. Flow folds in plastic metamorphosed limestone (after Balk).

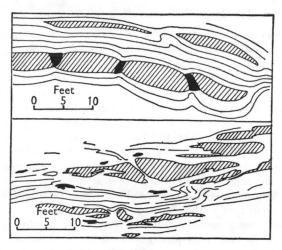

FIG. 330. Disruption of amphibolites during regional metamorphism. (*Above*), black indicates pegmatite partitions between dismembered amphibolite (lined) in Lewisian, Raasay; (*below*), melange of disrupted amphibolite (lined) in acid gneiss, Lewisian, Scourie.

its margins into hornblende-schist formed by differential movements along the contacts (Fig. 330).

Gneisses. At high grades, metamorphic rocks become plastic and capable of free recrystallisation. In these conditions they do not as a rule develop the very strong parallel structures characteristic of regionally metamorphosed rocks of lower grades; they therefore become gneissose or granular rather than schistose, regardless of composition. The development of the gneissose textures is generally accompanied by the appearance of considerable amounts of feldspar which is often segregated to produce the rough banding or lenticular structure characteristic of gneisses. This feldspar may be quite largely produced by reactions controlled by the rising temperature but, in addition, many gneisses contain feldspar formed by the metasomatic introduction of sodium or potassium; they are also often intimately mixed with veins, streaks or lenses of granitic or pegmatitic rock. In fact, the products of high-grade regional metamorphism are frequently *migmatitic*. We shall be dealing with the structure and origin of migmatites in the next chapter, but in order to complete our account of the sequence of regionally metamorphosed rocks, we give here an outline of the main types of gneisses and their general appearance.

Gneisses formed by high-grade metamorphism may contain

mineral assemblages characteristic of two metamorphic facies — the **amphibolite facies** characterised by the presence of plagioclase and hornblende in basic rocks, and the **granulite facies** in which plagioclase, hypersthene and diopside form the characteristic assemblage of basic rocks. Gneisses of the amphibolite facies are often rich in micas, hornblende or other inequidimensional minerals and may show a fair foliation; those of the granulite facies are made up very largely of minerals of granular habits and tend to be almost massive. In the field, the architecture of the gneisses is indicative of plastic flow. More rigid bands such as quartzites, limestones or basic rocks may be disrupted and separated into knots, or 'fish' engulfed in more plastic gneiss. Segregation-veins and lenticles made of quartz and feldspar often appear instead of the quartz-veins of lower grades.

A second class of gneisses, differing in origin and architecture from those so far described, is produced in many circumstances by deformation of pre-existing coarse-grained rocks. Examples of this class are the *flaser-gneisses* and *mylonite-gneisses* produced by dislocation-metamorphism (p. 530) and the *granite-gneisses* sometimes formed during the forcible intrusion of bodies of granite (p. 574). Similar rocks are commonly produced in terrains of regional metamorphism where an earlier generation of coarse metamorphic or plutonic rocks is subjected to renewed deformation and recrystallisation. Gneisses of this type often show evidence of cataclasis or granulation and are traversed by zones of shearing; they are texturally and structurally distinct from gneisses formed by straightforward regional metamorphism and may contain low-grade mineral assemblages appropriate to the conditions of the new metamorphism (Fig. 331).

Among gneisses formed by metamorphism in the *amphibolite*

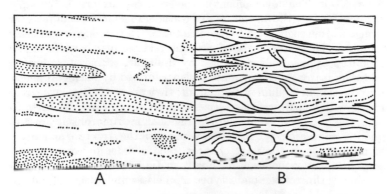

FIG. 331. Two types of gneissose foliation in the Lewisian. (*Left*), by plastic flow; (*right*), by cataclastic deformation.

facies, little need be said here. **Pelitic gneisses** are coarse, roughly-foliated or almost massive, generally showing feldspar in streaks or eyes. They may contain quartz, biotite, muscovite, garnet and kyanite or sillimanite; with rising temperature, muscovite is replaced by orthoclase or microcline. **Psammitic gneisses** commonly form massive pinkish rocks composed principally of quartz and feldspar. Pure quartzites become coarse-grained and glassy-looking, resembling vein-quartz in appearance. **Calcareous rocks** form coarse white or pink marbles, or patchy *calc-silicate gneisses* containing diopside, hornblende and basic plagioclase. **Basic rocks** are represented by granular *amphibolites* in which garnet or diopside is commonly present.

The **gneisses of the granulite facies** (Table V, p. 540) are considered to be formed not only at high temperatures but also under unusually high pressures — that is, at considerable depths in the crust. A characteristic feature of this facies is the scarcity of water and the (OH) radicle. Amphiboles and micas, though not entirely lacking, are subsidiary to the anhydrous pyroxenes and have in some regions been shown to contain less than their normal percentage of (OH). It appears that extreme heat and pressure drive off the remaining water in the metamorphic rocks and favour the development of 'dry' minerals. Other subsidiary results of the absence of water are the common scarcity of pegmatitic patches and the remarkable freshness of the minerals.

Quartz, orthoclase, garnet and sillimanite or kyanite, with minor amounts of biotite or hypersthene are the characteristic minerals of **pelitic gneisses** in this facies. **Calcareous rocks** contain calcite, diopside and basic plagioclase, while **basic rocks** form pyroxene-granulites made of plagioclase, diopside and hypersthene. A widespread sub-group of the granulite facies is the *charnockite series* in which the characteristic mineral is hypersthene. This series has a range of composition approximately the same as that of the plutonic rocks between gabbro and granites. The textures are granular and the component minerals include quartz, orthoclase and hypersthene in acid varieties and plagioclase, hypersthene and diopside in more basic rocks (Fig. 332); many of the minerals show distinctive properties, quartz, for example, being smoky blue in hand-specimen and crammed with microscopic hair-like inclusions. The origin of the charnockites is uncertain; some varieties may be produced by metamorphism of pre-existing plutonic rocks, others by migmatisation and others again by magmatic action. They appear to be formed under conditions where magmatic and metamorphic processes merge.

Finally, the unique rock *eclogite* should be mentioned. Eclogites are

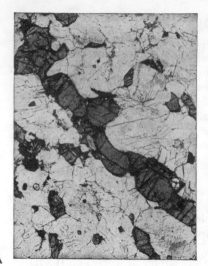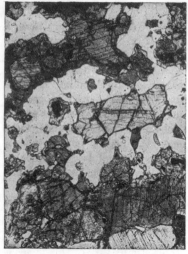

A   B

Fig. 332. Granulite Facies. A, charnockite, composed of hypersthene, feldspar and quartz, × 15; B, basic rock of the Granulite Facies, composed of pyroxene, garnet and plagioclase, × 15.

more or less equivalent to basalts in composition and are composed essentially of two minerals, the red magnesian garnet *pyrope* and a complex pale-green soda-bearing pyroxene *omphacite*. The origin of eclogites is again obscure. They are found locally in association with highly-metamorphosed rocks and in regions of great tectonic disturbance, and occur also as xenoliths in certain volcanic plugs such as the diamond-bearing kimberlite pipes of S. Africa which are believed to carry up material from great depths. They are among the densest known silicate rocks (density up to 3·6, compared with basalt, about 3·0) and it is thought by many geologists that they originate near the base of the crust or in the mantle (p. 24) and are carried to higher levels by magmatic or tectonic means.

TABLE V. GRANULITE FACIES

PELITES	PSAMMITES	CALCAREOUS ROCKS	BASIC ROCKS
quartz	quartz		
orthoclase	orthoclase		
plagioclase	plagioclase	basic plagioclase	**plagioclase**
garnet	*plus*:	calcite	
sillimanite or	garnet	diopside	**diopside**
kyanite	hypersthene	quartz	**hypersthene**
	sillimanite or		*plus*:
	kyanite		garnet
			olivine

540

ZONES OF REGIONAL METAMORPHISM

Having surveyed the rocks and mineral assemblages formed by regional metamorphism, we may now proceed to consider the distribution of these rocks in the crust, confining ourselves for the moment to areas where only a single phase of metamorphism has been at work. **Zones of regional metamorphism** can be mapped in the field like any other geological units, by distinguishing them according to characteristic minerals, textures or structures.

Much early thought on the arrangement of metamorphic rocks centred about the idea that metamorphism was related to depth of burial. The distribution of rock-types produced during the late Palaeozoic Hercynian orogeny in Europe led Grubenmann to recognise three great superposed zones which were, from above downwards:

(1) The *Epi-zone* characterised by slates and phyllites

(2) The *Meso-zone* characterised by schists

(3) The *Kata-zone* characterised by gneisses and granulites.

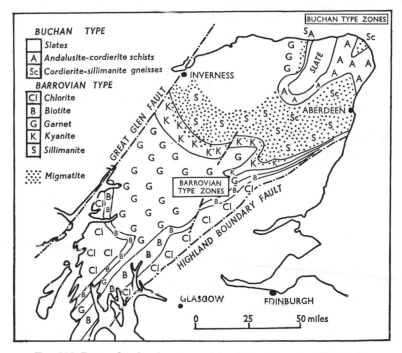

FIG. 333. Zones of regional metamorphism in the Grampian Highlands.

The concept of depth control in metamorphism seems, at first sight, a reasonable one, since in undisturbed regions of the crust both pressure and temperature increase with depth. It has been found, however, that in very many areas metamorphism of epi-zonal type passes laterally or even upwards into meso-zonal or kata-zonal metamorphism, and it is now evident that high-grade metamorphism can in suitable circumstances take place at quite shallow depths. With the abandonment of the idea of universal depth-zoning, it became necessary to establish the three-dimensional shapes of metamorphic zones from the evidence available in each separate region; no general laws can be formulated.

The depth-zones mentioned above were defined by their originators in terms of the general petrology of the characteristic rocks. A second method of zoning, which became widely adopted as a result of the work of Barrow in the Scottish Highlands, relies on the appearance of successive **index-minerals** in a key group of uniform composition. Barrow's investigations dealt with the late Pre-Cambrian Dalradian Series of the south-east Highlands and the key group selected by him consisted of pelitic rocks. In these rocks Barrow identified six zones, the zone-boundaries or isograds being marked by the incoming of the next index-mineral. The original **Barrovian zones,** and the slightly modified version adopted by later geologists, are as follow:

Index-minerals (Barrow)	Index-minerals (standard form)	Rock-type
1. Zone of digested clastic mica	chlorite zone	slates
2. Zone of biotite	biotite zone	slates and phyllites
3. Zone of garnet	almandine zone	schists
4. Zone of staurolite	staurolite zone	schists
5. Zone of kyanite	kyanite zone	schists
6. Zone of sillimanite	sillimanite zone	schists and gneisses, often migmatitic.

Barrow's zones were later extended by other geologists to cover a large part of the Dalradian outcrop in Scotland and were shown to form a regular pattern (Fig. 333). In broad terms, the zones are concentrically arranged around a core of sillimanite-bearing rocks which are flooded by granitic veins and patches referred to by Barrow as the 'Older Granite'; we should now call these sillimanite-gneisses migmatites. The higher grades of metamorphism are closely associated with the migmatites, while the low-grade rocks extend for many tens of miles beyond the centre of migmatisation. The arrangement of metamorphic zones presumably reflects in a general way the temperature gradient existing at the time of metamorphism and suggests that the geo-isotherms — surfaces of equal temperature — rose higher in the crust in the north-easterly region of extensive migmatisation than they did in the south-west part of the Highlands. Evidence concerning the attitude of the isograds in depth suggests, however, that there was not a steady increase of metamorphic grade with depth. In the south-east Highlands, the migmatites extend into the core of a great recumbent anticline facing towards the south-east. Towards the south-west, it has been suggested that rocks of garnet grade structurally overlie lower-grade biotite or chlorite-bearing rocks. The textures of the rocks and the relations of the metamorphic minerals to minor structures visible in the field show that movement and metamorphism went on together during the development of the Barrovian zones, and the effects of stress, together with the effects of the migration of migmatising emanations, may be responsible for the irregularities in the shapes of the zones. We shall see immediately that a rather different kind of metamorphic zoning was produced in the Dalradian as the earth-movements died away.

The Dalradian Series contains numerous bands of quartzite, limestone and impure calcareous rock in addition to the pelites providing the index minerals of the Barrovian zones; the series is also invaded by pre-metamorphic dolerite sills. It is therefore possible to effect *metamorphic correlations* by comparing the mineral assemblages produced in different parent rocks for each one of Barrow's zones. This exercise, of course, allows us to establish the metamorphic facies of the rocks in each zone, since metamorphism within a single zone took place under broadly uniform conditions. The chlorite- and biotite-zones may be said to belong to the greenschist facies, the garnet zone to the epidote-albite-amphibolite facies and the higher-grade zones to the amphibolite facies.

The index-minerals of the Barrovian zones do not invariably appear in the order found in the type locality. Garnet, for example, may appear before biotite, although this early garnet is often a species richer in manganese than the garnet characteristic of Barrow's almandine zone. Staurolite is often absent altogether, since it appears to require rocks of a rather specialised composition for its formation. Kyanite too is often absent and in some regions garnet, staurolite and kyanite appear almost simultaneously.

Elsewhere, an entirely different set of index-minerals may be developed. In the Dalradian Series itself, for example, pelitic rocks of the north-east region show a distinctive type of metamorphism designated by Read the **Buchan type** (Fig. 333). Here, the sequence of

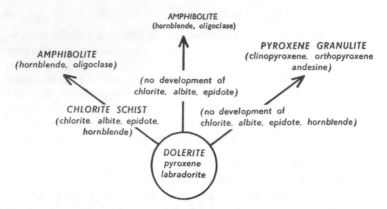

AMPHIBOLITE
(hornblende, oligoclase)

PYROXENE GRANULITE
(clinopyroxene, orthopyroxene
andesine)

AMPHIBOLITE
(hornblende, oligoclase)

(no development of
chlorite, albite, epidote)

CHLORITE SCHIST
(chlorite, albite, epidote,
hornblende)

(no development of
chlorite, albite, epidote, hornblende)

DOLERITE
pyroxene
labradorite

FIG. 334. Trends in the metamorphism of dolerites.

index minerals is: chlorite: biotite: andalusite-cordierite: sillimanite-cordierite. The rocks of the chlorite grade are slates and those of the sillimanite-cordierite grade are migmatitic gneisses. It seems probable that these rocks were formed over approximately the same range of temperatures as those of the Barrovian zones, since the two sequences begin and end with the same index-minerals, and we may therefore suppose that their special features are due to differences in pressure or in stress. The Buchan type of metamorphism was produced after the orogenic movements had mostly ceased and its mineral assemblages resemble those formed under static conditions as in many types of contact-metamorphism.

Variations comparable to those seen in the pelitic assemblages are revealed when the mineral assemblages of basic or calcareous rocks from different areas are compared. It is obvious that the trend of regional metamorphism varies from one area to another, a fact which seems reasonable in view of the number of independent controls; as an example, some of the trends of metamorphism in basic rocks are set out in Fig. 334.

In spite of the variations of mineral composition, certain features are common to most sequences of zones of increasing regional metamorphism. One is the increase in grain-size leading from slaty or phyllitic rocks to schists and finally to gneisses. A second is the prevalence of disruption and cataclasis at low grades and of plastic deformation at high grades. Lastly, the relationship between high-grade metamorphism and migmatisation should be emphasised. Barrow regarded the zones of the south-east Highlands as being in the nature of a gigantic aureole around the 'Older Granites'; and many later geologists have suggested that the heat and active solutions brought

544

into rocks which are being migmatised are essential factors in high-grade regional metamorphism. We shall consider this topic again later.

Regional metamorphism does not reach the same level of intensity in every part of an orogenic belt, and it may be useful to distinguish three rather different types of metamorphic province. In the first type, characterised by *slates and phyllites*, metamorphism seldom rises above the chlorite or biotite grade, and migmatites are not developed on a regional scale. This low-grade metamorphism is largely due to regional heating-up and deformation connected with orogenic movements. The Lower Palaeozoic rocks of the northern part of the Welsh basin, and the Devonian and Carboniferous rocks of Devon and Cornwall provide examples of dominantly slaty metamorphic provinces.

In the second type of province, which may be exemplified by the Dalradian and Moine Series of the Scottish Highlands, metamorphism *ranges from low to high grades*, and *migmatites* are developed in connection with the higher grades. The third type of metamorphic province is characterised by enormous areas of gneisses associated with minor developments of lower-grade rocks. Such *gneiss-provinces* are exposed only where prolonged erosion has laid bare regions once deeply buried and are seen, for example, in the Pre-Cambrian 'shields' of Africa, Scandinavia and Greenland. Many of the gneisses are probably of migmatitic origin, but the majority are so thoroughly reconstituted that no primary structures remain and their mode of origin cannot be firmly established.

POLYMETAMORPHISM

In orogenic belts, the crust remains unstable over long periods of time; phases of movement succeed one another, temperatures fluctuate and it is therefore not surprising that many rocks show evidence of having been metamorphosed more than once. *Polyphase metamorphism* results from successive but related phases of recrystallisation, separated by short time-intervals. *Polymetamorphism* involves two or more separate acts of metamorphism. Records of the earlier acts may be preserved as relict mineral assemblages, textures or structures which are progressively obliterated by the effects of later phases.

The rocks which provide the raw materials for a second phase of metamorphism are already metamorphic, and the nature of the final products depends on the structural and mineralogical characters of these parent rocks, and on the type of metamorphic process to which they are later subjected. Originally high-grade metamorphic rocks subjected to a new low-grade phase will suffer *retrogressive meta-morphism*, while low-grade rocks in the same circumstances will show relatively little change; no systematic classification of the effects of repeated metamorphism can be established, but we may mention a few examples of common polymetamorphic sequences.

The rocks of regionally metamorphosed terrains are often subjected to later local metamorphism at the borders of igneous intrusions or along dislocations. Examples of **contact-metamorphism superimposed on regional metamorphism** are supplied by both the contact-aureoles discussed in an earlier section. In the Insch aureole, for instance, the starting-point of the sequence of changes is a low-grade slate. The slaty texture and the characteristic chlorite and white mica of the slates are retained in the early stages of the new metamorphism when spotted slates are formed, but disappear when complete recrystal-lisation of the rocks takes place; the high-grade hornfelses show no evidence of polymetamorphism.

The superposition of **dislocation-metamorphism upon an earlier regional metamorphism** is seen in regions where the earth-movements contemporary with the original metamorphism continued as meta-morphism waned; in these circumstances, fracturing and thrusting succeed the more plastic forms of deformation. The metamorphic rocks of the Scottish Highlands, for example, are traversed by the Moine Thrust which brought about a dislocation-metamorphism leading to the production of mylonite-gneisses, mylonites and phyl-lonites (p. 528). Retrogressive changes converted the regionally-metamorphosed rocks, which are pelitic schists and granulitic psam-mites showing assemblages of the garnet or higher grades, to rocks containing much sericite, epidote, and chlorite, with only rare biotite and garnet. Where local metamorphisms, of either dis-location or contact type, are imposed on an earlier metamorphism, the relations of the two phases are as a rule clearly brought out by mapping. The metamorphism associated with the Moine Thrust, for instance, is limited to a zone alongside the thrust and can be observed to die away at a distance from the dislocation, while the earlier regional metamorphism extends over a much wider terrain.

Successive phases of regional metamorphism may be recorded in areas where the crust suffered more than one phase of heating. A complex example is provided by the island of Unst in the Shetlands, which is made up of a number of isolated blocks of metamorphic rocks brought together tectonically along thrusts (Fig. 335). We need not consider details, but may notice here that the westernmost block (the Valla Field block) shows the effects of two phases of regional metamorphism whose extent and characteristic minerals are shown

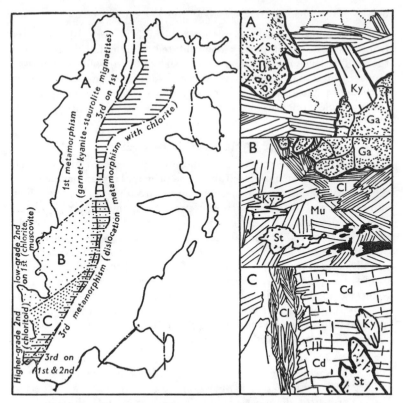

Fig. 335. Polymetamorphism, Unst, Shetlands. Map of Unst showing the distribution of the three metamorphisms in the western part
of the island: A, B, C, indicate positions of the specimens shown in
thin sections; Ky, kyanite; Ga, garnet; St, staurolite; Cl, chlorite;
Mu, muscovite; Cd, chloritoid; note relics of minerals of the first
metamorphism in B and C, and the chlorite-shear of the third
metamorphism in C.

on the map; a local dislocation-metamorphism is superimposed upon
both regional manifestations along the line of the thrust bounding
the block on the east.

Polymetamorphism of a special kind commonly takes place in the
basement underlying the sedimentary succession deposited in a
geosyncline. This succession often, though not invariably, rests
on much older rocks which have been metamorphosed in a previous orogenic cycle, and renewed orogenesis therefore subjects the
basement to a second sequence of metamorphic processes. Coarsely
crystalline rocks such as gneisses and granites in the basement

547

naturally react to the new metamorphism in a very different way
from the soft, incompletely consolidated sediments which overlie
them. The basement-rocks are often sheared, partially mylonitised
and subjected to retrogressive changes; reactions of this kind are seen
in the great Aar and Gotthard massifs of basement-rocks underlying
the Mesozoic sequences in the Alpine orogenic belt (Fig. 291).

METAMORPHIC FACIES

In describing the products of contact-, dislocation- and regional
metamorphism, we have mentioned the principal metamorphic facies
related to a number of metamorphic environments. We may now
summarise and complete such references to the metamorphic facies,
recalling first that all rocks of a single facies suffered metamorphism
under broadly similar temperatures and pressures and that variations
of mineral-composition within each facies are related solely to chemical differences (p. 519). Eskola, who formulated the modern concept
of metamorphic facies, recognised seven facies which he defined by
reference to diagnostic mineral-assemblages in *rocks of basic composition*. Later workers have extended and modified his scheme and
we give below a revised facies-classification based essentially on the
views of Turner and his colleagues.

(1) **Zeolite facies**: low temperatures and pressures, characterised
by a wide range of hydrated minerals including many zeolites.

(2) **Greenschist facies** (Table III): low temperatures, moderate
pressures, diagnostic assemblage albite-epidote-chlorite.

(3) **Albite-epidote-amphibolite facies** (Table IV): moderate temperatures and pressures, diagnostic assemblage albite-
epidote-hornblende.

(4) **Amphibolite facies** (Table IV): moderate to high temperatures and pressures, diagnostic assemblage plagioclase-
hornblende.

(5) **Granulite facies** (Table V): high temperatures and pressures,
diagnostic assemblage plagioclase-diopside-hypersthene.

(6) **Hornblende-hornfels facies**: moderate to high temperatures,
low pressures, diagnostic assemblage as for amphibolite
facies, but distinctive assemblages in pelitic and calcareous
rocks.

(7) **Pyroxene-hornfels facies** (Table II): high temperatures, low
pressures, diagnostic assemblage as for granulite facies but
distinctive assemblages in pelitic and calcareous rocks.

(8) **Sanidinite facies**: very high temperatures, low pressures,
diagnostic assemblage plagioclase-pigeonite-diopside.

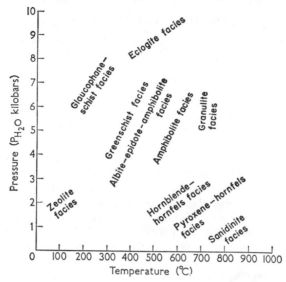

Fig. 336. Pressure-temperature diagram showing the possible relationships of the metamorphic facies, based on Fyfe and Turner.

(9) **Glaucophane-schist facies**: low temperatures, high pressures, diagnostic assemblage includes glaucophane in the absence of albite.

(10) **Eclogite facies**: moderate to high temperatures, probably very high pressures, diagnostic assemblage pyrope-omphacite.

Since the two principal environmental controls, temperature and pressure, can vary independently in the crust, the facies cannot be arranged in a linear series. Figure 336, based on Turner and Fyfe, suggests the possible relationships of facies on a pressure-temperature diagram. Examination of this figure will show that the associations of metamorphic facies which may be expected to develop during a period of rising temperature will depend in part on the *geothermal gradient*. Where high temperatures are reached at comparatively shallow depths, rocks of hornblende-hornfels and pyroxene-hornfels facies may be expected. Where pressures are higher for any given temperatures, whether as a result of deeper burial or of the operation of tectonic stresses, rocks of amphibolite and granulite facies may appear. The glaucophane-schist and eclogite facies may be associated with metamorphism under exceptionally high pressures. The scale of development naturally varies according to environment. The sanidinite and pyroxene-hornfels facies are almost restricted to contact-aureoles where high temperatures are generated locally by the influx of magma. Rocks of greenschist, epidote-amphibolite and amphibolite

549

facies may be developed in response to local metamorphism or regionally in connection with a general increase of temperature in the crust.

DATING OF METAMORPHIC ROCKS

A metamorphic rock presents special problems of dating, and the first essential is to establish what are the geological events concerned in its production which need to be dated. In the first place, the age of the parent rock, primary sediment or igneous intrusion must be determined. Fossils may sometimes survive a good deal of metamorphism and allow the rocks to be dated directly; but, as a rule, the question can only be settled by tracing the metamorphic rocks back into their unmetamorphosed equivalents whose age can be determined by standard methods. This of course may be easily done with contact-rocks in aureoles, and often with rocks in belts of dislocation-metamorphism but is much less easy where the great provinces of regional metamorphism are concerned. Here, the distances involved are so large that rock-sequences may change their sedimentary facies before the metamorphism dies out and, indeed, many metamorphic series have no identifiable non-metamorphic equivalents.

The second geological event with which we have to be concerned is the act of metamorphism itself. An upper age-limit is often given by the dating of an unconformable sedimentary series overlying the metamorphic rocks. More exact dating is sometimes made possible by establishing the connection between regional metamorphism and a given phase of earth-movement which can itself be dated. Again, where two metamorphic episodes have followed one another in poly-metamorphic rocks, the episodes can be separated by relating them to some geological event which took place between them; an example is illustrated in Fig. 337, in which a phase of intrusion of dolerite-dykes separated two episodes of regional metamorphism. Finally,

SCOURIAN

Metamorphism and migmatisation of granulite facies at deep levels in the crust

DOLERITE DYKE SWARM

Intrudes Scourian along parallel fractures formed at high level in crust

LAXFORDIAN

Earth movements, metamorphism and migmatisation transform Scourian and dykes at moderate levels in crust

FIG. 337. Timing in the metamorphism of the Lewisian. Two periods of metamorphism, the earlier dated 2600–2200 million years the later 1650–1450 m.y., are separated by an episode of dolerite dyke-intrusion.

dating of metamorphic rocks by means of isotopic age-determinations of radioactive minerals formed during the metamorphism (p. 49) is becoming of increasing value, and has been used to confirm the geological evidence in the example illustrated in Fig. 337. By using appropriate techniques, successive episodes of metamorphism may be dated and a complex geological history established.

FURTHER READING AND REFERENCE

General

Harker, A., 1952, *Metamorphism*, 3rd edit., Methuen.
Read., H. H., 1957, *The Granite Controversy*, Murby, London.
Turner, F. J. and J. Verhoogen, 1960, *Igneous and Metamorphic Petrology*, 2nd edit., McGraw-Hill.
Winkler, H. G. F., 1965, *Petrogenesis of metamorphic rocks*, Springer-Verlag.

Mineral assemblages

Bowen, N. L., 1940, 'Progressive metamorphism of siliceous limestone and dolomite', *Journ. Geol.*, vol. 48, p. 272.
Eskola, P., 1922, 'The Mineral Facies of Rocks', *Norsk Geol. Tidsskrift*, vol. 6, p. 143.
Francis, G. H., 1956, 'Facies boundaries in pelites at the middle grades of regional metamorphism', *Geol. Mag.*, vol. 93, p. 353.
Fyfe, W. S., F. J. Turner and J. Verhoogen, 1958, 'Metamorphic reactions and metamorphic facies', *Geol. Soc. Amer.*, Memoir 73.

Geology of metamorphic rocks

Balk, R. and T. F. W. Barth, 1936, 'Structural and petrologic studies in Dutchess County, New York', *Bull. Geol. Soc. Amer.*, vol. 47, pp. 685, 775.
Barrow, G., 1912, 'On the Geology of Lower Deeside and the southern Highland Border', *Proc. Geol. Assoc.*, vol. 20, p. 274.
Kennedy, W. Q., 1948, 'On the significance of thermal structure in the Scottish Highlands', *Geol. Mag.*, vol. 85, p. 229.
Pitcher, W. S. and H. H. Read, 1963, 'Contact-metamorphism in relation to manner of emplacement of the granites of Donegal, Ireland', *Journ. Geol.*, 71, 261–96.
Read, H. H., 1934, 'The metamorphic geology of Unst in the Shetland Islands', *Quart. Journ. Geol. Soc.*, vol. 90, p. 637.
——, 1933, 'On quartz-kyanite rocks in Unst, Shetland Islands and their bearing on metamorphic differentiation', *Miner. Mag.*, vol. 23, p. 317.
——, 1952, 'Metamorphism and migmatisation in the Ythan Valley, Aberdeenshire', *Trans. Edin. Geol. Soc.*, vol. 15, p. 265.
Teall, J. J. H., 1885, 'The metamorphosis of dolerite into hornblende-schist', *Quart. Journ. Geol. Soc.*, vol. 41, p. 133.

10

GRANITES, MIGMATITES AND ASSOCIATED ROCKS

INTRODUCTION

IN this chapter, we are concerned with the groups of rocks centred about the family of *granites*. These rocks, with the metamorphic rocks already dealt with, make up the Plutonic Series characteristic of the deep parts of the crust. They are entirely confined to areas with a continental type of crust and appear to derive much of their substance from the upper or sialic layer. Most of the granitic and allied rocks are found in the mobile belts, where they owe their origin to the conditions of high temperature and abnormal crustal activity prevailing during orogeny.

With the exception of the migmatites, the rocks to be described can be classified according to the same petrographical criteria as the igneous rocks dealt with in Chapter 7. Their places in the scheme of classification given in the Table on p. 391 are indicated by the names marked in italics. For descriptive purposes, the rocks can be grouped as follows:

(1) **Migmatites**: mixed rocks in which a metamorphic host is intimately mingled with granitic material.
(2) **Granites**: acid plutonic rocks.
(3) Minor intrusions associated with granites:
  (*a*) **Pegmatites and aplites,**
  (*b*) **Lamprophyres and appinites.**
(4) **Diorites**: intermediate plutonic rocks.

The most important of these groups is the granitic family which is as conspicuous in the Plutonic Series as the basalts are in the Volcanic Association. Daly estimated that granites and granodiorites were more than twenty times as abundant as all other plutonic bodies, and the sial as a whole is thought to be of broadly granitic composition. The essential minerals of the granite family are quartz, sodic plagioclase and potash-feldspar and a mafic mineral which may be biotite or less commonly hornblende — mineralogical variations within the family will be dealt with on a later page.

552

Granites show considerable variation in their mode of occurrence; details of their evolution will be considered later, and this preliminary statement is intended only to explain the nature of the problem. Broadly speaking, granitic material may occur in three forms, (1) in a *diffuse* form, in which the granite is mingled with pre-existing rocks to make migmatites, (2) in moderately homogeneous bodies which *replace* pre-existing rocks, either as a result of metasomatism or of melting of a part of the crust, and (3) in intrusive bodies which *displace* the country-rocks in the ways discussed in connection with the emplacement of magmatic intrusions (p. 396). In the migmatites and replacement bodies, granitic material is thought to have been generated more or less *in situ*. Where it is formed essentially in the solid by metamorphic and metasomatic changes, the process of granite-formation is termed *granitisation*. When it appears as a result of partial or complete melting of the parent rocks — that is, by the development of new magma — the process is one of *palingenesis*. The intrusive granites, on the other hand, are formed by the bodily migration of granitic material either in the form of magma or as a mush of solid grains lubricated by magma. These bodies may derive their substance from the migmatites and palingenetic granites, or from some independent source — intrusive granites may, for example, be produced by the differentiation or contamination of basic magma. The granites formed by all these different processes are petrographically often very much alike, and this fact has led to much controversy; it is now fairly generally agreed that granites originate in many ways and that the origin of any particular granite body can only be determined in the light of the local evidence.

With many granites are associated clusters of small intrusions — veins, dykes, sills and plugs — which range in composition from acid to ultrabasic. Granites intruded at shallow level in the crust may also be connected with volcanic centres at which rhyolites, andesites and other lavas are ejected. Many of these minor associates are un-questionably of magmatic origin and show structural forms and textures comparable with those discussed in Chapter 7. At the other extreme, migmatites and granites formed by granitisation grade into undoubted metamorphic rocks and show relict structures and crystalloblastic textures like those of the metamorphic rocks themselves. The granite family and its associates thus bridge the gap between metamorphic and igneous rocks. The other plutonic rocks dealt with in this chapter — the diorites — are often associated with granites in the field and may show rather similar variations in habit; they are, however, probably also of many different origins and some types would be better linked with the Volcanic Association.

MIGMATITES

The characteristic feature of the migmatites is the mixing in a single rock of two components derived from different sources. The *host rock* may represent any pre-existing crustal rock-type — since migmatisation takes place only at elevated temperatures, the host is invariably metamorphosed during the process. The *introduced component* of the migmatite migrates from outside into the host to combine with the pre-existing material; it may be supplied by a nearby body of magma or may rise from much deeper levels. The introduced material may migrate as a magma or aqueous solution of broadly granitic composition which is *injected* into the host during migmatisation, or it may take the form of a diffuse system of ions which migrates through the pore-fluids and is said to *permeate* the host; diffuse and dilute migrating materials of all sorts are covered by the conveniently non-committal term *emanations*.

The majority of migmatites show, in the field or in a good-sized hand-specimen, a streakiness or patchiness which reflects their mixed origin (Fig. 338). Very commonly, two partners can be recognised in the mixture — a darker and finer-grained rock of metamorphic aspect, and a light-coloured coarser-grained granitic rock made up largely of quartz and feldspar. These two partners can in a general way be identified as representing the host and the introduced material respectively, but it must be realised that reaction between the two components has generally modified the composition of each. Permeation by incoming emanations causes metasomatic alterations in the host, while the incoming material is itself modified by these reactions. The granitic parts of the rock may derive much of their substance from the host by the operation of metamorphic differentiation — indeed, some geologists attribute the formation of many migmatitic rocks largely to the segregation of granitic material from the host itself.

Migmatisation takes place in the crust when the appropriate emanations are introduced into rocks which are sufficiently reactive to combine with them; migmatites occur in the same environments as high-grade metamorphic rocks, appearing in the inner parts of contact-aureoles and in the high-grade zones of regional metamorphism. Many migmatites are formed under conditions of the amphibolite facies of metamorphism, but others are of the pyroxene-hornfels or granulite facies. Stress may play an indirect part in facilitating migmatisation by activating the host rocks and by providing tectonic planes which give easy access to migrating fluids.

A

B

FIG. 338. Migmatites. A, migmatised Lewisian amphibolite, Glenelg (Crown Copyright: by Permission of the Controller of H.M. Stationery Office); B, migmatised Moine psammitic gneiss, Glenelg (Crown Copyright: by Permission of the Controller of H.M. Stationery Office).

Migmatites developed under stress show tectonite fabrics comparable to those already described.

The effects of migmatisation on the chemical composition of the host vary with the original character of the host and with the composition of the introduced component. As a rule, the end-products of migmatisation approach granites in composition, though they often contain inclusions of strongly contrasted composition; migmatites derived from amphibolites may contain basic patches, those derived from quartzites contain siliceous nodules and so on. In many types of host, the most conspicuous mineralogical change brought about by migmatisation is the development of abundant new feldspar. This process of *feldspathisation* is believed to be due largely to the reaction of introduced alkalies with alumina and silica supplied by the host. The feldspars grow metasomatically and some-times form conspicuous porphyroblasts (Figs. 342, 344). Where soda is the principal introduced substance, oligoclase or albite is the main product of feldspathisation, and the migmatites tend towards a granodioritic or trondhjemitic end-product (Table I, p. 571); where potash predominates, orthoclase or microcline is the common feldspar and the migmatites become more strictly granitic in composition.

Migmatitic structures. The host rock provides a framework through which the incoming material migrates, and in the early stages of migmatisation, this framework controls the structure of the resulting migmatite. Pre-existing structures such as banding or schistosity may be preserved as relicts (Fig. 339) while partings such as bedding and cleavage may serve as channels for the passage of migrating materials (Fig. 339). The inherited pattern is modified both by chemical reactions — the growth of porphyroblasts, the segregation of eyes and veins of special composition and so on — and by the effects of stress contemporaneous with the migmatisation. As a result of these changes, the migmatites acquire a distinctive tectonic style characterised by folds of very plastic types and by many indications of plastic flow (Fig. 340); fracturing and cataclasis seldom accompany migmatisation. As migmatisation advances, and the granitic partner becomes dominant, the host is reduced to isolated and ghostly relics in the granitic matrix and the rocks become *nebulites* (Fig. 341). Finally, the inherited structures disappear, all indications of paren-tage may be lost, and the migmatite is reborn with a new structure as an *anatexite*.

At all stages, discordant, concordant or irregular *veins of granite, pegmatite or aplite* (p. 574) may criss-cross the migmatites in great numbers. They represent concentrations of incoming material as well as segregations from the host rocks. These veins show no signs of

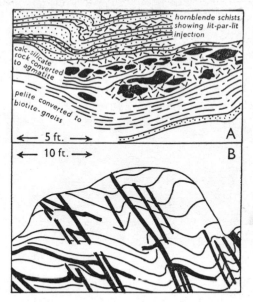

FIG. 339. A, control of migmatisation by original banding in the host, Lewisian, south Harris; B, control of migmatisation by structure, granitic sheets injected along an axial plane cleavage, Lewisian, Loch Laxford, Sutherland.

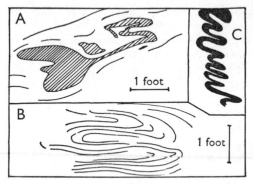

FIG. 340. Plasticity in migmatites; A, basic inclusion in acid migmatite, Lewisian, Scourie; B, flow folding in pelitic migmatite, Cleengort, Donegal; C, ptygmatic vein, Loch Coire, Sutherland.

Fig. 341. Migmatite, Inzie Head Gneiss, Aberdeenshire. Agmatite
in the upper part of the outcrop passing into nebulite in the lower part.

chilling and often fade into the granitic parts of the migmatite; a
characteristic form is the *ptygmatic vein* which follows a remarkably
sinuous course and is thought to be produced by injection into very
plastic country-rocks (Fig. 340).

The relationship between the two partners can be used to define a
number of different structural types of migmatite. Rocks in which
the host is penetrated by many parallel stripes of quartzo-feldspathic
material are said to show *lit-par-lit* structure. They are formed by the
injection or diffusion of incoming material along bedding or cleavage
and are widespread derivatives of flaggy psammitic or semi-pelitic
hosts (Fig. 342). Where the host rock is schistose, eye-shaped feldspar porphyroblasts or lenticles of quartz and feldspar, aligned in the
foliation, are commonly developed by permeation. These *augen-schists*
and *augen-gneisses* may develop from pelitic, hornblendic or calcareous schists (Fig. 342). They pass into irregularly streaked and
banded gneisses.

Where the host rock is homogeneous and its fabric isotropic,
permeation by feldspathising emanations may produce *permeation-
gneisses* in which the feldspar is uniformly distributed or is aggregated
in irregular patches. *Feldspar porphyroblasts* may also develop as
large hypidiomorphic crystals set almost at random (Fig. 344). Rocks

558

Fig. 342. Migmatites. A, Lit-par-lit gneiss: the host is a psammitic rock; note the biotitic selvages alongside the injections; B, Augengneiss: the host is pelitic.

of these types are often seen in contact-aureoles where the hosts are hornfelsic. Host rocks which resist migmatisation, especially those of basic and ultrabasic composition, tend to form *agmatites* in which the introduced material forms a network of veins penetrating and disrupting the host (Fig. 341). All the various migmatites in which the host dominates the structure pass finally into more homogeneous biotite-, hornblende- or pyroxene-gneisses containing hazy relicts of the host (*nebulites*) or occasional dark clots and streaks (*schlieren*) of modified host material.

Textures. The survival of relict structures in migmatites shows that these rocks, like the metamorphic rocks, remained essentially solid during their formation. The host material shows crystalloblastic textures comparable to those described in Chapter 9; the granitic partner is generally coarser in grain, hypidiomorphic granular in texture, and may be largely pegmatitic. There is as a rule no sharp boundary between the two partners. The contacts of quartzo-feldspathic eyes, streaks and bands are firmly welded and often transitional, and the grains interlock across them. It seems probable that the conditions of crystallisation were essentially similar throughout; the host rock was bathed in pore-fluids which passed continuously into the fluids of the granitic areas. Concentrations of volatiles gave rise to pegmatitic patches.

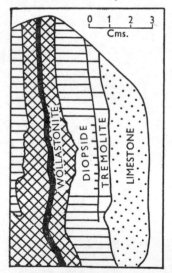

FIG. 343. Reaction zones along an acid vein (black) in limestone, Lough Anure, Donegal (after W. S. Pitcher).

Migmatitic textures are often distinguished by the abundance of evidence indicative of *reaction and replacement* — such evidence is of course seen also in rocks subjected to isochemical metamorphism, but in the changing chemical environment of migmatisation, continuous replacements are especially to be expected. Minerals in the host rock which were in equilibrium at the start of migmatisation tend to become unstable in the presence of the introduced material. Kyanite or sillimanite growing in a pelitic host may be converted to muscovite by the introduction of potash, calcite in a limestone may react with introduced silica to give lime-silicates and so on. In this way, pseudomorphs of early minerals may appear in the host and reaction rims may develop at contacts with granitic veins or patches (Fig. 343).

Feldspathisation, or the growth of new feldspar, usually as a result of the introduction of alkalies, involves the replacement of pre-existing minerals by acid plagioclase or potash-feldspar. This replacement can be most easily demonstrated where the feldspar grows as porphyroblasts (Fig. 344). The large feldspars are often sieved with inclusions of groundmass minerals which may be arranged in trails carrying the old structure of the host through the new crystal. The feldspar margins are often ragged, and delicate films of feldspar project outwards from the main crystal between the grains of the groundmass. The activity of alkalies during migmatisation is often reflected also by the replacement of one feldspar by another. Potash-feldspar often appears to be of later growth than plagioclase and may form a kind of cement at the margins of plagioclase grains, or may appear as rims around plagioclase porphyroblasts. Plagioclase replacing potash-feldspar gives rise to *myrmekite,* an intergrowth of plagioclase with vermicular droplets of quartz (Fig. 345); the quartz-inclusions represent silica expelled from the feldspar-lattice during the replacement of Si^{+4} by Al^{+3}. Oligoclase occasionally forms mantles around orthoclase porphyroblasts to produce compound grains of the type known as *rapakivi-feldspars* (Fig. 344).

Migmatites derived from the main types of host rocks. The starting-points in the sequences of changes induced by migmatisation are supplied by the structurally and chemically diverse association of metamorphic rocks which act as hosts. The end-products are banded

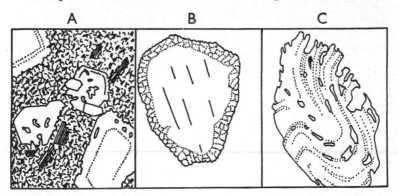

A   B   C

Fig. 344. Feldspar porphyroblasts in contact-migmatites. A, feldspar porphyroblasts in a biotite-hornfels enclave in the Trégastel granite, Normandy; B, rapakivi feldspar, oligoclase rim to orthoclase core, Dartmoor Granite, Cornwall; C, oligoclase porphyroblast with helicitic trails, Main Granite aureole, Donegal.

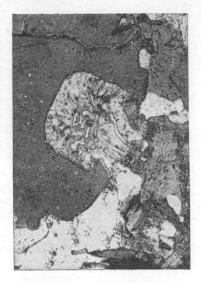

A

B

Fig. 345. Development of Feldspars in Contact-migmatites.
A, Margin of a feldspar porphyroblast showing unreplaced relics of
groundmass material, × 15; B, Myrmekite, oligoclase replacing
orthoclase with the disengagement of silica as quartz tubules, × 40.

or patchy gneisses or gneissose granites which, as a rule, show a
narrower range of variation than the parent rocks; migmatisation
brings about a *convergence* towards the general field of the granites,
and the changes in each rock-type are directed to making it approach
this field.

Pelitic rocks react readily to migmatisation and often pass into
gneisses while quartzites and calcareous rocks interbedded with them
remain more or less unmodified. Pelites are structurally easy to
permeate, schistose varieties in particular providing abundant
channels through which migrating fluids can pass, and they are
chemically less remote from the field of granites than is the majority
of metamorphosed sediments. Alumina and silica, the principal
components of feldspars, are present in quantity and comparatively
small adjustments of composition are sufficient to bring about
feldspathisation. The components in excess are alumina, iron and
magnesia which may migrate out of the host during migmatisation;
their fate is considered later.

In *regionally-metamorphosed terrains*, the first sign of migmatisation
in pelitic schists is generally shown by the development of eyes and
irregular streaks of coarse quartzo-feldspathic material, or of ovoid
feldspar porphyroblasts lying in the planes of schistosity. At the

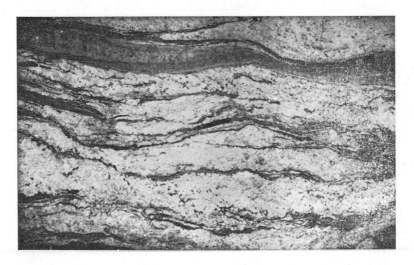

FIG. 346. Migmatisation of Pelites. (*Above*), development of nodes of feldspar in pelitic schist. (*Below*), biotitic relics of pelitic schist between quartzo-feldspathic streaks (from photographs by J. G. Ramsay).

margins of the feldspathic areas the minerals of the host rock often recrystallise to produce a selvage of large micas, sometimes associated with garnet, sillimanite or other aluminous minerals. As migmatisation proceeds, feldspar appears in the groundmass of the host and the quartzo-feldspathic folia multiply to produce a gneissose texture (Fig. 346). The original schistosity may be blurred by recrystallisation in the groundmass and give place to a less regular foliation. Where stress accompanies migmatisation, however, the micas retain a preferred orientation and the feldspathic areas often take the form of rods or spindles elongated in the direction of the lineation. Finally, the granitic folia become crowded together to produce a light-coloured gneiss, while the relics of the host are reduced to dark schlieren rich in quartz and biotite which wind their way between the feldspathic patches. The characteristic aluminous minerals of the host may recrystallise in the early stages of migmatisation and appear as characteristic minerals of the migmatitic gneisses. Thus migmatites in the sillimanite zone of the Barrovian metamorphic sequence of the south-east Highlands frequently contain sillimanite and garnet, while those of the Buchan district of north-east Scotland may contain sillimanite, garnet and cordierite (Fig. 333). As feldspathisation proceeds, however, the highly aluminous minerals tend to become unstable and are often replaced by muscovite, biotite or feldspar.

Hornfelsic pelitic rocks in *contact-aureoles* lack the strong directional structures of the schists and often give rise to granular-textured migmatites showing an irregular patchiness in place of the streaking or banding seen in gneisses derived from regionally metamorphosed schists. Large feldspar porphyroblasts are often developed with random orientation in the granular groundmass; French geologists use the expressive name *dents de cheval* for these crystals (Fig. 344).

Psammitic rocks are less sensitive to migmatisation than pelites. They are often massive, or are traversed only by widely spaced parting planes and consequently offer no convenient channels for the entry of emanations. Pure quartzites, moreover, are chemically remote from granite. They are made up almost exclusively of the single component, silica, and feldspathisation cannot take place without a considerable influx of material. Highly siliceous rocks are therefore *resisters* which tend to retain their original characters until an advanced stage in migmatisation (Fig. 347). Quartzites appear in migmatite complexes as very coarse glassy-looking rocks often forming bands which run almost continuously through a sea of gneisses derived from more permeable hosts. Impure psammites, which contain original feldspar and mica in addition to quartz, recrystallise

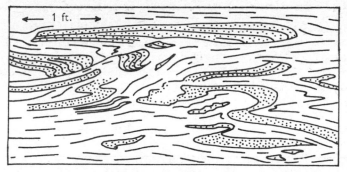

Fig. 347. Resisters in migmatisation: resistant siliceous ribs (dotted) in a migmatised pelitic matrix; note the disruption of the tougher ribs in the more plastic pelitic migmatites.

with little change of composition to give pinkish or buff-coloured siliceous gneisses with sugary granular textures. A *lit-par-lit* banding of siliceous and granitic layers results from the penetration of emanations along flaggy bedding-planes (Fig. 342).

Calcareous rocks are, like quartzites, slow to react to migmatisation, and calcareous migmatites seldom approach granite in composition. Coarse patchy calc-silicate rocks containing such minerals as diopside, hornblende, anorthitic plagioclase and sphene are formed by reaction between the limestone and the introduced material, and these rocks may pass into hornblende-gneisses or diopside-gneisses, or into amphibolites resembling metamorphosed basic rocks. Rapid variation is a characteristic feature of calcareous migmatites. Reaction-zones may appear at the borders of calcareous bands or along the contacts of veins (Fig. 343), and monomineralic clots of hornblende or diopside may be developed by metamorphic differentiation.

Basic rocks form compact massive bodies not easily permeated by incoming emanations. They commonly react to migmatisation by the development of a network of acid veins and thus pass into agmatites. The host rock may recrystallise with little change in composition, or it may be gradually feldspathised and pass into patchy dioritic migmatites made up of hornblende and andesine or oligoclase. At contacts with the acid material appinitic rocks with hornblendes a centimetre or more in length may appear (p. 583). Biotite is developed when potash is available, and garnet is a common accessory mineral. In some circumstances, inclusions of the host follow a different line of evolution. These inclusions may actually lose feldspar and turn into monomineralic knots of coarse hornblende; they are *basified* rather than granitised and survive as conspicuous dark bodies carried in the veining material.

565

In the field, several of the types of migmatites described above are generally found in association, their distribution depending on the conditions of migmatisation and the arrangement of the host rocks. Alternations of different kinds of host are reflected by the appearance of banded migmatites or by the occurrence of migmatites derived from one host containing bands or inclusions of rocks derived from another. In a sequence of interbedded pelites and psammites, pelitic gneisses may be seen to contain clearly-defined ribs of quartzite or fine-grained siliceous patches derived from impure psammites (Fig. 347). Resistant bands are commonly disrupted into strings of lenticles by movements taking place during migmatisation and these lenticles become enclosed in the more plastic gneisses as stream-lined inclusions around which the gneissose banding flows smoothly. In this way, the dominant migmatites come to carry relict bands or inclusions of resisters such as quartzites, limestones and basic or ultrabasic rocks.

On a larger scale, relics of resistant hosts may line up to form discontinuous bands which can be traced for several miles; these

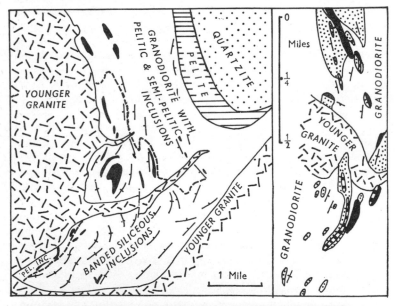

FIG. 348. Ghost-stratigraphy and ghost-structure, Thorr, Donegal (after W. S. Pitcher). (*Left*), map of the Thorr granodiorite, showing distribution and trends of the larger enclaves (black, limestone). (*Right*), detail of a group of enclaves in the Thorr granodiorite (dotted psammites, black limestone, barred metadolerite).

bands, with the variations in the migmatites themselves, define a *ghost-stratigraphy* and *ghost-structure* inherited from the country-rocks (Fig. 348). The survival in many migmatite areas of such inherited patterns demonstrates that the framework of the host rocks remained coherent throughout migmatisation; the patterns are, however, often deformed by contemporaneous movements and new structures of very plastic kinds are superimposed on them. When migmatisation is far advanced, the old patterns may be entirely destroyed and the migmatites are reborn as new rocks; this process is known as *anatexis*.

Migmatites and their geological setting. Migmatites are developed in regions of moderate or high temperature where the country-rocks are invaded by active emanations. The *migmatite-front* marks the outer limit of changes brought about by migmatisation and at this front the migmatites fade out into ordinary metamorphic rocks. Within the front the migmatite-complex — the varied association of migmatitic rocks — often shows a broad zoning which marks the stages of progressive transformation. Migmatites derived from the Moine Series of central Sutherland, for example, show an outer zone of veins, characterised by abundant granite, pegmatite and aplite veins but without appreciable permeation of the host, an intermediate zone of permeation and injection in which the host is the dominant partner, and an inner zone of gneisses in which granitic material is dominant and the host is reduced to relicts (Fig. 349).

Migmatites are found in two principal geological settings: they occur on a local scale in the contact-aureoles of certain granites and on a regional scale in many terrains of medium- or high-grade regional metamorphism. *Contact-migmatites* may make zones only extending a few hundred feet from the granite margin and appear also in rafts or xenoliths within the granite. Such rocks are seen at the contact of the Sea Point granite of Cape Town, where the host rock is a horn-felsed shale and within the Shap granite of Westmorland where the host consists of metamorphosed andesitic lavas. In these, and many other examples, the contact-migmatites are characterised by the presence of conspicuous feldspar porphyroblasts, in some instances showing rapakivi structure, and the associated granite contains similar feldspars; we shall return to this phenomenon later. The distribution of the contact-migmatites makes it seem clear that the feldspathising emanations producing them were derived directly from the neighbouring granite.

Regional migmatites form extensive complexes often hundreds of square miles in area and, as we have already seen, commonly lie at

T

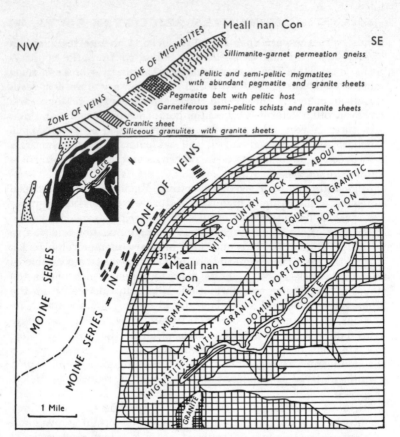

NW   Meall nan Con   SE

Sillimanite-garnet permeation gneiss

Pelitic and semi-pelitic migmatites with abundant pegmatite and granite sheets

Pegmatite belt with pelitic host
Garnetiferous semi-pelitic schists and granite sheets

Granitic sheet
Siliceous granulites with granite sheets

FIG. 349. Regional Migmatisation, Central Sutherland (after Read, H.M. Geological Survey). The main map shows the zones of migmatisation; the inset map shows the distribution of original lithological types, black pelites, dotted hornblende-gneiss, unornamented psammites. (*Top*), section of Meall nan Con (Ben Klibreck) showing zone of migmatites above zone of veins — the height of the section is about 2,500 feet and the vertical and horizontal scales are the same.

the centre of a broad system of zones of increasing regional metamorphism. In some areas the migmatite front is gently-inclined, and the emanations appear to have advanced from below upwards. In others, the migmatites form sheet-like bodies passing both upwards and downwards into less migmatised rocks; lateral migration of the migmatising fluids appears to be responsible for the formation of these bodies. An example is provided by the central Sutherland complex (Fig. 349) where the lower surface of the migmatite

568

complex can be seen to dip gently eastward on the slopes of Ben Klibreck.

Regional migmatites, unlike contact-migmatites, appear to be largely independent of bodies of homogeneous granite. The most extensive migmatite-complexes, which make the gneiss-provinces of high-grade metamorphism (p. 545), often contain only minor bodies of granite, and the composition and structure of these bodies suggest that they are themselves end-products of migmatisation. The regional migmatites, in fact, can more reasonably be regarded as the birthplace of new granites than as the byproducts of pre-existing granites. The source of the migmatising emanations must be looked for not in an intrusive magma but in the deeper and hotter parts of the crust.

Near the base of the crust in orogenic regions, the temperature may become so high that partial liquifaction takes place. A fluid containing the most easily mobilised components gathers in all interstices

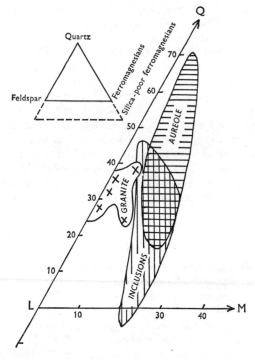

FIG. 350. Chemical changes in pelitic enclaves in the Dartmoor Granite (after D. L. Reynolds).

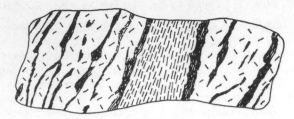

FIG. 351. Biotite selvages to granite veins in mica-schist, Sutherland.

and partings, and this fluid may be forced by orogenic pressures to move upward into new regions where it reacts with the country-rocks to produce migmatites. As we shall see later (p. 582), granitic material has the lowest melting-point of any common mixture of silicates, and the migrating material therefore consists of granitic fluids or of the active components silicon, sodium and potassium diffusing as ions. Analyses of migmatites from many localities show that the hosts are commonly enriched in these components during migmatisation (Fig. 350). At the same time, iron, magnesium and calcium are reduced by dilution and may also be expelled from the migmatites. The fate of any expelled material has been the subject of much controversy. On a small scale, there is evidence that the *cafemic* constituents (Fe, Mg, Ca) are concentrated in some surviving relicts of the host; examples are supplied by the basified hornblendic knots developed in basic migmatites (p. 565), by basified selvages at vein-contacts (Fig. 351) and by rims around inclusions. Some geologists regard these basic rims and knots as products of local *basic fronts* marking the migration of displaced cafemic material. Others see them as *subtraction-rocks* representing residual material concentrated by the mobilisation of more active feldspathic components — a basic behind rather than a basic front. On a regional scale, similar processes have been envisaged, but in the present state of knowledge their importance is difficult to assess.

GRANITES

Definitions. The granite family includes a number of species of light-coloured acid plutonic rocks which contain in varying proportions the minerals quartz, acid plagioclase and potash-feldspar and a ferromagnesian mineral which is generally biotite or hornblende. All these species can be loosely referred to as 'granite', but for petrographical purposes more exact definitions are required (Table I). The main divisions within the group are usually made on the basis of feldspar-content. The reduction and disappearance of quartz and the development of an intermediate plagioclase (andesine) provide transitions to the alkaline and intermediate families of syenites and diorites described on pp. 428, 584. The temperature at which crystallisation took place may also be expressed by variations in feldspar composition. *Hypersolvus* granites formed at high temperatures are characterised by alkali-feldspars carrying both K and Na (p. 102), while *subsolvus* granites are characterised by potash-feldspars and plagioclases with only limited solid solution.

TABLE I. SPECIES OF ACID PLUTONIC ROCKS, SHOWING RELATION TO SYENITES AND DIORITES

	Plagioclase$>\frac{2}{3}$ of total feldspar	Plagioclase $\frac{1}{3}-\frac{2}{3}$ of total feldspar	Plagioclase$<\frac{1}{3}$ of total feldspar
Quartz increasing ↑	{ GRANODIORITE { TRONDJHEMITE	ADAMELLITE	GRANITE
	{ TONALITE { QUARTZ-DIORITE		QUARTZ-SYENITE
No quartz	DIORITE (plagioclase =andesine)	MONZONITE	SYENITE (see Chapter 7)

Granite, s.s. is rich in potash-feldspar and is normally very acid, containing about 25 per cent of quartz and only a few per cent of biotite, or more rarely of amphibole or pyroxene (Fig. 352). The potash-feldspar of granitic rocks is commonly a *perthite* containing abundant films of plagioclase. Muscovite is often abundant and apatite, zircon, fluorspar, tourmaline and topaz are widespread accessories. *Adamellite* contains oligoclase and potash-feldspar in roughly equal proportions and is usually somewhat richer in ferromagnesian minerals than true granite. In *granodiorite*, plagioclase is the predominant feldspar and the mafic minerals, biotite or hornblende, form some 20 per cent of the rock. *Trondjhemite* is also plagioclase-rich, but is a pale felsic rock containing only a small amount of biotite. The plutonic species so far mentioned are often associated with finer-grained rocks of similar composition which form chilled marginal facies and minor intrusions. They can be included under the general names of *granite porphyries, microgranites and felsites* (Table on p. 391).

Textures. The granites are holocrystalline rocks which are coarse enough for the mineral grains to be distinguished with the naked eye. They show considerable variations in texture which reflect variations in the conditions of their formation. In the majority, irregular

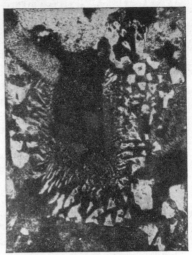

A   B

FIG. 352. Granitic Textures. A, granitic texture; quartz, orthoclase, plagioclase, scarce mica, polars crossed, × 15; B, granophyric texture, polars crossed, × 40.

hypidiomorphic granular textures (the 'granitic texture') are seen. The feldspars may show a squarish shape in cross-section but are seldom truly idiomorphic, and the remaining minerals form irregular grains with interlocking margins and frequent inclusions. Muscovite, when present, may build large flakes sieved with inclusions, and commonly replaces part of the feldspar. Other indications of reaction at late stages are supplied by patchy growths of potash-feldspar replacing plagioclase and cauliflower-shaped masses of myrmekite replacing potash-feldspar. Both feldspars are often filled with clouds of minute white micas or dusty kaolin.

The granitic texture described above is seen both in the granitic partners of many migmatites and in granites believed to be of intrusive origin. In some apparently magmatic granites, a more regular order of crystallisation is indicated by the occurrence of rectangular plagioclases, which may be zoned, in a granular matrix of interstitial quartz and potash-feldspar. The minerals here appear to have crystallised in order of their position in the reaction-series. In some varieties, the interstitial material is micrographic and these varieties pass into *granophyres* where the bulk of the rock is made up of micrographic intergrowths of quartz and feldspar (Fig. 352). In granophyres, the proportion of quartz to potash-feldspar is very constant, and is close to the eutectic proportions for a melt of the two minerals. It is probable that these rocks result from simultaneous

572

FIG. 353. Porphyritic Granites. A, Granite, Cornwall; B, Rapakivi granite, Finland.

crystallisation in a eutectic mixture, though similar textures may also be produced by the replacement of one mineral by another.

Porphyritic textures (Fig. 353), characterised by the occurrence of large feldspars in a finer-grained groundmass, are common, especially in small intrusive granites; in this respect the granites differ from the plutonic rocks described in Chapter 7 which are not as a rule porphyritic. The large feldspars are often idiomorphic, though in detail their margins are irregular. They may be made either of plagioclase or of potash-feldspar; *rapakivi-structure* is characterised by the occurrence of large ovoids in which a potash-feldspar core is mantled by a rim of small oligoclase grains. The origin of the large feldspars in granite has been much disputed. Some geologists regard them as phenocrysts analogous to those of lavas and small intrusions, and this view is supported by the fact that many porphyritic granites are associated with porphyritic dykes and sills. Other geologists have regarded the large feldspars as porphyroblasts grown in the solid; this view is supported by the occurrence of similar porphyroblasts in xenoliths and contact-migmatites. We shall return to this problem on a later page.

Finally, we may mention the rare and curious *orbicular granites*. In these rocks, and in the very similar *orbicular diorites*, the minerals appear to have crystallised in successive layers concentrically around a large number of nuclei (Fig. 360). The nuclei can sometimes be identified as small xenoliths; it seems probable that the distinctive structure is in some way connected with the presence of these inclusions, but the controlling factors are uncertain.

Planar and linear structures are developed from various causes in many granitic rocks. Migmatites, as we have seen, often show mimetic structures derived from the host and may also acquire a new foliation or lineation when formed under stress. *Flow-structures* produced by the planar or linear alignment of minerals and xenoliths are seen in certain intrusions. They reflect the movements of the magma and may be further emphasised by the continuance of magmatic pressures during consolidation. The first-formed marginal parts of the intrusion may then acquire so strong a foliation that they pass into *granite-gneiss*; such rocks are often associated with contact-schists rather than with hornfelses in the aureole.

PEGMATITES AND APLITES

During the crystallisation of granitic bodies, volatile substances are segregated in residual liquors which crystallise at a late stage to form veins in and near the granite. During the development of migmatites a volatile-rich fraction is mobilised and gathered into veins, patches

Fig. 354. Pegmatites. (*Above*), tourmaline-quartz pocket in pegmatite; (*Below*), tourmaline-feldspar pegmatite. (Ex Coll. G. P. L. Walker.)

and sheets. *Pegmatites* and *aplites*, the rocks formed from these volatile fractions, are therefore found in association with granites of all kinds. Both rocks consist essentially of quartz, with acid plagioclase and orthoclase or perthite; they contain large and varied suites of accessory minerals which owe their origin to the concentration of rare elements in the pegmatitic liquors.

Pegmatites and aplites are distinguished by their textures. The **aplites** are pale-coloured rocks of medium grain-size with a granular texture which gives them a sugary appearance. The **pegmatites** are characterised by extreme coarseness and variability of grain-size. Their larger crystals are seldom less than several centimetres in length and may exceptionally reach dimensions of many metres (p. 600). Some feldspars and accessory minerals may develop idiomorphic outlines and such species as tourmaline, beryl and topaz may form crystals of gem quality (Fig. 354). Graphic textures and frond-like or *plumose* growths of muscovite are seen in some pegmatites.

The accessory minerals vary according to the elements concentrated in the residual liquors. The pegmatites of a single granite usually all contain a similar suite of minerals, and the species present in the pegmatites may be found as minor accessories in the parent granite. There is usually also a family resemblance between the pegmatites of a group of granites belonging to a single orogenic belt; tin- and tungsten-minerals, for example, characterise the Cornish granites formed in the Hercynian orogeny, while these minerals are absent from the Scottish granites of the Caledonian orogeny (p. 600). Among the common accessory minerals, muscovite is almost always present, and may be accompanied by the pinkish lithium mica lepidolite. Topaz and fluorspar, containing fluorine in the crystal lattice, beryl carrying beryllium, and tourmaline carrying boron, together with garnet, are widespread, while cassiterite (SnO_2), columbite (a complex oxide containing tantalum), scheelite ($CaWO_4$) and uraninite and other radioactive minerals are developed in some provinces (Chapter 11). Aplites usually show a less varied suite of minerals than pegmatites, while both the aplites and pegmatites of migmatite complexes tend to be free from rare species, containing only such minerals as muscovite, tourmaline, garnet and biotite.

Pegmatites and aplites related to intrusive granites fill fissures in the outer parts of the granite and in the surrounding country-rocks. They appear to be formed by crystallisation from migrating liquors in the presence of abundant gaseous material, and their textures result from the activities of these volatiles which produce complex reactions and replacements. A single vein may contain both aplitic and pegmatitic varieties, sometimes arranged in rhythmically developed bands; the differences between the two varieties may depend principally on variations in the volatile content of the depositing liquors. At some distance from the parent rock, pegmatites and aplites become highly siliceous and pass into *quartz-veins* formed at lower temperatures.

Pneumatolysis and hydrothermal activity. The gaseous substances from which pegmatites are formed frequently react with the rocks through which they pass by a process known as *pneumatolysis*. As the temperature falls, the volatiles condense to give aqueous solutions from which the quartz-veins mentioned above are deposited. Reactions between these solutions and their country-rocks constitute *hydrothermal activity*. Pneumatolysis and hydrothermal activity each produce characteristic suites of minerals, including important metalliferous ore-minerals (Chapter 11).

THE GRANITE SERIES

Introduction. The characteristic habitats of granitic rocks are the deeper parts of the disturbed orogenic belts. The conditions in this environment are far removed from any that we know at the surface and have remained until recently particularly difficult to simulate in the laboratory. It is therefore not surprising that controversies over the origin of granite have continued without general agreement for more than a century. Of recent years, there has been a tendency to see the granite problem less as one capable of universal solution than as the sum of the problems provided by many individual granites, since it is widely agreed that there are, to use a much-quoted phrase, granites and granites.

It was stated on an earlier page that the granites, taken as a whole, bridge the gap between metamorphic rocks formed by transformations in the solid and igneous rocks formed by the consolidation of magma, and one of the principal points of contention concerns the relative importance of metamorphic as against igneous granites. At the one extreme, the diffuse granites or migmatites in which the host rock is often identifiable and a ghost-stratigraphy may be apparent, are considered by most geologists to have been formed by metasomatic processes which did not lead to dissolution of the solid framework; there is room for disagreement as to the part played by magmatic injection as against permeation by diffuse emanations and as to the extent to which melting of the most easily-fused fraction took place, but these points are not of great importance to us. At the other extreme, granite-bodies forming ring-complexes or occurring as

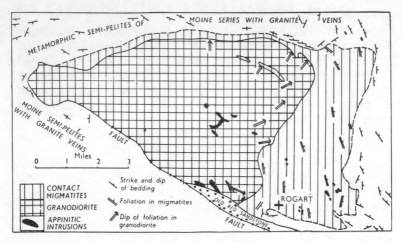

FIG. 355. Rogart Granodiorite, Sutherland (after Read, H.M.
Geological Survey).

integral parts of basic igneous intrusions are accepted by most
geologists as igneous and magmatic.

The diffuse migmatitic granites have already been discussed, and
may be exemplified by the Central Sutherland complex shown in
Fig. 349. By way of contrast, we may consider firstly a compact
granite which represents a forceful intrusion and secondly a granitic
ring-complex formed by permitted intrusion.

The **Rogart granodiorite of Sutherland** (Fig. 355) is emplaced in
regionally metamorphosed psammites and semi-pelites of the Moine
Series. Its contacts, modified in the south-west by faulting, are
broadly concordant, and appear to deflect the course of the regional
structures. The granodiorite itself is a coarse grey rock carrying both
hornblende and biotite and containing many clots and schlieren of
hornblende-rich rock. There is often a strong foliation and the
inclusions are aligned in this structure.

The country-rocks show no clear-cut contact-aureole, a fact which
may be due to the emplacement of the granodiorite before the rocks
had cooled down after regional metamorphism. There is, however, a
conspicuous belt of *contact-migmatites* along the northern and eastern
margin; within this zone the psammites and semi-pelites are converted into pinkish massive or *lit-par-lit* gneisses, and are invaded by
a network of biotite granite veins which extend beyond the zone of
permeation to form an external zone of veins. Clusters of small
appinitic intrusions (p. 583), themselves veined by granite, are found
in the migmatites and the granodiorite.

578

The form and relations of the Rogart granodiorite suggest that the body was intruded by pushing aside the country-rocks, distorting the pre-existing structural pattern and developing a strong foliation and lineation in the process. The marginal migmatites are thought to be due to the activity of an acid fraction squeezed out of the main body during consolidation.

The Rosses granite of Donegal (Fig. 356) provides our second example of an intrusive granite. This body is a *ring-complex* formed of three ring-intrusions emplaced as a result of the subsidence of a central plug (cf. pp. 397–9). All the three intrusions are made of granite, s.s., and are massive, pale-coloured rocks practically devoid of xenoliths. Swarms of microgranite and porphyry dykes are centred on the complex; one swarm cuts the older rings and is itself cut by the youngest intrusion, thus demonstrating the overlap in time of the major and minor intrusions.

The three granites are arranged concentrically, with the oldest at the outside and the youngest occupying the centre of the complex.

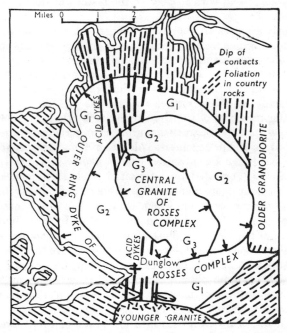

Fig. 356. The Rosses Ring Complex, Donegal (after W. S. Pitcher). G_1, G_2 and G_3 are successively younger granites intruded along ring fractures; dykes, thick black lines, were intruded between the times of G_2 and G_3.

The contacts are sharp, steep and often follow pre-existing joint-surfaces. The country-rocks surrounding the complex are grano-dioritic migmatites. They show no structural disturbance, the trend-lines in the migmatites running directly towards the contact and being sharply cut off. There is no migmatisation or contact-metamorphism. The minor intrusions chill against the migmatites and the youngest granite chills against its neighbour. Here, it is evident that we are dealing with intrusion of a magma with little surplus heat into country-rocks which had long passed the period of migmatisation and become cool and brittle.

The Granite Series. The numerous kinds of granite which have been mentioned in previous pages are not haphazardly distributed in the crust. If we study the granites of several orogenic belts, we find that certain types tend to recur in comparable parts of the belts and at comparable stages in their evolution. We recognise, in fact, a Granite Series whose starting-points are early deep-seated granites and whose final terms are late, often high-level intrusions — the words early and late being used with respect to the history of the orogenic belt concerned.

The early granites are represented largely by regional migmatites. These bodies are, as we have seen, developed in close connection with regional metamorphism, and are *autochthonous*, or formed more or less *in situ*, during or soon after the period of folding in the mobile belt. Where folding and migmatisation were roughly synchronous, the migmatites are said to be *syntectonic*.

The later members of the Granite Series are thought to be formed by the collection and migration of granitic material generated during migmatisation and palingenesis. This material may travel as a magma and give rise to igneous granites, or as a *migma* in which a mush of solid grains is lubricated by interstitial fluids. The bodies formed from either source are moderately compact and clearly separated from the country-rocks, in which they may induce contact-metamorphism. They displace the country-rocks by the mechanisms discussed in Chapter 7 and illustrated in the two examples shown in Figs. 355 and 356. *Parautochthonous* granites have travelled only a short distance from their place of origin; they are generally located in regionally-metamorphosed terrains and may be surrounded by a wide zone of contact-migmatites, such as is seen at Rogart. Granites which have migrated further are generally *late-tectonic* or *post-tectonic* in age. They may rise into low-grade or even unmetamorphosed country-rocks, and their associates may penetrate to the surface and give rise to acid or intermediate volcanic rocks. These relationships are diagrammatically expressed in Fig. 357.

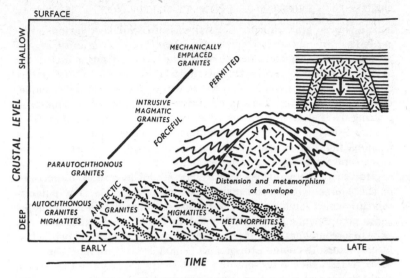

FIG. 357. The Granite Series.

An essential idea lying behind the concept of the Granite Series is that of the mobilisation and transport of material originally formed *in situ* in the crust. The migmatites and many great granite batholiths are thus considered to be plutonic bodies formed by *replacement* and not by displacement of the country-rocks; this view provides a means of meeting the most puzzling of all granite problems, the 'room problem', since it does not require the bodily introduction of enormous masses of material into the solid crust. Many other problems connected with the genesis of individual members of the Granite Series, however, remain unsolved. We may mention again the *dents de cheval* found in contact-migmatites and inclusions in certain small granites. These undoubted porphyroblasts are often found in association with a porphyritic granite carrying similar feldspars, as in the Sea Point and Shap granites. Many geologists have argued that since the feldspars in the country-rock are metasomatic, those in the granite must have a similar origin, and have concluded that the granite itself is a product of granitisation; this argument becomes more compelling when all the feldspars in question show rapakivi structure. In the present writers' view, the evidence of *dents de cheval* cannot by itself be taken to demonstrate the origin of the whole granitic body. A second problem still to be settled concerns the occurrence around certain parautochthonous or intrusive granites of marginal zones of basic plutonic rocks. These zones, seen for example

581

in the Newry granodiorite of north-east Ireland, are variously regarded as differentiates from the same magma as the granite, and as
products of a basic front formed as a result of granitisation on the site
of the granite body. Again, the final answer is lacking.

Since observations show that the continental crust is very variable,
it could be objected that the relative uniformity of the material
making up the Granite Series is not consistent with derivation from
the sial. Here, however, the findings of experimental work are
illuminating. Bowen and Tuttle have shown that solutions of quartz,
albite and orthoclase in the presence of water-vapour begin to
crystallise at temperatures which vary according to the proportions
of the components in the manner shown in Fig. 358. The eutectic
mixture which remains liquid to the lowest temperature contains the
three components in roughly equal proportions. Natural granites
poor in ferromagnesian minerals contain quartz, albite and orthoclase
in very much the same proportions (Fig. 358) and we may therefore
suppose that they represent the most easily melted fraction which
could be derived on heating from crustal rocks of varied composition.

Finally, we should recall that certain granites are found in non-
orogenic settings and are genetically, though not always petrologically,

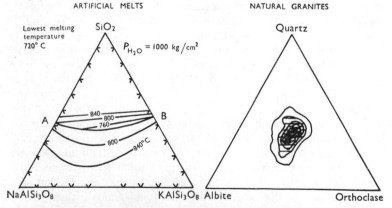

Fig. 358. The system $SiO_2.NaAlSi_3O_8.KAlSi_3O_8$, and its application
to natural granites (based on Bowen and Tuttle). (Left), diagram
showing the temperatures at which crystallisation begins in a quartz-
orthoclase-albite liquid, in the presence of water, at a water-vapour
pressure of 1000 kg/cm². Above AB, quartz appears first; below AB
feldspar appears first. The lowest temperatures of crystallisation are
shown by mixtures having a composition in the central part of AB.
(Right), composition of 571 natural granites containing less than 20%
of ferromagnesian minerals, expressed in terms of quartz, orthoclase
and albite. Note that the maximum falls in the position of the low-
temperature mixtures.

quite distinct from those of the Granite Series. Small quantities of granitic rocks, as well as acid minor intrusions and lavas, are formed by magmatic differentiation in *basic igneous provinces* (Chapter 7). Fair-sized intrusions of granite in such provinces are considered by some authors to result from melting of the country-rocks by the heat of the incoming basic magma; again, the evidence that granite represents a relatively easily-melted mixture lends support to this possibility. As examples of granites in basic provinces we can mention again the 'red rocks' at the roof of certain layered basic intrusions and the granites of Arran and Skye in the North Atlantic Tertiary province.

LAMPROPHYRES AND APPINITES

The lamprophyres and appinites are two groups of mafic rocks bearing alkali-feldspar which occur most commonly as minor intrusions in granitic provinces. The lamprophyres generally form dykes while the appinites more often form small bosses which may be grouped in clusters.

The *lamprophyres* are dark rocks characterised by the occurrence of phenocrysts of ferromagnesian minerals such as augite, brown hornblende or biotite. Feldspar is confined to the fine-grained groundmass and is generally orthoclase or a fairly acid plagioclase. Secondary minerals produced by the action of abundant volatiles in the magma are very common. Biotite is often patchily bleached, hornblende and augite may be altered to uralite, and talc, calcite and pyrite are widespread in the groundmass. The late-stage alterations characteristic of lamprophyres tend to give the rocks a dull earthy appearance. The various species of lamprophyre are distinguished mainly by the nature of the dominant ferromagnesian mineral. In *minettes*, biotite forms phenocrysts and orthoclase is the principal feldspar (Fig. 359); *camptonites* contain hornblende, augite and plagioclase, *spessartites* hornblende and plagioclase.

The *appinites* (Fig. 359) are cleaner-looking and coarser-grained than the lamprophyres. They contain a substantial amount (usually more than 50 per cent) of ferromagnesian minerals, which are associated with alkali-feldspars — orthoclase or acid plagioclase. The type appinite is made up largely of plagioclase and hornblende, the hornblende forming conspicuous prisms spearing at random through the pale feldspathic matrix. Other varieties contain abundant large flakes of biotite, while basic types are rich in augite or olivine.

The origin of the lamprophyres and appinites is not clearly understood and it is probable that similar rocks are formed by a number of

A   B

FIG. 359. A, Biotite-lamprophyre showing biotite phenocrysts in a
secondarily altered ground-mass, × 25; B, Appinite: a member of the
Appinite Suite, composed of biotite, pyroxene, sphene and plagioclase, × 35.

different processes. The field-association of the two groups with
granites of the orogenic belts suggests that the processes of regional
migmatisation and granite-formation may be connected with their
production; appinite intrusions are sometimes clustered about particular granites (e.g., the Rogart granodiorite) and appear to be
related to these bodies, while appinites formed *in situ* are seen occasionally among migmatites derived from basic hosts. Both appinites
and lamprophyres are frequently very rich in xenoliths of sedimentary
material which may contribute to their formation. Many appinites
have a pipe-form and their material may have been transported upwards by an explosive gas phase. In a totally different setting, basic
lamprophyres have been recorded from olivine-basalt provinces and
it should be noted that these dyke rocks are chemically similar to
certain feldspathoidal basalts of the same provinces.

DIORITES

A **diorite,** in the strict sense, is an intermediate plutonic rock composed of andesine and a mafic mineral which is usually hornblende.
Augite is sometimes an essential mineral and biotite and sphene are
commonly present. Diorites are generally coarse enough to present a
speckled appearance due to the scattering of dark minerals through
the pale feldspar grains; the dark minerals are often gathered into

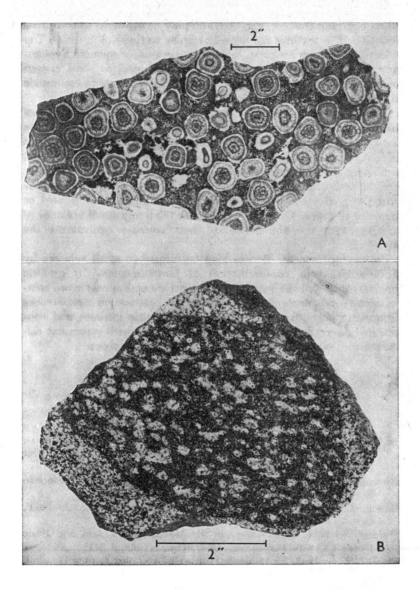

Fig. 360. Diorites. A, Orbicular Diorite; B. Diorite containing a feldspathised sedimentary xenolith.

585

small clots and clusters (Fig. 360) and may be arranged to produce a foliation. The textures are broadly similar to those of granites. The feldspar may form irregular, interlocking grains, or squarish hypidiomorphic crystals, while the mafic minerals tend to show ragged outlines. Orbicular diorites show growth of minerals in concentric zones, as already described (p. 574).

Diorites pass by way of *quartz-diorite* and *tonalite* (quartz-hornblende-biotite diorite) into granodiorites (Table I, p. 571); with the appearance of a more basic plagioclase and an increase in the content of ferromagnesian minerals they pass into gabbros. Though they hold a position intermediate between gabbros and granites, the diorites are decidedly less abundant than either of these groups and appear to be formed principally as secondary derivatives of more acid or more basic types. We may contrast the relatively small volumes of diorites with the abundance of their volcanic equivalents the andesites.

In basic provinces, diorites may be formed in small volumes by differentiation or contamination of basic magma. In granitic provinces, they make some small intrusions and appear more commonly as components of granitic masses. Migmatisation of basic rocks frequently leads to the development of dioritic gneisses and contamination of granite with basic material, or with somewhat calcareous sediments, gives mottled or patchy dioritic rocks.

FURTHER READING AND REFERENCE

Bailey, E. B., 1961, in 'The Geology of Ben Nevis and Glen Coe', *Mem. Geol. Surv. Scotland*. Deals with Glen Coe and Ben Nevis, the first ring-structures to be described.

Buddington, A. F., 1959, 'Granite emplacement with special reference to North America', *Bull. Geol. Soc. Amer.*, vol. 70, p. 671.

Cheng, Y. C., 1944, 'The migmatites around Bettyhill, Sutherland', *Quart. Journ. Geol. Soc.*, vol. 99 (for 1943), p. 107.

Holmes, A., 1931, 'The problem of the Association of Acid and Basic Rocks in Central Complexes', *Geol. Mag.*, vol. 68, p. 241.

Pitcher, W. S., 1953, 'The Rosses granitic ring-complex, County Donegal, Eire', *Proc. Geol. Assoc.*, vol. 64, p. 153.

——, H. H. Read and others, 1959, 'The Main Donegal Granite', *Quart. Journ. Geol. Soc.*, vol. 114 (for 1958), p. 259.

Read, H. H., 1931, 'The Geology of Central Sutherland', *Mem. Geol. Surv. Scotland*.

——, 1957, *The Granite Controversy*, Murby.

Reynolds, D. L., 1946, 'The sequence of geochemical changes leading to granitisation', *Quart. Journ. Geol. Soc.*, vol. 102, p. 389.

——, 1947, 'The association of basic "fronts" with granitisation', *Sci. Prog.*, vol. 35, p. 205.

Sederholm, J. J., 1923–34, 'On migmatites and associated Pre-Cambrian rocks of south-western Finland', I, *Bull. Com. Géol. Finlande*, no. 58, 1923: II, *ibid.*, no. 83, 1926: III, *ibid.*, no. 107, 1934. Three works by a geologist who had much to do with demonstrating the process of migmatisation.

Soper, N. J., 1963, 'The structure of the Rogart igneous complex', *Quart. J. Geol. Soc. Lond.*, 119, 445.

Tuttle, O. F., and N. L. Bowen, 1958, 'Origin of granite in the light of experimental studies in the system $NaAlSi_3O_8$–$KAlSi_3O_8$–SiO_2–H_2O', *Geol. Soc. Amer.*, Memoir 74.

Walker, F., and M. Mathias, 1946, 'The petrology of two granite-slate contacts at Cape Town, South Africa', *Quart. Journ. Geol. Soc.*, vol. 102, p. 499.

11

MINERAL DEPOSITS

MANY of the materials with which the geologist deals are of immense industrial and social importance — we need only mention such products as the natural fuels, water, building-materials and the ores of the useful metals to establish this opinion. But, as we have also said, there is no applied or economic geology that is different from general geology — the same geological rules are involved whether a rock is of value or not and it is only the emphasis that varies. The purpose of this chapter is not to give an exhaustive treatment of the useful minerals and rocks but rather to use them to recapitulate and summarise the geological principles that have been set out in the foregoing pages of this book. We propose to view the same phenomena from a different aspect.

Definitions concerning mineral deposits. Mineral deposits are those rocks and minerals that are of use to man and that can be worked at a profit. A broad two-fold division is often made into first, the *non-metallic mineral deposits* many of which are worked because of certain *physical* properties and second, the *metalliferous mineral deposits* worked essentially because they contain certain valuable *chemical* elements. This division obscures the fundamental pattern of mineral formation and is not followed here. A preferable classification is into *endogenetic* and *exogenetic* mineral deposits, a genetic classification applicable to rocks in general. *Endogenetic* rocks or deposits are those resulting from processes taking place or originating within the lithosphere; igneous rocks and their associated mineral deposits are endogenetic as are the metamorphic rocks and deposits. *Exogenetic* rocks and deposits are formed at the earth's surface where lithosphere, hydrosphere and atmosphere react on one another; they comprise the variety of sedimentary rocks.

Metalliferous mineral deposits are often called *ore-deposits*. An *ore* is material that pays to work for some metal. It is a mixture of the desired mineral, the *ore-mineral*, and unwanted minerals, the *gangue*. The metal content of the ore is its *tenor*; as examples, the tenor of a lead ore is on the average 6–10 per cent Pb, of a chromium-ore 35–50 per cent Cr, of a copper-ore 1·5–5 per cent Cu. Depending on the price of the metal, a deposit may be an ore one week and not the week after.

MINERALS OF MINERAL DEPOSITS

Many of the minerals making mineral deposits have been mentioned in Chapter 3 — examples are feldspar, garnet, rock-salt and dolomite. But the minerals of the ore-deposits — the ore-minerals of the common metals — have scarcely been touched upon. Even so, no detailed account, especially on the determinative side, of these can be given here, and the student must refer to the text-books of mineralogy for further information. A list of the common ore-minerals with their chemical compositions is given in the Table below. Common gangue minerals are quartz, calcite, dolomite, siderite ($FeCO_3$), barytes ($BaSO_4$), fluorspar, feldspar and garnet.

IMPORTANT ORE-MINERALS

ALUMINIUM, Al - - -	Bauxite, $Al_2O_3.2H_2O$
ANTIMONY, Sb - - -	Stibnite, Sb_2S_3
ARSENIC, As - - -	Mispickel or Arsenopyrite, FeAsS
BERYLLIUM, Be - -	Beryl, $Be_3Al_2Si_6O_{18}$
BISMUTH, Bi - - -	Native Bismuth, Bi
	Bismuthinite, Bi_2S_3
CADMIUM, Cd - - -	Greenockite, CdS
CHROMIUM, Cr - - -	Chromite, $FeO.Cr_2O_3$
COBALT, Co - - -	Smaltite, $CoAs_2$
	Cobaltite, CoAsS
COPPER, Cu - - -	Native Copper, Cu
	Cuprite, Cu_2O
	Chalcopyrite, Copper Pyrites, $CuFeS_2$
	Chalcocite, Cu_2S
	Covellite, CuS
	Bornite, Cu_5FeS_4
	Enargite, Cu_3AsS_4
	Chalcanthite, $CuSO_4.5H_2O$
	Malachite, $CuCO_3.Cu(OH)_2$
	Azurite, $2CuCO_3.Cu(OH)_2$
	Chrysocolla, $CuSiO_3.2H_2O$
GOLD, Au - - -	Native Gold, Au
	Sylvanite (Au, Ag)Te_2
	Calaverite, $AuTe_2$
IRON, Fe - - - -	Magnetite, Fe_3O_4
	Hematite, Fe_2O_3
	Goethite, $HFeO_2$, the main constituent of limonite
	Siderite, Chalybite, $FeCO_3$
	(Pyrite, FeS_2, worked for sulphur)
	(Pyrrhotite, Fe_nS_{n+1}, worked for nickel)

LEAD, Pb	- - -	Galena, PbS
		Anglesite, $PbSO_4$
		Cerussite, $PbCO_3$
MAGNESIUM, Mg	- -	Magnesite, $MgCO_3$
MANGANESE, Mn	- -	Pyrolusite, MnO_2
		Psilomelane, $MnO_2.nH_2O$
MERCURY, Hg -	- -	Cinnabar, HgS
MOLYBDENUM, Mo	- -	Molybdenite, MoS_2
		Wulfenite, $PbMoO_4$
NICKEL, Ni	- - -	Pentlandite (Fe, Ni)S
		Kupfernickel, NiAs
		Cloanthite, $NiAs_2$
		Garnierite, $H_2(Ni, Mg)SiO_3.H_2O$
SILVER, Ag	- - -	Native Silver, Ag
		Argentite, Ag_2S
		Cerargyrite, AgCl
TANTALUM, Ta -	- -	Tantalite-Columbite (Fe, Mn) $(Nb, Ta)_2O_6$
TIN, Sn -	- - -	Cassiterite, SnO_2
		Stannite, $Cu_2S.FeS.SnS_2$
TITANIUM, Ti -	- -	Rutile, TiO_2
		Ilmenite, $FeO.TiO_2$
TUNGSTEN, W -	- -	Wolfram (Fe, Mn)WO_4
		Scheelite, $CaWO_4$
URANIUM, U -	- -	Pitchblende, $2UO_3.UO_2$
		Torbernite, $Cu(UO_2)_2P_2O_8.12H_2O$
		Autunite, $Ca(UO_2)_2P_2O_8.8H_2O$
		Carnotite, $K_2O.2U_2O_3.V_2O_3.2H_2O$
VANADIUM, V -	- -	Patronite, VS_4
		Vanadinite, $Pb_3Cl(VO_4)_3$
		Carnotite, $K_2O.2U_2O_3.V_2O_3.2H_2O$
ZINC, Zn -	- - -	Zincite, ZnO
		Blende, Sphalerite, ZnS
		Smithsonite, $ZnCO_3$
		Hemimorphite, $Zn_4Si_2O_7(OH)_2.H_2O$
ZIRCONIUM, Zr -	- -	Zircon, $ZrSiO_4$

INVESTIGATION OF MINERAL DEPOSITS

A mineral deposit is, like all rock-occurrences, capable of being investigated and interpreted by standard geological methods. Its study in the field is therefore of fundamental importance. Geological maps on various appropriate scales have to be made of the region, with detailed maps of the deposit or ore-body itself. The complete exploration of the body may be accomplished by geophysical and geochemical investigations along the lines already indicated (pp. 36, 45) and supplemented by extensive drilling. Detailed field-work may reveal the relations of the deposit to the surrounding country-rocks or to adjacent igneous rocks. Geological structures obviously control the deposition of the valuable materials, and the regional and local structures of the country-rocks have to be determined. Structures presented by the deposit itself may also be of great significance.

The valuable minerals sought for may be determined in a number of ways. Many of them can be recognised on sight and the geologist interested in mineral deposits has to make himself familiar with the appearance and obvious physical properties of their constituent minerals. Chemical tests, such as those of blowpipe analysis, or more rigorous investigations, may be necessary, but cannot be dealt with here. The techniques of assaying, spectroscopy and X-ray investigations are employed in accurate determination of the minerals making the deposit. Finally, the methods, already described, of petrographic examination with the microscope yield information of great importance.

The ore-minerals, most of which are opaque, cannot be examined by transmitted light but are studied in *polished specimens* by *reflected light*. The polished specimen is prepared by embedding a piece of the ore in a suitable resin contained in a mould and then preparing a flat surface on the mounted sample by grinding. A final polish is put on the flat surface by rubbing on a lap sprinkled with a fine polishing powder. The mounted specimen is removed from the mould and is ready for examination. The microscope employed for the investigation of opaque minerals is fitted with a *vertical illuminator* by which light is thrown down on to the polished specimen and is reflected therefrom back to the eyepiece. The polished specimen can be examined by ordinary or polarised light and the relationships between the various ore-minerals present determined. Identification of these minerals is confirmed by hardness tests, etching by acids or by microchemical tests. In these latter, a small quantity of the mineral is scraped off and placed on a glass slip; it is then subjected to the usual chemical tests and the crystals or precipitates studied under the microscope.

Ore-deposition is often a complex process, involving a succession of replacements and depositions. *Replacement* is especially important and we give in Fig. 361 some examples of the criteria employed. These are the presence of residuals of the old mineral in the new, the preservation in the new mineral of structures and textures belonging to the old, the pseudomorphism of the old by the new, veining of old by new and other less conclusive criteria. The demonstration of replacement is often a difficult matter. Successive *deposition* of minerals in a cavity leads to a *crustification*, by the growth of different

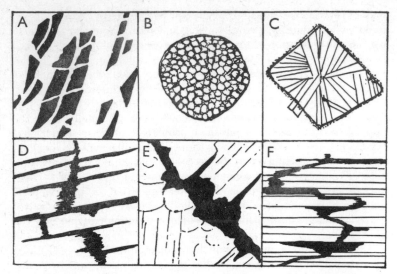

FIG. 361. Criteria of replacement. A, relics of blende (black) in chalcocite; B, replacement of woody tissue by silica, Rhynie chert, Aberdeenshire; C, replacement of andalusite prism by kyanite blades, Unst; D, thin section of staurolite showing replacement along fractures by chloritoid (black), Unst; E, replacement of several mineral grains by a vein of ore-mineral (black); F, ore-deposit replacing bedded limestone.

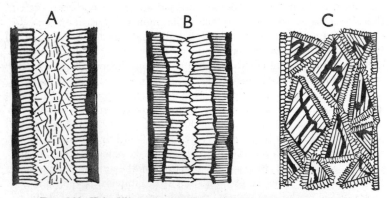

FIG. 362. Vein-filling. A, crustification, sequence of deposition is blende (black), quartz, fluorspar, barytes; B, comb-structure, sequence is blende (black), quartz, blende, quartz; vugs produced by incomplete filling; C, complex vein; breccia of limestone with replacement veins of galena (black) cemented by crusts of quartz, leaving vugs.

minerals in successive coats on one another (Fig. 362), and often to *comb-structure*, with the growth of good crystals inwards from the cavity-walls. The aim of the investigation of mineral deposits is that common to all geology — to unravel the history of the formation of the rock concerned.

CONCENTRATION IN THE FORMATION OF MINERAL DEPOSITS

In the formation of a mineral deposit, whether metallic or non-metallic, concentration of the useful material has taken place. We may recall, from Chapter 2, that nearly 99 per cent of the earth's crust is estimated to be made of eight elements, O Si Al Fe Ca Na K Mg, of which O and Si account for nearly three-quarters. Many of the metallic elements most important in industry are really scarce — Cu forming ·007 per cent of the crust, Sn ·004 per cent, Pb ·0016 per cent, U ·0004 per cent, Ag ·00001 per cent, Au ·0000005 per cent. It is obvious that some process of concentration must take place to make these elements accessible to man and the same commonly applies to useful minerals. This necessary concentration may occur in two environments which are, in fact, those of the endogenetic and exogenetic deposits already established. Processes within the crust, such as the solidification of a magma or the operations of meta-morphism, give rise to the endogenetic deposits. Surface-processes, such as deposition in a salt lake or sorting by river-action, produce the exogenetic mineral deposits. We examine these two great classes of mineral deposits in turn.

A. ENDOGENETIC MINERAL DEPOSITS

CONDITIONS OF ENDOGENETIC MINERAL FORMATION

It will be as well to consider the physical and geological conditions under which endogenetic mineral deposits are formed. Like many other minerals, ore- and gangue-minerals are deposited from a solution, whether this is liquid or gaseous, when with fall of tempera-ture and pressure, conditions become suitable. Whilst pressure is undoubtedly an important factor, temperature is much more so and it provides a basis for the genetic classification of many mineral deposits of this group. The temperature of formation is given in suitable cases by minerals which serve as *geological thermometers*.

Inversion-points provide the most useful indications of tempera-ture; at atmospheric pressure, quartz forms below 870°, and high-temperature quartz inverts to low-temperature quartz at 573° C, the two forms being recognisable by their different symmetries (p. 100). By observation it has been shown that the quartz in quartz-veins and

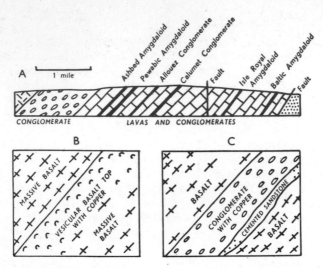

Fig. 363. Lithological controls of ore-deposition, copper deposits of the Lake Superior region. A, section showing the ore-bearing horizons (black); B, deposition in the vesicular tops of lavas and in the interstices of conglomerate.

some pegmatites formed below 573°, and that in most pegmatites and igneous rocks generally it formed above this temperature. Direct measurements of the temperature of flowing lavas or of the *melting-points* of minerals provide upper limits of their temperatures of formation. *Exsolution* of two minerals takes place at definite temperatures. *Liquid inclusions* in crystals at their time of formation completely filled the cavities in which they occur so, by heating experiments, the temperature of formation of the crystals can be found.

By the use of these criteria the ore-deposits of endogenetic origin can be grouped into high-, medium- and low-temperature types, as we see in a later page. Fairly typical assemblages of minerals characterise each group — magnetite, pyrrhotite, tourmaline, topaz, cassiterite, garnet, pyroxenes and amphiboles being of high-temperature formation; chalcopyrite, galena and blende of medium temperature; the tellurides, adularia feldspar, chalcedony (cryptocrystalline silica) and siderite of low-temperature formation.

Additional controls in mineral deposition may be provided by the *lithology* (Fig. 363) of the country rocks and especially by their textures and structures, since many ore-deposits are precipitated from solutions. Thus the permeability and porosity of the country-rocks and the presence of fractures and cavities in them may control ore-deposition. Alternations of pervious and impervious layers may

594

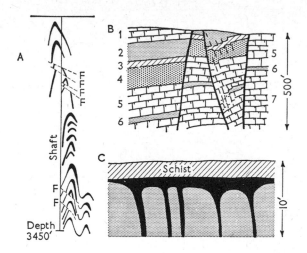

FIG. 364. Structural control of ore-deposition. A, saddle reefs, Bendigo (F = fault); B, fluorspar veins along faults (after Weller); C, veins along joints, with damming of ore-solutions at an impervious bed (after Spencer).

exert a profound influence on the location of ore-bodies. Bedding-planes and planes of unconformity may provide channelways for mineralising solutions. On a broader scale, the *geological structure* (Fig. 364) may be of the greatest importance for mineral deposition. Fractures such as joints, or brecciated zones along fault-belts may provide channels of easy access for ore-fluids. Tight folding in a series of competent and incompetent beds may create actual or potential spaces in the crests of the folds and thus promote the formation of *saddle-reefs*, illustrated by the famous gold-quartz deposits of Bendigo, Victoria (Fig. 364); in this example, however, reverse faulting, subsequent to folding, is now thought to be the main structural control.

IGNEOUS ACTIVITY AND ENDOGENETIC MINERAL DEPOSITION

The endogenetic mineral deposits are mostly related to that most active chemical and physical process going on in the crust, the formation and evolution of magmas (p. 401). Certain mineral deposits, such as those of chromite or feldspar, are integral parts of igneous rock bodies. Other deposits show a constant association with a certain type of igneous rock as, for example, tin-ores with granite. Some deposits are seen to be formed in connection with volcanic, fumerole or hot spring activity. Perhaps the best demonstration of

595

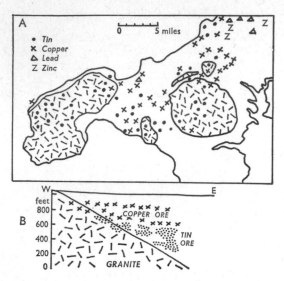

FIG. 365. Zonal arrangement of ore-deposits around the Cornish granites. A, general map; B, section in the St Day United Mine (after Fawns).

the genetic connection between igneous rocks and endogenetic mineral deposits is shown by the *zonal arrangement* of the ores around an igneous centre as illustrated in Cornwall (Fig. 365). High-temperature minerals are nearest to the igneous body, lower-temperature minerals farther out from the contact. The ideal sequence, never found complete, would be Sn and W; Au; Cu; Zn; Zn and Pb; Pb; Au and Ag, Sb and Hg.

In the account of the igneous rocks in Chapter 7, the course of crystallisation of magma was dealt with. The magma is considered to be a high-temperature mutual solution of silicates, oxides and volatile components. Such volatile components as H_2O, S, Cl, B, F and others act as transporters of the ore-elements. We may review the crystallisation of a magma as it affects the mineral deposits formed at each stage. First, the high-temperature heavy silicates crystallise out and with them or soon after them may be formed certain mineral deposits called *orthomagmatic*. With continued crystallisation, the volatiles and the remaining ore-elements originally dispersed throughout the magma become concentrated in the residual fluids, both liquid and gaseous, and these, on final consolidation, produce the high-temperature *pegmatitic-pneumatolytic* deposits. Some of the residual fluids may stream into the adjacent country-rock to form the contact-metamorphic or *pyrometasomatic* deposits by the replacement of

596

suitable country-rock—the temperature of formation of such contact deposits, as given by the geological thermometer minerals in them, is still high. With falling temperature, the final residual solutions, largely juvenile water, pass upwards from the igneous body through fissures in the country-rock and deposit their burden of ore- and gangue-minerals in the veins or lodes of the *hydrothermal* deposits, formed at low temperatures. We may use these various stages in the evolution of the magma to erect a classification of endogenetic mineral deposits.

Classification of endogenetic mineral deposits. The first division of the endogenetic mineral deposits is into (1) the *igneous* or *magmatic* or *primary* and (2) the *regional-metamorphic* or *secondary*. During regional metamorphism, new minerals of value may be produced by reconstitution of the components of the rocks, or concentrations may take place that make a mineral workable. In the previous section we have presented the basis for a classification of the primary deposits, so that our complete classification of the endogenetic mineral deposits is as given below. In this table some possible temperatures of formation have been given, and it will be noted that the hydrothermal group has been subdivided on their estimated temperatures of formation.

CLASSIFICATION OF ENDOGENETIC MINERAL DEPOSITS

(1) **Igneous, magmatic or primary**

    A. Orthomagmatic, 700–1500° C.
    B. Pegmatitic-pneumatolytic, ±575° C.
    C. Pyrometasomatic, 500–800° C.
    D. Hydrothermal.
        (i) hypothermal, 300–500° C.
        (ii) mesothermal, 200–300° C.
        (iii) epithermal, 50–200° C.

(2) **Metamorphic** c. 400° C.

ORTHOMAGMATIC MINERAL DEPOSITS

Concentration of minerals may take place in several ways and at different times during the crystallisation of magma. Heavy minerals crystallising early may accumulate by sinking under gravity to form true *magmatic segregations*, usually but not necessarily marginal in position in the igneous body into which the segregation grades. Deposits of this type may be represented by the chromite-deposits of the Bushveld igneous complex of South Africa (Chapter 7); here relatively thin and remarkably extensive and persistent bands of chromite intercalated in various types of gabbro, anorthosite or more

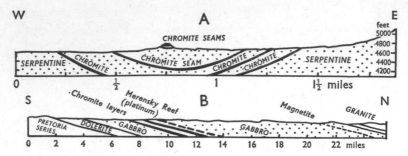

FIG. 366. Chromite deposits. A, section across the Great Dyke, Rhodesia (after Keep); B, section across part of the Bushveld Igneous Complex, South Africa, showing concentrations of chromite, platinum (Merensky Reef) and magnetite in gabbro (after Hall).

basic rocks, are considered to result from crystal accumulation under gravity (Fig. 366). Concentrations of early-formed minerals may not remain in their positions of accumulation but may be *injected* into the adjacent rocks as intrusive masses; the great magnetite deposits of Kiruna in Sweden may possibly be of this origin.

Other mineral deposits are formed by concentration later in the process of magmatic consolidation and may thus be related to the residual portions of the magma rather than to the early crystallisations. These *late magmatic deposits* include those formed from residual liquids, often injected into nearby rocks, and represented by ore-bodies of magnetite, often titaniferous, associated with basic igneous rocks — perhaps it may be shown eventually that the Kiruna deposit is of this origin. *Liquid immiscibility* is a process not much favoured in magmatic differentiation, but it appears to explain the formation of certain sulphide-deposits such as that of Insizwa, South Africa. It is believed that a concentration of metallic sulphides (Cu, Fe, Ni with Pt, Au, Ag etc.) may take place in a basic magma by their remaining liquid after the crystallisation of the rest of the magma as gabbro. The chief minerals involved are pyrrhotite, chalcopyrite and pentlandite. Such liquid fractions may of course be injected elsewhere before consolidation.

Some gemstones such as rubies and sapphires may crystallise from magmas rich in alumina, and it has been proposed that *diamonds* are crystallised from carbon-rich magmas, though this is disputed. Diamond is valued both as a gemstone and as an abrasive of the highest class for use in drill-bits and saws. It occurs in an ultrabasic igneous breccia (*blue ground*) which, at Kimberley in South Africa and elsewhere, forms vertical pipes drilled through horizontal rocks (Fig. 367). The process appears to combine volcanic-gas explosion

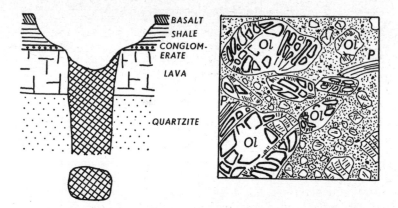

FIG. 367. Kimberlite. Cross-section and plan of a diamond pipe, Kimberley (after Du Toit); thin section of kimberlite showing crystals of serpentinised olivine and phlogopitic mica in a fine-grained base.

and magmatic upwelling. The diamond pipes may be 2000 feet or more in diameter and over 3,500 feet in depth, tapering to a carrot shape. As said, the origin of the diamonds is a matter for discussion: they may be crystallisations from a magma possibly contaminated with local carbonaceous shales or, more likely, derived from a deep-seated eclogite layer represented as xenoliths in the blue ground.

Perhaps we should, rather oddly, mention here the use of suitable igneous rocks in building and construction work. Fine-grained basic and intermediate rocks such as dolerites and andesites are used as *crushed stone* for concrete aggregate, etc. and coarse granitic and syenitic rocks provide valuable *dimension-stone* utilised in dressed blocks. Some of the latter, such as the syenite, laurvikite, from south Norway, take a high polish and provide *ornamental stone*. *Pumice,* because of its cellular character, is utilised as insulating material and in certain types of stucco, plaster and cement, or as an abrasive.

PEGMATITIC-PNEUMATOLYTIC MINERAL DEPOSITS

We have seen that with the continued crystallisation of the non-volatile components of the magma, the volatiles become concentrated in the final fluids, together with many elements originally dispersed throughout the magma. The final liquids may be squeezed into cracks and fissures in the parent igneous rock or in the adjacent country-rock and consolidate as high-temperature *pegmatite veins.* The *gases* of the magmatic residuals are hot and chemically active, composed of water-vapour and such elements as F, B and S capable of transporting ore-elements; when the conditions become suitable,

u   599

pneumatolytic mineral deposits may be formed. As we shall see in the next section, contact-metamorphic deposits may result from large-scale pneumatolytic action on suitable country-rocks. We now give examples of the pegmatitic-pneumatolytic mineral deposits.

Apart from the relatively unimportant 'ore pegmatites' the economic interest of the pegmatites is a consequence of their coarseness. Their feldspar may grow into very large crystals ready for quarrying for use in ceramics or glass-making; quartz provides material for abrasives; micas, in large 'books', are utilised in the manufacture of insulators in the electrical industries, and ground and scrap micas find a multitude of industrial uses. Among the non-metallic mineral deposits arising from concentration in pegmatites may be noted that of cryolite (Na_3AlF_6) used as a flux in the manufacture of aluminium from bauxite, and obtained from a pegmatite at Evigtuk in West Greenland. Spodumene ($LiAlSi_3O_4$), amblygonite [$Li(F,OH)AlPO_4$] and lithium mica, lepidolite [$KLi_2Al(Si_4O_{10})$ (OH,F)] are mined from pegmatites for the production of lithium salts; one crystal from the Black Hills, South Dakota, pegmatite yielded 90 tons of spodumene. Beryllium has recently become a very valuable metal; it is obtained from beryl ($Be_3Al_2Si_4O_{18}$) which occurs in large crystals in certain pegmatites. Zircon ($ZrSiO_4$) has been worked as large crystals in a weathered pegmatite; monazite [$(Ce,La,Yt)PO_4$ with ThO_2 and SiO_2], used as a source of thorium and cerium salts, is a primary mineral in certain granites and pegmatites from which it is concentrated by surface-processes, as we see later. Tantalite-columbite [$(Fe,Mn)(Nb,Ta)_2O_6$] is a constituent of pegmatites in the Black Hills and elsewhere. Apatite [$Ca_5(F,Cl)(PO_4)_3$] is worked in Kola, Russia, from concentrations in pegmatites and nepheline syenites.

Pneumatolytic mineral deposits may be illustrated by the classic *tin*-deposits of Cornwall now, regrettably, almost exhausted. Here the veins are associated with granites (Fig. 365) and the fissures filled with the ore-deposits run roughly parallel with the line of outcrop of the granite bosses. Quartz is the chief veinstone, associated with such boron and fluorine minerals as fluorspar (CaF_2), tourmaline (Al borosilicate), topaz ($Al_2F_2SiO_4$), axinite [$H(CaFeMn)_3Al_2B$ $(SiO_4)_{12}$], and apatite [$Ca_5(F,Cl,OH)(PO_4)_3$]. The adjacent country-rock is altered in suitable cases into a mixture of quartz, muscovite, tourmaline or topaz, called *greisen* (Fig. 368). Associated ore-minerals are wolfram and pitchblende ($2UO_3.UO_2$). Some of the tin-lodes are possibly of high-temperature hydrothermal origin. Mention has already been made of the zoning of the Cornish deposits (Fig. 365).

The production of greisen in the Cornish granites has just been

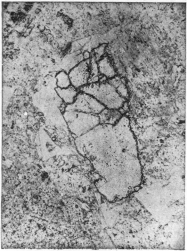

A   B

FIG. 368. Pneumatolysis. A, Tourmalinisation: tourmaline prisms developed, × 30; B, Greisenisation: topaz and muscovite developed, × 35.

noted; usually in greisen only a little tourmaline is present but in other modifications of the granites tourmaline is a major constituent. In this *tourmalinisation*, the original feldspars and micas are replaced by tourmaline to give a quartz-tourmaline rock (Fig. 368). Another pneumatolytic process associated with the Cornish granites results in the production of *kaolin* or *china-clay*, largely composed of the clay-mineral kaolinite [$Al_4Si_4O_{10}(OH)_8$]. Through the action of CO_2 and H_2O, the feldspars are converted into kaolinite, as represented in the equation below:

$$4KAlSi_3O_8 + 2CO_2 + 4H_2O \rightarrow 2K_2CO_3 + Al_4Si_4O_{10}(OH)_8 + 8SiO_2$$
orthoclase   kaolinite

The soft product is washed into tanks and the kaolinite, extensively used for china-ware and as a filler, is separated by repeated sedimentation. The association of cassiterite, tourmaline, topaz and other minerals of undoubted pneumatolytic origin supports the interpretation of the kaolin deposits as products of pneumatolysis, as do the great depths at which kaolinisation occurs and the existence of excellent china-clay beneath unaltered granite; the best china-clay occurs in the deepest pits. Other deposits of kaolin, as for example those in Georgia and South Carolina in the U.S.A., are produced by ordinary weathering and transportation processes, but this explanation is quite unacceptable for the great Cornish deposits.

601

PYROMETASOMATIC MINERAL DEPOSITS

Pyrometasomatic mineral deposits are typically developed at the contacts of *limestone* and *granodiorite intrusives*. High-temperature solutions carrying ore-components pass from the igneous rock into the country-rock and there produce *metasomatism* of suitable rocks with the deposition of ores. Geological thermometers indicate temperatures ranging between 500° and 800° C. Recrystallisation and reconstitution together with accessions from the magma produce a characteristic assemblage of minerals in typical deposits of this class: the ore-minerals are magnetite, hematite and pyrite, chalcopyrite and bornite, blende, galena, cassiterite, wolfram, scheelite, molybdenite, gold; the gangue-minerals are iron-rich silicates such as andradite garnet, hedenbergite, actinolite and olivine together with tremolite, wollastonite, epidote, zoisite, vesuvianite, diopside, plagioclase, fluorspar and micas. The iron-rich silicates make masses known as *skarns* (p. 526). The minerals of the pyrometasomatic deposits do not form simultaneously but yet show no definite consistent order: simple recrystallisation of the country-rock precedes reactions with magmatic accessions, as is to be expected from the emplacement and cooling history of the magmatic intrusions. The ore-deposit itself is a coarse granular mixture of skarn and ore minerals.

Pyrometasomatic ore-deposits occur especially in any zone resembling a roof to the intrusion, and are very irregular in shape (Fig. 369), though naturally the emanations have utilised any favourable paths, such as joints and bedding-planes. The classic example is that of the Morenci mining-field in Arizona where Waldemar Lindgren first demonstrated the movement of vast quantities

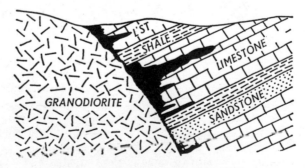

FIG. 369. Pyrometasomatism. Ore-deposit (black) formed at the contact of granodiorite, with preferential replacement of limestone of the country-rock.

of material into and out of the contact-zone. For example, Lindgren estimated that in a particular cubic metre of the deposit, at least 2·8 tons of material had come in and 1·8 tons gone out during the pyro-metasomatic process; the conclusion is the famous *law of equal volumes* in replacement processes.

HYDROTHERMAL MINERAL DEPOSITS

The final stage in the production of mineral deposits of magmatic origin is performed by hot *hydrothermal solutions* which may transport mineral matter great distances from the parent igneous centre. Such chemically active solutions leave the magma at a high temperature so that reaction with the country-rocks in their path readily takes place and *replacement-deposits* are formed. Any residual solution is thus continuously modified in composition and, moving still farther out, deposits its load when the temperature and the chemical environment become suitable. This deposition may take place in cavities and fissures as *lodes* and *veins* or between the grains of sediments or in other similar spaces as *impregnations*. We have subdivided the hydrothermal mineral deposits on the basis of the temperatures of their formation into high-, medium- and low-temperature deposits, the *hypothermal, mesothermal* and *epithermal*. This division is done by considering the mineral assemblages, both gangue and ore, found in any particular deposit. We deal briefly with famous examples of these three classes.

Among the **hypothermal deposits** we may first recall that some of the Cornish tin-wolfram veins are very likely of high-temperature hydrothermal formation — clearly there can be no rigid separation between related types. A classic high-temperature deposit is the Champion lode of the Kolar gold-field in India worked to a depth of nearly 9000 feet and occupying a fault-fracture in Pre-Cambrian rocks. Its walls are sharp, and especially rich portions of the lode — the *ore-shoots* — are considered to be controlled by drag-folds. The gold occurs in quartz with small amounts of metallic sulphides and with tourmaline, actinolite and biotite developed in the wall-rocks. Another famous hypothermal gold ore-field is that of Porcupine, Ontario, Canada, in which a plexus of veins occupies shear-fractures, and some replacement has also taken place. The quartz-veins carry gold, pyrite, tourmaline and carbonates. Great deposits of lead- and zinc-minerals are of hypothermal origin as, for example, in the Sullivan mine, British Columbia, and, more doubtfully, at Broken Hill, N.S.W. In the Sullivan mine, the massive ore-body *replaces* the bedded sedimentary rocks and is composed of silver-bearing galena and blende with minor amounts of cassiterite, tourmaline, garnet and actinolite. This great ore-body is clearly a high-temperature replacement. The famous Broken Hill lead-zinc area of New South Wales shows the galena-blende ore mixed with such high-temperature minerals as spinel, pyroxene, magnetite, garnet and the like. Some regard it as a replacement deposit along a sheared and folded zone in high-grade metamorphic rocks. Others argue that it is of syngenetic origin, the ores having been supplied from submarine volcanic sources and later, like the sediments, subjected to deformation and high-grade metamorphism.

In the **mesothermal deposits** the filling of fractures and cavities dominates over replacement. The Bendigo gold-quartz saddle-reefs, already referred to (Fig. 364), are localised at the crests of anticlines and in association with faults; in addition to the gold-quartz, the ore contains small amounts of pyrite, arsenopyrite, pyrrhotite and other sulphides, and the veinstone is dominantly dolomite. It is considered that much replacement has gone on at Bendigo, but clear evidence of cavity-filling is also available. Unlike the Cornish tin-lodes, those of Bolivia, which after Malaya produce most tin, are considered to be mesothermal in type. The veins are fracture fillings of cassiterite, quartz and pyrite with scarcer wolfram and metallic sulphides. The sequence of deposition of minerals shows successive formation from high temperature to low. The rich copper-area of Butte, Montana, is a system of steep veins filling a complex of fractures and faults of related origins. The chief copper-ores are chalcocite, enargite, bornite, chalcopyrite, tetrahedrite and covellite, other minerals present being quartz, pyrite and blende. Calcite, barytes, fluorspar and manganese carbonates and silicates occur as veinstones. In this exploited field, the minerals have been shown to be zonally arranged, the centre being characterised by chalcocite, an intermediate zone by enargite, bornite and chalcopyrite and an outer zone by blende, silver and manganese carbonates. Lastly, we may note the great pyrite deposits of Rio Tinto in Spain where gigantic lenses of pyrite occur in slates and volcanic rocks. Originally thought to be of mesothermal origin, these deposits are now regarded as due to replacement during the closing stages of acid vulcanicity.

The low-temperature **epithermal mineral deposits** can be illustrated first by the gold and silver telluride veins of the Cripple Creek area in Colorado. These famous veins are mostly located inside a Tertiary volcanic-breccia plug and were produced by deposition from hot solutions rising up from zones of volcanic disturbance created below the plug. The low-temperature feldspar, adularia, and jaspery quartz are among the veinstones. Cinnabar (HgS) occurs locally, and another typical epithermal deposit is illustrated by the cinnabar replacement-veins of Almaden in Spain. Finally, antimony-deposits, chiefly stibnite, are epithermal fillings, impregnations or replacements formed at low temperature and shallow depths.

METAMORPHIC MINERAL DEPOSITS

A mineral deposit already formed may, like any other rock, be subjected to the processes of metamorphism (Chapter 9) and receive new characters. Some ores acquire a schistose or granular texture, others may be improved by dehydration as, for example, in the production of magnetite and hematite ore-deposits from the limonitic hydrated oxides. It is possible too that during metamorphism a segregation of originally dispersed minerals may take place to give workable deposits. As we have seen, in metamorphism and migmatisation a good deal of regroupment of material may occur and purer and larger bodies of some particular mineral may thus be formed. It has been suggested that certain copper deposits are produced by the segregation during migmatisation of originally disseminated ores.

But in addition to such *metamorphosed deposits*, there is produced by metamorphism a valuable group of *metamorphic mineral deposits of non-metallic type*. We may briefly deal with the more important of these.

The *aluminium silicates*, Al_2SiO_5, sillimanite, kyanite and andalusite, are worked from concentrations arising by metamorphic diffusion, aided most likely by plutonic juices in migmatisation. At a temperature of 1545° C, these aluminium silicates are converted into mullite, $3Al_2O_3.2SiO_2$, and so provide high-grade refractories such as are required for the porcelain cores of sparking-plugs. Deposits of *asbestos*, in the commercial sense, include certain fibrous silicate minerals such as chrysotile, the fibrous serpentine which occurs in small veins in massive serpentine, asbestos proper, the fibrous member of the tremolite-actinolite series occurring in metamorphic rocks, and amosite the fibrous orthorhombic amphibole anthophyllite, $Mg_7Si_8O_{22}.(OH)_4$ produced by the metamorphism of basic or ultrabasic igneous rocks. The fibres of these mineral silicates are capable of being spun and are used to produce heat- and acid-resisting cloths, sheets, etc., brake-linings and insulating materials. We may mention here the deposits of *talc* [$Mg_3Si_4O_{10}(OH)_2$], usually in the massive variety *steatite* or *soapstone*, produced in lenses from rocks rich in magnesium, such as peridotite, gabbro or dolomite, during the processes of regional or dislocation metamorphism or by the action of waters of magmatic origin.

Emery, used as an abrasive, is a mixture of corundum, magnetite, hematite and spinel occurring as lenses in contact-metamorphosed limestones or basic gneisses, and as xenoliths in basic igneous rocks.

Corundum itself is worked in South Africa from the contacts of basic igneous rocks and intrusive pegmatites and is considered to result from desilication of the basic rock. The gem varieties of alumina, ruby and sapphire, have their primary home in contact-metamorphic limestones and other high-grade metamorphic rocks, as in Burma and elsewhere. Another abrasive is supplied by *garnet* which occurs in workable deposits in metamorphic and migmatitic rocks, where it has become concentrated by metamorphic segregation or under the influence of granitic juices.

Graphite, employed in the manufacture of crucibles and foundry-facings, occurs not only in fissure veins but as lenses in high-grade metamorphic rocks such as cordierite-gneisses. In Mexico, coal-seams of Triassic age are contact-metamorphosed by granite dykes and supply good graphite. Most graphite is probably of original sedimentary origin.

We may end this summary of metamorphic mineral deposits by recalling that many building-materials are of this origin, such as *slates*, ornamental stones such as *marbles* of various origins and types, and *serpentine* used for interior decoration. We may note here the increasing use of *vermiculite*, a variety of chlorite, as an insulating material.

SUPERGENE ENRICHMENT OF ORE-DEPOSITS

Before going on to consider the true exogenetic or surface-formed mineral deposits, we may conveniently examine here the changes in an ore-deposit that may be set in motion by weathering. We have already noted in Chapter 4 the chief characters of the processes that go on below and above the water-table (p. 145). Such processes operating on a deposit may profoundly affect its value as an ore. The changes arising from the action of descending waters are called *supergene enrichment*; by these a lean ore may be converted into one much more valuable.

We may illustrate the general process of supergene or secondary enrichment in a mineral vein by Fig. 370. The key level is that of the water-table existing at the time. Above this level, as we have seen in Chapter 4, oxidation is a dominant process. The primary minerals of the vein are oxidised and weathered out at the surface to produce the *gossan* in which, too, residual ore-minerals may become concentrated by surface-agencies. Below the gossan, the vein may be rendered comparatively barren of minerals due to *leaching* by descending solutions. These may react with the primary ore-minerals to give a zone of *oxidised ores* just above the water-table. Below this level is the important zone of *secondary enrichment* in which reaction between

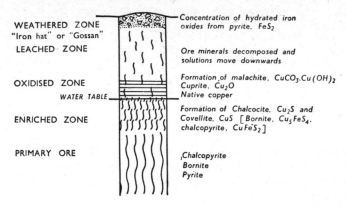

WEATHERED ZONE "Iron hat" or "Gossan"
Concentration of hydrated iron oxides from pyrite. FeS_2

LEACHED ZONE
Ore minerals decomposed and solutions move downwards

OXIDISED ZONE
Formation of malachite, $CuCO_3.Cu(OH)_2$ Cuprite, Cu_2O

WATER TABLE
Native copper

ENRICHED ZONE
Formation of Chalcocite, Cu_2S and Covellite, CuS [Bornite, Cu_5FeS_4, chalcopyrite, $CuFeS_2$]

PRIMARY ORE
,Chalcopyrite Bornite Pyrite

FIG. 370. Supergene enrichment in a copper lode.

primary ores and the descending solutions of oxysalts may result in the deposition of minerals with a greatly increased content of the useful metal. Below this zone the vein is in its *primary* condition, possibly there not having a high enough tenor of metal to repay working it.

An example of secondary enrichment of a copper lode containing chalcopyrite, bornite and pyrite is illustrated in Fig. 370. We see there the production of the gossan or 'iron-hat', rusty with hydrated iron oxides, formed from pyrite or chalcopyrite. Below the leached zone is the zone of oxidised ore-minerals with malachite [$CuCO_3.Cu(OH)_2$], cuprite (Cu_2O) and native copper (Cu). Below the water-table, in the zone of secondary enrichment, the chief minerals are chalcocite (Cu_2S), covellite (CuS), bornite (Cu_5FeS_4) and chalcopyrite ($CuFeS_2$). We can indicate the economic importance of supergene enrichment by listing the copper content of the relevant copper minerals of the different zones:

Malachite	57·3 per cent Cu	Chalcocite	79·8 per cent Cu
Azurite	55·1	Covellite	66·4
Cuprite	88·8	Bornite	63·3
Native copper	100·0	Chalcopyrite	34·5
Tenorite	79·85		

We can extend this example to display the supergene enrichment of some of the commoner ores. For instance, silver lodes may show the chloride, cerargyrite, in the gossan and oxidised zones, with native silver and rich secondary sulphides accompanying the primary ore, argentite, in the enriched zone below. Lead and zinc deposits show such oxyminerals as cerussite, anglesite and smithsonite in the upper parts with primary galena and blende below. Carnotite is an important oxidised uranium-ore mineral.

B. EXOGENETIC MINERAL DEPOSITS

Exogenetic mineral deposits formed by surface processes are in effect examples of sedimentary rocks accumulated according to the principles set out already in Chapters 4 and 5. Many of the exogenetic mineral deposits, such as the coals and the evaporates, have indeed already been described in detail and need only summary reference here; other deposits, such as petroleum, are given a slightly more full treatment.

It will be recalled that the sedimentary rocks in their widest sense comprise three classes, the residual deposits of weathering, and the true sedimentary rocks grouped into the detrital sediments classified by grain-size and the chemical-organic sediments classified by chemical composition. This same grouping can of course be applied to the exogenetic mineral deposits, with the results given in the table below.

EXOGENETIC MINERAL DEPOSITS

Weathering Residual Deposits

    Residual tin and gold, barytes, kyanite, phosphates, gemstones
    Bauxite and laterite, manganese deposits
    Residual iron-ores, ochres
    Residual nickel, zinc and cobalt deposits

Detrital Mineral Deposits

    Clays, sands and gravels, sandstones, foundry-sands
    Oil-shales, kaolinite
    Placer deposits, gold, platinum, cassiterite, diamond, ruby and
        sapphire, monazite, magnetite, ilmenite, thorianite, zircon, garnet
    Eluvial, stream- and beach-placers

Chemical-organic Deposits

    Carbonates, limestone, dolomite, magnesite
    Siliceous, diatomite, flint
    Ferruginous, siderite, iron-silicates, oxides, hydroxides, sulphides
    (Copper-deposits)
    Aluminous (bauxite and laterite)
    Phosphatic, phosphorite
    (Fertilisers generally)
    Evaporates, rock-salt, sodium sulphates and carbonates, borax,
        kernite, brines, anhydrite, gypsum, potassium-salts
    Carbonaceous, coals, bitumens.

RESIDUAL MINERAL DEPOSITS

The weathering of a rock may result in the concentration of a desirable original constituent by the removal of other and unwanted components. In this way, residual ore-deposits of tin and gold have been built up. Barytes ($BaSO_4$), kyanite (Al_2SiO_5), phosphates and gemstones are worked from residual weathering accumulations overlying the unweathered parent rocks. In these examples, the original valuable minerals have remained unchanged during weathering, but more often the usual chemical operations of weathering produce new minerals. Bauxite, the dominant ore of aluminium, and its iron-rich analogue, laterite, together with residual manganese hydroxides are examples, already described on p. 271, of such accumulations. An important group of iron-ores are of residual origin; primary iron-ores, such as siderite, pyrite and iron-silicates, disseminated through limestones or other rocks low in silica may be concentrated as hydrated iron oxides, as in Bilbao, Spain, in the Appalachians and especially in Guinea. Ochres, impuré iron oxides such as limonite, goethite ($HFeO_2$), or hematite, are concentrated by the weathering of rocks containing iron minerals. Residual nickel-deposits are produced in New Caledonia by the weathering of a nickeliferous serpentine derived from a peridotite; the nickel is present in garnierite, a hydrated nickel magnesium silicate. Certain zinc and cobalt deposits of oxidised minerals are weathered products of primary-vein minerals.

DETRITAL MINERAL DEPOSITS

Many of the detrital rocks are of great industrial importance. *Clay* is utilised in the manufacture of bricks, tiles and similar products. *Sands*, especially those well sorted and of angular grain, are used in concrete and mortar; pure quartz sands are used for glass-making. *Gravels* are dug in enormous quantities as aggregates for concrete. *Sandstone* is an important building-stone. Special types that may be recalled include the following: *foundry-sands* are sands with a small percentage of clay-bond employed to make moulds for castings; *fireclay* and *ganister*, the seatearths underlying coal-seams, are valuable refractories; *oil-shale* is mined for oil. Some *kaolinite* deposits as, for example, those of the United States, are detrital in origin and are valuable clays because they are free from impurities of iron hydroxides. The detrital deposits so far mentioned are essentially sedimentary rocks worked for their own sakes — a very important group of detrital mineral deposits are worked because a concentration of a special mineral has taken place. These are the placer deposits that we now examine.

Placer deposits result from the breaking up of the parent rock and the subsequent transportation and concentration of minerals which may exist in only small amount in the parent rock. Alluvial deposits are typical placer deposits, but some other types are included in the general term. The breaking-down of the rock is achieved by the ordinary processes of mechanical weathering (p. 127) and the comminuted material is moved by the transporting agents described in Chapter 4, gravity, river-waters, waves on a beach or the wind. The lighter components and those more easily destroyed by chemical or mechanical means are winnowed away and the heavier, tougher and more chemically resistant minerals are thus concentrated to form *placer* mineral deposits. Typical minerals of placers, with their specific gravities, are gold (12–20), platinum (21·46 pure), cassiterite (6·8–7·1), diamond (3·52), ruby and sapphire (3·9–4·1), monazite (5·27), magnetite (5·18), ilmenite (4·5–5), thorianite (9·3), zircon (4·7) and garnet (3·5–4·3). Depending on their place of formation, placer deposits can be divided into *eluvial* or hill-slope deposits, *stream*-deposits and *beach*-deposits (Fig. 371). We briefly note examples of these different types.

Eluvial placers are formed on hill-slopes where the material of the parent lode is broken up and moved downhill by creep (p. 149); lighter materials are washed or blown away or decayed, and the heavier ores are concentrated. Gold, cassiterite and gemstones are worked from eluvial deposits, especially important being the eluvial deposits of cassiterite in Malaya. *Stream-placers* are exemplified by many of the famous gold-deposits, such as those of California ('1849')

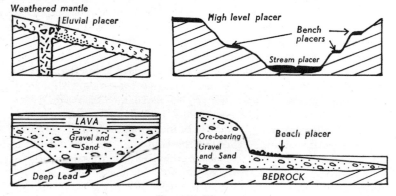

Fig. 371. Placers.

and the Klondike. Where the stream slackens, the heavy minerals of the load are deposited, as in the slack water on the insides of meanders. The gold is associated with 'black sands' of magnetite and ilmenite and also with heavy obdurate minerals such as garnet, zircon and monazite. *Bench-placers* occur in the gravels of the older river-terraces (p. 171) and *'deep leads'* are placers buried beneath later alluvial deposits or, in some places, lava-flows (Fig. 371). Platinum is worked from placers in the Urals, and cassiterite, 'stream-tin', in Malaya and the East Indies. Diamonds are obtained from placers in the Vaal and Orange river-valleys in South Africa and other gemstones from stream-gravels, as in the ruby mines of Burma. *Beach-placers* result from the action of waves and currents on mixed shore-material whereby the lighter grains are removed and the heavier, such as particles of gold, magnetite, garnet and diamond, are concentrated. A famous gold beach-placer is that of Nome in Alaska and other placers of this type occur on the beaches of Travancore, India, which supply ilmenite, zircon and monazite in large quantities. A great production of diamonds comes from the beach-placers of raised beach-gravels on the Namaqualand coast south of the mouth of the Orange river, where stream-placers also contain diamonds.

CHEMICAL-ORGANIC MINERAL DEPOSITS

The chemical-organic sedimentary rocks have been divided into the carbonate, siliceous, ferruginous, aluminous, phosphatic, saline and carbonaceous types (p. 246) and the economic importance of many of these rocks has been noted already. We may briefly recall the uses of the main industrial minerals and rocks of this class.

Among the *carbonate* rocks, the *limestones* are used as dimension-stone for building and as crushed stone for concrete aggregate. About three parts of limestone or chalk, mixed with one part of clay, give the raw materials for Portland cement, utilised in modern building in enormous amounts. Lime is made by heating a limestone and is employed in plaster and mortar-making. Travertine, the chemical limestone, is used in slabs for interior work. *Dolomite* and *magnesite* provide basic refractories desirable for certain metallurgical purposes, and dolomite, limestone and lime are employed extensively as fluxes.

The *siliceous* rocks of non-fragmental origin include diatomite and flint. The industrial uses of diatomite (p. 268) depend on its porosity and are chiefly as an insulating material, as a filler and as a filtering material. Flint is used in tube-mills and, in a calcined form, in the pottery industry.

Many important iron-ore deposits are comprised in the *ferruginous* sediments, as has already been noted on p. 269. Primary iron-bearing minerals of the parent rocks are broken up by weathering processes, the iron dissolved mainly by carbonated waters or humic or other organic acids, transported and deposited in sedimentary beds as siderite, hydrated iron-silicates, iron oxides or hydroxides or iron sulphides. We have already mentioned clay-ironstone, blackband-ironstones, bog iron-ore and the Jurassic bedded ironstones. In Alsace-Lorraine, oolitic iron-ores, mainly composed of limonite, make the famous 'minette' ores. Vastly more important are the naturally-enriched ores derived from Pre-Cambrian banded ironstones which often contain over 60% Fe and provide the world's main reserves of high-grade iron-ores.

It will be convenient to mention here the sedimentary *manganese* deposits, analogous to those of iron just dealt with. Besides, we may note that certain *copper*-deposits are held to be of sedimentary origin; the most famous of these is the Mansfeld Kupferschiefer in Germany of Permian age. The ore-bed is a thin extensive layer, a metre thick, of black marine shale with copper sulphides and other metallic compounds. Some authorities consider that the copper was derived from the weathering of distant copper-lodes in the drainage-basin, its transportation and deposition with the black muds in a Black Sea environment (p. 202). Sulphur bacteria are held to have taken a part in the deposition process. The technical term for the formation of an ore contemporary with the rest of the rock is *syngenetic*. Other geologists hold that the ore was introduced by hydrothermal solutions from an igneous source — it is *epigenetic*, formed later than the enclosing rock.

Among the *phosphatic* mineral deposits we may place certain bodies of *phosphorite* occurring in extensive thin beds intercalated with marine rocks of Black Sea facies (p. 202). The phosphate is derived from phosphorus-bearing primary minerals, such as apatite, and transported by streams into restricted basins where precipitation took place under anaerobic conditions (p. 202). Such marine phosphate beds are extensively developed in the Western United States and in Morocco. Phosphorus, together with Ca, K, N and often S, is essential for proper plant-growth, and soils need to be replenished in these components. Accordingly, and especially at this time, phosphates and other *mineral fertilisers* are of great social importance; we may deal with them as a whole here. From the naturally occurring phosphates, apatite and phosphorite, 'superphosphate' is manufactured. Lime is provided from powdered limestone which, besides feeding the plants, corrects the acidity of the soil and improves the soil-texture. Potash-fertilisers are produced from the evaporates mentioned in the next paragraph. Nitrates of direct mineral origin are obtained from the Atacama desert of Chile where soda-nitre or

Chile saltpetre ($NaNO_3$) occurs in evaporate deposits leached from surrounding volcanic rocks and preserved in the dry desert environment. A few per cent of nitre (KNO_3) occurs in the Chile deposits. Sulphur, in addition to its chemical use in the manufacture of superphosphate, is employed as a direct fertiliser and as an insecticide spray. It is provided by native sulphur or from sulphides and sulphates. The most important deposits of native sulphur are located in the cap-rock of salt domes, the sulphur occurring interlayered with gypsum from which, according to some, it is derived by reduction.

Many of the minerals used in the great chemical industry are *evaporates* or *saline* rocks of one sort or another formed by evaporation of the waters of saline lakes (p. 188). The chief of these minerals is *rock-salt*, *halite*, $NaCl$, readily identified by its taste and solubility. It occurs in extensive and thick beds at many geological horizons, as in the Silurian and Carboniferous of the United States, the Permian of Germany, the Trias of England and the Tertiary of Poland. Intrusive plugs of salt — *salt domes* — provide conditions suitable for oil accumulation (Fig. 165). Other sodium salts, the *sulphates* thenardite (Na_2SO_4), mirabilite ($Na_2SO_4.10H_2O$) and glauberite ($Na_2SO_4.CaSO_4$), the *carbonates* such as natron ($Na_2CO_3.10H_2O$) and trona ($Na_2CO_3.NaHCO_3.2H_2O$) are precipitated from the waters of alkali-lakes, as in the desert areas of the United States; these constituents have been leached out of the rocks of the drainage areas. Borax ($Na_2B_4O_7.10H_2O$) and kernite ($Na_2O.2B_2O_3.4H_2O$), the soluble *borates*, provide most of the 'borax' employed in a great variety of industrial processes; these minerals are obtained from playa-deposits formed by the drying up of appropriate saline lakes. Natural brines provide calcium chloride and magnesium chloride, together with bromine and iodine. *Anhydrite* ($CaSO_4$), another evaporate, is becoming increasingly important for the manufacture of sulphuric acid. *Gypsum*, $CaSO_4.2H_2O$, is employed in the manufacture of special cements, as an insulating material and more extensively for plasters, plaster-board and the like. As we have already noted, the most important use of the evaporate *potassium*-salts is as fertilisers, but some are employed in the chemical industry. The chief potassium-minerals occurring, for example, in the Stassfurt deposits (p. 272) are sylvine (KCl), carnallite ($KCl.MgCl_2.6H_2O$), kainite ($KCl.MgSO_4.3H_2O$) and polyhalite ($K_2SO_4.MgSO_4.2CaSO_4.2H_2O$).

Our final group of chemical-organic mineral deposits is the *carbonaceous* represented by the coals and the bitumens.

In foregoing chapters, we have seen that the *coal-series* of varying *ranks* of coal from peat to anthracite shows a progressive increase of carbon-content and decrease in volatiles, O, H and H_2O (p. 274 and

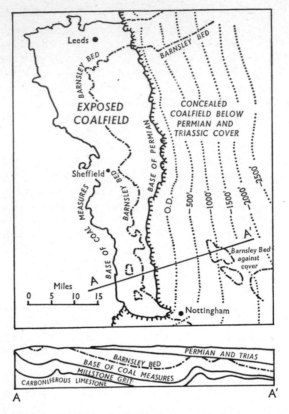

Fig. 372. The Yorkshire Coalfield: the exposed and concealed coal-fields in map and section. Dotted contours in the map indicate levels, in feet, of the base of the Permian cover (based on H.M. Geological Survey).

fig. 166). In the main system of British rocks containing coal-seams — the Carboniferous — a coal-measure rhythm of sedimentation is recorded as fireclay, coal-seam, shale, sandstone (p. 278, Fig. 169). After their deposition, the Carboniferous rocks were folded and denuded, the coal-bearing rocks being preserved in the synclinal areas as *coal-basins*. Across the denuded folds was deposited an unconformable cover, so that *concealed coal-fields* are found beneath these younger rocks — much of the present output of coal in Britain comes from the concealed coal-field of Yorkshire and Nottingham-shire, the conditions being shown in Fig. 372. In Fig. 373 are presented some factors affecting the coals of the South Wales Coal-field. Attention may be directed to the varieties of the coals (Fig.

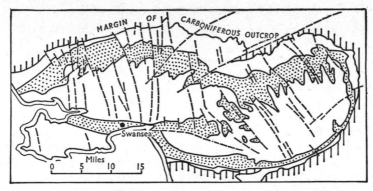

FIG. 373. The South Wales Coal-field. The effect of faults and folds on the outcrop of the Lower Coal Series (dotted) (after H.M. Geological Survey).

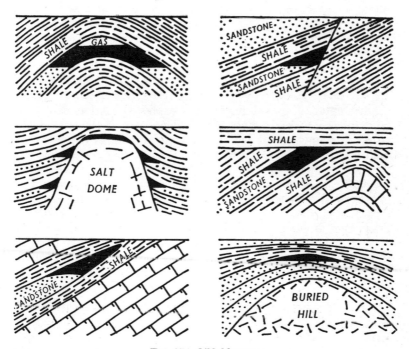

FIG. 374. Oilfield traps.

168) and the effects of faulting and folding on the availability of the coal.

Oil has been briefly noted and its manner of accumulation summarised (p. 279). We saw that oil and its associated hydrocarbons were derived from the *sapropelites*, marine muds containing much organic material. From these *source*-rocks, the oil migrates into *reservoir*-rocks of porous character, such as sands or fissured and jointed limestones (p. 148). When the reservoir-rocks are provided with an impervious cover and are suitably arranged, the oil may be *trapped* to form an *oil-pool*. Traps result in a number of ways — some of these have already been illustrated in Fig. 87 (Chapter 4) and others are given in Fig. 374. Important *structural traps* are produced by anticlines and domes, monoclines, faults and salt doming; *stratigraphical traps* are the result of unconformities, lensing, overlap and reflected buried hills.

METALLOGENIC EPOCHS AND PROVINCES

Many geologists dealing with mineral deposits, especially those of metallic ores, have emphasised the importance of the distribution in time and space of metalliferous deposits. *Metallogenic epochs* have been distinguished during which certain types of ore-deposits have been formed. But mineral deposits, as we have seen, are rocks just as much as any other rocks and must take their places in appropriate positions in the history of the earth's crust. Many mineral deposits are in reality minor phases of magmatic activity, others are the results of broad crustal movements expressed predominantly by other kinds of rocks. In short, mineral deposits of whatever kind, like all rocks, simply record acts in the *crustal drama*. In the next, and final, chapter of this volume we present these dramas in their entirety.

Before doing so, however, we may say a few words on *metallogenic provinces*. It is proposed by some ore-geologists that a dominant kind of mineralisation persists through several metallogenic epochs widely separated in time. If this were completely demonstrated, then most interesting discussions would ensue not only concerned with the genesis of ore-deposits but also with the origin and evolution of igneous and plutonic rocks and, indeed, with the whole of earth-history. Such a discussion is, unfortunately, for the future.

FURTHER READING AND REFERENCE

Determinative mineralogy
Dana, J. D., 1960, *Manual of Mineralogy*, 17th edit., Wiley.
Read, H. H., 1962, *Rutley's Elements of Mineralogy*, 25th edit., Murby.

Ore-deposits

Bateman, A. M., 1952, *Economic Mineral Deposits*, 2nd edit., Wiley.
Dines, H. G., 1956, Metalliferous Mining Region of South-west England, *Geol. Surv. Gt. Britain*.
Jones, W. R., and D. Williams, 1948, *Minerals and Mineral Deposits*, Home University Library.
Lindgren, W., 1933, *Mineral Deposits*, 4th edit., McGraw-Hill.
Park, C. F., and R. A. MacDiamid, 1964, *Ore deposits*, Freeman.

Coal-field geology

Trueman, A. E. (Editor), 1954, *The Coalfields of Great Britain*, Arnold.

Oil geology

Hobson, G. D., 1954, *Some Fundamentals of Petroleum Geology*, Oxford University Press.
Levorsen, A. I., 1966, *Petroleum Geology*, 2nd edit., Freeman.

12

A PATTERN OF EARTH HISTORY

Introduction

In the first pages of this book, geology was defined as earth-history, to be read from the rocks accessible to observation. In the foregoing chapters it has become apparent that these rocks are not formed haphazard; each records a circumscribed episode in a series of linked changes in crustal conditions. The interplay of geological processes is incessant; crustal movements, whether small and restricted or great and widespread, control the types and successions of sediments, the distribution of life-provinces, the activities of magma and volcanoes, and the deep-seated operations of metamorphism and plutonism. It has been merely a matter of convenience to deal with the production of the main rock-classes and their structural development in separate chapters — now, we have to consider how all geological processes re-act on one another, and thereby provide a pattern of earth-history.

Properties of the Stable and Mobile Zones of the Crust

In earlier chapters, we have repeatedly found a contrast between the geological products of crustal regions of differing stability. The sediments, for example, were classified on the one hand into those of the relatively stable continental masses and the platforms surrounding them, and on the other hand those developed in subsiding basins during phases of large-scale crustal movements. Not only the sedimentary facies but also the thickness of a sequence is influenced by the same factors. Stable areas accumulate, on balance, a restricted pile of sediment, and minor fluctuations in level may give rise to alternating phases of deposition and erosion. Unstable areas may accumulate successions of many thousands of feet during periods of subsidence, or may undergo rapid erosion, by which rocks once deeply buried are laid bare, during periods of uplift. Again, the characters of volcanic rocks are dependent on their crustal setting, certain basaltic assemblages appearing predominantly in the stable blocks and andesitic assemblages characterising belts of instability. Finally, metamorphic rocks, migmatites and most members of the granite series are developed on a regional scale only in the unstable belts.

The recognition of *stable* and *mobile* crustal regions thus expresses profound geological contrasts which are explored in more detail below. It should be remembered, however, that the terms are not used in any absolute sense. The stable areas as a whole are only relatively stable — if they remained totally unmoved, sedimentation, erosion and all other geological processes would come to a halt when equilibrium had been attained. They are frequently traversed by deep fractures and *zones of limited mobility* are developed in connection with these fractures. Moreover, the activity of any crustal segment changes with time; a new belt of mobility may develop in a previously stable area, and many old mobile belts, such as the Caledonian belt making much of north-west Britain, have become stabilised in the course of geological history.

The stable and mobile areas are contrasted also in their style of structures. *Stable areas* are affected principally by deep folds and associated fractures, that is, by flexures of very large radius registered by the elevation or subsidence of great areas. The rocks subjected to these disturbances are not converted into tectonites and show little or no small-scale deformation. The broad, slow movements producing structures of this type are called *epeirogenic* or continent-making.

Mobile areas usually appear as long and relatively narrow belts. Vertical movements of much greater extent than those affecting the stable regions lead to the formation of deep troughs, often filled with sediment, or of high mountain-belts, the former commonly evolving into the latter with the passage of time. These vertical movements expressed by distortion of the whole crust are accompanied by local and complex compressive stresses which lead to violent folding on short radii and to the development of great thrusts. Many of the rocks affected are metamorphosed under stress to become tectonites, while migmatisation and granite-formation begin in the deeper parts of the disturbed belt. The process by which the mobile belts evolve is called *orogenesis* or mountain-building.

THE STABLE AREAS

As we have said, the stable areas of the crust are not devoid of movement. Around the coasts of Britain, which forms part of the stable region of north-west Europe, raised beaches and submerged forests indicate small upheavals and depressions of relatively recent date, while minor earthquake-shocks, usually due to disturbances along old-established faults, are occasionally recorded. Movements of greater magnitude are demonstrated by the sedimentary successions

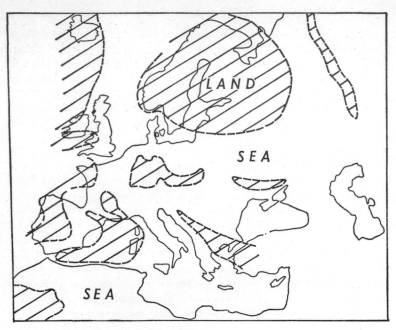

Fig. 375. The Cenomanian transgression in Europe, land areas lined.

built up on the continental shelves and within the continents themselves. A vast majestic depression is recorded in the transgressive series of sediments deposited in spreading epicontinental seas, as illustrated by the great *Cenomanian transgression* which drowned enormous low-lying areas towards the end of the Cretaceous period (Fig. 375). Elevation of the sea-floor gives rise to regressive sedimentary series as the shallow seas are drained off the land and may, of course, lead on to sub-aerial denudation and the development of an unconformity. These slow epeirogenic movements have been proposed as the bases for a division of geological history, a transgression and regression together making an ideal geological period.

On the continental parts of stable blocks, sediments of various facies may accumulate; they include arkoses formed by the decay of uplifted mountain masses, eolian and lacustrine deposits, coals, evaporates and tillites. The *Karroo sediments* of Southern Africa provide an illustration of a sequence formed by long-continued deposition in the interior of a relatively stable continental mass (Fig. 376). These sediments accumulated in great basins formed by gentle warping of the old metamorphic basement on which they rest. In the Karroo basin itself, the succession, entirely continental in facies, is

620

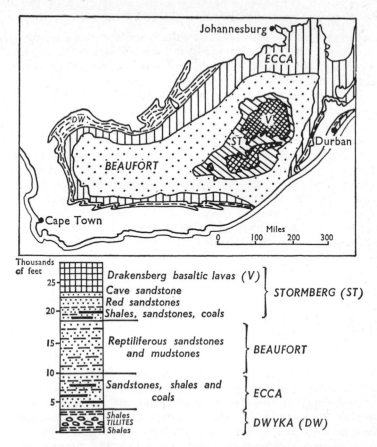

FIG. 376. The Karroo Basin, South Africa. The representative vertical
section is taken in the central part.

some 24,000 feet thick. It begins with a sequence of tillites, locally
resting upon a glaciated land-surface, and passes up into sandstones,
shales and coal-seams whose deposition continued from Permo-
Carboniferous to Jurassic times.

The thickness of the Karroo sequence gives a measure of the magnitude of epeirogenic movements. In the centres of the great basins,
the old floor must have been depressed to depths of several miles;
towards the margins of the basins the Karroo succession thins and
beyond their limits the basement-rocks probably remained exposed
and subject to erosion during Karroo deposition. The earth-movements must thus have involved a warping and distortion of the crust,

rather than simple elevation and subsidence, but this warping was on so broad a scale that it is hardly reflected in the local structures of the rocks: the Karroo sediments are over most of their outcrop virtually unfolded, and show very gentle dips.

Where no sedimentary successions have been formed, records of epeirogenic movements may be preserved by features of the surface-topography. Lake Victoria and Lake Kyogo in East Africa lie within a shallow basin of recent origin and their sinuous outlines indicate drowning of land resulting from a rearrangement of the drainage due to warping of the surface (Fig. 112). Again, old land-surfaces planed down by erosion during the Tertiary periods are found in East Africa to be tilted and distorted by later epeirogenic movements. In the Colorado Plateau of the western United States, recent elevation of thousands of feet brought about a rejuvenation of the drainage made apparent by the cutting of the Grand Canyon (p. 165).

The formation of warps by epeirogenic movements is achieved partly by broad flexuring, resulting in the formation of structural basins and domes, and partly by faulting; the more rigid basement-rocks are commonly fractured while the cover-rocks show gentle flexures or sharp monoclinal folds above the lines of faulting (Fig. 299). Where fault-movement and sedimentation went on together, drastic variations of thickness and sedimentary facies may be observed across the fault; thick deposits, often with conglomerates, slide breccias and slumped beds, appear on the down-faulted side, while the upthrow side may receive thin sequences or be subjected to erosion. An example of facies variation related to contemporary fault-movements is supplied by the Lower Carboniferous rocks of the Pennine region as already illustrated in Fig. 171. During Lower Carboniferous times a fracture-zone making the *Craven Faults* separated a relatively stable block in the north-east from a more rapidly subsiding region towards the south-west. South of the fault-zone, a succession of alternating shales and limestones totalling 5–6000 feet was laid down; reef-knolls formed by the accumulation of reef-building algae and corals more or less *in situ* recur at several levels, showing that the balance between subsidence and deposition kept the sea-floor at a shallow depth. On the north side of the Craven Faults, deposition began later, a zone some distance above the base of the Carboniferous resting with strong unconformity on a Lower Palaeozoic basement. The total thickness of Lower Carboniferous sediment is there only a few hundred feet, and less than half of this is of detrital origin. Massive limestones formed in shallow waters receiving little sand and mud are the dominant rocks, displayed especially in the Great Scar Limestone which makes a conspicuous escarpment to the south of Ingleborough.

The Karroo continental sediments mentioned above are topped by an enormous pile of basaltic lava-flows making the Drakensberg of Basutoland and are also invaded by related dolerite intrusions. It is estimated that the total volume of magma brought into the region was of the order of 100,000 cubic miles, of which by far the greater part was basic in composition. Similar *plateau-basalts* occur in the Deccan of peninsular India, another region which has remained stable through much of post-Cambrian times, and in the Paraná basin of Brazil, where they are associated with continental deposits of Karroo facies.

FRACTURE-ZONES OF LIMITED MOBILITY

Before passing on to consider the orogenic belts, we may examine certain interesting belts traversing the stable continents in which a *limited mobility* is evident. Strong vertical movements on fractures characterise these zones; the structural style is controlled by faulting and, as in the main parts of the stable regions already discussed, small-scale distortion and recrystallisation under stress are very restricted. The most spectacular examples of such zones of limited mobility are the great *rift-valleys* exemplified by the Rift-valley system of East Africa (Chapter 8, Fig. 305) which extends as a bifurcating series of narrow topographical depressions from the Jordan Valley to central Africa. In Europe a rift-valley system of similar type extends from Scandinavia through the valley of the Rhine to the Alps. In the ocean basins, comparable rift-structures follow the mid-oceanic ridge-systems for thousands of kilometres (Fig. 120). These fracture-systems provide some of the greatest tectonic units of the crust, extending for as much as one-sixth of the circumference of the earth.

The rift-valleys are bounded by parallel faults between which tracts of land, usually only 30–50 miles in width, are depressed; the floor of the Jordan Valley, for example, lies below sea-level while the scarps on either side rise steeply to heights of around 3000 feet. The rift-valley floors are often occupied by lakes and partially filled by sediment or volcanic products. Volcanic activity is frequently associated with rift-valleys and is commonly of a distinctive alkaline kind.

Both the extent of the rift-valleys and their connection with vulcanicity point to the occurrence of very deep fractures in the crust but, as we have already seen (Chapter 8), there has been disagreement as to whether the depression of the valley-floor is due to subsidence between normal faults or to the forcing down of a strip over-ridden by ramp-faults due to compression. The Rhine graben is usually accepted as a tensional structure bounded by groups of normal faults and other rift-valleys are now generally ascribed to a similar cause. It may be that the tension is associated with the formation of an arch of very great radius, the graben being comparable with the fallen keystone (Fig. 305); in East Africa, old land-surfaces are tilted upwards as they approach the scarps bounding the rift-valleys, and demonstrate that warping accompanied the faulting. We may note too, that the African rift-fault systems appear to be connected with the more widespread network of fractures formed in association with the basins and swells of the continental mass already considered.

Nevertheless, there are indications of compression along the rift-belts which still require explanation. The massif of Ruwenzori, on the borders of Uganda and the Congo, is an uplifted or horst block within the western rift-valley. It is made of metamorphic basement-rocks comparable to those making the walls of the rift, but its summit stands 10,000 feet above the rift-walls and appears to have been forced upward by a compression whose effects are also seen in a strong arching of an old land-surface. Geophysical surveys carried out in East Africa indicated that the rift-valleys are regions of negative gravity anomalies, that is, they are underlain by an excess of light material (p. 31); according to the principle of isostasy (p. 28), the valley-floors should tend to rise to compensate for this deficiency of mass and the fact of their continued subsidence is therefore ascribed by some geologists to the effects of compression in forcing down the central belt between thrust-faults.

Another style of structure produced by differential movements along fractures is illustrated by the *Basin and Range province* of the United States (Fig. 303). Here, fault-blocks uplifted and tilted in comparatively recent times form a number of parallel mountain-ridges running north and south. The feet of the uplifted blocks are clothed with piedmont-deposits, conglomerates, sandstones and other terrestrial rocks of similar facies produced by erosion of the elevated tracts, and lines of volcanic cones appear along some of the faults.

THE MOBILE BELTS

Introduction. In the true mobile belts, evidences of crustal instability are, as we have seen, innumerable. Metamorphic and granitic rocks clearly formed in the depths are exposed to view at the earth's surface and display on every scale structures indicative of internal distortion and bodily movement. Thick sequences of marine sediments are elevated into high mountains and enormous rock-masses are transported horizontally on thrust-planes over distances measurable in tens of miles. Folds, nappes and thrusts dominate the tectonic style, and the effects of deformation are recorded also in a multitude of minor folds, cleavages and linear elements and often in the whole fabric of the metamorphic rocks.

The *mobile belts of the present day* form, as we have already seen, two great systems, those of the *Circum-Pacific* and *Alpine-Himalayan* *belts*. Seismic activity is greater in these belts than in other parts of the globe and deep-focus earthquakes are, so far as is known, confined to their vicinity (Fig. 6, Fig. 17). Volcanic activity too is concentrated along the mobile belts (Fig. 255). Gravity anomalies, both positive and negative, have been recorded at many points and indicate that the crust is not in a state of isostatic equilibrium. Seismic data show that the M discontinuity at the base of the crust is displaced downwards beneath certain parts of the mobile belts, indicating a thickening of the crust in these localities. Many lines of evidence therefore point to abnormal mobility at the present day in the Circum-Pacific and Alpine-Himalayan tracts and show that the disturbance reaches down even below the base of the crust.

The mobile belts just mentioned are expressed at the earth's surface by topographical features of many kinds, and it is evident that geological processes of different sorts are taking place at different localities. We may mention first the *oceanic trenches* or deeps which are narrow, often arcuate grooves in the sea-floor, as exemplified by the *Tonga trench* of the south-west Pacific (Fig. 377); this depression, some 700 miles long and 35 miles broad, descends to a depth of over six miles below sea-level and nearly three miles below the general level of the sea-floor. Along the axis of the Tonga trench the M discontinuity appears from seismic evidence to be some 10 kilometres lower than is common in oceanic regions.

A second topographical form characteristic of the active mobile belts is that of *island-arcs* such as make the island-groups of Japan, the Philippines, the East Indies and the Caribbean (Fig. 377). Many island-arcs are simply lines of volcanoes, the land-areas being built up as a result of volcanic activity. These arcs are often closely associated with oceanic trenches and are frequently the site of positive gravity-anomalies (Fig. 19). Other arcs are more complex and include islands formed by the elevation of the sedimentary filling of a trench. These complex arcs, as exemplified by the eastern part of the Aleutians and the western part of the East Indies, may pass laterally into

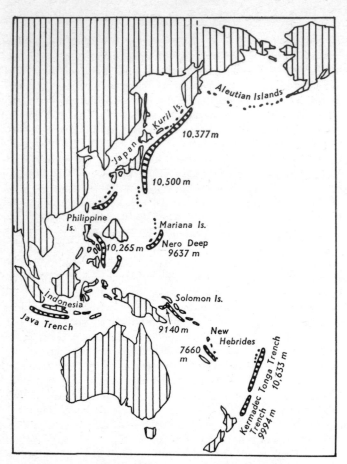

FIG. 377. Island arcs and oceanic trenches in the western Pacific; trenches are shown barred, depths in metres below sea level.

belts of high mountain-country. Many geologists have considered that the formation of oceanic deeps and island-arcs represents early stages in the orogenic processes leading to mountain-building. The *young mountain-belts* of the present day such as the Himalayas, the Alps and the Andes form long, often arcuate tracts of high ground. They are for the most part already deeply eroded and their geological structure and constitution can therefore be examined directly. It is considered that the aggregation of great masses of light materials in the folded sedimentary piles and granitic bodies of mobile belts leads, at a late stage in orogeny, to a compensating isostatic uplift and so to

626

the elevation of great ridges from which the mountain-belts are carved by erosion. The varying topographical forms exhibited by the mobile belts of today are thus seen as products of connected geological processes.

The Geosyncline. When the *sedimentary rocks* involved in the mobile belts are examined, certain remarkable facts are noted. Firstly, these sediments are often many times thicker than their equivalents on the stable platforms, and form piles equal to a substantial fraction of the normal thickness of the crust. For this to happen, the mobile belts must have been the site of prolonged subsidence. The bend in the crust which permitted such sediments to accumulate is a *geosyncline* which, with Bailey, we can define as a broad belt of profound subsidence. Whether or not a geosyncline becomes filled with sediment is decided by happenings in adjacent crustal regions — where these are low-lying or submerged, little detritus may be supplied, where they are elevated and subject to erosion, a copious supply of debris may be available. In any case, a geosyncline is likely to act as a sediment-trap, and its filling is often augmented by contributions from volcanic sources; we may recall the part played by vulcanicity in building the island-arcs referred to above. Secondly, the successions accumulating in geosynclines are often of a different facies from those laid down at the same time in shelf-seas on stable areas. Breaks in deposition are fewer and shorter in the subsiding trough, sorting and reworking of sediments are more limited and slumping is of frequent occurrence. Clastic and detrital sediments usually predominate over chemical and organic sediments and turbidite-deposits of greywacke-facies are widespread. On the less rapidly subsiding sea-floor beyond the geosyncline, deposition is often intermittent and the succession is broken by many diastems and minor unconformities; reworking of sediments results in good sorting and often leads to the production of rocks of orthoquartzite facies, while the stability of the sea-floor allows organisms to flourish and promotes the formation of limestones and other chemical-organic sediments. We may illustrate these generalisations and examine some of their limitations by brief reference to three examples, those of the Appalachian Mountains of eastern U.S.A., of Wales and of the Alps.

In the *Appalachian geosyncline*, filling of the downwarp began in late Pre-Cambrian or early Cambrian times and lasted, with interruptions due to phases of orogenic uplift, until the Permian period some 300 million years later. During this immense span, the places of maximum sedimentation shifted many times, so that the whole geosynclinal filling is really made up of a complex of elongated lenticles. In all, more than 40,000 feet of sediment were deposited, over

ten times the thickness of sediments of the same age laid down in
stable shelf-seas covering the interior of the American continent to
the west of the geosyncline.

Most of the sediment poured into the Appalachian geosyncline
came from the east, from a land-area sometimes named Appalachia.
As a result of the interplay of earth-movements, parts of the early
filling of the geosyncline were elevated into mountain ridges or
island-arcs while subsidence was still going on in adjacent regions;
erosion of these early mountains supplied much of the detritus filling
the later basins. The sediments of the Appalachian geosyncline are of
many facies, but as a gross generalisation it may be said that the

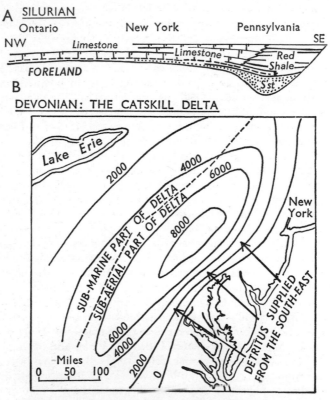

FIG. 378. Deposition in the Appalachian geosyncline. A, variation in
facies and thickness of the Silurian sediments (based on Kay); B,
isopachytes, in feet, of the Devonian sediments forming the Catskill
delta; arrows show the direction of transport of material to make the
delta (after Barrell).

early sediments included much sandstone, limestone and other carbonate rocks of orthoquartzite-facies, while the sediments from late
Ordovician onwards were predominantly clastic or detrital and often
approximated to greywacke-facies. The arrival of thick clastic
deposits can be correlated with the uplifting of new lands by orogenic
disturbances (Fig. 378). From the Devonian onwards, red rocks of
arkosic facies appear from time to time in the successions of the
eastern part of the Appalachians; these rocks are products of piedmont and flood-plain deposition in regions where earth-movements
or sedimentation carried the surface above sea-level. Through most
of the period of sedimentation, the stable region west of the geosyncline received successions in which thin sandstones and shales of
orthoquartzite-facies alternated with thick limestones and dolomites.
Only towards the end of the time did abundant detrital material
spread westward into the region. Volcanic contributions to the

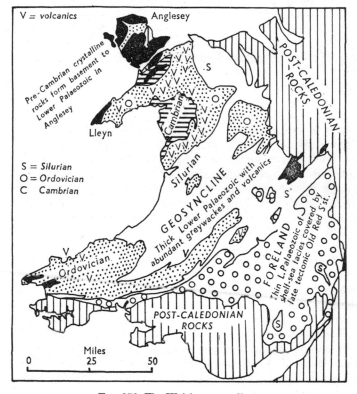

FIG. 379. The Welsh geosyncline.

geosynclinal filling included andesites, rhyolites, spilites and basalts formed during the Ordovician and Silurian; volcanic rocks are only of very minor importance in the shelf-area to the west.

The *Welsh geosyncline* (Fig. 379) began to fill up in late Pre-Cambrian or early Cambrian times and continued to receive sediment until its contents were forced up above sea-level at the end of the Silurian. The filling has a total thickness of some 40,000 feet, compared with the 5–10,000 feet of platform-deposits in the Welsh borders and English Midlands. The Welsh geosyncline is only one of a number of subsiding troughs formed during late Pre-Cambrian and Lower Palaeozoic times in the north-west of the British region, all the troughs belonging to the complex *Caledonian mobile belt.*

The sediments of the geosynclinal pile are overwhelmingly of greywacke-facies and at many levels include gritty clastic sediments such as the Lower Cambrian Harlech Grits. Graded bedding resulting from turbidity-current deposition is a characteristic sedimentary structure and slump-bedding, due to repeated sliding of sediment down the unstable sea-floor, is common, especially in the Silurian. Acid, intermediate and basic lavas, and welded tuffs, are interbedded with the geosynclinal sediments of late Pre-Cambrian and Ordovician age.

By contrast with the geosynclinal filling, the Lower Palaeozoic sequence of the stable Midland region is thin and incomplete. Over much of the region the whole Ordovician is missing and the Silurian rests with strong unconformity on a variety of older rocks. Well-sorted current-bedded sandstones and clean shales are interbedded with conspicuous limestones made largely of shell-debris; these limestones are exemplified by the Silurian Wenlock Limestone forming the conspicuous scarp of Wenlock Edge in Shropshire. Volcanic rocks are of very restricted occurrence. The contrasting environments of shelf and geosynclinal seas are reflected, as we have already seen (Fig. 210), in the faunas of the two regions. The shelf-deposits contain a rich *shelly fauna* characterised by a remarkable abundance of brachiopods, with trilobites and, at higher levels, corals and crinoids; the majority of these forms are shallow-water bottom-dwellers and some flourish only in clean waters. The geosynclinal deposits are largely of *graptolitic facies* characterised by sparse pelagic graptolites and by trilobites, but almost devoid of shelly or coral-bearing limestones.

As already emphasised, geosynclines are not to be thought of as simple, basin-like structures but rather as associations of several sub-parallel depressions in differing stages of development, which are separated by regions of less rapid subsidence. The complex *Alpine*

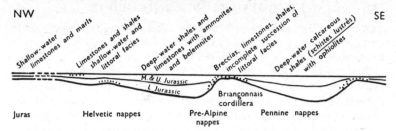

NW   SE

Shallow-water limestones and marls   Limestones and shales shallow-water and littoral facies   Deep-water shales and limestones with ammonites and belemnites   Breccias, limestones, shales, incomplete succession of littoral facies   Deep-water calcareous shales (schistes lustrés) with ophiolites

M. & U. Jurassic

L. Jurassic

Briançonnais cordillera

Juras   Helvetic nappes   Pre-Alpine nappes   Pennine nappes

FIG. 380. Diagrammatic section across the Alpine geosyncline in Jurassic times, showing the variation in environment and facies of the Jurassic sediments.

geosyncline of Mesozoic date provides a good illustration of this conception. From the distribution of sedimentary facies, Swiss geologists have shown that the geosyncline was made up of a number of longitudinal troughs separated by the so-called *cordilleras* which at certain times emerged to form ridges and island-arcs. We can examine the Jurassic sediments to demonstrate this conclusion (Fig. 380). On the north-western side of the geosyncline, the Jurassic sediments are of shallow-water facies and are made largely of limestones. Further south-east, the geosynclinal Jurassic forms a thicker, continuous sequence of deeper-water shales, black limestones and marly limestones. A shallow-water facies, marked by the occurrence of a thinner and less-complete succession of littoral and even some terrestrial sediments appears again in the vicinity of the Briançonnais cordillera, while to the south of this come on the sediments of the main trough — a thick pile of monotonous shales and calcareous shales continuous from the Jurassic to the Cretaceous and making the *schistes lustrés*. Associated with the schistes lustrés are thick masses of 'greenstone' — basic lavas and shallow intrusions making the so-called *ophiolites*.

We may note at this point that many sequences of geosynclinal sediments show evidence of deposition in moderately shallow water — indeed some are of orthoquartzite or 'shelf'-facies. This circumstance must indicate that subsidence and sedimentation more or less kept pace throughout the long period of deposition; the geosyncline was not a ready-made deep trough waiting to be filled. Moreover, the occurrence of breaks in the succession, of angular unconformities, and the widespread evidence of slumping and turbidity-current formation reinforce the impression of continued crustal unrest. The unrest culminates in one or more phases of violent upheaval and compression, the orogenic phases considered in the next section.

Igneous activity in the period of geosynclinal subsidence is attested

x

by the presence of both volcanic and intrusive rocks. There has developed a tendency to consider that the filling of the geosyncline is associated mainly with the uprise of basic magma, giving *ophiolites* such as those of the Alps. But we have seen that intermediate and acid lavas are widely developed in Wales and the Appalachians; the derivation of these types may be distinct from that of the ophiolites. Bodies of *serpentine* (p. 422) appear within the trough-filling in some geosynclines — in the Appalachians an elongated zone containing serpentines follows the thickest part of the succession. It is believed by some geologists that these masses are squeezed up into the geosyncline from a deep level beneath the M discontinuity disturbed by the orogenic processes.

OROGENESIS

As the geosynclinal basins deepen, the instability of the mobile belts increases. The basement of the geosyncline is depressed to depths approaching ten miles and the lower parts of its filling are thus carried down to regions of high pressure and increased temperature. On either side of the geosyncline the structural picture is very different. Here, the basement, covered only by a relatively thin veneer of shelf-sediments, still stands up to a high level in the crust and retains its normal rigidity. It is not surprising, therefore, that when tectonic forces compress the region there is a clear distinction between the reactions of the already disturbed, heated and weakened mobile belt, which now becomes the *orogenic belt*, and those of the more strong and stable *forelands* on either side. During orogenesis, the mobile belt is squeezed between the forelands and its rocks are driven upwards and outwards in great folds and thrust-sheets. The more deeply-buried rocks begin to recrystallise under the influence of heat, pressure and stress and in this metamorphic condition become increasingly mobile; the once rigid basement may be involved in metamorphism and reach a state of plasticity in which it can be interfolded with the sedimentary rocks of its cover. Migmatites and members of the Granite Series appear in the metamorphic region and it may be proposed that they originate as a result of the migration of active material from deep levels under the influence of the orogenic movements. We may explore some of these effects by considering the fate of the geosynclines already discussed.

In the *Appalachian orogenic belt* (Fig. 381), a *thrust-zone* is developed near the junction of the mobile belt with its western foreland. Along this zone, rocks of the geosynclinal facies are carried westward, for distances proved to be as much as thirty-five miles, over the thin

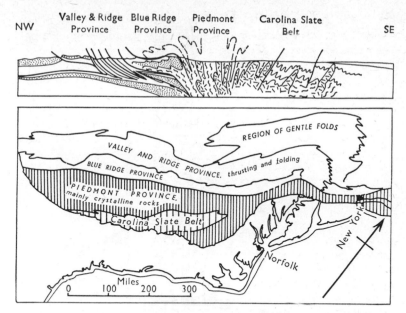

| NW | Valley & Ridge Province | Blue Ridge Province | Piedmont Province | Carolina Slate Belt | SE |

FIG. 381. Structure of the Appalachians, in section and map (based on P. B. King and the Tectonic Map of the United States).

shelf-sea succession of the foreland. Outside the thrust-front, the rocks are folded, as beautifully exemplified in the *Valley and Ridge province*. Here, regular anticlines and synclines corrugate the strata and run parallel for hundreds of miles. Within the thrust-front, in the *Blue Ridge province*, deformation and recrystallisation are more advanced; a slaty cleavage makes its appearance and the style of folding changes. Further east still, the *Piedmont province* consists of rocks now highly metamorphosed and invaded by granites. These rocks are considered by many American geologists to represent the most altered parts of the geosynclinal filling, together with the reactivated basement; but their high degree of alteration and the common destruction of any fossils they may have contained, make it difficult to elucidate their structure and stratigraphy. The Granite Series includes migmatites, syntectonic granites, post-tectonic plutons and high-level intrusions among which cauldron-subsidences are locally important.

The rocks of the *Welsh geosyncline* form, as we have noted, only a part of the *Caledonian orogenic belt* of Britain. Compression of this part of the geosyncline took place about the end of the Silurian and continued through early Devonian times. Sedimentation was brought

633

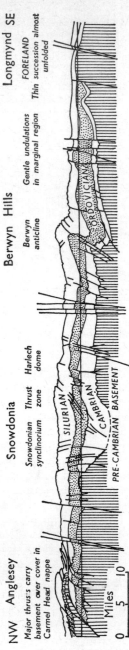

NW Anglesey   Snowdonia   Berwyn Hills   Longmynd SE

Major thrusts carry   Snowdonian   Thrust Harlech   Berwyn   Gentle undulations   FORELAND
basement over cover in synclinorium zone   dome   anticline in marginal region   Thin succession almost
Carmel Head nappe   unfolded

SILURIAN

CAMBRIAN

ORDOVICIAN

PRE-CAMBRIAN BASEMENT

Miles
0   5   10

Fig. 382. Structure of north Wales (based on a section by R. M. Shackleton).

to a halt by uplift, and an arcuate system of broad, open folds was formed roughly parallel to the margin of the geosyncline, with the accompaniment of a good deal of thrusting and disruption (Fig. 382). By contrast, the shelf-succession of the English Midlands remained virtually unfolded and sedimentation continued without interruption from late Silurian to early Devonian times, the facies merely changing from marine to terrestrial. Metamorphism in the Welsh region reached only a very low grade, the deeper rocks of North Wales being metamorphosed to slate grade and the remainder being practically unaltered. Migmatites are absent and granites are represented only by a few very small intrusions. In the older part of the Caledonian belt of north-west Ireland and the Scottish Highlands, on the other hand, the orogenic folding, which began much earlier than that of Wales, was accompanied by high-grade metamorphism, migmatisation and the production of a Granite Series. The Welsh geosyncline may thus be seen as a late and subsidiary structure in the evolution of the Caledonian belt.

But it is to the *Alpine orogenic belt* of the Alps that we should turn to obtain an example of extreme mobility. In early Tertiary times, the contents of the Mesozoic geosyncline were eviscerated to produce a pile of huge, far-travelled recumbent folds and nappes facing towards the northern side of the arcuate belt. The tectonic disturbance extended far out over the foreland and the relatively thin Mesozoic cover of the Jura Mountains was rucked up and driven north-westward over its basement, decollement taking place at a slippery horizon of evaporates near the base of the succession (Figs. 277, 286).

The western part of the Alpine belt (Figs. 383 and 384) shows, like the Appalachians, a number of parallel zones exhibiting different structural styles and broadly recording the effects of increasing mobility towards the interior of the belt. (i) To the north-west, the outermost zone is that of the *Jura Mountains* in which the cover was folded and fractured while the basement remained relatively undisturbed. This is followed (ii) by the low-lying *Swiss Plain*, occupying the site of a Tertiary basin of deposition in which detritus (the *Molasse*, see below) from the rising mountains accumulated. The next zone (iii) is that of the *Pre-Alps* which consists of the remnants of a pile of recumbent folds made of Mesozoic and Tertiary strata. These nappes are seen as klippes or thrust-outliers (p. 477) resting with tectonic junctions on the Helvetic nappes (iv) and the Molasse. The rocks of the pre-Alpine nappes are of a sedimentary facies which is out of harmony with that of the region where they are now found — the facies of the Jurassic, for example, resembles that of rocks laid down along the Briançonnais cordillera far to the south-east — and

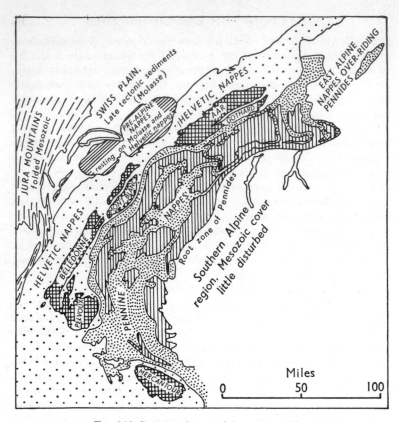

Fig. 383. Structural map of the western Alps.

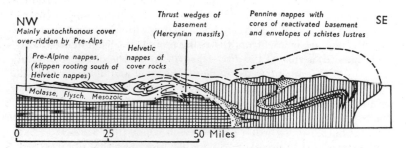

Fig. 384. Structural section across the western Alps.

636

this fact, together with the structural position of the nappes above those of the Helvetic zone immediately to the south-east, has led Swiss geologists to conclude that they must have travelled north-westward for fifty kilometres or more. Much of this forward travel may have been accomplished by sliding under the influence of gravity down the slope of the rising mountains.

To the south-east lie the *High Calcareous Alps* (iv) made up of recumbent folds, the *Helvetic nappes*, resting one above the other on thrusts. The rocks, which consist of Mesozoic and early Tertiary strata including much limestone, are greatly shattered but like all the rocks so far mentioned they are not metamorphosed. In the next zone (v), of the *Hercynian massifs*, enormous wedges of metamorphic and plutonic rocks belonging to the basement are thrust up. Between the wedges, the Mesozoic cover is preserved in tightly-compressed synclines. The rigid basement-rocks are often intensely sheared by the Alpine movements and towards the south they sometimes show evidence of polymetamorphism and the superposition of an Alpine structural pattern on an earlier Hercynian pattern.

To the south-east of the Hercynian massifs lies the zone of the *Pennine nappes* (vi), bounded by a line of strong thrusting. This zone is characterised by a highly plastic tectonic style which is largely due to the metamorphic character of the rocks. As before, a pile of nappes is arranged facing towards the north-west and with a root-zone in the south-east. The nappes are made of recumbent folds of schistes lustrés (p. 631) which suffered low- to high-grade syntectonic meta-morphism. Some folds are seen to have a *core* of pre-Mesozoic base-ment-rocks, squeezed out and reactivated during the Alpine move-ments and wrapped round by an *envelope* of schistes lustrés. This evidence of reactivation and distortion of the very rigid basement-rocks provides an excellent demonstration of the mobility attained by the crust during orogenesis. Evidence of activity at depth is also supplied by the occurrence of migmatites in the root-zone, and by the presence of late-tectonic granites intruding the lower nappes and the root-zone.

It will be noted that in all the zones so far mentioned, movement was directed towards the north-west side of the mountain-belt. Only to the south (vii) of the root-zone of the Pennine nappes, where the southern foreland of the mobile belt is approached, is there extensive evidence of movement in the opposite sense.

In the examples described above, we can distinguish variations in tectonic style across the width of the orogenic belt. In the foreland, the basement commonly yields by fracturing, and the cover-rocks may be peeled off and folded independently. At the margins of geosynclinal basins, the abrupt thickening of the cover produces a line of weakness which is often followed by enormous thrusts where basement and cover are driven outwards over the foreland. Examples of such *marginal thrust-zones* are the Moine thrust-zone of north-west Scotland (Fig. 292), the corresponding thrust forming the south-east Caledonian front in Norway and Sweden, and the Appalachian thrusts at the inner side of the Valley-and-ridge province. In the interior of the orogenic belt, the basement in non-metamorphic regions tends to yield along thrusts and shear-zones, and remains sharply distinguished from the less brittle cover. In metamorphic regions such as the Pennine nappes and the Scottish Highlands, the basement may be completely reconstituted by new metamorphism and migmatisation, and may become capable of plastic deformation. In these regions, basement and cover may become indistinguishable in metamorphic facies and tectonic style, and the unconformity between them may be obliterated.

An interesting example of the reactivation of the basement is provided by *mantled gneiss domes* first described by Eskola from a Pre-Cambrian orogenic belt in Finland. In this belt (Fig. 385), a

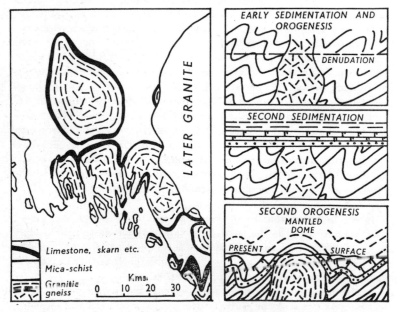

FIG. 385. Mantled Gneiss Domes. Map of typical gneiss domes in the Pitkyaranta region, Lake Ladoga, U.S.S.R.; sequence in the production of mantled gneiss domes (after Eskola).

distinctive succession of cover-rocks, locally with a basal conglomerate, was deposited unconformably on a previously metamorphosed basement containing synkinematic granites. During the new
orogeny, metamorphism and granitisation reactivated these base-
ment-granites and caused them to rise up as mobile bodies doming
and intruding the cover.

LATE OROGENIC EVENTS

As we have already seen, island-arcs and cordilleras begin to appear
within and at the margins of the basins of deposition even during the
geosynclinal phase of orogenic development. During the main orogenic phases, the geosynclinal pile is narrowed by compression and,
since the direction of easiest relief is generally upwards, the crests of
the folds begin to rise. The folded sediments form bundles of
dominantly light rocks which are commonly invaded by light
granitic material. As a result of this aggregation of material of low
density, isostatic readjustments take place which tend to raise the
whole belt and produce *topographic mountains*. The geosynclinal
seas are first restricted to narrow basins and finally expelled
altogether. Deposition continues in narrow belts of relative subsidence, the facies changing from marine to terrestrial, and erosion
begins to play a dominant part in shaping the surface-features of the
mobile belt.

During the early stages of the obliteration of the geosynclinal
basins deposition of *greywacke-facies* is the rule. The incoming of
these badly-sorted polymict sediments, often containing a high
proportion of coarse clastic material, appears to follow on the uprise
of the first cordilleras whose erosion-debris was shed into the basins
close beside them. Slumping and turbidity-current deposition reflect
the instability of the sea-floor, due both to the rapid piling-up of
sediment and to the mounting orogenic unrest. In the Alps, deposition
broadly of a greywacke-type is recorded by the Tertiary *Flysch*, a
thick series of argillaceous rocks, impure sandstones, breccias and
conglomerates with a sparse marine fauna, which in many places
follows the predominantly argillaceous and calcareous Mesozoic
successions. The Flysch represents material eroded from the rising
nappes, and is itself over-ridden by the Helvetic nappes. It is thus
clearly a *syntectonic* sedimentary formation. In the Welsh geosyncline,
as we have seen, greywackes were formed from the start of the period
of deposition; this early appearance of greywackes is probably due to
the fact that orogenic uplift had already begun in other parts of
the Caledonian mobile belt.

In the later phases, when the greater part of the mobile belt is

x2

carried above sea-level, erosion becomes more widespread and more rapid, and the facies of the sediments changes again. The *late-tectonic* and *post-tectonic* sediments are dominantly *arkosic*. They include polymict conglomerates, breccias, arkosic sandstones and shales, often brownish or red in colour, formed in *intermontane basins* in the environments of piedmont, flood-plain, lakes and deltas. In the Alps, the *Molasse* underlying the Swiss Plain is of this facies. Another example is the Triassic Newark Sandstone of the eastern U.S.A. formed from the debris of the Appalachian Mountains. The Devonian Old Red Sandstone of Scotland and the Welsh Borders is similarly related to the Caledonian orogenic belt; it carries a celebrated fauna of fresh-water vertebrates (ostracoderms, placoderms and fish) as well as some of the oldest-known land-plants. We may conveniently use the succession of strata which ends with the Old Red Sandstone in the Caledonian mobile belt of Britain as an example of the kind of sedimentation which may take place during the development of an orogenic belt (Fig. 386).

The late-tectonic sediments of a mountain-belt commonly rest with gross unconformity on rocks which are folded and often metamorphosed, migmatised and intruded by granites. It is obvious that after the plutonic processes had taken place, erosion must have bitten deeply into the newly-formed mountains before sedimentation was resumed. The main period of upheaval can be dated as taking place between the time of deposition of the youngest rocks involved in folding and metamorphism and that of the oldest rocks resting on the unconformity. In the Highland part of the Caledonian belt (Fig. 386) the youngest metamorphic rocks are certainly not younger than early Ordovician. The oldest rocks above the unconformity are uppermost Silurian and early Devonian, and widespread deposition did not start again until the Middle Devonian. On the Welsh borderland at the margin of the mobile belt, deposition was interrupted for much shorter periods, the main break being within the Devonian period.

Although the late-tectonic sediments did not accumulate until after the main phases of orogenic movement, it is plain that crustal disturbances continued during their formation. The great thickness of these deposits, sometimes going up to more than 10,000 feet, is in itself an indication of strong differential movements, since the floors of the basins of deposition must have subsided to make room for them; and it has been shown that tilting or movement of fault-blocks went on locally during their accumulation. Moreover, the sediments are often folded and faulted by *posthumous* movements.

Rocks of the post-orogenic stages are found to be *intruded by granites* late in the Granite Series of the orogeny concerned (p. 580).

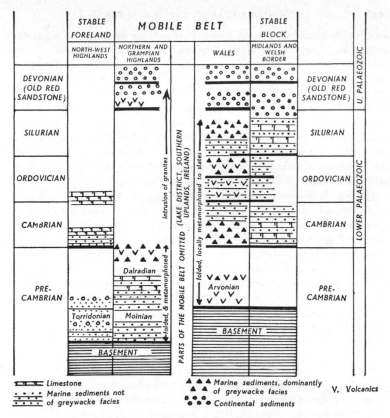

FIG. 386. Table of facies in the Caledonides of Britain.
(unconformity shown by thick line)

These intrusions represent some of the latest and most far-travelled of the material mobilised by plutonic activity in the orogenic belt. Caledonian examples are supplied by the ring-intrusions of Glencoe, Ben Nevis and Cruachan which penetrate Lower Old Red Sandstone lavas resting on metamorphosed Dalradian rocks. *Volcanic activity* of post-orogenic times is dominantly andesitic; this volcanic facies characterises both the embryonic stage of the island-arcs, as seen in Japan at the present day, and the later phase of mountain-belts as recorded at present in the Andean Cordillera of South America. Later, possibly very much later, when orogenic activity has died down and the mountain-block has reached a state of comparative stability, fracturing of the crust may herald the extrusion of plateau-basalts or alkaline rocks related to rift-faults. The drama of

641

geosynclinal sedimentation, mountain-building and degradation has been completed and a new crustal environment is established.

CAUSES OF OROGENY

Ancient orogenic belts of broadly the same age are found, like those of the present day, to have a world-wide distribution and, accordingly, it is reasonable to suppose that orogeny is due to a cause relating to the planet as a whole. What this cause is, is a matter for discussion, since no very satisfactory suggestion has yet been made; of the many proposals available we select three for consideration.

First is the *contraction-theory* of orogenesis. If the globe has cooled during geological history, then contraction of the inner shells could promote a crumpling of the crust as it accommodated itself to the shrinking interior. Both the subsidence of the geosynclines and the subsequent folding of their contents could be attributed to this cause, the shortening of the crust being taken up along the lines of weakness formed by the mobile belts. After orogeny had relieved the stresses, these slowly built up again until they reached a level at which a new orogeny took place — a periodicity of orogenic events would thus be accounted for.

Many objections have been brought against the contraction-theory. The earth is not proved to have cooled appreciably during geological history — the occurrence of sediments of glacial origin as far back as the late Pre-Cambrian suggests that there has been no significant change in surface-temperatures, and the energy released by radio-activity may even cause the crust to grow hotter. Contraction might however still result from compaction of the core or from polymorphic changes at deep levels. Another problem arises from the question as to whether the crust would be strong enough to transmit the stresses set up by contraction over distances of almost half the circumference of the globe, so that relief could be concentrated in the narrow and widely-spaced mobile belts and, moreover, the geophysical evidence of the contrast between the continental and oceanic crust would suggest that in such circumstances the crust would inevitably fail at the continental margin. A further difficulty concerns the adequacy of the probable amount of contraction to explain the observed shortening in successive fold-belts although this shortening is perhaps not as great as early estimates suggested.

Secondly, *convection-currents* in the mantle have been proposed as the prime cause of orogeny. There appears to be nothing inherently impossible in the idea that sub-crustal currents might be set up as a result of unequal cooling of sectors of the globe or of unequal heating due to radioactivity; we may note that vertical movements of the crust and the maintenance of isostatic balance would be impossible without some kind of flow in depth. According to the most favoured suggestions (see below), the downward flow of sub-crustal material from the line of junction of two convection-current cells may exert a drag on the crust, producing a geosynclinal downwarp and subsequently compressing the geosynclinal contents into a fold-belt. By this means the orogenic belt develops a deep root of crustal material which might serve to explain the negative gravity-anomalies recorded beneath oceanic trenches and certain parts of mountain-belts.

The last proposal concerning the cause of orogeny that we shall examine was an offshoot of the *theory of continental drift* which has been mentioned incidentally in earlier chapters. This theory as enunciated by one of its originators, A. Wegener, proposed that the thick masses of the continental crust are capable of drifting in the simatic substratum as ice-floes move in the sea. As the continents drifted, their prows or leading edges were buckled up to form, for example, the cordilleras of the western part of the Americas. A drift towards the equator compressed the contents of an east–west geosyncline to produce the Alpine-Himalayan belt. In the case of the Pacific fold-belts it can immediately be objected that the mountains are not made of buckled-up sial but of over-thick sediments. Moreover, Wegener's continental-drift theory provides no explanation of the resemblance between recently-formed fold-belts and those dating back to Palaeozoic and Pre-Cambrian times, since the main period of drifting was held to be post-Carboniferous. Although many objections can thus be raised to the mechanism favoured by Wegener, there is nevertheless a growing conviction among geologists that the processes of orogeny and continental drift are indirectly connected in that both are related to the same deep-seated cause. This cause, the operation of a system of convection-currents in the mantle (see above), may now be considered in relation to the major tectonic features of the crust as a whole.

CRUSTAL STRUCTURE AND MANTLE CONVECTION

The present-day crust exhibits two world-wide systems of structures — the system of *orogenic belts* on the one hand and that of *mid-oceanic ridges and rift-valleys* on the other. Both are associated with abnormal seismic and igneous activity and with evidence of high heat-flow: both are expressed by obvious topographical features and by peculiarities of structure which go down deep into the crust. The orogenic belts are compressional structures. The mid-oceanic ridges and the rift-valleys of the continents are probably tensional. The record of geological history makes it clear that the development and subsequent stabilisation of systems of orogenic belts have continued for nearly three thousand million years. Since the rift-systems are so largely oceanic, any fore-runners are unlikely to have left accessible records. But there is nevertheless evidence of the previous existence of tensional crustal features which may represent broadly comparable structures.

The scale and world-wide distribution of these structures suggest the operation of processes acting on a global scale. The same is

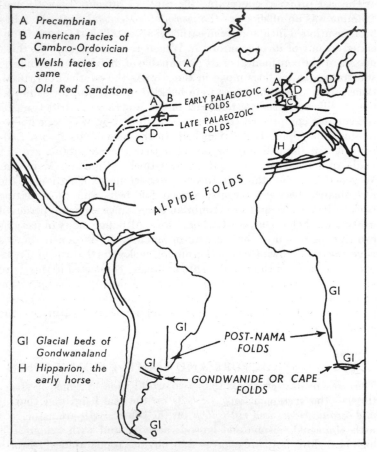

A   *Precambrian*
B   *American facies of Cambro-Ordovician*
C   *Welsh facies of same*
D   *Old Red Sandstone*

EARLY PALAEOZOIC FOLDS
LATE PALAEOZOIC FOLDS
ALPIDE FOLDS

Gl   *Glacial beds of Gondwanaland*
H   *Hipparion, the early horse*

POST-NAMA FOLDS
GONDWANIDE OR CAPE FOLDS

Fig. 387. Geological similarities on the two sides of the Atlantic (based on Du Toit and others).

clearly true of the vast horizontal displacements of masses of continental dimensions which are inherent in the hypothesis of continental drift. We may examine some of the evidence favouring such displacements before attempting to relate all the great crustal features to a common cause.

The *theory of continental drift* draws a great deal of its appeal from certain geological facts, among which we may select the following. First, there are remarkable correspondences in the geological build-up of the *lands on either side of the Atlantic*, as shown in Fig. 387. These correspondences would be explicable if the Atlantic had resulted from the formation of north-south fractures followed by a

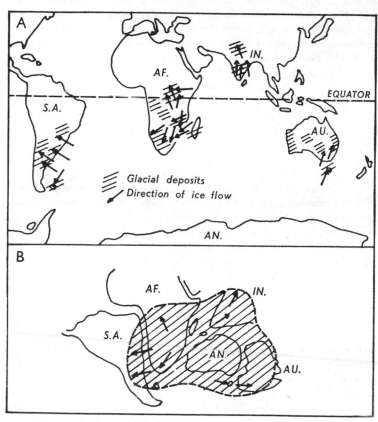

Fig. 388. A, the Permo-Carboniferous glaciation of Gondwanaland; B, hypothetical position of the continents at the time of the glaciation; the ice-sheet is lined.

westward drift which widened the gap between the sundered parts. Moreover, certain geological structures on either side of the Atlantic are, as they stand, obviously incomplete. The north-west Highlands and Outer Hebrides of Scotland represent a fragment of the stable block which acted as the western foreland of the Caledonian mobile belt. Both the basement and the cover-succession of this fragment must once have been vastly more extensive and it appears that their continuations must have been lost either by foundering in the ocean (see below) or by drifting.

Secondly, there are very detailed similarities in the rather peculiar geological history since late Carboniferous times of South America, South Africa, Australia, Peninsular India and Antarctica. These widely-separated regions formed part of a great land-mass termed *Gondwanaland*, on which was deposited a long sequence of terrestrial sediments exemplified by the Karroo of South Africa already dealt with. The Karroo succession began with widespread glacial deposits, and evidence of roughly contemporaneous glaciation is seen in most of the other fragments of Gondwanaland, both north and south of the equator (Fig. 388). As the continents are now placed, this evidence would indicate the spread of polar conditions over a vast area lying at present partly in tropical latitudes. This extraordinary distribution could be explained if the separated regions had, at the time of glaciation, been collected together around the current position of the South Pole and had later drifted apart to their present situations.

Thirdly, at about the time of the Permo-Carboniferous glaciation of Gondwanaland, coal-bearing strata deposited in tropical swamps and evaporates formed in a hot arid climate were laid down in the now temperate regions of North America and Europe. Again, these rocks indicate an *anomalous distribution of former climatic zones* with relation to the present poles; yet other examples are supplied by the distribution of Jurassic reef-building corals mentioned on p. 360, and by the occurrence of thick coal-seams in Antarctica and Spitzbergen. These anomalies may be explicable if it is supposed that the continental masses have in the course of time changed their position relative to the axis of rotation and climatic poles of the earth.

Fourthly, the *distribution of organisms* supplies some evidence bearing on the possibility of continental drift. Land-organisms, such as amphibia, reptiles, mammals, land-snails and insects, cannot be supposed to migrate freely across wide oceans, though accidental transport, for example by drift-wood, may account for some surprising distributions. Nevertheless, the occurrence of a high percentage of genera and species in common in the terrestrial deposits of widely-separated regions calls for explanation. Marked similarities of vertebrate faunas are shown by the sundered parts of the Karroo successions of Gondwanaland; the primitive Permian reptile *Mesosaurus*, for example, is found only in South Africa and the eastern part of South America. The Pteridosperm plant *Glossopteris* (p. 351) has been found in association with Permo-Carboniferous glacial deposits in South Africa, India, South America, Australia and Antarctica. To explain the occurrence of land-living organisms in widely-separated areas, appeal can be made in suitable instances to continental drift. An alternative mechanism invoked by some writers is migration over *land-bridges* — relatively narrow tracts of land or chains of islands — which formerly connected certain continental areas. The new knowledge concerning the form and structure of the ocean-floors makes the concept of land-bridges on the site of true oceans appear unlikely — as we have seen, the oceanic crust is thin and is almost lacking in the sialic layer, and there therefore seems no place in which foundered land-masses could be accommodated.

The theory of continental drift has received much support from a recent line of enquiry. *Palaeomagnetic observations* (p. 13), which deal with the 'fossil' magnetic fields of the earth, suggest that the magnetic fields in force when certain rocks were deposited did not agree in orientation with those of the present day. A lava from the Deccan Traps of peninsular India, for example, has a direction of magnetism, acquired when it consolidated, which is agreeable with its formation well south of the equator.

Palaeomagnetic studies of both lavas and sedimentary rocks suggest that the Indian sub-continent, situated not far from the antarctic polar regions during the Permo-Carboniferous glaciation, continued to drift northwards through much of the Mesozoic and Tertiary eras until it finally coalesced with the main mass of Asia. Comparison of the directions of magnetisation of rocks of the same age in Europe and in North America show divergencies which increase with age; these divergencies would be consistent with a westward drift of North America, opening up the Atlantic Ocean in Mesozoic and Tertiary times.

Further indications are provided by observations of the attitude of current-bedding in eolian deposits of the New Red Sandstone in Britain. These studies have been held to indicate that the *pattern of wind-directions* in the New Red desert is oblique to that which would be expected from comparisons with modern deserts. The observed pattern (Fig. 154) would be consistent with a northward shift of Britain accompanied by clockwise rotation of some 35° since Triassic times.

With these various types of evidence in mind, we may return to

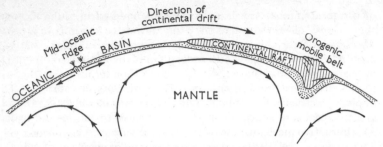

FIG. 389. Diagram illustrating a possible relationship between major crustal structures and a system of convection currents in the mantle.

the subject of convection-currents in the mantle. If the possibility that such currents may exist is admitted, it will be evident that they could exert forces on the crust in three rather different situations (Fig. 389). Where *rising currents* meet the base of the crust, they part and flow out tangentially away from the line of emergence. Frictional drag on the base of the crust favours *extension* while the heat and new mantle material brought from below provide a situation favourable to the generation of basic magmas. The mid-oceanic ridge-systems, with their accompanying basic vulcanicity and high heat-flow, may be the crustal structures formed above rising currents. *Descending currents* are produced where tangential currents meet and turn vertically downwards. The drag which they exert may be expected to cause compression and *shortening* and to thicken the crust into a root. The mobile belts, with their compressional structures, their deep roots and abundance of granitic materials mobilised from the deep parts of the crust, exhibit the features to be expected from zones situated above the lines of descending currents. Between the ascending and descending currents of the convection-cells, the forces exerted on the base of the crust would be *tangential*. Such forces, if powerful enough to move the thick rafts of continental crust, could supply the motive force responsible for *continental drift*. The continents should be moved away from the ascending currents, with consequent opening-up of ocean basins such as the Atlantic and Indian Oceans. These possibilities must clearly be tested against the evidence of geological history, a task which we shall attempt in a second volume.

THE CRUSTAL DRAMA

In the foregoing sections, we have considered the many kinds of earth-movement in the crust and have examined some of the processes

648

of sedimentation, erosion, igneous activity and plutonism which stem from them. We have now to assemble all this information to present the *crustal drama*, to use the Termiers' expressive title. This has a clearly distinguishable rhythm which has been repeated a number of times during earth-history.

The first act is the long *geosynclinal or pre-orogenic phase* in which the new mobile belts are marked out. Zones of weakness are developed, often at the margins of continental masses or between two such masses. Subsidence in these zones provides the *geosynclines* and sedimentary material begins to pile up in them; associated igneous activity gives basic and ultrabasic lavas and small intrusions (the *ophiolites*). The first sediments are commonly not of excessive thickness and may be orthoquartzitic in facies but, after some time, *disturbance* in the geosyncline and along its margins leads to the appearance of *island arcs* or *cordilleras* and, with the incoming of material from these new lands, *thick sedimentation of greywacke facies* is often initiated. Andesitic and rhyolitic lavas and tuffs may be associated with the greywackes.

At about the beginning of the geosynclinal phase, widespread epeirogenic movements may lead to a general slight depression of the stable blocks alongside the geosyncline. A *marine transgression* follows and a thin sequence of *shelf-sea sediments* is laid down, with a basal unconformity. A conspicuous example of such a transgression coinciding with geosynclinal subsidence is supplied by the *Cambrian transgression* marked in many parts of the world by the occurrence of Lower Cambrian basal conglomerates and sandstones resting unconformably on Pre-Cambrian rocks.

The second act of the drama is the *orogenic phase*, during which the contents of the geosynclines are compressed to give *folds, nappes and thrusts* of varying magnitude. The deeper parts of the sedimentary pile are *metamorphosed, migmatised and granitised*, and early members of the Granite Series appear as *syntectonic granites*. Orogenesis usually takes place in a number of short episodes which alternate with periods of relative quiet. The early episodes are recorded in the sedimentary successions by unconformities and by the incoming of coarse detritus. They work up to a climax which for a time may put a stop to sedimentation in much of the mobile zone.

The third act is the *late-orogenic or mountain-building phase* in which uplift takes place by isostatic adjustment assisted by fracturing and thrusting. Sediment worn from the newly-uplifted mountain chains is deposited in marginal and intermontane basins to give thick sequences of *arkosic facies*. Late members of the Granite Series penetrate these sediments as *intrusive granites* emplaced by various mechanical means. Vulcanicity produces dominantly *andesitic lavas* and pyroclastics. At depth, the plasticity induced by metamorphism dies away and the final movements are expressed by faulting. Gradually, in the *post-orogenic phase*, the fold-belt becomes stabilised, erosion and complementary sedimentation slow down and the abnormal tectonic and igneous activity finally ceases.

The late-orogenic uplift of the mobile belts is frequently accompanied by a more general emergence. The sea is shed from large parts of the stable areas and extensive new lands appear. Deposits of *continental facies* which, depending on climate and relief, may include arkoses, eolian sands, evaporates, lacustrine beds and coals, are laid down on these lands and provide some of the principal sequences of continental sediments in the stratigraphical column. The two famous European sequences of this type are the *Old Red Sandstone* deposited in the late stages of the Caledonian orogeny and the *New Red Sandstone* which followed the Hercynian orogeny and formed a blanket of deposits extending from north-west Europe to the margin of the Alpine geosyncline.

THE PATTERN OF EARTH-HISTORY IN TIME AND SPACE

THE OROGENIC RHYTHM

In the geological history of any reasonably sized area, there is recorded a succession of crustal dramas of the general type considered above. These successive dramas did not follow exactly the same course on each occasion, but they have enough in common for us to be justified in speaking of an *orogenic rhythm* affecting large sectors of the crust. Difficulties in establishing and correlating the details of this rhythm arise from the imperfections of the methods of geological dating and, where knowledge is scanty, it is easy to oversimplify the scheme. Orogenic events are not world-wide, and periods of geosynclinal subsidence in one region may coincide with periods of uplift in another; this fact is apparent from the make-up of the mobile belts of today which, as we have seen, include down-warped trenches, volcanic island-arcs and mountain-belts. Even within a more restricted area, the several orogenic episodes of one general period may be differently emphasised, so that the main unconformities fall at different stratigraphical levels. Accordingly, the classification of orogenic periods is a compromise, but for the Western European and North American, we can distinguish three great repetitions of the orogenic drama within the period dated by the fossil record. These are, from oldest to youngest, the *Caledonian, Hercynian and Alpine* 'cycles'. The main episodes of the orogenic phases recorded in Western Europe and North America are given in the following table:

TERTIARY	Pleistocene Pliocene Miocene Oligocene Eocene	MAIN ALPINE
MESOZOIC	Cretaceous Jurassic Triassic	LARAMIDE NEVADIAN
UPPER PALAEOZOIC	Permian Carboniferous Devonian	HERCYNIAN, APPALACHIAN
LOWER PALAEOZOIC	Silurian Ordovician Cambrian	LATE CALEDONIAN EARLY CALEDONIAN

The rhythmic repetition of orogenic dramas provides the basis for a division of geological time on a grander scale than that of the geological periods recognised in post-Cambrian times. This division is especially valuable in that it can be carried back into Pre-Cambrian time where the fossil-record fails, and can be made to provide a rough framework into which the events of Pre-Cambrian history will eventually be fitted. Since the ending of the Second World War, great progress has been made with the building-up of the succession of Pre-Cambrian orogenies and the dating of these orogenies in terms of millions of years by the investigation of radioactive minerals (p. 49); when this work is further advanced, we may hope to be able to piece together a history extending back over more than three thousand million years to the oldest dated rocks. The grandeur of this prospect makes it worth considering very briefly the evidence relating to the Pre-Cambrian orogenic rhythm.

THE PRE CAMBRIAN OROGENIC RHYTHM

In the first place, we can be reasonably certain that orogenic dramas of the type considered above took place in Pre-Cambrian times. The successions of sedimentary facies, the styles of tectonics, the metamorphic histories and sequences of granites seen in the Caledonian and Alpine chains can be matched in several Pre-Cambrian belts. The *Svecofennide belt* which crosses southern Finland and Sweden and is dated at about 1,800 million years supplies an example. In this belt, a thick sequence of greywacke-sediments is associated with abundant basic volcanics. Limestones and clean quartzites come in toward the margin of the belt. All the rocks are tightly folded and in some places cut by thrusts. They are regionally metamorphosed and migmatised and invaded by syntectonic and late-tectonic granites with a distinctive sulphide mineralisation.

Secondly, there is some evidence that Pre-Cambrian orogeny was, like that of later times, restricted to long and relatively narrow tracts. Marginal zones of thrusting and shearing have been described

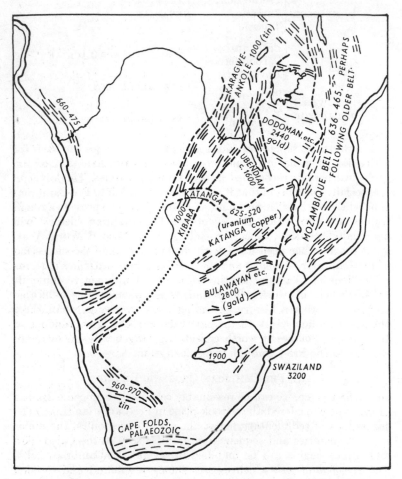

Fig. 390. Dated orogenic belts of Central and Southern Africa; structural lines based on Holmes (1950), dates from more recent publications.

in some few regions, and the folded and metamorphosed rocks of an orogenic belt can occasionally be traced laterally into undisturbed sequences on the adjacent foreland. In respect of form and history, the best-preserved Pre-Cambrian orogenic belts therefore resemble those of later times and it would appear that the doctrine of uniformitarianism can be applied to them.

Thirdly, a sequence of Pre-Cambrian orogenic periods can often be established on structural grounds. Each fold-belt has a fairly uniform structural pattern, the run of the main structures being as a rule parallel to the length of the belt. Later belts may show a continuous pattern crossing all earlier structures. In earlier belts the structures are cut off or distorted at newer orogenic fronts; they may reappear in the basement of the new belt, as Hercynian structures appear in the Hercynian massifs of the Alps. These relationships are illustrated for East and Central Africa in Fig. 390, which is a modified version of a classic map compiled by Holmes. The dates given for each belt are derived from the evidence of radioactive minerals and refer as a rule to minerals taken from pegmatites or other veins formed at a fairly late stage in the appropriate drama.

Finally, the recognition of a long sequence of orogenic dramas allows us to appreciate the range of variation in the orogenic rhythm. We may select one aspect of this variation for mention, since it is of particular economic importance — this is the contrast between the styles of mineralisation in different orogenic belts which is illustrated by the African region shown in Fig. 390. The gold-fields of Kenya and Rhodesia both lie in very old orogenic belts of east-west trend which Holmes regarded as possibly contemporaneous. Tin-ores in Uganda are associated with the Karagwe-Ankole belt, while the Copper Belt of Zambia and adjacent lands follows the late Pre-Cambrian Katanga belt which cuts many earlier orogenic structures. From evidence of this kind it is obvious that the seemingly academic study of geological structures may have profound practical implications; and once again, the sundered branches of geology meet in the elucidation of earth-history. As was said on the first page of this book, this is the prime aim of the geologist and will be pursued by us in a later volume.

FURTHER READING AND REFERENCE

Eardley, A. J., 1963, *Structural Geology of North America*, 2nd ed., Princeton Univ. Press.

Eastwood, T., 1946, *British Regional Geology, Northern England*, 2nd edit., Geol. Surv. and Museum. (Facies variations in the Carboniferous)

Eskola, P., 1949, 'The problem of mantled gneiss domes', William Smith Lecture, *Quart. Journ. Geol. Soc.*, vol. 104, p. 461.

Holmes, A., 1965, *Principles of Physical Geology*, 2nd edit., Nelson.

Jones, O. T., 1938, 'On the evolution of a geosyncline', *Quart. Journ. Geol. Soc.*, vol. 94, p. lx.

King, P. B., 1951, *Tectonics of Middle North America*, Princeton Univ. Press.

Poldervaart, A. (Editor), 1955, 'Crust of the Earth', *Geol. Soc. Amer. Special Paper 62.*

Potter, P. E. and F. J. Pettijohn, 1963, *Palaeocurrents and basin analysis*, Springer-Verlag.

Read, H. H., 1961, 'Aspects of Caledonian Magmatism in Britain', *Liv. Manch. Geol. Journ.*, vol. 2, p. 653.

Shotton, F. W., 1956, 'Some aspects of the New Red desert in Britain', *Liv. Manch. Geol. Journ.*, vol. I, p. 450.

Toit, A. L. du, 1937, *Our Wandering Continents*, Oliver and Boyd.

——, 1954, *Geology of South Africa*, 3rd edit., Oliver and Boyd.

Wegener, A., 1924, *The Origin of Continents and Oceans* (trans. J. G. A. Skerl), Methuen.

Willis, B., 1936, *East African Plateaus and Rift Valleys*, Carnegie Inst. Pub. 470.

Wills, L. J., 1929, *Physiographic Evolution of Great Britain*, Arnold.

'A symposium on continental drift', organized by P. M. S. Blackett and others, 1965, *Phil. Trans. Roy. Soc. Lond.*, Series A, No. 1088., Vol. 258.

INDEX